DILEMMAS
of the **Dollar**

COUNCIL ON FOREIGN RELATIONS BOOKS

Also by C. Fred Bergsten

World Politics and International Economics (co-editor)

Toward a New International Economic Order: Selected Papers of C. Fred Bergsten, 1972–1974

Toward a New World Trade Policy: The Maidenhead Papers (editor)

The Future of the International Economic Order: An Agenda for Research

Leading Issues in International Economic Policy: Essays in Honor of George N. Halm (co-editor)

Approaches to Greater Flexibility of Exchange Rates: The Bürgenstock Papers (co-arranger)

DILEMMAS
of the Dollar

The Economics and Politics
of United States
International Monetary Policy

Second Edition

C. Fred Bergsten

M.E. Sharpe
Armonk, New York
London, England

A COUNCIL ON FOREIGN RELATIONS BOOK

Library of Congress Cataloging-in-Publication Data

Bergsten, C. Fred, 1941–
Dilemmas of the dollar : the economics and politics of United States international monetary policy / C. Fred Bergsten.—2nd ed.
p. cm.
Includes index.
ISBN 0-87332-600-8 (alk. paper)
1. Foreign exchange—United States.
2. Balance of payments—United States.
3. International economic relations.
I. Title.
HG3863.B43 1996
332.4'5'0973—dc20
96-7104
CIP

HG 3863
.B43
1996

Printed in the United States of America

The paper used in this publication meets the minimum requirements of the American National Standard for Information Sciences— Permanence of Paper for Printed Library Materials, ANSI Z 39.48-1984.

∞

BM (p)   10   9   8   7   6   5   4   3   2   1

Comment

In *Dilemmas of the Dollar* Fred Bergsten offers a detailed analysis of what the dollar's role as the world's leading currency has meant for the U.S. economy during the last five decades. As Bergsten makes clear, the use of one's currency in international transactions presents the country of issue with a unique set of opportunities and challenges. Having to supply the rest of the world with continuous injections of dollars to meet global liquidity needs, the United States has been able to run continuous balance-of-payments deficits. Yet such a relaxation of the external constraint has to be managed in responsible fashion to assure stable exchange rates and effective adjustment processes. Bergsten provides us here with a masterful account of how this tension has confronted the United States with a variety of dilemmas since the end of World War II.

Published shortly after the collapse of the postwar dollar standard known as Bretton Woods, *Dilemmas of the Dollar* presents different scenarios for international monetary reform and assesses their respective implications for the United States. Twenty years later the book has lost none of its relevance. As correctly predicted by Bergsten, the market-dominated multicurrency system evolving since then has not worked well.

In a new chapter concluding this reissue, Bergsten makes the case for explicit target zones that would be managed by international policy coordination under the auspices of the International Monetary Fund. Anyone interested in the future role of the United States in the world economy will find this timeless classic an indispensable contribution.

Robert Guttmann
Hofstra University

To

Jenny,
in the hope that somehow she will reap
benefits sufficient to offset the costs to her of my writing this book.

Contents

Preface

The dollar had peaked as an international currency by 1968. It was decisively repudiated in 1973. Yet many noted economists have continued to proclaim the international dominance of the dollar and predict its perpetuation—just as many noted economists continued to observe a "dollar shortage" and forecast its perpetuation long after any such shortage had actually disappeared in the late 1950s. And the international monetary policy of the United States has sought to keep open the option of a world dollar standard despite the high and increasing costs such a role would levy on the United States if that system were to eventuate—just as the United Kingdom suffered high and increasing costs as it sought to perpetuate the role of sterling for at least half a century beyond its capacity to do so.

Such confusion is both understandable and predictable. The international monetary policy of the United States, including its approach to its balance of payments, is inextricably linked to the views of both government officials and outside observers, at home and abroad, concerning the international roles of the dollar. Yet there exists no comprehensive analysis of those roles, their effect on the United States, and what they suggest for U.S. policy. This vacuum too is understandable, because the roles of the dollar are complex and replete with dilemmas from the standpoint of both the United States and other countries throughout the world. But the vacuum must be filled, as part of the effort to provide an intellectual basis upon which to build a new monetary system. This book attempts to do so.

I originally conceived the book while working on international monetary problems in the Department of State during the mid-1960s. It became apparent to me at that time, when the United States first began to adopt active policies toward its balance of payments and toward reform of the monetary system, that we were drifting toward the creation of a dollar area with as many members as could be cajoled into joining—without any conceptual underpinning, and without any analysis of whether such an approach was in the long-term interest of the United States. It also became apparent that potentially tragic parallels existed between the historical evolution of the roles of sterling and the economic and political development of the United Kingdom, on the one hand, and the likely evolution of the dollar and the economic and political development of the United States, on the other. (The many books on sterling in the postwar period, by both British and foreign observers, came at least three decades too late—which adds to the parallel.) I therefore resolved to make an effort to shed sufficient light on the issues to help develop a sensible international monetary policy for the United States, particularly because international monetary policy seemed likely to have important implications for overall U.S. economic policy, and overall U.S. foreign policy, which would far transcend the narrow sphere of international monetary affairs.

The Council on Foreign Relations made the effort possible. I completed a first draft of the manuscript between late 1967 and early 1969, while in residence there as a visiting fellow. The final product was then delayed, but I believe vastly improved, as a result of my spending the first twenty-eight months of the first Nixon administration as Assistant for International Economic Affairs on the Senior Staff of the National Security Council. In June 1971, the Council on Foreign Relations took the exceedingly gracious step of renewing my fellowship so that I could spend most of the succeeding year revising the book, taking into account the dramatic changes that were occurring in the monetary system during that period. The Council also published a brief summary of the analysis in the book, and the policy conclusions and recommendations which it then contained, as its *Occasional Paper on International Affairs No. 2*, in September 1972. Further delay in this final publication was then occasioned by the need to incorporate the further changes in the monetary system which occurred in 1973, including the widespread advent of managed flexibility of exchange rates and the sharp rise in petroleum prices at the end of the year.

My first acknowledgements of help on the project, therefore, goes to those people associated with it through the Council. Miriam Camps made the whole enterprise possible by bringing us together. George Franklin, David MacEachron, and the Committee on Studies gave me initial encouragement and support—and were understanding far beyond the norm when my return to government service delayed the final product. Bayless Manning graciously renewed my fellowship. Rob Valkenier and Carol Kahn diligently edited the final product. Most of all, Bill Diebold helped immeasurably with his penetrating questions and advice, and his constant support.

As is the privilege of all Council fellows, I benefited from the advice of an outstanding study group. Robert V. Roosa was chairman of the group, and led its discussions intellectually as well as procedurally. All of us in this field owe a special intellectual debt to Robert Triffin, who first pointed to the need for fundamental monetary reform in the late 1950s, and I gratefully join the ranks of those who do. Edward

M. Bernstein and Fritz Machlup made their customary giant contributions. I received sage advice on the political implications of international money from Francis Bator and the late Henry Aubrey. Peter Kenen, Charles P. Kindleberger, Walter Salant, Rob West, and the late Emil Despres helped keep my economics straight. Dewey Daane, Bill Dale, Fred Deming, Alfred Reifman, Frank Schiff, Frank Southard, Willard Thorp, and George Willis bestowed the deep benefits of their practical experience and policy concerns as key officials currently or previously shaping international monetary policy. Al Costanzo, John Deaver, John Meyer, Andrew Overby, and Judd Polk did likewise from their vantage points in the private sector.

My final acknowledgments go to those who started me in international economics, and those with whom I share my current efforts in the field. Intellectually, my greatest debt of all is to Professor George N. Halm, who taught me the basics—and much beyond them —at the Fletcher School of Law and Diplomacy in 1961–63, and most helpfully commented on my manuscript at various stages throughout its development. My first boss in the State Department, Benjamin Caplan, both extended that education and provided me with the opportunity to participate actively at an early age on policy issues of great importance. And my postgraduate education and development of policy views could have had no better guide than Richard N. Cooper, in my view the finest international political economist in the world today, whose contributions to my own thinking as superior, colleague, and friend are reflected on almost every page of this book.

Finally, I wish to thank the Brookings Institution for making physical facilities available to me as a Brookings Guest Scholar to finish the book. I am also indebted to the unmatched intellectual qualities of the members of both the Foreign Policy and Economic Studies programs at Brookings, particularly Ed Fried and Lawrence Krause, for helping to sharpen my analysis greatly, and I look forward to many more years of pleasant and productive association with them. Janelle Jones and Karen Anderson did a yeoman job of typing the manuscript and managing my affairs throughout its preparation.

C. F. B.

Part I
The International Monetary System–Myth and Reality

The United States and International Monetary Reform

The Purpose of This Book

This book is about the effects of alternative international monetary arrangements on the national interests of the United States. Its method is to analyze the costs and benefits of the alternatives to the United States, by applying a number of economic and political criteria to each. Its objective is twofold: to deepen understanding of the impact of different monetary arrangements on the United States and to propose an approach to international monetary policy for the United States that will maximize the benefits for it.

The book thus differs markedly from almost all of the previous voluminous literature on international monetary issues. Most analysts have sought to explain the operation of the monetary system from a global standpoint, and virtually all proposals for reform have been based on global criteria, assuming implicitly that each individual country would benefit from a system that provided the best worldwide framework. To be sure, the United States has a major national interest in the effective functioning of the overall monetary system, and this book devotes much attention to that issue. But the economic and political interests of the United States go well beyond the smooth functioning of the system itself, to the specific nature of the very different kinds of conceivable international monetary arrangements. They are the focus of this book.

A second fundamental difference between this book and most other efforts in the field is its explicit effort to integrate economic and political considerations in order to maximize the usefulness of its analysis for policy-making in the real world. Numerous economists have developed elegant models of optimum adjustment devices and international reserve arrangements. A few political scientists have addressed the international monetary issue from the standpoint of its effect on overall relations among nations. But integration of the two approaches has been exceedingly rare, and is absolutely essential to understand the effects of the dollar's role in the past and the implications of its different potential roles in the future. This book attempts to develop such an approach.

The international roles of the dollar[1] are the vehicle for pursuing this analysis. The dollar's roles enabled the United States to run balance-of-payments deficits for two decades, and thus to acquire real resources from the rest of the world and avoid serious external financial constraint on either its domestic economic policy or its foreign policy. But the roles of the dollar also precluded effective adjustment of those deficits, generating unemployment in the United States and promoting tendencies toward protectionism and isolationism which raised major questions about the overall world role of the United States in the 1970s and beyond. The pervasive roles of the dollar both derived from and in turn promoted the globalist foreign policy of the United States, but they may have impeded necessary and desirable modification of that policy. As we shall see, these and other dilemmas deriving from the dollar's international roles have had pervasive effects on U.S. economic and foreign policies throughout the postwar period, and choices made concerning the dollar's future roles will continue to have an important impact on both for the foreseeable future.

Indeed, the viewpoint of this book is that U.S. international monetary policy can only be effectively understood through an analysis of the dollar's international roles, and of the perceptions of those roles and the outlook for them held by U.S. officials. Views about the dollar go far to explain why the United States has always opposed an increase in the official price of gold, even when it held by far the largest share of the world's stock; why, seemingly paradoxically, it promoted rivals to itself through the international use of other national currencies in the early 1960s and the creation of Special Drawing Rights in the mid-1960s; why it frequently opposed exchange-rate changes, even revaluations by surplus countries which would have helped the U.S. balance of payments, throughout most of the postwar period; and why, in what appears to be a total reversal, it has become an ardent advo-

---

1. The dollar plays several international roles: as a vehicle currency for private international transactions, as an intervention currency through which national monetary authorities affect the value of their own currencies in the foreign exchange markets, and as a reserve currency in which those authorities hold their monetary assets. These different roles have very different effects on both the United States and the international monetary system, and different sets of changes in the varying roles are both theoretically possible and quite conceivable in the real world. These differences will be elaborated throughout this book.

cate of exchange-rate flexibility in the 1970s. This book will assess U.S. international monetary policy through the focus of the international roles of the dollar—past, present, and potential. It covers much of the life cycle of the dollar as a key currency: its birth, its moderate expansion in the early postwar period and rapid expansion during the late 1960s and early 1970s, and its widespread repudiation by other countries in 1973.

This analysis of the dollar also has important implications for the functioning and future of the international monetary system. It is obvious that the dollar played a dominant role in the Bretton Woods system, which provided the financial basis of the postwar world economy from 1946 until 1971. In fact the evolution of the postwar monetary system can be conveniently viewed in the four phases marked by the different positions of the dollar. The first phase lasted through 1958, when the dollar was the *only* major convertible currency and the term "dollar shortage" best typified the international currency situation. The second phase lasted from 1959 until 1967–68, when *all* major currencies were truly convertible. The third phase ran until August 1971, with the dollar's convertibility into U.S. reserves (primarily gold) becoming increasingly nominal and the world splitting into de facto currency areas as a result. The fourth has been with us since August 1971, when the dollar has been the only major currency *not* convertible into the reserve assets of its national monetary authority and the international monetary system has quickly evolved in significant new directions—including the rapid ascendance to international prominence of several additional national currencies, particularly the German mark.

Significantly, the four major postwar phases of the balance-of-payments adjustment process are virtually identical with these four phases of the roles of the dollar. Until 1958, controls over international transactions—both capital and trade flows—were pervasive, and changes in those controls were the major mode of adjustment used by most countries. From 1959 until 1967–68 adjustment was largely eschewed in favor of financing of the surpluses (in Continental Europe) and deficits (in the United States and United Kingdom) which dominated. From 1967 to 1971, exchange rates once more began to change and controls over international transactions again began to proliferate. And, since 1971, flexible exchange rates and frequent changes of the parities which continued to exist have wholly transformed the adjustment process. The changing roles of the dollar thus provide a useful basis for analyzing all key aspects of the postwar monetary system, past and present.

Of even greater importance is the fact that different views about the roles to be played by the dollar in the future are a central issue, perhaps *the* central issue, in the efforts undertaken by national authorities around the world since 1971 to develop a stable successor to the Bretton Woods system. Debates about "convertibility" and new modes of adjustment are rooted in sharply divergent views about the future of the dollar. Some experts, particularly in the United States, but also to a surprising extent in other countries, wish to return to the dollar standard of the past—often without openly saying so. Others wish to eliminate completely the international roles of the dollar; having done so, part of this group would seek simply "to return to the charter of Bretton Woods," while others would seek an entirely new system instead. And others strike a more intermediate position.

This is partly because much of the debate about the international monetary system really centers on the distribution of income and political power, both among and within countries. There are a number of technically feasible solutions to the problems of balance-of-payments adjustment and international reserves. But the different solutions may have quite different effects on different countries, and different groups within countries. Because the focus of this book is the national interests of the United States, in both economic and political terms, it recognizes this reality and pays significant attention to it.

Thus the roles of the dollar are the organizing principle of the volume rather than the usual focus on the adjustment, liquidity and confidence problems—although each of those three issues will be carefully considered in the analysis of the dollar's roles. Indeed, it is the thesis of this book that the roles of the dollar were so central to "the Bretton Woods system" that any fundamental changes in that system can be achieved only through sweeping changes in the roles of the dollar. It is also a conclusion of this book that fundamental change would be very much in the national interests of the United States. In any event, it is clear that the implications of alternative new monetary arrangements can be understood—particularly from the standpoint of the United States—only in the light of thorough analysis of the effects of the roles of the dollar throughout the postwar period.

In addition, the monetary system which has been evolving in recent years, and even more so the system of the future, could be decisively affected by the international roles of new key currencies, particularly th German mark and perhaps also the Japanese yen. This study of the postwar roles of the dollar should expand understanding of the implications of such developments, from the standpoint of both the new key currency countries themselves and the system as a whole. Indeed, this book will draw general conclusions about the international roles of national currencies—which have, despite textbook references to a "gold standard" and "the Bretton Woods System," dominated international monetary affairs for at least a century.

Throughout this analysis of the effects on the United States of the international roles of the dollar, references are made to the effects on the United Kingdom, past and present, of the international roles of sterling. From this comparison emerges empirical evidence concerning the criteria which originally propel national currencies into international roles and their effects on the respective key currency countries. These patterns can be applied to the outlook for the evolution of new currencies in the future, and they do in fact derive additional (if very preliminary) support from the rapid international emergence of the German mark in recent years. The analysis of the international roles of national currencies in this book thus carries implications for future monetary arrangements beyond those which apply directly to U.S. policy and the dollar.

The Plan of the Book

This book is divided into three parts. Part I outlines the economic and political requirements which must be fulfilled by any effective international monetary system, and traces the way in which the pre-1914, interwar, and postwar systems have gone about doing so in practice as well as in theory. Both the conceptual and historical presentations focus on the pervasive roles played in those systems by national currencies, originally (but not solely) sterling and especially the dollar since World War II. Part I should provide useful orientation and background for the nonspecialist. The specialist can skip most of it. However, most economists will find new material in the discussion of the political underpinings of international monetary arrangements in the second half of Chapter 2. And my short history of the postwar period in Chapter 3 puts forth the original thesis that the "Bretton Woods system" can best be understood as a tripartite world comprising three evolving de facto monetary zones: a dollar area and a gold bloc along with the widely recognized sterling area.

Part II provides the analytical core of the book. Chapters 4, 5, and 6 assess the political and economic criteria which a currency must meet to achieve and maintain key currency status. The analysis is both conceptual and empirical, drawing on the British and American experiences of the past century. It attempts to provide a general theory of key currencies, and its conclusions pave the way for cost-benefit analysis of the effect on the United States of alternative international roles for the dollar by indicating what is required of the United States under such alternatives. It also paves the way for predictions about the evolution of new key currencies in the future.

Chapters 7 through 10 estimate the effects on the United States of the roles of the dollar, primarily under the monetary system which existed prior to August 1971. Chapter 7 assesses the net direct impact on the U.S. balance-of-payments of the dollar's roles: changes in foreign lending by U.S. banks, the interest payments and earnings which result. It will reach conclusions on the conditions under which the dollar's roles provide net financing for U.S. deficits, as well as on the direct welfare effects of those roles. Chapter 8 isolates the overhang, the dollar balances which exist at any time as a legacy of previous U.S. deficits, to see whether they add to the burden of external adjustment which the United States might face under particular circumstances. Chapter 9 examines the effects of the dollar's roles on U.S. adjustment to imbalances in its payments position. How much does the United States gain or lose by avoiding adjustment, which the roles the dollar frequently permit? How much does it gain or lose by the constraints on particular modes of adjustment levied by those same roles? Chapter 10 broadens the issue by assessing the importance of the dollar's roles to the United States through their impact on the functioning of the overall monetary system, looking at both the importance to the United States of an effective system and the impact of the dollar on achieving such a system. Part II concludes that the international roles of the dollar had begun to levy heavy net costs on the United States under the Bretton Woods system—just as the roles of sterling came to levy heavy costs on Britain when they were no longer supportable by its economic and political strength—and that a change in those roles had thus become highly desirable from a U.S. standpoint.

This analysis centers on the roles of the dollar in the Bretton Woods system, with the changes in its roles which have occurred since August 1971 treated in Part III as part of the analysis of alternative arrangements to replace Bretton Woods. Indeed, these chapters, plus the last section of Chapter 3, represent in part a history of how the "Bretton Woods system" worked in practice. There are three reasons for this focus. First, as the underpinning of the world economy for a generation, Bretton Woods is the base against which alternative arrangements are, quite properly, compared by virtually all observers. Second, many (if not most) observers both in the United States and elsewhere view Bretton Woods as an extremely successful system, at least in comparison to the alternatives which they perceive to be feasible, and seek to return as closely as possible to its basic precepts:

"fixed" exchange rates, a financial base in the dollar, an important role for gold, and steady consultation among governments in the International Monetary Fund and other bodies.

Third, no single "system" which can be analyzed as such has existed since August 1971. During that period, however, departures from the earlier arrangements have taken place which are highly relevant to our choices for the future, and provide valuable evidence against which to judge those alternatives. Floating exchange rates, with a great deal of uncoordinated intervention in the exchange markets by national monetary authorities, were the order of the day from August to December 1971. A parity system was restored at the Smithsonian meetings and lasted until March 1973, except for Britain from June 1972, but with the continued inconvertibility of the dollar into U.S. reserve assets it was a parity system which amounted to a pure dollar standard rather than the system envisaged by, and implemented at least partially under, Bretton Woods. Floats, first without much intervention and then with some initial steps toward multilateral surveillance of national interventions, then resumed primacy. These different post-August 1971 arrangements are analyzed in Part III, in the context of options for lasting reform, and are compared against the background of Bretton Woods to judge their merits and demerits from the standpoint of the United States.

The specialist should read Part II carefully. The nonspecialist may also want to do so, as it provides the conceptual underpinning for the policy discussions of Part III; but summaries of the major conclusions are provided at the end of each chapter, as noted in the table of contents.

Part III turns to policy alternatives, and should be read by specialist and nonspecialist alike (though chapter summaries are again available). Chapter 11 looks at the several alternatives for totally eliminating one or all of the international roles of the dollar. The substitution of a new national currency for the dollar, if one could be found which would qualify, would permit the elimination of all of the dollar's international roles. Freely flexible exchanges rates, without intervention by national authorities, would permit elimination of its reserve and intervention currency roles. Various versions of a "return to the gold standard," or the adoption of an international reserve asset (probably modelled on the existing Special Drawing Rights), would permit elimination of the dollar's reserve currency role. There are several ways to eliminate the intervention currency role alone. The effects on the United States of each of these approaches is analyzed.

Chapter 12 turns to the other extreme, the options for "crowning" the dollar as the sole basis for international monetary arrangements.

There are three ways in which, in theory, this could be done. First, the United States could force the world to a pure dollar standard simply by keeping it inconvertible into U.S. reserve assets—*if* there were no viable international alternatives to the dollar. (Since I argue that such alternatives *do* exist, I reject this "option" as unworkable and, in fact, conclude that its pursuit would be likely to produce a sharp diminution rather than an increase in the dollar's roles). Second, the United States could guarantee the value of external dollar holdings against any future depreciation, as the British did for official sterling holders in 1968, in the *hope*—or perhaps, through negotiations, with some certainty—that this would eliminate their reluctance to hold dollars. Third, the United States could resolve to fulfill all of the criteria for key currency status developed in Part II, and actually do so, so that foreigners would have no basis for doubting the value of their dollar balances or U.S. policy into the indefinite future. Again, the effects on the United States of each approach are assessed.

Chapters 11 and 12 present extreme alternatives for monetary reform—complete elimination of the dollar, and its total "crowning" —for several reasons. First, only such "pure" models can fully clarify the implications of each approach, especially for the United States, and the key differences between them. Second, "extreme" options once thought "dead" have regained prominence in the wake of the breakdown of the old system and the failure to replace it quickly with a new one. This is obviously true for floating exchange rates and for an inconvertible dollar standard, with or without the criterion of exchange-rate guarantees by the United States. It may also be true for gold (with the rapid escalation of its price in the free market and several steps by governments toward a similar increase in the official price) and for the emergence of a new key currency (with the rapid ascendance of the German mark). Third, and closely related, some of these "extreme" options have the support of some officials, as well as of many outside observers, and hence are serious contenders for future approval.

However, given the nature of international compromise at both the intellectual and political levels, less extreme outcomes are more likely to emerge from the interplay of market forces and bargaining among nations. Chapter 13 thus turns to the intermediate options for changing the international roles of the dollar: *limited* flexibility of exchange rates, the use of an international reserve asset to meet *part* of the world's liquidity needs, and the use of additional national currencies *alongside* the dollar. This discussion deals with such key questions as: *How much* flexibility, and for whom? *How great* a role for an international asset? *How great* a role for new key currencies? None of these approaches would deal definitively with the dollar, but all would have a major impact on it and hence on the national interests of the United States.

Finally, Chapters 14 through 16 pull together the several analytical strands of the earlier chapters and present overall policy conclusions. They will provide the gist of the book for the reader interested solely in policy, and provide references to the analytical material relevant to each conclusion. Chapter 14 calls for fundamental reform of the monetary system, and argues that such action is highly desirable from the U.S. standpoint. Chapter 15 proposes specific directions for reform which would be preferable from the U.S. standpoint: a high degree of flexibility of exchange rates, a sharp cutback in the international roles of the dollar, consolidation of as much of the dollar overhang as possible, avoidance of major reserve currency roles for other currencies, and primary reliance on an international asset for reserve purposes. It thus calls for a U.S. international monetary policy sharply different from the policy of the first postwar generation, and concludes that the successful advocacy of such a policy would carry major advantages for the U.S. economy and U.S. foreign policy for the 1970s and beyond.

2

The Economics and Politics
of International Money

The Economics of International Money

When a country faces an imbalance in its international payments position, it can respond in four possible ways or combinations thereof. First, it can finance the imbalance. A country in surplus can accumulate reserves or extend credit; a country in deficit can use reserves or borrow. Financing is an asymmetrical option: surplus countries can accumulate reserves and extend credits indefinitely; deficit countries must eventually run out of reserves and may also run out of borrowing possibilities.

Second, a country can alter the course of its domestic economy in an effort to adjust the imbalance indirectly. A surplus country can increase its growth rate, which will suck in more imports and reduce the incentive for its domestic industries to export (but may also attract capital because of increased profit opportunities). It can inflate, which will weaken the international competitiveness of its industries, perhaps by expanding its money supply and lowering its interest rates, thereby inducing capital outflows as well. A deficit country can improve its trade balance by checking internal inflation, and attract capital inflows by tightening its money supply and raising interest rates.

Indeed, some adjustment of this type takes place automatically as a result of the imbalance itself. The external demand that generates its trade surplus also pushes up the relative price level of the surplus country; capital inflows exert upward pressure on its prices and downward pressure on its interest rates; and the increase in incomes resulting from additional exports promotes increased imports. The opposite effects take place in deficit countries. However, these automatic tendencies cannot be counted upon to restore payments equilibrium. In fact, their effects can be fully offset through the sophisticated tools of economic management now found in most economies, and often will be if they conflict with other current aims of national policy.

12

Nevertheless a country can consciously use this approach to deal with an external payments imbalance.

Third, a country can seek to suppress its external imbalance directly by adopting selective measures aimed at particular classes of international transactions. A surplus country can reduce or eliminate its tariffs or other import restrictions, tax its exports to discourage them, subsidize private capital outflows and boost its foreign aid programs, or control capital inflows. A deficit country can erect new barriers to imports, subsidize exports, cut back its overseas government expenditures, forbid or discourage capital outflows, or adopt incentives for capital inflows.

Fourth, a country can seek to adjust the imbalance directly by changing its exchange rate. Revaluation by a surplus country raises the prices of its exports and reduces the prices of its imports. This should cut its trade balance by reducing foreign demand for its products and increasing domestic demand for imports. By raising total national income, revaluation will also increase demand for imports of goods and services (such as foreign travel). And by raising the value of domestic money, it may generate excessive liquidity in the economy, which will produce capital exports and reduce its attractiveness to foreign investment. Devaluation can similarly provide adjustment for a deficit country.

The entire debate about international monetary arrangements is over the priorities to be accorded these four different approaches. Some argue that countries should be forced to adjust immediately and that no financing should be available. Within that broad approach, some say that such adjustment should always take place through domestic economic changes, while others advocate that it take place wholly through exchange-rate changes. At the other extreme, some dispute the desirability of adjustment and opt instead for extensive financing. Some see dangers in both excessive financing and adjustment through either the domestic economy or the exchange rate, and accordingly call for widespread use of selective controls to suppress imbalances and avoid the need for either financing or real adjustment. In short, virtually all possible combinations evoke some support from serious observers.

The adjustment and liquidity problems are linked inextricably. In economic terms, adjustment and liquidity are perfect substitutes for each other, at least in the short run: the more one is available, the less the other is needed. In a world with an infinite amount of reserves available to all countries, none would have to adjust its balance-of-payments position. Conversely, if adjustment were somehow to take place automatically, no liquidity would be required. One crucial question is thus the trade-off between the two: How much liquidity should the system provide, and how much adjustment should it require?

This question cuts to the heart of the international monetary problem, because any of the approaches to adjustment may be painful for the countries involved. Policies required to deal with the balance of payments may conflict with policies required to meet other national objectives. A surplus country with full employment, for example, may be unwilling to expand its economy further to reduce the surplus because of the concomitant risk of inflation. A deficit country with unemployment may be unwilling to depress domestic demand, and/or raise its interest rates, because the employment problem would be exacerbated. Such situations, frequently referred to as "dilemma" cases, render indirect adjustment via the domestic economy particularly unattractive. There are of course "non-dilemma" cases in which such conflicts between the external and internal effects of domestic economic policy measures do not arise, and in which adjustment of external imbalance via the domestic economy may be perfectly acceptable and even desirable; but there is no reason to expect such cases to predominate.[1]

In addition, a surplus country may resist appreciation of its exchange rate, either through its own action or through depreciations by others, in view of the unfavorable effect on the competitive position of its exporting and import-competing industries and the unemployment that may result. A deficit country may not wish to let its exchange rate depreciate because losses of real national income would result and inflation would be fostered. Income is redistributed within a society whenever it adopts either type of exchange-rate change. Real adjustment is thus often distasteful to both surplus and deficit countries, and neither may wish to adopt policies necessary to effect it.

But there are also instances in which countries *want* to adjust their external accounts in order to *help* them deal with internal problems. A successful devaluation increases domestic employment and a suc-

1. Michael Michaely, *The Responsiveness of Demand Policies to Balance of Payments: Postwar Patterns* (New York: Columbia University Press, 1971), pp. 33–36, found that about 20 percent of the payments imbalances of countries other than the United States during 1950–66 represented "dilemma" situations. The United States also presented such a case when its deficits coexisted with sizable domestic unemployment in both the early 1960s and the early 1970s, although the latter case was more complicated because of the simultaneous existance of significant inflation, an "internal dilemma" to which we turn later.

cessful revaluation helps fight domestic inflation. In such cases, however, other countries may resist such adjustment efforts because of the adverse effects on them—the country initiating the exchange-rate change is, in essence, seeking to export its unemployment or inflation to someone else. Hence, others may either block the action in the first place, if they can do so, or render the action ineffective by emulating it. So an effective adjustment process must limit the scope for national actions as well as facilitate those which are needed.

In addition to the real economic costs of adjustment, which occur no matter who triggers it, countries often have further reasons to resist taking the initiative to achieve it. A surplus country can avoid inflation if a deficit country deflates, and vice versa. A surplus country can avoid complications for its own policy if it can avoid lowering its interest rates by virtue of an increase in interest rates by a deficit country. And a deficit country can avoid the political implications of "a failure of past policy" if a surplus country revalues instead of itself having to devalue. Thus countries often have strong incentives to try to get others to initiate adjustment, even if they are prepared to accept the real effects—and the real effects may differ, to some extent, depending on who takes the initiative. International agreement on sharing the international costs of adjustment and on how to do so in practice would be needed to permit an ideal solution to the adjustment problem.[2]

Here is the link to liquidity. If all countries resisted adjustment, it would be possible simply to finance imbalances indefinitely. But excessive financing could permit deficit countries to drain real resources away from surplus countries. This would redistribute international income in their favor and could cause excessive inflationary pressures in surplus countries. It explains why adjustment and liquidity may be perfect substitutes only in the "short" run; indefinite transfers of this type are likely to be unacceptable to the transferers. "Short" may turn out in practice to be quite long, however, because countries often like to run surpluses in their trade and payments balances despite the losses of real resources and the inflationary pressures that result and because some surplus countries—such as those oil exporters with huge payments surpluses and small populations—simply cannot absorb the real resources which their surpluses could finance.

2. The absence of such agreement is apparent from actual events. It was recorded explicitly in *The Balance of Payments Adjustment Process*, A Report by Working Party No. 3 of the OECD, August 1966, p. 26; and remains, as of this writing, despite the verbal agreements in the Committee of Twenty on the principle of "greater symmetry between surplus and deficit countries."

At the same time, insufficient financing for payments deficits could force countries to take precipitate measures harmful not only to their own national objectives but also to the welfare of the world—as, for example, in the case of new controls over trade and international capital flows or excessive exchange-rate depreciations. Indeed, it is quite likely that a monetary system which is short of liquidity *will* produce a proliferation of controls and competitive exchange-rate devaluations, including non-revaluations. A balanced international monetary system should thus provide enough liquidity to permit avoidance of undesirable adjustment policies, but not so much liquidity that inflation and unacceptable international resource transfers are promoted for lengthy periods of time. The definitions of "enough," "undesirable," and "lengthy" in this formulation are key elements in the differences in national attitudes toward international monetary arrangements.

The need for international liquidity goes further than just to finance current imbalances. Most countries want steady increases in their reserves over time to improve their capabilities to avoid being forced to adjust *future* payments imbalances precipitately, since such imbalances are likely to rise as the scale of international transactions rises in the absence of the adoption of some automatic adjustment mechanism.[3] The sharp growth in scale of international capital movements, which can cause huge swings in national payments positions, quite understandably adds to such desires. For example, the United Kingdom lost more than one-third of its total reserves in less than two weeks in June 1972. Unless total world liquidity is rising, increases in one country's reserves can take place only if there is a corresponding decline in another's. Since few countries have ever been willing to see their reserves decline by any sizable amount for any sustained period of time, the countries losing reserves would soon take counteraction to stop their losses and attempt to reconstitute their previous levels. If the adjustment process worked effecively, this might

---

3. Reserves probably need not grow as fast as the level of transactions; more likely they need to be keyed to the *variance* of annual changes in the level of, e.g., imports, which rises less rapidly than imports themselves; see H.G. Olivera, "A Note on the Optimal Growth of International Reserves," *Journal of Political Economy*, Vol. 77, No. 2 (March–April 1969), pp. 245–48. However, the variance of payments imbalances seemed to be rising at least in the late 1960s, so the need for increases in reserves might not slacken even if this more sophisticated concept were widely adopted; see G.C. Archibald and J. Richmond, "On the Theory of Foreign Exchange Requirements," *Review of Economic Studies*, Vol. 38, No. 2 (April 1971), pp. 245–63. A useful survey of this issue is Herbert Grubel, "The Demand for International Reserves: A Critical Review of the Literature," *Journal of Economic Literature*, Vol. IX, No. 4 (December 1971), pp. 1148–66.

be all right. If it did not, the widespread desires for increasing reserves could generate a sharply escalating series of restrictive internal and external policies, with a consequent slowing of world trade and economic growth and attendant political problems, unless the total amount of world liquidity is assured of rising over time. At the same time, countries do not wish to sterilize in the form of reserves too many resources that could be used elsewhere. Different countries have different views on this trade-off, and it is not at all clear how countries make their judgments on the issue, if in fact they make conscious judgments on it at all. Empirical analysis of the 1953–65 period indicates that the growth of the magnitude of swings in national payments positions, a reasonable proxy for estimating the desires of countries for reserve growth, averaged about 6 per cent annually for a broad cross-section of forty-six countries (excluding the United States).[4]

An insufficiency of liquidity can thus have a decidedly deflationary impact on the world economy by forcing precipitate adjustment of payments imbalances, and even by encouraging "adjustment" to build reserves where current imbalances do not exist. Too much liquidity, on the other hand, could permit postponement of needed adjustment and, hence, promote inflationary tendencies around the world.

In addition to the liquidity needs of national authorities for use in settling national balance-of-payments positions, adequate and internationally acceptable liquidity is also needed by private citizens who carry out international transactions. It would be needed even under a monetary system—such as one based on freely flexible exchange rates —which in principle required no official reserves at all. Since supplies of gold are sharply limited and since the international reserve assets (SDRs and IMF credits) cannot be used by the private sector, national currencies dominate this function.

Increasing amounts of national currencies will continue to be needed by traders and investors in private international finance as the volume of international transactions grow.[5] Efficiency is increased

---

4. M. G. Kelly, "The Demand for International Reserves," *American Economic Review*, Vol. LX, No. 4 (September 1970), pp. 655–67. For a variety of technical reasons, spelled out in my *Reforming the Dollar* (*op. cit.*), pp. 24–25, this figure would probably provide too low an estimate of needed reserve growth for any system in the future *with a similarly rigid adjustment process.*

5. An increasing velocity of money would also help this need. Indeed, it has already done so, partly through the Eurodollar market. See Fred H. Klopstock, "The Eurodollar Market: Some Unresolved Issues," *Princeton Essays in International Finance*, No. 65, March 1968, pp. 4–6.

by centralization of this transaction-currency function, by minimizing transactions costs and maximizing convenience, and so there is a tendency for a single national currency to play a large part of the role.[6] Because of the efficiency of relying heavily on a single national currency for private international finance, maximum use of a single national currency will also be optimal for intervention in the private foreign-exchange markets by monetary authorities—which is required in virtually all conceivable international monetary systems. In addition, some countries can always be expected to want to hold national currencies in their reserves—and some have done so for almost a century—for reasons discussed in detail in Chapters 4 and 5. In short, there is a strong tendency for national currencies to meet at least a part of the several international needs for liquidity, as we shall see more fully in Chapter 3.

The third aspect of the international monetary problem is the so-called confidence, or stability, issue. This is simply the modern equivalent of Gresham's Law and applies to both the official and private liquidity situations. When any monetary system contains more than one monetary asset, there is a possibility of shifts among the assets that could undermine the entire system. The reserves of national authorities are now held in a variety of forms: dollars, gold, marks, Special Drawing Rights (SDRs),[7] sterling, claims on the International Monetary Fund, and holdings of several other national currencies. The resulting potential for disruption was seen clearly in the sizable shifts from sterling into dollars and gold after Britain devalued in 1967. Gold, dollars, marks, sterling, and several other national currencies are also held widely by private citizens around the world, and shifts among them can thus both occur beyond the reach of the monetary authorities and cause private confidence problems even if the official holders insulate themselves—as they did from gold, in March 1968, by completely divorcing official from private gold trans-

6. See Alexander K. Swoboda, "The Eurodollar Market: An Interpretation," *Princeton Essays in International Finance*, No. 64, February 1964, pp. 8–11. Charles P. Kindleberger has also made this point in numerous places, for example, in "The Politics of International Money and World Language," *Princeton Essays in International Finance*, No. 61, August 1967, p. 3. There are no firm data on what share of world transactions are financed in particular currencies. An estimate of 20–25 percent for the dollar is derived from an analysis of the financing of Swedish trade in Sven Grassman, "A Fundamental Symmetry in International Payments Patterns," *Journal of International Economics*, Vol. 3, No. 2 (May 1973), pp. 105–16.

7. SDRs were designed to avoid the shiftability problem: they can be used only when a country meets a balance-of-payments "needs test" (except for a few minor exceptions).

actions after the massive rush into gold from all national currencies in 1967–68. The massive shifts from dollars into other national currencies in 1970–71 is the most dramatic recent example.

The adjustment, liquidity, and confidence issues have to be addressed by any international monetary system. There are three very different *ways* of doing so. The handling of these issues can simply emerge from the uncoordinated play of market forces among countries of relatively equal weight. Another way is domination by a single country. Or the issues can be consciously coordinated among at least the several major powers. History provides examples of all three types of systemic "organization." Before examining past and present systems in Chapter 3, however, we must first turn to the political considerations which motivate countries to take particular positions on each of these key international monetary issues. These political factors, which underlie the creation (de facto or de jure) of any international monetary system, must be discussed under the two broad headings: national goals, and national capabilities.

The Politics of International Money: National Goals[8]

Countries have two basic objectives in developing their international monetary policies, as they do in developing any aspect of their foreign policies: they want to minimize external constraints on their own actions, and maximize their gains from dealing with the rest of the world. This means, for example, that countries want to avoid being forced to adjust by others, but want to be able to adjust effectively when their own objectives call for that step. They can pursue these objectives through their own policies and by influencing the policies of others.

Within these broad limits, different countries have very different sets of specific goals and capabilities for achieving them. Some of these goals and capabilities are basically economic, some are basically political. They can change over time, although some lie surprisingly deep in national attitudes and behavior and thus have produced surprisingly similar underpinnings for each of the several monetary systems developed in the past. As they are basic to an understanding of what motivates countries to behave as they do on the international monetary scene, each will be analyzed in terms of how it affects national views on the three key international monetary issues:

8. For brief but penetrating earlier discussions, see Francis A. Bator, "The Political Economics of International Money," *Foreign Affairs*, Vol. 47, No. 1 (October 1968), pp. 51–67, and Charles P. Kindelberger, *Power and Money* (New York: Basic Books, 1970), especially Chapters 13–14.

1. What should be the trade-off between liquidity and adjustment?
2. How should liquidity be produced: by a non-national asset like gold or silver, national currencies like the dollar or sterling, or international assets like SDRs or IMF drawing rights?
3. How should adjustment be pursued: through macroeconomic internal policies, through selective controls on external transactions, or through changes in exchange rates?

In determining national goals, the first key element is the degree to which a given national economy is dependent on international transactions. A country which is relatively "open" to the world readily perceives that its national welfare relies importantly on the maintenance of a monetary system which avoids impediments to international transactions and disequilibrium exchange rates, because the resulting distortions carry significant costs for its economy.[9] Indeed, the costs are so significant that they cannot be permitted to persist for very long—and thus pre-emptive action should be taken if at all possible. By contrast, a country which is relatively "closed"[10] to the world economy can more easily afford such distortions, at a minimum delaying its response to them and perhaps avoiding them indefinitely.[11]

Open economies will thus generally prefer adjustment to financing, while closed ones will prefer financing. Within the spectrum of adjustment alternatives, open economies will have a relative policy preference for internal policy measures, less taste for exchange-rate changes, and will generally oppose controls. Closed economies will tend more toward controls and will certainly prefer exchange-rate changes to internal adjustment. Table 1 arrays the major countries

9. For the classic theoretical treatment of why such costs are much higher in open than in closed economies, and for some empirical estimates of the differences, see Harry G. Johnson, "The Costs of Protection and Self-sufficiency," *Quarterly Journal of Economics*, Vol. 79 (August 1965), pp. 356–72.

10. Note that the terms "open" and "closed" do not refer to whether the country follows a liberal or protectionist trade policy, but simply to its degree of international economic involvement. The analysis in the text does suggest a positive correlation, however, between the two types of openness.

11. When such closed economies are quite large, as is frequently the case, their own actions can seriously affect the functioning of the entire system and feed back through it to affect their own interests. Thus, very closed as well as very open economies have important interests in an effective system, but their time and policy preferences may be quite different. The main potential troublemakers may in fact be middle-sized countries, which are too small (or at least perceive themselves to be too small) to affect the system significantly themselves, but which are sufficiently closed to accept systemic shortcomings and noncooperative behavior.

Table 1

ECONOMIC OPENNESS RATIOS, 1960–64 AVERAGES
(In per cent of gross national product)

	Exports plus imports of goods and services	Exports plus imports of goods	Gross capital flows
Netherlands	.8745	.6834	.0879
Norway	.8530	.5048	.0589
Belgium	.7230	.5752	.0592
Switzerland	.6809	.5108	.1010
Sweden	.5248	.4266	.0326
Austria	.4956	.3833	.0383
United Kingdom	.4354	.2902	.0651
Canada	.4303	.3305	.0741
Germany	.3664	.2843	.0385
Italy	.3504	.2506	.0704
Spain	.2381	.1636	.0449
Japan	.2350	.1912	.0415
France	.2197	.1612	.0325
United States	.1010	.0659	.0205

Source: Adapted from Marina V.N. Whitman, "Economic Openness and International Financial Flows, *Journal of Money, Credit, and Banking*, Vol. I, No. 4 (Nov. 1969), pp. 748–49. Most of these ratios have risen in absolute terms, as shown for some countries in Table 18, but there is no reason to suspect significant changes in the ranking of the countries.

according to the degree of their openness to the world economy. The most open economies—the Low Countries, Switzerland, the Scandinavian countries, and among the middle-sized countries, Germany and Britain—have been the strongest advocates of liberal trade and free capital movements. The more closed economies, such as Japan and France, have been much more protectionist. The United States has also had perennially strong undercurrents of protectionism, which were largely overridden from 1934 through at least 1962 but which threatened to reappear in the 1970s.[12] Individual European countries may well become more protectionist toward the outside world as they coalesce into an expanded European Community, which, as a whole, is as closed to the world economy as is Japan (see Table 18).

The attitudes of some countries toward controls are also influenced by their peculiar historical experiences and cultural outlooks. The United States perceives its own economic success to be a result of

12. See C. Fred Bergsten, "Crisis in U.S. Trade Policy," *Foreign Affairs*, July 1971.

relatively unfettered free enterprise, maintains a deep concern for the inequities which inevitably flow from controls, regards bureaucracy with general distaste, and blanches at the programmatic problems of controlling such a huge economy. These views counterbalance the proclivity toward controls that might be expected in an economy as closed as is the American, though they do so more with regard to domestic adjustment options, such as incomes policies, than to controls limited solely to external transactions themselves. Germany abhors controls because of their use in the totalitarian politics of the Nazis, and because of a widespread perception that the postwar economic miracle resulted from the adoption of market economics in the late 1940s. These historical considerations reinforce the German opposition to controls based on the economy's openness.

A second key political factor is the economic policy preference of each country. Everybody wants both full employment and stable prices, but each country must accept a trade-off between the two. The trade-off is depicted by the "Phillips curve," which shows for each country how much unemployment is usually associated with how much inflation.[13] In addition to possessing different capabilities to effect this trade-off (discussed below because they are an important determinant of overall national adjustment capabilities), countries have different goals concerning it. Even if all national Phillips curves were identical, countries might well seek to locate at different points on them at any given time.

Historical and social factors often determine these preferences. Germany has placed very high priority on price stability in view of its traumatic experiences with hyper-inflation after each world war, which wiped out the value of its domestic currency, and its relative insulation from the later stages of the mass unemployment of the Great Depression. As a result, its labor unions were relatively docile throughout most of the postwar period and remain far less militant than unions in other countries. In addition, a large part of the German labor force in recent years has been comprised of foreigners with temporary work permits, so that any increase in "German" unemployment could be readily passed on to Turkey, Italy, Yugoslavia, and the other home countries of the imported workers. Indeed, the postwar

13. The classic source is A. W. Phillips. "The Relation Between Unemployment and the Rate of Change of Money Wage Rates in the United Kingdom, 1861–1957," Economica, New Series, Vol. XXV (1958), pp. 283–99. It should be noted that there is considerable debate among economists over the validity of "Phillips curves," even as descriptive tools, and even greater debate over the necessity of trading off more unemployment to get less inflation (or vice-versa) which they imply.

experience of Germany has been a brilliant success story of full employment and rapid growth, in which price stability *was* the major
internal economic problem. Most of the smaller countries of continental Western Europe have a similar postwar history and tilt toward
the German preference for anti-inflationary policies, though without
the extreme emphasis wrought in Germany by its history.

In contrast, the United Kingdom suffered from mass unemployment throughout the interwar period, and the United States was
severely racked in the Depression. Both have experienced severe unemployment and mediocre growth for prolonged periods in the postwar years. Neither has experienced runaway inflation, although the
rising prices of the early 1970s have given both a sharp taste of price
instability. Nevertheless, both tend to fear inflation less than unemployment, and accordingly are more likely to opt for expansionist
policies.

Countries whose priority is full employment will prefer to maximize the availability of international liquidity in order to minimize
the risk that they might have to tighten their own economies for
adjustment purposes. Countries more conscious of price stability will
opt for less liquidity and more adjustment instead. Price-conscious
countries may in fact be the least unwilling to revalue their currencies
because of the helpful anti-inflationary effects and because the chief
alternative when they are in surplus—additional internal expansion—
is directly inflationary. They may also use controls in an effort to
resist the liquidity effects of capital inflows to correct a deficit, and
they would be relatively willing to check internal growth. By contrast, countries which most fear unemployment would resist deflation,
opting instead for devaluation or controls.

These considerations lead countries to seek to impose their own
policy preferences on others. The rates of inflation in the system as a
whole can be held down if deficit countries adjust by deflating. The
rate of unemployment in the system as a whole can be held down if
surplus countries adjust by inflating. Britain constantly sought to promote U.S. inflation in the 1920s, and Germany constantly sought to
promote U.S. deflation in the 1960s. In practice, of course, this jousting may lead to the rejection of internal adjustment by both surplus
and deficit countries. If it does, then the systemic rate of inflation can
best be held down if the surplus countries revalue, and systemic unemployment can best be checked if the deficit countries devalue. In
principle, the choice should depend on whether the world as a whole
was facing excessive inflation or excessive unemployment. In practice,
however, the global preference is clear only in extreme situations such
as the Great Depression and, perhaps the global inflation of the early

1970s. The different national tastes just described thus are quite likely to promote policy conflict at most times.

Historic experience with inflation also has an effect on the liquidity choices of a country, by making its citizens wary of all paper money (and of governments, which are usually responsible for printing it). Thus, the United States, United Kingdom, and Japan make very little of gold and a show of willingness to trust a new paper asset like SDR. Continental Europeans, on the other hand, like gold. They are more leery of the use of national currencies and, perhaps even more so, of a synthetic money like SDRs as reserve assets.

A third difference lies in the basic foreign policy of different countries. Some countries are overtly mercantilistic, seeking consistently to run sizable trade and payments surpluses, and thus adding a major drive for net exports to their drive to build reserves.[14] Some pursue these mercantilist objectives for purely economic reasons, viewing export markets as essential for achieving economies of scale in production, and as providing job opportunities more reliably than the smaller (and perhaps more volatile) domestic market. Japan and Germany are the clearest examples but the United Kingdom may now also be in this camp—witness the focus of its overall foreign policy for a decade on obtaining entry to the European Community (EC) as the best hope for the British economy. Some countries remain mercantilist, however, for the broad foreign policy reasons that marked mercantilism as the reigning doctrine of economic thought before Adam Smith. They reason that large reserves and payments surpluses, which are key elements of international monetary power, enable them to exert leverage on noneconomic issues as well. France has always had this attitude, which reached its zenith under de Gaulle.

Some countries, by contrast, have traditionally not sought trade and payments surpluses. They have preferred to use their export and other current account earnings to acquire real resources from the rest of the world, including investments abroad, rather than to build up reserves. The United States and Britain, in earlier periods, are the classic cases of this anti-mercantilist approach. (France was a major foreign investor before World War I but lost most of its holdings by the Soviet take-over in Russia, and has since limited its foreign

14. The distinction between *trade* and *payments* surpluses will recur throughout this book. Classical mercantilist doctrine called for both. But trade surpluses provide jobs directly, while payments surpluses provide "only" the wherewithal—additional reserves—to avoid the risks of having to give up jobs at some later date. The United States, for example, lived with payments deficits for two decades but acted decisively—and understandably, to most other countries—when faced with the prospect of continuing trade deficits.

ventures largely to its colonies and, after their independence, the franc zone.)

The explanation for these fundamentally different approaches probably lies in the basic foreign policy of each country. The Uinted States and United Kingdom adopted their anti-mercantilist policies when they exercised a heavy political responsibility for world security and saw such policies as important economic means to help achieve their political ends. (As we shall see in Chapter 4, these policies and their political underpinnings are inextricably bound up with the key international roles of the dollar and sterling.) In periods before and after they exercised these responsibilities, they were far more prone to join the mercantilist jousting. The international political reasons seem particularly compelling because, as noted above, economic concerns in both countries usually center on unemployment more than on inflation and hence would add to the likelihood of mercantilist behavior on purely economic grounds.

Mercantilist countries want adjustment rather than financing if they are in deficit—preferably through devaluation—to enable them to recapture their desired trade and payments surpluses. Indeed, they seek undervalued exchange rates and may even be willing to accept domestic unemployment to achieve external surpluses. France is the clearest case in modern history, having established undervalued rates (which contributed heavily to subsequent systemic problems) in 1927, 1958, and 1969. Japan and Germany are its closest modern rivals, though the mercantilist zeal of both (particularly Germany) waned in the early 1970s as external policy was forced to focus on fighting inflation rather than on preserving the international competitiveness of domestic industries.

On the other hand, mercantilist countries fiercely resist taking any adjustment initiatives when they are in surplus. They generally prefer to finance deficit countries, even when weighed against adjustment initiatives by the latter. Their mercantilist desire to have ample liquidity for themselves generally leads them to support large-scale creation of global liquidity, as Japan has done. France's opposition to the creation of SDRs and external dollar balances was based on its objection to that *form* of reserve creation, combined with the view that, as a medium-sized power with little reluctance to devalue or impose controls to pursue its national aims, it would have little trouble in achieving trade and payments surpluses even within a system which caused major problems for most other countries.

By contrast, nonmercantilist countries accept financing for deficits rather than adjustment to them, and may even initiate adjustment when in surplus. Britain, for example, adopted a grossly overvalued exchange rate in 1926 and maintained one through most of the 1960s, thereby contribtuing much to subsequent systemic upheavals. But the clearest case was the United States prior to August 1971 (when it turned mercantilist, at least temporarily, with a vengeance): it actively adjusted its surplus of the early postwar period, and regarded with "benign neglect" both a reserve drain for over two decades and elimination of its trade surplus in both the late 1950s and early 1970s.

If all countries play the mercantilist game, any international monetary system is obviously subject to much trouble. Sizable increases in global liquidity might conceivably reconcile a widespread desire for payments surpluses. But even exceedingly generous liquidity growth would not necessarily satisfy the desire for *trade* surpluses, which can be met only by the existence of trade deficits elsewhere, and enough financing for the countries willing to run trade deficits to enable them to achieve payments equilibrium.[15]

As discussed in Chapter 3 the monetary system did in fact collapse when all major countries adopted mercantilist policies, for internal economic reasons, in the 1930s and again in 1971. We will also see that systems dominated by a single national power (Britain prior to 1914 and the United States throughout the first postwar generation) were effective only when that power rejected mercantilism. By doing so, such powers played the role of residual balancers, which permitted others to achieve their goals—and they received financing, primarily through the buildup of foreign holdings of their currencies, which permitted them to do so. The reversion to mercantilism by the United States in August 1971—which suggests a return to its policies of the 1930s but is incomparably more dangerous, both because U.S. relative power is now so much greater and because it represents such a sharp reversal from the "benign neglect" practiced until that date—thus raises major doubts about the viability of any system for the future.

Before we turn to what determines the capabilities of countries to achieve their goals, a few conclusions are evident. The first is that

15. This possibility underlies the primary argument, from the standpoint of the international monetary system, for linking reserve creation to development financing. If most of the industrialized countries seek trade surpluses, most of the lower income countries must run trade deficits which are quite sizable relative to their owned reserves. One way to reconcile the dilemma would be to distribute sufficient amounts of SDRs to the lower income countries to permit such trade patterns to develop. The alternative is a sharp increase in private capital flows from the industrialized to the lower income countries, but this would further increase the foreign debt burdens of the latter and hence might be unacceptable to them.

there are few consistent patterns among the goals sought by individual countries. It is particularly interesting to note that the large EC countries—Britain, Germany and France—have different views among them on every issue. The Phillips curve preferences of the United Kingdom are similar to those of France, but different from those of Germany. Britain is aligned with Germany *vis-à-vis* France in terms of economic openness. But it stands between the other two in terms of proclivity toward controls, an issue on which the smaller and more open countries join Germany *vis-à-vis* France. Germany and France are close together on mercantilist economics, however, with Britain (and the smaller countries) less inclined in that direction. Similarly, Japan and the United States align differently with various European countries on different issues—though Japan and France display consistently similar patterns. All these variations of course produce a constantly changing pattern of alliances on individual issues.

A second conclusion is that there appears to be some convergence of the goals of the major countries. The prolonged and extremely rapid price rises in the United States since 1966, and in Britain throughout the 1960s and early 1970s, have tilted policy concerns in both countries more toward inflation, relative to unemployment, than has generally been the case in the past. As already noted, the United States, like Britain long before, has shifted toward the mercantilism consistently practiced by most others throughout the relevant past. The European Community, by expanding its membership, has become a much more closed economy than any of its constituent parts were before. Three large economic centers—the United States, the European Community, and Japan—have thus become remarkably similar in terms of the key criterion of "openness." The pressure of events has forced both Germany and the United States to accept some controls over their international transactions, and has probably reduced the abhorrence of each toward such measures for the future.

The effect of most of these convergences is indeterminate, however. The emergence of a closer identity of anti-inflationary concerns may be integrative and help solve systemic problems, perhaps by cutting back on excessive liquidity creation. But it may also be disintegrative if countries seek to export inflation to each other through competitive revaluations, just as they previously sought to export unemployment to each other through competitive devaluations. The U.S. entry into mercantilist competition—which means that it joins the scramble for trade surpluses and reserves, and reduces its willingness to use its foreign economic policy to pursue broad systemic objectives—may be disintegrative and exacerbate policy conflict. Indeed, *divergent* attitudes toward mercantilist objectives would ease systemic problems as they did throughout the period of U.S. "benign neglect." The emergence of closer agreement on the acceptability of controls may foster more international agreement, but agreement along such lines may not solve any of the underlying problems and could even make them worse. Even more important, the movement of the three big economic powers toward greater similarity, as relatively closed economic structures, could either produce similar attitudes and hence solid bases for agreement or be disintegrative because the costs of nonagreement are reduced by the fact of being closed.[16]

These convergences raise one other critical point. Countries obviously cannot use their external economic policies both mercantilistically and to fight inflation at the same time, since the former calls for surpluses and the latter for deficits. The ideal solution is thus for different sets of countries to have sharply different problems at the same time, some with unemployment and some with inflation, so that both sets will be happy for the former to run surpluses and the latter to run deficits. (Indeed, there is a minority interpretation that preoccupation with inflation explains why the United States was prepared to run payments deficits that for so long enabled other countries to satisfy their desire for surpluses.) But a steady succession of such happy coincidences can hardly be counted on, and indeed is rendered increasingly unlikely by the apparent *reduction* in cyclical differences that arises from the continuing growth of international economic interdependence. So the result may be the worst of all worlds: countries vying to export inflation to each other during world booms, and to export unemployment to each other during world slowdowns. In these cases, the outcome would turn largely on the capabilities of individual nations to pursue their objectives, to the analysis of which we now turn.

The Politics of International Money: National Power

The international monetary capabilities of individual countries are functions of both their economic and political power. Some countries have little or no international monetary power. Others have enough to permit them to avoid external constraints on their behavior (negative power). Some may in addition have sufficient power to block actions desired by others (veto power). Finally, some may also be

---

16. Two theoretically possible convergences would clearly help resolve systemic conflict: rejection of mercantilism by all countries, and the breakup of present economic units into much more open economies. Both obviously run counter to present trends.

able to influence or even determine the behavior of others (positive power).

Again, the first key element is a country's size. Both the sizes of its Gross National Product and the volume of its trade, capital movements, and other international transactions are vitally important. Countries with large GNPs, which are also usually relatively closed to the world economy, can most easily remain aloof from international pressures. As we have seen, they can most easily afford external disequilibrium and thus resist real adjustment; accordingly, they have a great deal of negative power.

Countries with a large volume of international transactions are able to affect other countries and the entire system significantly, and hence wield positive power. They can deny exports of goods and capital, cut off markets, or seize foreign investments. If their volume of transactions is sufficiently large, they can even throw the major costs of adjustment onto other countries by their own actions—for example, pre-1914 Britain is viewed by some analysts as having been able to make other countries lower their export prices by raising its own bank rate, which had the effect of raising their costs of maintaining inventories and orderly marketing procedures.

The inherently strongest power position is that of a country which is relatively closed to the world economy yet which accounts for a large share of international economic transactions, wielding both negative and positive power as a result. The United States is the obvious prototype. The European Community as a group, however, already accounts for a larger share of world trade than does the United States, and its firms may be less open to the outside world than are U.S. firms when both trade and investment are considered. It is true that the EC remains significantly more open than the United States in absolute terms and thus probably possesses more positive than negative power. Germany and Japan are the individual countries which rank closest behind the United States in this matrix. The German export level now matches the American, but Germany remains much more open and the volume of Japan's international transactions is still much less. The U.S.S.R. wields sizable negative international economic power because of its closed economy, but little positive power because of the low level of its international transactions. France, though less extreme on both counts, is next closest to this end of the spectrum.

Conversely, small (and thus usually open) countries are deeply affected by the world economy and usually have little power to withstand external events except at high cost. (Their political desire for "symmetry" with bigger countries thus adds to their desire to see adjustment prevail over financing in the system as a whole, which they already prefer on economic grounds, as outlined above.) Their economic weight is so small that they also can have little effect on other countries. Again, the size of a country's GNP is more important in determining its ability to withstand external influences (negative power), while the size of its external sector is more important for its ability to influence others (positive power). Some of the smaller European countries have more positive than negative power, because of the very high levels of their world trade (Netherlands) and financial involvement (Switzerland) relative to the size of their internal economies, but they can use that positive power only at great risk because their lack of negative power makes them so vulnerable to retaliation.[17] The oil exporting countries have apparently acquired enough positive power in the middle 1970s to more than offset their near-total absence of negative power.

A large part of the struggle for international monetary power represents an effort by smaller countries to narrow the structural gap caused by disparate national size. The gap can be narrowed only in two ways. A country can achieve extremely rapid growth of GNP and external transactions relative to the larger country, as did the United States relative to Britain and France in an earlier period and, more recently, the European Community and Japan relative to the United States. Or the smaller states can combine, as did the gold bloc against the sterling area in the 1930, the sterling bloc and the European Payments Union against the United States in the early postwar period, and, more recently, the European Community and the oil exporting countries. (Some of these steps were taken explicitly for international monetary reasons, while the international monetary power effects were merely by-products for the others.) These steps may frequently pay off, because large countries can wield great international economic power only if the size disparity is very great, as was the case with the United Kingdom in the nineteenth century and with the United States in the early postwar period. Small countries are powerless only if they are truly infinitesimal, and the history of economic development clearly shows that at least some of

17. Karl Deutsch, *The Analysis of International Relations* (Englewood Cliffs, N.J.: Prentice-Hall, 1968), p. 32, points to the "range of power"—the difference between the highest reward a country can get, and the most severe punishment it can suffer—as an important determinant of power. Such a range in the monetary area is by far greater for small and open countries, which have both much to gain and much to lose from the world ·conomy, than for large and closed countries.

the "trailing" economic powers are always in the process of catching up with the erstwhile leader. In addition, jousting for relative superiority among the group of middle countries is another major goal in the race for international monetary power, particularly if the objective of narrowing the lead of a dominant power appears hopeless because that lead is so overwhelming.

The second key element of a country's international monetary power is its international political position, which relates closely to its military power. This too is partly a function of national size, since a country can more easily develop major political power on a sizable economic base. However, many large countries have limited military power (Germany and Japan since 1945), and some smaller countries have developed relatively important political roles. In this nuclear age, for example, China, which is quite small in economic terms, wields a great deal of military and hence political power. The larger security and foreign policy objectives of a country thus intertwine with its underlying economic capabilities in determining its international monetary power.

But different countries translate their political power into monetary power to significantly different degrees. Some may view their international economic goals as sufficiently important to pursue them through the use of their international political power, as did Britain and other imperialist nations in an earlier epoch. Some may place such high priority on security concerns, and pay such little attention to international economics, that they neither want to use political power to pursue economic objectives nor are organized to do so. Indeed, like the United States throughout the earlier postwar period, they may use economic policies primarily in support of their security objectives.

A country with less international power often finds itself dependent upon a country with greater power. As a result, it may be required to take international monetary measures dictated by the power on which it depends. Many members of the sterling area, particularly smaller states such as Kuwait and Hong Kong in times past, depended on the British navy for their security and held their reserves in sterling as a major quid pro quo. It is no accident that the largest dollar holders are Germany and Japan, despite the significant differences between their economic goals and those of the United States; both have relied on the latter for their security throughout the postwar period. Indeed, the most important postwar step in insulating the United States from external pressure on its reserves was the explicit pledge by Germany—the most persistent surplus country in the world—not to use any of its dollars to buy U.S. gold, which was an implicit quid pro quo negotiated in 1967 for the maintenance of unchanged American troop levels in Germany. Some smaller countries which depend on U.S. protection and aid, such as Korea and Taiwan, have adopted similarly (if not such explicitly) "cooperative" international monetary policies.

These political and security factors underlie all economic relations among nations, but their importance changes over time as world tensions ebb and flow. Political factors may dominate economic relations during periods of extreme international insecurity, particularly during wars, including Cold War. They become less important when international tensions are low.

In addition, few countries coordinate their security and international economic policies on a daily basis. Different officials are responsible for the two broad areas of policy. They may be unfamiliar with the other area, too constrained simply by the demands on their own time to work actively on both, implicit parties to nonaggression treaties in which they keep out of each other's business, and afraid to take on issues within the other's sphere for fear of losing and undermining their positions in their own sphere of influence.[18] Thus it is much more likely that political power will be brought to bear *ad hoc* on individual issues of great importance which come to the attention of top officials (including heads of state) than on the more routine (even if quite important) daily business which characterizes international economic relations.

In addition, crises arise so rapidly that even the best organized country will find it difficult to mobilize its political leverage in time to help. A politically powerful country can best utilize its leverage on an economic issue if that issue requires negotiations over an extended period of time. The best examples from recent U.S. history are the monetary-trade crisis in the fall of 1971, which was eventually settled by heads of state; the SDR negotiation, in which President Johnson took a personal interest; and several of the military offset negotiations with Germany. In marked contrast are several failures: to get Germany to revalue at the Bonn conference in November 1968, where the United States saw a major issue but did not have time to mobilize much of a campaign; to make any significant headway in 1970 on reforming the system to get greater flexibility of exchange rates, which never received a high-level political push; and after September

18. See Morton A. Halperin, *Bureaucratic Politics and Foreign Policy* (Washington, D.C.: Brookings Institution, 1974).

1972, when U.S. proposals for comprehensive systemic reform suffered similar political neglect.[19]

Countries which seek to use their international political power for economic objectives, and organize themselves to do so, can thereby provide a boost for their international monetary power. But the narrowly international monetary elements of international monetary power may thus play a dominant role in everyday business in this field, as well as an important role in all such relations. Five different considerations are involved: the level of a country's reserves, its ability to create money,[20] its ability to get credit, its ability to block the creation of international money or granting of credit to others, and its ability to run payments surpluses through adjustment of its own policies at acceptable costs. The importance of each differs sharply depending upon the nature of the international monetary system at any given time. We consider each in turn.

Large reserves permit a country to delay adjustment of a payments deficit. If underlying forces are working in the direction of eventual restoration of equilibrium, reserves may enable it to avoid altogether taking any steps solely for balance-of-payments reasons. Even if they are not, large reserves permit a country to adopt measures which will achieve adjustment gradually and hence avoid economic and political shocks. The advantage of large reserves is greatest in a monetary system in which adjustment is difficult, like the Bretton Woods system. It is least in a system where adjustment is rapid, like the pre-1914 "gold standard" or the post-1918 and post-March 1973 worlds of flexible exchange rates. We can already begin to see why the United States strongly supported the Bretton Woods system when it held two-thirds of world reserves, but had become an ardent advocate of exchange-rate flexibility by 1973 when its reserves, relative to its international transactions, were among the lowest of any major industrialized country.

Large reserve levels do not always correlate with national size. To be sure, the most extreme instance of a country whose reserves were so large that it could resist adjustment indefinitely was the United States in the early postwar period, largely as a result of the "golden

---

19. Shared attitudes on the economic exigencies of the moment, rather than any use of U.S. political leverage, seem to have motivated the agreements to realign parities in February 1973 and to abandon the defense of fixed rates in March 1973.

20. These first two considerations are stressed by Eugene A. Birnbaum, *Gold and the International Monetary System: An Orderly Reform*, Princeton Essays in International Finance, No. 66 (April 1968), especially pp. 5–6.

avalanche" which descended upon it as fears of war and an undervalued dollar produced massive capital flight from Europe in the late 1930s, and of its overwhelmingly superior economic position immediately after the war. As late as 1950, it possessed two-thirds of the total gold reserves of the non-Communist world.

Other large countries have not been in similar situations, however. Britain was the major manager of the pre-1914 monetary system on reserves which, at least in 1913, were far smaller than those of the United States, Russia, and France, and roughly equivalent to those of Italy, Germany, Austria-Hungary, Japan, and even India and Argentina.[21] But, as noted, adjustment was rapid at that time. The U.S.S.R. today has limited reserves and hence limited international monetary power, which may indicate one reason (in addition to obvious security motives) for its reluctance to join the non-Communist international monetary system.[22] About 1967, when it was becoming the third largest economy and fourth largest trading nation in the non-Communist world, Japan had gross reserves of only $2 billion, which were more than offset by its short-term liabilities to U.S. and Eurodollar banks.

The relationship of reserves to the size of a country's international transactions is more important than the relationship to its GNP, because the size of payments imbalances can be expected to correlate roughly with the value of these transactions, and the basic purpose of reserves is to finance such imbalances. The power of reserves to forestall adjustment flows mainly from this relationship. In the early 1970s, Switzerland has by far the highest ratio of reserves to imports among the major countries, and Spain and Portugal also rank high in this regard. The oil countries are already able to exert sizable power through their huge reserves (relative to their needs) and will be increasingly potent in the future. The Scandinavian countries, especially Sweden and Denmark, have the lowest ratios. The United States, from its previous position of extreme supremacy, is virtually at the bottom of the list, well behind Germany and Japan. (See Table 2 for details.)

The value of a country's reserves in augmenting its international monetary power depends in part on their quality. Gold is generally

---

21. Peter H. Lindert, *Key Currencies and Gold*, 1900–1913, Princeton Studies in International Finance, No. 24 (1969), pp. 10–11.
22. Its reluctance is increased by the possibility that its doing so would presumably require it to sell its gold at the official price, instead of the much higher free-market price, which would take away the increase in international monetary power that the U.S.S.R. achieved since the market price moved upward in the early 1970s.

Table 2

RESERVE ADEQUACY OF SELECTED COUNTRIES, 1974
(In millions of dollars)

Country	Reserves[a]	Imports (c.i.f.)	Months of Imports Covered
1. Saudi Arabia	14,285	3,473	49.3
2. Venezuela	6,529	4,042	19.4
3. Iran	8,383	5,974	16.8
4. Libya	3,616	3,140	13.8
5. Switzerland	9,011	14,422	7.5
6. Portugal	2,354	3,988[b]	7.1
7. Germany	32,399	68,885	5.6
8. Spain	6,485	15,329	5.1
9. Austria	3,430	9,025	4.6
10. Australia	4,269	12,425	4.1
11. Brazil	5,252	15,708[b]	4.0
12. Norway	1,929	8,396	2.8
13. Japan	13,519	62,033	2.6
14. Netherlands	6,958	34,540[b]	2.4
15. Belgium	5,345	29,703	2.2
16. Italy	6,941	41,064	2.0
17. Canada	5,825	34,483	2.0
18. France	8,851	52,904	2.0
19. United States	16,058	107,996	1.8
20. United Kingdom	6,939	54,143	1.5
21. Sweden	1,735	16,220	1.3
22. Denmark	935	9,848	1.2

[a] Gold reserves valued at official price of $42.22 per ounce.
[b] Third quarter of 1974, annual rate.
Source: *International Financial Statistics*, April 1975.

viewed as being the least risky of present reserve assets, and the sizable premium for commodity gold in the private market enhances the traditional attraction of gold as an asset. Foreign-exchange holdings are generally viewed as less reliable, and indeed the value of both of the major reserve currencies was cut by sizable amounts in the 1930s and again in recent years. The gold value of SDRs is fully guaranteed, but the SDRs have no intrinsic value and depend on the maintenance of international monetary cooperation. Furthermore, only 70 per cent of them can in fact be regarded as true reserves under the original SDR rules, since 30 per cent of those actually used must be "reconstituted" at the IMF within five years.

The effects on each nation's monetary power of the decline in U.S. reserves throughout the postwar period, and the low level of British reserves prior to World War I, were offset to a sizable extent by the ability of both countries to create international liquidity through the widespread foreign acceptance of dollars and sterling as official reserve assets, and as private stores of value and media of exchange. U.S. liquid liabilities to all foreigners approached $100 billion in early 1973 —virtually all of which were accumulated in the postwar period—and hence provided an equal level of financing for U.S. foreign expenditures. Like gross reserves, the contribution to a country's international monetary power of the capacity to build up foreign liabilities relates directly to the difficulties of achieving effective adjustment under the prevailing monetary system.

Even reserve currency countries cannot create liquidity unilaterally, however. There must be willing (or coercible) holders for such balances to develop. Thus the power of a country to create its own money depends both on the economic attractiveness of such balances to others, which has thrust the mark into prominence in the early 1970s, and on its own political role, such as the security leverage exercised over Germany by the United States, to which reference has been made. (This whole issue is discussed in depth in Chapters 4–6.) An elimination of the reserve currency role of the dollar would of course reduce one key aspect of the international monetary power of the United States, just as a decline in the price of gold would sharply reduce the power of countries (including the United States) which held most of their reserves in that form.

Other important countries can influence the creation of world reserves through their votes on increases in IMF quotas and, since 1969, the creation of Special Drawing Rights. No country, however, including the United States, has ever had enough voting power in the IMF to control these decisions unilaterally. The United States does have enough votes to *block* such creation of world reserves, and can also veto efforts to create liquidity through an increase in the official price of gold. (Britain also had the latter veto power until 1970.) If it votes *en bloc*, the European Community can now exercise similar power. Indeed, this is the *only* way in which the EC can effectively block the creation of world reserves, which suggests that it would maximize its international monetary power under any system of relatively fixed exchange rates if SDRs were the primary monetary asset of such a system. The less developed countries, if they could agree to act together, could also exercise such a veto.[23]

23. Creation of SDRs requires a weighted vote of 85 per cent. A "uniform increase in par values," i.e., an incresae in the official price of gold, can be blocked by any country possessing 10 per cent of the total weighted rate. The United States now possesses about 22 per cent of weighted IMF votes; Britain, 9 per cent; and the enlarged EC, almost 30 per cent.

Blocking power over the creation of international liquidity is particularly important for surplus countries which want to force deficit countries to adjust rather than finance their deficits—perhaps in an effort to check world inflationary pressures. (Of course, as we have seen, some deficit countries, rather than adopt anti-inflationary measures, might devalue or adopt additional controls and thereby exacerbate world inflation instead.) In addition to doing so through the Fund, they could refuse to accept dollars, for example, and instead bring adjustment pressure on the United States: directly, as long as the dollar was convertible into U.S. reserve assets; indirectly by forcing dollar depreciation through the foreign exchange markets, as many of them had begun to do even before the U.S. actions of August 1971. In response to the first approach, a key currency country can suspend convertibility, as the United States did in August 1971. If it were unwilling to let its currency depreciate in value, however, its only recourse in the face of foreign sales of its currency would be to resume convertibility and to try to restore sufficient payments equilibrium to support it.

Two related aspects of international monetary power are a country's ability to obtain credit, or to block others from obtaining credit unless its own conditions are met. Some would argue that the creation of reserve currency balances is simply a special case of receiving credit, since interest is paid on them and they represent claims on the issuing authority. However, such "credits" have no fixed maturities; and, indeed, some foreign-held dollars may never be redeemed with U.S. reserve assets, partly because other countries may never want to give them all up, partly because the United States may never be willing (or even able) to convert them into alternative reserve assets. In addition, about one-half of the foreign private dollar holdings, and about 10 per cent of the official holdings, are in the form of demand deposits and do not draw interest in normal times. Accordingly, I classify reserve currency holdings as "owned reserves" of the holders, and distinguish between them and credits. Others would classify SDRs as credits, because countries have to pay interest on the "net use" of them, but I would accept this only for the 30 per cent of such assets which, under the original SDR rules, must be "reconstituted" at the IMF within five years of their use.

The ability to obtain credit depends on the credit-worthiness of a country, its importance in the monetary system, and its willingness to accept policy "guidance" from the lender. Unlike firms and individuals, however, industrialized countries as such do not borrow abroad to augment their working capital or to finance new investment. Most do so only to finance an overall payments deficit and avoid adjustment thereof, or as part of an adjustment program to assure that there is sufficient support to assure its success. Thus their success in attracting credit depends primarily on whether other countries want to help them avoid adjustment, and hence avoid the effects of such adjustment on themselves, or can use the leverage provided through the credit to extract a particular policy approach.

Such lending should be generally forthcoming if the world faces generally deflationary pressures and high unemployment. In the recent years of pervasive inflation, it is more likely that lending has been limited to countries sufficiently important to seriously disrupt the system by taking precipitate adjustment initiatives of a type uncongenial to the lender—such as devaluing, which would add to world inflation, rather than deflation, which would help counter it. Thus there is a high positive correlation between the ability of a country to attract credit and its importance in international monetary relations.

The massive credits extended to Britain throughout the 1960s were of this type, aimed first at enabling it to avoid devaluation and then at making the devaluation work in order to avoid a larger or a second devaluation. France could readily obtain credits because of fears that any devaluation it undertook would be excessive, and bring major pressure on other deficit countries (mainly the United States and Britain) as a result. The credit packages for the lira initiated by the United States in 1964 and by Germany in 1974 were based on fears that an Italian devaluation or trade controls could trigger widespread speculation against other currencies, including the dollar, and jeopardize the system. The lender can often attach conditions that will force the deficit country to take adjustment initiatives other than devaluations, particularly internal anti-inflation measures, which might act more slowly and hence require the credit to tide it over. The IMF attached such conditions to its loans to Britain *after* the 1967 devaluation, and thereby helped assure the success of the policy in eliminating British deficits for a while.

This assumes of course that countries in a position to extend credits possess similar views about the desirability of preserving the existing system, and agree that credits will help do so. Countries which disagree with either assumption, perhaps because they view the existing system as prejudicial to their interests, may try to block such credits instead. France abstained from some of the major credit packages to the British (and also dropped out of the gold pool) as part of its campaign in the mid-1960s to topple the reserve currency system, which it viewed as providing "exorbitant privileges" at least to the United States.

A major country could probably hold up or even block IMF credits, even if it did not possess enough votes to exercise a formal veto. However, it cannot block bilateral credits or an *ad hoc* multilateral credit package constructed by several willing donors. Indeed, the extensive network of international credit which developed during the 1960s—centered on the series of bilateral swaps between major foreign central banks and the Federal Reserve System—provided a convenient way to provide *ad hoc* financing and hence get around any insistence on adjustment, or on the form of international liquidity, by international minorities.

Finally, even without large reserves and recourse to foreign financing, a country can possess a good deal of international monetary power if it is able to adjust its payments deficits at relatively low cost. In such a position it will be able to avoid overt constraints from other countries. Conversely, a country which cannot adjust quickly and effectively becomes subject to considerable outside constraints on its actions. Of course, the need to adjust may already represent something of a constraint, so this element of monetary power is less than that which enables countries to avoid adjustment altogether by virtue of their liquidity capabilities.

Adjustment, it will be recalled, can take place either indirectly through altering the course of the domestic economy, or through measures aimed directly at the external accounts—exchange rate changes or selective controls. As the main cost of internal adjustment to a deficit country is the lost output and unemployment which may result from deflation, a country which could significantly dampen its price rises without causing much unemployment would have a potent adjustment tool.[24] The tool would be most potent in a fixed-rate system in which countries relied on internal measures to achieve adjustment.

Countries differ widely in the shapes of their "Phillips curves," which depict the relationship between unemployment and inflation in each that can be expected on the basis of past experience.[25] How-

---

24. The main cost of internal adjustment of a surplus country is the extra inflation which results; a country which could expand its economy without causing much inflation would be relatively efficient in eliminating surpluses. However, the ability to eliminate surpluses efficiently does not provide international monetary power, while the power to eliminate deficits efficiently does.

25. For a comparison of the Phillips curves in eleven key countries, see Eric Spitaller, "Prices and Unemployment in Selected Industrial Countries," *IMF Staff Papers*, Vol. XVIII, No. 3 (November 1971), pp. 528–67, from which the data in the text are drawn.

ever, there is striking similarity between the additional amounts of unemployment generated by similar reductions in inflation rates in the key countries. Cutting the rate of price increase from 5 to 4 per cent, for example, raises unemployment by 0.25–0.3 percentage points in all countries with comparable data—France, Japan, Sweden, Britain, the United States—except for Canada, where the increase is 0.6 percentage points.

When the rate of price increase drops from 4 to 3 per cent, Germany (and apparently Italy, although its data are not strictly comparable)suffers the smallest increase in unemployment (0.3 percentage points) and Canada again suffers most (0.7 points), with most countries clustered around 0.5 points. The United States (and Italy again) suffers least as inflation recedes from 3 to 2 per cent (0.4 points), with Canada again worst off (1.2 points) and others clustered around 0.6–0.8 points. (See Table 3 for the details.)

Table 3

COMPARISON OF NATIONAL "PHILLIPS CURVES"
(In 1970)

Is associated with an increase in unemployment in:	*A reduction in the rate of inflation from:*		
	5 to 4 per cent	*4 to 3 per cent*	*3 to 2 per cent*
Germany	na	0.6 to 0.9	0.9 to 1.7
United Kingdom	1.9 to 2.2	2.2 2.7	2.7 3.3
Japan	1.2 1.45	1.45 1.9	1.9 2.6e
France	1.7 2.0	2.0 2.5	2.5 3.1
Sweden	1.4 1.65	1.65 2.1	2.1 2.9
Italy*	3.2 3.5	3.5 3.8	3.8 4.1
United States	4.2 4.5	4.5 5.0	5.0 5.4
Canada	3.5 4.1	4.1 4.8	4.8 6.0

na—not available.
e—estimated
*—data not fully comparable.
Source: Erich Spitaller, "Prices and Unemployment in Selected Industrial Countries," *IMF Staff Papers*, Vol. XVIII, No. 3 (November 1971), p. 550.

However, these similar *changes* take place at very different *levels*. Reducing price increases to 3 per cent takes German unemployment only to 0.9 per cent and Japanese unemployment to 1.9 per cent, whereas it takes French and British unemployment to 2.5–2.7 per cent and U.S. and Canadian unemployment to 4.8–5.0 per cent. Similar disparities in absolute terms exist as the rate of inflation is cut to lower (or raised to higher) levels. To be sure, there are significant differences in national definitions and the rates of unemployment deemed "acceptable" by different countries. But Germany and Japan, to a lesser extent, surely possess some additional international monetary power because they can match or beat the price-rise performance of other countries, a key aspect of international competitiveness, at significantly lower levels of domestic unemployment.

A second key element in achieving "adjustment power" through internal policy is the leverage of domestic income and price changes over changes in the external accounts. Such leverage can be expected to be greatest in open economies such as the Netherlands, where imports account for over 40 per cent of GNP. On the other hand, changes in domestic income have less leverage over the balance of payments in a closed economy such as the United States where imports amount to about 7 per cent of GNP.

The relationship between the responses of open and closed economies to *changes* in domestic growth rates is less clear, although relatively open economies appear to have generally higher "income elasticities of demand for imports." For example, Italian, Belgian, and Swiss imports can be expected to grow about twice as fast as the growth of their internal economies, German imports about 1.8 times as fast, British and U.S. imports about 1.5–1.7 times as fast, and Japanese and Canadian imports only about 1.2 times as fast.[26] All other things equal, this means that Italy could cut its import growth by two-thirds more than could Japan through identical percentage cuts in internal growth rates.

Price elasticities determine the responsiveness of trade flows to price changes caused either by domestic economy policies or by changes in exchange rates.[27] By contrast with income elasticities, price elasticities of demand for imports are likely to be higher in closed than in open economies. The reason is that imports represent a smaller share of the economy to begin with and thus have much more room to change in response to changed circumstances. For the same reason, foreign price elasticities of demand could be expected to be higher for the exports of small economies, which are usually relatively small factors in the world market, than for the exports of large econ-

26. H. S. Houthakker and Stephen P. Magee, "Income and Price Elasticities in World Trade," *The Review of Economics and Statistics*, Vol. LI, No. 2 (May 1969), pp. 115, 125.
27. The two kinds of price elasticities were found to be quite similar by Helen B. Junz and Rudolf R. Rhomberg, "Price Competitiveness in Export Trade Among Industrial Countries," *American Economic Review*, Vol LVIII, No. 2 (May 1973), pp. 412–18.

omies which are large factors. Both conclusions must be highly qualified by the "all other things equal" condition, which *inter alia* does not hold because of the sharp difference in the composition of exports and imports of the different countries—in some instances there are much larger shares of relatively price-inelastic food and raw materials than highly price-elastic manufactured goods. Small countries are usually relatively open, and large countries relatively closed; but Britain and Germany are considerably more open than Japan and France, and the correlation is by no means precise.[28]

The economy with maximum "adjustment power" through domestic policy changes would thus be one in which (a) price rises could be cut at relatively little unemployment expense, but which (b) was extremely open so that the cutbacks in income exerted major leverage; which had (c) a high income-elasticity of demand for imports and (d) a high price-elasticity of demand for imports, and (e) faced a high foreign price-elasticity of demand for its exports. The limitations of present data make it impossible to assess with confidence how different countries compare on a combination of these criteria, but Table 4 pulls together the ranking of seven major countries on these five criteria. With no effort made to assign weights to the different

Table 4

MAJOR COUNTRIES RANKED IN ORDER OF THEIR CAPABILITY
TO ADJUST VIA DOMESTIC ECONOMIC POLICY

	Phillips curve trade-off	*Openness*	*Price elasticity of imports*	*Price elasticity of exports*	*Income elasticity of imports*	*Total*
Germany	1	3	3	5	1	13
Sweden	3	2	3	7	5	20
France	4	5	7	1	3	20
United States	7	7	2	2	2	20
Canada	6	1	1	6	7	21
Japan	2	6	4	5	6	23
United Kingdom	5	4	6	4	4	23

28. All empirical work to date on these price elasticities must be used with great caution. Houthakker and Magee, *op. cit.*, do find much lower price elasticities of import demand for Italy, Britain, and Germany than for the United States and Japan (but they also find high elasticities for Belgium, Canada, and Switzerland). However, they find higher price elasticities of demand for the exports of some of the large countries (the United States, Germany, Britain) than for some of the smaller countries.

criteria or to take account of the magnitudes of difference between the ranks on each criterion, Germany appears to have the best overall "adjustment power" from domestic policy, while all the other major countries are clustered closely together.[29]

Adjustment can also be obtained through measures aimed directly at the external accounts. "Adjustment power" through exchange-rate changes, for example, should accrue to countries which faced high price-elasticities of demand for their exports and imports, but which were relatively closed so that such changes would have little effect on their domestic economies (especially when compared with the scale of internal adjustment needed to achieve a comparable external effect). Phillips curve trade-offs and income elasticities of demand for imports could both be much less important here, and their effects are in fact captured in the openness variable.

On this (very rough) compilation, the United States has by far the greatest potential "adjustment power" (see Table 5). In addition, the level of U.S. reserves relative to the level of its international transactions has become among the lowest of the industrialized countries in the 1970s, so it could withstand pressure to adjust only through continued use of the dollar for financing. The international monetary power of the United States is thus greatest in a system which relies

Table 5

MAJOR COUNTRIES RANKED IN ORDER OF THEIR CAPABILITY TO ADJUST VIA EXCHANGE RATE CHANGES

	Openness	Price elasticity of imports	Price elasticity of exports	Total
United States	1	2	2	5
Japan	2	4	5	11
France	3	7	1	11
Germany	5	5	3	13
United Kingdom	4	6	4	14
Canada	7	1	6	14
Sweden	6	3	7	16

29. Since Germany has been in steady surplus, there is no way to test whether its adjustment policy preferences when in deficit would in fact reflect this comparative policy advantage. As noted in footnote 24, the ability to adjust effectively to surpluses—which has been the German "problem"—does not represent international monetary power.

either on the dollar for financing,[30] or at least in large part on the exchange-rate mechanism to achieve payments adjustment. Indeed, any country would be expected to promote the development of a monetary system which provided the broadest possible scope for whichever mode of adjustment it could carry out most effectively.

A major paradox arises at this point, however. Prior to 1971, the United States was the very country which resisted exchange-rate adjustment most tenaciously throughout the postwar period, despite the decline in virtually all other aspects of its international monetary power—including its size advantage, its political leverage over its allies, and the steady erosion of its reserves—and despite the adjustment leverage available to it from changing its exchange rate. We shall see in Chapter 9 that the key currency roles of the dollar played a major role in constraining the United States from such adjustment and inducing its policy-makers to shy from this option. Thus the dollar's roles placed a major constraint on the exercise of its international monetary power at the same time they added to that power by enabling it to create financing for its deficits—one of the "dilemmas of the dollar" that are the focus of this book.

International monetary power is thus based on a combination of a country's size, its world political power, its ability to finance payments deficits, and its ability to eliminate deficits effectively. A country can satisfy its primary policy objective, avoidance of forced adjustment, by financing its deficits through the possession of large reserves, by maintaining a key currency role, by running payments surpluses without major cost to its other national objectives, or by possessing enough negative power simply to remain aloof from such pressures and being willing to accept the consequences of such noncooperation. If forced to adjust, a country can minimize the costs to it by promoting a monetary system which facilitates the kind of adjustment—via domestic macroeconomic policy or via direct external measures, primarily exchange-rate changes—in which it has a comparative advantage. Conversely, a country can minimize the power of other countries by draining their reserves, denying them key currency status

---

30. Key currency countries can also be viewed as having a special sort of "adjustment power," through their ability to attract larger inflows of liquid capital than can other countries through a given interest-rate change. Lindert, *op. cit.*, demonstrated that Britain could do so prior to 1914, and the phenomenon explains the U.S. official settlements surpluses in 1968–69 in the face of a booming domestic economy and a deteriorating current account. It is a matter of taste whether such inflows are viewed as financing or adjustment, but they clearly add to the power of a key currency country.

or credits, and by fostering a system which minimizes the scope for adjustment techniques in which they have a comparative advantage. We turn next to an analysis of how different national goals and capabilities have blended to form the several different kinds of international monetary systems that history has produced.

3

The International Monetary System:
Past and Present

Any international monetary system must be organized in one of three ways, or some combination of them, as noted in Chapter 2. One possibility is uncoordinated exercise of market forces and sovereign national policies. Another is dominance by a single country with sufficient power to do so. A third is effective international coordination of national policies, the highest form of which could be global integration. The most likely combination is dominance by individual countries within one or more groups of countries, and either uncoordinated or coordinated relations among the groups.

The organization of the international monetary system, at any particular point in time, depends on the interplay of national goals and capabilities discussed in Chapter 2. This chapter begins with a quick survey of the systems which developed in the past, and then turns to a more detailed analysis of how the system has worked in practice in recent years. Throughout, particular attention will be paid to the international roles played by national currencies, and particularly the evolution of the dollar.

Before 1914: The "Gold Standard"
Legend has it that prior to 1914 the international monetary system was based purely on gold and internal economic adjustment. Countries supposedly adjusted their internal economies rapidly in response to gold flows, deflating (as gold flowed out) to boost their trade surpluses and inflating (when gold flowed in) to reduce them. The pervasiveness of these "rules of the game" in fact induced countries to act pre-emptively, by raising or lowering their interest rates when gold flows were anticipated. Exchange-rate changes and controls over international economic transactions were forbidden. Thus "effective" adjustment took place "automatically," and little official liquidity was needed.

In fact, the "gold standard" was never based solely on gold.[1] Silver was the dominant monetary metal throughout the first half of the nineteenth century, and remained the major reserve asset of such key countries as Germany and France until the 1880s. The monetary use of gold *within* countries declined sharply throughout the nineteenth century and accounted for less than 10 per cent of domestic money supplies by 1913. It was not until about 1880 that enough major countries pegged their currencies to gold externally to constitute even a de facto "standard." By that time, however, the international use of national currencies had also become important. By 1913, in fact, foreign exchange accounted for about 20 per cent of world reserves—a higher share than in all but the last year or so before the collapse of the interwar "gold exchange standard," which, according to the conventional wisdom, was much more heavily reliant on the key currencies. And foreign exchange represented a significant share of the reserves of a larger number of countries before World War I than after.[2]

Indeed, the world prior to 1914—like the world between the wars and after World War II—was far from monolithic in terms of its monetary allegiances. Only two countries, the United Kingdom and the United States, held only gold. Many major countries held large amounts of silver and are often viewed as being on a "limping" gold standard. (Some less important countries, including China, held *only silver.*) Most major countries held large amounts of foreign exchange and hence were on a gold exchange standard. With this group, some held mainly sterling; some, Reichsmarks; and some, French francs. Some switched from one basis to another. Some formed regional monetary groupings, most notably the Latin Monetary Union comprising France, Belgium, Switzerland, Italy, and Greece. So even the "gold standard" system exhibited a wide range of national preferences for different reserve assets.

It is also a myth that exchange-rate changes were unknown in this period. Some countries around the periphery of the system (including Spain) did not peg their exchange rates at all. Devaluations were frequent, especially in Latin America. It is a myth that countries let external pressures determine their internal policies. Downward wage

1. See for example, Arthur I. Bloomfield, *Monetary Policy Under the International Gold Standard 1880–1914*, Federal Reserve Bank of New York, October 1959, and Robert Triffin, *The Evolution of the International Monetary System: Historical Reappraisal and Future Perspectives*, Princeton Studies in International Finance, No. 12 (1964).
2. Peter H. Lindert, *Key Currencies and Gold: 1900–1913*, Princeton Studies in International Finance, No. 24 (1969).

adjustments were extremely small in the few cases in which they did occur, and it appears that domestic economic policy changed in response to the requirements of external balance less than half the time.[3] It is also a myth that adjustment was achieved solely (or even primarily) through changes in trade balances; capital flows were much more important as an equilibrating factor in both the short and longer terms.

However, it is true that no major country changed its exchange rate during this period. And the only major applications of direct controls were by the United States (in the mid-1890s) and Russia (as a result of the Russo-Japanese War),[4] although manipulations of the gold points (equivalent to today's exchange-rate margins) and various changes in other monetary operations served the same purpose at times. So we must ask what combination of events made such an adjustment process possible.

The first explanation is that official reserves grew steadily and quite rapidly at least from 1880 through 1913. The data are far from adequate, but the best available suggest that world holdings of gold and foreign exchange reserves grew by about 7 per cent annually during this period, from about $1.2 billion in 1880 to about $6.5 billion in 1913, and by almost 10 per cent annually during its last decade.[5] (See Table 6.) The increases appear to have been distributed fairly widely among countries. Indeed, only Denmark of ten countries surveyed by Bloomfield experienced a decline in the ratio of its reserves to imports over the period as a whole, and several (including the U.S.) experienced sizable increases.[6] The gross reserves of each of the three key currency countries—Britain, France, and Germany—rose steadily. Thus, pressures for rapid adjustment, which would prompt the application of controls but also force exchange-rate changes, were significantly cushioned by the growth of owned reserves.

The second explanation is that the economies of all of the major countries exhibited a high degree of congruency, both cyclically and secularly, because of the close interrelationships among them. All of the major economies were in Europe; even the United States and

3. Bloomfield, *op. cit.*, pp. 47–51, found such "neutralization" present in 60 per cent of his total observations for this period.
4. Arthur I. Bloomfield, *Short-Term Capital Movements Under the Pre-1914 Gold Standard*, Princeton Studies in International Finance, No. 11. (1967), pp. 29, 84–85.
5. Gold production varied sharply during this period, rising rapidly in 1848–72 and 1892–1913, but slowly in between. Central banks, however, acquired a far greater share of the new output in the lean production years—by vastly expanding the use of paper money in domestic circulation—and were thus able to maintain the steady growth of their reserves.
6. Bloomfield, *Short-Term Capital Movements*, pp. 31–32.

Table 6

WORLD RESERVES PRIOR TO WORLD WAR I
(In billions of dollars)

	1880	1885	1903	1910	1913
Gold	1.0	1.3	2.6	4.2	4.9
Foreign exchange	0.2	0.3	0.8	1.5	1.6
Total	1.2	1.6	3.4	5.7	6.5
Silver	0.6e	0.7	1.0e	1.1e	1.2
Total	1.8	2.3	4.4	6.8	7.7

e—Estimated by author from sources shown.
Sources: Arthur J. Bloomfield, *Short-term Capital Movements under the Pre-
1914 Gold Standard,* Princeton Studies in International Finance, No.
11, July 1963.
Robert Triffin, *The Evolution of the IMF: Historical Reappraisal and
Future Perspectives,* Princeton Studies in International Finance, No. 12,
June 1964.
Peter H. Lindert, *Key Currencies and Gold, 1900–1913,* Princeton
Studies in International Finance, No. 24, August 1969.

Japan were still peripheral. All of these European countries are relatively open to international transactions even today, unlike the United
States and Japan; during that period they all were even more open to
international trade—and especially to capital movements at both long
and short term.[7] As a result, the three major powers in the system—
Britain, Germany, and France—were together in the expansion or
contraction phase of the business cycle an amazingly high 83 per cent
of the time from 1880 through mid-1914, as contrasted with such
confluence only 45 per cent of the time from mid-1919 to mid-1932.[8]
  The automatic stabilizers triggered by payments imbalances, which

  7. Ratios of exports to gross domestic product were as follows, for 1913 and
     1970, respectively: United Kingdom, 16.7 and 16.2; France, 20.0 and 16.0;
     Japan 16.7 and 11.2. The Federal Republic of Germany shows a slightly
     higher ratio for 1970 than all of prewar Germany shows for 1913, but we
     would expect the territorial changes to make modern Germany much more
     open. Alfred Maizels, *Industrial Growth and World Trade* (Cambridge:
     University Press, 1963, pp. 428–29 and 531.) Net foreign investment by
     the United Kingdom exceeded 5 per cent of its estimated national product,
     or about 40 per cent of net national investment, during 1900–13. The
     comparable figures for France and Germany ranged between 1.5 and 3.5
     per cent, and 7.5 and 10 per cent, respectively. These figures compare with
     net foreign investment by the United States, during 1946–66, of 0.4 per
     cent of national product and 4.7 per cent of net national savings. Lindert,
     op. cit., pp. 1–2.
  8. Oskar Morgenstern, *International Financial Transactions and Business
     Cycles* (Princeton, N.J.: Princeton University Press, 1959), p. 45.

work through both incomes and prices,[9] thus had quite a powerful effect in triggering adjustment. Dilemma cases—in which internal and external needs conflict and adjustment must come through the exchange rate—were probably quite infrequent. The high degree of national economic synchronization also meant that changes in the rate of unemployment and in price levels moved together among the major countries. Indeed, in the absence of statistics, synchronization may have been thought to be higher than it really was, and it must always be remembered that policy is determined by perception. The potential conflict among the different objectives of national economic policy was reduced by the fact that people in one country could not observe much better unemployment or price performances in other countries. Discount-rate changes, the major policy instrument then in use, were highly and positively correlated among the major countries.

Most important, national authorities had not yet become responsible for preserving domestic full employment, or even price stability. Hence there were few efforts to offset the adjustment impulses of the highly synchronized international business cycle. This absence of governmental adoption of responsibility to pursue a variety of national economic goals goes far to explain why cyclical synchronization promoted effective adjustment before 1913, whereas, as pointed out in Chapter 2, such synchronization may today cause major problems as countries seek to export unemployment or inflation while all are facing the same problem.

Corresponding to the absence of governmental adoption of numerous policy targets, techniques of monetary management had yet to become very sophisticated. External assets exceeded domestic assets in the portfolios of most central banks, making them extremely sensitive to changes in reserves. Indeed, most central banks—the managers of national currencies, to the extent they were managed—were privately owned, and they worried more about their own liquidity and earnings than about public policy. Fiscal policy barely existed. The simple target of preserving a fixed exchange rate dominated policy and was not "undermined" by active manipulation of other policy instruments. The traumatic experiences of the twentieth century with inflation and mass unemployment, which both underlie the different

9. Payments deficits, especially if they result from lagging foreign demand for a country's exports, reduce domestic income and hence reduce domestic inflationary pressures, and also reduce the domestic money supply as the monetary base contracts with the loss of reserves, all of which in turn improve the country's competitive position and help eliminate the deficit. The opposite effects occur for surplus countries, especially if the surplus results from booming foreign demand for their exports.

national policy preferences that exist today and compelled governments to take a far more active economic policy role, were still to come. Even if dilemma cases had occurred frequently, they might therefore still not have produced controls and exchange-rate changes.

Finally, the high degree of openness of the key economies made exchange-rate changes and controls over external transactions relatively costly ways to adjust, compared to changes in internal economies. The biases against controls were reinforced by the intellectual ascendancy of laissez-faire economics, and by the illustration of the successes of this doctrine in the world leadership of the United Kingdom.

To preserve a fixed exchange rate, countries were willing to alter their monetary policy—mainly to attract and repel private capital. Such private capital movements, uninhibited by official controls, were encouraged by the widespread confidence in fixed parities. Hence they were able to play a major role in supplementing official reserves to finance imbalances—and to give major countries time to let their external balances adjust indirectly as a result of changes in their domestic economies. The capital imported by major countries frequently came from the less developed countries of the periphery, and the cutbacks in their capital exports were at the expense of the same group, so both adjustment and financing for the larger countries often forced instability (and parity changes) on the smaller.

Underlying these relatively convergent economic goals were relatively convergent political relationships. As is well known, the period between the Napoleonic Wars and World War I represents the archetypal balance-of-power political system, in which there were no permanent enemies. Britain was the most powerful single country, and it effectively played the role of balancer among the major continental countries, all of whom thus had a major incentive to retain good relations with it. Given the importance of international economic relations to the United Kingdom, this clearly required cooperation with Britain on international monetary matters. Outside Europe, the nineteenth century was the age of imperialism in which Britain extended its rule (and the use of sterling) to many additional countries around the globe.

As in political and security matters, however, Britain was careful in its monetary relations not to try to assert hegemonial dominance over the major countries themselves, and hence force them to join against it. Indeed, contrary to another myth—that sterling dominated the prewar monetary system—France and Germany both became major key currency centers by 1900. Each was in fact dominant financially in its own sphere of political influence: France in Russia and elsewhere in

Eastern Europe, Germany in Central Europe.[10] In addition, both France and Germany possessed much larger gross reserves than did the United Kingdom, and hence had greater monetary power on this criterion. On the other hand, Britain still accounted for a far larger share of world trade and capital movements than any other country, though Germany, in particular, had narrowed the British lead greatly by 1913. In addition, Britain had superior ability to attract short-term capital, even from Berlin and Paris, through changes in its monetary policy and through moral suasion. (Berlin and Paris were, in turn, able to attract capital from the periphery.) This financial power enabled the United Kingdom to run balance-of-payments surpluses when its domestic economy was booming, by attracting sufficient capital to offset the deterioration of its current account, whereas neither France nor Germany was able to do so. And, on a global basis, sterling was much more widely held than the other two key currencies. The United Kingdom clearly possessed the greatest individual monetary power, if not by the overwhelming margin often attributed to it.

Relations among the three centers were governed largely by the similarities of their economic structures and national economic goals, as outlined above, and were relatively harmonious. The *gross* reserves of each center were rising, and as there were no data on their liquid liabilities to show that they were running balance-of-payments deficits on today's definitions, there were no major crises of confidence in any one of them which upset systemic stability. In fact, France helped the United Kingdom on several occasions, through direct loans and discounting of British bills, in direct contrast to its decidedly uncooperative behavior toward the same country in 1928–31 and the mid-1960s.

The Interwar Period: A "Gold Exchange Standard"
World War I drastically altered the international monetary system. All three key countries of the prewar years were deeply affected. Germany was shattered by defeat, then rent by hyperinflation which reduced the mark to one trillionth of its former value, forced to become the world's largest international debtor, and branded a political pariah. France was severely undermined both economically and politically even in victory, losing the bulk of its foreign investment in the wake of the Bolshevik revolution and traumatized both by a feel-

10. Lindert, *op. cit., passim.* His data (pp. 18–19) show that, in 1913, foreign holdings totaled $455.5 million in England, $575.1 million in France, and $152.3 million in Germany. Holdings by European countries alone accounted for $262.1 million in France, $115.5 million in Germany, and only $76.4 million in England.

ing of continued insecurity toward Germany and national humiliation at relying for victory on its allies. The United Kingdom was also weakened, cashing in a large share of its foreign investments to finance the war. Two of the other important prewar actors, Russia and Austria-Hungary, no longer existed for international monetary purposes.

Of greatest importance, however, was the emergence of the United States as the world's leading political and economic power. Only the United States really emerged from the war as a "winner," without significant costs of blood or treasure offsetting the triumph. U.S. business and finance became involved overseas in a major way for the first time, as the United States swiftly replaced Britain as the world's largest creditor country. American reserves were the world's largest already in 1913, but in 1918 they approached 40 per cent of the world's total and, by 1923, 45 per cent. It was the only major country able to meet the universal objective of keeping its currency pegged to gold in the early postwar years. As a result of all these changes, the dollar became a key international currency.

Some of the countries which remained neutral during the war also managed to emerge relatively well off. Japan was rapidly establishing its ascendance in the Far East. Switzerland, the Netherlands, and Scandinavia were relatively unscathed as well.

A dramatic shift in national economic capabilities emerged from all these changes. Power was de-centralized from its relatively homogeneous European base. New actors appeared, some old ones disappeared, and a major new power emerged. The three key currency countries of the pre-1914 system were all weakened relative to that new power, and their power positions relative to each other changed sharply as well.

Yet, despite these radical changes, the prevailing policy objective of most countries was to return to the prewar monetary system and even their prewar exchange rates. The British never even considered a different rate for sterling despite the cataclysmic effects of the war and its aftermath, and as late as 1927 many leading French officials wanted to return to the prewar franc parity despite the sharp depreciation which had occurred in the interim. Virtually all countries sought to restore the prewar monetary system on the basis of the "gold standard" which they thought had existed before the war, a view that prevailed throughout the entire period despite depression and deepening political tensions. As usual in public policy matters, understanding badly lagged behind reality and the major effort was devoted to fighting the previous battles. Though it takes us far ahead of our story to do so, it is worth noting the striking parallel with the early 1970s—

when there remains a nostalgic desire on the part of many to return to the Bretton Woods system, despite the radical changes in the underlying structure on which it was built and operated.

In fact, at least three monetary "systems" existed in the interwar period.[11] Freely floating exchange rates and gold dominated the immediate postwar years. From about 1922 until 1931, countries increasingly pegged their exchange rates, and national currencies resumed the important role in world reserves which they had established prior to 1914. After 1931, the "system" broke up into several components centered on sterling, the dollar, and gold, in which reserves were held in these different forms and adjustment among the major countries was sought through controlled floats and direct controls over international transactions. (Some cooperation among the United States, the United Kingdom, and the members of the gold bloc was achieved in the late 1930s, but made little impact on the actual functioning of the system, though it persisted until the outbreak of the second war effecively terminated international monetary arrangements once more.)

World reserves were generally viewed as inadequate immediately after World War I. The inflation bred by the war had sharply raised price levels, in all countries and for all commodities except gold. As a result, gold production declined by one-third from 1915 to 1922 and the real value of gold reserves declined sharply. In addition, the war had led to liquidation of virtually all of the reserve currency balances built up before 1914, which had totaled about 20 per cent of total reserves. Finally, short-term capital movements, which had performed a major equilibrating function in the world of immutable parities and convergent economic trends before 1914, played a disequilibrating role in the new world of freely floating exchange rates and widely divergent economies. Instead of reducing the need for official liquidity, they increased it.

The pervasive desire of most countries to return to their prewar gold parities ruled out considerations of increasing the price of gold, especially since Britain—which more than any single country still controlled that price—was particularly avid to restore the old parity. Apparently no consideration was given to what the Articles of Agreement of the International Monetary Fund labelled in 1944 a "uniform change in par values"—raising the price of gold without changing the exchange rates between national currencies. Indeed, countries

11. The data used in the text are from the two basic works on this period: William Adams Brown, Jr., *The International Gold Standard Reinterpreted* 1919–1934 (New York: National Bureau of Economic Research, 1940) and Ragnar Nurkse, *International Currency Experience* (Princeton, N.J.: Princeton University Press, League of Nations, 1944).

in this period thought in terms of gold parities rather than exchange-rate relationships with other currencies.

The desire to "economize on gold" led to the recommendations of the Genoa Conference of 1922 for resumed use of national currencies as international reserve assets—under certain safeguards, which were forgotten even as the use of these currencies developed anew.[12] By 1924, official accumulation of foreign exchange reached 25 per cent of total European reserves (excluding the United Kingdom); it rose to a peak of 42 per cent at end of 1928. In addition, important non-European countries held sizable amounts of sterling. All told, practically every country in the world except the United Kingdom and United States, the two reserve centers, and Canada, held sizable quantities of foreign exchange. So it was a major source of the growth of total world liquidity in this period. The holdings were in both dollars and sterling, though no data exist to reveal how much of each, but the whole trend was widely viewed as a British plot to enable sterling to reassert its prewar parity—a view buttressed by the leading role played by the British Chancellor of the Exchequer in pushing the Genoa Resolutions, and his willingness to accept a provision of those Resolutions which absolutely forbade exchange-rate adjustments by reserve centers.[13]

Owned reserves were supplemented in two important ways during the middle and late 1920s. Private lending, particularly from the United States to Europe, resumed on a massive scale and played a major equilibrating role. And official cooperation between central banks led to several packages of short-term credits to help defend parities, foreshadowing the sophisticated system of swaps which developed in the 1960s.

France, which had become by far the largest holder of foreign exchange, began to convert its sterling into gold after 1928. This move alone had a major impact in reducing world reserves by reducing the reserves of the United Kingdom, the key currency center. The French

12. For a trenchant critique of the practices which subsequently developed, see "The Gold Exchange Standard," BIS, Monetary and Economic Department, CB 60, Papers Relating to the Gold Standard Prepared for the World Economic Conference, London, 1933. The author was Dr. Karl Blessing, later President of the Deutsche Bundesbank after World War II, who played a major role in the "gold exchange standard" of the later period. He particularly criticized the practice of holding reserve currency balances with private instead of central banks, which made it difficult for the authorities to know the size of their liabilities and to influence them, and the destructive policies of France—both of which recurred in the 1960s!

13. "Genoa Financial Commission Report," *Federal Reserve Bulletin*, June 1922, p. 678.

move was particularly perfidious, because France had built its foreign exchange holdings after 1926 in order to achieve a grossly undervalued exchange rate. (Frenchmen later rationalized that they never intended to maintain these reserve currency balances, but did not voice that position at the time.) Italy was the only other country which converted significant amounts prior to the unpegging of sterling from gold in 1931, although Germany had made sizable conversions earlier. In the year *following* the British float, however, virtually all foreign exchange holdings by monetary authorities outside the sterling area were liquidated—their percentage of total European reserves dropped below 9 per cent by September 1932.[14]

Simultaneously, however, the desire for liquidity was beginning to be met by increases in the price of gold. The first step was the British abandonment of sterling's gold parity. When the cycle of devaluations of the early 1930s was completed, after the United States and then finally France and the other continental European countries moved, the price of gold had been increased substantially in terms of all national currencies—writing up the purchasing power of gold holdings and stimulating a doubling of gold production in just seven years, from 1931 to 1938. Indeed, the depreciations of the 1930s restored the exchange-rate relationships among the major currencies close to their pre-1931 level; the major long-term effect of the cycle was the increase in the gold price. (A few countries switched from sterling into French francs rather than gold in the early 1930s, and France became a reserve center on a limited scale again for a while, but this phase ended as France too headed toward eventual devaluation.)

In effect, competitive depreciation was thus a method of increasing world liquidity. However, the increase turned out to be excessive. By the late 1930s, talk turned to the possible need for a *reduction* in the price of gold to help combat world inflation.[15] Indeed, the "golden avalanche" which descended on he United States in the late 1930s partly represented speculation against such a dollar revaluation. Thus the liquidity arrangements of most of the interwar period, with the exception of the middle 1920s, turned out to be a dismal failure both

---

14. The phenomenon of a sharp move out of a reserve currency *after* it is devalued, which runs counter to *a priori* logic but will be explained in Chapter 5, was repeated after the sterling devaluation in 1967, and to some extent after the dollar devaluation of 1971 and especially 1973.

15. See, for example, Frank D. Graham and Charles N. Whittlesey, *The Golden Avalanche* (Princeton: Princeton University Press, 1939), esp. chap. IX.

in providing proper amounts of reserves and in doing so by means which were widely accepted and hence likely to remain stable.

The adjustment arrangements turned out to be just as bad. The huge dislocations wrought by the war made it impossible for any of the European countries to restore fixed exchange rates at its conclusion. They were all forced to let their rates float freely, and sharp divergences from the prewar cross-rates quickly appeared as the result of their different rates of inflation and sharply varying needs to import working capital. It is a measure of the strength of conventional monetary orthodoxy that short-term capital movements in the immediate postwar period tended to move exchange rates toward their prewar relationships, but attitudes changed quickly as the new situation became apparent and speculation began to accelerate the depreciations of many currencies. Despite this, national monetary authorities in some key countries—including the United Kingdom and France—took little active part in the exchange markets. However, most of them concluded that the capital movements triggered by the floats themselves added greatly to their already enormous difficulties. Free floating thus seemed to represent a highly ineffective adjustment mechanism and many authorities vowed that they would never permit it again, a vow on which they made good in the 1930s.[16] Indeed, the keen postwar desire to restore fixed parities was heightened by this experience with floating.

Beginning in 1923, the major countries began to "stabilize" to escape the uncertainties which they associated with flexibility. The return to fixed rates was completed when Germany repegged to gold in 1924, Britain did so in 1925, and France did so de facto in 1926. Unfortunately, all three major countries repegged at rates which bore little relationship to the economic reality of the time. A host of lesser countries, including Japan as late as 1930, made the same mistake.

Nostalgia for pre-1914 stability, but primarily the desire to establish sterling irrevocably as the center of the "new" gold exchange standard,

---

16. S.C. Tsiang, "Fluctuating Exchange Rates in Countries with Relatively Stable Economies: Some European Experiences After World War I," *IMF Staff Papers*, Vol. VII, No. 2 (Oct. 1959), pp. 244–73, concludes that the exchange rate instability resulting from speculative activity in the United Kingdom, France, and Norway was due to ineffective monetary policy rather than to anything inherent in the flexible exchange rate. (The same argument has been made by many observers of the ultimate failure of the Canadian float in the early 1960s). It is thus not surprising that the monetary authorities of the time concluded that it was rate flexibility which was the major villain.

persuaded the British to peg sterling at its prewar parity.[17] Indeed, this remains the clearest case in history where the lure of playing a key currency role levied devastating costs on the key currency country. The resulting gross overvaluation could only be defended by maintaining mass unemployment, an obviously unstable condition that led to the breakdown of the entire system in 1931.

On the other hand, France, wanting a rate that was economically viable and would permit it to regain international economic power, repegged at a grossly undervalued level and built huge trade surpluses. Its payments surpluses were even larger, as liquid capital that had flowed out of the depreciating franc to London in the early 1920s returned to Paris after the "stabilization." As a result, France raised its reserves far above those of any other European country and even brought them within about $1 billion of the United States by the end of 1928. Paradoxically, an apparently stable system could be restored because of the congruent views of the two key countries: France wanted an undervalued rate, and Britain was willing to accept an overvalued rate. But the fixed-rate regime which began again in the mid-1920s thus did so on a wholly unstable base and, to make matters worse, it contained no mechanism at all for changing exchange rates without virtual chaos. Yet such changes soon became necessary both because of the initial misalignment and because of the divergent economic paths of the key countries in the late 1920s, with the United States inflating while Britain was deflating and France was relatively stable. In short, there was no adjustment process.

As a result, the system did break down shortly. Numerous peripheral countries floated early in the depression. Britain abandoned convertibility in 1931; many sterling countries went with it, and the sterling area was formalized a year later. Most other European countries abandoned parity shortly after Britain. To avoid the ills which they associated with the free floats of the early 1920s, most of the floaters managed their rates actively in the 1930s—and many sought to improve their national competitive positions by forcing depreciation of their currencies in the exchange markets. The result was a highly unstable, and indeed viciously competitive, international monetary regime.[18]

Of particular importance was the U.S. departure from gold in 1933, and the eventual massive devaluation of 1934—in which the United

17. D.E. Moggeridge, *The Return to Gold 1925* (Cambridge, England: University Press, 1969), *passim*, but esp. pp. 85–86.
18. For a detailed history, see Charles P. Kindleberger, *The World in Depression, 1929–1939* (London: Allen Lane, 1973).

States raised the price of gold to $35 per ounce from its previous parity of $20.67. Unlike the other countries, it was not forced to move either by payments deficits or by low reserves; it was in payments surplus throughout the early 1930s and its reserves remained the world's largest. Indeed, despite the domestic boom, the United States had deliberately avoided deterioration of its trade and payments position in the late 1920s by sterilizing the monetary effects of its external surpluses, by sharply raising its tariffs, and by insisting that payments continue on both German reparations and the interallied debts. Its devaluation was motivated solely by a desire to alleviate domestic unemployment in the United States, to help it recover from the Great Depression. (Again we note a striking parallel with more recent events. The U.S. devaluation of 1971 was aimed largely at reducing domestic unemployment, though it was "justified" by the external deficit which the United States was running at that time.) France and the rest of the European gold bloc countries clung to their gold parities longest, using exchange and import controls to do so; but they finally devalued in 1934–35 after their previous undervaluations had become overvaluations (with the British and American moves) and deepened their internal economic woes.

Through their abandonment of gold parities and manipulations in the exchange markets via exchange and trade controls, the major countries sought to achieve competitive advantages both to boost domestic employment and to maintain their reserves. Germany was of course the extreme case of using controls to pursue economic, and through them political, objectives. But all of the other major countries, through their newly created "exchange stabilization funds," intervened actively in the exchange markets. "Dirty floats" were the order of the day in contrast to the "clean floats" of the early 1920s. No coordination of these measures took place among the major countries, and even the cooperative procedures which had developed during the late 1920s broke down. The results prompted the phrase "beggar-thy-neighbor-policies," which remains today the most severe charge that can be levied against a nation's international economic policies. Small countries sought refuge by pegging their exchange rates to the major countries on which they were most dependent economically and/or politically.

The measures adopted did have some degree of success *in the short run.* By moving first, Britain was able to temper the effects on it of the world depression and to pull around it more tightly than ever those foreign countries which most complemented its economic needs. The United States obtained at least a mild export stimulus from its devaluation. France and the rest of the gold bloc, by repeating the

British error of 1925–31 in clinging far too long to an erroneous parity and using controls instead of devaluing, felt the full force of depression. Germany used its economic policy to further its control over Central and Southeast Europe and prepare for its effort to seek domination of all Europe. As already noted, however, the overall exchange-rate pattern by 1936 was about the same as before the cycle of devaluations, so the only long-term effect was a perhaps excessive increase in the price of gold.

The major countries finally saw the wisdom of restoring some degree of cooperation when, in 1936, the United States, Britain, and France (later joined by the other gold bloc countries)[19] reached the so-called Tripartite Agreement, to provide a broad framework for preserving exchange-rate stability among the major centers. Until the outbreak of World War II, the international monetary system remained divided into these three basic components: the sterling area, and the informal gold and dollar areas. In addition, outside the basic "system," and much like the Communist countries today, Germany dominated Central and Southeastern Europe and Japan dominated its military possessions in the Far East.

Thus the international interwar monetary results differed vastly from those of the prewar years. One central reason was the adoption by all major countries of new policy targets. Before 1914, nations aimed primarily at preserving their gold parities, and assumed little or no responsibility for promoting full employment or price stability. But the recessions, hyperinflations, and exchange-rate floats of the early postwar period changed all that, and the mass unemployment of the depression ended it forever. (The forced floats, despite their perceived shortcomings, also demonstrated that life was possible without fixed rates.) Dilemma cases, such as the British combination of mass unemployment with payments deficits and the American combination of rapid inflation with payments surpluses, became prevalent. The degree and complexity of economic difficulties was much more severe and in most countries overwhelmed the sentiment (though it remained strong) for re-establishing fixed parities as the chief goal of economic policy. Beneath all these new economic goals lay funda-

19. The gold bloc of the interwar period consisted of France, Belgium, Italy, the Netherlands, Poland, and Switzerland. It was formalized in July 1933 through a statement by these six countries which called for "free functioning of the gold standard" as the basis of existing parities, when of course the "gold standard" had already been abandoned by virtually all other countries, and the sterling area had already begun to evolve formally. We will see later a striking continuity between this interwar gold bloc and the de facto gold bloc which emerged during the postwar period.

mental political insecurities, which prompted each country to view national autonomy—for purely national security reasons—as a desirable goal of economic policy.[20]

In addition, the role of governments had taken a quantum leap upward as they managed the first "total war" in history, and in the process "completely and ruthlessly" organized the economic lives of nations.[21] Laissez faire economic policy died in 1914, and it was only natural that national governments would use their new capabilities to meet the priority problems of the subsequent years.

Different national policy preferences emerged as a result of the differences in national economic and political experiences. Germany and other Central European countries were traumatized politically by defeat, and economically by inflation. The United States, Britain, and France suffered from severe recession and then depression. These different experiences, contrasting sharply with the synchronous development of the key countries before 1914, produced destabilizing rather than stabilizing capital flows. Germany, France, and Britain all sought to restore their destroyed or tarnished political power; the deep enmities of the interwar years between the victors and vanquished, and the deep distrust among the victors, are the backdrop to that period.

In addition to these changes in goals, the underlying power positions of the key countries had changed radically, as noted at the outset of this section. Britain, no longer able to dominate even to the degree that it had before 1914, weakened itself disastrously through a policy which sought to re-establish that dominance. After 1926, France may have even held more monetary power than Britain, due to its larger reserves and current surpluses. The greatest power of all was the United States, but it opted out of political cooperation with Europe when the Senate rejected the League of Nations, and it ran into difficulties at home, first with inflation and then with depression, in the late 1920s and into the 1930s.[22]

These vast differences in both goals and capabilities precluded

20. E.H. Carr, *The Twenty Years' Crisis, 1919–1939* (London: MacMillan, 1939), esp. pp. 121–23.
21. Carr, *op. cit.*, p. 114.
22. Brown, *passim*, and numerous other writers see the existence of two financial centers, the United States and Britain, as one of the key reasons for the failure of the interwar system. However, the recent empirical discoveries of Lindert, cited in Chapter 1, suggest that Britain also had serious competition from France and Germany before World War I. The issue is thus why U.S.-U.K. competition in the interwar years was a problem while U.K.-French-German competition in the prewar years was not. The text is addressed to that question.

meaningful international economic cooperation. Continental Europe, especially France, viewed the "gold exchange standard" as a British power play, and the three major reserve currency holders of the period—France, Germany, and Italy—all viewed that system only as a temporary "halfway house" en route to their going back to gold when they were able to do so. All of Europe viewed U.S. gold sterilization as a destructive act, and resented the aggressive entry of U.S. financial institutions into competition with their own. Germany, of course, viewed the whole reparations issue as a major source of international conflict. The erstwhile allies viewed U.S. demands for repayment of wartime loans as impossibly uncooperative, especially when U.S. sterilization policy and tariff protection obviated any possibility of effecting the transfer through increased European trade surpluses. France wanted to recoup national pride for having had to rely on the Anglo-Saxons to drive back the Germans. What little cooperation did exist was based on the slender reed of personal relationships between a few individuals, and largely broke down when one of them became ill or passed from the scene.[23] The London Conference of 1933 was a fiasco and the Tripartite Agreement was a minimal attempt at cooperation. In short, conflict among nations, on both economic and political grounds, replaced the relative harmony which had prevailed before 1914 and would probably have undermined any monetary system however constituted.

The Postwar Period

Like World War I, the Second War also caused wrenching changes in the world monetary system. The United States and the Soviet Union emerged as the only world superpowers. After momentary flirtations with opposite courses of action, the United States remained fully engaged in world affairs while the U.S.S.R. withdrew from all economic cooperation with the West. All three Axis powers lay prostrate and occupied. The two chief European economic protagonists of the interwar years, Britain and France, were again battered in victory.

The Second War greatly accelerated the world trends triggered by the First War: superpower world involvement for the United States, the achievement of superpower status coupled with economic disengagement by the U.S.S.R., the weakening of all of Europe relative to both, the prostration of Germany relative to France and Britain. It thus completed the shift from a Europe-based monetary system of

23. See Stephen V.O. Clarke, *International Financial Cooperation: 1929-1931* (Federal Reserve Bank of New York, 1967).

relatively synchronous economies, with a balance of economic power, to a global system of widely disparate economies under the dominance of a single economic giant.

Compared with the chaos which followed immediately after World War I, however, the world took the enormous stride forward of consciously organizing its economic system. The Articles of Agreement of the International Monetary Fund (IMF) were to govern international monetary relations, and the Fund was to manage them. The International Bank for Reconstruction and Development (IBRD) was set up to finance postwar reconstruction, and only limited efforts were made to levy reparations on the losers of the war or to collect interallied debts incurred during the period of hostilities. The Charter of the International Trade Organization (ITO) was to govern world trade relations with the Organization itself as the manager; and the General Agreement on Tariffs and Trade (GATT) was substituted when the Charter proved too ambitious to be acceptable.

With respect to international monetary relations, the Bretton Woods arrangements sought to prevent recurrence of the problems which had plagued the interwar period. The creation of a body of rules and an institution to implement them aimed at avoiding uncoordinated national actions, especially trade controls and competitive depreciations. The system was to be based on fixed exchange rates in order to avoid both the dirty floats of the 1930s and the destabilizing capital flows triggered by the free floats of the early 1920s. Exchange-rate changes were permitted, however, when the international community agreed that a "fundamental disequilibrium" existed.[24] This was a significant improvement over the gold standard norm of rejecting every notion of such adjustment techniques, and the proscriptions at Genoa—the closest interwar analogue to Bretton Woods—against exchange-rate changes by reserve centers. It was the operational reflection of the key principles recognized in the Articles that the international system should not dictate the internal economic policies of member countries, but that the system as a whole had an interest in the parities of each of its members. In addition, countries wisely avoided the post-1918 desires to return to prewar parities, regardless of whatever might be required by the real economics of the new situation.

The Articles of Agreement, under the "scarce currency" clause, also

24. Any country was also permitted to change its original par value by 10 per cent without Fund approval, because Keynes viewed the British error of 1925 as of about that magnitude and sought to pre-empt any international complications which would otherwise arise if similar errors were made in the future.

provided the possibility of discrimination against a surplus country if it would neither lend nor adjust, because otherwise the adjustment pressures would fall entirely on deficit countries. Capital controls were explicitly envisaged in the arsenal of measures to prevent destabilizing flows, but new trade controls were prohibited except when the international community agreed that a country needed to impose them for balance-of-payments reasons. Provision was made for a "uniform increase" in the price of gold to permit an increase in world liquidity without going through the agonies of the 1930s. The Fund itself was a source of credits to augment owned reserves. Transitional arrangements permitted countries to maintain controls and inconvertible currencies for a time after the war to avoid any premature effort to return to "normal," as occured after World War I. The true power positions of individual countries were recognized by providing for weighted voting on all Fund decisions. The United States, rejecting its interwar isolationism, played the major role in the creation of the institution.[25]

These were dramatic improvements. The simple fact that such a code and institution were developed at all is of great historical significance. The Articles provided a basis for meeting many of the postwar problems. Throughout the period, international trade and investment have boomed and global economic prosperity has grown and spread as never before in the history of mankind. So criticism of the new mechanism, particularly with the advantage of hindsight, may seem churlish.

Yet the Fund itself quickly proved unable to handle the problems which developed. It made no provision for increasing owned reserves effectively. Its credit facilities were too small. It provided no leadership in achieving adjustment, and even impeded that process. Conventional wisdom has it that the United States filled the gap unilaterally. U.S. deficits provided the reserve growth sought by other countries through the dollar. The United States extended credit when credit was needed. U.S. deficits enabled the other industrialized countries to meet at least a large part of their mercantilist desires for trade as well as payments surpluses and hence avoid any need to

---

25. The British (Keynes) plan would have been superior to the American (White) plan on many of these issues. In fact, in retrospect we can see that the United States would have fared better under the British plan than under its own, if only because it would then have financed European reconstruction with loans via the Fund, instead of Marshall Plan grants, and hence would have had recourse to sizable assets with which to finance its own subsequent deficits, which would have been far less contentious than the continuing expansion of its own dollar liabilities.

adjust. Many observers thus refer to the postwar monetary system as a "dollar standard," in which the dollar was the primary reserve asset and most countries pegged their exchange rates to the dollar.

This is a fairly accurate picture of what happened prior to 1958. Even then, however, different countries adopted different attitudes toward the dollar and U.S. dominance of the system. There was never a monolithic "dollar standard," even during the period of "dollar shortage," under which all countries behaved similarly toward the dollar and toward the United States. These differences in attitudes became stronger after 1958, when the major European currencies returned to convertibility and the U.S. deficits became much larger. The differences intensified throughout the 1960s, finally forcing de facto inconvertibility on the dollar in the latter part of the decade and de jure inconvertibility in 1971.

In my view, the unitary system created at Bretton Woods in fact broke up—not into a unitary system based on the dollar—but into a tripartite system containing a dollar area, a sterling area, and a gold bloc. To be sure, these monetary zones were based on different degrees of formality, and their nature shifted quite differently over time. But the de facto members of the three areas adopted clearly different attitudes and policies toward virtually all international monetary issues. The system which developed was in fact not unlike the tripartite division of the world along similar (dollar-sterling-gold) lines in the 1930s, or even the tripartite division among groupings based on sterling, the French franc, and the German Reichsmark prior to 1914. In my view, the evolution of the postwar monetary system can best be understood in terms of this approach.[26]

The Tripartite Nature of the Postwar International Monetary System
The allegiance of countries to different monetary groupings can be observed in two ways. The first is the maintenance of a fixed exchange-rate relationship between a country's currency and that of the reserve center of the area. The second is a country's pattern of reserve holdings; members of a currency area hold their reserves primarily in the currency of the reserve center of the area. If a country both maintains a fixed relationship between its currency and that of the center coun-

26. The "key currency" approach was the main rival to the Bretton Woods approach during the wartime planning period. See especially John H. Williams, "Currency Stabilization: The Keynes and White Plans," *Foreign Affairs*, Vol. 21, No. 4 (July 1943), pp. 645–58. The one postwar analysis which uses this analytical framework to any significant extent is Gunther Ruff, "A Dollar Reserve System as a Transitional Solution," *Princeton Essays in International Finance*, No. 57, Jan. 1967.

try, and holds all of its reserves in the center's currency, it is clearly of a member of the given currency area. This is the traditional pattern of the sterling area.

There are less clearcut situations, however. A country may "join" a currency area after it has already accumulated sizable reserve assets other than those of its new center country, and continue to hold them. A country may hold its reserves in a key currency but let its exchange rate fluctuate vis-à-vis that same key currency country, as did Canada in the 1950s. In such cases, it may still be accurate to classify a country as a member of a "currency area." In general, the mode in which reserves are held is a more important indication of "currency area membership" in a world of fixed exchange rates, which relies more heavily on financing than on adjustment; and the maintenance of a fixed exchange-rate relationship is a more important indicator in a world of flexible exchange rates, which relies on adjustment rather than financing.

Parities between particular countries can be maintained through parallel changes in their exchange rates vis-à-vis other currencies (as in the common floating of most sterling countries after 1931, or of the several European countries clustered around the German mark from early 1973), or by joint defense of an existing parity between them (as through the area-wide exchange controls of the sterling area after 1932); these are the "adjustment indicators" of national monetary allegiance. In addition, parities can be maintained through sizable financing between the countries, as in the preferential treatment accorded sterling countries in the London capital market and the holding of sterling by those countries in lieu of conversions into British reserves.

A large number of countries pegged their exchange rates to sterling in the early postwar period and maintained area-wide exchange controls, thus maintaining the formal sterling area relationships which had developed in the interwar period.[27] Most other countries pegged their exchange rates to the dollar, which is one reason why some observers have viewed the world as being completely on a "dollar standard." These observers, however, confuse the *method* of pegging with the *purpose* of pegging. To be sure, a country will peg to a cur-

27. A small number of (mainly African) countries developed similar relationships with France and Portugal, but the "franc zone" and "escudo zone" were never large enough to be important separate elements in the international monetary system. They are ignored in this analysis.

rency to which it intends to keep its rate fixed. But the opposite is *not* true: a country will not necessarily keep its rate fixed to a currency to which it pegs. Pegging decisions may be based simply on convenience or cost considerations, and most non-sterling countries have pegged to the dollar throughout the postwar period because it offered the largest and most convenient financial markets. But many of these countries changed their dollar parities one or more times— whereas few sterling countries ever changed their sterling parities while remaining in the sterling area. Indeed, only twenty-five of the fifty-three countries which were pegging to the dollar in late 1973 had kept their dollar *parities* intact through the U.S. devaluations of 1971 and 1973, and six of them changed their dollar parities later in 1973.

The "adjustment indicator" of monetary allegiance is thus the maintenance of ties between exchange rates, with or without explicit policy coordination to maintain those ties. The waning importance of sterling can be seen in the sharp reduction in the number of countries, from 1931 to 1949 to 1967 to 1972, which followed the British devaluations.[28] The decline of the dollar can be seen by the fact that thirteen countries which emulated its devaluation in 1971–72 did not do so in February 1973 (although there were four which followed the reverse pattern), and that several additional countries did not follow its subsequent depreciation after March 1973. In fact, no major financial power—except, curiously, several of the newly rich Arab oil countries—was even pegging its exchange rate to the dollar by late 1973. The rising importance of the mark can be seen by the number of important countries which began to peg to it after most rates were freed to float in March 1973: Belgium, Denmark, France, the Netherlands, Norway, Sweden and, de facto, Austria and perhaps Switzerland. Table 7 roughly arrays the IMF members in terms of their pegging practices in late 1973.

The second indicator of monetary allegiance is a country's pattern of reserve holdings. As already noted, both dollar area and gold bloc countries may peg their currencies to the dollar. But dollar area members make the bulk of the changes in their total reserves by accumulating or selling dollars. They either have high "foreign exchange

28. For the trend from 1931 to 1967, see Benjamin J. Cohen, *The Future of Sterling as an International Currency* (London: Macmillan, 1971), pp. 191–95. Only twelve countries (Bangladesh, Barbados, Fiji, The Gambia, India, Ireland, Malawi, Mauritius, Sierra Leone, Sri Lanka, Trinidad-Tobago) were floating with sterling by late 1973.

Table 7

PEGGING ARRANGEMENTS OF IMF MEMBERS, LATE 1973

To The Dollar (54)		To the Mark (8) (Eurofloat)	To Sterling (13)	To French Franc (12)	None (23)
Followed both U.S. devaluations (25)	Other (29)				
Bolivia	Algeria	Austria	Bangladesh	Cameroon	Afghanistan
Costa Rica	Argentina	Belgium	Barbados	Central African Republic	Australia
Dominican Republic	Burma	Denmark	Fiji	Chad	Brazil
Ecuador	Burundi	France[2]	Gambia	Congo	Canada
El Salvador	Egypt	Netherlands	Guyana	Dahomey	Chile
Greece[1]	Ethiopia	Norway	India	Gabon	Colombia
Guatamala	Ghana	Sweden	Ireland	Ivory Coast	Finland
Haiti	Iran	Switzerland	Malawi	Mauritania	Germany[2]
Honduras	Iraq		Malta	Niger	Italy
Iceland[1]	Jamaica		Mauritias	Senegal	Japan
Indonesia	Jordan		Sierra Leone	Togo	Korea
Israel	Libya		Sri Lanka	Upper Volta	Lebanon
Kenya[1]	Kuwait		Trinidad-Tobago		Malaysia
Liberia	Malagasy				Morocco
Mexico	Mali				New Zealand
Nicaragua	Nepal				Portugal
Panama	Nigeria				Singapore
Paraguay	Pakistan				South Africa
Peru	Rwanda				Thailand
Philippines	Saudi Arabia				United Kingdom[2]
Sudan	Somalia				United States[2]
Tanzania[1]	Spain				Uruguay
Thailand[1]	Syria				Vietnam
Uganda[1]	Tunisia				
Zaire	Turkey				
	Other (cont.)				
	Venezuela				
	Yemen				
	Yugoslavia				
	Zambia				

[1] Changed their dollar parities after March 1973.

[2] Center of currency area.

Source: International Financial Statistics, November, 1973.

68

ratios," or steadily increase their foreign exchange ratios, or both. The foreign exchange ratios of gold bloc countries are very low.[29]

The operational stress is on the country's use of dollars at the margin, the relationship between *changes* in its foreign exchange holdings and *changes* in its total reserves. Countries "joined" or "left" the dollar area at different stages in the buildup of their total reserves, and so have showed sharp differences in the overall percentage of their reserves represented by dollars—although dollar area countries generally show far higher foreign exchange ratios than gold bloc members show. Those which were dollar area members from 1945 (or even before), such as many Latin American countries, had very high foreign exchange ratios throughout the period and obviously could not show sizable increases therein. Some countries which "joined" at a late date, such as Germany, already had large gold holdings and thus lower though rising— foreign exchange ratios. Full members of the dollar area settle all of their surpluses and deficits in dollars.

Table 8 arrays the foreign exchange ratios of the 27 countries with the largest reserve holdings in the world, which accounted for 88.3 per cent of global gold and foreign exchange holdings at the end of 1971.[30] The table focuses on the four different time periods which

29. The "foreign exchange ratio" simply describes the percentage of a country's reserves held in the form of foreign exchange. The higher this ratio, the more attached is a member to a currency area. The ratio can range between o (if the country holds no foreign exchange) and 100 (if it holds no gold). It would be desirable to determine separate "dollar ratios" and "sterling ratios" and "mark ratios" to distinguish further the activity of countries such as Australia, which moved from the sterling area into the dollar area, but data permitting such comparison are not publicly available. The dollar and sterling areas essentially fused in 1968 anyway, as will be discussed shortly in the text, when the bulk of the sterling balances acquired dollar-value guarantees and the United Kingdom began to take all of its reserve increases in dollar form.

30. The table compares only national gold and foreign exchange holdings and excludes the two other components of owned reserves—SDRs and IMF positions—for two reasons. First, countries share in initial SDR allocations and increases in IMF quotas on the basis of their relative Fund positions and have no control over these increases in their total reserves unless they (a) have enough power to block SDR and regular quota allocations in the first place or (b) opt out of the SDR allocations after they have been decided. Second, surplus countries have limited control over changes in their SDR holdings and IMF positions, which are determined by IMF decisions under the SDR "guidance" procedure and Fund policy on "currencies to be drawn" when deficit countries use their SDRs and IMF credits. There are minor exceptions to these generalizations. On occasion, countries (including France) have objected to the use of their currency —and hence an increase in their Fund position—by the Fund. And, on at least one occasion, a country (Italy) converted its dollars into an increase in its Fund position.

Table 8

FOREIGN EXCHANGE* RATIOS OF THE WORLD'S LEADING
FINANCIAL POWERS, 1948–MARCH 1973
(Reserves in millions of dollars)

| | 1948 | | | |
	Gold	Foreign Exchange	Gold +FX	FX Ratio
Gold Bloc				
Austria	50	12	62	.193
Belgium	624	328	952	.344
France	548	5	553	.009
Italy[1]	96	328	424	.773
Netherlands	167	166	333	.498
Portugal	236	303	539	.562
Switzerland	1,387	274	1,661	.164
Dollar Area				
Brazil	317	441	758	.581
Canada	401	610	1,011	.603
Germany[2]	—	295	295	1.000
Israel	—	103	103	1.000
Japan	3	81	84	.964
Mexico	42	36	78	.461
Norway	53	88	141	.624
Saudi Arabia	na	na	na	na
Spain[3]	111	10	121	.082
Sweden	81	152	233	.652
Thailand	77	138	215	.641
Turkey	167	30	197	.152
Venezuela	323	36	359	.100
Sterling Area				
Australia	88	1,177	1,265	.930
Egypt	54	1,353	1,407	.961
India	256	3,099	3,355	.923
Ireland	17	408	425	.960
Libya	na	na	na	na
Malaysia	—	112	112	1.000
Reserve Centers				
United Kingdom	1,596	398	1,994	.199
United States	24,399	—	24,399	.000

* Includes *all* holdings of foreign exchange. As discussed in text, data on the currency composition of foreign exchange holdings are not available. This table thus assumes that *all* foreign exchange holdings are either dollars (for "dollar area countries") or sterling (for "sterling area countries"). Thus it ignores *inter alia* the rapid buildup in mark holdings in the last period and the shift of some sterling countries into dollars.
FX—foreign exchange.
na—not available.

	1957				1967		
Gold	Foreign Exchange	Gold +FX	FX Ratio	Gold	Foreign Exchange	Gold +FX	FX Ratio
102	407	509	.799	695	667	1,362	.489
915	227	1,142	.198	1,480	782	2,262	.345
581	64	645	.099	5,234	874	6,108	.143
452	1,027	1,479	.694	2,400	2,221	4,621	.480
744	312	1,056	.295	1,711	556	2,267	.245
461	289	750	.385	699	516	1,215	.424
1,706	192	1,898	.101	3,089	607	3,696	.164
324	152	476	.319	45	142	187	.759
1,100	746	1,846	.404	1,015	1,269	2,284	.555
2,541	2,572	5,113	.503	4,228	2,873	7,101	.404
2	56	58	.965	46	646	692	.933
23	805	828	.972	338	1,453	1,791	.811
180	273	453	.602	166	325	491	.661
45	139	184	.755	18	608	626	.971
16	12	28	.428	69	670	739	.906
101	5	106	.047	785	315	1,100	.286
219	257	476	.537	203	499	702	.710
112	209	321	.651	92	893	985	.906
144	124	268	.462	97	22	119	.184
720	735	1,455	.505	401	398	799	.498
126	1,195	1,321	.904	231	928	1,159	.800
188	277	465	.595	93	102	195	.523
247	695	942	.737	243	419	662	.632
18	278	296	.939	25	403	428	.941
—	43	43	1.000	68	313	381	.821
—	251	251	1.000	31	394	425	.927
1,554	720	2,274	.316	1,291	1,404	2,695	.520
22,857	—	22,857	.000	12,065	2,345	14,410	.162

[1] Moved into dollar area temporarily circa 1964–66. See text.
[2] Joined dollar area 1967. See text.
[3] Joined dollar area 1970. See text.
[4] Virtually all of the increase in the dollar value of gold reserves between August 1971 and March 1973 derived from the increase in the official dollar price of gold rather than increases in the volume of gold held.
Source: IMF, *International Financial Statistics*, various issues.

Table 8—*Continued*

FOREIGN EXCHANGE* RATIOS OF THE WORLD'S LEADING
FINANCIAL POWERS, 1948–MARCH 1973
(Reserves in millions of dollars)

	August 1971			
	Gold	Foreign Exchange	Gold +FX	FX Ratio
Gold Bloc				
Austria	752	1,283	2,035	.630
Belgium	1,584	852	2,436	.349
France	3,523	3,366	6,889	.488
Italy[1]	2,884	3,064	5,948	.515
Netherlands	1,889	404	2,293	.176
Portugal	907	715	1,622	.440
Switzerland	2,909	3,672	6,581	.557
Dollar Area				
Brazil	46	1,266	1,312	.964
Canada	792	3,539	4,331	.817
Germany[2]	4,076	11,147	15,223	.732
Israel	43	583	626	.931
Japan	679	11,069	11,748	.942
Mexico	184	552	736	.750
Norway	34	974	1,008	.966
Saudi Arabia	127	978	1,105	.885
Spain[3]	498	2,139	2,637	.811
Sweden	200	642	842	.762
Thailand	81	772	953	.810
Turkey	127	381	508	.750
Venezuela	391	647	1,038	.623
Sterling Area				
Australia	259	2,164	2,423	.893
Egypt	85	93	178	.522
India	243	651	894	.728
Ireland	16	786	802	.980
Libya	85	2,364	2,449	.965
Malaysia	58	722	780	.925
Reserve Centers				
United Kingdom	558	3,502	4,060	.862
United States	10,209	248	10,457	.023

March 1973[4]				1948 to 1957			
Gold	Foreign Exchange	Gold + FX	FX Ratio	Gold	Foreign Exchange	Gold + FX	FX Ratio
881	1,797	2,678	.671	52	395	447	.883
1,781	1,836	3,617	.507	291	−101	109	<0
4,260	5,683	9,943	.571	33	59	92	.641
3,483	1,986	5,469	.363	356	699	1,055	.662
2,287	2,354	4,641	.507	577	146	723	.201
1,136	1,444	2,580	.559	225	−14	211	<0
3,513	4,363	7,876	.553	319	−82	237	<0
56	4,573	4,629	.987	7	−289	−282	1.024
927	4,305	5,232	.822	699	126	835	.162
4,964	25,045	30,009	.834	2,541	2,277	4,818	.472
46	1,376	1,422	.967	2	−47	−45	1.044
891	16,059	16,950	.947	20	724	744	.973
209	801	1,010	.793	138	237	375	.632
41	1,138	1,179	.965	−8	51	43	1.186
130	2,726	2,856	.954	16	12	28	.428
602	4,457	5,059	.881	−10	−5	−15	.333
244	1,635	1,879	.870	138	105	243	.432
99	1,107	1,206	.917	35	71	106	.669
151	1,498	1,649	.908	−23	94	71	1.323
472	878	1,350	.650	397	699	1,096	.637
313	5,218	5,531	.943	38	18	56	.321
103	48	151	.317	134	−1,076	−942	1.142
293	629	922	.682	−9	−2,404	−2,413	.996
19	898	917	.979	1	−130	−129	1.007
103	2,849	2,952	.965	—	43	43	1.000
70	876	946	.926	—	139	139	1.000
900	4,266	5,166	.825	−42	322	280	1.150
11,651	8	11,659	.000	−1,542	—	−1,542	.000

73

Table 8—*Continued*

FOREIGN EXCHANGE* RATIOS OF THE WORLD'S LEADING
FINANCIAL POWERS, 1948–MARCH 1973
(Reserves in millions of dollars)

	1957 to 1967			
	Gold	Foreign Exchange	Gold +FX	FX Ratio
Gold Bloc				
Austria	593	260	853	.304
Belgium	565	555	1,120	.495
France	4,653	810	5,463	.148
Italy[1]	1,948	1,194	3,142	.380
Netherlands	967	244	1,211	.201
Portugal	238	227	465	.488
Switzerland	1,383	415	1,798	.230
Dollar Area				
Brazil	−279	−10	−289	.034
Canada	−85	523	438	1.194
Germany[2]	1,687	301	1,988	.151
Israel	44	590	634	.930
Japan	315	648	963	.672
Mexico	−14	52	38	1.368
Norway	−27	469	442	1.061
Saudi Arabia	53	658	711	.925
Spain[3]	684	300	984	.304
Sweden	−16	242	226	1.070
Thailand	−20	684	644	1.030
Turkey	−47	−102	−149	.684
Venezuela	−319	−337	−656	.513
Sterling Area				
Australia	105	−267	−162	1.648
Egypt	−95	−175	−270	.648
India	−4	−276	−280	.985
Ireland	7	125	132	.946
Libya	68	270	338	.798
Malaysia	31	143	174	.821
Reserve Centers				
United Kingdom	−263	684	421	1.624
United States	−10,792	2,345	−8,447	>1.000

	1967 to August 1971				August 1971 to March 1973[4]		
Gold	Foreign Exchange	Gold + FX	FX Ratio	Gold	Foreign Exchange	Gold + FX	FX Ratio
57	616	673	.915	129	514	643	.799
104	70	174	.402	197	984	1,181	.833
−1,711	2,492	781	>1.000	737	2,317	3,054	.758
484	843	1,327	.635	599	−1,078	−479	>1.000
178	−152	26	<.000	398	1,950	2,348	.830
208	199	407	.488	229	729	958	.760
−180	3,065	2,885	>1.000	604	691	1,295	.533
1	1,124	1,125	.999	10	3,307	3,317	.996
−223	2,270	2,047	>1.000	135	766	901	.850
−152	8,274	8,122	>1.000	918	13,898	14,816	.938
−3	−63	−66	.954	3	793	796	.996
341	9,616	9,957	.965	212	4,990	5,202	.959
18	227	245	.926	25	249	274	.908
16	366	382	.958	7	164	171	.959
58	308	366	.841	3	1,748	1,751	.998
−287	1,824	1,537	>1.000	104	2,318	2,422	.957
−3	143	140	>1.000	44	993	1,037	.957
−11	−121	−132	.916	18	335	353	.949
30	359	389	.922	24	1,117	1,141	.978
−10	249	239	>1.000	81	231	312	.740
28	1,236	1,264	.977	54	3,054	3,108	.982
−8	−9	−17	.529	18	−45	−27	>1.000
—	232	232	1.000	50	−22	28	<.000
−9	383	374	>1.000	3	112	115	.973
17	2,051	2,068	.991	18	485	503	.964
27	328	355	.923	12	154	166	.927
−733	2,098	1,365	>1.000	342	764	1,106	.690
−1,856	−2,097	−3,953	.530	1,442	−240	1,202	<.000

represent the four phases of the postwar monetary system. It presents a clear picture of two different sets of countries: one with a much stronger preference for dollars or sterling, and hence with high foreign exchange ratios; the other with a much stronger preference for gold, and hence much smaller foreign exchange ratios.[31] A "hard core" of six to ten countries, which has always accounted for a large percentage of total world reserves (and, since 1969, a majority of the world's gold reserves), obviously preferred gold throughout this period. The "membership" of the group shifted throughout the period; for example, Germany and Spain are included under "dollar area" because they had moved into that grouping in the later periods, but both were gold bloc countries with low foreign exchange ratios through most of the 1960s. It is interesting to note the continuity of preferences for gold in the membership of the interwar and postwar gold blocs: Belgium, France, Italy, the Netherlands, and Switzerland were the most important in each.

The degree to which these preferences for gold were exercised changed dramatically. They were fully manifest during the first period, through 1958, as gold bloc countries took the bulk (63 per cent) of their reserve increases in gold *despite* the slow growth of world gold holdings in general. They intensified during the 1960s as the weakening of the dollar became increasingly apparent, with gold bloc countries taking 75 per cent of their much larger surpluses in gold. (The figure rises slightly if Germany and Spain are included in the gold bloc for this period.) But the preferences for gold became virtually absent (except for Belgium and the Netherlands) as dollar convertibility became largely nominal after 1967.

Chapters 4–6 will analyze in detail why countries choose to hold different monetary assets at any given point in time, and the reasons why the dollar became the center of a widespread—but by no means universal—monetary area in the postwar period. Here we simply list the operating "rules" which reflected the "membership" of countries in the different monetary areas as a necessary backdrop to completing this summary discussion of postwar monetary history. It is also worth repeating that the degree to which these "rules" were implemented by different countries shifted over time as the dollar area moved through its several phases.

The first "rule" of any dollar area is that "member countries" finance their payments imbalances, with both dollar and nondollar

31. In interpreting the ratios, it must be remembered that even gold bloc countries have maintained working balances in dollars because of the near-universal use of the dollar for intervention purposes.

countries, by changes in their dollar balances. A second "rule" was a corollary of the first: the United States, as the center of the area, stood ready to settle in gold any deficits originally settled in dollars by dollar area members ('including itself). Japan financed its payments deficits in dollars, which might then be presented to the United States for conversion into gold if the initial settlement was with a gold bloc country. Japan did not have to settle is imbalances in nondollar assets unless, of course, it ran out of dollars and needed to draw on any other reserves which it might hold.

The U.S. role was thus, in practice, not unlike the traditional British role at the center of the sterling area. There was one important difference, however. Britain generally settled its own imbalances outside the sterling area with reserve assets in the first instance, rather than by building up sterling liabilities. The reason is that Britain defended a fixed parity for sterling in the exchange markets (against the dollar) whereas the United States did not. This defense was carried out mainly by private British banks, which filled their needs for foreign exchange by buying dollars from the Bank of England in return for sterling. So a sterling parity has always been maintained by direct sales of reserve assets by the Bank of England.

By contrast, the dollar parity was traditionally maintained in the first instance through dollar accumulations by other countries, in view of the intervention currency role of the dollar. These surplus countries then had to take an active initiative to convert their dollars into U.S. reserves. As a result, the United States was not always called upon to use its gross reserves to finance deficits of the dollar area (including itself), whereas the United Kingdom was almost certainly called upon to use its gross reserves to finance any sterling-area deficits.

This discussion highlights the absence in the dollar area, due to its relative informality, of one element which was a long-standing feature of the sterling area: reserve pooling. As noted above, the United States has had to draw on its gold stock to finance Japanese deficits, and hence U.S. gold reserves could fall even when the United States itself was not running a payments deficit.[32] But there is no direct addition to the U.S. gold supply when Japan runs a payments surplus with the nondollar world. The loss to the United States from the absence of such pooling, however, was limited because of the global use of the dollar as an intervention currency. A

32. In practice, such occasions were quite infrequent. The history is analyzed in detail in Chapter 8.

Japanese surplus with France is financed initially by a shift of dollars from France to Japan. France would thus either run down dollar balances which it held temporarily, which would otherwise have been converted into U.S. gold shortly anyway, or have to replenish its dollar working balances by selling gold to the United States. Indeed, France did sell $925 million of gold to the United States as late as 1968–69 for precisely this reason.

One implication of these "rules" is that dollar area countries do not buy gold from the United States to augment their own gold holdings, although this rule was formalized only with Germany.[33] However, dollar countries had no need to do so from the standpoint of financing their current deficits anyway, because, as just noted, the U.S. stood ready to convert into gold any deficits which they might have run with nondollar countries and settled initially in dollars. Since this "rule" applied only at the margin, dollar area members did not have to sell to the United States gold balances which they had accumulated previously, although there have been a few instances in which dollar area countries, mainly Canada and a few Latin American countries, have sold gold to the United States when they did not need to do so to finance their own payments deficits. In addition, dollar area countries—such as Germany in 1969—have run short of dollars for intervention purposes and sold gold to the United States to replenish them.[34] But the general absence of gold sales to the United States by dollar countries indicates that no such requirement ever existed.

It should be noted further that there have been some breaches of even the existing marginal rule. As Table 8 indicates, a few countries added to their gold holdings during their periods of membership in the dollar area. However, none did so to a very large degree, particularly after 1957, and most of their increases came from IMF sales and their shares in the distributions of the gold pool when it was a net buyer of gold in the early 1960. In addition, Germany and

33. See the letter of March 30, 1967, from Bundesbank President Blessing to Federal Reserve Chairman Martin, the supporting letter of the same date from Chancellor Kiesinger to Blessing, and the official U.S. statement on the subject in Department of State press release No. 104, May 2, 1967. In an interview published posthumously, in *Der Spiegel* of May 1971, p. 82, Blessing confessed "a sense of personal guilt" for signing the letter, and concluded that "the dollars which came in to us should without any reservation have been converted to gold," but recognized that "the letter which I wrote at that time is unfortunately still valid today."

34. In that particular case of this German gold sale, of $500 million, the United States agreed that Germany could repurchase the gold without violating its commitment cited in note 33. However, Germany has not done so.

Spain joined the dollar area late in the period and their gold purchases pre-dated their "membership."

The Evolution of the Tripartite System

The passage of the postwar monetary system through its four phases can best be explained through the changes which took place in the relationships among the three groups of countries just described, and in the international roles of the dollar which basically determined those relations.

First came the period of "dollar shortage," extending from the end of World War II through 1957. The dollar was the only major currency (except for the Swiss franc and the floating Canadian dollar) which was freely convertible, both into other national currencies and into reserve assets of the issuing country. Gold holdings and IMF positions rose slowly, and sterling holdings remained roughly constant (although they changed hands a good deal). Virtually all countries sought all the dollars they could get, but a number of countries also bought gold from the United States at frequent intervals as the gold bloc began to take shape. The U.S. payments deficits of this period were largely "demand-generated," and were, if anything, frequently too small in terms of the equilibrium needs of the system. Because enough dollars and new gold were not available, the European Payments Union was created to provide additional credits to facilitate the liberalization (on an intra-European basis) of European trade and payments.

The adjustment process in this period was dominated by the U.S. effort to run sufficiently sizable deficits to meet world demand for dollars.[35] The effort included large U.S. aid, which was often "reverse tied" to procurement abroad, large U.S. military expenditures overseas, promotion of travel abroad and private foreign investment by U.S. firms and banks, and acceptance of trade discrimination and nonreciprocal trade agreements.

Other surplus countries (especially Germany in the later 1950s) adjusted by accelerating the reduction of their trade and exchange

35. These "deficits" were often viewed as "surpluses" on contemporary definitions. For an amusing description of how the U.S. position in 1951 was viewed first as a surplus of $5 billion and then later, after twenty changes in definitions over eleven years, as a deficit rising to almost $1 billion, see Fritz Machlup, "The Mysterious Numbers Game of Balance-of-Payments Statistics," in his *International Payments, Debts and Gold* (New York: Charles Scribner's Sons, 1969), pp. 144–47. This period provides some of the best evidence why payments balance and payments equilibrium can be two quite different concepts.

controls. Deficit countries maintained widespread controls, and hence suppressed their payments disequilibria. After the devaluations of 1949 restored rough equilibrium among the exchange rates of the major countries, there were no more parity changes in this period. Nor did any major countries alter their domestic policies in the direction called for by their external positions, with the exception of the United Kingdom and Japan,[36] both of which generally had internal needs that required policies similar to those which helped restore payments equilibrium as well as very low reserves.

During this period, countries were free to compose their reserve portfolios in any way they wanted. Gold bloc countries were under no pressure, either from the United States or from concern for the stability of the system, not to buy gold from the United States. Many did so, and the world was truly on a "gold exchange standard," but U.S. gold holdings were higher at the end of 1957 than at the end of the war. At the same time, countries which wanted dollars (and sterling) could add whatever balances they could earn. This period provides the best evidence of the real reserve asset preferences of the various countries, and the tripartite system had developed along reasonably clear lines by its conclusion. Table 8 shows that virtually all of Continental Western Europe was in the gold bloc, the sterling area of the interwar period remained basically intact, and Japan and Scandinavia had joined a large number of less developed countries in holding most of their reserves in dollars.

The three monetary areas which emerged made sense in terms of the economic linkages among the countries which comprised each. (The reasons why the various countries adopted these different attitudes, which are crucial to an understanding of the postwar monetary system and the role of key currencies, are analyzed in depth in Chapters 4–6.) They were relatively compact, or at least proximate, geographically—except for the sterling area, which had always been geographically far-flung and was already beginning to wither partly for that reason. But the gold bloc comprised most of Europe, and the dollar area comprised mainly the Western Hemisphere and much of East Asia. The system was thus quite like the tripartite regime which had emerged in the 1930s, and not unlike that in the Europe-centered world prior to 1914.

The second phase of the postwar system ran from 1958 until about 1967–68. It was ushered in by the return to convertibility of European currencies at the same time that the Six created the Common Market, which were major steps toward cutting the huge economic and political lead held until that time by the United States. The

36. Michaely, op. cit., esp. pp. 33–37.

sizable French devaluation of 1958, the only major parity change between 1949 and 1967, provided France with an especially potent competitive position upon entering this phase. (The resumption of convertibility was the closest postwar parallel to the interwar "stabilization" returns to gold parities by the major Europeans in 1923–26.) This was the only postwar phase in which all major currencies have been fully convertible.[37]

The dominant feature of the period was the fundamental change in the international role of the dollar and the U.S. balance-of-payments position. The United States was no longer comfortable with the gold losses occasioned by the coincidence of its payments deficits with the continued surpluses of gold bloc countries. Some other countries no longer anxiously sought dollars, or even wanted to hold more, and some thought world liquidity was growing too fast. But some countries continued to seek dollars and happily hold all they earned, and some thought world reserves were growing too slowly. So it was ambiguous whether the U.S. deficits were still demand-generated, or whether they were at least partly supply-generated, and therefore whether anything—and, if so, what—should be done about them. The period can best be labeled a "gold-dollar standard."

The United States first responded by attuning domestic macroeconomic policy at least partly to the needs of the balance of payments—a classic "gold standard" adjustment approach. However, the specific macroeconomic measures chosen by the Eisenhower and Kennedy administrations differed to some extent. The Republicans chose the classic method of deflating, balancing the budget, and tightening money, despite the underutilization of domestic resources. The Democrats, on the contrary, sought adjustment mainly through the improved competitive position and capital flows which they avowed would result from "getting the country moving again." However, partly because of the balance of payments, they too hesitated for a time in proposing needed tax cuts and kept interest rates high. They also made a major concession to monetary orthodoxy through "Operation Twist," which sought to avoid liquid capital outflows without impairing domestic investment by keeping short-term interest rates high and long-term rates low.[38] The other lines of attack in this period were to cut the foreign-exchange costs of gov-

37. The Japanese yen did not become technically convertible until 1964, but had in practice become so several years earlier.
38. See Theodore Sorensen, *Kennedy* (New York: Harper & Row, 1965), esp. pp. 405–08, and Arthur Schlesinger, Jr., *A Thousand Days* (Boston: Houghton Mifflin, 1965), esp. pp. 652–65, who quotes Kennedy as saying that the two things that "scared him most" were nuclear war and the payments deficit.

ernment programs, by tying foreign aid and overseas military expenditures to procurement in the United States, and by negotiating military sales agreements with Germany and other allies. To this point, all of the measures adopted were applied across-the-board to all foreign countries.

There seemed never to be any serious consideration of devaluation, despite the existence of substantial unemployment and hence the existence of a dilemma case which in fact seemed to call for just such a step. There were three reasons. First "dollar shortage" continued to set the intellectual framework of the period, and it was regarded as inconceivable that other countries would let the United States cut the rate of the dollar; as we shall see in detail later, they could prevent devaluation of the dollar against their currencies simply by maintaining the price at which they intervened—via the dollar—in the exchange markets. Second, and closely related, there was widespread confidence—at least in the United States, and probably abroad as well—that the U.S. deficits were temporary phenomena which would soon move back into equilibrium.[39] Third, and also closely related, the United States continued to view its foreign economic policy as an integral element of its security policy, which during this very period was facing the height of the cold war through such events as the Berlin crisis of 1961 and the Cuban missile crisis a year later. Continued U.S. support for its allies, particularly in Europe, thus remained at the core of foreign policy—and even the hint of devaluation could throw off-course both U.S.-European relations and confidence in the European economies. Devaluation, if even considered at all, was decisively rejected.

These three factors fused with, and reinforced, the desire to maintain and expand the key currency roles of the dollar. Devaluation would hurt U.S. relations with other countries and shatter confidence in the outlook for the U.S. balance of payments, but it would also undermine the dollar in international finance. To be sure, much of the U.S. concern over undermining the dollar related to a sincere, and largely correct, concern that serious systemic instability would result from such a train of events. But the international roles of the

39. This confidence gained support from the publication of Walter S. Salant et al., The United States Balance of Payments in 1968 (Washington, D.C.: The Brookings Institution, 1963), which foresaw a sizable U.S. surplus, or, at worst, a small deficit by 1968. With the advantage of hindsight, we can see that the Brookings authors greatly underestimated the outflow of U.S. private capital throughout the 1960s. But their projections of the current account were right on track until the Vietnam-induced inflation commenced in 1965–66, and they can hardly be blamed for failing to foresee the escalation of conflict in Southeast Asia and the failure of U.S. economic policy to compensate therefor.

dollar were also perceived as highly desirable from a U.S. standpoint, and thus worth some costs to defend.

The main thrust of the international monetary policy of the Kennedy and Johnson administrations was thus an unending series of efforts to achieve additional financing for U.S. deficits. The major component of that effort was to promote the reserve currency role of the dollar. As early as 1962, the United States took two steps in that direction. First, it instigated the gold pool to provide a stronger defense against the possibility of another speculative increase in the price of gold in the London market. Such an outbreak in 1960 had raised expectations of a dollar devaluation, which would undermine the key currency position of the U.S. currency. Second, it called for other currencies to assume key currency roles alongside the dollar, which would legitimize this role for the dollar by making it nominally open to others as well and presumably expand its financing potential.

But as the United States now concluded that it had a "balance-of-payments problem" only when gold bloc countries ran surpluses and tapped its reserves, it also began to use specific levers to bring countries more or less formally into the dollar area. The process began with the United Kingdom in the early 1960s. Britain had previously been one of the major buyers of U.S. gold, but it bought no more as it relied increasingly on the United States to marshal international support for the continually ailing pound. Canada stopped buying gold when it had to start relying on U.S. financing, both public and private, after it repegged its exchange rate in 1962. Italy accumulated dollars for a time in the mid-1960s after the United States produced a rescue package for the lira in 1964. And Germany, the most persistent surplus country in the world throughout the postwar period, formally renounced its right to convert dollars into U.S. gold in 1967 to avoid the risk of U.S. troop withdrawals. Not surprisingly, the countries which most firmly resisted such U.S. pressures and formed the hard core of the gold bloc were precisely those countries which had clung longest to gold in the interwar period: France, Switzerland, Belgium, and the Netherlands.

In addition, a number of dollar area members (and even a few nondollar countries) began in the middle 1960s to switch their dollar holdings from short-term to long-term U.S. assets to help the American payments position as reported on the "liquidity" definition, which was widely used then.[40] Some bought bonds which were not im-

---

40. Most of these transactions had no effect on the "official settlements" balance. The U.S. "official settlements" balance can be improved by shifts of dollars from monetary authorities to commercial banks, but there is no evidence that central banks ever followed this policy for purposes of window-dressing the U.S. balance-of-payments figures.

mediately convertible into U.S. reserve assets.[41] Some made large shifts of short-term dollar balances into "long-term" (i.e., over one-year original maturity) time deposits and certificates of deposits in U.S. banks, which are treated "above the line" on the liquidity definition and hence served to reduce the magnitude of the published deficit on that concept.[42] Some countries—and especially the international lending institutions—also bought large amounts of non-guaranteed U.S. government agency bonds, which also "counted" as helping the published liquidity position, but there are no published data on the purchasers of these assets. These shifts became so large that the outgoing Johnson Administration could report a U.S. surplus on the liquidity definition in 1968, due to well over $2 billion of statistical window-dressing in that year alone, at a time when the underlying U.S. external position was beginning to deteriorate badly.

Not surprisingly, virtually all of the countries which cooperated with the United States in these ways were dollar area members. (Australia was in the process of moving into it from the sterling area.) The dollar area thus did begin to experiment with measures to bolster the payments position of the reserve center, at least as presented publicly, on the view that the published data themselves had a major effect on confidence in the dollar *and* provided monetary officials in other countries with an excuse to remain in the dollar area. There was considerable similarity between these steps and the reserve pooling and discriminatory trading arrangements of the Common-

41. The published data do not distinguish between those bonds which were convertible and those which were not, but they totaled $1.7 billion at their 1968 peak. Canada held $1.3 billion of the 1968 total, and purchased another $1.3 billion of these bonds in 1970 and 1971.

42. Such shifts totalled about $800 million in 1966, $900 million in 1967, and $500 million in 1968. In addition, some international and regional organizations invested both the proceeds of their borrowing in the United States, and some of their own reserves, in such assets. Published data do not permit a precise analysis of which countries made such shifts, but close estimates can be made from inspection of the relevant table of the *Treasury Bulletin*, February 1972, p. 101, which shows the following countries as major holders of long-term claims on U.S. banks at the end of 1968, when they reached their peak of $3.2 billion:

	(in millions)		(in millions)
Japan	$658	Mexico	$168
IBRD	432	Korea	88
IADB	314	Australia	68
"Other" Asia	451	Philippines	67
Argentina	284	Venezuela	44
Israel	241	Taiwan	43
Thailand	201	ADB	31

wealth-sterling area, which helped the British balance-of-payments position for many years.

The United States sought financing from nondollar countries during this period, but the devices which had to be used with them were markedly different. Gold bloc countries agreed to swap arrangements, purchases of Roosa bonds, creation of the General Arrangements to Borrow (GAB) to augment the leading capacity of the IMF, and increases in the size of IMF quotas. All of these lines of credit carried relatively short-term maturities or exchange-value guarantees, however, in contrast to the indefinite maturities and absence of guarantees on dollar-area balances. Thus they were clearly less advantageous to the United States.

The U.S. approach to adjustment shifted abruptly during this period from the global application of macroeconomic measures and reductions in government overseas expenditures to the selective use of capital controls. These controls were selective both in terms of payments items and of countries to which they applied. Not surprisingly, all of the countries just listed as contributing to the apparent improvements in the U.S. balance-of-payments position enjoyed favored treatment under these U.S. capital-restraints programs. The favored treatment of the international lending institutions was also undoubtedly related to their dollar area "membership."

The first U.S. measure was the Interest Equalization Act (IET). Effective from July 1963, it raised for borrowers in foreign countries covered by the tax the cost of floating loans in the United States with maturities exceeding one year. In 1965, the tax was extended to term loans from U.S. banks as well. Exemption from the tax was originally provided for all borrowers in less-developed countries, thereby including some dollar area members and some which were not, all new Canadian issues, and Japanese issues up to $100 million per year. (Japan subsequently lost its limited exemption.) Thus some developed dollar area members (such as the Scandinavian countries, Japan, and Germany) were covered by the tax, while some less developed dollar countries were not. In practice, however, most of the covered dollar countries had no desire to borrow in the United States and did not need exemption. Japan had an exemption as long as it did need it. Germany's formal adherence to the dollar area came almost four years after the inception of IET, and exempting it as a quid pro quo would have been both unnecessary economically and extremely embarrassing politically. And eligible nondollar countries (such as New Zealand) were dissuaded from borrowing in the United States even when they were *willing* to pay the tax. Thus the dollar area discrimination of the IET was much tighter de facto than de jure.

Under the "voluntary cooperation program" that limited U.S. direct investment outflows from 1965 through 1967, a distinction was made simply between "developed countries" (including most of the oil producers), which were covered, and less developed countries, which were not. Canada was not covered by the program during 1965, its first year of operation, but was in 1966 and 1967. When the direct investment program became mandatory in 1968, three categories of countries were set up, and dollar area discrimination became more clear-cut. Flows to the less developed countries were treated most liberally; an intermediate group was comprised of Canada (subsequently completely exempted), Japan, Britain, Australia, and New Zealand; and most of Western Europe plus South Africa were hit hardest. (Spain was moved from the most restricted to the intermediate group in 1970, as a quid for its belated move into the dollar area.) Two aspects are especially noteworthy: the complete exemption of Canada, the closest dollar area member, and the reflection of the evolution toward dollar area membership of three sterling countries, including Britain itself. However, some dollar countries (including Germany and Sweden) were in the tightest category.

There were no exceptions under the voluntary program on foreign lending by U.S. banks administered by the Federal Reserve Board, except for Canada after early 1968. However, less developed countries were originally supposed to receive priority treatment second only to export credits, and a third priority was originally accorded to Japan and Britain. Exemptions under the program on long-term lending by nonbank financial institutions, also administered by the Board, parallelled those under the IET since it mainly covered foreign security issues.

The discrimination applied during this period by the Untied States in its balance-of-payments programs thus recognized the existence of the dollar area but did not do so systematically, due to the informality of the area—and the lack of awareness of its existence even throughout the U.S. government. The components of the program were inconsistent in their country application: the IET (and the related Federal Reserve program for nonbanks) had an LDC exception and limited Canadian (and originally Japanese) exceptions; the voluntary Commerce Department program had a general LDC exception and a Canadian exception in its first year; the mandatory Commerce program exempted Canada, treated all LDCs most liberally, and grouped Japan, Britain, Australia and New Zealand in a middle category; and the Federal Reserve program exempted Canada and provided a secondary priority for all LDCs and a tertiary priority for Japan and Britain.

The underlying conceptual basis of both U.S. liquidity and adjustment policy in this period was recognition of the existence of the two distinctly different monetary areas, the gold bloc and the dollar-sterling area. Two types of new liquidity arrangements were sought: window-dressing statistical operations with dollar area colleagues, and increases in real financing with gold bloc countries—either by inducing countries to shift from the gold bloc to the dollar area, or by providing new modes of inter-area financing. The adjustment efforts sought to concentrate on gold bloc countries, and dollar holders were frequently exempted or provided favorable treatment. The United States, subtly but surely, used its economic and political bargaining leverage, which remained immense, to bring key individual countries into an increasingly recognizable dollar area. To some extent, it used the carrot of concessions, especially preferential treatment under its new capital controls, but did not go nearly so far as Britain had done with trade discrimination—in the Ottawa Agreement in 1932 creating Commonwealth preference—and systematic lending preferences to achieve maximum membership of the sterling area. More visible was the stick of possible reprisals, in a few cases (such as Germany) in broad political and security areas but primarily in the monetary field itself, playing on the growing fears of systemic instability and the widely held view that the United States could "destroy the system" by suspending dollar convertibility. As part of its policy, it was willing to adopt measures aimed at reducing its deficit, or which at least appeared to be seriously aimed at doing so, as evidence of its willingness to accept some share of the responsibility for initiating adjustment. And since it continued to sell gold to those countries which insisted on it, a hard-core gold bloc resistant to U.S. pressures and systemic risks developed openly.

The dollar area which evolved in this period was a geographical anomaly. The most obvious oddities were Germany and Italy (for its brief stay in the area), which were not only closer economically to their neighbors than to the United States but members of a Common Market which included charter members of the gold bloc. An equally odd member was the United Kingdom, the reserve center of another currency area. Even some of the less developed countries in the dollar area, such as some of the oil countries, were much closer economically to Europe than to America.

The sterling area had been equally far-flung geographically, but all of its members—for historical reasons—did have closer economic ties to Britain than to any other major power. And as its similar ties were loosening, in part because of new economic groupings and patterns of trade and investment which were developing around the world, the United States began formalizing a dollar area on even shakier grounds —in the same kind of defensive reaction that led Britain to formalize the sterling area in 1932. In the typology of Susan Strange,[43] the dollar had moved from being a "top currency," chosen by others purely because it was so attractive, to being a "master currency" which was held by some because they were so dependent on the United States and a "negotiated currency" which required specific quid pro quo for others to go on holding it. Thus the new dollar area looked highly unstable even as it was being formed.

During this second postwar period, the other major countries followed the American lead. They sought extra financing when in deficit and relied increasingly on tightening capital controls—on outflows when in deficit, on inflows when in surplus—and even on trade controls when they needed to adjust. Countries became even less willing than in the 1950s to attune domestic policy to external needs. Exchange-rate parities again became sacrosanct—as before 1914, but with conditions far different from those which made the fixed-rate system work reasonably well before 1914—even when changes were clearly needed, as in the British (and perhaps Italian) case on the downside and the German (and perhaps French and Dutch) case on the upside. The inadequate German and Dutch revaluations in 1961, the only parity changes in the whole period, emphasize the point. Suppression of imbalances through financing and controls thus bottled up growing disequalibria and set the stage for moving into the third postwar phase—the "crisis zone."[44]

The third phase began with a series of major events in 1967–68 and lasted until the United States formally declared the dollar inconvertible into its reserves in August 1971. This phase was a de facto dollar standard, and Table 8 shows a sharp upward leap in the marginal foreign exchange ratios of even some of the most perennial gold bloc countries (France, Switzerland) during this period. The dollar was not crowned in 1967–68 because of its own strength, however. Indeed, the basic U.S. balance of payments and internal economy were

---

43. *Sterling and British Policy* (London: Oxford University Press, 1971), esp. Chapter 1.

44. This artful term was coined by Lawrence H. Officer and Thomas D. Willett, "A Note on the Stability of a Reserve-Currency System," *Quarterly Journal of Economics*, Vol. LXXXIII (1969). I view it as applying best to the period outlined in the text.

weakening rapidly. New restraints were placed on the balance of payments in early 1968. The dollar was crowned because one of its rivals (gold) became too strong, the other (sterling) finally expired, and no new rival had yet emerged.

The first key step, already mentioned, was the German renunciation of gold conversions in early 1967. This was the first revelation that the United States felt so threatened that it had to get a country *explicitly* to join the dollar area, and that it was willing to take the risks inherent in using the leverage of its military position to do so. The move was particularly important to the U.S., because Germany was the major surplus country of the period and had financed most of its surpluses with gold during 1957–67.

Next, the British devaluation in 1967 failed to restore confidence in sterling and again triggered—rather than prevented—a massive move out of the currency by official holders. This "diversification" was stopped only by the Basel arrangements of 1968, which gave sterling countries a dollar-value guarantee on virtually all of their sterling reserves and hence effectively brought them into the dollar area.[45] In addition, the private gold speculation which followed the devaluation of sterling threatened to force the United States to suspend the gold convertibility of the dollar. As the United States made clear that it would do so rather than devalue the dollar or agree to a uniform increase in the official price of gold, the major countries at the Washington meeting of financial officials in March 1968 agreed to free the price of gold in the free market and—much more importantly—to refrain from bringing any more gold into official reserves. There were also reports of tacit agreements to avoid any reshuffling among countries of existing gold reserves, i.e., for gold bloc countries not to buy gold from the United States, although some purchases of limited magnitude did take place during the succeeding third phase.

In essence, the dollar area—led by the United States, but with important support from Germany and others—overpowered the gold bloc in the crunch. France, having dropped out of the gold pool in a futile effort to fan the speculative flames in 1967, did not even attend the critical Washington meeting. There was simply no effective alternative to the dollar at the time. To be sure, the pending final agreement on SDRs provided a measure of face-saving for the gold bloc countries other than France (which opposed SDRs, too), but their

45. Britain explicitly recognized the end of the sterling area in mid-1972 when it extended the coverage of its exchange controls to sterling countries. Exception from those controls had been the major remaining benefit of membership in the area. Britain also let the Basel guarantees expire at the end of 1974.

actual creation was still two years away and they would play no role in the private markets anyway. The agreement was also facilitated by the new U.S. payments restrictions adopted in January 1968 and the repeated pledges by U.S. officials that a tax increase to cool the American inflation was coming, but the payments measures had no real adjustment effect and the tax increase was still very uncertain (and did not eventuate for several more months). It was a classic triumph for inertia, though it accelerated by that very fact the changes in the system—in the opposite direction—which, we shall see in Chapters 4–6, were bound to develop in any event as a result of basic changes in the underlying economic and political circumstances.

In this way the tripartite system of 1958–67 dissolved, with sterling merged with the dollar and gold no longer available to provide reserve growth. Final agreement was reached almost simultaneously on the SDR scheme, in principle to provide for growth in world reserves to replace both gold (additions of which to the system were now banned) and dollars. This set of 1967–68 agreements delayed for three years the de jure termination of dollar convertibility and created a twilight third phase of the postwar system, in which the tripartite world of the two previous decades became a near-global dollar area simply because countries had virtually no choice but the dollar.

U.S. payments policy moved sharply toward "benign neglect" in this twilight phase, as might have been expected with the sharp reduction in the threat to U.S. reserves and the explicit elimination of any rivals to the dollar. The specifics included the Nixon administration's hands-off policy on direct responses to inflationary price and wage developments, steady liberalization of the existing capital controls, firm statements that no restraints on foreign travel would again be contemplated (as they were in 1968 by the Johnson administration), relaxation of aid-tying, reduced pressure on Germany and other allies to offset U.S. military expenditures, absence of pressure on Germany or Japan (or anyone else) to revalue despite their large surpluses, changes in Federal Reserve regulations which initially had the effect of reducing capital inflows, and the unwinding of the earlier statistical window-dressing which had improved the published balance-of-payments data.[46] Perhaps most important, during this period the United States ceased its efforts to reform the monetary system after having pushed hard for Special Drawing Rights from 1965 to 1968

46. The Nixon administation did not adopt a pure form of "benign neglect," which would have meant elimination rather than moderation of all the selective measures which it inherited, partly for domestic political reasons (aid-tying and military offsets) and partly for international psychological reasons (the capital controls).

and having begun to push for greater flexibility of exchange rates in 1968

Foreign acceptance of "benign neglect" was eased for a while by the large U.S. official settlements surpluses in 1968–69, due to the extremely tight U.S. monetary policy which accompanied full employment and excessive domestic demand; U.S. agreement in late 1969 to let limited amounts of gold from new South African production into the monetary system; and the creation of SDRs from 1970. The results of the policy were to shift the burden of adjustment completely to other countries, and many of them responded when the United States returned to large deficits after 1969. Canada floated in 1970. The Germans, Dutch, Swiss and Austrians appreciated their exchange rates in early 1971. Indeed, had Japan revalued as well, the de facto dollar standard might well have endured for a good deal longer.

But the United States decided in August 1971 that the dollar standard did not meet its national needs. As a result of persisent domestic unemployment, the Japanese failure to adjust, the development of a trade deficit and massive payments deficit, and the growing threat of congressional support for protectionist trade policies which derived great strength from all three developments, the United States decided—for the first time since 1934—that it wanted real adjustment instead of financing. It sought such adjustment through a sizable devaluation, and decided that it could achieve one only through a lengthy, well-publicized negotiation—which required the suspension of dollar convertibility into U.S. reserves to prevent demands on them as the negotiations proceeded. As a result, any dollars henceforth generated by U.S. deficits had to be held abroad, and the trend toward a global dollar standard begun in 1967–68 reached its zenith—simply because countries now had no other choice. The measures of August 15, 1971 represented a total policy reversal for the United States, from "benign neglect" of its balance of payments to aggressive pursuit of sizable trade and payments surpluses. By making the dollar the only major currency inconvertible into the reserves of its issuing country, the U.S. action ushered in the fourth phase of the monetary system in the postwar period—and clearly signalled the total reversal in the position of the dollar, which had been the only convertible currency in the first of those periods and shared convertibility status with the other major currencies during the second.

Concerns over domestic unemployment dominated this U.S. policy shift. The rate of unemployment was already high, especially with the next Presidential election only fifteen months away. In addition, a wage-price freeze had become absolutely essential to control inflationary psychology, but carried the usual risks for employment characteristic of any anti-inflationary policy. Yet Richard Nixon had already gone quite far, for a Republican President, in defining his "balanced budget" on the full-employment concept and actually permitting a huge deficit, and felt unable to adopt further major fiscal stimuli without excessively offending his conservative supporters. Thus the foreign sector was an inviting target for action, especially when it could be demonstrated that a devaluation—which could be fully justified on balance-of payments grounds—could generate over 500,000 jobs and cut the rate of unemployment by 0.7 percentage points. So the August 15 package included the suspension of convertibility and a plea for that devaluation, with an import surcharge and proposal for new export incentives to assure some employment gains even if the devaluation were not achieved or proved to be inadequate.

The second key factor was the emergence of the first U.S. trade deficit since 1888. In addition to "justifying devaluation," and thereby providing a cover for the employment goal just outlined, the shift seemed to some to symbolize a diminished U.S. competitive ability which could undermine its overall foreign policy and perhaps even national security. The support which a trade deficit lent to advocates of protectionist trade policies reinforced this broad foreign policy concern. Economic and foreign policy reasons thus combined to produce the abrupt policy change.[47]

The stated purpose of the move, of course, was to restore equilibrium in the U.S. balance of payments. Yet it is worth noting that U.S. gold losses were actually smaller in 1970–71 than in 1967–68, even as the published deficit ballooned, and there is no evidence of any queueing to accelerate them. (The only foreign move was a request by the British for exchange-rate guarantees for part of their dollar balances, which would *never* have produced a U.S. gold loss, and would have been strictly parallel to the guarantees which the U.S. always required on sterling while helping the British during their payments crises in the 1960s.) So the de facto dollar standard, based on limited gold convertibility of the dollar, became a pure dollar standard not because of any collapse of the dollar overhang when foreigners panicked at the risk of a dollar devaluation, as predicted for so long by Robert Triffin and others, but because the U.S. changed its basic balance-of-payments goal, seeking a trade surplus and the concomitant reduction in domestic unemployment rather than financing for what-

47. For a more detailed analysis of the decisions of August 15, 1971, see C. Fred Bergsten, "The New Economics and U.S. Foreign Policy," *Foreign Affairs*, January 1972.

ever level of payments deficit it might run. As usual, it was domestic politics rather than foreign policy which forced dramatic changes in long-standing international arrangements.

In systemic terms, however, the U.S. action was quite similar to the British action of September 21, 1931. Both formally ended a "gold exchange standard" by suspending the convertibility of the key currency into that country's reserve assets, and floating the currency toward a depreciated level which would restore its trade position and create jobs at home. Both took a number of countries with them. Both ushered in an era of near-universal floating exchange rates, with a few countries (again, mainly the old gold bloc but this time clustered around Germany in a new mark zone) clinging to internal fixity. Both left some other major countries with overvalued exchange rates and triggered early competitive depreciations by other key countries. (It took the markets only six months to force Britain to reverse the overvaluation of sterling which derived from the Smithsonian Agreement.) Both triggered an accelerated proliferation of national controls and raised serious threats of accelerating tendencies toward trade protectionism, which already existed. Both could trace at least some of their difficulties back to the overt efforts of France to undermine the key currency and to run large payments surpluses by maintaining an undervalued exchange rate. Most important for each nationally, both had stayed overvalued far too long out of concern for maintaining the status of their currencies, at the cost of heavy domestic unemployment, and had failed to recognize the need to align their international financial roles with the sharp declines in their overall economic and political power positions. Most important for the system, both ended forever their respective dominance—the United Kingdom in 1931 opened the door to dollar ascendancy; the United States in 1971 opened the door to an SDR standard, the rise of the mark, or perhaps a multiple key currency world, the choices among which we shall explore later in this book.

For the purposes of this analysis, the most important development in this fourth phase of the postwar monetary system is the widespread repudiation of the dollar. I have noted that the events of 1967–68 turned the world into a near-global dollar area, and the events of 1971 completed that process by ending even the nominal convertibility of the dollar into U.S. reserve assets. In each case, "countries then had no choice but the dollar" as long as they sought to maintain fixed exchange rates and hence finance their external surpluses and deficits. In fact, however, countries had another choice: they could reject fixed exchange rates and opt instead for a system based on adjustment rather than financing. In this way, they could reject the dollar.

Virtually every major country in the world adopted this approach in March 1973. Even a second devaluation had failed to restore confidence in the dollar, which continued to depreciate. Inflationary pressures continued to derive from the continued rapid buildup of dollar balances in virtually all countries after the first devaluation (see Table 8). All major countries thus explicitly left the dollar area, letting their exchange rates henceforth fluctuate against the dollar and ending the dollar buildup. (A partial exception was Japan, which de facto maintained a parity with the dollar for some time after March—but which did so by *selling* huge quantities of its dollar holdings rather than accepting any more dollar increases.) Even when the dollar depreciated after its second formal devaluation to levels which were widely viewed as "grossly undervalued," no central banks entered the market to buy dollars. The "pure dollar standard" thus lasted only eighteen months.

In addition, Europe responded by attempting to develop an independent monetary zone within which the members of the Common Market would keep their currencies tied closely together and float as a unit vis-à-vis the dollar. The United Kingdom and Italy quickly found themselves unable to maintain fixed rates even within this limited group, however, and floated independently.

The remaining European countries, including some non-members of the Common Market, retained the "joint float" essentially by pegging their currencies to the German mark. In addition, a number of countries around the world began holding marks in their reserves. By mid-1973, the mark had already far surpassed sterling as the world's second most important currency, and was growing by far the most rapidly. Thus the second manifestation of the repudiation of the dollar was the emergence on the international financial scene of the German mark.

The third manifestation was the beginning of a restoration of the international monetary position of gold. In early 1974, the two-tiered system adopted in 1968 was amended to permit countries to sell their gold reserves in the private markets—at a price far higher than the official price of $42.22 per ounce. Shortly thereafter, it was agreed that countries could value their gold reserves at "market-related prices" for purposes of using them as collateral against borrowings; Italy soon did so for a loan from Germany. And, in December 1974, the United States and France agreed that any country which wanted to could revalue its overall monetary reserves by valuing all of its official gold at market prices; France immediately announced its intention to do so, and several countries which held little gold in their reserves (notably Iran and Iraq) protested the move. From the systemic standpoint, this trend represented further repudiation of the dollar—perhaps with a changed attitude on the part of the United States, which after all continued to hold by far larger gold reserves than any other country.

To be sure, these developments had already begun to occur in the previous phase of the postwar monetary evolution. As indicated above, the U.S. "benign neglect" which attended the advent of de facto dollar inconvertibility after 1967–68 had triggered frequent floats and revaluations by individual countries (Canada, Germany, the Netherlands, Switzerland, Austria) well before the de jure suspension of convertibility in August 1971, and the mark was already assuming a prominent international financial role. And these systemic changes were not caused wholly by foreign reactions to the dollar. The other major countries had finally understood their own renewed strength, and no longer felt it necessary to lean on the United States. The onset of world-wide inflation made revaluation a much more attractive policy option, in terms of its domestic effects, than it had been since the onset of the Great Depression. But the wholesale repudiation of the dollar came only when the dollar became wholly nonconvertible, was devalued twice, and lost the basic foundation of key currency status with the runaway U.S. inflation of 1973–74.

This repudiation of the dollar was eclipsed for a while, after early 1974, by the deep concern of all oil-importing countries—and hence virtually all of the heretofore major financial powers—over how to finance the sizable deterioration in their current account positions caused by the rise in the price of oil. Indeed, antipathy toward the "dollar overhang" largely disappeared, at least from traditional sources, in the scramble for *any kind* of financing. And the increased emphasis on economic security, as well as the increased fear of deep global economic stress, re-strengthened the relative position of the United States as a safe (and large energy-*producing*) haven, as before 1939. But the developments cited above which indicate repudiation of the dollar—flexible exchange rates, the rise of the mark and other national currencies, the restoration of gold— indicate that the basic trend continues, albeit perhaps at a slower pace and in a less politically charged environment. We turn now to an analysis of why these changes occurred, and what they imply for U.S. international monetary policy in the years ahead.

Part II
The International Roles of the Dollars

4

Attributes of a Key Currency:
The Internal Economics

We must determine the specific requirements for a key currency before we can analyze the effects of the dollar's roles on the United States. First, the costs of a key currency role can be estimated only if these requirements are understood: the costs may be substantial if the country is required to meet additional policy targets, if some of its outstanding targets must be adjusted, or if the number of policy instruments available to it is reduced. Second, the analysis should reveal whether the requirements support each other or are mutually inconsistent, and hence whether a system based on such roles is stable or unstable. Third, the criteria will enable us to judge whether the other members of the international monetary system are behaving in a manner that permits successful exercise of the key currency roles by the center country, let alone whether it and the system as a whole are obtaining the benefits which can be derived from them.

It will also be necessary to assess the relative importance of the individual criteria. Some may merely be functions of a certain international monetary milieu and could be dispensed with under alternative systems. Some may be necessary to *achieve* key currency status but not to maintain it since history amply demonstrates that tradition and inertia bear heavily on monetary practices; indeed, it is much easier to *remain* a key currency than to become one, and it is even quit difficult to *stop* being one. We will try to find the combination of criteria which would be both necessary and sufficient to maintain key currency status under different monetary arrangements.

The three major roles of the dollar—as a transactions currency, an intervention currency, and a reserve currency—are closely linked. Some observers have argued that elimination of any one of them would seriously impair the others,[1] and it is true that any wariness on the

1. See the statement of Robert V. Roosa in Roosa and Fred Hirsch, "Reserves, Reserve Currencies, and Vehicle Currencies: An Argument," *Princeton Essays in International Finance*, No. 54, May 1966, pp. 4–5. Roosa did concede, however, that over a period of decades "it may turn out" that a currency could play a vehicle role "without also serving as a reserve currency" (p. 3).

part of foreign central banks in accepting dollars may indeed reduce the attractiveness of dollars to private users. Most observers agree that the reserve currency role could not exist without the vehicle currency role (which combines the transactions and intervention roles), but would deny the converse. Some would go even further, and argue that the elimination of the reserve currency role—if carried out in a cooperative way—would actually promote the vehicle currency role.[2]

Most analyses of the attributes required of a key currency country have been purely economic.[3] But no one has attempted to define the

2. See, e.g., the statement by Hirsch, *op. cit.*, p. 5.
3. Several authors have made systematic efforts to compile lists of the attributes required of key currency countries. Each, however, has failed either to distinguish between the attributes necessary for vehicle currency and reserve currency status; to rank the criteria for each in the order of their importance; to determine which of them are necessary and sufficient under the present international monetary system and various possible alternative systems; or to include vital political elements. See Robert Z. Aliber, "The Costs and Benefits of the U.S. Role as a Reserve Currency Country," *Quarterly Journal of Economics*, Vol. LXXVIII, No. 3 (August 1964), p. 443 and Chapter 3 of his *The Future of the Dollar as an International Currency* (New York: Frederick A. Praeger, 1966); Herbert G. Grubel, "The Benefits and Costs of Being the World Banker," *National Banking Review*, Vol. 2, No. 2 (December 1964), p. 190, John Karlik, "The Costs and Benefits of Being A Reserve Currency Country," unpublished Ph.D. thesis at Columbia University, pp. 45–59; Peter B. Kenen, *Reserve Asset Preferences of Central Banks and Stability of the Gold Exchange Standard*, Princeton Studies in International Finance, No. 10, 1963, p. 68; Raymond F. Mikesell, "United States as World Banker," *National Banking Review*, Vol. 4, No. 4 (December 1966), pp. 145–46; Robert V. Roosa, *The Dollar and World Liquidity* (New York: Random House, 1967), p. 29; U.S. Treasury Department, *Maintaining the Strength of the United States Dollar in a Strong Free World Economy*, January 1968, p. 21, Cohen, *op. cit.* Criteria for the vehicle currency function are discussed by James Tobin, "The Future of the Dollar as International Money," Carl Snyder Memorial Lecture, University of California, Santa Barbara, March 23, 1965, reprinted in *Guidelines for International Monetary Reform*, Reuss Subcommittee Hearings, part 2, Supplement, 1965, p. 222, and Alexander Swoboda, "Vehicle Currencies and the Foreign Exchange Market: The Case of the Dollar," in Robert Z. Aliber, ed., *The International Market for Foreign Exchange* (New York: Praeger Publishers, 1969), pp. 32–40. Criteria for maintenance of an "international money market" were outlined by William A. Brown, Jr., *The International Gold Standard Re-interpreted 1914–1934* (New York: National Bureau of Economic Research, 1940), pp. 599ff. Implicit lists of criteria are included in George Halm, "Special Problems of a Key Currency in Balance of Payments Deficit," *Factors Affecting the U.S. Balance of Payments*, Compilation of Studies for the Reuss Subcommittee, 1962, pp. 545–48 and William A. Salant, "The Reserve Currency Use of the Dollar: Blessing or Burden to the United States," *Review of Economics and Statistics*, Vol. XLVI, No. 2 (May 1964), p. 166.

overall world role which a country must be both capable of and willing to play in order to assume a key currency role, something all known monetary systems have required. This and the next two chapters will demonstrate that the international role of national currencies depends on the *degree* of national dominance of their countries of issue, the cooperation extended by other countries, and the attitudes and national goals of the key currency country.

The numerous financial and economic criteria that are critical to the calculation are considered in detail in the next two chapters. Political power alone is not enough to produce a key currency, though one question we will want to investigate is whether the required economic attributes are likely to exist only in a country which also meets the political requirements—both perhaps stemming from similar causes, and reinforcing each other. In any event, the economic factors must be seen in the broader political context, the subject of this chapter.

The World Role

A country must play a major part in world affairs politically if it is to achieve key currency status. A basic reason is that a key currency must provide a safe depository for foreign funds, and national military (and hence political) strength is generally required for it to do so.

There are two deeper reasons, however. First, a country probably must achieve some dominance before other sovereign states, at least important ones, will readily accept widespread use of its currency, particularly as a reserve asset. Second, and probably more important, no country would have the self-confidence, and concern for the functioning of the entire system, to be willing to expose itself to the risks of key currency status unless it had sufficient overall leverage with other countries to minimize those risks. To be sure, for short periods a currency may be widely sought purely because it is financially attractive, and then its country of issue may perceive little or no risk in playing an international role. But key currency status develops only over a lengthy period of time during which it is almost certain that purely financial attractiveness will wane at some points; then, partly in response, both countries holding the currency and the country of issue will harbor serious doubts about the wisdom of the enterprise. So the two conditions cited are necessary if any nascent key currency is to survive long enough really to merit the title.

The two major key currency countries in history developed on the basis of being the two most impregnable bastions of national security: Britain prior to World War I, and the United States after World

War II.[4] Britain's competitors were undermined by the Napoleonic Wars, revolutions, and the limited wars of the nineteenth century. Only after peace had returned to the continent for several decades could Germany and France achieve sufficient power to play the regional key currency roles outlined in Chapter 3. The absence of international political leadership between the wars—indeed, the jousting among Britain, France and America—correlates with the absence of currency leadership during that period. After World War II, America's rivals were laid prostrate by the war itself, and then their existence was threatened by the cold war. In recent years, however, the return of relative world political stability coupled with the resurgence of a number of important economies, especially Germany and Japan, has again opened the door to a multiplicity of key currencies. It is noteworth, for example, that exposed Germany could not qualify so long as the cold war persisted—but in 1968, even when the Soviet Union invaded Czechoslovakia, there was little capital flight from Germany. Switzerland is also something of a political bastion because of its geography and its successful preservation of neutrality. Its currency is widely sought. But its inability to play a world political role —as well as its small size, which is closely related—renders it unwilling to take on the risks associated with being a key currency country.

This is not to say that countries seek world political roles in order to achieve key currency status. But broad political involvement around the world leads to economic involvement; trade and finance do "follow the flag" to a large extent.[5] For example, the great rush of U.S. investment into Western Europe in the late 1950s and 1960s was made possible by two earlier political programs: the Marshall Plan, which helped Europe recover economically (and offered insurance to

---

4. Robert Mundell agrees: "The success of the pound was closely tied up with the security domain of the British Empire and the success of the dollar was and is contingent on the security umbrella of the U.S. . . . because these credit monies, unlike their predecessor full-bodied gold monies, had to be immune from political disturbances, especially war." See his comments in Harry G. Johnson and Alexander Swoboda, eds., *The Economics of Common Currencies* (London: George Allen and Unwin, 1973), p. 168.
5. Some of the closest students of the relationship between international economic and political development share this conclusion. The late Henry G. Aubrey, *The Dollar in World Affairs: An Essay in International Financial Policy* (New York: Praeger Publishers, for the Council on Foreign Relations, 1964), concluded that the U.S. world military role led inexorably to its widespread economic role (p. 12), and that the political and economic roles are linked inextricably (p. 29). Strange, *op. cit.*, p. 47, concludes that the British acquisition of empire and development of a key currency role for sterling were "highly inter-active."

U.S. companies against many economic and political risks which they might face in Europe), and the U.S. security commitment in NATO, with its highly visible manifestation in four U.S. divisions in Germany, which made Europe safe from the threat of external aggression. Both the private U.S. investments and the preceding government programs contributed, in turn, to the U.S. balance-of-payments deficits, which required external financing, and hence to the development of the reserve currency role of the dollar. In the British case, such far-flung outposts as Hong Kong, Malaysia, and Kuwait maintained fealty to sterling to preserve the protection afforded them by the British navy[6] —and left sterling (either de jure or de facto, by requiring dollar guarantees for their balances) when the British reduced or abandoned their security commitments in recent years. In both cases, the political involvement clearly came first and the financial role followed.[7]

Once in place, international economic involvement in turn increases the interest of the key currency country in maintaining as much political dominance as possible. The degree of this interest, however, depends on the importance of the international economy to the key currency country. Britain always relied heavily on world trade and foreign customers for The City, which has had great political power within Britain. A leading chronicler of Britain's nineteenth century economic history has concluded that "Britain's widespread commercial interests . . . dictated considerable efforts towards maintaining peace and order in the world."[8] Even in recent years, Britain preserved its military roles in Hong Kong and the Persian Gulf well beyond their scheduled termination in the late 1960s largely for financial reasons.

On the other hand, the United States has not until fairly recently viewed the world economy as very important for its own well-being. Hence its overall foreign policy has been little affected by narrow considerations of economic self-interest although, to be sure, the United States reaped many economic benefits from the postwar system—

6. The British government recognized officially in the White Paper on the Basel arrangements in 1968 (p. 2) that sterling countries had been "diversifying" their reserves in the 1960s *inter alia* because of "an increase in [other] political . . . links with the non-sterling world."
7. Susan Strange, *op. cit.*, p. 44, notes the long time-lag between British political involvement in many parts of the world and the commencement of British financial involvement. U.S. private interests seem to have been a bit quicker in the postwar period, although neither U.S. international banking nor direct investment abroad got going on a really sizeable scale until a decade after official involvement in NATO and the Marshall Plan.
8. Albert H. Imlah, *Economic Elements in the Pax Britannica* (Cambridge: Harvard University, 1958), p. 6.

many of which we will analyze in Chapters 7–10. The U.S. "offset" arrangement with Germany in 1967, however, provides an example of how international economic involvement provides a temptation for a key currency country to seek to maintain political dominance. Germany feared that its only alternative to the commitment not to buy U.S. gold was a reduction in the U.S. troop level. Overall U.S. military policy—and hence U.S. foreign policy toward all of Europe, including the U.S.S.R.—could therefore have become circumscribed by the fear of a collapse of the German share of the dollar overhang. This could have represented a serious policy constraint had the U.S. government (a) wanted to cut troops in Europe for strategic or political reasons, which it did not, and (b) not wanted to suspend dollar convertibility, which it did. But it demonstrates that global economic involvement can induce global political involvement, and suggests that a reduced economic role may be necessary to permit a reduced political role.

In addition, the private sector is likely to play a major role in the foreign economic involvement of most countries. When trouble arises, it will often call on the home government, which will thus face growing domestic pressure to maintain the global capability necessary to give effective support.[9] At the same time the international roles of the currency, by enabling the reserve center to avoid forced adjustment, can help the government maintain the capability and combat isolationist pressures at home. As we will see later, however, there are some circumstances in which the international roles of the currency *promote* such pressures and undermine this capability. The political and economic elements are mutually reinforcing.

9. The revisionist historians claim that these pressures dominated U.S. foreign policy in the early postwar period, and would vehemently reject my conclusion that U.S. foreign policy has been little affected by considerations of narrow economic self-interest. See, e.g., Joyce and Gabriel Kolko, *The Limits of Power, 1945–1954*. However, the Kolkos repeatedly recognize that neither the Congress nor the business community was willing to support administration initiatives which were supposedly taken on their behalf— leading one to ask who were the conspirators who pursued U.S. economic interests under the guise of "national security." Even more important, they do not recognize the prevailing view of the time that the economic collapses of the early interwar period and, especially, the Great Depression, laid the foundation for political chaos and war that followed—and that a failure to restore an effective world economy could do so again, even if a particular threat (which soon turned out to be the U.S.S.R.) could not always be pinpointed. In more than six hundred pages on U.S. foreign policy in the decade after World War II, the Kolkos never once mention Munich—an incredible omission which demonstrates the vapidity of their views. In my view, this line of analysis is much more likely to apply to U.S. policy in the 1970s and beyond than in the period which it covers.

In the financial field, the private sector plays the leading role in fostering the use of key currencies. Such currencies are basically "elected" by the markets; de facto government "ratification" is a necessary but subsequent step. Several currencies in the process of market "election," such as the German mark and especially the Swiss franc, have in fact been retarded in that process by their governments. This observation supports our earlier conclusion that a country's overall world role determines whether it is willing to see its currency play a key currency role and proceed with such "ratification." Countries such as Germany and Switzerland have clearly attracted key currency attention and have most of the economic attributes. They are able, but they have not been willing. Similarly, at least one country— France, in the interwar period and perhaps again in the middle 1960s —has been willing, for political reasons, but not able. Only the United States and Britain, on a global basis, have been both able *and willing*. The explanation lies in the overall world roles played by these countries. This is especially true for the United States, which did not have overwhelming external economic interests, as did Britain.

These world roles depend largely upon the general international system which prevails at a certain point in time. A particular international system is usually based on the security considerations of the major powers, the primary focus of world politics. Economic and financial arrangements are derivative sub-systems. The capabilities and interests of major countries influence systemic development itself, fostering a milieu which in turn provides them with a certain scope for activity. The economic and financial capabilities of a major country thus derive in part from an international system which it had a major role in "constructing" itself, and—even more important— from its willingness to play a particular financial role related to its more general international goals.

Modern history has encompassed two relatively well-defined international systems. One was the balance-of-power system which prevailed prior to World War I. The other was the bipolar system of the first ten to fifteen years after World War II. The interwar period and the present are less clear-cut, but are more closely akin to multipolar systems than either of the historical archetypes.[10] The interwar and present periods differ sharply, of course, because of the direction from

---

10. For a sophisticated refinement of the system into "muted bipolar," "polycentric," and "multipolar" layers, see Stanley Hoffman, *Gulliver's Troubles, or the Setting of American Foreign Policy* (New York; McGraw-Hill, for the Council on Foreign Relations, 1968), Chapter II.

which they moved toward multipolarity: the interwar period from a balance-of-power system which broke down into world war, and the present from a bipolar system wholly dominated by the nuclear superpowers. In addition, in the interwar period, the strongest potential "pole"—the United States—retreated toward disengagement from world affairs, whereas all the important "poles" at present are deeply involved.

British supremacy was the key to the success for the balance-of-power system in preventing global war for a century.[11] Britain achieved supremacy by a willingness to side with whichever of the continental powers was in a weaker power position at the time; this did not "restore the balance," but in fact tipped the scales in favor of Britain's alliance of the moment, thereby deterring conflict. As a result of shifts from one alliance to another, Britain effectively kept Europe divided and prevented any other power from achieving dominance.[12] In addition, by its known willingness to play the balancing role if the price were right, Britain was able through skilful diplomacy to extract major concessions from those who coveted its support.[13] And, more importantly, it was able to keep disputes among the other powers limited to Europe and thereby preserve freedom for its own imperial exploits around the world, which were universally considered at that time a major source of its overall power.[14]

Britain was able to use this dominant political power to sponsor the

---

11. E.H. Carr, *The Twenty Years' Crisis, 1919–1939* (London: Macmillan, 1949), esp. p. 232.
12. In his classic *America's Strategy in World Politics* (New York: Harcourt Brace, 1942), p. 105, Nicholas Spykman concluded that "A divided and balanced continent is a prerequisite to the continued existence of the Empire, and a divided continent means British hegemony." Alfred Pollard, "The Balance of Power," *Journal of the British Institute of World Affairs*, Vol. 2, (March 1923), pp. 61–62, agreed that "The balance of power in Europe was, in fact, a directive according to which Europe was to provide the balance and Great Britain to have the power."
13. Hans J. Morgenthau, *Politics Among Nations*, 3rd ed. (New York: Random House, 1961), p. 194.
14. Pollard, *op. cit.*, concludes that "the advantage to us of the balance of power in Europe was that it released us from a similar incubus anywhere else." One of the leading historians of the period adds that "British policy may be said to have thrown its weight from time to time onto the European scales in order to secure virtual immunity for her overseas designs." He also notes that "peace was never concluded without substantial additions being made to Britain's colonial empire," which reveals how Britain often used the bargaining leverage cited in the text. R. W. Seton-Watson, *Britain in Europe, 1789–1914* (Cambridge University Press, 1955), p. 36.

liberalization of world trade. This was of great importance to it economically because of its heavy dependence on foreign goods and because freer trade meant more income for Britain as the world's leading industrial power.[15] Success in this endeavor in turn required improved means of international payments, especially among private parties but also between monetary authorities, and accelerated the demand for international use of a national currency. Britain's financial and economic capabilities enabled sterling to play such a role even beyond the areas of British political dominance.

At the same time, the economic interest in expanding trade and international finance, and its broader "milieu goals,"[16] induced Britain to permit sterling to realize its capabilities. The use of sterling as a key currency maximized the flow of world transactions, and hence British economic welfare, thereby also maximizing Britain's capability to preserve its political power and security. But Britain also had great faith that laissez faire economics would promote world peace, and part of Britain's power in this period derived from the global influence of its economic thinkers and economic policy.

In the interwar period, the United Kingdom was unable to resume playing the key currency role effectively. Its overall power position and financial and economic capabilities had been jarred by World War I and the collapse of the balance-of-power system to the extent that Britain could never again achieve world dominance. Nevertheless, it continued to pursue its milieu goals. Britain tried to restore sterling's international roles and compounded the mistake by adopting erroneous policies in pursuit of the unobtainable goal.

At the same time, the United States, whose rising world capabilities had been dramatically revealed by World War I, turned away from assuming leadership. Despite its rejection of membership in the League of Nations, the United States became engaged in fairly widespread dealings with Europe during the 1920s, in large part because of the reparations loans to Germany and the inter-allied debts. As a result, the dollar was fairly widely used internationally during the

---

15. At the same time, Imlah, *op cit.*, p. 14, dates the rapid industrialization of *other countries* from 1824, when Britain began its trade liberalization policy. Such progress abroad of course greatly increased the scope for trade, and increased world welfare. Over the longer term, however, it also probably accelerated the decline of Britain's economic leadership and hence the key currency role of sterling.
16. Arnold Wolfers, *Discord and Collaboration* (Baltimore: Johns Hopkins Press, 1962), p. 74, defines "milieu goals" as "shaping conditions beyond their national boundaries" in the image of the countries setting the goals.

1920s.[17] But the United States retreated to virtually total isolationism in the early 1930s with the Smoot-Hawley tariff and the devaluation of the dollar in 1933–34 for purely internal reasons. As a result, the international roles of the dollar were almost eliminated for a time.

The abrupt about-face of U.S. planning for, and policy in, the post-World War II period laid the basis for the development of the dollar's key currency roles as we know them today. The United States stood globally dominant, economically as well as militarily, at the end of the war. Shortly, however, recovery of the Soviet Union produced the bipolar system which prevailed for more than a decade.

The development of this system had two effects. First, it was inconceivable that countries implacably opposed to the United States and grouped around the Soviet "pole"—the U.S.S.R. itself, the Eastern European countries, Communist China at that time, North Korea, and later North Vietnam and Cuba—would hold balances in the United States. The reason is obvious: political hostility would constantly jeopardize the safety of their dollar assets.[18] Some countries

17. The data are fragmentary, but it appears that foreign official dollar balances totaled about $1 billion in June 1927 and that official sterling holdings may have totaled about $2 billion at the same time. Hal B. Lary and Associates, *The United States in the World Economy* (U.S. Dept. of Commerce, 1943), p. 115, and Nurske, *op. cit.*, pp. 235–236. Alan Day, *The Future of Sterling* (Oxford: The Clarendon Press, 1954), p. 33, put it most succinctly: "The single, most outstanding feature of this environment [the international monetary system in the interwar period] was the relative rise in the position of America and the relative decline in that of Britain." Robert V. Roosa noted that "the dollar moved up alongside sterling during the interwar period," in "Outlook for United States Balance of Payments," Hearings, Joint Economic Committee, Subcommittee on International Exchange and Payments, December 13, 1962, p. 119; the statement is broadly correct, although *the value of foreign-held liquid dollars did not come to exceed foreign-held liquid sterling until after sterling's devaluation in 1949.* There was heated opposition to any key currency role for the dollar from the New York Federal Reserve Bank, however, which totally rejected the concepts of the Genoa Resolutions. See Stephen V.O. Clark, *Central Bank Cooperation, 1924–1931* (New York: Federal Reserve Bank of New York, 1967), pp. 38–39, and William A. Brown, Jr., *The International Gold Standard Reinterpreted, 1914–1934* (New York: National Bureau of Economic Research, 1940), p. 1187. The Board of Governors of the Federal Reserve System, on the other hand, actually encouraged the reserve currency use of the dollar by guaranteeing bankers' acceptances purchased for foreign central banks by U.S. commercial banks, greatly increasing the attractiveness of these instruments to the foreign monetary authorities. Lary, *op. cit.*

18. The presence of the Eurodollar market—where the United States cannot effectively control foreign dollar holdings—became an important mitigating factor in the early 1960s. A number of East European countries do hold

were thus ruled out of a dollar system for broad political reasons. By contrast, Britain's pivotal role in the balance-of-power system had led to shifts in its alliance and adversary relationships. No implacable enmities developed, and all countries were potential holders of sterling. Even at the outbreak of World War I, Germany, Austria-Hungary, and Italy held foreign exchange assets in London.[19] And Russia had even floated a loan on the London money market while its troops were fighting British troops in the Crimean War.[20]

Second, hostility between major nations begets alliance systems and intra-alliance hegemony. Political and military dominance by one power may be acceptable as protection against another power. (In the nineteenth century system, the United Kingdom was at once the "protector" of each other major power against the rest and so could generalize widely its "intra-alliance" hegemony.) This increases the likelihood that dependent allies will accept economic and financial dominance by the politically and militarily dominant power: India with regard to sterling both pre-1914 and during World War II, virtually all of Eastern Europe with regard to the ruble after World War II. Indeed, some of the major dollar holders—including Germany and Japan, the two largest—were motivated importantly by their political and military reliance on the United States; at a minimum, they could justify their holdings to domestic critics by pointing to the overriding need to avoid intra-alliance difficulties.

In addition, overseas military expenditures by the dominant power help generate the balance-of-payments deficits which are necessary for an expanding key currency role. As such expenditures are essentially noneconomic, they may be harder to transfer in the form of real resources (devaluation by the sending country increases their costs, for example) and hence are more likely than other overseas expenditures to produce deficits. The causality runs the other way as well: a

dollar balances, although not directly in the United States. But this development at least partly reflects the reduced cohesion of the "Soviet bloc" —the move from a "tight bipolar" toward a "loose bipolar" world system —and the resulting growth of political and economic ties being forged between Eastern Europe and the West. No such developments have yet occurred vis-à vis the Asian Communist countries, so the general point made in the text remains valid for them.

19. At the end of 1913, Germany's foreign exchange assets totaled $50 million, about 15 per cent of total German reserves, of which about $14 million are known to have been held in London. Italy's holdings also totaled $50 million and a similar percentage of its total reserves, but only $6 million were clearly in England. Austria-Hungary held about $17 million in foreign exchange, including $4 million in England. See Lindert, *op. cit.*, pp. 18–19.

20. Imlah *op. cit.*, p. 10.

dominant power with large foreign political expenditures must have a ready way to finance the payments deficits which may result, and an international role for its currency is one way to do so.

Intra-alliance hegemony also increases the willingness of the dominant power to see its currency play a major international role, since it naturally wishes to support the economies of its allies. The dominant power's desire for trade and payments liberalization, and the creation and maintenance of an effective monetary system, is also part of its pursuit of milieu goals. Such goals include the emergence of strong allied economies based on principles congenial to the dominant power, and are important political objectives in its competition with other major powers. They are substitutes for the quest for "possession goals," the historical objective of great powers, which has become particularly risky with the advent of nuclear weaponry. As well as presenting an image of success, successful economic development contributes to the military and political capabilities of the allies and the alliance as a whole. One phase of the economic development of allies is a build-up of their monetary reserves, and it would be surprising if the dominant power would not be ready to assist in this process as well.

These political objectives were decisive for the United States since, unlike the United Kingdom, it did not have an overwhelming interest in the expansion of international trade and finance for domestic economic reasons. As leader of the postwar crusade against Communism, and as an integral part of its policy of containment, the United States sought strong allies built in its own image. It was convinced, based on the experience of the interwar period, that economic weakness sowed the seeds of political instability and jeopardized world peace. So its security goals played a major role in the willingness of the United States to see the dollar play a key currency role.[21] Both the United States and United Kingdom in their hegemonial periods, however, were confident that their economic dominance rendered them immune from harm in the process, and would bring them economic profit from it as well.

21. Political goals also importantly affected Britain's sterling policy at a key point. After World War II, there was widespread pressure—including from the United States—for blockage of at least a large part of the sterling balances which had been built up during the war, to protect both Britain and systemic stability. India was one of the major sterling holders, however, and Indian independence—the viability of which would have been jeopardized had India's reserves been largely blocked—was a major goal of British foreign policy at the time. So Britain accepted the continued costs of the sterling overhang at least partly for this reason. See Richard N. Gardner, *Sterling-Dollar Diplomacy* (New York: McGraw-Hill, expanded edition, 1969), p. 326.

Indeed, key currency countries must place higher importance than other countries do on their milieu goals, relative to narrowly national economic considerations. The reason for this is that de facto management of the monetary system is another political requirement for key currency status; some country must be a balancer to make the system work until international management becomes far more successful than it has been heretofore. The importance of milieu goals to key currency countries induces them to play such a balancing role. But their importance is now declining in the United States, even as the importance of international economic transactions is rising. In consequence, the United States is now far less willing to be the systemic balancer. Nevertheless, there is reason to believe that its sense of global responsibility (and its relatively closed economy) will keep it ahead of other countries on this score, to some extent, indefinitely.

Political and military dominance thus underlies economic and financial dominance, the prerequisite for key currency capability and for the willingness of a great power to play such a role. The abatement of the balance-of-power system eliminated Britain's role as "balancer," reduced its international power, and decisively eroded its international monetary capabilities although the English failed to perceive these shifts, and act accordingly, for almost fifty years. The evolution of the postwar world from bipolarity to multipolarity has similarly reduced the scope for U.S. dominance.

It is true that a politically powerful country need not exercise its financial dominance by establishing a key currency. But if others seek to use its currency widely, it would have to make a conscious decision to prevent that development. Such a decision would be inconsistent with the country's overall approach unless it was prepared to place its power behind a workable substitute, which would almost certainly be less favorable to its national interests in the short run and would be more difficult to set up.

The United States did place its power behind the *creation* of the International Monetary Fund to govern the postwar monetary system. However, the IMF, as constituted at Bretton Woods, never provided comprehensive mechanisms for liquidity and adjustment, and the United States rejected the Keynes plan for an International Clearing Union which would have done so far more effectively. In addition, the United States—while it was itself a surplus country—gutted the IMF of much of its (limited) capability to foster adjustment by rendering inoperative the "scarce currency clause," its only lever against surplus countries.

In effect, the United States used the IMF as a multilateral cover for its national dominance—which of course also had the merit for other countries of providing a cover for their impotence, and some actual protection against the United States. It decided to handle the issues unilaterally, and usually did so quite generously and quite well. However, in the process it created a system based on the dollar and U.S. hegemony rather than on the IMF and international cooperation. This accurately reflected the power realities of the time but left major problems for the future. Achievement of key currency status does require a choice by the dominant country, at least to the extent of rejecting the possible alternatives, and it is a mistake to say—as many commentators and officials do, for understandable if erroneous political reasons—that the United States "did not seek the reserve currency role, but had it thrust upon us."

A country's overall world role is thus vital if its currency is to play a major international function. The *degree* of its dominance also relates closely to the *extent* of the key currency's role. Total hegemony, as in the case of the United States in the non-Communist world in the immediate postwar period, would be most compatible with global vehicle currency *and* reserve currency use. Regional dominance alone —as in the cases of Germany and France before 1914, Britain in the Empire and in the Commonwealth from about 1932 forward, or France and Portugal within their colonial territories—would be consistent with use limited to a specific monetary area.

The Decline of Dominance

We have explained that a country is likely to achieve economic and financial dominance only if it achieves political and military dominance, with the extent of the former relating to the latter. Now we must test the symmetry of the proposition: need a country's financial power decline as its overall world power declines?

As the political dominance of Britain and the United States declined, so did their financial dominance. Britain created a defensive sterling area in 1932, intensified the exchange controls of the area in the early postwar period, and was finally forced to negotiate a series of highly disadvantageous guarantee arrangements after 1968 (the Basel agreements) to prevent total collapse of what remained of it. The United States created a de facto dollar area with growing intensity and growing instability from the early 1960s, and finally declared the dollar inconvertible into U.S. reserves for all countries, as outlined in the last chapter. But no correlation proves causality, and we must see whether there are firm reasons to expect financial power to decline along with political power.

Hegemonial powers need loyal allies. But helping to build up the military and economic power of allies reduces political and economic dominance, which is the foundation of hegemony. The United Kingdom promoted rapid economic recovery on the Continent after the Napoleonic Wars by permitting the major European power to float huge loans in the London capital market. The United States helped rebuild its allies through Marshall Plan aid and other ways, and in Europe with support for their joining together in the Common Market. The international framework thus changed as a result of the efforts of the hegemonial power itself. Here is a major internal contradiction of the key currency system—a "political corollary" of the "Triffin paradox," which hypothesizes the instability of a key currency system for technical financial reasons—and a reason why the needed dominance of the center country is likely to be transitory, and hence unstable.

There is a closely related financial reason for the correlation between political and financial decline. The center country's broad international goals and the requirements of its key currency position are likely to produce payments deficits. But one of the chief bases of international financial power, as we saw in Chapter 2, is the level of a country's reserves and its current balance-of-payments position. Adequate reserves or current surpluses enable a peripheral country to negate the efforts of a reserve center to influence its policies, for example, through the leverage of foreign aid. If a peripheral country's position becomes strong enough, it can positively affect the policies of the reserve center in some circumstances—for example, through changes in its reserve asset composition. The key currency country, however, deliberately permits—even fosters—a decline in its reserve position and a buildup of the reserve positions of its strongest allies, the middle powers. Hence there will inevitably be a relative power shift to the latter. (For similar reasons, the loose bipolar system is considered by most political analysts unstable and inherently contradictory on the political and military front.)

Another reason for declining U.S. dominance in today's world stems from the growing doubt that the Communist countries will launch military attacks against anybody, and the resultant "devaluation of the currency of alliance."[22] Hence the real leverage of the United States over both its allies and foes is reduced except in the highly unlikely cases of life or death. Indeed, political factors become smaller in the overall economic power equation during a period of détente as compared to a period of hot or cold war. So even the country with the greatest political power, which the United States

22. R. N. Rosecrance, "Bipolarity, Multipolarity, and the Future," *Journal of Conflict Resolution*, Vol. X, No. 3 (September 1966), p. 325.

clearly remains, can get less economic (or other) mileage from its power. Other countries can get more mileage, at least on economic issues, from their purely economic power. Only the United States can still deal directly with Moscow (or even Peking) on the great strategic issues. Yet it now finds itself increasingly dependent on its allies, as in the monetary negotiations in the fall of 1971, but possessing decreasing leverage over them and faced with narrowed options *because* of its size. This paradox is the basis of Hoffmann's conclusion that the United States is seriously disadvantaged by its great power position in the world today, and hence must sharply curtail its goals and the means to achieve them.[23]

The financial decline of the dominant power is also promoted by the behavioral changes of other countries. The increasing confidence of the leadership of other countries, as their global positions became relatively stronger, induces them to speak more independently in all fields. They would maximize their relative power position by joining forces and forming a second "pole" within the monetary system. This was a major objective of the sterling bloc and of the European Payments Union after World War II. The European Community has already done it to some extent, and is attempting to do so further through "economic and monetary union."

In the political world, the superpower retains its military deterrent and thus its ultimate source of dominance. But it can never use its nuclear might against a recalcitrant ally. (It can probably never use it against a superpower adversary either, because of the cataclysmic effects.) The United States also has a "financial deterrent": it can freeze foreign assets in the United States (dollar balances of earmarked gold held here by foreign monetary authorities).[24] Like the nuclear deterrent, this financial deterrent could only be used once (on a broad scale) and would totally wreck the system for the future. Hence it is virtually as unthinkable as its military analogue. And

---

23. Hoffmann, *op. cit.*, p. 67. There are many interesting similarities between these costs of the overall U.S. world role and the costs to the U.S. international financial position of the key currency role of the dollar—such as dependence on the cooperation of other members of the system, and the narrowing of policy options.

24. Milton Gilbert, long the chief economist of the Bank for International Settlements, reported in 1968, in "The Gold-Dollar System: Conditions of Equilibrium and the Price of Gold," *Princeton Essays in International Finance*, No. 70, that the possibility of dollar blockage by the United States is an important reason for many countries to hold gold in their reserves. They view themselves as "sole masters" of their gold reserves, which is important because "every major country" gives some weight to the "war chest" motive for holding gold.

foreigners can avoid even this remote risk by holding the key currency outside the jurisdiction of the key currency country, i.e., in the Eurodollar market.

The United States also has the ability to declare the dollar inconvertible into U.S. reserve assets and announce an unwillingness to defend any exchange rate for the dollar, as it did on August 15, 1971. This deterrent helped enable the United States essentially to ignore its balance of payments for many years, particularly in the "crisis zone" after 1967, since other countries did not wish to trigger the formal cessation of U.S. convertibility. Adoption of formal inconvertibility was indeed very serious. It ran counter to the traditional "milieu goals" of the United States and signified a major abrogation of its world leadership role. Confidence in U.S. policy will be extremely difficult to restore as a result. The actual use of the deterrent indicated a perception by the government that its leadership role has already been seriously threatened by the deterioration of its external trade and payments position—and some of the basic political requirements for key currency status were badly undermined by the move itself.

But the world economy has continued to function. U.S. suspension of de jure convertibility was not Doomsday. The world power of the United States is, of course, not based entirely on the nuclear deterrent, and its financial power was never based entirely on this financial lever. But an important part of what remained of its hegemonial financial position within the non-Communist world was based on the *threat* to declare the dollar inconvertible into U.S. reserve assets if pushed too far, and this threat played a major role in achieving systemic change sought by the United States as recently as the institution of the two-tiered gold system in 1968. The fact that the lever has now been used sharply reduces one source of U.S. power, both because other countries are unlikely to permit themselves to be subjected to it again and because the results of the action were far less damaging than most people had imagined they would be.

Despite all these reasons for expecting a decline in financial dominance along with a decline in overall political dominance, key currencies clearly tend to retain strong international positions long after their capabilities wane. Indeed, their position may continue to expand after their political roles begin to decline. In the 1920s and recently, when the power of Britain and the United States waned relative to that of other countries in the broad, political sense described in this chapter, the use of sterling and the dollar, respectively, continued to grow at least in absolute terms.

There are several reasons for this apparent anomaly. First, the use of a currency may continue to grow in *absolute* terms while its *share* of total international use of national currencies is declining along expected lines. The demand of the system as a whole for key currencies may be increasing fast enough to offset in absolute terms the decline in relative dominance of the center country, or the growing demand by countries over which its dominance has waned. The Reichsmark and the French franc began to compete seriously with sterling in the last decade or two before World War I; the dollar and the franc ate into sterling's role in the early interwar period; and the Deutschemark, Swiss franc, and SDRs began to take a greater share from the dollar at the margin in the late 1960s. Yet the absolute role of each of the existing key currencies continued to grow. Second, it is far more difficult to *become* a key currency than to remain one. A new currency must acquire all the needed attributes to move in even if the existing currency falters badly, and even if the key currency country decides that it no longer wants to accept the costs involved. This absence of rivals is the basic explanation of the continued rise of the dollar in the late 1960s and early 1970s. Third, inertia and tradition play major roles in monetary matters. Very fundamental changes—such as the floating devaluations of Britain in 1931, and the United States after August 1971—may be necessary to change perceptions. Fourth, it is quite likely that the world's contemporary perception of these broad changes may differ from what we can see with hindsight, or may develop only with an appreciable time lag, especially since the waning power is likely to make a major effort to hide its decline as long as possible.

Nevertheless, it is clear that a declining overall world role for a country produces a declining world financial role for its currency. The financial decline will probably take place with a time lag, and will be noticed only at the margin at first. But the proposition that the world political role is a prerequisite for key currency status appears symmetrical, and hence clearly a central feature in assessing the viability of any national currency to play major international roles.

In the early 1970s there emerged a sharp contrast between the political power position of the United States and the international roles of the dollar. Its power had declined markedly. But the roles of the dollar had multiplied, in absolute terms. The paradox was explained by the time lag and by the absence of rivals which could immediately supplant the dollar, though several were already seizing an increasing *share* of world finance. The situation was one of fundamental political disequilibrium and was inherently unstable.

There is of course the possibility that the relative military and political power of the superpower may differ from its relative economic power.[25] This is certainly the case for the United States in the 1970s. It will remain the military leader of the non-Communist world by an overwhelming degree, due to its nuclear capability, large conventional forces, and overall economic size—although the importance of this leadership is declining. But it has slipped well behind some of its major political allies on such international economic measures as level of reserves, share of world trade, and even per capita income, and its share of each continues to fall—though its relative independence from oil imports gives it more economic security than most of its major allies, and hence restores some of its relative economic power. In such a situation, the superpower, if it is well organized bureaucratically, can use whichever component of its power position has eroded less to pursue its goals in another area. The 1967 "offset" arrangement with Germany, wherein the United States achieved a major financial breakthrough with the leverage provided by its military position, is again a prototype. On the other hand, U.S. weakness was demonstrated by the ability of its allies to force a solution to the crisis in the fall of 1971 in return for supporting the new U.S. initiatives toward Moscow and Peking.

There are problems with this "linkage" approach. As much of international economic relations is carried on solely by economic officials, the economic power position alone may be determinative, although the overall position is always in the background. In addition, much international economic decision-making occurs in crisis periods of very short duration when it is very difficult or even impossible to mobilize a nation's political power—such as threatening to cut U.S. troop levels. For example, the United States was far more able to use its political leverage in the extended SDR negotiations and the exchange-rate crisis in the fall of 1971, which afforded opportunities for Presidential action at meetings with heads of state and through regular correspondence, than in a crisis situation such as the Bonn conference of late 1968 and even the March 1968 meeting in Washington which created the two-tiered system.

Finally, and most substantively, security issues are usually far more crucial than international economic issues. It would usually be a serious mistake for the United States to threaten the use of security measures to achieve economic gains, since its bluff might be called and it would then either have to back down or take steps injurious to its own defense interests. If Germany had not agreed in 1967 to hold

25. For an analysis, see Harold van B. Cleveland, *The Atlantic Idea and Its European Rivals* (New York: McGraw-Hill, for the Council on Foreign Relations, 1966), esp. p. 158.

onto all of its further dollar accruals, it is doubtful that the United States would have cut its troop levels—and even more doubtful that they should have been cut as a result of the failure to achieve an economic accord. As for the administration's goal of using a "better offset agreement" to mollify Congress, it is clear that few Congressmen ever even became aware of the German pledge; Senator Mansfield and his supporters were certainly not deterred by it from citing economic justifications for their proposals, revealing once more that their real motives for cutting troop levels had little to do with finance.

Foreign Cooperation

The final political criterion for key currency status for one country is adequate behavior by other major countries. As already noted, a key currency country must be prepared to manage the monetary system, but it cannot always do so alone. Four possibilities exist in terms of possible responses from others: passivity, active cooperation, active hostility to its key currency status, and actual competition for such a role.

At root, two factors motivate the response of non-center countries to the key currency. One is their concern with systemic stability, which is of course disrupted if the key currency itself becomes unstable. Only for the largest countries, however, is such a concern likely to outweigh narrowly national considerations, because only they can affect the system sufficiently through their own moves to feel feedback on their own interests.[26] In 1973, Germany and Japan—as measured by the size of their trade and dollar reserves—clearly fit this category, but several others (Canada, Switzerland, France) probably did so as well. As we saw in Chapter 3, the system's entry into the "crisis zone" in 1967–68 dominated all other factors in determining the international monetary policy of all major countries.

The second motivation of non-center countries is their perceived degree of direct dependence on the center country itself, in both political and economic terms. For example, Germany continues to view its national security as relying on U.S. troops and the U.S. nuclear deterrent. Japan relies on the deterrent. Canada relies on the U.S. market for its exports, and for much of its capital. Such countries may not want the United States to reduce its balance-of-payments

---

26. H. A. Hagemann, "Reserve Policies of Central Banks and Their Implications for U.S. Balance of Payments Policy," *American Economic Review*, Vol. LIX, No. 1 (March 1969), found that national size was a significant factor in determining national foreign-exchange ratios even in the 1955–65 period, when systemic considerations were not nearly as evident as they later became.

deficits for fear that the adjustment measures adopted would impinge directly on needs of theirs which are far more important to them than U.S. external financial equilibrium.

To predict who is likely to cooperate with the United States, respond passively, or actively oppose it, we can array countries along a spectrum which shows their systemic concerns and their dependence on the center. From the standpoint of the reserve center, the ideal combination is a country large enough to feel systemic responsibility and highly reliant on the reserve center, politically or economically. Germany is the prototype today, with Japan and Canada following fairly closely. The worst combination is a country with a power position sufficient to do damage but insufficient to foster in it a feeling of systemic responsibility, combined with a high degree of political and economic independence from the center. France is the present prototype, as it was in the late 1920s, muted only to the extent that it still relies on the United States for its ultimate security—in circumstances which it firmly believes will never arise.

There are trade-offs, however, between the two considerations. In the postwar period, even countries with systemic concern could buy gold without hurting the system—but their dependence on the United States precluded several from doing so anyway. In the "crisis zone," even countries which were completely independent of the United States did not buy gold from it, because they would have undermined the system by doing so. So a high risk of systemic breakdown replaced U.S. political and economic dominance as the major U.S. lever in protecting its international monetary position.

Beween these two extremes, however, the requirements of the center country for "acceptable behavior" by others shift over time. During a period of hegemonial dominance, such as the United States experienced in the early postwar period, passive foreign acceptance of the key currency role suffices. When dominance declines, as for the dollar in the 1960s and particularly in the 1970s, active cooperation is needed; competition makes life difficult; and overt hostility can seriously undermine the center's ability to continue. ("Crisis zone" considerations may make hostility unlikely, but do not obviate the reserve center's need to avoid it.) If a key currency country becomes simply one of several leading powers, or even more so if it slips from the top ranks, it will need quite active support from others, including its key currency competitors—as did Britain throughout both the interwar and postwar periods—and overt hostility, as the French policy toward sterling in 1928–32, will cripple it badly.

In the decade or so before World War I, as just noted, both the Reichsmark and the French franc cut sharply into the international roles which presumably—because no firm data for the earlier period exist—were previously dominated by sterling. There was little active cooperation among the three centers, but neither was there open competition. Indeed, each dominated in a fairly clear geographic area —Germany in Central Europe, France in Russia and the Balkans, Britain in the rest of the world. Russia shifted balances from Berlin to Paris, trying to play off Germany and France, but apparently had little success in generating competition between them. Relations among the three reserve centers were governed by the "gold standard" framework accepted by all countries at that time. Systemic friction was avoided by the adherence of each to implicit rules concerning the sphere of its financial influence and its relationship to its main rivals.

For the first half of the interwar period, no national currency dominated. The resulting uncertainties led the leading monetary historian of the period to conclude that the "decentralization of the system" added to its difficulties and ultimately to collapse.[27] However, there was no overt rivalry for key currency status between the United States and Britain, and indeed the former actively supported the British position—at times, even at serious cost to itself. Much more damaging was the active French opposition to such status for either Anglo-Saxon country and its aggressive efforts to undermine at least Britain as soon as its own financial position became strong enough in the late 1920s to do so.[28]

In the 1960s the dollar received active cooperation from most of the other major countries, whether members of the dollar area or gold bloc. However, the competition for key currency status inherent in the continued international use of sterling contributed to the instability of the international monetary system and hence to the difficulties of the dollar. Sterling's weakness made some direct contributions to strengthening the dollar, as capital moved from Britain to America and countries moved from the sterling area into the dollar area. But it also contributed to the fragility of the overall system, and it frequently triggered major crisis, culminating in its

27. Brown, *op. cit.*, p. 805. Day, *op. cit.*, p. 31, refers to it as "an uneasy and half-realized dyarchy," since "the war had destroyed the absolute dominance of the pound but did not substitute that of the dollar." He concludes, however (p. 27), that much more fundamental difficulties were the basic causes of the collapse and that a "two-centre system . . . could operate as smoothly as the single-centred system" if the same conditions (especially an efficient adjustment process) existed.

28. Charles P. Kindleberger, "The International Monetary Politics of a Near-Great Power: Two French Episodes, 1926–1939 and 1960–1970," *Economic Notes*, Vol. I, No. 2–3 (1972), pp. 30–41.

own devaluation in November 1967, the massive private run on gold which followed, and the subsequent dissolution of the sterling area.

The emergence of the mark as a key currency in the late 1960s and especially in the 1970s shifted more dollars into German official reserves and may have slightly increased German uneasiness, but raised no systemic problems at first because of the German pledge to hold onto the dollars. Once exchange rates began to float, however, the structural portfolio adjustment from dollars into marks (and other national currencies, to a lesser extent) provided steady downward pressure on the dollar. The French attack on the dollar (and sterling to a lesser extent) in the mid-1960s caused the United States to initiate wide-ranging capital controls and finally decide to support the creation of a new international money to supplement the dollar.[29]

In theory, currency monopoly by a dominant political power is probably the most stable basis for any international monetary system. However, there is no *a priori* reason why duopoly, or even monopolistic competition among relative equals, cannot work as well. Indeed, such competitive situations existed without causing major problems prior to 1914 and again in the early postwar period. But they broke down in the late 1920s, under overt attack, and—again partly due to overt attack—weakened the system which was finally broken down by unilateral U.S. action in 1971. It is therefore clear that satisfactory "rules of the game," or at least firm understandings, are necessary if the required degree of international cooperation is to be assured in such situations. Competition from "non-national" sources—his-

---

29. The French wanted gold, of course, instead of SDRs. This is a paradox of French, particularly Gaulist, policy. The French wished to dethrone the dollar but did not realize that an international money like SDR could do so as well as gold. Indeed, they failed to realize that SDR could do so *better* from their *political* standpoint, in view of the likelihood of achieving an EC veto over all major SDR decisions and the French capacity to dominate EC policy in the monetary area. (This in turn makes one wonder whether conservative economics and a desire for real political power, or the gold hoards of French voters and sadistic desire to force the United States to devalue—which might have been viewed by de Gaulle as the greatest possible political "defeat" for the United States, although it was viewed by the Nixon Administration as a great political "victory" when accomplished in 1971—were more important in determining French policy.) In fact, the French strategy of dethroning the dollar would probably have backfired had the tactic of defeating the SDR succeeded, since France would have gotten an even more completely dollar world instead of a gold revaluation. The most that can be said for Gaullist monetary power is that it had only the timing wrong; had it concentrated its dollar sales around the time of the sterling devaluation and private gold run in 1967–68, instead of "wasting" them in 1963–65, it just might have added sufficiently to the monetary panic to tip the balance against the United States.

torically from gold and silver, and now from SDR as well—also raise the basic stability question and require clear understandings on relative roles.

The need for cooperation by other countries points to a final political requirement for a key currency. It must adopt a posture of confidence consistent with its objective degree of dominance, and present an image of strength commensurate to the position it wishes to retain. It must do so judiciously and without offending other countries,[30] but failure to present an image of strength when the strength was present would unnecessarily undermine the key currency and the system. Great presentational skill is thus required of its representatives. On the other hand, attempts to present such an image when the underlying strength no longer existed would reflect an effort to maintain dominance when it was no longer possible. One signal that dominance has slipped is emergence of a need on the part of the center country for more *active* cooperation by other powers. There must be consistency between actual relative strength and official posture, or it would be difficult indeed to elicit such cooperation from the other members of the system.

Summary
International political power is clearly a prerequisite for key currency status. The two great key currencies of history developed in response to the adoption of a world political role by their countries of issue. Such a correlation is probable both because a country would be unlikely to accept the risks of key currency status unless it had broad systemic interests engendered by its security and political, including "milieu," objectives, and because other countries are likely to accept economic leadership only from countries which also provide political leadership. The extent to which a key currency role is then feasible depends on a mix between the degree to which such a role is deemed important for the economic self-interest of the center country, and the degree to which overall international tensions push both center and peripheral countries in such a direction for essentially security purposes. Correspondingly, international power takes on a much greater "economic" content during periods of relatively harmonious international relations, and military power becomes less necessary to thrust a country toward key currency status under such conditions. But no cases yet exist of the development of a key

30. Since "the mere possession of great power always creates a presumption of arrogance, even when the power is used with restraint and discrimination." Hoffmann, *op. cit.*, p. 345.

currency not coupled with global political engagement, and several potential key currencies have failed to achieve as significant a position as more purely economic factors would suggest because of their countries' limited world roles.

At the same time, this very world involvement tends to undermine the status of the key currency country itself. The same broad goals which thrust it into the international scene in the first place will tend to weaken its own financial position and induce it to build up rivals, which will inevitably challenge its own supremacy one day. So there is a fundamental contradiction underlying the development of a key currency system, from the political side, which renders it unstable over the long run. Alternatives to the key currency approach have always been open to politically dominant countries, but none have so far had adequate foresight to adopt them.

Finally, the correlation between political and financial leadership appears to be symmetrical: they decline as well as rise together, though usually with a significant time lag during which the center country will frequently be tempted to use its remaining political power to shore up its declining financial position—though yielding to such temptations will generally be unwise for both financial and security reasons. The decline may be masked for some time by a variety of factors, such as continued *absolute* growth of the declining currency at the same time that its *share* of world finance is falling. And world demand for national currencies assures the perpetuation of the role of each until a new one is elected by the market to take its place, usually in the wake of some rather decisive revelation of the weakness of the *ancien régime*.

Part of the reason behind the rise and fall of key currencies is the concomitant political ebb and flow of other countries. As others gain greater political power and thus self-confidence, they will tend to move from passive acceptance of key-currency hegemony to active competition with the key currency and perhaps even overt hostility toward it. The speed with which they move along this continuum will be determined both by their direct dependence on the key currency country and the extent of systemic responsibility which they feel. Without at least a modicum of cooperation from other politically relevant countries, any key currency will be in trouble—even if it employs its major financial weapons, which often turn out to be usable only once and are far less potent than is often believed.

5

Attributes of a Key Currency: The External Economics

In addition to the political criteria, a country must fulfill certain economic requirements to achieve and maintain key currency status. A more extensive list of economic attributes is needed for reserve currency than for vehicle currency status, and we shall try to distinguish carefully between the two. We shall also rank and weight the criteria in an effort to determine which represent a sufficient set to preserve (or achieve) each role.

As was demonstrated in Chapter 2, virtually any practicable monetary system will need national currencies at least for international vehicle use, and strong tendencies exist for their use as reserve assets as well. The attributes of any single national currency must thus be compared with the attributes of other potentially contending currencies and non-national assets, not against any absolute standard, to see whether it qualifies for these roles. Particularly with regard to the reserve currency role, the varying attitudes of different foreign monetary authorities must be taken into account in assessing whether a center country will find its currency widely acceptable; such differences in fact lie at the heart of the decisions of countries to "join" different currency areas.

Indeed, the attitudes of foreign holders, both private and official, determine the requirements of the center country. To some extent, then, an effort to assess these requirements is an exercise in the psychology of traders, investors, speculators, and monetary authorities and can never reach definitive conclusions. Nevertheless, I shall assess each of the possible requirements conceptually and then inject (with a number of cautionary remarks) the evidence revealed in several econometric studies.

The Fundamental Requirement: Confidence in Convertibility
The economic attributes of a key currency must be seen at several levels. Most immediately evident are those required directly by

potential foreign holders: liquidity of the asset, safety of its principal value, and yield.[1]

Most monetary authorities probably regard the attributes in roughly that order. As the primary purpose of their reserves is to finance future deficits in their national balance-of-payments positions, liquidity is the primary criterion. In addition, most monetary authorities have great incentive to avoid losses, because they must then seek compensating appropriations and have their "failures" exposed.[2] Safety of principal is thus also exceedingly important. Yield should not be as important. Official institutions in many countries have little incentive to maximize earnings, because their legislation requires that such earning be turned back to the government.[3] In addition, the primary concern of monetary authorities in at least the major countries should by systemic stability, which should constrain them from seeking to maximize earnings through rapid shifts among different reserve assets.

Most private holders, on the other hand, place greater emphasis on earnings. They are willing to take greater risks in pursuit of appreciation of principal as well as higher yield, and face no constraints from systemic responsibilities. They may also seek to maximize their returns by evading taxes. So yield is a relatively more important attribute for a transactions currency than for a reserve currency, while safety of the

1. For a slightly different categorization, covering the same points, see Robert Z. Aliber, "Gresham's Law, Asset Preferences and the Demand for International Reserves," *Quarterly Journal of Economics*, Vol. LXXXI, No. 4 (November 1967), pp. 628–38.

2. Gilbert, *op. cit.*, p. 6, argues that gold bloc countries "are concerned primarily to avoid risk to their balance-sheet positions." The losses charged to the Bundesbank under the accounting system of that time led it to argue strongly against the mark revaluation which eventually took place in 1961, although such "losses" apply of course to *all* of a country's reserve assets when it itself revalues; this is a different issue from defending oneself against "losses" imposed by the devaluation of another country whose currency you are holding.

3. Charles P. Kindleberger concludes that "central bank accounting is not consistent with the national interest of most countries" because of both the absence of incentive for profit and the incentive to avoid losses. He suggests that the motivations of the monetary authorities be balanced by permitting them to accumulate interest earned on foreign exchange holdings as a special reserve against the risk of devaluation, a proposal which becomes increasingly important as exchange rates are changed more frequently to achieve adjustment. See Kindleberger, "International Monetary Arrangements," University of Queensland, 1966, p. 18. Some countries have in fact begun to move toward such a system. Richard N. Cooper has referred to the policy implications of this accounting symmetry—its bias against exchange-rate changes—as "the tyranny of the accountants."

asset—at least over a longer period of time—is somewhat less important for that purpose.

At a second level, a basic requirement to meet all three criteria is confidence in the external convertibility of the key currency. The currency is not liquid internationally if it cannot be converted. Its yield is also sharply reduced in real value if it cannot be converted—though the value is not eliminated if the holder has liabilities in the same currency, or future plans for using it. Convertibility at a given moment is not sufficient; there must be confidence that it will be maintained over the time horizon relevant to the potential holder, which is probably longer for most official than for most private holders. And confidence must be maintained at home as well as abroad, since today's networks of rapid communications assure rapid transmission of any domestic faltering of faith. This criterion would be violated by the application of widespread exchange or quantitative controls to a key currency, either by the center country itself or by other countries, or by anticipations that such controls might be applied in the near future.[4]

The general point, however, only raises questions. *Into what* must convertibility be assured? At *what prices?* The answers to the two are inextricably related.

The price issue is the more important of the two. All the analysts of the key currency issue cited above call explicitly or implicitly for fixity of the rate at which dollars can be converted into other reserve assets. All, however, were discussing the dollar's role in the context of an international monetary system based on fixed exchange rates. Under such a system, maintenance of confidence in a fixed parity clearly is of high importance for a key currency in all its roles.[5] Under

4. It is reported that New Zealand threatened to leave the sterling area when the United Kingdom extended its restraints on capital exports to developed sterling area countries in 1965–66. Fred Hirsch, *Money International* (Garden City, N.Y.: Doubleday, 1969), p. 332. When the United Kingdom ended completely its discrimination in favor of borrowing by sterling countries, in mid-1972, Malaysia and Singapore publicly announced in response that they would henceforth peg their currencies to the dollar instead of to sterling.

5. Former Chancellor of the Exchequer Reginald Maudling has said, to the contrary, that "I see no reason why a floating pound should not continue to act in this (reserve currency) role." However, he supported the statement only by referring to the agreement of Commonwealth countries to remain tied to sterling even had it floated upon its return to convertibility, as was seriously contemplated by the British government from 1952 until 1955. So he was talking only about reserve currency status within a currency area floating as a unit against the rest of the world. See Maudling's interview in *The Banker*, Vol. 118, No. 508 (June 1968), p. 421.

a system where *all* rates are floating, the analogue is maintenance of confidence in the least amount of instability. In any system, private traders and monetary authorities alike will place a high premium on assurance of capital value. The liquidity, safety and yield criteria all naturally promote such an attitude. Borrowers of the currency will not wish to risk an increase in their debt burden through an appreciation of the currency, so the tendency of holders to seek the currency most likely to rise in price will have an important offset, which points to relative stability as the key. And there are major economic gains from preserving a fixed point of monetary reference and a relatively stable store of value, which neither rises nor falls very much over time.

There are two ways for a key currency country to assure holders on this score. One is simply to guarantee the balances against any changes in this value, and to make up any losses on them resulting from devaluation of the key currency. The other is to preserve market confidence that the exchange rate will not change, either because there will be no need for it to do so or because the country would reject devaluation in favor of other measures if faced with a need to adjust its payments position. The classic historical case is the British refusal after World War I even to consider returning to convertibility at any parity other than that which had existed (with a few brief exceptions at the time of the Napoleonic Wars) since 1717—despite the advice of Keynes and others that such a rate would overvalue sterling by 10–12 per cent.[6] The U.S. refusal to consider devaluing the dollar in the late 1960s, particularly at the time of the gold crisis of March 1968, is the contemporary analogue.

An existing intervention currency has greater prospects for price stability than all other currencies, other things being equal. This is so because an intervention currency, within the margins around parities in a system of fixed exchange rates, can fluctuate toward any other currency only one-half as much as the latter can move in relation to any third currency—in other words, any two nonintervention currencies can move to their respective ceiling and floor *against the intervention currency*, leaving it in the middle between them. This is one reason why *achievement* of key currency status adds to the capability of a currency to *maintain* that status.

In the Smithsonian Agreement of December 1971, the widening of

6. The fascinating story of this British decision, which clearly reveals the importance to it of restoring the key currency role of sterling, is chronicled in D. E. Moggridge, *The Return to Gold 1925* (Cambridge: University Press, 1969).

the margins from 0.75 per cent on either side of parity to 2.25 per cent increased the absolute magnitude of this advantage for the dollar. The subsequent decision of the European Community countries to limit the fluctuation of their currencies to one-half the permitted global margin, however, meant that none of them could fluctuate more toward each other than they could toward the dollar as long as they kept this "snake in the tunnel." Hence the EC move sharply reduced this important advantage for the dollar. Indeed, any EC currency which became *the* intervention currency in their regime would achieve *greater* stability than the dollar on this score, because it could then fluctuate against any other EC currency only one-half as much as could any two other EC currencies against each other.

Actual devaluation clearly undermines a currency's ability to play a key international role. This may seem paradoxical, because devaluation strengthens a country's competitive capability and should help restore its currency's role—at least if confidence in the new parity is widespread. And the obviously excessive devaluation of the dollar of 1934 did lead shortly to a renewal of the dollar's roles. However, that dollar restoration was the product both of the coming war in Europe and of the grossly excessive amount of the devaluation, which led the markets to regard gold as then greatly overvalued.[7]

In general, the key short-run issue in devaluation is whether the new parity is credible. Doubts on this score motivated the accelerated "diversification" of reserves by sterling area countries *after* November 1967 and forced Britain to negotiate the Basel arrangements in 1968. Continued talk about the need for another U.S. devaluation precluded a return to confidence in the dollar after December 1971, and the second devaluation of February 1973 appeared to justify such attitudes. Indeed, devaluations can be expected to hurt the balance of payments of the devaluing country for the first quarter or two, as imports become more expensive before supply and demand responses can effect basic changes in production and consumption patterns. Unless a devaluation is obviously excessive, doubts that it will restore equilibrium are likely to dominate for at least a while after the event.

For the longer run, the realization that a key currency *can* be devalued is perhaps the most fundamental factor likely to erode its attractiveness in a system based on a presumption of fixed exchange

---

7. We shall see in Part III that a huge revaluation of the official price of gold might again promote international use of the dollar, if carried out in terms of all currencies. The discussion here refers to devaluations of the dollar against other national currencies, with or without an increase in the price of gold. As noted in Chapter 3, the devaluations of the 1930s left exchange rates virtually unchanged and resulted *only* in an increase in the price of gold.

rates. Such a step shatters the illusion that the key currency is an impregnable bastion of stability. It causes asset holders throughout the world to reassess their portfolios. Even if the new exchange rate looks solid for the moment, it has become clear that the key currency country can—and, more importantly, *will* devalue if its own needs dictate.[8]

This is why Britain, wanting to retain sterling as the world's leading currency, accepted so many sacrifices to restore the prewar parity of sterling in 1925, and sterling never regained a truly global role after Britain suspended gold convertibility and floated its exchange rate in 1931. Even the regional role which remained for sterling was finally undermined by the devaluation of 1967, and Britain had to extend formal dollar-value guarantees on most of the outstanding reserve balances to avoid wholesale defections from the remaining sterling area.

The dollar first developed as a key currency during and immediately after World War I, when it was the only major currency to maintain a fixed parity. Its role virtually disappeared when the dollar depreciated in 1933–34, but resumed when the dollar was again pegged to gold while other major currencies continued to float or seemed likely to require devaluations. The postwar dominance of the dollar emerged when it was the currency with the longest-lived parity of all countries. Confidence in the dollar was bolstered by the requirement that only Congress could change its exchange rate, such an awkward procedure that it added to the unlikelihood of such a step ever being taken.[9] The role of the dollar could hardly be the same as in the past now that the presumption of fixed-price convertibility has been shattered. This is true especially since several major countries have not devalued for a long time: Germany and Japan since their postwar stabilization, the Netherlands and Belgium since 1949, Switzerland since the 1930s.

Once a key currency *is* devalued, the reassessment by holders of that currency tends to justify movement out of it. As we shall see in detail in Chapter 8, every key currency develops an "overhang"—a large

8. One politically astute observer capsulized the situation well by referring to the devaluation as "the dethronement of the dollar," in a chapter entitled "The Dollar's Fall From Pre-eminence." See Henry Brandon, *The Retreat of American Power* (Garden City, N.Y.: Doubleday and Co., 1973), pp. 218–46.

9. Switzerland is the only other country whose legislature has historically had to approve a change in parity. Indeed, Max Iklé, in Aliber, ed., *The International Market for Foreign Exchange*, p. 255, indicates that this problem partly explains why the Swiss did not follow the German-Dutch revaluation in 1961. Swiss law was changed to permit parity changes to be made by the government, however, just in time for the revaluation of May 1971.

stock of outstanding liabilities—during its key currency tenure. Once doubts arise about the future stability of such a currency, this over-hang provides a steady source of downward pressure against it which will reinforce the doubts triggered by the devaluation in the first place. This will be true even if the new exchange rate looks stable, or even undervalued, in terms of current balance-of-payment trends, as the United States discovered after February 1973. The sterling over-hang led to just such movements after November 1967, and the dollar overhang did so after August 1971 and, especially, after February 1973.

For *vehicle* currency purposes, the answer to "convertibility into what" is easy in the short run: convertibility need be only into other national currencies.[10] Even the dollar was never directly convertible into U.S. gold reserves for private holders.

For the longer run, however, both private and official holders tend to look for assets whose price outlook is the least unstable among those which meet the minimum liquidity qualifications. The willing-ness of the monetary authorities of a country to limit the price fluctu-ations of its currency may thus play a critical role in the acceptability of that currency. Since they can do so only by defending their cur-rency in the exchange markets through the use of their national reserves, convertibility into those reserves probably plays an exceed-ingly important, if indirect, role in the acceptability of a particular national currency even for vehicle purposes. (This criterion would obviously have little effect if *all* exchange rates are viewed as equally unstable, but this situation is unlikely to arise in practice.) The pri-vate sector probably has little concern for which particular assets are used by the monetary authorities of a key currency country, and look primarily to the credibility of their commitment to limit fluctuations in the price of a given currency.

For *reserve* currency purposes, the answer to "convertibility into what" depends on the nature of the prevailing international monetary system. A basic distinction must be made between a system whose reserve assets assumed their international roles solely through the his-torical evolutions of market forces, and a system whose assets became accepted through conscious international decision. In a market-determined system, any single reserve asset must be interconvertible with any other reserve asset in the system to be acceptable to all countries. When the system is negotiated, this need not be the case.

---

10. R. S. Sayers, *Modern Banking* (Oxford: Clarendon Press, 1960), 5th ed., p. 123, avers that the convertibility of sterling into any other currency in the world was "much more useful" than its convertibility into gold, al-though he does not distinguish between the vehicle and reserve currency roles.

Sterling's reserve currency role in the pre-1914 period developed while its determination to assure convertibility into gold was unquestioned. The United Kingdom viewed gold convertibility (at the pre-war parity) as absolutely essential to restoring sterling's role after World War I. Sterling relapsed when the United Kingdom was off the gold standard in the early 1920s and again after 1931. (The reserve use of sterling grew again only under the negotiated monetary conditions attending World War II, and the negotiated conditions set up by the Basel arrangements in 1968 which made sterling into a surrogate for the dollar.) The Genoa Conference of 1922, which issued the first organized call for international use of national currencies as reserve assets, emphasized the importance of gold convertibility by suggesting that its maintenance be an absolute requirement for any country playing a reserve currency role in the proposed gold-exchange-standard system.[11]

U.S. officials (before August 15, 1971) and numerous nongovernment authorities have frequently cited the necessity of dollar convertibility into *gold* as a criterion for reserve currency use of the dollar.[12] This partly reflected the fact that the international monetary system has for the past century or so been based largely on gold, and gold convertibility has exercised a psychic mystique as a result. The dollar's reserve currency use developed during and after World War I, when it was the only major currency to remain on the gold standard. It dwindled almost into oblivion from 1932 to 1934, when the price at which gold convertibility would be maintained for the dollar (rightly) came under suspicion. It expanded due to *voluntary* growth of foreign holdings from the renewal of credible gold convertibility in 1934 until such convertibility came under suspicion in the mid-1960s. And the failure of other strong currencies to attract widespread international use in the postwar period is partly explained by the fact that no currency other than the dollar was convertible into gold.

More important, however, was the fact that gold was the *only* reserve asset held by the United States throughout most of this period, and hence the only asset used to retain the fixed exchange rate for the dollar. "Gold convertibility" was thus the conventional description of "a fixed exchange rate for the dollar." The mark and several other currencies, none of which are convertible into gold as was the dollar, have begun to play important key currency roles

11. Resolution 11 of the Genoa Financial Report, quoted in *Federal Reserve Bulletin*, June 1922, p. 679.
12. See, e.g., the U.S. Treasury Department, *op. cit.*, p. 21, and Roosa *op. cit.*, p. 29.

because their exchange rates look stable relative to alternative assets. History suggests that the role of the dollar could only decline once it became inconvertible into U.S. reserve assets. This was particularly true while other currencies remained convertible into the reserves of their monetary authorities, as was the case from December 1971 until March 1973, but holds in any event since the dollar was declining from a position of pre-eminence. Indeed, even the vehicle role was likely to be undermined once foreign monetary authorities refused to accept dollars because of their nonconvertibility into U.S. reserve assets, as happened when most of the major countries moved to flexible exchange rates in early 1973.

Convertibility into gold would certainly be unnecessary in an international monetary system in which gold no longer played an important monetary role.[13] But even with gold still in the system, it was explicitly decided in the SDR negotiations not to provide gold convertibility for them. There is no way to get gold for SDRs: a country can only use SDRs to finance a balance-of-payments deficit, not to alter the composition of its reserve assets; it cannot sell SDRs to the IMF for gold; it cannot use SDRs to buy gold in private markets, since private persons cannot hold SDRs; and, with the suspension of gold convertibility for the dollar, the only currency previously convertible into gold, there is no indirect channel from SDRs into gold unless a country were to violate the two-tiered gold system.

SDRs are not automatically convertible into dollars either. They may be so converted, but only if a country designated by the IMF to receive SDRs chooses to provide dollars for them.[14] Of course, SDRs can be converted indirectly into dollars if the country using SDRs converts whatever currency it receives into dollars for subsequent market use.

13. M. A. G. van Meerhaeghe, "The IMF Twenty Years On," *Economia Internazionale*, Vol. XXI, No. 1 (February 1968), p. 114, argues that gold convertibility sometimes did the dollar "more harm than good" by providing an alternative asset to rival it. He is simply saying, however, that the elimination of gold from the system would tend toward crowning the dollar—which is of course true, and was especially true at the time he made the comment. If gold is in the system, the overwhelming evidence supports the case made in the text that the dollar is strengthened by convertibility into that alternative asset.

14. Dollars are not automatically convertible into SDR either. They can be so converted only if both the country holding dollars and the United States agree to do so, as indeed happened, chiefly with Belgium and the Netherlands, for a total of $640 million in 1970–71. The United States suspended its willingness to make any further transactions of this type as part of its overall suspension of dollar convertibility into U.S. reserve assets on August 15, 1971.

The SDR is a successful asset, despite the absence of gold convertibility, because it is a _negotiated_ international money. The limits to SDR convertibility are not only fully understood; they were incorporated by design to avoid dangers which were perceived by its creators to be greater than the advantages of endowing it with all the attributes of other assets.

By contrast, the convertibility status of the dollar became increasingly unclear as the 1960s progressed. As the outstanding volume of dollar reserves came to exceed U.S. gold (and eventually all U.S. reserves) by ever larger amounts, the United States negotiated several alternatives to gold convertibility—swap arrangements, Roosa bonds, sales of SDRs, use of its IMF position—which provided at least partial exchange rate guarantees for their holders. (An extension of such arrangements or some other negotiated conditions could reestablish the reserve currency role of the dollar, as we shall see in Chapter 12.) However, such negotiations only covered small parts of the dollar holdings of a few countries. Thus there resulted an uneasy situation in which the dollar remained fully convertible into gold de jure, but de facto became increasingly a negotiated reserve asset of which large amounts were neither realistically convertible into gold nor subject to any negotiated arrangement. It was this uncertain limbo which lay beneath the increasing shakiness of the reserve currency role of the dollar and of the system as a whole.

The question of convertibility of a reserve currency "into what" is thus answerable in either of two ways. If the existing monetary system rests on market forces and purely economic incentives, a reserve currency must be interconvertible with all of the other reserve assets in the system to be fully acceptable. If the system is based on negotiated agreements, a reserve currency need be convertible only to the extent determined in the negotiations. A new reserve currency for the future, such as a European unit or the Japanese yen, could emerge in either of these two ways: it could become fully interconvertible with all other non-negotiated reserve assets in the system and develop a reserve role purely through its financial attractiveness, or it could be designated as a reserve asset with convertibility attributes agreed by all countries.

The market approach, however, creates the confidence problem previously described: the multiplicity of competing assets in the system. This mode of developing a key currency generates an internal systemic contradiction and thus requires negotiated safeguards to prevent resulting problems just as an approach negotiated from the outset would require. A negotiated solution to the liquidity problem, with or without reserve currencies, is necessary to avoid systemic problems.

Indeed, it may well be better to avoid any monetary roles for reserve currencies than to permit them to exist without negotiated understandings as to their roles, including the convertibility obligations of the reserve currency country.

The questions of what assets a key currency must be convertible into, and at what price, are thus determined by the international monetary context at a given time. The Bretton Woods system, being based on fixed exchange rates and gold, required convertibility into gold (and perhaps SDR) and fixed exchange rates for any reserve currency—particularly since there was one, the dollar, which met such criteria. A system of freely flexible exchange rates would by definition require no convertibility into national reserve assets, so the outlook for relative price stability would become the dominant consideration. After two dollar devaluations, however, that criterion will almost certainly dominate any system that is set in place for the future anyway, since the previous leader has been decisively dethroned. Accordingly we turn now to the underlying attributes necessary to assure confidence in the price stability of a particular currency.

The most immediate attribute is the external economic and financial position of the key currency country, which is the subject of the rest of this chapter. This discussion covers a country's different liquidity ratios, which change as a result of the level and structure of its current balance-of-payments position. The external financial position in turn rests fundamentally on domestic economic criteria, such as growth and the preservation of relative price stability, which will be discussed in Chapter 6 along with the several structural criteria for key currency status, such as the size of a country in the world economy, the capacity of its capital markets, and the attratciveness of its interest rates.

In addition to analyzing these attributes conceptually, we shall draw on the several efforts that have been made to determine the motivations of monetary authorities through the use of econometric techniques.[15] Each sought to learn why some of the major countries held

---

15. Peter B. Kenen, *Reserve-Asset Preferences of Central Banks and Stability of the Gold-Exchange Standard*, Princeton Studies in International Finance, No. 10, 1963; Margaret L. Greene, *Reserve-Asset Preferences of Central Banks*, International Economics Workshop, Columbia University, 1966; H.A. Hagemann, "Reserve Policies of Central Banks and Their Implications for U.S. Balance of Payments Policy," *American Economic Review*, Vol. LIX, No. 1 (March 1969), pp. 62–77; John H. Makin, "The Composition of International Reserve Holdings: A Problem of Choice Involving Risk," *American Economic Review*, Vol. LXI, No. 5 (December 1971), pp. 818–32. The Greene study updated and improved the Kenen study, so the latter will not be considered independently in the text.

larger or smaller portions of their reserves in gold or in foreign exchange, or why they increased or decreased these portions at the margin. The studies thus provide some evidence against which the conceptual analysis can be tested. Table 9 indicates the countries observed, variables tested, and results of the studies. There have also been two econometric efforts to test why private foreigners hold foreign exchange,[16] which will be used as well.

These studies can provide only limited help, however. First, as they compare only gold and foreign exchange holdings, they shed no light on holdings of different national currencies. They could not possibly do so, in view of the absence of the necessary data. Second, their observations cover early time periods, the most recent running through the first quarter of 1968. Hence they encompass at best a part of the "crisis zone" period in which concern for systemic stability loomed large, perhaps dominantly, in the reserve asset choices of many monetary authorities. (This is also an advantage, however, in that it provides a better test of the "true desires" or monetary authorities.) Third, the observed behavior of monetary authorities (even outside the "crisis zone") may reveal nothing more than least-bad choices among a series of poor alternatives, and hence little about whether the underlying system is stable in either economic or political terms. Fourth, some of the variables tested may often be only the surface symptoms of underlying economic trends. Expectations of an increase in the price of gold, Makin's key variable, may be based on declines in the U.S. liquidity ratio, or current U.S. balance-of-payments deficits, which may in turn reflect poor U.S. price performance. The discovery that a forward premium in the private gold market, or even the U.S. balance-of-payments position, is a significant factor in foreign portfolio decisions may not tell us very much about what truly motivates them. Fifth, many of the variables deemed important in my analysis, particularly the political factors but also such economic factors as the efficacy of capital markets, either cannot or have not been quantified.[16a] None of the econometric effects approaches the scope

16. Moredechai E. Kreinen and Roy F. Gilbert "The Demand for Foreign Currency Holdings by European Banks," *Southern Economic Journal*, Vol. 38, No. 1 (July 1971), pp. 101–04, and B. J. Cohen, "A Survey of Capital Movements and Findings Regarding Their Interest Sensitivity," in *The United States Balance of Payments: Hearings*, Joint Economic Committee, Washington 1963, pp. 153–91.

16a. For an effort in this direction, see Lawrence H. Officer, "Reserve-Asset Preferences in the Crisis Zone, 1958–67," *Journal of Money, Credit and Banking*, Vol. 6, No.2 (May 1974), pp. 191–211.

Table 9

ECONOMETRIC ESTIMATES OF SIGNIFICANT FACTORS
DETERMINING FOREIGN EXCHANGE HOLDINGS OF
MAJOR COUNTRIES

	Variable Tested by	Austria	Belgium	Canada	Denmark	France
Country tested by:		H,M	G,H,M	G,H,M	M	G,H,M
Interest rates	G,H,M	M*(11)	G,M (6)	G	M(3)	G,M* (10)
U.S. balance-of-payments position (liquidity definition)	H,M				M	M
Country's total reserves	G,H		G,H (4)	H(5)		G,H (6)
Expected return on gold	M	M(3)	M (12)	M(2)	M(5)	M(6)
U.S. prices	M					
Changes in foreign exchange holdings	H			G		G
U.S. liquidity ratio (gold/liabilities to official holders)	H	H(4)	H(10)	H(7)		H(2)
U.S. short-term private assets	H					
U.S. short-term liabilities to private foreigners	H	H		H		H
U.S. long-term foreign assets	H					
U.S. long-term liabilities to foreigners	H					
Foreign assets of other country's commercial banks	H					
Foreign liabilities of other country's commercial banks	H		H	H		
IMF credit tranche position of country	H					H

G=Greene study with data for 1957-June 1964. See footnote 15, p. 134, for full citations.
H=Hagemann study, with data from about 1955-65.
M=Makin study, with data for July 1961-March 1968.
*Wrong sign.
Figures in parentheses indicate ranking for that variable.

Germany	Italy	Japan	Nether-lands	Spain	Sweden	Switzer-land	United Kingdom
G,H,M	G,H,M	H,M	G,H,M	H,M	G,H,M	G,H,M	G,M
G*,M	G,H,M	M(1)	G,M*	M(4)	G,H,M	G,M	G,M*12
(8)	(5)		(9)		(2)	(7)	
		H	M*				
H(7)	G		G,H(3)	H(2)	G,H	G,H	G
					(1)	(8)	
M(10)	M(9)	M(1)	M*(13)	M(7)	M(4)	M(11)	M(8)
G	G		G		G	G	G
H(6)	H(1)	H(9)	H(8)	H(3)	H(5)	H(11)	
					H		
	} H						
		H					
} H		} H					
					H		

needed to test all of my variables. Sixth, and perhaps most important, foreign attitudes and behavior are more likely to be conditioned by *expectations* of future developments than by current or recent developments. Such expectations are of course unquantifiable, since even the actual results from future time periods would not tell us what the relevant decision-makers thought would happen at the moment of decision. Finally, the studies are not wholly comparable because they used different dependent and independent variables, and because their country coverage and observation periods were not identical.

In addition, the coefficients of the significant variables may tell us even less about the motives of the countries involved than the discovery of the significance itself. For example, Makin's equations show that the Swiss foreign exchange ratio is determined less by the anticipated return on gold than are the ratios of most countries. However, Switzerland is a premier member of the gold bloc, and its basic policy is to hold gold *whatever* the market outlook for the gold price. Thus its ratio changes little in response to *changes* in gold market prices. Indeed, high coefficients for this variable probably indicate either that the countries involved straddle the gold bloc and dollar area, or are the result of large one-shot shifts from one area to the other. Nevertheless, we will refer to the econometric results where they apply to the variables under discussion.

The Liquidity Ratio
The external financial position of a country is the immediate determinant of foreign perceptions of the outlook for stability of its currency. A country's external position has four distinct but closely related features: (a) its liquidity ratios, which compare its quick assets and its quick liabilities; (b) its overall balance-of-payments position, which determines changes in its liquidity ratios; (c) its international investment position, which compares its total foreign assets and liabilities; and (d) the structure of its balance of payments, which determines whether its overall international investment position will rise or fall. Hagemann's econometric study, the most comprehensive effort to date, found that the U.S. liquidity ratio was the major determinant of the foreign exchange ratios of all eleven countries which he studied. By contrast, only one of Hagemann's countries and two of Makin's seemed to be affected *in addition* by the current U.S. payments position.

Every country, as we saw in Chapter 2, wants reserves sufficient to protect it from being forced to adjust to future payments deficits with such speed that it will have to abandon, or even moderate, its economic or foreign policy objectives. A key currency country, however.

may have an additional criterion in assessing the needed level of its gross reserves: "backing" for its liabilities to foreign residents. If it does, the cost of holding these extra reserves—it is probably best measured simply by current market interest rates, which indicate roughly the opportunity cost of the resources that are being tied up—must be set against the financing provided by the foreign dollar accruals in assessing the net financing which the roles of the dollar provide for the United States.

Whether the center country has such an additional requirement in practice depends on the nature of the existing monetary system. In a pure dollar standard, with the world fully reliant on the dollar and no other reserve or vehicle assets in existence, the United States would need reserves neither to "back" its outstanding liabilities nor to finance its current deficits. On the other hand, if the world were suddenly to reject any increases in its dollar holdings, the United States would need enough reserves to cover all of its current deficits. If in addition the world rejected its present dollar holdings as well, the United States would need 100 per cent backing for those dollars to avoid being forced into inconvertibility. In practice, the situation is always likely to lie in between these extremes because of the different views of different countries and the shifting payments constellation among them. The appropriate liquidity ratio for the reserve center should therefore be one part of the negotiations that are needed to preserve stability for any international monetary system based even partly on national currencies. In the face of the uncertainty which prevails in the absence of such negotiations, the key currency country must decide whether to err in the direction of holding excessive reserves or take a chance of being caught short.

The "backing" criterion looms very large in foreign assessments of whether a center country's reserves are sufficient to permit it to continue playing a key currency role, both because the level of reserves needed to finance current deficits is so uncertain and because the center can finance much of its current deficits without using its reserves at all. At the same time, the key currency country will certainly not lose sight of its two-fold need for gross reserves, and others will quickly remind it once any serious uncertainties arise about the future of the currency.

A consensus emerged in the late 1960s that the United States would *not* sell its gold "down to the last bar" to redeem outstanding dollars, due to its need to retain at least some of its reserves against the contingency of future payments deficits which might have to be financed with reserve assets. The development of this consensus was accelerated when the United States itself began talking about the need to increase its reserves, as it did when arguing for sizable SDR creations in 1968–69 and indicating that it planned to hold at least part of its allocations rather than "spend them profligately."[17] It is thus conceptually wrong to consider all of a center country's reserves as "backing" for its external liabilities, and its liquidity ratio must be high enough to allow for at least some use of its assets to finance potential current deficits.

Three major questions must be answered to derive operationally significant liquidity ratios for a key currency country: What assets can it count? What liabilities must be "backed"? And what is an acceptable ratio between the two? There seems to be no reason to expect systematic differences between the views of official and private foreigners on these issues. Indeed, private foreigners will try to anticipate the policy views of officials, since one of their main concerns about foreign currencies is the price at which their own authorities will buy those currencies from them, thereby providing them with an effective exchange-rate guarantee. Similar answers probably apply to the vehicle and reserve currency roles.[18]

A country's gross international assets comprise varying degrees of liquidity and availability to its monetary authorities. Almost all conventional analysis treats only the liquid reserve assets actually owned

17. Former Secretary Fowler testified to this as early as May 1968: the United States would "welcome growth in our reserves" because they "are now no more than average among all Fund members when measured against the size of our imports or our total international transactions—even before allowing for the special features of our short-term liabilities" See Attachment A to his statement to the House Banking and Currency Committee on the SDR Amendment to the IMF Articles of Agreement, May 1, 1968, p. A-12.

18. Only the availability of data on the various categories of assets and liabilities permit them to be disaggregated in any calculation. The United Kingdom prior to 1914 was judged by its overall international asset position, rather than any compartmentalization of assets or liabilities, since data were available only on an aggregate basis. As we shall see, a key currency country almost inevitably develops a stronger long-term than short-term position, so such a comparison would be more favorable for it. The lack of data thus served U.K. and world needs admirably. Thomas Balogh, *Unequal Partners* (Oxford: Oxford University Press, 1963), Vol. 2, p. 40, concludes that "if Bank of England liabilities had been scrutinized, on the sort of basis on which the U.S. gold reserves are now [1963] scrutinized, and compared with changes in various liabilities, the Bank of England would have been confronted with an immediate run and the expansion of the world economy under the leadership of Great Britain would have been brought to a halt." This conclusion receives strong support from the fact that the final crisis which forced Britain to float in 1931 was triggered at least partly by the publication, two weeks earlier by the MacMillan Committee, for the first time of a complete picture of the international liquidity position of sterling.

by a country's monetary authorities as unambiguously "countable" as "backing" against foreign holdings of its currencies. Even within this "inner ring," however, distinctions must be made. Gold is considered the safest and most liquid of any reserve asset, especially when it carries a high price premium in the private market.[19] SDRs are dependent on continued international cooperation as they have no private market value. In addition, 30 per cent of them must be reconstituted within five years and hence represent credit rather than "owned reserves."

If the United States were the only reserve center, the reserve currency situation would be clear: it could not count any other currencies as backing for the dollar, and all other countries could count dollars in their reserves. At present, however, the increasing international use of several other currencies complicates the issue. Since the external liabilities of all centers are "backed" only fractionally, the value to each of holding the others' currencies will vary with confidence in the currency being held. The exchange value of some of these holdings, such as those acquired under swaps, are guaranteed and should thus be considered as solid as gold and SDRs; indeed, this is often done by netting out both sides of the swaps from a country's liquidity ratio. But foreign exchange holdings, particularly of a "secondary" reserve currency (sterling) by the "primary" reserve currency country (the United States), are likely to be considered as less eligible "backing."[20] The problem is compounded by the possibility that these particular reserves might be subjected to national controls, and that their prices might change more readily than the prices of gold or SDRs. At the outer edge of this inner ring are any other relatively liquid foreign claims of the monetary authorities, such as the Roosa bonds held by several countries to help finance U.S. deficits in the 1960s, and the

19. While the United States maintained a "gold cover" for the domestic money supply, some regarded only the remaining "free gold" as clearly available for international use, despite the clear authority of the Federal Reserve to waive the requirement and the repeated assurances of the U.S. government that it would do so if necessary. The gold cover was completely abolished in March 1968—just before the collapse of the gold pool—to help assure foreign officials that the gold *could* be used internationally. Only Switzerland now maintains a gold cover for its currency, which could immobilize some of its reserves from international use.

20. Sir Roy Harrod's proposal in 1968 that the United States and United Kingdom hold each other's currencies "up to generously defined limits" as part of a North Atlantic monetary arrangement would thus have been of only marginal help to their extra-area positions. See his *Dollar-Sterling Collaboration: Basis for Initiative* (London: Moor House, February 1968), p. 65.

foreign securities commandeered by the British government from its citizens to help finance both world wars.[21]

A center country of a currency area might of course be able to draw on the "inner ring" assets of the other members of the area to bolster its own reserves. In the sterling area, the gold and dollar reserves of all member countries were long pooled under the control of the United Kingdom[22] and thus showed up in any compilation of "U.K. reserves." The United States, however, has received only minimum reserve pooling from the dollar area.[23] Any formalization of a dollar area might include reserve pooling, which would expand the front-line assets available to the United States to meet extra-area deficits in exchange for an increase in intra-area liabilities. Such pooling would significantly benefit the most meaningful U.S. "liquidity ratio," and improve the dollar's current standing.

The second ring in the series of concentric circles of reserves includes credits available to the monetary authorities. "Gold tranche" drawing rights at the IMF are first, because they are available automatically as long as the IMF itself exists and have 3–5 year maturities. Swaps are next. They can be mobilized quickly in large amounts but have very short maturities, and countries have often attached policy conditions to their agreement to activate. In addition, they are subject to bilateral cooperation; the United States suspended its central role in the swap network for a time after August 1971. Conditional drawing rights at the Fund follow in order: they also have 3–5 year maturities, but require increasingly stiff policy commitments from the borrower and, at a minimum, take time to mobilize.

The third ring encompasses the liquid claims of the private sector, particularly the commercial banks, which could in time of crisis be made quickly available to the monetary authorities. Some observers

---

21. In one of the rare instances where "official reserves" are rigorously defined, however, sterling area countries "counted" some of their longer-term and/or less liquid claims on the United Kingdom for purposes of determining the extent of the dollar-value guarantees which the British would extend to them under the Basel arrangements in 1968.
22. Although there never appears to have been any pooling of SDR allocations, which is one more indicator of the disintegration of the area by 1970. Three of the largest traditional holders of sterling—Kuwait, Libya, and Hong Kong —did not even participate in the original SDR scheme.
23. Such support has come mainly from Canada. It has sold gold to the United States and to Italy to mop up Italian balances of U.S. dollars, sold foreign exchange drawn from the IMF to the United States to enable it to reduce its dollar liabilities, and sold both gold and SDRs to the United Kingdom in 1972 to avoid a larger drain on the United States in the context of Britain's debt repayment to the IMF.

would exclude this category, because mobilization of private assets for official defense of an exchange rate would imply both a crisis situation and controls—hardly a situation to inspire confidence in a key currency. Private liquid assets should be regarded as quasi-backing, however, on more subtle grounds: the private sector could sell them off, either voluntarily or under government inducement, and hence rather quickly reduce the external liabilities of the key currency country.[24] The U.S. government now implicitly treats liquid claims of its private sector as national assets by moving them "below the line" in its "net liquidity" measure of its payments position.[25]

The same treatment could apply to nonliquid assets, in principle, although they could be mobilized only over a longer time period unless larger losses were accepted. The British never included their sizable portfolio of U.S. securities in their reserves, and in fact took several years to "liquify" them in the mid-1960s, although foreign holders of sterling were doubtlessly aware of this "secondary reserve," and the British did absorb some of the sterling balances held by Argentina and Uruguay in 1947 by selling them U.K. investments there. The United States induced its citizens to become net sellers of sizable amounts of outstanding foreign securities through the Interest Equalization Tax in 1963. In addition, in the mid-1960s, the United States successfully sought debt prepayments from the European recipients of earlier Marshall Plan aid.[26]

So far we have discussed only the *stock* of assets available to the center country. Their flow may be at least as important. We have already noted that steady increases in their reserve levels seem to satisfy countries psychologically that "all is well." By analogy, steady growth of the key currency country's assets, however defined by different foreign observers, may be more important to those observers than the level of the outstanding stock. The steady growth of the gross

---

24. See H.R. Heller, "The Transactions Demand for International Means of Payment," *Journal of Political Economy*, Vol. LXXVI, No. 1 (January/ February 1968), pp. 141–45.

25. See David T. Devlin, "The U.S. Balance of Payments: Revised Presentation," *Survey of Current Business*, June 1971, p. 24.

26. The economic status of Marshall Plan countries had improved much more sharply in a short period of time than can be expected of most of the more recent aid recipients, however, and loans to countries in weak financial positions could probably not be "counted" under any circumstances. The structure of U.K. foreign claims, many of which were on primary producing countries heavily in debt and hit by the first wave of the depression, was an important element in the *collapse* of confidence of sterling in 1931. See David Williams, "London and the 1931 Financial Crisis," *Economic History Review*, Vol. LIV, No. 3 (April 1963), p. 523.

reserves of all three key currency countries in the pre-1914 period, even as their liabilities grew more rapidly, may have been a key factor in the stability of that system. Certainly the steady decline of U.S. gross reserves after 1958 was a major factor undermining confidence in the dollar.

The "right answer," on either stock or flow grounds, would be a weighted average lying somewhere between the two extremes of gold bloc and dollar area preferences. It is impossible to say just where it lies without full knowledge of the thought patterns of the foreign holders and potential holders whose confidence in the currency is the crux of the matter.[27] Such knowledge is never available, however, and the center country must therefore lean toward the conservative extreme—accepting the costs of so doing—to avoid jeopardizing the stability of the system. The only satisfactory answer is really to poll foreign holders to see what assets they deem acceptable as "backing" and, as we shall see, what liabilities they would count and what ratio should be maintained between them—or negotiate the issue with them, to reach an understanding compatible with continued international use of the key currency. Such polling or negotiation would be practicable only with monetary authorities, but this would suffice for the United States under any system in which it remained passive in the exchange markets, since foreign private dollar balances could then become a claim on U.S. reserves only via foreign monetary authorities.

The problem is even more difficult on the liability side:[28] decisions must be made about maturity, type of holder (official, private, international organizations, etc.) and nationality of holder (gold bloc, dollar area, sterling area). Conceptually, a distinction should be made between liquid liabilities, which can be presented for conversion at

---

27. Hagemann's evidence indicates that only five countries (Belgium, Germany, the Netherlands, Spain, Switzerland) looked only at the U.S. gold stock during the period of his inquiry (through 1968). Several countries (Austria, France, Italy, Sweden) also seemed to consider U.S. private short-term assets as well. It is interesting that gold bloc and dollar area members are found in both groups.

28. None of the numerous students of the adequacy of international reserves has adjusted gross reserves for liabilities. Three addressed the issue specifically, and concluded that there were no ready criteria for excluding or including any of the various classes of liabilities. See Weir Brown, *The External Liquidity of an Advanced Country*, Princeton Studies in International Finance, No. 14, 1964, p. 3; T. J. Courchene and G. N. Youssef, "The Demand for International Reserves," *Journal of Political Economy*, Vol. LXXV, No. 4, Part I (August 1967), p. 408; Peter B. Kenen and Elinor R. Yudin, "The Demand for International Reserves," *Review of Economics and Statistics*, Vol. XLVII (1965), p. 242.

very short notice, and all others. Unfortunately, there is no way to implement this concept statistically. Some "short-term" deposits are virtually illiquid, since they are held as cover against insurance premiums or as compensating balances against loans from banks in the key currency country.[29] Some "long-term" liabilities are quite liquid, such as common stocks and bonds. Even non-liquid liabilities could become a claim on the assets of the center country over time, and could do so even in the short run if their owners were willing to accept liquidation losses in order to escape the currency. And it has often been pointed out that, in the absence of comprehensive exchange controls, domestic residents could export huge amounts of a currency if confidence were to wane sharply.

Another tricky question is how to differentiate among key currency liabilities to monetary authorities and to private foreigners. Again the data do not permit perfect distinctions, mainly because a number of central banks place reserve currency balances in the Eurocurrency market rather than directly with U.K. and U.S. banks, and these holdings show up in the U.S. and U.K. statistics as liabilities to *private* foreigners (the banks in the Eurodollar market) rather than to the monetary authorities.[30]

Conceptually, of course, private holders can at any time sell their holdings of a convertible currency for foreign exchange. Private dollars can thus readily move into official hands and become a claim on U.S. reserves. Indeed, the view that both private and official dollar balances threatened U.S. reserves was the conceptual basis for the dominant "gross liquidity" definition of the U.S. balance-of-payments position from the mid-1950s until at least the mid-1960s. And the view may have been largely correct during the earlier period when market fac-

29. The concept of compensating balances was applied to reserve currency holdings as early as 1905, when British banks required the government of Japan to hold such balances in London if it wanted financing for its war against Russia. Lindert, *op. cit.*, p. 32.

30. The IMF, in its *Annual Report* for 1973 (p. 36), identified official holdings of Eurodollars at $14.6 billion at the end of 1972 and also reported an unidentified residual component of world reserves, which probably included some more, of $12.7 billion. This compares with an official U.S. figure for liabilities to private foreigners of about $21 billion, implying that the dollar holdings of truly private foreigners had become quite small even after allowing for some multiple credit creation through the Eurodollar market (which produces a larger total for foreign dollar assets than for U.S. dollar liabilities to foreigners). There are several less important reasons for the discrepancies as well. For a careful discussion, see Ralph C. Bryant, "Dollar Balances and the U.S. Balance of Payments, A Conceptual Review," unpublished Ph.D. dissertation, Yale University, 1966, pp. 251-55.

tors totally dominated the conversion decision of foreign monetary officials.[31]

As the monetary system moved deeper into the "crisis zone," however, the actions of monetary authorities became greatly affected by the knowledge that efforts to exercise their conversion rights could force the key currency country to devalue or suspend convertibility and thus disrupt the existing system. Foreign monetary authorities became a buffer between foreign private dollar holdings and U.S. reserve assets, which are threatened *only* when the key currency holdings reach official hands.

Since the mid-1960s, as just indicated, a large proportion of the dollars recorded in the U.S. data as liabilities to private foreigners were really owned by foreign monetary authorities. These holdings may well continue to grow, despite the agreement of European central banks to stop the practice, because numerous non-European countries with large reserves—including, but not limited to, the oil exporters—continue to view the Eurocurrency market as optimally combining the economic attractions of reserve currency balances and avoidance of the political risks of holding such balances directly in the key currency countries. As a result, it can be argued that the U.S. liquidity ratio should now include U.S. liquid liabilities to "private" foreigners, at least as presented in the U.S. statistics.[32]

The crucial question for the United States is again the attitudes of foreign monetary authorities. If they are willing to hold whatever key currency balances accrue to them, the center country need not worry about its liabilities at all. Whether they are willing to do so depends on the nature of the system and whether the other countries involved are members of the dollar area or of the gold bloc.

Even in the absence of negotiated understandings, however, a key currency country might reasonably regard with concern only its liquid liabilities to official and private holders in countries outside its currency area, beyond levels clearly required by them as working balances. It could regard as "safe" its liquid (and other) liabilities to

31. Paradoxically, the concept disappeared only in 1971—when conversions of dollars into other currencies by private foreigners were greater than ever before. However, the bulk of these dollars could clearly not have been converted into U.S. reserves, so the abandonment of the concept in terms of depicting the degree of *realistic* threat to the reserves is defensible.

32. Guido Carli, Governor of the Bank of Italy, "The Eurodollar Market and Its Control," lecture given to the Swiss Institute of International Affairs, Zurich, Feb. 14, 1972, pp. 10–11. In principle, the United States would not need to count *all* of its liabilities to private foreigners; the ideal approach would be to include only the Eurodollar reserve holdings of foreign officials, as reported by them to the IMF.

countries within its currency area. There are always difficulties in deciding which countries to include in the dollar area, and a conservative approach should be followed in any such judgment for the United States. Inclusion of U.S. liquid liabilities to all countries, however, as traditionally done, presents a misleading picture. The only definitive solution in determining what assets were to "count" would be to poll foreign monetary authorities to get their views regarding the future of their dollar holdings.[33]

There is one difficulty in this approach. As pointed out in Chapter 3, a key currency country may have to use its owned reserves to finance the deficits of overseas members of its currency area, as well as its own payments deficits, with countries outside the area. It is quite possible that some of the reserve currency balances held by currency area members, as well as private holdings in those countries, will at some point be transferred outside the currency area and become a likely claim on the reserves of the center country. Indeed, the United States could be in payments balance, or even in surplus, but face a drain in its reserves if other dollar countries were in deficit with gold bloc countries. The center country thus needs to pay attention to the balance-of-payments trends of members of its currency area, as well as its own balance of payments and liquidity ratio, in assessing the probability of pressures developing in the exchange market. The sterling area always did so explicitly. The "dollar area" never did so, perhaps because the easiest way to do it in a predominantly dollar world was simply to focus on the balance-of-payments trends of the few gold bloc countries. But unless it is expected that dollar area countries will run consistent deficits with the rest of the world, there is no need to treat their dollar holdings as liquid or imminent claims on U.S. reserves.[34]

The final question is what ratio between assets and liabilities, each properly defined, must be maintained by the key currency country. The higher the required ratio, the higher the cost imposed on the country. Safest would be a ratio greater than 100 per cent by the absolute amount of the key currency country's expected need to use reserves to meet fluctuations in its current balance of payments. Such a ratio would at all times make it perfectly obvious that every outstanding dollar could be exchanged for some other U.S. reserve asset,

33. Hagemann found that only Belgium, Germany, the Netherlands, Spain, and Switzerland seemed to look solely at U.S. liquid liabilities to foreign monetary authorities. Austria, Canada, France, Italy, and Japan seemed to look also at its liquid liabilities to private foreigners.
34. This issue is treated at length in the analysis of the dollar overhang in Chapter 8.

and that even the perception of the United States of its own "minimum" needs to finance future payments deficits would not interfere with such conversions.[35] Maintenance of such a ratio, however, would obviate the possibility of any net dollar financing for U.S. payments deficits.

A simple 100 per cent ratio—which would be less onerous—has appeared important in the U.S. case in the past, although it has been defined in importantly different ways. Each of the three post-convertibility gold rushes—late 1960, early 1965, and late 1967–early 1968—occurred at a time when one of the key ratios between U.S. reserve assets and dollar liabilities dipped below 100 per cent, and each produced important policy reactions by the United States to deal both with its own balance of payments and with the inadequacies of the monetary system.

In 1960, the ratio of total U.S. reserves (mainly gold) to total liabilities to all foreigners, official and private, dropped below 100 per cent (Table 10, line 1). For the first time the published data showed that U.S. reserves had become insufficient to redeem all outstanding dollar balances, private and official. This ratio was particularly important at that time, prior to any thoughts of instituting a two-tier system for gold, because foreign private dollar balances did represent an indirect claim on U.S. gold. Its importance was heightened by the exclusive use of the gross liquidity definition of its balance-of-payments position by the U.S. government.

As a result, some countries began to seek guarantees for their dollar reserves. As indicated in Chapter 3, the United States responded in part by boosting the key currency roles of the dollar and in part by lining up new financing arrangements with gold bloc countries. President Kennedy, in early 1961, sought to help that process by announcing the first U.S. balance-of-payments program in an effort to restore confidence that the dollar parity would be maintained.[36]

In 1965, the ratio of U.S. reserves to short-term dollar holdings of foreign official agencies dropped below 100 per cent (Table 10, line 2). This ratio was particularly important psychologically. Since only official holders could buy gold directly from the United States, they represented the most obvious immediate threat to its reserves. For the first time, the data revealed that U.S. reserves were insufficient to redeem those dollar balances which, under its policy of thirty

---

35. Day, *op, cit.*, pp. 163–64, called in 1954 for a simple 1 : 1 ratio, at a minimum, for the United Kingdom. Germany maintained a ratio exceeding 1 : 1 in the early 1970s, as the mark became a key currency.

36. The importance of the fall of the liquidity ratio in President Kennedy's decision to adopt such a program is recorded in Sorensen, *Kennedy*, p. 406.

Table 10

KEY U.S. LIQUIDITY RATIOS: 1960–73

	1960	1961	1962	1963	1964	1965	1966	1967	1968	1969	1970	1971
1. Total U.S. *reserves* to (a) liquid liabilities to all foreigners plus (b) nonliquid liabilities to official foreigners	0.92[a]	0.82	0.71	0.64	0.57	0.52	0.48	0.42	0.41	0.37	0.31	0.18
2. Total U.S. *reserves* to liabilities to official foreigners	1.63	1.48	1.26	1.11	1.00	0.93	0.93	0.77	0.85	1.00	0.59	0.24
3. Total U.S. *liquid assets* (including private) to liabilities to official foreigners	na	na	na	1.22	1.17	1.03	1.05	0.88	0.99	1.15	0.69	0.31
4. Total U.S. *assets abroad* to total U.S. liabilities to foreigners	2.09	2.00	2.08	2.02	2.02	2.05	2.08	1.94	1.81	1.74	1.71	1.47

	1972	1973
1.	0.16	0.16
2.	0.21	0.22
3.	0.31	0.33
4.	1.34	1.39

na—not available.
[a] Was 1.11 in 1959.

Source: *Survey of Current Business*, Vol. 54, No. 8, Part II (August 1974), pp. 5–6; and Vol. 52, No. 10 (October, 1972), p. 21, 23.

149

years' standing, the United States avowed that it stood ready to convert into gold at the request of the holder.

This time, the response was two-fold. President Johnson announced by far the most severe balance-of-payments program to date in February 1965, extending controls to the entire capital account, to seek confidence that the dollar would not have to be devalued. And in mid-1965 the United States took a major international initiative to seek agreement to create a new international money, which led to the SDR decisions some two to three years later, to suggest to the world that it would not have to rely on the dollar forever (and to bolster the reserves of the United States itself).

In mid-1967 the ratio of *all* liquid U.S. assets (official *plus private*) to foreign official dollar holdings dropped below 100 per cent (Table 10, line 3). In addition, the ratio of total U.S. reserve assets to total dollar liabilities to foreign official agencies dropped *decisively* below 100 per cent. The data then clearly suggested that the United States could not redeem all officially held dollars even by mobilizing all of the liquid holdings of its private sector.

This time, the United States enacted a still tougher balance-of-payments program: reaffirming its intention to raise taxes, placing mandatory controls on capital outflows, and even proposing to Congress a tax on foreign travel expenditures by Americans. The goal was still to persuade the world that the dollar would not be devalued. And it took three systemic steps to protect the dollar. In March, it succeeded in getting foreign agreement to abandon the gold pool and institute the two-tiered system instead, and to make final the SDR negotiations. And, in June, it sponsored the Basel negotiations which ended the run on U.S. gold by countries leaving the sterling area.

It would, of course, be an overstatement to attribute each of these modern gold rushes fully to the U.S. liquidity position portrayed by the published U.S. data. Other factors intervened, including French political decisions in 1965 and the sterling devaluation in 1967–68. In late 1960 and early 1965, however, there were no tangible trigger points for the rushes. The dipping below critical 100 per cent thresholds by the United States' international liquidity ratios must have been an important element in engendering concern about the dollar and setting off the runs for gold.

The concept of fractional reserves, which has become commonplace in national banking systems throughout the world, should in logic apply internationally as well.[37] As already noted, the center currency

37. George N. Halm, *op. cit.*, pp. 554–56, argues that "there is no fixed relationship between backing percentages and confidence, just as there is under normal circumstances no reason to assume the impossible [simultaneous

gets no net balance-of-payments financing—the major gain for it of key currency status—if such a concept does not apply. And as our discussion of private and public holdings of key currencies has indicated, many of them are unlikely to be liquidated even in a major crisis. But the domestic analogy cannot be counted on, because the reserve currency is not legal tender internationally as it is domestically. The United Kingdom dominated the pre-1914 gold standard with a fractional reserve behind sterling, but the fraction was quite high and the absence of published data hid even this fact from the world.[38] Hagemann's estimates do not reveal what level of reserve ratio, if any, is particularly likely to cause problems. And the history of the dollar in the postwar period obviously indicates that nervousness sets in, in many quarters, when the liquidity ratio (however defined) drops below 100 per cent.

Views on the subject differ, however. Gold bloc countries probably require backing closer to 100 per cent—but their views are not very important in this context, because they do not hold very many dollars anyway (except for working balances). Dollar area countries require much smaller backing, perhaps even zero, and their views are very important because they hold the vast bulk of foreign dollars. The required U.S. liquidity ratio is a function of the distribution of world dollar holdings among these two groups of countries, which skews it sharply toward a very low level. In a crisis, however, even apparently solid "dollar countries" could panic. The only true solution to this problem would be the creation of an international lender of last resort and a system of international insurance against "failure" of the bank, to parallel the two cornerstones of an effective domestic banking system.

---

conversion of all claims into gold] will be attempted." Even Miroslav Kriz, a more conservative observer, concludes that "this country's gold stock need not be so large as to cover all our liabilities to foreign governments and central banks—not to mention those to foreign private bankers, merchants, and investors." See his "Gold: Barbarous Relic or Useful Instrument?" *Princeton Essays in Finance*, No. 60, June 1967, p. 17.

38. It is difficult to construct just what this ratio was, because of shortages of data. In 1913, we know that Bank of England gold holdings totaled $165 million and its sterling liabilities to official holders were $432 million (Lindert, *op. cit.*, p. 37) so that the *Bank's* liquidity ratio was about 40 per cent. Including the $200 million or so in gold held by 76 other British banks at the time, however, the ratio is close to 100 per cent. The ratio had presumably been declining up to that time, since official sterling balances seemed to have risen steadily from about 1895 while Britain's reserves rose only gradually. Lindert, *op. cit.*, p. 39, estimates that the U.K. payments deficit averaged about $21 million annually from 1900–1913 on the equivalent of today's official settlements definition.

Both could readily be provided by building on present institutions. The swap network, which aims to halt runs on a national currency, could provide over $18 billion in temporary support to the United States after its magnitude was increased in mid-1973. It is entirely analogous to the discount privileges which private banks have through the Federal Reserve System, and the partial exchange-rate guarantees on the swap activations are similar to the protection provided by the Federal Deposit Insurance Corporation. Larger amounts and longer maturities for the swaps, and more comprehensive exchange-rate guarantees, could make the system foolproof since any sizable run on the "key currency bank" by private holders would have to be reversed shortly to permit financing of ongoing economic transactions. The major monetary authorities would have to abstain from joining such a run, of course, but agreement to do so would be an integral part of any agreement to activate the swaps if someone else started a run.[39]

A fractional international reserve system could thus be made to work, with only marginal modifications in present policy. Proper publicity of the arrangements would be exceedingly important, since private holders would have to be made aware both of the liquidity ratio that had been agreed was "necessary" and of the new safeguards to protect the system. Such safeguards and agreement could only be reached through negotiations among at least the major countries on the proper role in the system for the reserve currency. Without such changes, such a system will always be danger-prone.

The Balance-of-Payments Position

The second aspect of a country's external position which affects its key currency status is its current balance-of-payments position. The econometric efforts of Hagemann and Malkin found that only one of eleven and two of thirteen major countries, respectively, seemed to change their foreign exchange ratios in response to the current U.S. payments position (gross liquidity definition) apart from any effects

---

39. On this entire subject, see numerous statements by Charles P. Kindleberger. In his "Testimony Before the Senate Committee on Banking and Currency on the Bill to Remove the Gold Cover for Federal Reserve Notes," January 11, 1968, pp. 9–10, he notes that short run inelasticity of the U.S. money supply produced the panics of 1873, 1884, and 1907. These developments finally produced the rediscount features of the Federal Reserve Act, which have consequently been largely superseded by open-market operations. A lender of last resort was required to provide the necessary money in a crisis. If an international central bank were to develop over time, its open-market operations could supersede the "rediscount facilities" which are now provided through the swap networks (and which could themselves be internationalized through the IMF or other institutions).

it might have on the U.S. liquidity ratios. However, after the liquidity ratio (defined most narrowly) dipped below 100 per cent, we would expect foreign observers to focus more heavily on the current U.S. payments position. Indeed, a high correlation did exist before 1968 between U.S. gold sales, perhaps the best simple indicator of foreign confidence in the dollar, and the official settlements deficit.[40] After 1968, the correlation disappeared as "crisis zone" considerations dominated.[41]

Whether the payments position is important directly, or only indirectly through its effect in changing the U.S. liquidity ratio, we must ask, "What is payments equilibrium for a center country?" Many people associate "equilibrium" with "zero balance," but such an association is probably incorrect in most key currency cases.[42] "Equilibrium" must take into account the needs and desires of the entire system, no less than those of the center country. There are three possibilities for center-country equilibrium: persistent surplus, persistent deficit, or persistent balance. Taking into account the needs of the system, which may change radically from one time period to

40. A formula derived by Paul Høst-Madsen, "Gold Outflows from the United States, 1958–1963," *IMF Staff Papers*, Vol. XI, No. 2 (July 1964), pp. 248–59, in which the independent variables were the U.S. official settlements position and changes in the monetary gold stock, predicted U.S. gold losses of $11.5 billion for 1958–67 compared with actual sales of $11.2 billion.

41. Curiously, Tower and Willett, *op. cit.*, the originators of the "crisis zone" approach, speculated that the current payments position became more important in that period because the "hopelessness" of the liquidity ratios made current U.S. deficits a much more important key currency criterion. They seem to have underestimated the importance of their own concept.

42. First of all, a "zero balance" can mean many different things, depending upon the definition of "balance." The United States has used numerous official definitions, and others are used by other countries and/or by international organizations. The United States government now focuses on three official definitions. The "basic balance" includes trade in goods and services and long-term capital movements. The net liquidity balance adds short-term nonliquid private capital, SDR allocations, and errors and omissions; "below the line," along with changes in U.S. official gross reserves and liquid foreign claims of the U.S. private sector, it thus includes changes in U.S. liquid liabilities to *all* foreigners. The official reserve transactions balance includes "below the line" changes in U.S. liabilities (liquid and nonliquid) to foreign monetary authorities, along with gross reserve changes. The United States could thus be in net liquidity deficit even if it was not losing gross reserves and even if foreign monetary authorities were not accumulating dollars, so long as private foreigners were. On the other hand, a zero official settlements position would be fully compatible with increased dollar holdings by private foreigners, no change in U.S. gross reserves, and no change in foreign official dollar holdings.

another, a case can be made for each alternative as representing equilibrium for a key currency country.

Two close students of the British case conclude that "the really fundamental conditions [for sterling's roles] were that . . . *sterling was always useful and sterling was always available,*" which really means "that there was no fundamental disequilibrium in the world payments system, so that the demand for sterling and the supply of it always tended to be adjusted to one another."[43] This obviously puts major emphasis on the structure of the system. Significantly, neither observer concludes that this equating of supply and demand generated any particular result in the U.K. external accounts. U.K. holdings of "bullion and specie" rose by small amounts in most years during the nineteenth and early twentieth century, but fell in a good number as well.[44] It appears that the United Kingdom ran deficits on the official settlements definition averaging about $21 million annually during 1900–1913.[45]

The dollar's career as a key currency also encompasses a mixture of payments positions. The United States was in surplus immediately after World War I, but moved into deficit throughout the 1920s when the roles of the dollar were expanding. These roles, after nearly disappearing in the first half of the 1930s when the United States was in surplus, went through a strong resurgence during the second half of the decade despite the fact that the surpluses were even larger. After World War II, the United States was again in surplus at first, through 1949; was consistently in deficit from 1950–65; was in official reserve transactions' surplus but liquidity deficit during 1966–69; and then moved into large deficit on all definitions in 1970–71.

The following chart depicts the possible combinations between (a) the center country's payments position and (b) changes in holdings of the key currency by the rest of the world. World holdings of the key currency are rising any place above the horizontal axis, declining anywhere below it. The gross reserves of the center country are rising any place to the right of the vertical axis, declining to its left. It is thus in payments surplus any place southeast of BB', in deficit any

---

43. Sayers, *op. cit.*, p. 121, and Day, *op. cit.*, p. 20; italics in original.
44. There were declines in ten of the years from 1880 to 1913 and 31 years throughout the 1816–1913 "century." Imlah, *op. cit.*, pp. 70–75. Imlah himself concludes (p. 11) that there "was a remarkable degree of equilibrium in the British balance of payments" throughout the nineteenth century, with "only a modest net inflow of gold and at no time an excessive accumulation of it." He defines balance in terms of gold movements only.
45. Lindert, *op. cit.*, p. 39.

place northwest of it. There are 17 possible combinations, represented by the 8 octants, 8 points along the axes and diagonals, and the origin.

The chart demonstrates that world key currency holdings can rise whether the center country is in surplus (Octant I), balance (along segment OB'), or deficit (Octants II–IV). Holdings can also fall even if it is in deficit (Octant V). *Gross* world reserves can of course rise as a result of the center country's payments position only if it is in deficit (Octants II–IV), and will fall if it is in surplus (Octants I, VI–VIII). The United States has experienced life in all eight octants, as shown on the chart.

Payments surpluses would improve the key currency country's liquidity ratio, provide assurance against oversupply of the currency, and maintain its attractiveness. Surpluses could coexist with expanding use of the currency as a reserve asset and increases in gross world reserves, as long as the gross reserves of the key currency country were growing more quickly than the foreign-held dollar reserves (Octant I). This would mean that foreigners were selling other reserve assets to acquire dollars, as in 1934–40, 1948, and 1957. It would imply a growing world dollar standard, one result of which would be a redistribution of world nondollar reserves to the United States.

On the other hand, U. S. surpluses might also generate reductions in world dollar holdings and hence in total world reserves. Such surpluses could be financed partly by U.S. reserve increases (Octants VII–VIII), as in 1930, 1932, 1941, 1946–47, and 1949, and hence only partly by decreases in foreign dollars (and world reserves). Or they could be accompanied by U. S. reserve losses, and hence reductions in world dollar holdings that exceeded the U. S. deficit (Octant VI), as in 1931 and 1933. This would produce a decline in total world reserves, and a redistribution of nondollar reserves away from the United States.

Persistent deficits, on the other hand, always decrease the liquidity ratio. They normally provide increased world holdings of the key currency (Octants III–IV, the United States in most recent years, including 1970–72). In most years, U.S. reserve losses have accompanied such foreign-held dollar buildups. However, U.S. deficits can occur without reducing the center country's gross reserves (Octant II), as in 1926, 1929, 1951–52, and 1956. In addition, U.S. deficits do not *assure* additions to gross world reserves; see Octant V, which was the U.S. case in 1925, 1928, and 1965, when both U.S. reserves and world dollar reserves dropped.

A position of balance would straddle these problems. The United States could provide additional dollar balances on a one-to-one basis for any increases in its gross reserves, meeting foreign demand for

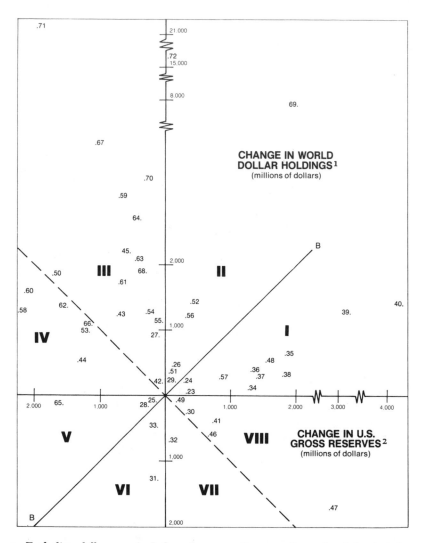

1. Excluding dollars acquired through swap actions, 1961–72, by deducting the reserves in U.S. holdings of convertible currencies; including amounts shown by the United States as "other readily marketable liabilities to foreign official agencies" and "non-liquid liabilities to official foreigners," 1962–1972.
2. Excluding holdings of convertible foreign currencies, 1961–72, since most were acquired through activation of swaps.
Note: "World dollar holdings" includes foreign commercial credits to the United States prior to 1947, but these amounts were probably small.
Sources: For 1923–59, U.S. Department of Commerce, *Balance of Payments Statistical Supplement*, Rev. Ed., pp. 1–4; for 1960–72, *Survey of Current Business*, June 1973.

dollars without impairing its liquidity ratio. On the other hand, it could permit its reserves to decline along with any reductions in foreign dollar-holdings, to avoid declines in the reserves of the rest of the world.[46]

Which of these positions represents equilibrium can be discerned only in the light of the prevailing monetary system. If assets other than the key currency are unable to provide sufficient growth in world transactions balances or gross reserves to meet the desires of other countries, then it is desirable for world holdings of the currency to grow. Such growth in *total* world reserves could occur via an "Octant I solution," with the reserve center in surplus. This would constantly improve the center country's liquidity ratio as well as build foreign reserve currency balances, and presumably avoid any instability arising from a decline in the center's liquidity ratio. Like any steady surpluses, this would mean a steady increase in the center country's share of world reserves. However, it would mean an even greater increase in the center's share of the non-reserve-currency reserves of the world—and it would provide no *net* growth in reserves for the rest of the world. At some point, in fact, it would result in the transfer of all non-reserve-currency reserves to the center country and would have to cease. It is thus an unstable solution.

Deficits financed by increases in world key currency balances (i.e., in Octants II–IV) are clearly in the world's interest in such a situation. The obvious problem is that prolongation of such deficits (or even balances along OB) impairs the key currency country's liquidity ratio. This is the famous "Triffin paradox."[47] The system must thus

46. A position of balance could lead to shifts in reserve composition in either direction: with increasing world use of the key currency (along OB[1]) and U.S. accumulation of an increasing share of nondollar world reserves, or with decreasing use with a corresponding drain of gross reserves from the center country (along OB). Both would affect the reserve center's liquidity ratio unless it started at an even 100 per cent, with an important difference. Equal increases in both reserve holdings and currency liabilities would improve the center country's liquidity ratio from a starting point *below* 100 per cent, and reduce it from a starting point *above* 100 per cent. Equal decreases in gross reserves and liabilities would have opposite effects. A center country concerned that its liquidity ratio was less than 100 per cent could thus "afford" to run a balanced payments position only if international use of its currency were growing, and it was restoring its own gross reserves by similar amounts. It could not accept reductions in foreign holdings of its currency, matched by declines in its own gross reserves, even though that would represent payments balance, because it would also represent a declining liquidity ratio.
47. First outlined in Robert Triffin, *Gold and the Dollar Crisis* (New Haven: Yale University Press, 1960).

either (a) include some safeguards for the center country, such as those discussed in the last section, or (b) provide a substitute to meet world liquidity needs. If neither is done, the key currency country will at some point simply become unable to continue running deficits and will have to chose between putting its payments position into balance (along OB', not OB) or surplus, even if such a step would not produce equilibrium, or take unilateral steps to protect itself against the absence of world agreement on the role it should play.

If the world decides to place reliance on the key currency to meet liquidity needs and takes the requisite steps to that end, it becomes possible for the center country to run deficits without fear that a deterioration of its liquidity ratio will at some point produce a crisis. Since the active membership of the internatonal monetary system has a like interest in avoiding such a crisis, such agreement should be forthcoming if the premise is widely accepted.

If, on the other hand, there is a world decision to shift at least some reliance for reserves to another asset, such as the SDR, there are several possibilities for the "proper" position of the key currency country. If the world decides that *no* further increase in the reserve use of the currency is desirable, it must treat its current balance of payments as would any other country—requring balance over time if it is unwilling to see a permanent decline in its owned reserves—and also worry about the balances already outstanding (the "overhang"), especially if they have already produced a shaky liquidity ratio.[48]

If the world desires some continued increases in the use of the currency for reserve purposes, safeguards need to be erected to the corresponding extent. These increases could take place with the key currency country in any of the three possible balance-of-payments positions through agreement on whether the increases were to provide additions to world gross reserves (requiring a key currency balance or surplus). The center country's willingness to continue to play a key currency role would of course be influenced by this decision.

There is thus no *a priori* "right" payments position for a key currency country. The U.S. position has varied over all of the octants. The desirability of any particular position depends on the existing monetary system, including aggregate world desire for new liquidity. Once a currency has achieved key currency status and is circulating

---

48. A complete elimination of the international use of the key currency, including outstanding balances, would have to include a negotiated arrangement on them as outlined in Chapter 11. Otherwise, safeguards would have to be erected against their causing difficulties, as in the Basel arrangements for sterling.

around the world, it can then run balances or even surpluses and still retain an international position indefinitely. Deficits are much more likely—though not necessary, as we have just seen—if it is to play an expanding role, in view of the desires of other countries to build their reserves.

A distinction must be made between the vehicle and reserve currency roles. The vehicle currency role of the dollar could expand with the United States in balance or even in surplus on the official settlements definition, and in deficit only on the net liquidity definition. For both uses to increase, however, and for the dollar to make a net contribution to gross world reserves, the United States would have to be in deficit on *both* definitions. But the key point for *all* purposes is that instability is likely to result if no agreements are reached on the proper balance-of-payments target for the key currency country. To be stable in any situation, except one clearly dominated by a single nation, any system based even partly on such currencies must be a negotiated system.

The final question about the payments position of a key currency country concerns the *magnitude* of surpluses or deficits which might be required to maximize the smooth functioning of the international monetary system if the currency is to go on expanding as an international asset. The larger the surplus, the more likely (although not certain) would be the diminution of its key currency role. In addition to the likely reduction of outstanding balances that would result directly, consistent surpluses would imply the possibility of eventual appreciation of the currency; borrowers would then be reluctant to acquire liabilities in it, and it could not play a two-way role in international capital movements. If the key currency country is to run deficits, there are three choices concerning magnitude: the size of the deficits could be unlimited; they could be limited in some agreed, regulated way; or they could be limited without prior agreement by the action of the key currency and/or other countries with sufficient capabilities to do so.

A number of observers made estimates of the equilibrium position for the U.S. balance of payments during the latter years of the Bretton Woods system. All were on the deficit side, and all tacitly assumed that the deficits must observe some limits. None, however, foresaw international agreement on the limit, and thus tried to guess the level that would fall within a de facto "allowable" range. Kindleberger, Despres and Salant judged in 1966 that the United States could run gross liquidity deficits of *at least* $1.5 billion to $2.0 billion annually for a long time, and probably much more, *provided* their analysis of the United States as the world's financial intermediary was accepted. They recognized that equilibrium might move to a lower level, however, if European capital markets were to develop more rapidly and hence reduce European dependence on the United States for long-term capital.[49] On the conservative side of the spectrum, Kriz estimated that the deficits could run at about $1 billion "after we have shown determination to deal with the deficit."[50] Tobin, in 1965, estimated that annual liquidity deficits averaging $1.5 billion would be acceptable and that most of them would be "financed" by private foreign demand for dollars.[51] Edward M. Bernstein suggested that equilibrium was probably about $1 billion on the official settlements definition before the creation of SDRs, but "much less now."[52] All of these judgments were of course based on the international monetary system that existed at the time they were made—prior to the SDR agreement, the two-tiered gold system, the suspension of gold convertibility of the dollar, or the move to more flexible exchange rates.

The most important estimate of the U.S. equilibrium position was made by the international community as a whole when it decided the amount of SDRs to be allocated in 1970–72, the first "basic period." In deciding to create SDRs at a rate of $3.5 billion in 1970 and $3 billion in 1971 and 1972, it assumed that foreign official holdings of dollars would rise by $0.5 billion to $1.0 billion annually by virtue of an official reserve transactions deficit of this magnitude for the United States in 1970–72.[53] The consensus, however, was only implicit; no firm agreements were reached concerning U.S. or foreign behavior to assure such a result—and, of course, actual events turned out to be widely different.

49. See "The Dollar and World Liquidity—a Minority View," *The Economist*, February 5, 1966, p. 528, where they concluded that "an annual growth in *Europe's* dollar holdings averaging perhaps $1–1.5 billion to $2 billion a year or *perhaps more* for a long time is normal expansion for a bank the size of the United States with a fast-growing world as its body of customers." Kindleberger individually added that, in his judgment, the United States could run a liquidity deficit "of $1.5 to $2 billion for . . . perhaps a generation without endangering the dollar, provided my analysis has been accepted." See his "International Monetary Arrangements," The English, Scottish and Australia Bank Ltd. Research Lecture of 1966, delivered at the University of Queensland, July 25, 1966, p. 10.
50. Miroslav Kriz, *op. cit.*
51. And hence official settlements deficits would be very small. Tobin, *op, cit.*, p. 224.
52. Edward M. Bernstein, "Fifty Years of U.S. Balance of Payments Statistics," *Survey of Current Business*, Vol. LI, No. 7, Part II (Anniversary Issue, 1971), p. 21.
53. And that other sources of reserves, including gold, would rise by $0.5 billion. See the "Proposal by the Managing Director on the Allocation of Special Drawing Rights for the First Basic Period," in IMF, *International Reserves: Needs and Availability* (Washington, D.C.: 1970), pp. 500–501.

The "unlimited" possibility must be differentiated between principle and practice. If key currency deficits are not too high, a principle that they have no limit may appear to exist; but if they rise too far, the "principle" may come under attack.

U.S. gross reserves were higher at the end of 1959 than at the end of 1945, and even rose throughout the 1951–57 period. In this sense, the U.S. liquidity deficits—which averaged $1.5 billion—in 1950–57 were apparently within any de facto limit which might have existed at that time. The efforts of the U.S. government to prevent even larger conversions of U.S. gold during the early 1960s appear to validate former Under Secretary Roosa's comment that, during that period, the United States abused its reserve currency role—but that such abuse is certainly not an inherent characteristic of a reserve currency country.[54] As long as there is no agreement that the deficits can be unlimited, it is best to consider any deficits which do not encounter negative foreign reaction—principally, conversion of dollars into gold in the U.S. case—as simply not having reached the unregulated limit. The limits might also remain unreached because the key currency country is itself reluctant to run deficits sufficient to meet world demand for its currency.[55] Unlimited key currency deficits permissible by *agreement* are compatible only with a pure reserve currency system wholly dominated by the key currency country.

Key currency deficits limited by agreement would presumably allow for their desired contribution to world liquidity.[56] This "allowable deficit" would take account of special factors in the key currency country's payments position which responded to foreign desires sufficiently so that other countries did not require a transfer of real resources to offset them, such as U.S. military expenditures for NATO. It would also take into account the desire of some countries to add to their dollar reserves.

However, four caveats must be registered. First, countries other than a key currency center could undertake such internationally desirable

54. See Roosa and Hirsch, *op, cit.*, p. 5.
55. Richard N. Cooper implies that the United Kingdom may have been in this position in the 1920s, failing to perceive the potential foreign demand for sterling and hence accepting heavier-than-needed domestic unemployment to support its overvalued exchange rate. See his analysis in *The Economics of Interdependence* (New York: McGraw-Hill, for the Council on Foreign Relations, 1968).
56. Walter Salant, in "Does the International Monetary System Need Reform?" in J. Carter Murphy, ed., *Money in the International Order* (Dallas: S.M.U. Press, 1965), pp. 3–32, defines long-run equilibrium for a financial center country in a growing world economy as "a deficit equal on average to the long-run increase in foreigners' desire to hold liquid assets denominated in the financial center's currency.

transactions and not be expected by their trading partners to "balance" them in a conventional payments sense. They could get compensatory financing by means other than creating liquid liabilities in their own currencies. Only the two key currency countries have in fact played such roles in the past, however, and our earlier discussion suggested that the same kind of overall world role which would promote the kinds of transactions cited is critical in providing a country with both the capabilities and the willingness to play a key currency role. It is therefore doubtful that other countries would undertake the type of responsibility cited here without at the same time moving toward key currency status, roughly in proportion to their overall world roles.

Second, there are ways to "offset" the international financial effects of internationally agreed activities, such as U.S. expenditures in NATO, other than through deficits in the reserve center's balance of payments. Indeed, Germany "offset" U.S. military expenditures wholly through its own military expenditures in the United States during 1961–66. Long-term German loans, which became part of the U.S.-German offset agreements thereafter, also improve the U.S. payments position on all definitions. Thus, just as key currency status is not necessary for a country to exercise such internationally desirable functions, so the internationally desirable functions need not be financed through the use of key currencies.

Third, the key currency balances accumulated by foreign monetary authorities to meet their own reserve desires derive partly from the exercise of the internationally desirable functions. The two categories thus cannot be cumulated to derive the "allowable deficit." In fact, overlap between the two contributes to acceptance of the "allowable" from the vantage points of both liquidity and adjustment, appealing to different decision-makers in the foreign countries involved.

Fourth, center country deficits might in practice still not provide the "right" amount of liquidity. Indeed, the U.S. deficits of 1970–72 far exceeded the "allowable" implicit in the SDR allocation decision. Nevertheless, agreement on an "allowable deficit"—which would reflect a world consensus on equilibrium for the reserve center—would go far to reconcile the liquidity and adjustment problems and reduce the severity of each. For the center country, adjustment would then be required toward a certain agreed level, not willy-nilly toward zero (on some definition) or some other figure which its policy-makers *guess* would be "allowable."

Indeed, the focus of discussion in the exchange rate negotiations triggered by the U.S. suspension of gold convertibility in August 1971 should have been the desired equilibrium position of the U.S. balance of payments. The original goal of a $13 billion improvement in its position, put forward by the U.S. government, included a forecast that such a swing would produce a $2 billion surplus (official reserve transactions basis) for the United States. Other countries finally agreed to a set of exchange rates which was estimated to produce only a $9 billion U.S. improvement, and leave it roughly in balance instead of surplus.[57] So the exercise provided no consensus on the future equilibrium level for the U.S. balance of payments, as well as fresh evidence of the need for such a view as a basis for virtually all of the major decisions confronting the international financial community.

The possibilities of either limited or unlimited deficits, pursuant to international agreement, would provide a stable payments environment for a key currency country. A third possibility, deficits limited by foreign attitudes but with no understanding about where the limit was, is by contrast a highly unstable environment—and has been the situation throughout the postwar period. Different foreign countries have different views about the permissible size of the key currency deficits; hence the global "allowable" would shift with the constellation of foreign payments surpluses between gold bloc and dollar area countries. The views of individual countries could also shift over time with changes in political power relationships and in such economic variables as the degree of world inflation or deflation inducing them to shift from one area to the other. The "allowable" could shift over time even if the payments constellation were constant. Thus it is incorrect to think that there is some single and immutable payments "threshold" beneath which deficits are acceptable and beyond which they are not.

The key currency country might read incorrectly the attitude of foreign countries, since they would generally not be spelled out publicly or even privately in any detail. Even if it read the foreign views correctly, it might forecast incorrectly the foreign payments constellation. As a result of the uncertainty, deficits would probably be either too large or too small even though the de facto "allowable" would certainly be a range rather than any single point.[58] The system could not function sustainably under either type of error, which equate with

57. Bank for International Settlements, *Forty-second Annual Report*, June 1972, pp. 28–29.
58. Although the range might be rather small. Francis Bator, "International Liquidity: An Unofficial View of the U.S. Case," *American Economic Review, Papers and Proceedings*, May 1968, notes that "under the 1965 rules of the game (i.e., pre-SDR) . . . there was no room at all between the devil and the deep blue; no profile of U.S. deficits or surplus could reduce the betting odds on trouble to a comfortable level."

"dollar glut" and "dollar shortage," respectively. Given the uncertainty about the acceptability of the deficits to foreign monetary authorities, private confidence in the key currency could easily be shaken and trigger crises. It is this manifestation of the gold exchange standard which Triffin has rightly criticized as unstable and dangerout, not the inherent role of national currencies as international money.[59]

Thus, if a key currency country is to run deficits, the international monetary system must provide a stable basis for it to do so. The most important criterion is that there be agreement among all major countries—including the key currency country itself—about what should be, over time, the average range of the deficits. Equilibrium can only be defined internationally.

The International Investment Position and the Balance-of-Payments Structure

The next question is whether a country must seek a certain structure in its balance of payments to qualify for key currency status. If it must do so, another policy target is added to the overall payments criterion. On the other hand, the structure criterion could substitute for the overall payments criterion. In either case, the target represents a policy cost only if the required structure differs from the structure the country would want to run in any event.

Some observers argue that a key currency country must continually run a current account surplus and be a net capital exporter.[60] This raises three questions: Why should it be in current surplus? Why should it be a capital exporter? What should be the relation between

59. The BIS contemporarily criticized the pre-1932 gold exchange standard in precisely the same terms: because of the way it operated, not because of the system itself. See "The Gold Exchange Standard," BIS Monetary and Economic Department, Papers Relating to the Gold Standard Prepared for the World Economic Conference of 1933, p. 22. Bryant, *op. cit.*, p. 367, notes perceptively that "the question of the future of the reserve-currency role of the dollar is logically prior to the problem of determining 'appropriate' balance of payments policy targets for the United States." His statement needs amendment only to encompass the question of *all* future international roles of the dollar.

60. Kenen, *op. cit.*, p. 68, and Aubrey, *op. cit.*, p. 261, take the position that a key currency must possess a steadily growing net international investment position, which is a better way to describe this "liquidity ratio." And this must be what Roy Harrod, *Reforming the World's Money* (New York: St. Martin's Press, 1965), p. 51, has in mind when he says that "two conditions are needed for a currency to become a reserve currency, namely (i) that it should be thoroughly strong and (ii) that its country should be in substantial deficit."

the current and capital accounts? We must also ask whether a key currency, in addition to or instead of running a current account surplus, needs to run a trade surplus.

We have already reached three conclusions about the economic requirements of reserve currency status: (a) that maintenance of a strong liquidity ratio is an important immediate indicator of the ability of a center country to maintain convertibility, but (b) that there is no clear agreement on what assets and liabilities "count" in the liquidity ratio or what it should be, and (c) that payments deficits will usually produce a deteriorating liquidity ratio for the center country. Indeed, this is the traditional "Triffin paradox," which he argues will doom any reserve currency system from its very birth.

There is, however, a way to avoid the dilemma. A reserve center could run payments deficits, as conventionally defined, but *avoid* deterioration in its "liquidity ratio," if (a) *private* short-term assets and *long-term* assets and liabilities were "counted" in deriving the ratio and (b) the center's balance-of-payments structure comprised current account surpluses of sufficient size to permit net outflows of long-term capital plus outflows of private short-term capital, which together were of greater magnitude than its net short-term capital inflows (which represent primarily the buildup of foreign reserve and vehicle holdings of its currency) plus its reserve losses. For example, even if other countries wanted to build their overall reserves by adding $3 billion to their dollar balances annually, the United States could run official settlements deficits of a like magnitude but still build its "liquidity ratio" by exporting $4 billion of net long-term capital plus private short-term capital—if its current account surplus totaled just $1 billion.[61]

The first issue is thus whether a large number of monetary authorities would be willing to "count" private short-term assets of the United States plus net long-term assets in assessing its ability to preserve the fixed-price convertibility of the dollar into U.S. reserve assets. Hagemann in fact found a very high cross-sectional correlation between U.S. gold losses and declines in U.S. short-term private foreign assets, suggesting that the rest of the world as a whole does view such assets as part of the most relevant U.S. liquidity ratios. He also found that four of his eleven countries (Austria, France, Italy, and

---

61. This formulation leaves open whether U.S. liabilities include only those to official holders or those to private foreigners as well. If only official dollars "count," then *net* outflows of short-term capital would be reduced by the amount of the inflow from private foreigners. If both "count," gross short-term outflows would be set against them. The net result in absolute terms, though not in ratios, would be the same.

Sweden) did in fact consider such short-term assets, and that two (Italy and Japan) appeared to consider the net long-term position. So one-half of his countries apparently took this somewhat broader view of the U.S. liquidity position. It is particularly noteworthy that this group includes two countries (Austria and Italy) which have vacillated between the dollar and gold, and whose views on the current U.S. position have thus been particularly important for the dollar at particular points in time.

Such views are quite logical, since we saw in Chapter 2 how the widespread mercantilistic attitudes of the present period focus heavily on the current, and even the trade, account. Certainly it is true that the current account provides a clearer picture of a country's competitive ability than its overall balance of payments, especially when the latter fluctuates as sharply as is now routine due to movement of liquid capital. Finally, the possession of large foreign assets by the reserve center provides a ready way for other countries to retaliate if it ever *were* to block foreign liquid balances, and hence reduces further the likelihood that such a step would ever be taken.

Some recent experience also supports the importance of the current account. In 1966 and 1968–69, the United States ran large official settlement surpluses, both due to large inflows of liquid money. But both periods were followed shortly by the two greatest "dollar crises" of all time: the gold hemorrhage of late 1967–early 1968, and in 1971 the even bigger flight from the dollar and U.S. suspension of convertibility. So foreigners apparently viewed the liquidity ratios and the current account, which were deteriorating in this period, as much more important indicators of the health of the dollar than the official reserve transactions balance.

It will be recalled that short-term private assets and foreign security holdings are much more likely to "count" in determining the liquidity ratio than foreign direct investments, for several reasons. Short-term private balances are of course quite liquid, and the monetary authorities can induce their liquidation quite easily—as the United States did, in 1965, to both bank claims and the foreign liquid balances of U.S. corporations. Foreign securities are also much more readily available to the monetary authorities, and have in fact been sequestered by the British authorities twice in the past. Foreign securities are much more marketable than direct investments, and hence could be more rapidly sold off without significant loss—by the monetary authorities, if they did sequester, or by the private holders if forced or induced to do so by the authorities, as in the United States through the Interest Equalization Tax since 1963. (The IET did not directly induce sales of foreign securities, but it impeded purchases of new foreign securities and hence induced *net* sales.)

Both forms of investment are politically more palatable in the host country than direct investment, and hence more likely to be considered sympathetically in assessing the center's position. And, for the same political reason, they are much less likely to be sequestered and rendered totally unavailable to the center country. All in all, short-term claims and foreign securities *are* much more liquid than foreign direct investments, and thus *are a* much more logical candidate for inclusion in a reserve center's "liquidity ratio." In a cross-sectional analysis of 18 countries in 1964, Hagemann discovered that U.S. *direct* investment abroad seemed to deter foreign dollar-holdings while long-term *portfolio* investment seemed to promote them.

Foreigners might also be willing to "count" these assets in assessing the U.S. liquidity ratio if they strengthen its current account. If the United States were *not* steadily increasing its net international creditor position—because its overall payments deficits were comprised of a current deficit and a capital inflow, or a deficit for both—it would encounter growing net interest *payments* which would, over time, weaken its current account. The United Kingdom relied heavily on its investment income for years, including most of the period of sterling's dominance.[62]

In assessing whether a distinction should be made between direct and portfolio investment for these purposes, we thus also need to assess whether they have significantly different effects on the center's current account. Direct investment generally has a higher yield, but it also has greater effects on other components of the investing country's balance of payments, notably the trade account. There is fierce controversy over the magnitude and even the direction of these effects: private industry argues that such investment is necessary to retain foreign markets and preserve at least some of the exports of the investing country, while labor argues that such investment displaces exports by the investing countries by an amount virtually equal to the new foreign production which results. We simply do not know enough at the moment to provide a definitive answer to the question. Most observers agree that foreign direct investment, over time, makes a net contribution to the balance-of-payments strength of the sending country. However, the net gain may on the average not begin to

62. The United Kingdom's *balance* on interest and dividends consistently provided most of its current account surplus (or exceeded it) from about 1825. Imlah, *op. cit.*, pp. 70-75.

appear for as long as eight years, or even longer.[63] If this is true, they do not provide much greater help for the U.S. current account than does foreign portfolio investment, where a 20-year loan at 5 per cent becomes a net gain for the balance of payments in about ten years and where short-term loans to foreigners, especially if they finance additional U.S. exports, can do so much more quickly. So there seems to be no basis on present evidence to discriminate in favor of direct investment for balance-of-payments reasons.

There is also the special case of foreign portfolio claims of the center country's government, which are the financial manifestation of foreign aid loans. Hagemann's cross-section analysis suggests that a peripheral country's willingness to hold foreign exchange is also determined by any such assistance it may receive from the center.[64] To be sure, this is primarily a political effect—though it is also "economic" in the sense that the peripheral country will avoid liquidations of reserve currency holdings because the center might then reduce its aid levels or at least tighten its aid conditions. (This effect is much more likely for less developed than for major industrialized countries.) In addition, relatively rapid mobilization of these assets by the center is also possible if the debtor countries have progressed, as when the United States received several billion dollars of prepayments in the early 1960s from previous recipients of Marshall Plan aid.

One can even speculate that the British—abetted by the absence of disaggregated data—were able to "get away with" the relatively low liquidity ratio of the Bank of England before 1914 by virtue of their huge and growing portfolio of short-term foreign claims and foreign securities, some of which were indeed subsequently commandeered by the government and used to defend the exchange rate of sterling. One can also note that the dollar began to run into trouble *after* the United States consciously began to limit its short-term claims abroad

63. The best study so far of this issue for the United States concludes that the average "payoff period" is eight years; G. C. Hufbauer and F. N. Adler, *The Trade Impact of U.S. Manufacturing Activity Abroad*, Treasury Studies in Tax Analysis No. 1, 1967. The best study for Britain finds an average "payoff period" of fourteen years. See W. R. Reddaway *et al.*, *Effects of United Kingdom Direct Investment Overseas: Final Report* (Cambridge, Eng.: University Press, 1968). Both studies have been roundly criticized, however, and their results must be viewed with great caution.
64. The U.K. White Paper on the Basel Facility (p. 2) supports this point by noting that sterling countries diversified their reserves in the 1960s in part because of "their growing reliance on non-sterling sources for investment and aid."

and run down its net holdings of foreign securities, at the same time creating no barriers against continued plant and equipment investments abroad by U.S. firms and providing no concrete inducement for foreign firms to make direct investments in the United States. Both sets of measures accelerated the trend of direct investment to increase its share in overall net U.S. foreign investment—and, on this line of analysis, may have reduced support for the international roles of the dollar as a result.

If it is true that the U.S. "liquidity ratio" is much more important to foreign dollar holders than the current U.S. payments position, and if it is true that even some gold bloc foreigners are apt to "count" U.S. short-term assets and holdings of foreign securities in that ratio, then the United States should have been limiting direct investment and avoiding controls on short-term claims and portfolio investment after 1963 rather than doing the opposite—even within the general approach of seeking adjustment through the application of controls. Indeed, the most illuminating balance-of-payments presentation might then be to group direct investment with the current account in a modified "basic balance," with all other capital movements treated separately. Any surplus in this modified basic balance would then equate to the net growth of U.S. foreign assets which "counted" in determining the most meaningful U.S. liquidity ratio.

The notion that long-term foreign assets *should* be included in the key ratios of the center country receives strong support from the school of thought which regards the United States as an international financial intermediary, accepting short-term deposits and extending long-term credits because its liquidity preferences are different from, and complementary to, those of other countries (particularly in Europe). Indeed, advocates of this school would consider changes in the overall international investment position of the United States alongside the conventional measures of its balance of payments in assessing the current state of its international financial strength. It is acceptance of the intermediation concept on which Kindleberger and others roughly conditioned their estimates, cited above, that the United States could go on running sizable payments deficits on the conventional concept for many years. This school, however, makes no distinction between foreign portfolio and foreign direct investment by the United States, and therein may lie one of its weaknesses in terms of winning widespread foreign acceptance.

There is thus strong reason to suspect that the growth of its private short-term foreign assets and its net foreign long-term investment position, perhaps with direct investment excluded, is an important criterion for a key currency in preserving its status. Indeed, the dollar began to run into real trouble and entered the "crisis zone" when its international investment position began to decline, after 1966, after remaining virtually unchanged throughout the earlier 1960s (line 4 of Table 10). This in turn, particularly for a key currency country which is likely to run payments deficits, requires sizable current surpluses.

The empirical evidence supports the thesis that key currency status and a position as a net capital exporter proceed together, although it does not demonstrate that net capital exports are a necessary prerequisite of key currency status. The United Kingdom built up large overseas investments *before* its currency became widely used as a reserve currency, although presumably it was already being widely used as a vehicle currency during the earlier periods. The stagnation of sterling as a key currency since 1945 has paralleled its decreasing role as a net exporter of capital. The use of the dollar as both a vehicle and reserve currency grew hand in hand with the United States becoming a net capital exporter after World War I. It disappeared when the United States became a net capital importer again in the early 1930s, and its re-emergence later in that decade when the United States was *not* a net capital exporter can be attributed to the political environment then existing. The dollar's roles developed more strongly than ever after World War II, in company with massive and growing U.S. capital outflows, but continued to grow in more recent years even when net U.S. capital exports fell. France became an important capital exporter, mainly at long term, prior to 1914 when its franc became an important international currency. (No data are available to test the same proposition for Germany.) The empirical correlation between the two roles is highly suggestive, even if causality is not proved.

The final structural issue is whether a key currency needs to be specifically supported by a strong trade surplus, in addition to (or instead of) a strong current account surplus. A strong trade balance might be viewed as the clearest external manifestation of a strong competitive position. It might thus be deemed the best "international" proxy for some of the underlying domestic criteria to be discussed in the next chapter—dynamic growth, increasing productivity, maintenance of price stability—or at least as the best readily available approximation, since precise trade data are released much more rapidly than precise current account data. Such considerations presumably motivated the U.S. Treasury to say in 1968 that "the keystone of a sound international position for the United States and the dollar is a substantial trade surplus." And the focus of the effort to achieve a sizable devaluation of the dollar in the early 1970s was clearly to regain a large trade surplus.[65]

If the maintenance of key currency status required the United States to run trade surpluses, it might well be imposing an *extra* policy target on the country; for secular trends suggest that the United States may, over the years ahead, move gradually into trade deficits of increasing size. One argument is that, since the United States is becoming increasingly a producer of services, relative to its own demand structure, its comparative advantage is declining in the entire goods sector; that a smaller share of national output is available for export; and a larger share of national demand for goods may be satisfied by imports.[66] Another is that U.S. firms are likely to produce an increasing share of their total output through their foreign subsidiaries as more industries move to an advanced stage in the "product cycle" where products become standardized and cost considerations dominate locational decisions.[67]

There are several important conceptual and empirical flaws, however, in the notion that a key currency country must run a trade surplus. We have already demonstrated that it is *current account* surpluses which enable the key currency to build its international investment position. Investment income is the most reliable source of current account strength and so is at lease as important as trade surpluses. Furthermore, a strong trade position, by itself, demonstrates very little about the competitive strength of the country. Any country can run trade surpluses by depressing domestic demand, by subsidizing exports, or by restricting imports. None of these approaches, all of which were tried by the United Kingdom during the 1960s, is sustainable: economic waste and political reality now rule out sustained unemployment, while economic inefficiency and international repercussions rule out sustained trade controls. (A trade surplus generated by unemployment would also conflict with one of the important domestic criteria, discussed in Chapter 6, and a surplus generated by controls would violate an important requirement for a key currency.)

65. However, that same objective could have been motivated more by the effort of the moment to reduce the high level of U.S. unemployment than to preserve the key currency status of the dollar, or indeed any international financial objective, as indicated in Chapter 3. See C. Fred Bergsten, "The New Economics and U.S. Foreign Policy," *Foreign Affairs*, Jan. 1972, especially pp. 200–204.
66. Lawrence B. Krause, "Are Exports Becoming Irrelevant?" *Foreign Policy*, No. 3 (Summer 1971), p. 67.
67. Raymond Vernon, "International Trade and Investment in the Product Cycle," *Quarterly Journal of Economics*, May 1966.

The empirical problem is that the United Kingdom ran trade surpluses in only five years during the period from 1796 to 1913 when sterling was the leading world currency.[68]

A strong trade position at full employment without controls would no doubt contribute to the world esteem accorded a key currency. But the United States can clearly run a sizable and growing current account surplus without a trade surplus. A trade surplus cannot be considered a necessary condition for key currency status for the dollar in the United States.

If this conclusion is correct, the U.S. government may have been misguided to stress so persistently the importance of a trade surplus as a key sign of fundamental strength in the dollar. It may have been a mistake to present the data in such a way as to inflate the trade surplus by including aid-financed sales in the export figures and by valuing imports on an f.o.b. rather than c.i.f. basis.[69] By so doing, it has raised serious foreign fears over *increases* in the U.S. trade surplus. Partly as a result, foreigners always reacted negatively to any suggestion of U.S. measures to improve its trade balance—including such mild steps along "border tax" lines as were suggested by President Johnson on January 1, 1968—until that balance, as officially defined by the U.S. government, shifted into deficit in 1971. The United States may thus have tightened the straitjacket on its adjustment policy options for an analytically dubious benefit.

Summary

The cardinal test of the key currency status of any national currency is the degree of foreign and domestic confidence in its future price stability, relative to competing assets—mainly other national cur-

68. Imlah, *op. cit.*, pp. 37–38 and 70–75. As already noted, Britain ran sizable current account surpluses throughout this period.
69. Calculating imports on an f.o.b. basis *is* analytically preferable. However, other countries are able to portray a weaker trade (though not current account) position than actually exists by valuing imports c.i.f. Hence they can more easily justify measures to improve it. There is one important argument for presenting a picture of a strong U.S. trade balance outside the context of the balance of payments: that it helps in the preservation of a liberal trade policy, by strengthening the case that liberal trade benefits the United States. It is true that this argument carries some political impact. However, its economic foundation is nonsensical: increased imports help the United States, and retaliation against its exports would hurt it, whether it started from surplus or deficit. In addition, overall adjustments —such as exchange-rate changes—are the only way to go about improving the trade balance anyway; protectionist trade policies would not do so. The best remedy to this political problem is to expose its untenable intellectual foundation.

rencies for vehicle purposes, and including non-currency assets such as gold and SDRs for monetary authorities. In a system of fixed exchange rates, this requires confidence in continued convertibility of the key currency into all other reserve assets in the system at the current price. In a system of flexible exchange rates, it requires confidence that the key currency will not depreciate, and probably (due to the effect on borrowers of the currency) that it will not appreciate very much either.

Both the conceptual analysis of this chapter and the empirical results of several econometric studies suggest that the key elements in generating such foreign confidence are the various "liquidity ratios" of the center country: the ratios between its reserve assets and foreign liabilities. However, different countries adopt different views toward which assets and liabilities should be "counted" in this calculation, and what constitutes an appropriate ratio between them. Gold bloc countries could be expected to take the most restrictive approach on each count, and dollar area countries to be the most relaxed.

In the absence of negotiations explicitly directed to these issues, however, the center country will be highly uncertain about what it has to do to avoid jeopardizing its key currency position. In turn, the system will be unstable to the extent that it relies on the key currency (or currencies) placed in such a position. This was in fact the situation of the "Bretton Woods system" throughout its life, which became particularly acute in the 1960s—particularly when the various U.S. liquidity ratios passed psychologically critical points in 1960, 1965, and 1967. It was this manifestation of the international use of national currencies which Triffin and others criticized as producing systemic collapse, not anything inherent in such a practice—though both history and political factors suggest that it would be extremely difficult, in practice, to reach the negotiated agreements necessary to permit key currencies and systemic stability to coexist peacefully.

In any event, the center country will have to maintain a sufficiently strong liquidity ratio to preserve the needed confidence in its currency. Its current balance-of-payments position is important chiefly as it affects its different versions of this ratio; indeed, history shows that key currency status is compatible with a wide combination of balance-of-payments positions of the center country and changes in total world reserves. The most common payments position for a center country whose currency's international roles are expanding, however, is a deficit. As usually defined, this in turn leads to a deterioration in its liquidity ratios defined to include only short-term assets and liabilities—and hence trouble for both the center country and the entire system, to the extent that it relies on the key currency (or currencies).

The dilemma could be resolved, however, if countries would focus not on the liquidity ratios defined so narrowly but rather on the center's international investment position, including its long-term foreign assets and liabilities. This would permit the center both to expand its short-term liabilities and to add to world reserves through its key currency function without weakening foreign confidence in the stability of its exchange rate. And there is both historical and empirical evidence to suggest that confidence in the dollar began to decline markedly only after the U.S. liquidity ratio, as thus broadly defined (and perhapse thus better referred to as the U.S. international investment position), began to deteriorate in the late 1960s.

Thus a key currency country may well have to maintain a balance-of-payments structure comprising current account surpluses and net capital outflows. If international use of its currency is to grow, the capital outflows will have to exceed the current account surplus—and the stability of such an arrangement will depend, in turn, upon the willingness of the bulk of the other major countries in the system to accept such a structure in the payments position of the center. There appears no need, however, for the center to run a trade surplus for key currency reasons.

6

Attributes of a Key Currency: The Politics

We have just assessed a variety of the external economic attributes required of a key currency country as the most direct indicators of whether confidence can be maintained in the relative stability of its currency and its international status retained. In turn, however, these external attributes rest on the domestic economy of the key currency itself. It is they which ultimately determine the strength of a key currency, and whether it can achieve or maintain a major international role.

This chapter analyzes two aspects of the requisite internal economics. The first, which may prove decisive in the short run, is the set of indicators of a country's current economic strength: its rate of economic growth and its ability to maintain relatively stable prices. The second aspect comprises the more permanent economic factors which "qualify" a country for international status in the first instance: its size in the world economy, which determines to an important extent both the weight which it can bring to bear on others and the degree to which it can remain aloof from external influences, and its savings and investment structure, which go far to determine the capacity of its capital markets. We might think of the first set as "flow" variables, the second set as "stock" variables.

Finally, this chapter will conclude with an effort to pull together the analyses of Chapters 4–6 to reach conclusions about the relative importance for the achievement and maintenance of key currency status of the various political, external economic, and internal economic attributes. This sets the stage for Chapters 7–10, which will attempt to assess the costs and benefits to the Unied States of the roles which the dollar has played in the monetary system heretofore.

Economic Growth
The two most important indicators of the outlook for the U.S. current account and overall balance-of-payments positions, and hence

for the key liquidity ratios, are economic growth and the maintenance of relative price stability.

Growth is cited less frequently by students of the key currency question than other economic factors.[1] Nevertheless, dynamic growth maximizes the likelihood that the resources which can be acquired directly for the currency being held will be desirable at all times. Since the productive resources of any country are the ultimate "backing" of its currency, ongoing "product leadership" is an important attribute for a country whose currency is to play a major international role.[2]

This direct effect is secondary, however. It would be of central importance only if currencies were not convertible into each other. With convertibility, balances in a single currency are claims on resources anywhere, not just claims on resources in its country of issue. This is why confidence in continued convertibility is absolutely essential for a key currency.

Dynamic growth is important primarily because it is critical for long-term maintenance of a strong external economic position. Without it, devaluations become likely both because of lagging productivity (as in Britain before 1967) and because of domestic pressures to use the exchange rate to reduce unemployment (as in the United States in 1933 and 1971). Because this point is widely recognized in the financial world, few countries would add willingly to their holdings of a currency backed by a relatively stagnant economy. It is a more important consideration for the reserve currency than for the vehicle currency function, because of the longer time horizons of most official holders, but it is also important for the latter function because growth greatly enhances the attractiveness of equity participation in a national economy by private foreign investors.

Rapid growth may increase imports more than exports in the short run, hurting the country's trade and current account balances. This

1. Mikesell, *op. cit.*, pp. 146–48, does regard a strong domestic economy, including high employment and rising productivity as well as price stability and a strong current account position, as more important than gold convertibility. See also U.S. Treasury Department, *op. cit.*, p. 21.
2. Britain's world leadership in manufacturing in the early nineteenth century is a case in point. Balogh, *op. cit.*, p. 25, concludes that "The rise of London as the centre of an international economy was based on Britain's mercantile supremacy as an Imperial Power and her industrial leadership as an initiater of mechanised mass-production." Another view along the same lines is taken by Jean-Jacques Servan-Schreiber, "Alarmed Voice of a New Europe," *Life*, May 17, 1968, p. 49: "U.S. know-how, business methods, and brain power are all too potent. They are the real foundations of the dollar and they are superior."

is particularly true for the United States, since its income elasticity of demand for imports exceeds the income elasticity of demand of the rest of the world for U.S. exports. Indeed, on this calculation alone, the United States could only grow about three-fifths as fast as the rest of the world if it were to avoid a secular deterioration in its trade balance.[3]

However, rapid growth also tends to increase capital inflows and discourage capital outflows. The reasons are that such growth makes the outlook for profits more attractive at home than abroad, and rapid growth usually requires relatively high interest rates to control the concomitant inflationary pressures. The overall balance of payments, including short-term capital flows, is quite likely to improve. Indeed, the U.S. balance of payments has been strongest (on the official settlements definition) in recent years when unemployment was low and economic growth was booming (1966, 1968–69), mainly because such conditions trigger tight domestic monetary policy. It has been weakest when growth was sluggish and monetary policy was easy as a result (1970–71).[4] The issue in the short run is whether foreign holders look more closely at the current account or the official settlements position—and we concluded in the last section that most of them seem to focus on the former. Dynamic growth can contribute both ways, however, by strengthening the official settlements position in the short run and the current account in the long run.

In addition, maintenance of a strong economy is necessary to enable a country to provide the real resources needed to maintain a world role, as discussed in Chapter 4. It would be impossible to fund a level of military expenditures adequate to maintain a strong world political role, for example, without adequate domestic growth, particularly with the increasing competition of domestic needs. Indeed, rapid growth of resources is needed in most countries to preserve a sufficiently tranquil domestic society to permit pursuit of any active foreign policy.

The stagnation of sterling's reserve currency role in the postwar period is vivid testimony to this conclusion.[5] The United Kingdom

3. Houthakker and Magee, *op. cit.*
4. A strong *positive* correlation between U.S. domestic growth and balance-of-payments surpluses was found in the pre-1914 period and for the 1950s by Jeffrey G. Williamson, *American Growth and the Balance of Payments, 1820–1913* (Chapel Hill: University of North Carolina Press, 1964).
5. The same factor may have been crucial in the fall of sterling in 1931. Williams, *op. cit.*, p. 523, cites the relative incompleteness of Britain's recovery after World War I as one of the "more important" elements in the loss of faith in London, which contributed to the "final" sterling crisis in 1931.

has grown more slowly than any other major country during this time, and much of its balance-of-payments difficulty and the related withdrawal from its world political role can be traced to that deficiency. At the same time, the currencies of Germany and Japan, where dynamic growth rates have been sustained throughout the postwar period, are now being sought widely for international use. Domestic economic strength is clearly an important condition for achievement of key currency status.

The U.S. case mildly supports the conclusion that growth is important, but suggests that other domestic economic factors may be even more important. Wider use of the dollar corresponded to relatively strong U.S. growth in the 1920s. The international demise of the dollar corresponded to the deepening U.S. recession of the early 1930s, which compared unfavorably with the relatively shallow decline of economic activity in Britain at the time. In the postwar period the dollar was avidly sought at least until 1958, even though U.S. economic growth was not particularly impressive prior to 1961. This relatively slow growth was widely regarded as "natural" for a mature economy undamaged by the war, however, and an image of dynamic growth was artificially maintained because the other major countries were still going through their reconstruction phases. The United States grew impressively from 1961 through 1968; but the reserve currency role stagnated after 1964, while vehicle currency use continued to expand. (Reserve currency use skyrocketed in 1970–72, but this was due to "crisis zone" considerations and was little related to underlying U.S. performance.)

The rapid U.S. growth of the 1960s can be divided into two phases, which goes far to explain its otherwise inconsistent effects on the international roles of the dollar. In the 1961–64 phase, excellent price stability was also achieved. In the post-1964 period, inflation loomed as an increasingly important problem and there were ever more calls for *restraint* in the growth rate. The correlation between the two phases and the shift in the fortunes of the dollar, especially as a reserve currency, suggest that another element in the domestic economic picture, price stability, plays a highly important role.

Price Stability

There are several reasons why maintenance of reasonable price stability is an extremely important attribute for a key currency country. At a minimum, it is probably necessary to assure steady economic growth. In addition, relative price stability strengthens a country's international competitiveness and its external economic position.

The price performance of the center country also has a major impact on *world* price stability, and hence on these same macroeconomic factors in all countries—especially those closely aligned to the center. Excessive inflation in the center country means excessive inflation in the world, and excessive deflation in the center threatens world recession.[6] Foreign willingness to hold dollars, and keep their exchange rates pegged to the dollar, implies that neither excessive inflation nor deflation is being exported to them through such channels.

On the other hand, price stability for a key currency far superior to that of most other countries would also create important problems. It would promote balance-of-payments surpluses for the center country. It would promote appreciation of the key currency, which would make foreigners wary of borrowing it and hence reduce its availability. It would generate low interest rates, due to low inflationary expectations, and make holdings of the currency less attractive. Modal price performance may therefore be optimal for a key currency country.[7]

Relative price stability also enhances the attractiveness of any store of value, and currencies are one of the clearest cases in point. As already noted, safety of principal is probably the most important consideration of monetary authorities in the determination of their reserve asset preferences, and similar motives play an important role in the decisions of private bankers and traders. A currency which is able to maintain its purchasing power relative to other available assets—and whose authorities appear willing and able to promote such stability—takes a major step toward qualifying as a key currency. This same stability, through its effect in strengthening a country's external position, reduces sharply the possibilities of devaluation of the currency and adds to its prospective safety as a store of value.

Price stability is also important because of the biases of the financial decision-makers, both in private life and in official positions, who do so much in determining the internaitonal role which currencies are to play. Many financial men, by virtue of their own experience and training, place relatively greater weight on price stability than on

6. For precisely this reason, Mundell has proposed unambiguous assignment of U.S. monetary policy to the policy target of *world* price stability. See his "The Crisis Problem," in Robert A. Mundell and Alexander K. Swoboda, eds., *Monetary Problems of the World Economy* (Chicago: University of Chicago Press, 1969), pp. 343–50. The degree of world price influence of a key currency country depends partly on its size, which is discussed in the next section.

7. Tibor Scitovsky, *Money and the Balance of Payments* (New York: Rand McNally, 1969), esp. pp. 177–78.

some of the other objectives of economic policy, such as growth and full employment. The generalization may be truer for Continental European than for Anglo-Saxon countries, as discussed in Chapter 2, which adds to the global bias since financial men generally have greater influence on policy in Continental Europe. As a result, price stability may assume more weight in assessing a currency by those whose judgments are most critical than it would in some "objective" and more balanced view of economic targets.

The historical record supports the conclusion that price stability is an important criterion for a reserve currency. Sterling was considered highly stable throughout the pre-1914 period, and the Bank of England was known to be both willing and capable of maintaining such stability.[8] British prices have been much less stable in the postwar period, however, and sterling's reserve currency role has stagnated.

The United States, on the other hand, had the best price record of any major country during World War I and the interwar period, when the dollar became a key currency. It had virtually the best record in the early post-World War II period, during which the dollar rose to ascendancy. Relative U.S. price stability was especially marked in the 1958–64 era, when increases in the dollar's roles were greatest. The rapid price increases which began in 1965 and continued into the early 1970s, on the other hand, correlate closely with the growth of foreign official doubt about the dollar, which played a major role in fomenting the crises of both 1967–68 and 1971.

The Swiss situation again helps prove the point: its franc, the only Continental currency to be widely sought for international use over the years, has maintained a better price record—both over the long sweep of history and more recently as well—than any other currency on the Continent. Absence of a history of stable prices helps to explain why some of the other major European currencies have not previously achieved key currency status. The historical experience of Germany and France, for example, has created reluctance to hold marks or francs, and can probably be overcome only by a quite sustained period of stable prices in each country. The events of May 1968, after ten years of good price performance, would appear to justify such a view with regard to France. Germany has now maintained an impressive degree of price stability for a generation, how-

---

8. Day, *op. cit.*, p. 17. U.K. prices were at least as stable as those of other major countries for which data are available for the 1814–1913 period (the United States, Germany, France, and, in later years, Italy) and in most periods more so. See the collection of such data in Robert Triffin, *The Evolution of the International Monetary System*, Princeton Studies in International Finance, No. 12, June 1964, p. 13.

ever. Coupled with its historically determined antipathy toward inflation and the collapse of U.S. price stability in the early 1970s, it now looks the most likely bastion against inflation of any of the major countries.

The Domestic Economic Criteria: A Comparison

Thus, two aspects of a domestic economy, dynamic growth and relatively stable prices, are important determinants of whether a country is equipped to play a key currency role. A country qualifies best if it achieves and maintains both rapid growth and stable prices: as did Britain in the nineteenth century, the United States in the early interwar period and in the early 1960s, and Germany throughout most of the postwar period. It is most likely to lose its position if it is faced both with slow growth and with rapid inflation, as was the United Kingdom throughout most of the postwar period and the United States in 1970–71.

The close correlation between price developments in the United States and changes in the dollar's reserve currency role suggests, however, that price stability is the more important of the two criteria. In fact, a center country may have to retain relatively high price stability at the cost of higher unemployment to avoid deterioration of its key currency position. It thus may face pressure to choose a point on its Phillips curve which conflicts with its purely domestic objectives. The pressure is compounded since many officials conscious of price stability may view exuberant economic growth with some suspicion, due to the attendant risks of inflation and weakness in at least the current account of the balance of payments.

This problem adversely affects the ability of a key currency country to pursue national policies independently. It has become increasingly acute for the United States in recent years, as its Phillips curve has shifted outward. Inflation in the early 1970s in the United States tended to run about 1.5 per cent higher at any given level of unemployment than it had as recently as a decade ago, owing to structural changes in the labor force.[9] To meet any given norm of price stability, the United States would thus have to accept a good deal more un-. employment than in the past. Such a norm could of course be based on purely domestic considerations, but pressures for it could also

9. At the "full employment" level of 4 per cent, inflation ran at about 3.25 per cent in 1960 but at 4.75 per cent at the end of the decade. See George L. Perry, "Changing Labor Markets and Inflation," *Brookings Papers on Economic Activity* 3, 1970, pp. 411-41, and Charles L. Schultze, "Has the Phillips Curve Shifted? Some Additional Evidence," *Brookings Papers on Economic Activity* 2, 1971, pp. 452-67.

come from foreign dollar-holders or prospective dollar-holders.[10] Maintenance of a key currency role for the dollar has thus become more costly for the United States on this count, a very critical one in domestic economic and political terms.

National Size

Finally, several structural elements of a country's domestic economy are requisite for key currency status: its importance in the world economy, the importance to it of the world economy, and the capabilities of its capital markets.

It is quite evident why a national currency attains widespread international use when its home country comes to play a major role in world economic transactions, whether through purely economic motives or in the wake of national political designs. It is quite convenient for private traders and bankers to hold balances in a currency in which a large part of their business must be transacted. Then, once such balances begin to be built up in a few countries, economies of scale provide incentives for expanding the value of transactions carried out in that currency throughout the world, and its convenience value rises.[11] There is very rough evidence that a key currency may tend to finance a share of world trade at least equivalent to the share in world trade of its country of issue.[12]

In the middle 1960s, the dollar was clearly a more efficient vehicle for foreign-exchange transactions than any other currency. The margins between buying and selling rates were lower for the dollar than for other currencies. The volume of dollars which could be traded without affecting the exchange rate was two to five times as great as the volume of other currencies which could be so traded. Brokerage fees on dollar transactions ranged from 10 per cent to 50

---

10. Rates of inflation have risen in other countries too, and it is possible that Phillips curves have shifted as markedly as has that of the United States. Unfortunately, no studies of such changes have been made. And it should be noted that other countries, particularly in Western Europe, and Japan have been much more successful than have the United States and United Kingdom in insulating their international competitive position from internal inflation; indeed, their indicators of export prices have risen less than their indicators of domestic prices, whereas the opposite has been true for the United States.

11. See Harold Demsetz, "The Cost of Transacting," *Quarterly Journal of Economics*, Vol. LXXXII, No. 1 (February 1968), pp. 33–53.

12. With most of the rest, in countries with convertible currencies, financed in local currency. See Grassman, *op. cit.*, and the Danish data cited therein.

per cent of the fees for transactions in other currencies in the major foreign exchange markets.[13]

The demand for a key currency by foreign private sectors is central to its role as an intervention currency. When a foreign country is in deficit, its residents will seek to buy foreign exchange—mainly the key currency—from the monetary authorities. The latter, who must provide the needed foreign exchange to maintain their own exchange rate, save themselves the cost of converting other assets into the key currency if they maintain a stock of it on hand. Convenience therefore motivates both the vehicle currency and intervention currency uses of a foreign currency whose country of issue is an important factor in international trade and capital movements. The degree of such use is determined for individual countries largely by the closeness of their economic ties with the center country.

The two global reserve currencies have emerged when their countries of issue played a dominant role in global trade and capital movements. British imports reached an overwhelming 42 per cent of other countries' exports in 1800 and were still at 17 per cent in 1913, but had diminished to 9 per cent in 1967. Its share of sterling area trade, although it has also diminished greatly, remains at least twice as high as its global share and hence correlates with sterling's continued (though also declining) role with members of the area. The dominance of the United Kingdom in international financial flows was even greater: as late as 1913 the gross long-term creditor position was 41 per cent of the world total[15] and must have been even higher earlier. Its share, including short-term capital, was undoubtedly even greater, given the dominance of London's bill of exchange in trade finance.

The dollar began to play its international role as the U.S. share of world trade grew throughout the interwar period, and of course reached overwhelming proportions after 1945 when its major competitors lay prostrate in the aftermath of the war. The U.S. trade share has naturally declined since that time—though its share of world exports dipped only from 16 per cent in 1950 to 14 per cent in

---

13. The data, which were provided by the various central banks, are brought together in Alexander K. Swoboda, "Vehicle Currencies and the Foreign Exchange Market: The Case of the Dollar," in Robert Z. Aliber, ed., *The International Market for Foreign Exchange* (New York: Praeger Publishers, 1969), pp. 30–40.
14. Imlah, *op. cit.*, p. 191.
15. United Nations, *International Capital Movements during the Inter-War Period*, 1949, p. 2.

1970—but the share of international financial transactions probably continued to increase at least until the capital restraints imposed for balance-of-payments reasons slowed gross movements of capital to and from the United States.

In the late 1960s and early 1970s, international use of the German mark closely paralleled the growth of German trade, which had virtually reached the level of U.S. trade (at the exchange rates prevailing in mid-1973) by 1972. But history also suggests that the presence of an important international economic position is not a sufficient condition for the development of a key currency. Germany, for example, became a larger factor than the United Kingdom in world trade (and perhaps even in total international transactions, since Britain has restricted its capital outflows for many years) long before the mark began to be widely used. Japan has now also passed the United Kingdom as a world trader, but the yen is not yet widely used. In earlier periods, French trade and capital movements had a high share in the world total. But these currencies have not achieved key currency status, except for France within the franc zone and Germany (until recently) within Central Europe—where both did dominate the flow of international transactions. The answer is fourfold: economies of scale promote the widest international use of a single currency; the country whose relative dominance is greatest will most naturally supply that single currency; there are political and economic criteria other than size which must be met if a currency is to achieve widespread international use; and, perhaps most important, the "reigning" key currency tends to retain the dominant role until cataclysmic events (such as the sterling action of 1931 and the dollar actions of 1971–73) blast loose the fundamental inertia of monetary systems and open the doors to possible successors.

In addition to the "carrot" with which national size endows a currency, it provides a "stick." Sufficient national size enables a country to bring down the entire monetary system, or force other countries simply to accept its unilateral actions, and thus provides it with extra leverage to preserve its key currency roles. We called this "positive international monetary power" in Chapter 2. During the pre-1914 and early postwar periods, respectively, Britain and the United States could have severely damaged the entire system by devaluing and/or abandoning gold convertibility. Even after both had declined somewhat, their adoption of both measures in 1931 and 1971, respectively, jarred the systems severely. It is a measure of the durability of key currencies that even the sterling devaluation of 1967 had important systemic effects.

Even after the current U.S. liquidity ratio had dipped below 100 per cent and the first post-convertibility gold crisis took place in 1960, the United States apparently had sizable benefits from its perceived capability to do systemic damage. Greene found that, under otherwise similar conditions, the nine countries which she studied were buying $1.7 billion less gold annually in 1961–64 than in 1957–60. The main changes occurred with Germany, Italy, and Britain. Her numbers may be a bit high, because her time period caught Italy's brief life in the dollar area and pre-dated the bulk of France's conversions, but do reveal important shifts by at least a few key countries.[16] In March 1968, the implicit U.S. threat to suspend convertibility played a major role in achieving agreement to abandon the gold pool and adopt the two-tiered system for gold. Throughout the late 1960s and early 1970s, the deterioration of all the U.S. liquidity ratios and numerous other factors would have led us to expect much larger gold conversions had it not been for "crisis zone" conditions. Indeed, on the basis of his analysis of 1955–65, Hagemann concluded—with Triffin —that the dollar overhang and the system were bound to collapse unless the United States put its payments position into balance quickly—and, of course, they did not. In short, national size and the related economic and financial power are critical for key currency status.

Independence from External Constraints

The second significant aspect of size is the relative importance of external transactions to the domestic economy of the country—in economic terms, its degree of "openness." Superficially, it might appear that the economies of key currency countries should be closely geared to international transactions, since they might then be considered most likely to pursue policies consistent with the interest of the international community.[17] Foreign antipathy to any hint of "benign neglect" of its balance of payments by the U.S. government seems to reinforce this view. And the usual textbook description of the experience of the United Kingdom supports it as well; in the pre-1914 period, Britain is often seen as adjusting its internal policy to external variations as a matter of course.

This view is erroneous, however. In fact, a key currency must be

---

16. Hagemann, on the other hand, found sizable changes in reserve composition policy only for France, Spain and Italy at the time of the 1960 crisis, and no dramatic departures in 1965.
17. Mikesell, *op. cit.*, p. 145, argues that the center country must attune its policies to international stability and growth. Mundell, as noted earlier, goes even further in proposing that *world* price stability become the target of U.S. monetary policy.

based on an economy that is affected to only a minimal extent by external transactions.[18] The reason is that a key currency country should be strong enough to pursue its domestic economic policy without regard to the vagaries of external events—"negative international monetary power," to use the terminology of Chapter 2. It can meet such a criterion if it can effectively reject domestic adjustment to external imbalances, either because external transactions play a small part in the country's overall economic picture or because its dominance in the world economy is so great that it can effectively throw the burden of adjustment onto other countries. Such economic independence minimizes the pressures on the center country from erroneous economic policies and economic disaster elsewhere in the world, and makes its currency a safer haven standing above all others. This is not to say, of course, that there must be no constraints on a key currency country derived from the outside world; it must meet the numerous criteria required for maintenance of its center status. The point here is that its domestic economy must be able to avoid undue *direct* repercussions from foreign events. The revival of dollar strength in the wake of the oil embargo in late 1973, because the United States was the major country least dependent on imported oil—despite the fact that the embargo was aimed primarily *at it*—is the latest case in point.

In addition, a number of foreign countries will seldom if ever want the center country to alter its internal or external economic policies in response to its balance-of-payments position. It is only other major countries, which are themselves reasonably immune from international repercussions or otherwise easily able to pursue their own economic objectives, which object to "benign neglect." In fact, most countries probably will always place priority on maintaining the level of their exports and capital inflows—which would be jeopardized by any of the adjustment options which the center might choose. Even in his cross-section study of eighteen of the most developed countries, Hagemann found that the existence of current account deficits on *their* part, the share of their exports which went to the reserve centers, and their reliance on aid and private capital inflows were significant factors in determining their own foreign exchange ratios. In a sense, this consideration is the opposite side of the national size criterion: adjustment by a dominant country will throw unwelcome costs on *other* countries, which will oppose its adjusting as a result. The degree of aloofness which a center country can preserve on this account will vary directly with its economic proximity to other countries, and is

18. Karlik, *op. cit.*, pp. 78–79, agrees.

another key determinant of why countries "join" a particular currency area.

The experience of the United States, where external events have historically played an almost negligible role in formulating domestic economic policy, supports the conclusion that "aloofness" is an important key currency criterion. External economic developments have traditionally had such a small direct impact on the American economy that they have had little macroeconomic impact, and only a few countries have put pressure on the United States to alter that situation. As far back as the 1920s, the dollar developed as a key currency just at the time the United States was becoming the first country ever to proclaim publicly that its economic policies aimed to neutralize the internal effects of its balance-of-payments position. In the postwar period, Michaely's study of the responsiveness of domestic macroeconomic policy in nine major countries confirms that, except perhaps for interest rates in the early 1960s, the United States remained wholly aloof from the pressures of the balance of payments.[19] The 1933–34 devaluation was an effort to help restore domestic growth; the U.S. balance of payments was in surplus (even on today's liquidity definition) in every year from 1930 to the outbreak of World War II.

However, this U.S. aloofness to external events has been breaking down rapidly. Chapter 10 will outline in detail the increasing U.S. reliance on external events. Here it suffices to note that the U.S. devaluation of 1971, and its follow-on in 1973, were motivated by concerns that its external position was significantly increasing U.S. unemployment and, by throwing trade into deficit, was jeopardizing overall U.S. foreign policy. The United States was still not *forced* to devalue by outside events, but the internal effects of those outside events had become so important that it could no longer afford "benign neglect." In addition, a sizable share of the sharp increase in U.S. inflation in 1973–74 was imported (partly as a result of those same devaluations). In short, another of the U.S. key currency criteria is declining sharply.

A close interpretation of the British case prior to 1914 also supports the view that "aloofness" correlates positively with key currency status. Britain was willing to tighten monetary policy in response to external developments during that period, but most of the real burden

19. Michael Michaely, *The Responsiveness of Demand Policies to Balance of Payments: Postwar Patterns* (New York: Columbia University Press, 1971), esp. pp. 252–75. The only other countries to remain so wholly aloof were Germany and Sweden.

of the adjustment was borne not by the United Kingdom itself but by the rest of the world. The United Kingdom was able to attract foreign capital in sufficient size and with sufficient speed to balance its accounts promptly, so that the tight monetary policy did not much affect internal British economic activity.[20]

In addition, numerous observers have argued that Britain so dominated the international economy of that time that the principal balance-of-payments effect of its bank rate changes was on the price of its commodity imports. By tightening monetary policy, the United Kingdom reduced the supply of funds available to foreign suppliers to finance inventories and increased the cost of such financing. These suppliers were therefore forced to liquidate their commodity inventories and cut prices; accordingly, Britain's import bill declined.[21] When the United Kingdom tried to reacquire a key international role for sterling in 1925 by *catering* to international requirements, by adopting a grossly overvalued exchange rate, it achieved some short-term success but quickly ran into trouble and saw its role diminish sharply—and the world economy crumble—by 1931. Once the United Kingdom could no longer meet the "aloofness" criterion, sterling could not effectively play a key currency role.

Both the United States and the United Kingdom, in the periods of international dominance of their currencies, have thus been able to hold their domestic economies largely aloof from external events. (The only other country in the past 150 years to possess such capabilities was the Soviet Union, which decided not to participate in the international monetary system after World War II but has played a key currency role in the area of its domination since that time.) To the extent that the United Kingdom could not maintain total aloofness, because external transactions did play an important role in its economy, it must be remembered that the reserve currency roles of sterling and the dollar occurred in extremely different historical contexts. British dominance occurred in a "gold standard" world in which countries attached high importance to adjustment of their pay-

20. Lindert, *op. cit.*, pp. 36–57. See also Williams, *op. cit.*, who concludes (p. 519) "that the pre-1914 British domestic economy hardly responded at all to changes in bank rates."
21. See Peter Kenen, *British Monetary Policy and the Balance of Payments, 1951–1957* (Cambridge: Harvard University Press, 1960), pp. 59–62. Lindert, *ibid*, however, finds evidence of such a relationship for only a minority of observation periods in his analysis of changes in British monthly import prices. Day, *op. cit.*, p. 21, notes that increases in U.K. interest rates, the major instrument used, did "slightly dampen economic activity in Britain" but also concludes that "the real burden of British payments adjustment was borne by the peripheral countries."

ments imbalances and were willing to do so through internal policy changes. Its susceptibility to some adjustment pressure was acceptable domestically, while its ability to shift the burden to others provided sufficient "aloofness." The United States, on the other hand, acted in a world where international considerations in most countries were clearly subordinated to domestic goals, and where international payments imbalances often made the conflict between external and internal requirements painfully apparent. So Britain's somewhat greater susceptibility to external effects, compared with that of the United States, was fully in keeping with its milieu and did not detract seriously from its key currency status. And the inability of Switzerland, and even of larger countries such as Germany and Japan, to avoid sizable domestic repercussions from external developments, at least without widespread controls which violate another key currency criterion, has traditionally been a major limitation to their qualification as key currency countries—but this limitation is rapidly becoming less important, relative to the dollar, as the U.S. economy becomes increasingly reliant on the world economy.

The importance of this criterion of size (and aloofness) for a key currency country, like that of a world political role to which it closely relates, may also shift over time. In a "fair weather" period when reasonable harmony prevails in the international economy, external disturbances would be less likely to upset the center country—so its aloofness would be less important. In a stormy period, however, such as the fifty years from Sarajevo through at least the chilliest of the cold war years, and as resuscitated by the energy crisis from late 1973, the "safe haven" requirement may be much more important.

National independence from external events has one further dimension: it is necessary for a country to be *willing* to permit its currency to play a large international role. This is so because such a role will increase the host country's economic openness, perhaps increase the number of targets of its economic policy or reduce its instruments for coping with them, and hence tend to increase potential policy conflicts within the country—even if on balance the roles provide the country with net benefits.

Herein lies another potential dilemma in the key currency role: an increase in the role will lead to a diminution of the independence criterion, which in turn will make the country both less capable and less willing to continue playing it. Domestic politics might thus preclude the possibility of sustaining a key currency role even if it started. The events of May 1968 in France were caused at least in part by the Gaullist emphasis on price stability, which was at least partly motivated by a desire for the franc to play a much greater international role. Indeed, macroeconomic policy in the United States has become significantly affected by external events. The general tax increase of 1968 was finally adopted by the Congress partly because of the monetary crises extending from late 1967 through early 1968; and "the necessity for dealing with the international financial problem promptly . . . tipped the scales" in favor of adoption of wage-price controls in 1971.[22] The willingness to play the key currency role has also diminished, in general, as a result of the pressure it has brought on the United States to choose a point on its Phillips curve different from the dictates of the domestic economy and to avoid devaluation even when such a step was needed to restore external equilibrium and avoid increases in domestic unemployment.

The risk of further international economic entanglement may be a major reason why some major countries have been unwilling to play a key currency role.[23] The Swiss, who are heavily reliant on international trade and capital movements, have stated as much. This reinforces our earlier judgment that a country's world political role is crucial to its assumption of key currency status. Given the aloofness of its economy from external events, the United States (like the Soviet Union) could have dispensed with any entangling involvement in the international economy. Some of the most important external constraints on the United States derive from the roles of the dollar in the international monetary system, which it accepted but did not need for economic reasons.

The constraints come mainly from "playing by the rules of the game," rather than from other countries. For example, by seeking to negotiate military offset agreements and by restricting the use of its foreign aid, the United States accepted significant constraints on its foreign policy to demonstrate that it was not pursuing a policy of "benign neglect." Similarly, it accepted restraints on the international activities of its banks and corporations by placing restrictions on their capital outflows, and even proposed restraints on foreign travel by its citizens. It did all this, instead of seeking to devalue the dollar, despite the high degree of "adjustment power" which we saw in Chapter 2 that it has through the exchange-rate mechanism, and accepted significant domestic criticism to do so. Thus the *exercise* of aloofness was clearly declining even before August 1971. And the inability of the United States to remain aloof was demonstrated most vividly in late 1971—paradoxically, as a result of its belligerent "unilateral" move which broke all the existing rules—when it revealed its

22. *Annual Report of the Council of Economic Advisers*, 1972, pp. 67–68.
23. Swoboda, *op. cit.*, p. 21.

dependence on other countries to achieve a change in the exchange rate of the dollar, which it decided was necessary to pursue its own vital economic and foreign policy interests.

It is of course true that the United States gains economically from involvement in the world economy, as will be shown in detail in Chapter 10. It is also true that its willingness to accept the rules, and play by them, was encouraged by its apparent ability to preserve a large measure of independence even *with* world involvement, and by some of the gains to it from the dollar's roles, to which we turn shortly. But at the root of its voluntary abandonment of jealously guarded impregnability in the postwar period, in direct contrast to its behavior in the interwar years, must have lain a concept of a world role for the United States which required it to accept such a potential cost in order to achieve broader goals. No other explanation is satisfactory.

Savings Flows and Capital Markets

Another structural requirement for key currency status is highly developed financial markets. Such markets are necessary to meet the needs of foreign (as well as domestic) currency holders, since the very nature of some of their transactions—trade, finance, and investment outlets for private holders, intervention use for official holders—requires them to move quickly in and out of assets denominated in the key currency without incurring sizable losses.

A market which can provide the needed range of investment instruments with regard to yield, maturity, and liquidity will probably develop only if domestic savings in a country are sufficiently large.[24] Some countries, such as postwar Germany and Japan, have generated large savings flows, which have not, however, led to the creation of large pools of investment media that provide the basis for highly developed capital markets. In both cases, the absence of significant government debt obviates the existence of the safest and most liquid of securities markets.[25] So the availability of a large savings *flow* is not a sufficient condition for such developments; a large stock is needed as well.

But a large flow of savings is also important to provide capital for the new investment which is the *sine qua non* for the achievement

24. Foreign capital played a large role in improving the London market, which, in turn, became even more attractive to foreign capital. This is one more example of the process through which the *achievement* of key currency status fosters the *maintenance* of key currency status.
25. Kenen, *op. cit.*, p. 68, cites the need for a large short-term public debt, presumably for this reason, as a key currency criterion.

and maintenance of dynamic economic growth. Much of the United Kingdom's sluggish postwar growth is due to shortage of investment, in part due to inadequate domestic savings. Some of the resurgence of U.S. growth in the early 1960s can be traced to the inauguration of the investment tax credit and accelerated depreciation allowance in 1962, and similar measures were re-instituted in 1971 in an effort to promote higher growth once more.

Sizable domestic savings are also needed to make credit available to foreigners at a reasonable price, which is an important criterion for growth of the vehicle use of a currency.[26] Some observers in fact extend the "dominance" theme · to this issue, arguing that the world's leading capital exporter is most likely to achieve key currency status.[27] Some technical reasons can be advanced to support this view. Borrowers will find it convenient to hold unused portions of loans in the currency in which they were extended; indeed, two key steps in the development of the use of national currencies for reserve purposes were Russia's decision to hold the bulk of its German borrowing in Berlin in the 1890s, and Germany's decision to hold most of the proceeds of the Dawes reparation loan in dollars in 1924. Countries are often required to hold compensating balances in the currency loaned, and they can save transactions costs by maintaining a reserve in that currency against amortization and interest payments. The economies of scale involved in maximum utilization of a single currency do suggest a close relationship between dominance in the key currency and capital exporting roles, and key currency status itself probably accelerates capital exports.[28]

There is also a subtle reason why capital exports are needed to preserve reserve currency status. When other countries get into balance-of-payments trouble, they are prone to turn to the center country—the *de facto* manager of systemic stability—for help. Italy

---

26. Paul Einzig, "The Declining Use of Sterling as a "Trading Currency," *Westminster Bank Review*, May 1968 p. 2.
27. Day, *op. cit.*, p. 15; Imlah, *op. cit.*, p. 7; Brown, *op. cit.*, p. 600.
28. Strange, *op. cit.*, esp. Ch. 4, argues that sterling's roles have led to a "hypertrophy" of foreign direct investment by Britain. Robert Z. Aliber argues that the key currency role of the dollar is a major factor leading to U.S. foreign investment, because the dollar carries less exchange-rate uncertainty and hence lower interest rates. (Aliber developed this theme before the exchange-rate upheavals of 1971–73.) He notes that the rise of U.S. foreign investment and the rise of the dollar as an international currency coincided, and that a similar correlation occurred between U.K. foreign investment and the international roles of sterling. See his "A Theory of Direct Foreign Investment" in C. P. Kindleberger, ed., *The International Corporation* (Cambridge, Mass.: MIT Press, 1970), pp. 17–34.

did so in 1964, despite a recent agreement among the EC countries to provide medium-term credits to each other; and the British and others frequently did so even when the United States was itself in heavy deficit. If the United States had then been unwilling to provide the requested capital, it could not have expected other countries to finance the United States by acquiring dollars when it had a similar need. Indeed, in grateful response Italy actually "joined" the dollar area for a while after the 1964 loans from the United States—just as Germany had "joined" the "dollar area" in 1924 as a result of large United States loans.

The money markets necessary to facilitate investments of large amounts of foreign capital also enable countries to become leading capital exporters. On the other hand, there is no *a priori* reason to assume that such a savings position will assure an *excess* of current domestic savings over domestic needs and hence produce *net* capital exports.

The requirement of gross capital exports relates to the previous criteria concerning a country's size in the world economy and its own economic openness. If its current savings flow is large in world terms but small in domestic terms, the country can provide large amounts of capital to other countries *without* a serious diminution of domestic investment and hence domestic growth. The United Kingdom again provides the classic case: by lending abroad in some years prior to 1913 as much as 40 per cent of its domestic savings, it may have seriously short-changed its domestic economy, sowing the seeds of a deterioration in its competitive position which led eventually to a decline in the world role of its currency.[29] The United States, on the other hand, has been able to supply much larger amounts of capital to the world with a much smaller impact on its domestic investment. And shortages of savings in most other industrialized countries preclude them from being willing to encourage, or in some cases even permit, foreign investment in appreciable magnitudes.

The savings position of a country is thus highly important in permitting it to meet, at the same time, the national independence and capital exporter criteria. It also provides a corollary of the contradiction suggested in the earlier discussion: If a key currency country expands its foreign investment at a rate greater than it expands its

29. Keynes was the original proponent of this view. For more recent arguments, see Andrew Shonfield, *British Economic Policy Since the War* (Harmondsworth: Penguin Books, 1959, rev. ed.), p. 274, and Max Nicholson, *The System: The Misgovernment of Modern Britain* (London: Hodder and Stoughton, 1967), pp. 53–54. Many other analysts of the British experience totally reject this conclusion.

domestic savings, at some point it may begin to undermine its domestic economy by exporting too large a share of its capital resources. The share of U.S. investment devoted to overseas expansion has risen steadily, from 9.4 per cent in 1950 to over 14 per cent in 1970, and is likely to continue to rise in the absence of controls to stop it, so similar problems could be in the offing for the United States.

Finally, the stock and flow of a key currency country's savings are important because of their implications for its level of interest rates, which in turn may be an important factor in determining foreign holdings of a key currency. It has been argued that the opportunity for earning interest is an important element in the decision of some countries to hold foreign exchange in their reserves,[30] and of private citizens to hold transactions balances in foreign currencies. The important policy issue is not the existence of interest payments, however, but whether *changes* in interest rates produce significant *changes* in such holdings in both the public and private sector.

There are two studies of foreign exchange holdings of private foreigners alone. The most recent, which is limited to commercial banks in seven European countries, suggests that a 1 per cent increase in Eurodollar interest rates might raise their holdings of foreign currencies (mainly, but not wholly, dollars—and perhaps Eurodollars rather than dollar holdings *in the United States*) by as much as $0.75 billion to $1 billion.[31] The only explicitly significant and sizable findings were for Germany ($287 million) and Italy ($129), however, with the remainder of the aggregate figure based on the heroic assumption that Germany could be regarded as representative of the United Kingdom and France. The study revealed very small effects for Austria, Denmark, the Netherlands, and Norway, and a perverse effect for Belgium.

A much earlier study, conducted at the Federal Reserve Bank of New York in 1963, estimated that "substantial" increases in interest rates could reduce switches of dollars from private to official hands by $600 million to $700 million annually. A footnote suggested that "substantial" might mean "one-half of one per cent" or even less in some circumstances, and "larger" in others. The study recognized,

---

30. Milton Gilbert, *op. cit.*, p. 4, says that "reserves would be almost entirely in gold" if no interest rates were paid on dollars. This may be something of an overstatement because of "crisis zone" considerations and because currencies expected to appreciate (the dollar in the late 1930s, the mark and Swiss franc in recent years) might be held anyway, but it is probably true over any lengthy period of time.
31. Kreinen and Roy F. Gilbert, *op. cit.*

however, that "we cannot yet estimate by how much interest rates must change to generate a given size capital flow."[32]

Relative interest rates may thus be an important factor in private foreign dollar holdings, but we have a very imprecise notion of how important. The conscious British effort to avoid rundowns of foreign sterling balances by maintaining high interest rates on sterling suggests, however, that they are widely regarded as important.

The three econometric studies which compare reserve currency balances (mainly dollars) with other reserve assets (mainly gold) yield contradictory results. Greene found a high degree of significance for interest rates in eight of nine countries (excepting only Germany). Makin found significance in eight of thirteen, but high significance only for five. The most comprehensive study (Hagemann) found them significant for only two countries (Italy and Sweden). All three studies revealed interest rates as significant for Italy and Sweden, but only two other countries (Belgium and, surprisingly, Switzerland) were deemed significantly affected by this variable in even two studies. The results for official holders are thus even more uncertain.

Finally, we have several studies which have assessed the changes in U.S. liabilities to all foreigners, private and official, in response to changes in interest rates. This is the most reliable kind of study because of the statistical imprecision between the two categories outlined above, and because the high degree of complementarity between official and private dollars means that recorded changes in one might simply reflect changes initiated by the other.

Stein has estimated that, in the absence of speculative pressure, a U.S. Treasury bill rate one percentage point below the U.K. Treasury bill rate reduced the annual inflow of foreign capital to the United States in the early 1960s by $185 million—from $850 million to $665 million.[33] Using the stock-adjustment approach, Branson found for the same period a reduction of $496 million in foreign capital flows to the United States resulting from a reduction of one percentage point in United States interest rates and an increase of one point in Canadian rates.[34] Using data from more recent years, Branson and Hill have estimated that a change of one percentage point in the short-term differential causes a shift of about $2 billion in U.S. liabilities to all foreigners over three quarters, and a continuous flow

32. Cohen, *op. cit.*, pp. 193, 205–8.
33. Jerome L. Stein, "International Short-Term Capital," *American Economic Review*, Vol. LV, No. 1 (March 1965), p. 65.
34. William H. Branson, *Financial Capital Flows in the U.S. Balance of Payments* (Amsterdam: North-Holland Publishing Co., 1968), p. 172.

of about one-tenth that size per quarter.[35] Miller and Whitman, using a slightly different approach, obtain smaller figures: stock-adjustments of $1.2 billion if foreign rates rise by 1 per cent and $0.8 billion if U.S. rates rise, with continuous flows of only about 2 per cent quarterly in addition.[36]

No firm conclusions can be drawn from these disparate and sometimes contradictory findings. Two general results appear, however: that large amounts of money probably do shift in and out of dollars as a result of changes in interest rate differentials, and that the bulk of these shifts are likely to be triggered by private moves among different currencies rather than by official moves between national currencies and gold. The maintenance of an attractive yield is an important criterion for a key currency, but much more so for its function as a transactions currency than for its intervention and reserve currency uses.[37]

There is of course no simple determinant of interest rate differentials. At a given time, they are dominated by cyclical considerations. For secular purposes, they are presumably lower in a country with a relatively high stock and flow of national savings—such as the United States—and higher in a country which experiences high rates of inflation. Here are two more potential dilemmas among the criteria for key currency status: (a) sizable savings are needed to provide the requisite capital markets but tilt the scales toward lower interest rates, which discourage key currency balances; (b) relatively high rates of inflation promote high interest rates and hence attract such balances, but undermine the basic price stability criterion.

There is one further dilemma relating to the interest rates of a key currency country. On the other hand, high rates are helpful in maintaining balances. On the other, they discourage foreign borrowing in the currency and hence make it harder to meet the gross (or,

35. William H. Branson and Raymond H. Hill, "Capital Movements Among Major OECD Countries: Some Preliminary Results," *Journal of Finance,* Vol. XXVI, No. 2 (May 1971), pp. 283–85. If the long-term interest rate differential also changed by one percentage point there could be an additional flow of $1 billion. And if the velocity of money in the United States changed along with the change in U.S. interest rates in the way that it has done traditionally, $1.3 billion more would shift as well (in five quarters).

36. Norman Miller and Marina v.N. Whitman, "A Mean-Variance Analysis of United States Long-Term Portfolio Foreign Investment," *Quarterly Journal of Economics,* Vol. LXXXIV, No. 2 (May 1970), pp. 175–96.

37. An interesting exception was the IMF decision in 1958 to sell a large quantity of gold to the United States specifically to get an interest-bearing asset which would provide some income for it. (Later IMF gold sales were motivated more by the U.S. desire to window-dress the size of its gold stock.)

even more so, net) capital exporter criterion.[38] The only way to reconcile this dilemma would be for a reserve center to subsidize interest rates on loans to foreigners, and/or pay higher rates to foreign depositors. The United States has in fact done the latter; it has paid higher rates to foreigners directly, in exempting foreign monetary authorities from the interest rate ceilings of Regulation Q; and it did so indirectly, until recently, by exempting U.S. banks from reserve requirements on the deposits of their Eurodollar branches, which could thus pay more to attract foreign deposits.

Summary and Conclusions of Chapters 4–6
Our analysis suggests that several basic distinctions must be made in assessing the relative importance of the various attributes of a key currency. First, some of the traits are fundamental and would apply under virtually any conceivable international monetary system, whereas some are functions "merely" of a specific system. Second, all criteria must be considered relative to other national currencies, since a vehicle currency is required in virtually any conceivable international monetary system, and relative to other reserve assets (gold and SDR as well as other national currencies). Third, the relative importance of a certain criterion may change over time, because of changes not only in the nature of the system but also in the degree to which other criteria are being met. Fourth, some attributes are required for reserve currency status which are not required for vehicle currency status. In our effort to summarize the conditions that seem necessary to preserve key currency status, we will thus start with the more comprehensive requirements for the reserve currency role and subsequently discard those which seem unnecessary for the more limited vehicle function.

Several structural requirements head the list. First, the relative size of a country in the world is of overwhelming importance for the international roles of its currency. This is so both because of the economies of scale which derive from transacting in such a currency, and because size goes far in determining how much power the country has to disrupt other countries and hence deter them from taking actions inimical to its interests. Second, a key currency country must also be able to maintain a high degree of independence of national action, particularly in periods of international political and economic uncertainty. Thus it can assure other countries that it will not be

38. Cohen, *The Future of Sterling as an International Currency*, failed to recognize this problem when he included the contradictory criteria of "cheap credit" and "high interest rates" in his requirements for key currency status.

deflected by dangerous outside forces; that it will not take frequent actions which hurt them, out of concern for its own narrow interests; and that it will be willing to accept the hazards of a key currency role and sustain the role domestically. It can fulfill this criterion either through being a very closed economy, like the United States in the early postwar period, or by being able to force the real burden of adjustment onto others, like the United Kingdom before 1914. Third, it must possess a high stock and flow of savings to provide attractive capital markets for foreign deposits, to finance adequate domestic growth, and to maintain a base for capital exports. Fourth, it must avoid exchange controls, or similar devices to achieve the same ends. Such controls must be either pervasive and hence violate the fundamental requirement of key currency convertibility, or partial and hence widely viewed as ineffective substitutes for eventual devaluation—which would also violate the basic fixed-price convertibility requirement.

Then come the dynamic elements, which must be seen at several levels. Foreign holders are concerned *directly* with the liquidity, safety, and yield of their assets. The liquidity and safety criteria are met, in part, by the structural requirements for good capital markets and no exchange controls just discussed. In addition, however, these criteria require confidence in maximum price stability of the currency, for convertibility into other currencies for private holders and other reserve assets for monetary authorities. Such confidence, for monetary authorities, can be based on explicit and credible exchange-rate guarantees by the reserve center. Otherwise, confidence requires that the key currency will not be devalued, either because it is forced to do so by market pressures or because the key currency country decides that its national interests would be served by such a step. This in turn depends on views of the center country's external economic position—which includes its liquidity ratios, and the current overall position and structure of its balance of payments, which change those ratios. At the base of the pyramid lies the country's domestic economic performance, which fundamentally determines its external results.

In the absence of credible exchange-rate guarantees, or explicit understandings in the system permitting more lenient conditions, the center country must probably maintain (a) a liquidity ratio of 100 per cent against all currency holdings in countries outside its own currency area and (b) a small fractional reserve against holdings within its currency area to hedge against net deficits by members of the area and departures from the area by individual countries. If the currency area is not clearly defined, of course, the center must lean toward 100 per cent "backing" against a wider range of foreign balances. Indeed, declines below 100 per cent in some of the key ratios on a *global* basis apparently played a major role in triggering the "dollar crises" of 1960, 1965, and 1967. And the only completely safe position for the reserve center would be a reserve ratio in excess of this weighted average, which itself applies solely to the "overhang," by enough to provide adequate financing for any foreseeable future deficits it might run that could not be handled by the acquisition of additional liabilities. Fractional backing would be fully tenable only under explicit understandings to that end, with automatic discount facilities (via the swap network) and deposit insurance (via exchange-rate guarantees) to back them up.

As part of this "perfectly safe" position, the United States would have to define its liquidity ratio as the relationship between its reserve assets and the dollar holdings of the relevant foreign monetary authorities—which exceed recorded U.S. liabilities to such authorities to the extent that they hold dollars in the Eurodollar market, rather than directly in the United States. A realistic view of foreign attitudes, both conceptually and empirically, suggests that the U.S. liquidity ratio should include the short-term assets of the U.S. private sector; its net position on long-term portfolio capital (excluding direct investment); and its liquid liabilities to all private foreigners.

Both liquidity definitions of the U.S. balance-of-payments position, particularly the "gross liquidity" definition which prevailed prior to 1971, are thus extremely misleading. The most relevant U.S. balance-of-payments need is a sizable surplus on current account plus direct investment. This is particularly true if foreign holdings of dollars need to grow for transactions and/or reserve purposes, requiring a liquidity (or even official settlements) deficit without redistributing non-dollar reserves steadily toward the United States, and if concerns about possible dollar revaluation are to be avoided. Sizable current account surpluses are the only way for the United States simultaneously to provide such increased liquid dollar balances and build its most important liquidity ratio. (If there is no systemic need for increased dollar holdings, this condition is of course relaxed.) Within the current account, there is no additional need for a trade surplus for international financial reasons.

The most important internal economic attribute underlying a key currency is modal price performance. Excessive inflation would threaten the preservation of convertibility, make interest rates too high to maintain capital exports, and impart an inflationary bias to the world economy. Excessive price stability would imply payments surpluses, thus reducing foreign currency balances directly; possible appreciation of the currency, making foreign borrowing in it un-attractive; and low interest rates, deterring foreign balances vis-à-vis other reserve centers. The relative stability of modal performance should usually be enough to preserve confidence in the country's competitiveness and to preserve it as a store of value.

The other important domestic attribute is dynamic growth, which is necessary for long-term strength of the current account (and hence avoiding devaluation in the long run), and usually helps the official settlements position in the short run. It is also necessary to provide adequate domestic resources for the world political role, another key currency criterion as outlined in Chapter 4.

Two main differences emerge between the reserve currency and vehicle currency requirements. The latter require confidence in con-vertibility only into other national currencies, while the former re-quires confidence in convertibility into other reserve assets (now gold and SDR) as well—although the breakdown of the latter could jeopardize the former if, for example, as happened in 1973, monetary authorities became unwilling to accept additional dollars because of their non-convertibility into U.S. reserve assets at a known price. Second, as vehicle currency holders have shorter time horizons and higher profit incentives than reserve currency holders, they worry more about yield and less about the longer term outlook for the center's world political roles, liquidity ratios, balance of payments, price stability, and the like. Nevertheless, the criteria for the two roles are broadly similar—perhaps surprisingly so.

Our analysis has also brought out some of the reasons why key cur-rency status tends to expand and to perpetuate itself. The key cur-rency role itself generates added international political involvement by the center country, which adds to the political attributes needed to play the role and to the desire to maintain key currency status to help finance it. An intervention currency can only fluctuate one-half as much as other currencies in the exchange markets, and is thus relatively more stable. The strong and growing international invest-ment position needed for key currency status generates growing cur-rent account income, which in turn permits further growth of the international investment position and improvement in the key liquidity ratio. And foreign deposits and borrowings help further the development of the center's capital markets, so that they can qualify even better to backstop a key currency role in the future. We might therefore expect the use of EC currencies by other EC countries for intervention purposes, to maintain the narrower band which they have repeatedly sought to institute, to lead over time to their growing use outside the EC as well.

Finally, the analysis has brought out a number of dilemmas in the key currency requirements. There is the familiar Triffin paradox that the (narrowly defined) liquidity ratio will deteriorate and eventually undermine the key currency, as a result of the very payments deficits it is required to run to meet systemic needs. Equally basic, the requirements that the reserve currency be convertible into all other reserve assets creates the fundamental confidence problem in the system. Politically, we saw in Chapter 4 that the milieu goals of a center country, some of which it expresses through the key currency roles, include strengthening its major allies and hence undermining the very political and economic dominance (including its relative size in the world economy) on which its key currency role rests. In purely economic terms, the national independence criterion is similarly eroded by the country's growing international involvement due to the currency roles; most specifically, it may be required to demonstrate a price performance that violates its own employment targets, and could be especially costly for the United States in view of the adverse shift of its Phillips curve over the last decade. That shift itself raises the possibility of a further dilemma, since the price performance needed for key currency purposes, might now require a growth rate sufficiently lower than in the past to undermine the criterion of dynamic domestic growth. Even the control of inflation has contradictions: it lowers interest rates, which both deters deposits and encourages foreign borrowings. Finally, the need to maintain balance of payments equilibrium may at times conflict with the needs to preserve fixed-price convertibility (and avoid exchange (or even capital) controls. All of these dilemmas, if left to play themselves out, are of course costly to the key currency country.

More broadly, the attributes requires for key currency status levy costs on the center country only if they represent *additional* policy targets. Some of the attributes do not, at least for the United States: a sizable role in the world economy.[39] the maintenance of rapid domestic growth, a large stock and flow of savings, and superior capital markets. But some may require economic policy changes, at least on some occasions: the general need to remain aloof from external disturbances even when the national interest calls for response to them, the specific avoidance of exchange-rate changes and ex-

---

39. In the past, however, other countries have grouped together at least partly to increase their power position relative to the United States. Examples are the sterling area and the European Payments Union. In these cases, the "size" requirement *did* represent an additional policy target.

change controls, the provision of capital exports, walking the tight-rope of overall payments deficits coupled with current account surpluses, even the maintenance of convertibility itself, and achievement of modal price performance (which might preclude higher or lower price rises, either of which might on occasion be desirable). Overall foreign policy may also be altered by the need to maintain a major world role to preserve key currency status, and by the need to seek foreign financial cooperation. As noted above, fewer of these additional policy targets are required to maintain the vehicle currency role than to maintain the reserve currency role.

Whether these costs make key currency status a national liability depends on how they, and the other costs which derive from the actual exercise of the key currency role, compare with the benefits which such status confers. Let us now turn to a comparison between these costs and benefits to see whether the United States should seek to remain a reserve center, or should seek to seize the current transitional phase of international monetary arrangements to get out of the key currency business altogether.

7

The Direct Effects on
the U.S. Economy of
the Dollar's International Roles

The international roles of the dollar have several direct effects on the U.S. economy. The existence of a large volume of dollars held outside the country influences monetary conditions in the United States. The earnings of numerous U.S. banks and firms are affected by the external roles of the dollar, which thus alter national income. This chapter analyzes both phenomena.

In addition, the international roles of the dollar have direct effects on the balance of payments, which in turn directly affect U.S. welfare. Foreign earnings and the willingness of foreigners to acquire dollars provide external financing for the balance of payments, permitting the United States to run larger deficits or smaller surpluses than would otherwise be possible. The international roles of the dollar thus permit the United States to acquire real resources from the rest of the world, which reduce inflationary pressures in the United States. At the same time, however, the roles may themselves directly increase the payments deficit—for example, because foreign monetary authorities and private citizens seek additional dollar balances, and because the interest paid by the United States on the outstanding dollar balances may exceed the earnings of U.S. banks and firms attributable to the dollar's roles. This chapter estimates the direct effects of the dollar's roles on the U.S. balance of payments, to complete the analysis of the direct effects of the international roles of the dollar on the U.S. economy.

Chapters 8, 9, and 10 will then analyze the indirect results of the dollar's roles: whether the dollar overhang generates additional constraints on domestic economic policy; whether the roles of the dollar frustrate effective payments adjustment by circumscribing the policy options available to the United States; and whether they support the maintenance of an effective international monetary system. Integration of the direct and indirect effects will then enable us to reach an overall judgment as to whether these roles have represented a net benefit or net cost to the United States in the past, and as to their net effects under the possible alternative systems in the future which will be considered in Part III.

The Direct Effect on Domestic Economic Policy

Changes in foreign holdings of dollars can produce shifts in the domestic U.S. money supply.[1] Traditional gold standard theory required "automatic" adjustment to a payments deficit, mainly through losses of reserve assets by the deficit country with a consequent reduction in its money supply. To meet the overriding objective of maintaining domestic full employment, such adjustment has long been avoided by virtually all countries through eliminating or at least reducing the link between reserve assets and the domestic money supply. But to the extent that U.S. deficits are financed by dollar accruals abroad, which are then deposited in the United States, the deficits would have no contracting effect on the U.S. money supply anyway and would not even require offsetting monetary policy to avoid effects on the domestic economy.[2] This "marvelous secret of a deficit without tears"[3] for a reserve center is viewed by its critics as the fatal defect of the gold exchange standard.

In this and the following chapters, we shall assess whether such "deficits without tears"—which can only result from the expansion of the key currency roles of the dollar—do in fact represent a net benefit for the United States. Here the issue is simply whether the existence

---

1. All concepts of the U.S. money supply include deposits of foreign banks in U.S. banks, and exclude Eurodollar deposits (dollar deposits in non-U.S. banks). There is some controversy over the appropriateness of this distinction, but it has relatively little effect on the issues discussed in the text since there is a rough degree of equality between both the amounts, and changes in, foreign bank deposits in the United States and dollar deposits in foreign banks.

2. The United States was in fact one of the last countries to break the link between reserve assets and domestic monetary policy, abandoning the requirement of a fractional gold cover for its currency in March 1968 under the pressure of heavy gold losses. However, the authorities had always made it quite clear that they could and would suspend the gold cover requirement if necessary to meet their international obligations to convert foreign official dollars into gold—without having to reduce the domestic money supply. The financing of U.S. payments deficits through foreign accumulations of dollars undoubtedly delayed the formal step of abandoning the gold cover by rendering it unnecessary until that time.

3. Jacques Rueff, *The Age of Inflation* (Chicago: Henry Regnery 1964), p. 117. Rueff, however, views the reserve centers as "victims" rather than as beneficiaries of the process.

of a large and growing stock of foreign-owned dollars, which is made possible only by the past and continuing key currency roles of the dollar, help or hurt the U.S. economy. This stock is exceedingly large: the Eurodollar market totaled about $100 billion at the end of 1972, and deposits in the foreign branches of U.S. commercial banks exceeded $60 billion. It has been estimated that about 10 per cent of all dollar-denominated financial market assets were held by foreigners by that time.

The main policy issue here is whether the existence of this large external stock of dollars can upset internal U.S. monetary policy. If it can, national economic independence from international events will be undermined. Since such independence is a key currency criterion, its undermining would reduce both the capability and the willingness to go on playing the roles, as well as levy more general costs on the United States. The issue is particularly acute when the U.S. policy objective is to tighten credit. Money can always be created to offset capital outflows, but it is much more difficult to counter inflows. The remainder of the discussion will focus on this case.

In the credit crunches of 1966 and 1968–69, U.S. banks did in fact borrow heavily from their foreign branches and other foreign banks.[4] Such borrowing was necessary if they were to meet the demand for credit from their clients, because U.S. interest rates had exceeded the Regulation Q ceilings which they could pay to domestic lenders. This triggered massive liquidation of the certificates of deposit which the banks had previously issued. However, offsetting borrowing from foreign sources was possible because Regulation Q did not apply to foreign lenders, and the absence of reserve requirements and FDIC charges even enabled the banks more easily to afford the higher interest rates necessary to attract funds.

The size of this borrowing can be very large. For example, U.S. banks borrowed almost $7 billion from their own foreign branches alone in 1969. This amounted to 50-100 per cent of the total increase in the domestic money supply in 1969 ($6.3 billion to $15.8 billion, depending on which definition is used). However, some observers argue that the increase in one U.S. bank's reserves as a result of this borrowing is generally offset for the banking system as a whole by a

4. The eleven large banks with London branches offset about 90 per cent of their runoff of certificates of deposits through Eurodollar borrowings in 1966, and 115 per cent of such runoffs in 1968. During such periods, they got 20–33 per cent of their total funds from the Eurodollar market in contrast to its normal 10 per cent share. Andrew F. Brimmer, "Eurodollar Flows and the Efficiency of U.S. Monetary Policy," a paper presented at the New School for Social Research, New York, March 8, 1969 pp. 6–11.

reduction in the reserves of another U.S. bank, whose foreign branch has lost deposits to the foreign branch of the first bank. On this view, the only net effects of these transactions on the money supply occur when (a) foreign central banks intervene in the process through gold transactions or activation of the swap network, in which case the Federal Reserve usually knows of the step immediately and can act accordingly, or (b) U.S. residents hold increasing portions of their cash assets abroad, producing changes in the velocity of domestic currency circulation and the traditional relationships between the U.S. money supply and the economy.[5]

Through whatever route, however, it is clear that these shifts of Eurodollars to the United States significantly tightened money in Europe. They must therefore have created some pressures to ease money in the United States, both in real terms and because the maintenance of a steady stream of business loans by the big banks with best access to Eurodollars could undercut the Federal Reserve's restrictive effects psychologically.[6] The Board itself concluded in 1969 that these inflows required countervailing action. In June, Chairman William McChesney Martin tried moral suasion by writing to member banks that "solicitation or acceptance of deposits at foreign branches for purposes unconnected with foreign or international transactions is particularly inappropriate at the present time, when a restrictive monetary policy is in effect."[7] Later in 1969, the Board applied reserve requirements to the foreign borrowings of U.S. banks and hence increased their cost. In 1971, it began to eliminate the Regulation Q ceiling on interest payments to domestic lenders and thereby reduce the need for U.S. banks to resort to Eurodollars.

It is of course true that the Federal Reserve could always offset the effects of Eurodollar shifts through compensatory open market operations if it adequately anticipated the shifts or moved quickly in

---

5. See, for example, William E. Gibson, "Eurodollars and U.S. Monetary Policy." *Journal of Money, Credit, and Banking* Vol. III No. 3 (August 1971), p. 662. Edward M. Bernstein, "The Eurodollar Market and National Credit Policy," *Quarterly Review and Investment Survey*, Model, Roland and Co., First Quarter, 1969, concluded even more strongly (p. 18) that "there is no evidence that credit policy has been less effective merely because of Eurodollar borrowing by U.S. banks." He sees a redistribution of credit availability within the U.S. banking system in favor of the large banks with European branches, and a transmission of high U.S. interest rates to Europe, as the major results of the Eurodollar shifts.

6. Governor Brimmer, *op. cit.*, expressed concern over "the ability of the dozen or so large banks with London branches to deflect and delay the efforts of monetary policy by resort to Eurodollars."

7. *Federal Reserve Bulletin*, June 1969, p. 562.

response to them. The Federal Reserve would of course usually be aware of the coming impact of official gold transactions and swap activations, but even in such cases foresight can never be perfect. In any event, the U.S. authorities concluded that their national policy jurisdiction was inadequate to cover the international domains over which the banks they supposedly controlled could operate. As a result, they expanded their arsenal of policy measures to enable them to prevent, as well as offset, the effect of changes in foreign holdings of dollars. Their action testifies to the possibility that these balances can have an effect on monetary policy which would represent a cost to the U.S. economy.

Even after the Federal Reserve broadened its array of policy instruments to deal with Eurodollars, however, they have caused important problems for U.S. monetary policy. The Board anticipated heavy dollar reflows to the United States after the exchange-rate realignment at the Smithsonian meeting in December 1971, and hence managed the "purely domestic" money supply more restrictively in early 1972 than was consistent with its own targeted objectives. But the reflow failed to materialize. As a result, U.S. monetary conditions were left tighter than the Board itself deemed desirable.

In addition, the very purpose of the measures adopted by the Federal Reserve to cut the costs to domestic monetary policy is to reduce inflows of foreign capital to the United States. This in turn reduces the likelihood of foreign finacing for U.S. balance-of-payments deficits, and thus reduces one of the major benefits of the dollar's roles—yet one more dilemma of the dollar.[8] And the need to adopt the measures itself conflicts with the aloofness criterion for a key currency country.

Any country of course faces some conflict between the external and internal effects of its monetary policy when dealing with a "dilemma" adjustment situation. Capital inflows induced by tighter money will always offset to some extent its disinflationary domestic consequences, and outflows induced by easier money will dissipate to some extent its expansionary effects. Since any country is subject to this problem, we must ask how much of it can be legitimately treated as a cost of any of the key currency roles of the dollar.

---

8. In late 1970, however, the Federal Reserve tried to slow the *outflow* of capital to the Euromarkets by raising its marginal reserve requirements, against any such borrowings in excess of reserve-free base levels, which would deter banks from repaying Eurodollar borrowings if they foresaw a need to reconstitute them later. The new policy tool thus provides a means for affecting the U.S. payments balance in both directions, though it had little effect in deterring repayments during the 1971 crisis period.

No precise answer can be given. Several non-key currency countries, notably Germany and Switzerland, have frequently been subjected to the same phenomenon. Because these countries are so much smaller, the capital flows have clearly had greater effects on their internal economies than on the United States. It is also true that U.S. banks would always be able to attract some foreign capital to cope with domestic monetary tightness, whether or not the dollar was a key currency.

But the great amount of volatile international capital which is prepared to move frequently in search of higher yields still moves primarily between the two existing money markets where large investment facilities are always available: New York and the Eurocurrency market, both of which developed in large part as a result of the international acceptability of the dollar. The volume of funds constantly invested in those markets clearly does reflect the international roles of the dollar. In addition, virtually any shifting by major monetary authorities involves the dollar. A sizable part of any undermining of U.S. monetary policy generated by movements of externally owned capital can thus be legitimately treated as a cost of the international roles of the dollar.[9] Further support for this conclusion is provided by the fact that much of the vigorous opposition of most Continental monetary authorities to any international use of their currencies is based on the concern that such use would upset *their* domestic monetary policies.

These costs must be charged in part to the reserve currency role, since Eurodollar shifts by U.S. banks affect U.S. monetary policy most clearly when official intervention comes into play, and in part to the vehicle currency role. They could only be quantified by estimating, in specific cases, the extra amount of U.S. inflation (or deflation) caused by changes in the level of balances and then calculating in turn its effect on national welfare. Any such calculations would be extremely tenuous, not least because of the absence of a general theory of inflation, and they will not be presented here. The measures adopted by the Federal Reserve since 1969 suggest that the costs will henceforth be smaller than would otherwise have been

9. Indeed, a large part of the costs levied on other countries, such as Germany or Switzerland, are also due to the roles of the dollar. This can generate some political costs for the United States when these countries attack U.S. policy as the cause of their own internal economic problems (as the German Minister of Economics and Finance did during the 1972 election campaign in Germany), which can also be attributed at least in part to the roles of the dollar.

the case, but continued growth of the Eurodollar market could more than offset this reduction. Only total elimination of the international roles of the dollar would eliminate these particular costs.[10]

Finally, it should be noted that the phenomenon described here as a social cost to the United States might understandably be regarded by some as a benefit. Some banks, particularly those with large networks of foreign branches in the Eurodollar market, have been able to meet the needs of their best customers—often large business firms—by attracting just those foreign balances which serve to undermine domestic monetary policy. This is a clear example of the well-known divergence between social and private welfare, however, and may help explain why banking and big business have tended to support the maintenance and expansion of the dollar's role in international finance more vigorously than have other sectors of American society. It is of course theoretically possible that shifts in foreign dollar deposits have offset the mistakes of the Federal Reserve and "improved" U.S. monetary conditions—though even the harshest critics of the Federal Reserve would presumably seek a more orderly way of improving its performance.

Seigniorage

A second direct effect of the international roles of the dollar on the U.S. economy operates through its effect on private U.S. banks and corporations. It is often claimed that the United States extracts "seigniorage" from the international roles of the dollar. Seigniorage originally referred to the command over real resources available to a sovereign from his monopolistic privilege of coining money. As applied to the world economy today, semantic and conceptual problems have clouded the issue badly. Seigniorage encompasses both the global social gain of substituting paper money for commodity money, through a saving of real resources, and the gains to a particular mone-

10. The part of the "problem" caused by deposits of national monetary authorities in the Eurodollar market could be solved by requiring all central banks to hold their reserve currency balances in the country of issue. Such a proposal was made by the BIS to the London Economic Conference in 1933, with respect to continuing the gold exchange standard at that time, for similar reasons. See Blessing, p. 30. Agreement along these lines was reached by the Group of Ten central banks in 1971, but most such holdings by central banks were always from countries outside the Ten anyway, and continue to rise rapidly (in other national currencies as well as in dollars). See IMF, *Annual Report*, 1973, p. 39.

tary authority from exercising monopoly power over money issuance.[11] Pursuing this second aspect, some observers have defined "seigniorage" to include all of the benefits accruing to the United States from the roles of the dollar, through enabling it to run larger deficits in its overall balance of payments.[12] Others construe the term more narrowly, limiting it to the direct financial return to the United States of financial operations, denominated in dollars, by U.S. banks and firms.[13]

Definitions are always to some extent a matter of taste, but the narrower view of "seigniorage" is both closer to the original meaning of the term and much more useful operationally. Since the broader approach would define "seigniorage" as encompassing all of the benefits to the United States of the dollar's roles, it would also have to encompass all of the costs to the U.S. of those roles—which has clearly not been done by any of its proponents.[14] So I shall use "seigniorage" solely to denote the *direct* economic effects of the dollar's roles on U.S. financial transactions, which are only one portion of the total costs and benefits.

On this concept, seigniorage is available if a country "appropriates real resources through the issue of noninterest-bearing debt, through

11. Harry Johnson, "A Note on Seigniorage and the Social Saving from Substituting Credit for Commodity Money," in Mundell and Swoboda, eds., *op. cit.*, pp. 323–26. Johnson also distinguishes between the current and capital aspects of seigniorage, the former consisting of the increase in aggregate national absorption permitted by the benefits of money creation and the latter consisting of the yield on additional investments permitted by the cumulative effects of this money creation over time.

12. See, for example, Cohen, *op. cit.*, pp. 35–37, and Chapter 5; Serge-Christophe Kolm, "Les Etats-Unis beneficient-ils du droit de seigneur?" *Kyklos*, Vol. XXIII, Fasc. 3 (1970), pp. 425–45; Aliber, "The Costs and Benefits of the U.S. Role as a Reserve Currency," p. 446.

13. Ronald I. McKinnon, "Private and International Money: The Case for the Dollar," *Essays in International Finance*, No. 74 (April 1969), esp. p. 20, Herbert G. Grubel, "The Distribution of Seigniorage from International Liquidity Creation," in Mundell and Swoboda, eds., *Monetary Problems in the World Economy*, pp. 269–70; and Alexander K. Swoboda, "The Euro-Dollar Market: An Interpretation," *Essays in International Finance*, No. 64 (February 1968), pp. 11–13, who notes the broader definition but focuses on the narrower, which he refers to as "private" or "denomination" seigniorage.

14. Indeed, Cohen *op. cit.*, p. 37, proceeds erroneously to compare the gross seigniorage gains to Britain of sterling's roles *only* to U.K. interest payments on its foreign sterling liabilities—not to the other costs of sterling's roles, which he addresses later in his book, but conceptually divorces from "seigniorage." In addition, he treats as "seigniorage" such broad effects as the reserve pooling of the sterling area, but excludes from it the invisible earnings of "the City" of London—the U.S. equivalent of which is a major element in my own analysis of U.S. seigniorage.

the suppression of interest rates, or through the exercise of reserve requirements."[15] The United States does each of these three to some extent, though to a decreasing degree as a result of the development of the Eurodollar market.

Between 10 and 50 per cent of total U.S. liquid liabilities to foreigners are usually in the form of noninterest-bearing demand deposits.[16] Since these are the dollars voluntarily held as working balances by private foreigners and monetary authorities, no U.S. coercion is involved. Nevertheless, U.S. banks earn interest when they re-lend the dollars and the United States as a whole gains seigniorage as a result. Part of the noninterest-bearing foreign deposits in the

Table 11

U.S. SHORT-TERM LIABILITIES, BY TYPE OF LIABILITY: 1963–74
(In millions of dollars, at year-ends)

Year	Demand Deposits			Other Deposits			Share of Total Deposits	
	Official	Private	Total	Official	Private	Total	Demand	Other
1963	1,402	5,595	6,997	11,065	3,268	14,333	32.8	67.2
1964	1,591	6,558	8,149	11,629	4,122	15,751	34.1	65.9
1965	1,535	6,515	8,050	11,531	4,491	16,022	33.4	66.6
1966	1,679	8,149	9,828	10,861	5,531	16,392	37.5	62.5
1967	2,054	9,456	11,510	11,973	5,748	17,721	39.4	60.6
1968	2,149	12,171	14,320	9,169	6,744	15,913	47.4	52.6
1969	1,930	18,467	20,397	9,146	9,243	18,389	52.6	47.4
1970	1,652	14,073	15,725	17,681	7,136	24,817	38.8	61.2
1971	1,620	8,707	10,327	38,059	5,249	43,308	19.3	80.7
New Series:[a]								
1971	1,327	5,059	6,386	37,692	9,584	47,276	11.9	88.1
1972	1,591	6,613	8,204	38,409	12,669	51,078	13.8	86.2
1973	2,125	9,084	11,209	41,794	14,076	55,870	16.7	83.3
1974	2,951	10,913	13,864	50,106	27,570	77,676	15.1	84.9

[a] Series changes primarily due to reclassification of some liabilities of U.S. banks to their foreign branches and of U.S. agencies and branches of foreign banks to their head offices.

Source: *Treasury Bulletin*, April 1975, p. 95.

15. McKinnon, *op. cit.*, p. 20.
16. See Table 11. The ratio was only about 10 per cent on June 30, 1972—$7.2 billion of $70.1 billion—because total liabilities were inflated and the private component deflated by the continuing uncertainty about the dollar. It exceeded 50 per cent—$20.4 billion of $38.8 billion—at the end of 1969, when private foreign demand for dollars was very high due to the tightness of U.S. monetary policy.

United States, however, are the deposits of foreign branches of U.S. banks at their head offices—only about 10 per cent of all private deposits in mid-1972, but much higher ratios earlier in direct correlation with the higher percentage of *total* U.S. liquid liabilities in noninterest-bearing forms—and deposits of foreign banks in their U.S. agency banks. The head offices pay no interest to their foreign branches, but the branches themselves pay European market interest rates—which are often higher than U.S. rates—to attract the funds, and thus contribute smaller earnings or larger losses than otherwise to the parent corporation. Thus the head office does pay interest *de facto* on these loans, perhaps at a higher rate than it would on its domestic deposits, and both the balance-of-payments and seigniorage gains to the United States are reduced as a result. In mid-1972, the seigniorage gains represented only the interest earnings on the $5.7 billion on noninterest-bearing deposits of foreigners other than the branches of U.S. banks, or perhaps $300–400 million. When private foreign demand for dollars was near its peak at the end of 1969, this stock totaled only $7.9 billion, which would have generated interest earnings of about $600–700 million.

On all *interest-bearing* dollar deposits, the fierce competition among U.S. banks, and between them and foreign Eurodollar banks, assures interest rates very close to market equilibrium levels and hence limits sharply the seigniorage obtained on their dollar loans by U.S. banks.[17] Indeed, both the U.S. government (through Roosa bonds) and U.S. banks (through long-term certificates of deposit) have often paid *higher* interest rates to attract foreign deposits. The government has also given exchange-value guarantees, with a potential future cost that was realized when the dollar was devalued, to stretch out the maturity of the U.S. foreign debt (and to window-dress the official balance-of-payments statistics, as outlined in Chapter 3).

The United States has also held down domestic interest rates through Federal Reserve Regulation Q, which places a ceiling on the rates U.S. banks may pay on deposits with them. However, the ceiling does not apply to the dollar deposits of foreign monetary author-

---

17. The low-interest 10-year loans made to the United States government by Germany in 1969 and 1970, under the 1969 military offset agreement, are an exception, which also provided low-cost financing for part of the U.S. budget deficits. However, these loans did not reflect the key currency role of the dollar. Indeed, they represented an alternative to continued reliance on those roles in their traditional form; in view of its 1967 commitment not to buy gold from the United States, Germany would otherwise have kept the dollars in Treasury bills and earned market interest rates on them.

ities (and most international institutions). With regard to private holders, the ceiling normally exceeds money market rates and has little effect. In periods of unusually tight U.S. monetary policy such as 1966 and 1968–69, however, market rates have exceeded the ceiling and the big U.S. banks replaced their massive runoffs of domestic deposits with foreign-held dollars. But they did so mainly through attracting foreign deposits to their foreign branches, which were also not bound by Regulation Q. Thus Regulation Q holds down interest rate payments only to private foreigners who make deposits directly with U.S. banks, instead of with their foreign branches, during periods of very tight money in the United States. The amount involved totaled less than $6. billion at its peak at the end of 1969; Regulation Q may have suppressed the interest rate payable by two percentage points at that time, for a U.S. seigniorage gain of perhaps $100–150 million.

Indeed, Regulation Q effectively *increased* the rates paid on foreign deposits by pushing U.S. demand for money into the Eurodollar market. The main result, as indicated in the preceeding section, was an undermining of U.S. monetary policy or at least a requirement for compensating action by the monetary authorities, rather than seigniorage for the United States, since Regulation Q forced U.S. banks to pay more for foreign deposits—perhaps more than they earned in re-lending the money to their domestic customers, particularly after the Federal Reserve imposed reserve requirements on foreign deposits in late 1969. The suspension in June 1970 of the Regulation Q ceiling on large deposits with maturities of 30–89 days began to reduce this effect.

The U.S. government levies no reserve requirement on foreign dollar-holders. (It has frequently pressured foreign governments to maintain dollar balances in return for continued security arrangements and aid, but this extremely important aspect of the issue gets to the broader question of financing overall U.S. deficits rather than narrow seigniorage effects.) Individual U.S. banks, however, require compensating balances—the conceptual equivalent of reserve requirements—on many of their loans to foreigners, as on many of their domestic loans. No estimates of such balances are available, but they add to the extraction of seigniorage by the United States to the extent that they relate to the international roles of the dollar.[18]

18. Some state laws require foreign-owned insurance companies to maintain contingency reserves in the United States against policies issued to U.S. residents. These transactions are essentially unrelated to the international role of the dollar, however.

It has also been argued that U.S. direct investments abroad take place partly because of a "currency premium" which the market attaches to the dollar, enabling U.S. firms to capitalize the same stream of expected future earnings at a higher rate than could firms in other countries.[19] This "currency premium" allegedly exists because fewer exchange-rate uncertainties attach to the dollar than to any other currency and because its use saves transactions costs, both of which are due to the international roles of the dollar. Whether or not U.S. firms were motivated to invest abroad by the existence of such a "currency premium," this analysis suggests that they also derive a kind of seigniorage from the dollar. As noted in the last chapter, historical comparisons do demonstrate close correlation between foreign investment and key currency positions.

However, events since 1971 would seem to have laid to rest any notion of such a "premium" on the dollar. In any event, such a premium on any currency would not accrue solely, or even necessarily primarily, to the nationals of the country issuing that currency. Non-U.S. firms can, and do, borrow in dollars. U.S. firms can, and do, borrow in marks and other foreign currencies. The internationalization of the world capital market, and particularly the development of the Eurobond market, has eroded any seigniorage available to U.S. firms just as the internationalization of the money market has eroded the seigniorage available to U.S. banks. So it is doubtful whether U.S. firms have extracted much seigniorage on their direct investment from the international roles of the dollar. Even if they did, the additional investment would in fact be costly both to the U.S. balance of payments (at least in the short run) and to the most relevant liquidity ratio, and thus could undermine the international roles of the dollar even as the firms were benefitting from them.

It thus appears that the amount of seigniorage extracted by the United States from the international roles of the dollar is relatively small. It includes small amounts stemming from the absence of interest payments on some foreign dollar deposits ($300–400 million in mid-1972, a few hundred million dollars more at earlier dates); the suppression, via Regulation Q, of interest rates paid on private foreign balances held directly in the United States (perhaps another $100 million at most); the requirements of some banks that foreign (as well as domestic) borrowers maintain compensating balances; and

19. Robert Z. Aliber, "A Theory of Direct Foreign Investment," in Charles P. Kindleberger, ed., The International Corporation (Cambridge, Mass.: MIT Press, 1970), esp. pp. 28–31.

perhaps some additional gains to U.S. direct investment abroad. The total could hardly exceed $1 billion per year; it is probably much smaller and, in view of the growing competition of the Eurocurrency and Eurobond markets, declining rather than growing as time passes.

The Banking Sector

We turn now to an effort to quantify the effects of the dollar's international monetary roles on the U.S. balance of payments. If we assume that all foreign deposits in the United States reflect those roles,[20] the net effect on the balance of payments depends, in the first instance, on· what share of these deposits is reloaned to foreigners. No precise calculation is possible because of the fungibility of money. However, except for periods of extremely tight money in the United States when foreign deposits were re-lent primarily to domestic customers, there was a very high correlation between increases in loans to foreigners and increases in foreign deposits in the United States prior to February 1965, when the Voluntary Foreign Credit Restraints (VFCR) were applied to U.S. banks and the Interest Equalization Tax was applied to term bank loans. This relationship was much closer than the correlation between changes in loans to foreigners and in all loans by the banking system.[21]

Foreign claims of U.S. banks expanded by 90 per cent of the total deposits they received from foreigners during 1958–65 (excepting the

20. There is no way to determine the additional effects of the dollar's roles on the foreign earnings of U.S. banks. Cohen, *op. cit.*, pp. 129–35, estimates that about one-third of the foreign earnings of U.K. banks relate to the international roles of sterling. There are no U.S. data equivalent to the U.K. data, provided by the Bank of England, on which his estimates are based. It would seem that a higher percentage should apply to U.S. overseas banking earnings, however, because a large share of U.K. earnings derives from their dollar operations, and U.S. banks would have no alternative into which to shift such a large share of their operations.

21. Arthur B. Laffer, "Short-Term Capital Movements and the Voluntary Foreign Credit Restraint Program," unpublished, 1969, found no net effect on the U.S. official settlements balance during the first two years of restraints on outflows by U.S. banks. See also Allan H. Meltzer, "The Regulation of Bank Payment Abroad, Another Failure of the Government Balance of Payments Program," in George P. Shultz and Robert Z. Aliber, eds., *Guidelines, Informal Controls and the Market Place* (Chicago: University of Chicago Press, 1966), pp. 183–206. Laffer and Meltzer agree that the controls reduced foreign lending by U.S. banks, but that private foreign deposits in the United States declined even more. Thus the program did reduce the gross liquidity deficit, which was the focus of policy at the time, but may have actually hurt the more important official reserve transactions balance.

domestic tight money year of 1959),[22] the only "normal" period since the advent of wide currency convertibility. Since 1965, the relationship has been distorted by the extremely tight domestic monetary conditions of 1966 and 1968–69, the VFCR, and speculation against the dollar. The close correlation between changes in claims and changes in deposits did reappear in 1970, the most "normal" year since 1964.

These close ties between inflows and outflows can readily be explained by the existence of different monetary conditions in different national money markets. Interest rates are generally higher outside the United States, so U.S. banks are generally willing to pay the higher rates of interest needed to attract and hold foreign deposits only if they know they can re-lend the funds to other foreigners at similarly higher rates. These tendencies have been strongly reinforced institutionally by the development of foreign departments in the major U.S. banks, operating in large part in the Eurodollar market through their foreign branches. Unless faced by overriding domestic needs, as in 1966 and 1968–69, or limited by controls, as was the case from 1965 to 1974, they will be permitted by top management to re-lend to their own clients (i.e., foreigners) the money they have borrowed abroad, and seek to raise money from their clients to make loans to other clients. The money is, in fact, *not* wholly fungible due to the compartmentalization between the foreign and domestic divisions of the operating banks. In a return to more "normal" times, it is thus plausible to expect a continued close correlation between foreign lending and foreign borrowing by U.S. banks.

If changes in foreign deposits in U.S. banks and in their loans to foreigners are roughly equal over time, the net effect on the balance of payments is simply the net interest differential on the change in

---

22. The r^2 for this simple regression was .961. Laffer, *op. cit.*, found a similar relationship between the reductions of U.S. bank claims and liabilities after the inauguration of the VFCR. It is surprising that this relationship has not been more widely recognized. Most students of U.S. capital movements, however, have looked at the inflow and outflow sides separately and searched for independent causes for each rather than relating them to each other. Such an approach may have been discouraged by the unusual treatment of these items in the balance-of-payments. Outflows of U.S. capital were treated "above the line" until 1965, while all inflows of foreign deposits were treated "below the line." At that time, deposits of private foreigners were moved "above the line" on one of the two official concepts, and all of the new definitions instituted in 1971 treat the two items in parallel fashion.

the outstanding stock.[23] The interest differential between foreign interest-bearing deposits in U.S. banks and loans to foreigners by those banks is normally about one percentage point.[24] It will be recalled, however, that from 20 to 40 per cent of the foreign claims are in the form of noninterest-bearing demand deposits (after adjustment for the reduced earnings of U.S. banks from their foreign branches in lieu of direct interest payments on the deposits of those branches). Thus the increase in net interest earnings of U.S. banks is greater than one percentage point on the total increase in banking claims and liabilities. If the banks pay 5 per cent on their foreign deposits and charge 6 per cent on their foreign loans, for example, their net gain—and the net gain to the balance of payments—would be $20–30 million on every net increase of $1 billion in both claims and liabilities.

These calculations, however, are based on "normal" years when U.S. monetary conditions were not extremely tight, when there were

23. Robert Roosa focused attention on this aspect of the key currency issue when he told a Congressional subcommittee in 1962 that U.S. earnings from its international banking function "greatly exceed the interest we pay." See his statement in "Outlook for the U.S. Balance of Payments," Reuss Subcommittee, *Hearings*, December 12–14, 1962, p. 119. In principle, one should also consider the difference in their feedback effects on other items in the balance of payments. There has been empirical work on the feedback effects of trade flows on these capital movements, but none on the feedback effects of the capital movements on trade flows. The work that has been done suggests that U.S. claims rise with U.S. exports, and that U.S. liabilities rise with foreign exports. American exports have been declining slowly as a percentage of world exports, liabilities seem more sensitive than claims to changes in trade flows, and the U.S. surplus has been steadily declining. Increases in trade flows thus probably lead to faster growth of United States liabilities than of claims. This would partially explain the buildup in dollar working balances held by private foreigners throughout the postwar period, but it does not permit us to draw any conclusions about the net effects of bank claims and liabilities on the U.S. trade balance. See Branson and Hill, *op. cit.*, pp. 280–81; Laffer, *op. cit.*, p. 15; Branson, *Financial Capital Flows in the U.S. Balance of Payments*, pp. 82, 92; Martin F. J. Prachowny, *A Structural Model of the U.S. Balance of Payments* (Amsterdam: North Holland, 1969), p. 88.

24. The Department of Commerce has indicated that it used a spread of 0.25 to 1.40 percentage points for the first three quarters of 1973. It also assumes that the banks include their costs and charges for ancillary financial services in their interest rates, and hence makes no separate estimates for them. Herbert Grubel, "The Benefits and Costs of Being the World Banker," *National Banking Review*, Vol. 2, No. 2 (December 1964), p. 192, was thus wrong to credit the international roles of the dollar with additional earnings (albeit small ones) on this score.

no controls over the foreign lending of U.S. banks, and when there was no widespread speculation against the dollar. All of these elements have been absent since 1965. As a result, U.S. dollar liabilities had grown to more than $80 billion by the end of 1972, of which only about $8 billion did not bear interest, and far exceeded the $15 billion of foreign claims of U.S. banks. So the balance-of-payments effect of the one percentage point differential in favor of U.S. lenders has been swamped by the excess of liabilities over claims, by about $3 billion per year. In short, there is now a sizable direct cost to the U.S. balance of payments from the legacy of the past exercise of the international roles of the dollar.

This balance-of-payments cost in any given year is only offset if net U.S. liabilities grow by the corresponding $3 billion, to finance the net cost itself. Yet the two are likely to grow in tandem in "normal" periods, and liabilities are likely to grow faster than claims only if claims are controlled, the dollar is under speculative attack, or U.S. monetary policy is unusually tight in response to excessive inflationary pressures—none of which conditions are likely to support such growing international roles for the dollar. But even if liabilities did grow significantly faster to provide the needed financing, the net interest cost would rise correspondingly and require even larger increase in net liabilities in the future—a dynamically unstable situation.

These costs clearly suggest an effort by the United States to eliminate the legacy of its key currency functions of the past. They also suggest that it would be a mistake for the United States to agree to maintain *present* levels of outstanding liabilities without leaving foreign residents free to add *to* their level of dollar balances. Of course, it is possible that the "needed" $3 billion or so per year would be accumulated and maintained by private foreigners without any addition to the dollar holdings of foreign monetary authorities. Since private foreigners hold virtually all of the noninterest-bearing demand deposits, they are the more desirable depositors from the U.S. standpoint anyway. The United States might thus be able to avoid additional balance-of-payments cost from the interest rate effects of the dollar's international roles by retaining the vehicle currency function and letting the reserve currency function stagnate.

This analysis has so far considered only banking flows, and one cannot go too far in compartmentalizing the private capital account. Other private U.S. capital outflows also may have reflected the presence of foreign deposits in the United States, especially in the recent "abnormal" years when they were under less rigid control than bank outflows, especially since some of them (particularly direct investment) are less deterred by tight domestic monetary conditions.[25]

In the simplest case, a U.S. commercial bank might re-lend its foreign deposits to a U.S. investment bank or firm, which might then use the money to purchase a foreign security or make a direct investment abroad. Money's fungibility assures us that such financial intermediation will take place, if normally through less easily detectable means. Indeed, the relationship between foreign liquid investments in the United States and U.S. long-term investments abroad is the heart of the "financial intermediation" thesis, which explains the persistent U.S. balance-of-payments deficit as primarily a result of this very phenomenon.[26] The thesis focuses on the differences in "liquidity preference" between Europe and the United States. European savers allegedly prefer highly liquid assets and hence invest at short term in the United States, because the desire of European borrowers to incur long-term liabilities will be met only (or at least more cheaply) by American lenders. This result is reinforced by greater competitiveness and lower costs among U.S. financial institutions than among their European competitors. Capital thus flows to the United States in short-term form and back to Europe at longer term.

The advocates of the financial intermediation thesis admit that we do not know the direction of causation of these capital flows. It is conceivable either that U.S. capital outflows generate increased liquidity abroad, much of which is deposited in the United States, or that the foreign demand pattern primarily determines both short-term inflows and long-term outflows.[27] The proponents of the thesis

25. Indeed, Cohen, *op. cit.*, pp. 99 ff., attributes to the international roles of sterling a stock of U.K. foreign investment equal to *total* U.K. sterling liabilities, presumably on the notion that this stock was built up only because Britain could finance its payments deficits by increasing its sterling liabilities. He may have reached this judgment on the basis of Britain's decision to sell off some of its overseas private assets to finance both world wars. But even such an historical approach flatly contradicts his own conclusion that U.K. liabilities grew rapidly only during World War II—a period when its foreign private investment was declining. Much more relevant, however, is the obvious fact that the future elimination of the international roles of sterling would clearly not force the United Kingdom to liquidate an equal amount of its foreign investment.

26. Emile Despres, Charles P. Kindleberger, and Walter S. Salant, "The Dollar and World Liquidity—A Minority View," *The Economist*, February 5, 1966, pp. 526–29.

27. See especially Walter Salant "The Balance of Payments of a Financial Center" in Fellner, Machlup, Triffin, et al., *Maintaining and Restoring Balance in International Payments* (Princeton, N.J.: Princeton University Press, 1966), pp. 177–96.

have provided one piece of statistical support for their theoretical model, which suggests that about 25 per cent of foreign direct investment by U.S. firms—about $1 billion annually in recent years—produces foreign liquid deposits in the United States.[28] In addition, such a firm opponent of most of the financial intermediation thesis as Triffin concedes that "American investments in Europe are, in part at least, the reflection as well as the cause of the accumulation of liquid assets by Europeans in the United States."[29]

On the other hand, the several careful analyses of the U.S. capital account already cited uncovered no relationship between U.S. banking liabilities and foreign investment by U.S. firms.[30] In addition, there is widespread agreement that the *motivation* for the direct investment outflows comes almost entirely from the U.S. investors: the liquid dollars that are eventually banked by some Europeans—not necessarily the sellers of the direct investment assets—have no causal effect on the U.S. outflows of long-term capital, even if they constitute a part of the intermediation process. And the coincidence of increases in liabilities with increases in direct investment may simply mean that U.S. direct investors hold part of their working balances in the United States before using them on a particular project. For our purposes, it suffices to note that U.S. direct investment outflows are not a consequence of foreign deposits here and should not be included in the calculation of the costs and benefits to the United States deriving from the international roles of the dollar in the sense just discussed.

Other Direct Effects on the Balance of Payments

The vehicle currency role of the dollar presumably brings earnings additional to those of U.S. banks. Unfortunately, very little data exist on which to base estimates of these earnings—in contrast to the situation in Britain, where active debate on the international roles of sterling since 1957 has produced a number of private and official studies of the subject. The estimates in this section are thus particularly hazardous.

28. Laffer, *op. cit.*, p. 15.
29. See his "The Balance of Payments and the Foreign Investment Position of the United States," *Essays in International Finance*, No. 55 (September 1966), p. 9. Triffin also questions whether foreign official dollar balances in the United States can be viewed as part of the process of financial intermediation. He is answered by Kindleberger, "International Monetary Arrangements," The English, Scottish and Australia Bank Ltd. Research Lecture of 1966, delivered at the University of Queensland, July 25, 1966, p. 10, and Salant "The Balance of Payments of a Financial Center" *op. cit.*, pp. 186–87.
30. Branson, Branson and Hill, Prachowny, *op. cit.*

Foreign insurance and reinsurance activities of U.S. firms might be prompted by the international use of the dollar. In 1972, net receipts from these activities totaled $162 million.[31] No explicit data on insurance have even been published, but a maximum of $20–25 million annually has been estimated by trade sources. Even the small contribution of these activities to the U.S. balance of payments may not be closely related to the international roles of the dollar, so nothing will be included for them in our calculations.[32]

It has also been suggested that U.S. exports bring higher prices because of the services available in New York to the importer.[33] One could in fact go further and assert that the superior financial services of the United States, which at least in part reflect the dollar's international roles, generate additional U.S. exports so that the gains far exceed the earnings on the services themselves. Both possibilities should be covered more than adequately by adding to our estimates a gain of $700 million—roughly 1 percent of U.S. exports in 1973.[34]

So far we have considered only receipts by U.S. residents (banks, insurance companies, etc.) from foreigners. In addition, U.S. banking and other financial institutions have, like manufacturing and other industries, increasingly ventured abroad. In 1966, direct investment outflows for "banking and other finance" totaled $329 million against income and related receipts of $135 million.[35] This category was one

---

31. Information supplied by the Office of Business Economics, Department of Commerce. The U.S. balance of payments also includes premiums paid by U.S. residents to foreign reinsurers, and losses recovered thereon, but these activities are unrelated to the international roles of the dollar.

32. Cohen, *op. cit.*, p. 135, estimates that U.K. insurance earnings are based on the "established position, reputation, efficiency, and contacts" of its firms and are totally unaffected by sterling's international roles. This would probably be more true for Britain, with its well-established international insurers than for the United States, but no more than a small fraction of the U.S. firms' earnings could be attributed to the dollar's roles.

33. Grubel, *op. cit.*, pp. 192–93. The presumption is that the charge for services is added to the price of the export in such a way as to enhance, or at least not detract from, its competitiveness. The gains which accrue in the form of earnings on export credits extended by banks have been covered in the previous section.

34. Cohen, *op. cit.*, p. 126, "follows standard procedures" by excluding any such effects from his calculations for sterling. He does so simply because no estimates are available. However, he notes that several observers, including the U.K. government, have referred to the existence of such effects, and his zero estimate is no more scientific than a positive guesstimate.

35. Department of Commerce, *U.S. Direct Investment Abroad, 1966,* pp. 49, 104, 153. In 1972, direct investment in the insurance industry totaled $25 million while income receipts totaled $112 million.

of the fastest growing areas of U.S. foreign investment, due to the explosion of the Eurodollar market and international banking during that period, and it would not be surprising to find that annual outflows had reached $500 million with income at perhaps $200 million in the early 1970s. The key currency roles of the dollar—including the restrictions on U.S. capital exports to defend those roles—undoubtedly contributed to the inducement to U.S. banks to invest abroad, to maximize the potential earnings available to them through financing third-country trade and Eurodollar transactions. The roles must therefore be charged with perhaps one-half the short-term balance-of-payments costs of the net annual outflow, perhaps $150 million in 1972.[36]

Finally, it will be recalled that a key currency country can most directly maintain foreign confidence in its fixed-price convertibility by extending exchange-value guarantees on foreign holdings of its currency. The dollar's roles thus levy on the United States the contingent costs of restoring the value of foreign holdings in the event of a dollar devaluation to the extent that it guarantees the value of such holdings in terms of SDRs, gold, or another currency.[37] The United States has heretofore extended such guarantees only on swap drawings and Roosa bonds. As a result of the 1971 devaluation, it incurred a liability estimated at $172 million on these debts—implying that about $2 billion, or 3 per cent of foreign dollar holdings (4 per cent of official holdings) carried guarantees.[38]

---

36. Over the longer term, of course, the U.S. balance of payments may benefit from this—like most other—private foreign direct investment, at the point when the cumulative return on a given outflow exceeds the original outflow. Indeed, there is less possibility of harm to the trade balance from net export diversion in the case of such investment by banks than in the case of manufacturing firms. But, equally, there is less possibility of net export creation to offset the net financial outflow which continues to exist.

37. All countries guarantee the gold value of holdings of their currency by the IMF and several of the international lending institutions, and have a similar contingent liability on their net use of SDRs. These obligations stem solely from membership in the institutions, and have nothing to do with the international status of the currency in question.

38. Background documents on the Par Value Modification Bill submitted to the Congress by the Secretary of the Treasury, Feb. 9, 1972, pp. III–3. The United Kingdom had through 1974 a much higher contingent liability on outstanding sterling reserves, since as part of the Basel arrangements of 1968 it guaranteed the dollar value of each sterling country's sterling holdings that exceed 10 per cent of its total reserves, which could amount to virtually the entire sterling balances. The potential importance of that guarantee was reduced somewhat by the dollar devaluations of 1971–72, since the United Kingdom guaranteed the dollar value of the overseas sterling *at*

Conclusion

The several direct economic effects of the international roles of the dollar on the U.S. balance of payments are summarized in the following tabulation. For purposes of demonstrating the evolution over time, it compares the effects which policy-makers could anticipate in 1973 with those which could have been anticipated at the end of 1960 and at the end of 1968. The three-month Treasury bill rate in each year[39] is used to estimate interest payments, and it is assumed that lending rates by U.S. banks in each case averaged one percentage point higher.

Several conclusions derive from this analysis. First, the United States will need short-term inflows of about $2.5 billion annually to have reasonable assurance that the net direct effects of the roles of

	1960	1968	1973
		(in millions of dollars)	
Net interest earned/paid on existing stock of bank loans/ monetary liabilities	−200	−500	−3,000
Net interest earned/paid on next year's increase in bank loans/monetary liabilities (assuming $1 billion of each in a "normal" year in which the volume of each grows by roughly equal amounts)	20	25	22
Additional export earnings	200	350	700
Foreign direct investment by U.S. financial companies, net	—	−100	− 150
Contingent liability against dollar devaluation[a]	—	−200	− 100
Total	0	−425	−2,500

[a] Based on 5 per cent devaluation and actual amount of dollars guaranteed at that time.

---

the time of the arrangements; the dollar devaluation thus gave the United Kingdom a "credit" against an equal sterling devaluation against the dollar before the guarantees would be exercised. That credit was "used up" by the sterling depreciation from mid-1972, however, and Britain increased the dollar value of the guarantee in 1973.

39. 1960, 3 per cent; 1968, 5 per cent; 1971, 4 per cent.

the dollar, past and present, do not hurt the balance of payments. It is certain that any *reduction* in foreign dollar balances would hurt the balance of payments. There is no possibility for the United States to derive indirect economic benefits from the roles of the dollar, such as the reduction of pressure for adjustment of payments deficits, until the direct economic costs of those roles are offset. It has thus been erroneous for some time to think, as many apparently still do, that any buildup in foreign holdings of dollars demonstrates that the dollar's roles provide financing for U.S. payments deficits.

Second, the comparison over time demonstrates that the net direct effects of the key currency role have been moving adversely for the United States. In the absence of increases in foreign holdings of dollars, these figures suggest that the balance had already shifted to net costs in the early 1960s and had begun to significantly hurt U.S. interests by the late 1960s. The figures are only estimates, of course; but as they were derived on a consistent basis, one can have a high degree of confidence in the trend, which is clearly negative for the United States. Confidence in the conclusion that the overall effect has become negative should be strengthened by the fact that the high net interest costs. are reasonably firm estimates, whereas the high earnings figures for additional exports are much more conjectural.

Third, as noted above, the cost-benefit ratio is dynamically unstable. The United States can preserve net balance-of-payments benefits from the current roles of the dollar only if its liabilities grow significantly faster than its claims. Such increases, however, are likely to increase the net interest cost of the outstanding stock of claims and liabilities. Thus, greater net inflows may be needed in succeeding years to preserve net benefits, and the $2.5 billion needed annually in 1973 could grow over time.

Fourth, the United States would obviously gain most in the short run by eliminating the interest costs of the outstanding balances and retaining both its portfolio of foreign claims and the possibility of attracting net inflows in the future. It would also gain, however, and probably shift the net calculation back to positive, if it could eliminate or reduce the interest payments stemming from the reserve currency role while retaining the vehicle currency role. Most of the interest payments on the present dollar balances accrue to official holders, because they hold both a greater share of total balances and a greater share of their balances in interest-bearing form. In addition, most of the non-banking gains from the dollar's roles presumably derive primarily from the transactions function of the dollar. Some of these earnings might even be retained if the dollar's roles were eliminated completely. Nevertheless, complete elimination of the roles would be better from the U.S. standpoint (on these calculations alone) than would continuation of the status quo, unless the United States could be assured of net annual inflows exceeding $2.5 billion in the short run and a pattern of foreign deposits and interest rates that would avoid dynamic instability for the long run—a highly unlikely coincidence.

Fifth, the interest rate issue will be crucial in any U.S. judgment about the future roles of the dollar. An agreement simply to consolidate the present balances at present interest rates would not, on these direct financial criteria alone, appear attractive if the arrangement encompassed a concomitant prohibition on future increases in U.S. net liabilities to help finance the balance-of-payments effects of the interest payments themselves. This would be particularly true if the arrangement also provided for U.S. guarantees of the value of the dollars in terms of gold, SDRs, a weighted average of other currencies, or some other international yardstick. Such a provision would increase the contingent costs to the United States of the dollar's roles by virtually the full amount of the guarantee, since a very small proportion of present U.S. liabilities carry any such provisos. Indeed, a consolidation at market interest rates with full-value guarantees would increase, rather than cut, the future costs to the United States of the dollar's past key currency roles.

Welfare Effects

The contribution to U.S. welfare of these financial activities of U.S. banks and firms, stemming from the international roles of the dollar, is limited. The reason is that, in most of the cases, the resources used to earn foreign exchange have alternative domestic uses; the social gain from their present international employment is simply its excess over the domestic alternatives. Virtually all of the services analyzed here could probably be used domestically. If the marginal cost of supplying the services to foreigners were close to zero, it would also be close to zero for the marginal use domestically and thus the returns would be similar. The presence of separate foreign departments in some banks and companies suggests that the marginal cost is not zero, but neither would it be significant in terms of the overall GNP.

U.S. banks presumably make higher profits on their foreign loans than on the domestic loans they can extend at the same time, or else the banks would not undertake them—although even here there is a possible exception where the large banks borrow at excessively high cost, through their foreign branches, to meet loan demand from their domestic corporate customers. On the generous assumption that the banks' margin on foreign loans exceeds their margins on domestic loans by 0.5 per cent, about $80 million would be added to U.S. welfare from the present stock of bank assets, and the gain would rise by $5 million annually if the stock rose by $1 billion annually.

In the case of non-bank services, it is possible that the additional domestic supply would depress domestic prices slightly. Allowing for a 5 per cent differential,[40] the welfare gain to the United States of the perhaps $1 billion of present maximum gross earnings on provision of non-banking services to foreigners, related to the key currency roles of the dollar, is about $50 million annually.

The U.S. welfare gain on foreign investment undertaken by U.S. financial firms, at least partly to exploit additional potential gains from the international position of the dollar, would be the difference between the rate of return abroad after foreign taxes and the best available domestic return. Data permitting precise quantification of this differential are not available; however, it would seem most unlikely to exceed three percentage points, allowing for a slight reduction in domestic return if the capital had been invested domestically. On the estimated stock of $3 billion, this would represent a welfare gain of perhaps $100 million.

The welfare effect of these specific manifestations of the key currency roles is thus about $200 million, less than one-fiftieth of one per cent of GNP. On these grounds alone, the maintenance or even rapid expansion of the international roles of the dollar could hardly be supported very vigorously by any sectors of American society.

In addition to the specific welfare effects, however, there is an aggregate effect on U.S. welfare of the deficit-financing potential of the international roles of the dollar. We have concluded above that foreign dollar balances will have to grow by at least $2.5 billion annually in the future to offset the *adverse* effects which the international roles of the dollar now levy directly on the U.S. balance of payments. If foreign dollar balances were to exceed that rate of growth, the roles of the dollar would enable the United States to run deficits in its overall balance of payments. This would have both a direct and an indirect effect on U.S. welfare. Directly, it would permit the United States to absorb real resources from the rest of the world. Indirectly, it would enable the United States to avoid adjustment of its payments position —the costs of which in practice are virtually certain to exceed the reduction in absorption concomitant to the elimination of the payments deficit, because of the imprecision of adjustment measures even in the best of circumstances. The aggregate effect on U.S. welfare of

40. As did Grubel, *op. cit.*, p. 192.

the roles of the dollar is thus best measured by the costs of adjustment which are avoided through their financing for U.S. deficits, which is the subject of the next chapter.

In passing, however, it is interesting to estimate the *absolute* magnitudes of the increases in U.S. welfare which were made possible by the deficit-financing roles of the dollar in the past.[41] Virtually all of the $80 billion of liquid U.S. dollar liabilities to foreigners which had accumulated by the end of 1972 can be treated as providing such financing.[42]

It is of course impossible to link this financing directly to any specific component of foreign spending by Americans—imports, tourist expenditures, military expenditures, foreign aid, direct investment, bank loans or other short-term capital exports. Prior to the massive dollar buildup of 1970–72, it is probably most appropriate to link the financing with private capital outflows since such outflows were the primary target of the government's efforts to reduce the payments deficits. The average yield on these investments ranged between 10 and 15 per cent, while the average interest payments by the United States on the dollar liabilities ranged between 1 and 6 per cent. The net annual return to the United States on the first $50 billion of foreign dollar accruals had reached about $500 million by 1969—slightly more than 0.5 per cent of GNP. The value of the assets acquired in the process would also represent a tiny share of total U.S. wealth, although it is by no means negligible in absolute terms.

In 1970–72, both the nature and the magnitude of the welfare effects changed. A great deal of the huge buildup in foreign-held dollars simply reflected outflows of short-term U.S. capital, with the only gain to the United States being the small interest-rate differential in

41. Here we use "welfare" in the strict economic sense of maximizing the returns, valued in real dollars, from a given level of material input. In periods of high unemployment, of course, national "welfare" in a broader sense may suggest a wholly different focus for economic policy. Payments deficits thus "benefit" the U.S. most clearly during periods of full employment and excessive inflation, when additional imports and capital outflows relieve the pressure on the domestic economy, but are much more ambiguous during periods of high unemployment because an alternative exchange rate might "contribute more" by creating more jobs than it cost by reducing the terms of trade.

42. Robert Z. Aliber, *The Future of the Dollar as an International Currency* (New York: Praeger Publishers, 1966), p. 45, argues that it is inappropriate to count *all* of the foreign-held dollars as enabling the United States to increase its consumption because it held larger reserves than otherwise to "back" the foreign holdings. I concluded in Chapter 5, however, that any such additional holdings must have been quite small.

its favor. But a large part also reflected the sharp deterioration in the trade balance, which in turn was largely due to the overvaluation of the dollar. American consumption of imports was thus increased by the ability of the United States to finance its continuing payments deficits with dollars. Even if as much as one-half the total increase in imports in 1971 ($5.8 billion)[43] could be so explained, however, the resulting figure would be less than 0.5 per cent of total U.S. personal consumption expenditures in that year ($662 billion). And GNP *declined* as a result of the decline in U.S. net exports, a highly unwelcome development in a period of high unemployment such as existed at that time. Largely as a result, this larger magnitude of "benefit" from the dollar's roles proved to be unsustainable for any significant period of time.

So the direct welfare gains to the United States of the payments deficits financed by the dollar have been extremely small in the past, even when the deficits became very large and involved the trade balance as well as foreign investment. They have, nevertheless, represented a benefit from the international roles of the dollar which could apparently be sustained at a modest level. But we shall see in Chapter 9 that this consideration is swamped by the more relevant concern of the costs to the United States of adjusting if the dollar financing were not available.

Finally, it remains to allocate these balance-of-payments and direct welfare effects between the reserve and vehicle currency roles of the dollar. We can divide the interest payments on foreign deposits at least roughly between official and private holders at any given time, although the distinction in the published data is inaccurate (due to Eurodollar deposits of official holders, which the U.S. data record as U.S. liabilities to *private* foreigners) and shifts occur quite rapidly between the two categories. Most of the private earnings and expenditures—the additional export earnings and the foreign investment by financial institutions—relate primarily to the vehicle currency role, and many of them would probably continue if the reserve currency role were totally eliminated. Some of the foreign branches of U.S. banks do receive Eurodollar deposits of foreign monetary authorities

43. Which would encompass both the lower prices in overvalued dollars and higher volume of imports which resulted. Use of such a figure squares with the official estimate that the devaluation of 1971–72 would improve the U.S. balance of payments by $8–10 billion, since the objective of the policy change was to eliminate the imbalance which had existed before 1971 as well as the imbalance which developed additionally during that year. It is slightly higher than the terms-of-trade effect which will be derived in Chapter 9 as likely to flow from a U.S. devaluation of such magnitude.

(the total amount of which reached $6.6 billion in early 1972), which is of course a reflection of the reserve currency role, but it is doubtful that many of them base their investment plans on that consideration. All of the contingent liability against devaluation must be charged to the reserve currency role, since the guaranteed assets (swaps and Roosa bonds) are held only by officials. But the only way to allocate the foreign loans of U.S. banks, which we concluded are closely related to their foreign deposits, is on a *pro rata* basis between reserve and vehicle currency deposits.

The result is that the total balance-of-payments cost of the dollar's roles, based on the division of dollar balances between official and private holders at the end of. 1972, can be attributed to the reserve currency role. Indeed, the vehicle currency role comes out slightly positive. This result is highly sensitive to the official-private mix of outstanding dollars, but even a significant reconstitution of private foreign dollar balances would leave by far the greater costs with the reserve currency role.

Appendix: A Comparison with the United Kingdom

There have been several detailed attempts to assess the contribution of the "City of London" to the British balance of payments, which provide an interesting comparison with the results of the foregoing analysis for the United States. The most exhaustive private efforts concluded that the City earned $518 million at the prevailing exchange rate in 1963,[1] and about $600 million to $800 million in 1967.[2] The official estimates put the 1965–68 average at $600 million as well.[3]

These totals, however, are not comparable with my results for the United States. The British studies did not attempt to separate those effects relating primarily to the role of the key currency from the overall myriad of activities of the City; they failed to include some of the effects clearly flowing from sterling's roles; and they failed to distinguish between the balance-of-payments and welfare returns of the items they did cover. As a result, these studies grossly overstated the contributions which the City makes to the U.K. balance of payments.

First, they included certain items clearly not related to sterling's roles. Bank earnings from Euro*dollar* transactions and commissions from handling security issues denominated in *dollars* hardly reflect the roles of

1. William M. Clarke, *The City in the World Economy* (London: Institute of Economic Affairs, 1965).
2. Committee on Invisible Exports, *Britain's Invisible Earnings* (London: British National Export Council, 1967).
3. Central Statistical Office, *United Kingdom Balance of Payments*, 1969. The Committee of Inquiry on Decimal Currency, in its September 1963 report, Command 2145, estimated such earnings at $420 million in 1961.

sterling as an international currency. Earnings from shipping brokerage and the London commodity markets derive from Britain's historical maritime and trading roles, and are now affected only marginally by the position of sterling. Most of these activities in fact thrived throughout the period when sterling was inconvertible outside the sterling area, belying their reliance on the currency.[4] Two observers have estimated that Britain would lose only 20–30 per cent of the gross earnings of the City as (erroneously) calculated here—or about $150–$200 million—if sterling were to go out of the international business altogether.[5]

Second, even the alleged gross gains are clearly not balance-of-payments figures. They include, as their component, as much as £85 million of foreign earnings of British insurance companies and Lloyd's of London, most of which are not remitted to the United Kingdom. The companies remitted only one-third of their estimated earnings in 1956, and Lloyd's has built up a sizable trust fund (which totaled $463 million in 1963) in the United States by leaving its earnings abroad.[6] Another problem is that the insurance estimate employs a rate of underwriting profit which represents an average over a thirty-year period (1 per cent), whereas *losses* averaging over 3 per cent were registered in each year from 1956 through 1964.[7] A large part of this "contribution" of the City is thus not realized in the balance of payments in any current sense.

Third, the U.K. studies exclude some major items which clearly stem directly from sterling's international roles. Most noticeable is the exclusion of interest paid on foreign deposits in London, except for a minuscule part of the total labeled "normal banking deposits."[8] The omission

4. Clarke, *op. cit.*, p. 136, estimates that U.K. foreign earnings from shipping brokerage doubled between 1946 and 1956, and that foreign earnings from the commodity market at least tripled during the same period.
5. Cohen, *op. cit.*, p. 141, estimates a loss of less than 20 per cent of the City's gross earnings—£60 million of the £310 million annual average for 1965–68. The main losses are from the banks (£25 million) on interest earnings, £5 million on their foreign investment, £5 million on miscellaneous services amounting to about one-third of their gross foreign earnings. The merchant and brokerage sectors would also lose about one-third of their earnings (£15 million and £10 million, respectively). There would be no effect on insurance earnings. Andrew Shonfield, *British Economic Policy Since the War* (London: Penguin Books, 1958), p. 158, foresaw a similar pattern and a loss of less than one-third of total earnings a decade earlier. And the Radcliffe Committee on the Working of the Monetary System Report (London: HMSO, Command 827, August 1959), p. 241, thought that the earnings "would not be perceptibly less."
6. Clarke, *op. cit.*, p. 126.
7. *Ibid.*, pp. 73–74.
8. £150–200 million of a total of £5 billion at the time of Clarke's writing, *ibid.*, p. 129. However, earnings on sterling loans to foreigners were taken into account, and Clarke notes that "London's banks and institutions are in reality financing some of their business by making full use of foreign deposits," *ibid.*, pp. 129–30.

of these interest payments obviously results in a large overstatement of the *net* contribution of sterling's international roles to the U.K. balance of payments. The studies also count the earnings of the overseas branches and subsidiaries of U.K. banks, but exclude the capital outflows from Britain to increase the level of such activities.

Cohen has rectified the first and part of the third of these errors, and has subsumed the second, by regarding all insurance earnings as independent of sterling's roles. He concludes that the net direct effect of sterling's roles on the U.K. balance of payments is negative by about $100 million annually, and that their direct welfare benefit is positive by about $100 million.[9] I regard the former figure as too low, because it excludes capital outflows for further expansion of the banks' overseas network. I regard the latter as far too high because it "very generously," in Cohen's own words, judges that the international returns on these services are three times as great as the resources would earn domestically. This is certainly not true for the margin on bank loans, which provide the bulk of his welfare effects.

These studies of sterling carry some interesting implications for the dollar. Cohen's figures suggest, perhaps surprisingly, that Britain suffers much smaller direct balance-of-payments costs from the roles of sterling than does the United States from the roles of the dollar.[10] The contrast is even greater when we note that the U.K. figures exclude any additional export earnings due to sterling's roles, while the U.S. figures for 1971 estimate $500 million from that source.[11] Cohen's conclusion also suggests that these direct earnings are much more important to U.K. than to U.S. welfare, being one-half as great in an economy one-eighth as large. This difference is even greater, again, if the U.S. gain for export earnings is regarded suspiciously, though it should be reduced for Cohen's overstatement of the degree of welfare gains from the banks' international activities. Nevertheless we might expect such a difference, in view of Britain's long history of relying much more heavily than the

---

9. Cohen attributes virtually all of this benefit to the transactions role of sterling. This conclusion results from his flawed methodology of separating bank earnings from interest payments, however, because less than one-half of total sterling liabilities reflect the transactions role.
10. Strictly speaking, his data are for 1965–68 and the U.S. data for those years showed a roughly similar result. However, the United Kingdom ran payments surpluses during most of the 1969–71 period while U.S. dollar liabilities (and hence net interest payments) rose sharply. So it is roughly acceptable to compare the earlier U.K. data, which encompass the peak period of sterling's difficulties with the later U.S. data, which cover the peak year of the dollar's troubles. Both may thus be too high in absolute terms, but should be comparable.
11. The Committee on Invisible Exports, *op, cit.*, did make an alternative calculation including a $100 million benefit to U.K. exports from the effects of the City. Addition of this sum to Cohen's figures, or even part of it, would of course make the U.S. comparison even worse.

United States does on its financial community.[12] Thus the United States would appear to have a far greater interest than the United Kingdom has in getting rid of the key currency system, because it both suffers higher balance-of-payment costs and enjoys smaller welfare gains from the international use of its currency.

On the more specific estimates, both U.S. bank earnings and interest payments are about ten times as great as their British counterparts— roughly in line with the difference in size of the two economies, but throwing some doubt on the standard generalization that sterling still finances 20–30 per cent of world trade. Cohen attributes larger gains from sterling for miscellaneous U.K. financial services (bank services, merchanting, brokerage) than I attribute from the dollar for the United States, which would be in line with Britain's much greater historical and current involvement in such activities.[13] As already noted, I also attribute some U.S. export earnings to the dollar's roles, while Cohen excludes such estimates for Britain.

Finally, the sterling studies also demonstrate that the United Kingdom has been able to maintain an impressive level of gross foreign earnings in areas related to the role of its currency despite the stagnation of that role throughout the postwar period. The invisible earnings have grown quite slowly in recent years but they have by no means disappeared; except in a few cases where reasons other than changes in the role of sterling are readily apparent, they have not even declined.[14] But they also suggest that stagnation in the growth of the international use of a currency may contribute to stagnation in that country's earnings on services related to the currency's uses.

12. Similarly, the United Kingdom "suffers" much more than does the United States from the related effect of the key currency roles in promoting financial rather than business careers—which Hirsch, *Money International*, p. 327, regards as another cost to Britain of the roles of sterling.

13. For example, Lloyd's and other U.K. firms wrote over 60 per cent of worldwide marine insurance in 1970, while U.S. firms wrote only 25 per cent, according to a 1971 speech to the LOSS Executive Association by Mr. John B. Ricker, Jr., Chairman of Marine Office—Appleton Cox.

14. Paradoxically, the earnings rose rapidly during the 1946–56 period despite the inconvertibility of sterling outside the sterling area, but grew by barely 2 per cent year since the return of sterling to convertibility in 1958. The rapid increase in the early postwar years probably reflects largely a return to the "normal" level prevailing before 1939, however, rather than any significant development of "new" markets. Certainly this is true in the cases of banking and insurance, which were either completely disrupted or rigidly controlled during the war.

8

The Threat from the Overhang

As Chapter 7 has shown, one legacy of the international roles of the dollar in the past is a quantifiable direct cost on the U.S. balance of payments, which had reached $2.5 billion per year by 1973; further, the large volume of expatriated dollars can add to these costs by adversely affecting U.S. monetary policy. To get a complete picture, we must next assess the *indirect* effects of the dollar's roles on the balance of payments, and through it on U.S. welfare.

On the one hand, the roles of the dollar could increase the adjustment burden. The dollar overhang[1] could descend and force adjustment on the United States, either by depreciating the exchange rate of the dollar directly or by inducing alternative U.S. adjustment measures to avoid the costs of such depreciation. In addition, under any system in which the United States sought to maintain a fixed exchange rate for the dollar, collapse of the overhang could levy political costs as the United States sought to avoid being forced to adjust, perhaps by opting out of its systemic commitments. All of this could occur even if its current payments position were in balance. And the dollar's roles could themselves prevent the United States from adopting efficient adjustment policies. On the other hand, increases in foreign dollar holdings could provide net financing for future U.S. deficits—by rising more than the $2.5 billion needed annually to neutralize the present direct costs of the dollar's roles—and hence reduce the adjustment required.

Each of these questions must be analyzed in turn. This chapter will analyze the overhang, and whether perceptions of it are likely to constrain policy. We want to know whether the existence of the overhang *adds* to the direct costs to the United States of the international roles of the dollar developed in Chapter 7.

---

1. The term "overhang" connotes impending doom and is inaccurate if applied to all outstanding dollar balances, because, as this chapter will demonstrate, many countries are perfectly happy to hold dollars even under the least stable circumstances. The term will be used nonetheless because of its convenience and general acceptance.

Surprisingly, most previous analysts have failed to analyze the over-hang systematically. Some assert that it is the major source of global international financial difficulties, and that its collapse was inevitable.[2] Others argue that the United States "simply" has a balance-of-payments problem, and that the overhang would cause no difficulties if the current deficit were eliminated or at least reduced sufficiently, because confidence in the dollar would then preclude any foreign uneasiness about it. The objective of this chapter is to assess the severity of the overhang problem.

The overhang of foreign dollar balances has two parts: (a) the transactions balances held by private foreigners and the intervention balances held by monetary authorities, which primarily reflect the vehicle currency role, and (b) the reserve currency balances held by foreign monetary authorities. Under fixed exchange rates the private overhang could affect U.S. reserves only via foreign monetary authorities. The reason is that, since 1934, the United States has not intervened actively to defend the exchange rate of the dollar.[3] Banks and other operators in the markets thus could not tap U.S. reserves directly. Private foreign-held dollars could draw down U.S. reserves only if they first were added to the official overhang, and were then converted by official holders into U.S. reserves. Thus the reserve currency role of the dollar protected the United States against possible costs of the vehicle currency role.

This situation changed dramatically with the widespread adoption of flexible exchange rates in early 1973. Under flexible rates, central banks no longer stood ready to buy dollars at a fixed, or indeed any, price from their private sectors. Thus the "private overhang" could henceforth affect the dollar directly by forcing its depreciation in the exchange markets. In addition, the large stock of private foreign dollar holdings which had been created through the Eurodollar market and hence did not represent direct U.S. liabilities now became a threat to the dollar, whereas they had not been one during the previous system under which the dollar could be threatened only via reserve

2. For the classic theoretical case, see the numerous writings by Robert Triffin, beginning with *Gold and the Dollar Crisis, op. cit.* For empirical support based on data through 1965, see Helmut A. Hagemann, "Reserve Policies of Central Banks and Their Implications for U.S. Balance-of-Payments Policy," *American Economic Review*, Vol. LIX, No. 1 (March 1969), pp. 62–77.
3. The United States did intervene in the markets to a minor extent after 1960, but its intervention was marginal to the maintenance of the dollar parity. Any new convertibility policy in which it converted dollars into SDR or gold, or any other reserve assets, would not change the basic point as long as the United States remained passive in the exchange market.

currency balances. The move to flexible rates thus removed the dollar's insulation from the private overhang.

Indeed, private foreign dollar holdings undoubtedly contributed to the depreciation of the dollar caused by the dollar overhang in the second quarter of 1973. During that period, the U.S. balance of payments was in surplus on the official reserve transactions definition: foreign official holdings of dollars declined by about $1 billion. However, the weighted average exchange rate of the dollar depreciated in the foreign exchange markets against the German mark, the Swiss franc, and other Continental European currencies. The only explanation for this anomalous combination of a U.S. payments surplus and a weakening dollar is a "marking down" of the dollar through selling pressure generated by the dollar overhang.[4] So the overhang may have a more direct impact on the U.S. economy under flexible exchange rates than it did under fixed parities.

As a result of its suspension of the convertibility of foreign dollar balances into U.S. reserves on August 15, 1971, however, the United States no longer faced the risk of reserve losses from the overhang.[5] Indeed, under a system in which all exchange rates float freely with no intervention, the overhang can technically be reduced only through net foreign purchases of U.S. goods or assets, i.e., a U.S. payments surplus. In a sense, however, this action and the subsequent widespread adoption of flexible exchange rates heightens the importance of the overhang as a policy issue for the United States and for the international monetary system. As just noted, private dollar balances now have a more important direct effect on exchange rates with the removal of foreign reserves as a buffer between them and the United States. Shifts in the reserve-asset preferences of the world's monetary authorities also now have an immediate effect on exchange rates. And a number of key policy issues regarding the overhang were immediately raised by the events of 1971–73. Is the present overhang a sufficiently serious threat so that the United States should not resume asset convertibility until it is eliminated? Is any

4. There was a small U.S. deficit on the liquidity concepts, reflecting a buildup in *private* foreign dollar balances, but it could hardly explain the sharp decline of the dollar during this period.
5. Many analysts attribute the decision to suspend convertibility largely to the risk of collapse of the overhang. I rejected this conclusion in Chapter 3, pointing to the moderate level of U.S. reserve losses which preceded the step and interpreting the action as motivated primarily by concern over the effect of the overvaluation of the dollar on U.S. jobs. To the extent that the action was motivated at all by external considerations, it was the sharp deterioration of the current trade balance and not any fear of the overhang which triggered the action.

overhang such a problem that its re-creation should be resisted under any circumstances, despite the persistent tendencies toward the international use of national currencies? Or is it really no problem at all? Or is it a problem only under some particular relationship between the reserves of the center country and the size of the overhang; and does a deterioration in the liquidity ratio of the center country increase or decrease the problem? Or must we distinguish between the different components of the overhang, both functionally (reserve vs. intervention vs. transactions balances) and geographically (dollar-sterling area vs. gold bloc) in deciding what to do about it? These questions are central both to the immediate reform of the existing monetary system (because of the present overhang) and to the structuring of the new system which is to replace it (because of the possibility that new overhangs, either from the dollar again or from other currencies, will develop in the future).

Actual Conversions from the Overhang: The Theory
The existence of the dollar overhang can generate four types of costs to the United States. We have already discussed three which affect it directly: the problem for the management of domestic monetary policy of a large supply of currency outside the country; the interest payments on the overhanging dollars, which are only partly recouped by the tendency of U.S. financial institutions to re-lend these foreign deposits to other foreigners; and the cost of compensation to holders of guaranteed portions of the overhang when the dollar is devalued. All of these costs would disappear if the overhang were eliminated.

These considerations are swamped, however, by the possibility that conversions from the overhang, or fear thereof on the part of U.S. officials, will require balance-of-payments adjustment measures *additional* to those required by the current payments position. Under a regime of convertibility of foreign official dollars into U.S. reserves, such measures would be motivated in the first instance by a desire to avoid reserve losses, and the discussion will frequently be couched in terms of such losses. Ultimately, however, the U.S. concerns with extensive sales of foreign dollars would be (a) the real economic costs to the United States of the resulting depreciation of the dollar and (b) the instability which could result for the monetary system as a whole due to rapid and unregulated depreciation of its most important currency. These concerns exist whether or not the dollar is convertible into U.S. reserve assets. Thus, under most of the foreseeable circumstances, the United States would oppose foreign dollar sales from the overhang cited in the preceding paragraph. On the other hand, if it can avoid conversions from the overhang simply by maintaining equilibrium in its current payments position, it does not have an additional policy target and does not need an additional policy instrument.

Under the Bretton Woods system, or any system of fixed parities, the existence of the overhang means that changes in U.S. gross reserves can be less favorable than its current balance-of-payments position on either the liquidity or official reserve transactions definitions. Since changes in reserves bring the most immediate pressure to bear on U.S. international monetary policy—and perhaps the only international pressure sufficient to force it to action, given the relative closed nature of the U.S. economy, the costs of any significant forced action, and the difficulty of reaching intra-U.S. government agreement to act[6]—their effect can be determinative. The United States might then be saddled by the overhang with an additional policy target—the avoidance of such conversions, which often translates rhetorically into "maintenance of international confidence in the dollar." As discussed in Chapter 5, this could in practice mean efforts to improve the U.S. liquidity ratio—with no additional policy instrument with which to achieve the target.[7]

Under any system of flexible exchange rates, the existence of the overhang can lead to net foreign sales of dollars which will depress the exchange rate of the dollar below the level called for by the current competitive relationship between the United States and other countries. Such sales are the counterpart of dollar conversions into U.S. reserve assets under fixed exchange rates. Indeed, they are in practice more likely to occur because their systemic implications

6. On the problem of achieving intra-U.S. agreement, in general, see Henry A. Kissinger, *The Troubled Partnership* (New York: McGraw-Hill, for the Council on Foreign Relations, 1965), *passim*, and the growing literature on bureaucratic politics. In the monetary context, see John Kenneth Galbraith, "A Political and Administrative View of the U.S. Balance of Payments," *Review of Economics and Statistics*, 1964, p. 119, and the hints by Robert V. Roosa in *The Dollar and World Liquidity* (New York: Random House, 1967), pp. 28–29. The United States can of course take international monetary action when it thinks it can serve its domestic economic or foreign policy needs by doing so, as in the devaluations of 1934 and 1971, whether or not external pressures exist.

7. The "redundancy problem," which suggests that the United States need have no international monetary policy target at all, because there can be only $n-1$ exchange rates in a world of n countries and the United States as nth country because the dollar is the key currency of the system, would then be "solved" by adding this requirement to the world total of policy targets rather than by leaving the United States with a "free variable." See Robert A. Mundell, "The Redundancy Problem and the World Price Level," Appendix to Chapter 13, *International Economics* (New York, Macmillan, 1968), pp. 195–98.

are far less severe—although there remains a constraint against dollar sales for countries which do not want their currencies to appreciate against the dollar, hurting their competitive position in international trade. A "collapse of the overhang" thus takes different forms under fixed or flexible exchange rates, but levies on the United States the two kinds of costs cited above in either case.

Part of the overhang, can "collapse" for three reasons: shifts of dollar balances from dollar area to gold bloc countries; shifts of countries from dollar area membership to gold bloc membership; and marginal increases in the gold ratios of countries already in the gold bloc. Each of these shifts could be expected to produce net sales of dollars which previously were willingly held. (In the present world of managed flexibility of exchange rates, "dollar area" membership of course means that a country holds the bulk of its reserves in dollars, not that it pegs its exchange rate to the dollar. Indeed, a couple of "gold bloc" countries in terms of reserve composition have since early 1973 in essence pegged their exchange rates to the German mark.)

It is possible that individual dollar area countries other than the United States might move into persistent deficit and be willing to see their reserves decline over time. If these deficits simply led to shifts to other dollar area countries, there would be no pressure on the dollar from the overhang; this is a basic reason for seeking maximum size for a currency area. If the shifts are on balance to the gold bloc, however, net dollar sales could result even if the United States itself were in balance or surplus.

Given the available data, the existence of this condition can only be detected indirectly by comparing the aggregate payments position of gold bloc countries, the overall balance-of-payments position of the United States, and changes in net world reserves.[8] If gold bloc surpluses exceed current U.S. deficits by more than the addition to net world liquidity, we can infer that the overseas dollar area is in deficit, transferring dollars to the gold bloc, and the overhang would be threatening the dollar as a result.

Most countries are reluctant to let their reserves decline very much for very long. In fact, most of them desire steady growth in their holdings. Nevertheless, sustained losses by individual dollar countries could well occur over given periods of time. Germany, Japan, and several of the oil-exporting countries are the dollar holders most

---

8. See Table 12. As outlined in Chapter 3, the sterling area merged with the dollar area for all practical purposes from 1968 and is thus not treated separately thereafter.

likely to countenance reserve declines.[9] They would certainly finance any payments deficits they might run with dollars. And at least part of the German-held dollars would be quite likely to move to gold bloc countries, since Germany's continental EC partners would generally be the main beneficiaries of such deficits and are at present all members of that "currency area." No other major dollar countries appear likely to accept large reserve declines.

The second case would occur when countries shift their "membership" from dollar area to gold bloc, and then sell off at least some of their dollars as a result. Shifts in area membership can occur because individual countries decide that their reserve center is no longer maintaining the attributes which preserve their confidence in the currency (especially if there are no guarantees against devaluation losses); because changes in the pattern of a country's international economic relations are taking place, with one financial center gradually assuming a more dominant role than the one which had previously been most important; or because of "pure politics."

All three factors played a role in the gradual dissolution and final collapse of the sterling area. The lack of confidence in the new sterling parity after the November 1967 devaluation, coupled with the realization that sterling *could* be devalued, was probably the immediate cause of the Basel arrangements. However, long-term shifts in trading and financial patterns were a major underlying cause for numerous countries, such as Australia. And politics entered with the sale of sterling by several Middle Eastern countries in mid-1967, because of alleged British support for Israel in the Six Day War.

In the third case, which existed under the Bretton Woods system, a gold bloc country could decide to reduce further the dollar component of its reserves. It might do so because of a downward revision of its estimated need for working balances, perhaps because it had estimated incorrectly that in the near future it would have to be using the dollars acquired through recent surpluses to finance deficits. Or if yields on dollar assets declined, the opportunity cost of holding gold would also fall and possibly promote increases in gold ratios.[10] Or it might do so for political reasons.

---

9. Indeed, some Japanese officials indicated in May 1972 that Japan actively sought to reduce its reserves to $10 billion (from a level of about $16 billion at that time, which shortly became even larger) in order to forestall pressures from the United States and others for additional adjustment measures. Japanese reserves did fall by more than $6 billion in 1973.

10. See Chapter 5. In a later version of one of the econometric analyses referred to here, "Reserve Asset Preferences Revisited," in Peter B. Kenen

Table 12

THE STRUCTURE OF INTERNATIONAL PAYMENTS: 1958-74
(In millions of dollars)

	1958	1959	1960	1961	1962	1963	1964	1965	1966	1967	1968
Sources of additions to world reserves[1]											
U.S. official reserve transactions deficit	3,040	1,542	3,403	1,348	2,650	1,934	1,534	1,289	−219	3,418	−1,641
Net change in monetary gold	735	−145	135	830	420	940	620	1,015	−950	−1,400	−570
Net change in IMF reserve positions	245	692	320	588	−363	145	215	1,221	954	−583	740
Net change in SDRs	—	—	—	—	—	—	—	—	—	—	—
Total	4,020	2,071	3,858	2,766	2,707	3,019	2,369	3,525	−215	1,435	−1,471
Uses of additions to world reserves											
Gold bloc reserves[2]	2,283	1,222	1,563	2,523	1,356	1,195	1,783	2,156	810	1,684	−2,722
Sterling area payments position with nonsterling countries	364	498	−1,092	468	938	456	−1,786	−785	−608	−918	4
Outer dollar area reserves[3]	1,373	351	3,387	−225	413	1,368	2,372	2,154	−417	669	1,251
(of which): Germany	(682)	(−1,089)	(−2,242)	(131)	(−207)	(694)	(232)	(−453)	(599)	(124)	(−1,795)
Canada	(112)	(−9)	(−40)	(287)	(271)	(56)	(278)	(146)	(−334)	(−16)	(329)
Japan	(234)	(385)	(502)	(−283)	(356)	(36)	(−39)	(133)	(−33)	(−89)	(876)
Latin America	(−695)	(−210)	(−80)	(−260)	(−490)	(480)	(130)	(425)	(−100)	(180)	(480)
Others	(1,040)	(854)	(763)	(−100)	(373)	(102)	(1,771)	(1,903)	(−549)	(438)	(−2,229)
Total	4,020	2,071	3,858	2,765	2,759	3,096	2,399	3,525	−256	1,423	−1,471

240

Table 12—*Continued*

	1969	1970	1971	1972	1973	1974
Sources of additions to world reserves[1]						
U.S. official reserve transactions deficit	−2,702	9,839	29,765	10,340	5,304	8,070
Net change in monetary gold	190	−1,950	2,030	−335	4,315	570
Net change in IMF reserve positions	238	971	−801	−29	574	3,388
Net change in SDRs	—	3,414	2,718	3,053	1,193	221
Total	−2,274	12,274	33,712	13,029	11,386	12,249
Uses of additions to world reserves						
Gold bloc reserves[2]	−157	3,585	8,783	3,705	3,132	2,490
Sterling area payments position with nonsterling countries	4	4	4	4	4	4
Outer dollar area reserves[3]	2,431	9,689	24,929	9,324	8,254	9,759
(of which): Germany	(−2,819)	(6,481)	(4,782)	5,128	9,362	−748
Canada	(60)	(1,573)	(1,022)	349	−282	57
Japan	(748)	(1,186)	(10,520)	3,005	−6,119	1,273
Latin America	(560)	(1,175)	(945)	3,965	5,866	5,144
Others	(3,882)	(−726)	(7,660)	−3,123	−573	4,033
Total	−2,274	12,274	33,712	13,029	11,386	12,249

[1] Excluding the United States.   [3] Derived as residual.
[2] See Table 12a for details.   [4] Included with outer dollar area after 1967.

Sources:
(1) For U.S. balance of payments, *Survey of Current Business*, various issues.
(2) For sterling area balance of payments, *United Kingdom Balance of Payments 1967*.
(3) For other items, *International Financial Statistics*, various issues.

Conversions by gold bloc countries in any single year may simply represent "reconstitution" of the gold ratios they wish to maintain over time, however, and which they had maintained in the past. All surpluses are accumulated (by countries other than the United States) first in the form of foreign currencies acquired through exchange market intervention, and the authorities may wait a while before convert-

and Roger Lawrence, eds., *The Open Economy: Essays on International Trade and Finance* (New York: Columbia University Press, 1968), p. 377, Margaret Greene did find "clear but weak evidence of interest-rate sensitivity on reserve-asset compositions," for all of the gold bloc countries which she studied (Belgium, France, Italy, Netherlands, Switzerland—and the United Kingdom, which at that time was still the center of the sterling area) but to only one (Sweden) of the four dollar area countries (the others being Canada, Germany, and Japan).

Table 12A

TOTAL RESERVES OF GOLD BLOC COUNTRIES: 1957–74
(In millions of dollars)

	1957	1958	1959	1960	1961	1962
Austria	523	678	697	716	846	1,081
Belgium	1,148	1,553	1,306	1,506	1,813	1,753
France	645	1,050	1,736	2,272	3,365	4,049
Italy	1,479	2,278	3,120	3,251	3,800	4,068
Netherlands	1,056	1,561	1,442	1,861	1,955	1,943
Portugal	750	599	640	637	552	681
Switzerland	1,898	2,063	2,063	2,324	2,759	2,871
Total	7,499	9,782	11,004	12,567	15,090	16,446
Change in period	na	2,283	1,222	1,563	2,523	1,356

	1963	1964	1965	1966	1967	1968
Austria	1,228	1,317	1,305	1,326	1,478	1,504
Belgium	1,978	2,222	2,334	2,350	2,590	2,187
France	4,908	5,724	6,343	6,733	6,994	4,201
Italy	3,619	3,824	4,800	4,911	5,463	5,341
Netherlands	2,102	2,346	2,416	2,448	2,619	2,463
Portugal	732	871	938	1,077	1,234	1,363
Switzerland	3,074	3,120	3,444	3,545	3,696	4,293
Total	17,641	19,424	21,580	22,390	24,074	21,352
Change in period	1,195	1,783	2,156	810	1,684	−2,722

	1969	1970	1971	1972	1973	1974
Austria	1,530	1,751	2,343	2,719	2,873	3,430
Belgium	2,388	2,847	3,473	3,870	5,100	5,345
France	3,833	4,960	8,253	10,015	8,529	8,851
Italy	5,045	5,352	6,787	6,079	6,434	6,941
Netherlands	2,529	3,234	3,796	4,785	6,547	6,958
Portugal	1,445	1,504	1,945	2,312	2,839	2,354
Switzerland	4,425	5,132	6,966	7,488	8,078	9,011
Total	21,195	24,780	33,563	37,268	40,400	42,890
Change in period	−157	3,585	8,783	3,705	3,132	2,490

Source: *International Financial Statistics*, various issues.

ing to see if their gains are simply transitory or whether they will be maintained.[11] If the lag carries over the end of a year (or even quarter), the actual conversions may give the appearance of coming

11. Greene, *op. cit.*, p. 363, was able to improve her "explanations" of foreign reserve-asset preferences for almost all countries by introducing a lag of one quarter to allow for reduction of foreign exchange balances to "desired" levels.

from the overhang. This is true, in a strict sense, but they are such a short-lived part of the overhang that it would be misleading to consider them as such. If we knew precisely the desired working balance levels of gold bloc countries, we could calculate the maximum threat from this segment of the overhang at any point in time.

The final possibility concerns the shift of foreign dollar holdings from private to official hands. American statistics would treat such a shift as increasing the official reserve transactions deficit, so that subsequent conversion of the dollars by the monetary authorities acquiring them would simply represent current financing for the deficit on that concept. However, the liquidity definitions treat foreign private and official dollar holdings alike. The shift from private to official hands would thus have no effect on the current calculation on *that* concept, and sales of the dollars would produce a loss of reserves in excess of the current liquidity deficit or depreciation of the dollar in the exchange markets. As such, it can be seen as a collapse of part of the (private) overhang.

Interest rate considerations can trigger large shifts of privately held foreign dollars into the few money markets which can accommodate them, and to monetary officials in those countries. Nonspeculative flows of private foreign capital into and out of the dollar may also be determined by the level of U.S. imports and the outflow of capital from the United States. The rate of import growth affects only the rate of growth of foreign deposits in the United States, however, and the overhang would not be touched except in the unlikely event of a sustained decline in the level of imports. On the other hand, there has been a close correlation between bank outflows and inflows, as discussed in Chapter 7, except in periods of extremely tight money in the United States or speculative activity. Thus another of the criteria for a key currency country—that it be a consistent gross exporter of capital—may in fact be a major determinant of changes in private foreign balances here. If the net claims of U.S. banks on private foreigners are reduced, it can be expected that private foreign dollar deposits in the United States will also be reduced. Such operations would represent simply a *pari passu* extinguishing of the two sides of a single banking arrangement, however, and would not represent a shift of foreign dollars from private to official hands; rather it would be an improvement in the U.S. balance of payments on the liquidity definition, financed by a reduction in U.S. liquid liabilities to private foreigners. So it would not pose any threat to the dollar, though in a strict accounting sense it would be a "collapse" of part of the overhang.

There is also the possibility of such shifts for speculative reasons, which follows from our earlier conclusion that the maintenance of confidence in the dollar's convertibility into other national currencies at a stable price is a primary requirement for continued vehicle currency status. Stein estimated that speculative pressures sufficient to depress the forward exchange rate of the dollar one percentage point below the expected level, given the interest rate differential, could generate an outflow of $1 billion of private foreign capital (in addition to deterring the expected inflow of $850 million under nonspeculative conditions with no interest rate differential) in the early 1960s. While the analysis of the speculative effect is itself speculative, and Stein's "speculative" variable admittedly includes nonspeculative factors, there is no doubt that the effect could be sizable when dollar depreciation became a real possibility—as has been clearly seen in the early 1970s. Again, only some part of the speculative outflow would lead to dollar accumulation in gold bloc reserves and hence to pressure on the dollar. The amount would be partly determined by the relative strength of other currencies when the speculation developed; if the mark were strong and Germany still in the dollar area, the effect would be much less than if the movement were into Swiss francs. But the existence of the private overhang does add to the pressure on the United States to maintain conditions conducive to confidence in a stable exchange rate for the dollar.

Of the four possibilities for conversions from the overhang, all can produce a short-term problem. But the reconstitution of "normal" gold ratios by gold bloc countries and isolated departures from the dollar area by individual countries are purely short-term problems with finite limits. On the other hand, a long-term problem could arise either because outer dollar area countries with large reserves were expected to run persistent balance-of-payments deficits which led to gold bloc surpluses, or because a few countries with large dollar holdings (or a large number of smaller countries) were expected to leave the dollar area over time, or because the development of additional vehicle currencies presaged a secular shift out of dollars by private (and perhaps official) foreigners.

The proper policy response by the reserve center differs as to whether the problem is short- or long-term, just as policy responses to current deficits should differ depending on whether they are likely to be temporary or chronic. For example, the United States should be much more eager to seek a negotiated consolidation of the dollar balances if it foresees continuing selling pressure than if it expects merely one-shot, albeit sizable, sales reflecting short-term factors. At present, it is certainly conceivable that the dollar overhang will descend over time and by sizable amounts: many countries (including Germany) may wish to leave the dollar area as the United States no longer maintains the needed key currency attributes, especially as they now see that the dollar *can* be devalued and as their trade becomes increasingly oriented toward Europe and Japan instead of toward the United States; Japan and/or Germany may run payments deficits for a while, which would redistribute dollar reserves to gold bloc countries; virtually all gold countries clearly hold more dollars than they need as working balances, or want; and it is quite possible that private dollar balances will fall as the mark and other new vehicle currencies increasingly cut into the previous U.S. position.

There is the usual practical problem, in addition to the conceptual one. A key currency country might not accurately perceive its problem as long-term, and try to meet it simply on a short-term basis. Conversely, it might read a short-term movement as a long-term trend and seek consolidation when it could continue to reap net benefits from the currency's roles. The problem of discerning whether sales from the overhang are one-shot phenomena or the beginning of a trend is, of course, additional to the problem of discerning whether underlying problems of the current balance of payments reflect short- or long-term difficulties.

Faced with the possibility of a continuing descent of the overhang, the reserve center would have to make a critical policy choice. Either it would have to take steps to assure the world that it would continue to meet the criteria for a key currency (primarily through bolstering its liquidity ratio and improving its own balance-of-payments position over the longer run), or do something directly affecting the balances themselves—by way of a multilateral consolidation thereof, or by the opposite unilateral alternative of guaranteeing their value. (It can also buy time by repudiating their convertibility altogether, as the United States did in 1971, but over the longer run this probably increases the magnitude of the overhang shifts and the pressure on the dollar which they generate.) An effort to restore confidence in the currency would reflect a decision to try to maintain its international roles and avoid the expected long-term descent of the overhang. So would a guarantee of the overhang, by the country of issue, the option which was in fact chosen by the British in 1968—despite avowals to the contrary. On the other hand, a multinational consolidation or repudiation would signal an effort to eliminate at least the historical legacy of those roles. These options are discussed in depth in Part III.

The short-term problems which can derive from collapses of parts of the overhang are often more dramatic than the more serious long-term trends, as they may well be the source of a "crisis" in the foreign exchange markets. They may result from temporary deficits by outer dollar area countries, coupled with gold bloc surpluses (temporary or permanent); one-shot sales, reflecting an isolated shift of membership from the dollar area to gold bloc; or temporary private selling of dollars. All of these are water over the dam once they have occurred, and there is no reason why they should trigger major policy responses by the reserve center. Surmounted crises may entail a small cost for the reserve center if it needs to smooth out the impact of the conversions by borrowing (perhaps via the swap network or from the IMF) at interest rates higher than it was paying on the liquidated balances.[12] But a major cost would result only if the center were panicked into adopting costly adjustment policies beyond those required by the needs of the current balance-of-payments position and by the *long-term* outlook for the overhang. Before looking at whether an unwarranted *fear* of future conversions has erroneously triggered U.S. policy actions in the past, or could do so in the future, we need to review the actual history of the dollar overhang to see if they substantiate the conceptual approach just outlined.

The Historical Record: U.S. Gold Sales and the Overhang
The record of U.S. gold sales over the era of postwar convertibility (1958–71) reveals very few conversions from the overhang. In two years (1966 and 1968), there were gold sales while the official reserve transactions position was in surplus.[13] In one year (1965) gold sales exceeded the U.S. deficit on the official reserve transactions definition (by a very small amount). With these exceptions, *aggregate* U.S. gold sales can be fully explained as partial financing for *current* deficits, not due to conversions from the overhang. The data are in Table 13.[14]

However, conversions from the overhang by individual countries

12. See John Letiche, "International Liquidity: Synthesis and Appraisal," *American Economic Review*, Vol. LVIII, No. 2 (May 1968) p. 645, and Robert Mundell, "The Cost of Exchange Crises and the Problem of Sterling" and "The Crisis Problem," Chapters 19 and 20 of his *International Economics* (New York: Macmillan, 1968).
13. In 1969, U.S. gold purchases were smaller than the total official reserve transactions surplus. Such a "collapse" of the overhang for purposes of financing a U.S. payments surplus does not raise the problem of U.S. reserve losses under discussion here, although it does raise questions of how the United States can be assured of receiving reserve assets when it runs a surplus and hence be in a position to finance subsequent deficits with assets.
14. It is too early to analyze clearly the effect of the overhang on the dollar under a system of flexible exchange rates. It appears, however, that the dollar may be systemically undervalued for a while, in terms of the current competitive position of the U.S. economy, because of a portfolio adjustment by both private and official holders (taken as a group) from dollars into other national currencies, particularly the mark. See C. Fred Bergsten, "New Urgency for Monetary Reform," *Foreign Policy*, 19 (Summer 1975).

Table 13

U.S. GOLD SALES AND PAYMENTS DEFICITS: 1960–71
(In millions of dollars)

	1960	1961	1962	1963	1964	1965	1966	1967	1968	1969	1970	1971
Gold sales to foreigners	1,969	970	833	392	36	1,322	608	1,031	1,118	−957	631	843
Less: estimated gold pool transactions	—	—	387	−329	−618	−150	−80	879	835	—	—	—
U.S. monetary gold sales	1,969	970	446	721	654	1,472	688	152	283	−957	631	843
Basic balance	−1,155	20	−979	−1,262	28	−1,814	−1,614	−3,196	−1,349	−3,011	−3,059	−9,374
Net liquidity balance	−3,665	−2,229	−2,845	−2,571	−2,745	−2,493	−2,148	−4,685	−1,610	−6,122	−3,851	−22,002
Official reserve transactions balance	−3,403	−1,348	−2,650	−1,934	−1,534	−1,289	219	−3,418	1,641	2,702	−9,839	−29,765

Sources: *Survey of Current Business*, and *Treasury Bulletin*, various issues.

247

could be concealed in the overall data. If there were such cases, the overhang might still be considered a threat to U.S. reserves. It is therefore necessary to look at individual countries which brought gold from the United States during this period. The relevant data are in Table 14.

First, we consider the aggregate cases of 1965, 1966, and 1968. Gold sales to foreign monetary authorities totaled $1.5 billion in 1965, slightly greater than the official settlements deficit of $1.3 billion. The gold bloc countries taken together had an aggregate surplus of $1.7 billion in 1965, slightly more than the U.S. deficit alone but about $0.7 billion less than the U.S. deficit combined with the increase in world reserves from the increased availability of gold.[15] Hence their conversions significantly exceeded their "need" to buy gold from the United States, and did represent conversions from the overhang.

An inspection of the geographical distribution of gold sales reveals that these conversions primarily represented reconstitution by a few gold bloc countries of gold ratios which had declined in the previous year or two. Three countries purchased gold beyond the level of their current payments surpluses and accounted for the reduction in the overhang: Austria, France, and Spain. Austria bought $100 million, although its total reserves were virtually unchanged for the year. In 1963 and 1964, however, it had accumulated a like amount of dollars rather than maintain only a normal level of dollar working balances. France bought almost $300 million more than "justified" by its current surplus. However, it had accumulated over $400 million million in dollar form in 1964, and large amounts in each previous year as far back as 1958. Hence it was simply reconstituting the gold portion of its reserves. Spain bought $180 million in gold, while its total reserves actually fell by almost $100, but it had accumulated over $300 million in dollars in 1964.[16]

15. In 1965, there was a general increase in IMF quotas. The gold "losses" of IMF member countries for this purpose are not deducted, since they were simply offset by an increase in automatic drawing rights on the Fund itself.
16. The Spanish case has an additional aspect. Spain apparently held sizable sterling balances until around 1963, when it sold them because of irritation over a unilateral change by the United Kingdom in its exchange-value commitments under the European Monetary Agreement (which had succeeded the European Payments Union). Part of the conversions from sterling were into gold but part into dollars, some of which were in turn not converted into gold until 1965. So the Spanish case might be interpreted as a shift from at least partial membership in the sterling area to the gold bloc, through dollars and with a partial two-year lag. As noted previously, Spain later shifted into the dollar area (in 1970).

Table 14

RESERVE CHANGES AND GOLD PURCHASES FROM THE UNITED STATES
OF MAJOR GOLD BLOC COUNTRIES: 1958–71 (In millions of dollars)

	1958	1959	1960	1961	1962	1963	1964	1965	1966	1967	1968	1969	1970	1971
Austria:														
change in reserves	154	19	19	129	236	148	88	−6	22	151	26	27	220	400
gold from U.S.	84	83	1	—	143	82	55	100	25	—	−4	—	—	—
Belgium:														
change in reserves	405	−247	200	307	−60	217	252	112	16	240	−403	201	459	352
gold from U.S.	329	39	141	144	63	—	40	83	—	—	58	—	—	110
France:														
change in reserves	405	686	536	1,093	684	859	816	619	390	261	−2,793	−368	1,127	2,625
gold from U.S.	—	266	173	—	456	518	405	884	601	—	−600	−325	129	473
Italy:														
change in reserves	728	872	195	548	269	−449	205	976	110	553	−121	−329	286	899
gold from U.S.	349	—	—	−100	—	—	−200	80	60	85	209	76	—	—
Netherlands:														
change in reserves	530	−97	421	95	−12	156	247	67	32	171	−156	66	705	263
gold from U.S.	261	30	249	25	—	—	60	35	—	—	19	—	50	25
Spain:														
change in reserves	−40	143	332	345	159	102	366	−104	−204	−156	50	132	535	1,177
gold from U.S.	−32	—	114	155	146	130	32	180	—	—	—	—	−51	—
Switzerland:														
change in reserves	165	—	261	434	113	203	46	124	80	231	377	63	706	1,284
gold from U.S.	215	−20	324	125	−102	—	81	50	2	30	50	25	50	175
Memorandum:														
Total gold purchases from U.S., these 7	1,206	398	1,002	350	706	730	473	1,412	688	115	−268	−224	176	783
Total U.S. monetary gold sales	2,294	998	1,969	970	446	721	654	1,472	688	152	283	−957	631	843

Source: *International Financial Statistics*, and *Treasury Bulletin.*

249

In addition, the French conversions were at least partly attributable to political motivations—de Gaulle's "gold war." The same may be true for the Spanish conversions, since Spain was at that time seeking French sponsorship for EEC membership and may have thought that a clear policy of independence from the United States—especially when contrasted with the "subservience" of other EEC applicants, notably Britain, which was already moving toward "joining" the dollar area—would be helpful to that end. The 1965 experience with the overhang can thus be attributed to reconstitution of gold ratios by gold bloc countries, with a heavy dose of politics thrown in to affect the timing. But it clearly had a finite and limited scope, since gold bloc countries by definition hold few dollars. This conclusion was amply demonstrated within a few years by France's need to *sell* gold in 1968–69 to acquire currencies and by subsequent currency drawings from the Fund by both France and Spain.

The 1966 case was different. Gold sales to foreign monetary authorities totaled about $700, while the U.S. figures showed an official settlement surplus of $266 million. There is thus an apparent spread of almost $1 billion dollars. The "real" spread was less by about $500 million, however, because there was apparently an increase of that magnitude in foreign official placements in the Eurodollar market.[17] On the other hand, the United States on balance bought about $150 million of gold from dollar area countries during the year, so the real "spread" was about $650 million.[18]

About $200 million of the difference can be explained by a further reconstitution by France, again with political overtones. The remaining U.S. gold loss could have resulted from either of two causes. Even though it was in overall surplus, the United States could have been in bilateral deficit with gold bloc countries. Such a situation would reflect the basic asymmetry facing a reserve center, which may have to finance its deficits with reserves but whose surpluses may be financed by running down its liabilities. However, the United States does not appear to have been in deficit in 1966 with France, the main purchaser of its gold that year.[19]

The other possibility is a deficit of the outer dollar area with the

17. IMF, *Annual Report*, 1973, p. 36. It will be recalled that a shift of foreign official dollar balances into the Eurodollar market is recorded in the U.S. data as a reduction in U.S. liabilities to official holders and an increase in U.S. liabilities to private foreigners.

18. The total gold holdings of national monetary authorities fell sharply in 1966 but were financed cooperatively by the gold pool members, and apparently none of the non-U.S. members "refinanced" its own gold losses from the United States.

19. IMF, *Balance of Payments Yearbook*, Vol. 19, shows France running a small bilateral deficit with the United States in 1966.

rest of the world. Table 12 shows that such a deficit did occur and totalled about $400 million—explaining the remaining difference. Beyond the aggregate data, it is virtually impossible to determine which outer dollar area countries may have been involved in 1966. In any year many of them are in surplus with the gold bloc and many in deficit, so that one would have to look at time series even to derive inferences about the marginal shifts which moved the entire area into deficit. Since the area as a whole was in surplus in all years but two since 1958, neither of the factors involved in the small 1966 "descent" should have been regarded as serious by the U.S. authorities.[20]

In 1968, U.S. gold sales to foreign authorities were approximately $300 million while the official reserves transactions position was in surplus by $1.6 billion. About $1.5 billion of the difference can be traced to a further buildup of Eurodollar balances by foreign officials, however, so the conversion from the overhang was only about $400 million—not much for a year which began with the greatest gold rush of all time, and forced the abandonment of the gold pool and the freeing of the free market price in March.

There were two major factors in the 1968 conversions. First, there was further "reconstitution" of almost $300 million by gold bloc countries: about $200 million by Italy, and smaller amounts by Belgium and the Netherlands. These were, again, limited in scope and no cause for alarm.

Second, there also were U.S. gold sales of about $300 million to countries departing from the sterling area. The biggest buyers were Singapore, Ireland, Iraq, Malaysia, and Kuwait. It might have been expected that these sterling countries would have moved into gold

20. Triffin argued at the time that, during 1965–67, there were massive conversions of dollars which imperiled the entire international monetary system and the United States. He fully recognized, however, that virtually all of these "conversions" represented financing of the current surpluses of gold bloc countries and did *not* result from a collapse of the overhang: "From the end of 1964 through mid-1967, [foreign countries] converted the entirety of their current reserve gains ($4.4 billion) and some ($0.2 billion) of their previously accumulated foreign exchange holdings into gold ($2.4 billion) and claims on the IMF ($2.1 billion)." Robert Triffin, "Neither Gold Nor the Dollar," *The New Republic*, January 27, 1968, p. 24. It is obvious that the "conversions" of *current earnings*—which can be regarded as "conversions" only in the trivial sense that virtually all balance-of-payments surpluses initially accrue to countries other than the United States in the form of foreign exchange—were virtually the whole story. The excess has already been explained as reconstitution of gold ratios which Austria, France, and Spain had let decline in previous years. And global foreign official holdings of dollars (including near-liquid assets) actually rose in 1965, fell only $800 million in 1966, and rose again by almost $3.5 billion in 1967.

by buying it directly from Britain, the holder of the reserve pool for the sterling area. However, they shifted instead from sterling into gold through dollars. The United Kingdom apparently argued that its gold reserve had become too slender to tap—it had shrunk below $1.3 billion at the end of 1967—and induced countries leaving the area to take dollars instead, which they could then use to buy gold from the United States. In essence, it was the overhang of *British* dollars which was collapsing—and most of those dollars had been provided by the United States and other countries under the massive lines of credit made available to protect sterling during that period, some of which were earmarked precisely against a drawdown of sterling area balances. It was thus U.S. dollars which were largely financing the purchases of U.S. gold, through the outer sterling area and then Britain itself.

These conversions thus stemmed basically from the dissolution of the sterling area. The United Kingdom suffered from a gradual movement of countries out of the sterling area until 1967–68, as noted above, due mainly to the weakening of trade and financial ties between Britain and individual sterling countries relative to their growing ties with the United States, Japan, and continental Europe—a weakening of the "national size" criterion. In addition, the historically inverse correlation between the U.K. and overseas sterling area payments positions, which was one of the primary economic bases of the sterling area, had weakened significantly since the 1950s.[21] Since both trends seemed permanent, they alone—as well as Britain's failing capacity to meet many of the key currency criteria—should have initiated much earlier U.K. efforts to shed sterling's roles. But wholesale defections from the sterling area were finally triggered by uncertainty about the future parity of sterling, which continued after the U.K. devaluation of 1967, combined with the demonstrated reality that sterling could be devalued. Further "diversification" of the remaining sterling balances was clearly coming, as a result of both the short-term concern about the stability of sterling and the culmination of longer-term trends away from the close economic and political ties of several sterling countries to the United Kingdom.

So the United Kingdom clearly faced a long-term problem, and needed to act accordingly. But the United States also faced a problem. Britain still had sizable dollar holdings, many of which could well be converted in the future as the outer sterling area countries

---

21. See Richard N. Cooper, "The Balance of Payments," in Richard E. Caves, ed., *Britain's Economic Prospects* (Washington, D.C.: Brookings Institution, 1968), pp. 182–83.

continued to "diversify," and the United States was likely to go on losing reserves as the sterling area dissolved. Britain decided to respond by giving dollar-value guarantees on the bulk of the remaining sterling balances, and the United States pushed hard for what became the Basel arrangements to back up the British guarantees with a package of multilateral credits and took a large share of the package itself. (To help bring in the European creditors, the United States made several concessions on the remaining loose ends of the two-tier gold arrangements, which were being concluded at the same time.) In this way the United States also properly sought a long-term solution to deal with a potential long-term collapse of part of the dollar overhang.

Two more aggregate cases should be mentioned. In both 1961 and 1964, aggregate gold bloc surpluses exceeded the U.S. official reserve transactions deficits, which raised the possibility of conversions from the overhang (see Tables 12 and 13). In 1961, these surpluses exceeded $3 billion while the U.S. official reserve transactions deficit was only about $1.35 billion. New gold production added over $0.8 billion to world reserves, however, and Britain sold $400 million worth of gold (although the sterling area as a whole was not in deficit for the year), so U.S. gold sales were under $1 billion. Even gold bloc countries seek at least small increases in their foreign exchange holdings to build their working balances, and some of the reconstitution that took place in following years also reflected the failure of these countries to finance the usual percentage of their surpluses with gold in 1961.

In 1964, gold bloc surpluses of almost $2 billion exceeded the U.S. official reserve transactions deficit of about $1.5 billion, but U.S. monetary gold sales were only $654 million. Gold bloc countries again financed most of their surpluses from net additions to world monetary gold holdings ($0.6 billion) and U.K. gold losses ($0.35 billion). Again they built up their dollar balances temporarily, converting some of them into U.S. gold during the following year. Since over one-half of the U.S. deficit in 1964 occurred during the fourth quarter, the carryover of gold purchases into 1965 was not unusual.

These cases, incidentally, reveal the importance which changes in world monetary gold holdings had on the demand for gold from the United States in the pre–March 1968 period.[22] Changes in gold plus

22. Høst-Madsen, *op. cit.*, p. 250, concluded that the United States could have incurred annual liquidity deficits of "a little more than $1 billion" in the early 1960s, without losing gold, partly because annual additions to world gold reserves averaged about $460 million.

SDR, or SDR alone, would presumably have similar effects on any international roles of the dollar in the future. The greater the amount of new nondollar liquidity coming into the system, the less likely are conversions from the overhang triggered by outer dollar area deficits with the gold bloc or perhaps even nondollar "reconstitution" by gold bloc countries. A reserve currency country thus has a national interest in the growth of world reserves from sources *other* than its own currency—which explains part of the U.S. support for SDRs from the mid-1960s—at the same time it fears that the competitive effect of such growth may hurt its national interests.

There were a few other cases where specific gold bloc countries bought gold in excess of their current surpluses in years when aggregate U.S. gold losses were less than the current U.S. deficit (see Table 14). All of them fit the pattern already described in which the conversions represented reconstitution of previous reserve asset compositions. Austria made such conversions in 1959, from dollars earned during 1958. Belgium did so in 1959 and 1960, the Netherlands in 1959, Switzerland in 1958, 1960, and 1964 from dollars earned in the preceding years, and Spain in 1963 from dollars earned in 1959–61. France did so only in 1965–66, as discussed above.

The one case of a country moving from dollar area to gold bloc is Italy, if one sees it as having been in the dollar area from 1964 to 1966. Italy's foreign exchange ratio had risen from 31 per cent at the end of 1963 to 44 per cent in 1965, after the United States in early 1964 organized a major rescue package for the lira when Italy's balance of payments temporarily shifted into large deficit. The Italian ratio began to decline in 1966, however, and by the end of 1970 had fallen back to 30 per cent—and it bought gold from the United States in both 1968 and 1969, despite running overall payments deficits in both years. The ambiguity in categorizing such a country obviously reflects the lack of institutionalization of the gold bloc and the dollar area, and points out the difficulty in using the concept; a policy-maker in 1965 might have erroneously "counted on" Italy to finance its payments surplus with dollars. *Ex post facto*, it is simply a matter of taste whether to pick 1966 as the year in which Italy shifted back to the gold bloc, after a short life in the dollar area, or to treat its gold purchases as reconstitution of its gold ratio of several years earlier. At the time, however, the United States could easily have made the mistake of regarding Italy as in the dollar area to stay.

Prior to 1962, the United States also made large gold sales to the United Kingdom. As the holder of the reserve pool for another currency area, it tended to finance virtually all of the surpluses of the area with gold. Even in years when the sterling area was in deficit,

Britain might buy gold from the United States to maintain a high gold ratio among its remaining reserves. In addition, some of the U.K. gold purchases prior to the formation of the gold pool in 1961 reflected the Bank of England's intervention in the private gold market, the gold losses from which were then replenished from the United States. Some of the U.S. sales to Britain thus really met private demand.

Since late 1964, the United Kingdom has not tried to maintain a high gold ratio. An increasing percentage of its reserves during the three-year period before the 1967 devaluation, and for some time thereafter, was mortgaged to its foreign short-term creditors and the International Monetary Fund. All of these debts bore interest, and the net cost to Britain would have been extremely high had it held gold. In addition, it realized that any large gold purchases could upset the gold market and contribute to the overall shakiness of the international monetary system—in which sterling itself was the weakest link.

Finally, and most important, the United Kingdom was heavily reliant on the United States for credit and for help in mobilizing international support for sterling. Any gold purchases from the United States during this period would have been unthinkable. The run on U.S. gold by other sterling countries in 1968, as described above, already came pretty close to violating this precept. After the United Kingdom was forced to give dollar-value guarantees on the bulk of its sterling liabilities under the Basel arrangements in 1968, it quite properly decided to hold virtually all of its reserves in dollars on the time-honored banking principle of matching up assets and liabilities. It is for these reasons, rather than any underlying national desire to change, that Britain (and the sterling area with it) was forced into de facto merger with the dollar area.

The postwar history of the *private* overhang reveals steady increases in each year from 1948 through 1969, with the exception of declines of under $100 million in 1953 and 1960, and then massive declines in 1970 and 1971. There were also several shorter periods when there were rather sharp declines, such as July 1960—January 1961 ($857 million), May–September 1962 ($583 million), and the first quarter of 1967 ($673 million); each, however, was followed immediately by a resumption of the long-run trend.[23]

The 1960–61 decline was due almost entirely to speculation against

---

23. Declines also frequently occur each November-December due to the window-dressing activities of some foreign banks, which are reversed after the turn of the year. They are ignored here.

the dollar. From June 1960 through February 1961, the actual forward exchange rate of the dollar was well below the rate predicted by the differential between U.S. and U.K. Treasury bill rates. The average difference was about 0.6 per cent, which provided the basis for Stein's analysis, supported by subsequent events, that such a difference would explain virtually all of the withdrawals.[24] The "discount" on the dollar disappeared shortly after President Kennedy presented the first comprehensive U.S. balance-of-payments program, "helped" immeasurably by the long-expected revaluation of the mark in early March and the associated advent of a sterling crisis which culminated that summer.

The decline in the second half of 1962 was related to renewed speculation against the dollar in the wake of the devaluation of the Canadian dollar and the sharp decline in the U.S. stock market in June. This flurry was halted largely by President Kennedy's reaffirmation to Europe, via Telstar, of U.S. determination to maintain the parity of the dollar.[25] Neither the 1960–61 nor the 1962 decline appears related to relative monetary conditions in the United States and abroad.

Monetary conditions in the United States go a long way toward explaining the decline of early 1967, however. Instead of dropping toward year's end, as usual, private foreign dollar balances climbed by almost $800 million in the fourth quarter of 1966—almost entirely because U.S. head offices imported Eurodollars from their foreign branches to meet domestic demand for loans to counter the credit crunch of 1966. With a return to more normal domestic monetary conditions in the first quarter of 1967, the U.S. banks reduced their liabilities to their foreign branches by over $600 million (and by another $650 million in April and May), explaining virtually the entire overall decline.

Much the same pattern prevailed in 1970, but on a much larger and more prolonged scale. Excessively tight money in the United States triggered massive borrowings ($6.3 billion) by U.S. banks from their foreign branches, offsetting an almost identical buildup in loans ($7 billion) by the banks to their foreign branches in 1968 and accounting for a large share of the net drawdown in private "foreign"

24. The data are presented in Stein, *op. cit.*, p. 59. Kenen, *op. cit.*, p. 157, concluded that interest rates at this time did have an effect on outflows of U.S. captial although he regarded his conclusions as "not decisive."
25. See the "Treasury and Federal Reserve Foreign Exchange Operations" reports in the *Federal Reserve Bulletin*, Sept. 1962 and March 1963.

dollar holdings for the year. Similar borrowing by U.S. banks from their foreign branches accounted for a similar portion of the private "foreign" runoff in 1971, though they were of a smaller absolute magnitude ($3.5 billion through the first three quarters) since the existing stock of previous loans to the branches had been largely exhausted in 1970. Other private foreign holdings also declined as a result of the relatively easy monetary conditions in the United States. Speculation against the dollar, which proved to be well-placed, certainly played a part in the decline at least in 1971—but a surprisingly large share of the total shift can be attributed solely to interest rate differentials and the other effects of tight US monetary policy.

Most important, however, these reductions in private dollar balances did not lead to comparable conversions into U.S. reserves. There has been a high degree of complementarity between foreign official and private holdings, on a global basis, and the monetary authorities in virtually all countries have apparently concluded that most reductions in private dollar balances are likely to be temporary phenomena.[26] Hence they have simply held them, pending a rebuilding of working balances by the private sector. Indeed, as U.S. annual reserve losses *never* exceeded the corresponding net liquidity deficit, it is clear that the total overhang, private plus official, never "collapsed" even in any single year. Private and official dollar balances have never declined together in a single year, reinforcing the conclusion that the two are highly complementary.

U.S. Policy Toward the Overhang in the Past

The historical record thus indicates clearly that the overhang did not cause much of an economic problem for the United States in the past, when the dollar was convertible into U.S. reserve assets. Despite continued warnings of intensifying degree, the overhang never collapsed. It did not do so in the early years of the gold exchange standard, when the U.S. gold stock was sufficiently sizable that large conversions could in fact have taken place. It did not do so after the system entered the "crisis zone." It did not even do so in 1970–71, in the face of huge U.S. payments deficits and a massive shift of dollars from private to official hands. The several years in which the overhang did decline all occurred during the middle 1960s, a period

---

26. See Ralph C. Bryant, "Dollar Balances and the U.S. Balance of Payments," unpublished Ph.D. thesis, Yale University, 1966, pp. 304–16.

in which the United States also adopted a series of balance-of-payments "programs" largely to avoid even larger conversions.

One can thus again discern three distinct periods in the evolution of a key currency. In the first phase, its liquidity ratio and ability to meet the other key currency criteria are so strong that others have little or no incentive to convert. In its latter phases the ratio is sufficiently weak that others have an incentive not to convert for fear of wrecking the system, being blamed for doing so, and perhaps forcing unwanted appreciation of their own exchange rates. There is a middle period, however, in which the overhang may be a real risk to the center country.[27]

But U.S. policy feared the overhang through all three periods, and took policy measures to deal with it. We must therefore ask whether these measures were unneeded and therefore levied costs on the U.S. because of erroneous views concerning the overhang, or whether it was the measures which prevented the overhang from becoming a problem. In either case, of course, the measures levied costs on the U.S. economy which must be set against the benefits to it of the continuing key currency roles of the dollar.

U.S. policy clearly erred in thinking that relatively high U.S. interest rates were needed to keep the overhang from collapsing, since it is now quite clear that (a) very few official dollars move as a result of interest rates and (b) moves of private dollars in response thereto are temporary, and likely to remain in foreign reserves until shifted back into private hands. And the presence of the overhang clearly pushed some U.S. policy-makers toward the conservative side in formulating economic policy. It provided an additional argument in favor of caution in the intra-governmental decision-making machinery, particularly with regard to keeping interest rates high.[28] It apparently played a role in bringing on the recession of 1960–61, and

27. Otmar Emminger agrees, arguing in 1967 that "the gold exchange standard *in its present phase* provides additional pressure for discipline." See his "The Gold Exchange Standard, Reserve Currencies and International Monetary Reform," an address to the European Luncheon Club of the British Council of the European Movement, Jan. 25, 1967, p. 9.

28. John Kenneth Galbraith argues that the balance-of-payments situation— specifically buttressed by the existence of the overhang, because of the widespread view that U.S. interest rates affect the level of foreign dollar balances —gave opponents of low interest rates their "most telling argument" in the face of conflicting domestic requirements in the early 1960s. See his "The Balance of Payments—A Political and Administrative View," *Review of Economics and Statistics*, Vol. XLVI (1964), pp. 118–19.

delaying the return to full employment in the early 1960s.[29] These U.S. policies of the early 1960s were therefore unnecessary, and indicate the excessive impact which fear of conversions from the overhang can have on policy.[30]

In addition, all the U.S. balance-of-payments "programs" were adopted, in part, because of fears that the overhang would collapse. Both the 1961 and 1963 programs occurred at a time when there had been no significant conversions from the official overhang, however. In addition, both programs focused on raising interest rates although, as just pointed out, such steps were unnecessary to avoid problems from the overhang.

29. Henry C. Wallich, a member of the Council of Economic Advisors under President Eisenhower, "Government Action," in Seymour E. Harris, ed., *The Dollar in Crisis* (New York: Harcourt, Brace & World, 1961), pp. 98–100, notes that the threat of gold losses (which include conversions from the overhang, as well as financing for current deficits) "lent considerable force" to the arguments for a balanced budget for fiscal 1960, which helped nip recovery in the bud and generate the recession. Richard N. Cooper, a member of the Council staff in the early Kennedy administration, puts it even more strongly: "The United States took deflationary measures in the severe budget of 1959 largely as a result of balance of payments considerations." See his "Comment," *Journal of Political Economy*, Vol. LXXV, No. 4, Part II, Supplement (August 1967), p. 542. Cooper also notes that the public attitude toward gold losses "played a major role" in the cautious Kennedy policies toward much-needed domestic expansion, supporting the point made by Galbraith in the previous footnote. With regard to the Kennedy administration's policies and the overhang, one outsider saw the failure to reduce the unemployment rate to 4 per cent as "directly attributable to the large short-term capital obligations of the United States which the key-currency status had brought about." See Herbert Grubel, "The Benefits and Costs of Being the World Banker," *National Banking Review*, Vol. II, No. 2 (December 1964), p. 203. Theodore Sorensen, *Kennedy, passim,* supports these conclusions.

30. The belief of the authorities that interest rates *did* have an effect on the private overhang is reflected in the writing of Robert Gemill of the Board of Governors of the Federal Reserve System. See his "Interest Rates and Foreign Dollar Balances," *Journal of Finance*, September 1961, esp. pp. 371–75. But Gemmill himself did not find much correlation between deviations from trend of private foreign dollar balances and interest rate differentials, and admitted that "a substantial portion of the decline [in the balances from mid-1960 to early 1961] could have been accounted for by speculative movements." His policy conclusion (p. 376) was: the sum which might be moved ("less than $1 billion") was so small relative to the U.S. payments position that as long as there was confidence in the dollar, major changes in U.S. reserves were likely to result only from changes in its current payments position, and the role of the United States as a reserve center did not, at the time anyway, "appear to impose significant restrictions on the range of domestic financial policies which this country is able to pursue."

The February 1965 program, which introduced widespread capital restraints, was mainly triggered by the French and Spanish purchases of 1962–64. Virtually all of these conversions reflected current U.S. deficits, however, and (except on the already discredited gross liquidity definition) the current position was improving markedly: 1964 saw a trade surplus of $6.7 billion, the largest of the entire post-reconstruction period, and basic balance; and the official reserve transactions deficit had fallen sharply in both 1963 and 1964, as was pointed out by President Johnson in his balance-of-payments message. Fears of conversions from the overhang must therefore have been a major motivation for the program, along with a belief that further improvement of the official reserve transaction and liquidity balances would help avert them. But our analysis shows that there had been virtually no conversions from the overhang prior to 1965, and those which had occurred were simply reconstitutions of previous gold ratios by gold bloc countries, which had limited scope and were unlikely to be determined by U.S. action. Indeed, such conversions took place on a sizable scale (by France, Spain, and Austria) for the first time soon *after* the program was announced, and continued until they had restored their desired gold ratios.[31]

The January 1968 program was based on fear of a collapse of both the private and official overhangs in the wake of the sterling devaluation of November 1967 and the gold rush by private buyers which succeeded it. Again, there had been no recent purchases of U.S. gold from the overhang—none at all since the French had finally reached their desired gold ratio in 1965—and the United States had lost less gold to monetary authorities ($152 million) in 1967 than in any year since sizable deficits began in 1958. There was a critical international monetary problem, to be sure, but it was systemic in nature—the growing view that a world liquidity shortage would force an increase in the official price of gold. The answer to the problem was thus systemic in nature, and was indeed achieved in March 1968 by the institution of the two-tier gold system and the Stockholm agreement on SDRs ten days later. The problem of collapses from the dollar overhang due to the dissolution of the sterling area had not even begun, but it too was of course a systemic problem and was subse-

---

31. The major effect of the 1965 measures was to reduce U.S. short-term claims on foreigners and liquid U.S. liabilities to private foreigners by similar amounts. Thus it had no net impact on either the official reserve transactions balance or the most important liquidity ratio (or even the net liquidity balance, though it was not in use at the time), and provided no significant support for the international roles of the dollar either.

quently dealt with in mid-1968 by a systemic measure—the Basel arrangements.

Even as late as August 1971, when dollar convertibility had become largely nominal, the Nixon administration claimed publicly that it reversed its economic policy and adopted a wage-price freeze in large part to prevent a collapse of the overhang.[32] But it is clear that there had been no conversions from the overhang, despite huge deficits in the current U.S. payments position, and were no signs of impending collapse in the future.

These various measures were adopted because there was a widespread belief that the best way to prevent collapse of the overhang was to bring the current payments position into equilibrium. This view was held despite the fact that there has been no consistent relationship between foreign gold conversions and the size of the U.S. deficit, let alone conversions from the overhang and that deficit. The reason, in part, is that increases in private foreign holdings of dollars played a sharply varying role in financing the liquidity deficit. But we could hardly expect to find a consistent systemic relationship, because the distribution of surpluses which mirrors the U.S. *current* deficit is the basic determinant of reserve losses. When gold bloc countries run the surpluses, the losses are a high percentage of the deficit; when dollar area countries run them, most of the deficits are financed by foreign holdings of dollars. For the overhang, however, conversions arise only from the four sources already mentioned: overseas dollar area (ODA) deficits coupled with gold bloc surpluses beyond those equivalent to the current U.S. deficit; country shifts from dollar area to gold bloc; one-shot increases in gold bloc countries' gold ratios; or dollar sales by private foreigners which wind up in gold bloc reserves. Therefore, achievement of balance in the U.S. current payments position will prevent conversions from the overhang *only* if it pre-

32. As indicated throughout this book, I reject the validity of this claim. For testimony on the decisiveness of external considerations in the Nixon New Economic Policy of August 1971, explicitly including the overhang, however, see p. 4 of the *Economic Report of the President*, 1972, and pp. 167–69 of the accompanying *Annual Report of the Council of Economic Advisors*. Some administration officials have claimed that the United Kingdom triggered the U.S. actions by seeking to convert all of its dollars into gold on August 13, 1971. In fact, the United Kingdom sought only a gold-value guarantee on part of its dollar assets—just as the United States had insisted on such a guarantee on *all* the sterling it held "to help the British" during the prolonged sterling crises of 1964–67. Neither the British nor any other major country bought gold in the period immediately preceeding the U.S. suspension of convertibility, and there is no evidence that any were planning to do so.

vents one or more of these four developments. The successive balance-of-payments program adopted by the United States in the 1960s can thus be judged successful only if they contributed to doing so.

The first possibility is that U.S. deficits induce deficits in other dollar area countries, at least part of which generate additional surpluses in gold bloc countries. If this were true, a reduction of U.S. deficits would reduce the threat from the overhang. (If ODA countries simply pass on their current dollar earnings to gold bloc countries, the overhang is not affected; the U.S. deficit would be matched by a gold bloc surplus through a triangular payments pattern.) Two analytical steps are required to see whether this pattern holds: to find whether U.S. deficits do in fact generate deficits in ODA countries, and whether ODA deficits generate additional gold bloc surpluses.

In the aggregate, however, we find a fairly high degree of complementarity between the payments positions of the United States and the ODA and an even higher degree of complementarity between *changes* in their position—as should be the case for a currency area.[33] This suggests that, at least in the aggregate, deteriorations in the U.S. position relate to *improvements* in the ODA position. In no year has a deterioration in the U.S. payments position been accompanied by a deterioration in the ODA payments position. The high degree of U.S.-ODA complementarity suggests that the main offset to an improvement in the U.S. payments position will be a deterioration in the ODA position, not in the gold bloc position, and hence will have only a minor effect in reducing the overhang by drawing down any dollars held beyond working-balance needs in that area.

This overall relationship might not hold for individual countries, however. There is little hard evidence, but one study suggests that three dollar area members—Japan, Sweden, and Denmark—have in the past tended to experience import increases greater than their

33. See Table 12. There was a simple correlation of −0.37 between the payments position of the United States and the ODA for the 1958–67 period. By coincidence, this is precisely the same correlation found by Cooper, "The Balance of Payments," p. 182, between the trade balances of the United Kingdom and the outer sterling countries in the 1950–59 period, which provided a continuing rationale for the existence of the sterling area at that time. The correlation presented here is even more relevant, because it is between *payments* balances rather than simply *trade* balances. I found a much better fit between *changes* in U.S. and ODA payments positions, where the simple correlation was also much stronger at −0.61.

export increases over the short run.[34] If their *overall* payments positions react similarly, if their reaction to increased earnings from the
United States parallels their reactions to aggregate earnings increases, and if some part of the induced deficits accrue to gold bloc
reserves, then increases in the U.S. deficit might lead to transfers
from that part of the overhang held by these countries. Available
data do not permit comprehensive study of the geographical distribution of the added expenditures, but the study just mentioned reveals
the share of four gold bloc countries (Belgium France, Italy, Netherlands) in their marginal imports in the 1950–62 period at 16.5 per
cent for Sweden, 9.6 per cent for Denmark, and 2.4 per cent for
Japan.[35]

Combining the overall "reflection ratios" and marginal import
shares, this particular study concluded that the trade balance of the
four gold bloc countries studied (Belgium, France, Italy, Netherlands) would be improved by 21 per cent of the expansion of exports
of Sweden, 20 per cent of Denmark, 15 per cent of Japan, 12 per
cent of Germany, 7 per cent of Canada, and 6 per cent of Norway.
These percentages would probably be increased, at least for the
European dollar area members, by the updating of the data and by
the inclusion of the other major bloc countries (Switzerland, Austria,
and Portugal). The payment ratios would probably be further increased by the importance of Switzerland in capital movements and
by all of the countries in tourism. But we would still not know
whether the combined effects of an increase in the earnings of individual ODA countries would generate overall deficits in their position which would transmit dollars to the reserves of gold bloc countries. The same study, which is limited to trade effects, does suggest
that such a result occurred in the case of Japan, to a very small
extent,[36] and not in any of the others, and the dramatic shift in

34. Rolf Piekarz and Lois Ernstorff Steckler, "Induced Changes in Trade and
    Payments," *Review of Economics and Statistics*, Vol. XLIX, No. (Nov. 4,
    1967), p. 520. Note that these are trade, not *payments*, balances. Neverthe-
    less, they suggest possible swings in the latter. In the early 1960s, Japan may
    also have borrowed in the United States to finance *ex ante* deficits, and hence
    generated additional pressure on U.S. reserves.
35. Piekarz and Steckler, *op. cit.*, p. 521.
36. *Ibid.*, p. 524, concludes that a one-unit increase in U.S. imports from Japan
    would lead to a 1.25 unit deterioration of the Japanese trade balance. Since
    15 per cent of Japan's marginal imports come from the gold bloc countries
    studied, a figure which should be adjusted upward as noted in the text, a
    pass-through to the gold bloc of about 5 per cent of the marginal increases
    in U.S. imports from Japan might be expected.

Japan's international position since the period covered by this study throws doubt on the present validity of even this conclusion.

The sketchy evidence which is available thus throws serious doubt on the possibility that deterioration in the U.S. payments position generates improvements in the gold bloc payments position through induced losses of *outstanding* dollars by dollar area countries, or that improvement in the U.S. position will induce reserve gains by the ODA. In the aggregate, such losses or gains appear highly unlikely on any significant scale. An improvement in the U.S. payments position is thus unlikely to be required to forestall conversions from the overhang via this route.

The second possibility, that improvement in the U.S. balance of payments might induce countries not to leave the dollar area, is much more likely. In the broadest sense, U.S. failure to continue to meet the key currency criteria outlined in Chapters 4–6 might persuade countries to "give up" on the dollar. If the dollar appeared likely to depreciate too much in terms of gold bloc currencies, countries which were members of the dollar area, and especially those which had important economic relations outside the area, might be unwilling to accept the decline in value of their (dollar) reserves.

Excessive U.S. inflation might especially induce countries to shift to the gold bloc. If intra-bloc exchange rates remained fixed while inter-bloc adjustments were achieved by exchange-rate changes, a member country would have to accept "imported inflation" from the United States if it remained in the currency area but could let its exchange rate appreciate if it went outside. It might have a similar reaction if it deemed inflows of capital from the United States to be excessive, and again might prefer either to let its exchange rate appreciate relative to the dollar or to escape the discriminatory arrangements which favored such inflows.[37] Canada, the major country most closely tied to the U.S. economy, has in fact floated its exchange rate on two separate and prolonged occasions—mainly because of long-term capital inflows from the United States in 1950, mainly because of U.S. inflation and short-term capital inflows in

37. The discriminatory favoritism could, however, presumably be "escaped" without a shift out of the dollar area. Germany never "benefited" from such favored treatment, for example, and apparently never had any desire to do so. Several other dollar countries which did not receive favored treatment, however, such as Norway and Sweden, probably would have preferred to get it—and some gold bloc countries, such as Belgium and Spain, when it still fit that category, explicitly requested favoritism. Spain in fact shifted from the gold bloc to the dollar area in return for being shifted to a more favorable category under the U.S. direct investment controls in 1970.

1970. It is possible that countries which appreciated their exchange rates under such circumstances would continue to hold their reserves in dollars, as Canada has done, but the likelihood of their leaving the dollar area in its financial sense is heightened if they leave it in its adjustment sense.

The limited data available, from earlier years, provide little evidence that countries have in fact moved away from the dollar because of U.S. deficits. Of eleven countries tested through 1965, including four of the major dollar area countries (Germany, Japan, Canada, Sweden), Hagemann found that only Japan tended to reduce its foreign exchange ratio in response to U.S. liquidity deficits.[38] Using data through March 1968 for thirteen countries, including the same four dollar countries plus Denmark, Makin found that only France and Denmark tended to reduce their dollar ratios in response to U.S. liquidity deficits; Japan no longer appeared to do so.[39] Of course, smaller dollar area countries are less likely to be inhibited by crisis zone considerations than are large countries, so these findings do not dispel the possibility of sales from the oevrhang in response to large U.S. deficits. A country might also be tempted to leave the area if it disapproved of being "forced to finance" U.S. foreign policy which it did not support or, conversely, if it failed to receive U.S. support for its own policies.[40]

The third case, an increase in the gold ratios of countries already in the gold bloc, can occur for several reasons. It is certainly possible that fears about the future stability of the key currmecy, and hence the currcnt payments position, might have an impact on "reconstitution" decisions and contribute to conversions from the overhang. A U.S. move into surplus might also draw down the overhang directly, and hence reduce the potential for such reconstitution, although I have just shown that most of the foreign deterioration would take place in the ODA and that little effect on the overhang could be expected on that score.

---

38. Hagemann, *op. cit.*, p. 69.
39. John H. Makin, "The Composition of International Reserve Holdings, A Problem of Choice Involving Risk," *American Economic Review*, Vol. LXI, No. 5 (December 1971), p. 827. The Netherlands tended to *increase* its dollar ratio when the U.S. liquidity deficit rose, displaying a sense of major systemic responsibility even though it is a small country.
40. The decisions of Malaysia and Singapore to leave the sterling area were clearly related to Britain's abandonment of its military commitments to them. This, of course, relates broadly to the decline in Britain's world political role, a major reserve currency attribute. The formal entry of Germany into the dollar area was directly related to the maintenance of U.S. forces in Germany.

I have also suggested that deterioration in the United States payments position, by threatening confidence in the future stability of the dollar, can induce private shifts into other assets. All the major crises before 1971, however, were almost wholly movements out of sterling or other currencies *into* dollars and other assets, or of various national currencies into gold, with very little shifting from dollars into other currencies. (A partial exception was the large movement into marks in early 1969, but this was almost wholly speculation on a mark revaluation rather than on a dollar devaluation). Furthermore, the major pre-1971 "dollar crisis"—in March 1968—was quelled not by any new U.S. payments measures, despite the widespread awareness that the U.S. deficit had skyrocketed, but by a change in the rules of the international monetary system. And the adoption of the two-tier gold system itself minimized, if it did not eliminate, the likelihood of renewed movements from dollars into gold in the future. From early 1970 through mid-1971, of course, there was a large movement of dollars from private to official foreigners, partly due to correct anticipation of the eventual dollar devaluation.

It is thus quite possible that a widely perceived outlook for improvement in the current U.S. balance of payments, by reducing concerns over the likelihood of an eventual change in the dollar's convertibility at fixed prices, will avoid selling pressure from the overhang. The U.S. balance-of-payments "programs" of the mid-1960s, to a significant extent, altered perceptions in this direction for at least short periods (despite their small real effects) and hence may have helped avoid conversions. The United States was apparently able to convince foreign officials that the latest "program" was sufficient to deal with the problem, or at least provide those officials with arguments of sufficient plausibility to that effect that they could credibly argue the case at home—and perhaps even convince their private sectors that stability was likely. The foreign officials may well have been part of an implicit conspiracy in promulgating such views, both because their more sophisticated knowledge of the issues made them aware of the difficulties of truly solving the problems within the existing system and because some of them liked the U.S. deficits sufficiently well that they did not really wish to see them eliminated.

Leverage

The overhang does of course provide foreign holders of dollars with a certain amount of additional leverage over U.S. policy.[41] Germany,

41. President Kennedy clearly thought so. See Sorenson, *Kennedy*, pp. 401 and 570, and Schlesinger, *A Thousand Days*, p. 611.

holding $25 billion *in dollars,* clearly possesses greater leverage vis-à-vis the United States, all other things being equal, than it would if it were simply running current balance-of-payments surpluses. And given the importance of the overhang to the entire international monetary system, as well as its political significance in symbolizing the dominance of the dollar, it was inevitable that the United States would become increasingly subject to "multilateral surveillance" of its policies.

At the same time, however, the existence of the overhang also adds to U.S. leverage. Long before August 1971, most foreign monetary officials had become well aware that the United States might under certain circumstances use its "financial deterrent"—a gold embargo plus willingness to let the exchange rate of the dollar float —if the demand for gold conversions became too great.[42] In order to preserve the gold convertibility of their dollar balances, the exchange rates between their currencies and the dollar, and international monetary stability generally, foreign officials started to err on the side of caution, at least after the institution of the two-tiered gold system in 1968. Even some gold bloc countries, such as Switzerland, did not convert all the dollars they accrued as a result of current imbalances. Similarly, dollar area countries were inhibited about leaving the area—especially Germany, whose agreements with the United States on the subject were explicit. Small actual conversions by peripheral countries thus became unlikely to snowball, and in fact might have even further deterred others. Paradoxically, the existence of the overhang may have given the United States extra leeway in its balance-of-payments policy, once the system had entered the "crisis zone," precisely because of the dollar's international roles.[43] Indeed, the most significant fact about the overhang in 1971 was that it did *not* collapse.

42. David Kelley in "Two-Tier Gold: Who Was Right?" *The Banker,* Vol. 118, No. 505 (July 1968), p. 601, notes on the basis of interviews with European central bankers that the U.S. Treasury had convinced European central bankers in 1968 that "gold would be embargoed in case of a run on the dollar." Further evidence of this conviction came at that time from Franz Aschinger, "Das Problem des Wahrungsgolde," *Neue Zürcher Zeitung,* August 17, 1968, who anticipated such an embargo if the U.S. gold stock were to fall to $10 billion. Events in 1971 proved him to be remarkably accurate, although the United States instituted the gold embargo *without* the development of any significant new demand for gold.
43. Harry Johnson noted in 1967 that "the gold reserve policies of the European countries in the recent past have been carefully designed to put pressure on the United States by threatening an international liquidity crisis without actually either bringing such a crisis about or running the danger of so doing, and there is little probability of such a crisis occurring because it is in the interest of no country that it should." See his "Theoretical Problems of the

These opposing tendencies changed over time, however. Up to some point, clearly until 1959 and perhaps into the early 1960s, there were no foreign fears of a U.S. embargo on conversions—but, for much of this same time, neither would the United States have been very concerned about reserve losses resulting from them. There may have been a period in the middle 1960s, before the overhang exceeded U.S. reserves, when net leverage tipped in favor of foreign dollar-holders—and the "programs" in these years were caused at least in part by foreign pressure for the United States to "do something" about its balance of payments. But when the U.S. gold stock fell below the level of foreign dollar holdings, the credibility of the deterrent increased sharply, and the pendulum had probably shifted the other way at least by 1967. The relatively small U.S. gold losses to foreign monetary authorities in 1967 and 1968, despite the ballooning of the deficit in 1967 on any definition to its highest level since 1960, and the U.S. ability to dictate the institution of the two-tier gold system in early 1968, bear out this conclusion.[44] Even more striking was the tiny share of the huge deficits of 1970–71 financed by gold sales. Once the possibility of an embargo approached, the likelihood of conversions receded.

There is an intermediate case, however, where *individual* foreign dollar holders may retain a leverage advantage, particularly if they are not large enough really to undermine the system. If one or a few countries began a series of conversions, each of them not too large and/or spread over time, the United States would probably find it difficult to justify an act as drastic as an embargo. Even as far back as 1965–66, France and Spain would probably have been unable to

International Monetary System," *Pakistan Development Review*, Spring 1967, pp. 23–25. This conclusion was by no means invalidated by the events of either 1968 or 1971; the 1968 crisis was due to private speculation on gold, which the officials tried to hold back far too long, and in 1971 the United States decided that its *own* interests called for suspension of convertibility with very little pressure on U.S. reserves from the overhang, or even from dollars generated by its massive current deficits.

44. In 1967, Treasury gold sales to foreigners slightly exceeded $1 billion. Almost $900 million, however, represented the U.S. share of the losses of the gold pool and hence represented private gold purchases (although not a "collapse" of the private overhang, since private foreign dollar holdings rose by over $1.5 billion for the year as a whole, half of which came in the fourth quarter when the major monetary upheavals began). Only Italy, Switzerland, and Belgium among the major countries bought gold from the United States—and the amounts were small, much less than their overall surpluses for the year. In 1968, $0.9 billion of the total $1.3 billion of U.S. gold sales to foreigners went through the pool before it was abolished on March 17.

complete their conversions had many others followed suit. The United States could be victimized by "salami tactics," although the opportunity for such "free riding" probably recedes as the system moves further into the crisis zone, paradoxically increasing its stability.[45] Although no general conclusion on this subject can command full confidence, it is most likely that individual (especially smaller) foreign countries still wielded additional leverage over the United States before the suspension of convertibility in 1971, whereas the galaxy of foreign dollar-holders taken together, or even a large group of them such as the European Community, did not do so to a very significant degree. In short, monetary leverage appears to center on small creditors and large debtors.

This suggests that multilateral surveillance carried out through international organizations with wide membership, such as the OECD, IMF, BIS, or Group of Ten, did not influence U.S. policy as much as bilateral pressures from individual dollar holders backed up by threats (explicit or implicit) to buy gold from the United States if no action is taken. The U.S. national interest, on this criterion at least, thus lies in maximizing the use of multilateral surveillance of the monetary system so that each country is held responsible by all other major countries for the impact of its actions on the system.

Summary and Outlook

We can use the foregoing analytical framework to assess the outlook for both the existing overhang and the possible re-creation of new overhangs even if the present one is eliminated or significantly reduced. Both will play an important role in my conclusions regarding the needed reforms of the international monetary system, and particularly the interest of the United States in those reforms.

While the dollar remains inconvertible into U.S. reserve assets, the overhang cannot of course represent any threat to those reserves. The United States may, however, have to restore at least some measure of convertibility in any reformed system. And even when the dollar is inconvertible into U.S. reserves, significant conversions from the overhang can produce sizable depreciation of the dollar. In some circumstances, the United States might welcome such an event. In other circumstances, however, particularly when it has restored full employment and still faces sizable inflationary pressures, such forced depreciation would be highly unwelcome because

45. Officer and Willett, *op. cit.* Some "nibbling" at the U.S. gold stock did continue right up to the suspension of convertibility in August 1971.

it would reduce domestic welfare and undermine the objectives of internal economic policy. Precipitate dollar depreciation, caused by foreign "dumping" of dollars on the exchange markets, could also seriously upset the stability of the entire monetary system, *inter alia* fostering new capital controls, which would undermine the major U.S. interest in systemic stability (analyzed in Chapter 10). In addition, U.S. payments surpluses in such a milieu would clearly be financed by a rundown in its dollar liabilities rather than an increase in its gross reserves, and would relegate the United States to an increasingly weakened international financial position—in terms of the relationship between its level of reserves and its growing level of international transactions—despite the external strength which it would have generated. Finally, the continued existence of the overhang will continue the control of other countries over the exchange rate of the dollar, whereas we shall see in Chapter 9 that a major U.S. international monetary objective must be to regain control of that policy instrument.

The crucial question for the United States about the present overhang, under any monetary system, is whether it is (1) stable or (2) likely to collapse in amounts sufficient to undermine U.S. policy goals, or to cause sufficient displeasure in other major countries to have the same policy effects. Chapters 4–6 concluded that the ability of the United States to meet the key currency criteria, from both a political and a economic standpoint, has been waning rapidly and will continue to do so in the future. In terms of the conceptual framework presented in this chapter, this has two implications. It means that an increasing number of countries will wish to leave the dollar area. And it suggests that there may indeed be a secular shift away from dollars to other national currencies for private transactions use in international finance, so that the complementarity between private and official dollars which prevented collapse of the "private overhang" in the past may no longer prevail.

The very size to which it has grown has implications for the other two ways in which the overhang could collapse. It is clear that nondollar countries now hold far more dollars than they need as working balances. Indeed, total gold bloc holdings of all foreign exchange, still mostly dollars, exceeded $20 billion by mid-1973, so that excess alone probably approaches total U.S. reserves. So new "reconstitutions" by nondollar countries could alone have a major effect on U.S. reserves and/or the exchange rate of the dollar.

In addition, the sharp growth of their dollar holdings in recent years suggests that several dollar countries might now be willing to run sizable payments deficits for a while—even if they still seek steady secular growth in their reserves over the longer term. In mid-1972 Japan stated a desire to cut its reserves sharply, and in fact did so in 1973. German reserves far exceed German reserve targets. A number of countries with lower incomes have also experienced sharp reserve growth, and could run off some of these gains in pursuit of their development plans.

Finally, a number of countries have in recent years actively sought appreciation of their exchange rates to help them combat internal inflation. Germany, Australia, Sweden, Austria and Norway are among those which have done so. Hence there now appears to be much less reluctance around the world to lose reserves in terms of domestic economic consequences. Indeed, some countries, such as Japan in 1973, have aggressively sold their reserves to keep their exchange rates from depreciating. As long as inflation remains a major problem for individmual couunllries, such sales of reserves—mainly dollars—will remain a real possibility. The sizable increases in the reserve levels of many countries, as described in the preceding paragraph, enable them to carry out such policies.

So shifts of dollars from dollar to nondollar countries are now much more likely than in the past, compounding the problem of excess dollars already held by most nondollar countries and increasing the probability of sales from the overhang. It thus appears that both the United States and most other countries, particularly those which do not wish to be in the dollar area in the future, have a major interest in eliminating the problems caused by the present overhang.

Again, the United States should learn from the British experience. After World War II, which had triggered the development of the sterling overhang that persists to the present, there were numerous opportunities for Britain—pushed by the United States—to fund the sterling balances. Because of its desire to preserve the international roles of sterling and its political objectives in some of the key sterling countries (especially India), it decided against such an effort.[46] As a result, its economic and foreign policy faced an additional serious constraint until 1968, and Britain then had to accept highly unfavorable "consolidation" conditions in the Basel arrangements rather than the much better arrangements envisaged right after the war.

For reasons similar to their intent in dealing with the present overhang, all countries have an interest in avoiding re-creating the overhang problem in the future. It is true that the overhang may

46. See Richard N. Gardner, *Sterling-Dollar Diplomacy*, pp. 325–28.

cause no serious problems for the key currency country in its early phases, and therein lies the subtle lure to enter a role from which it becomes exceedingly difficult to turn back. And the overhang may cause no serious economic problems for the center country in the final stages of a fixed rate system, because conversion becomes impossible without destroying the system, but sizable systemic and political problems result instead. In an intermediate period, however, such as the United States experienced in the middle 1960s, the overhang may also cause serious problems for the center country—or at least raise the specter of real problems with sufficient plausibility to levy costs on that country as a result. And even more serious problems from the overhang may emerge under flexible exchange rates. The case against developing new overhangs, from the standpoints of both the center country and the system as a whole, is thus very strong.

9

The Dollar and Adjustment of the U.S. Balance of Payments

The United States, we have seen, may be able to run payments deficits without losing reserve assets because foreigners *want* to increase their holdings of dollars, or because, for narrowly national or systemic reasons, they may also be *willing* to accept additional dollars beyond the amounts they actively seek. Whatever the reason for the buildup of foreign-held dollars, they provide the United States with some clear benefits. As indicated in Chapter 7, they have permitted it to absorb real resources from the rest of the world equal roughly to the total of accumulated U.S. liquid dollar liabilities to foreigners, which reached $80 billion by the end of 1972. The real gain to the United States from that buildup of foreign dollars, however, was the avoidance of the costs of the adjustment measures which would otherwise have had to been taken, if those adjustment measures would have run counter to other U.S. policy objectives.

It is possible, however, for the dollar's international roles to generate adjustment costs for the United States if the roles themselves constrain the means by which it can adjust. This cost would loom particularly large when the United States *wanted* to adjust, to meet internal or external objectives beyond balance-of-payments equilibrium itself. There is also the possibility that the additional financing provided by the dollar simply postpones adjustment, in which case it provides a net benefit for the United States if the gains from postponement exceed the eventual adjustment cost, but a net cost if the larger action eventually required is greater than the sum of smaller actions taken earlier—all properly discounted for the time bought. To assess these effects, we must know the costs to the United States of adjustment through the different means available, to assess both the value to it of avoiding adjustment through dollar financing and the extent of the problems caused by the dollar's roles if they constrain its adjustment options. This chapter provides such an assessment.

273

Effective adjustment affects all countries, regardless of which takes the *initiative* to act. The United States may "take no action," but feels real economic effects when Germany revalues or Britain imposes an import surcharge. The United States thus *avoids* adjustment only if *all* countries fully finance their surpluses and thereby fully finance U.S. deficits. To be sure, the costs of adjustment differ, depending on who takes the initiative, because of the greater diffusion of the economic effects when others act, and the possibly significant difference in domestic political effects. In any case, we must know the costs to the United States of adjustment via the various possible methods, whether initiated by it or by others.

For a deficit country, the adjustment alternatives include: slowing down the domestic economy; a loosening of fiscal and a tightening of monetary policy to achieve simultaneously the country's domestic and international economic goals (the "policy mix" approach); incomes policies; selective measures aimed at specific external transactions; and exchange rate depreciation. For a surplus country, the opposite approaches are available. Some of these measures may of course be adopted for purely domestic reasons, such as the need to restrain price increases. If they help achieve balance-of-payments adjustment at the same time, there is no additional cost to the economy from the adjustment requirement. (We have frequently referred to cases where the same measures can promote both internal and external equilibrium as "non-dilemma" cases.) Our concern in this analysis will be only with those *additional* measures adopted *purely* for balance-of-payments reasons. Various combinations among the different methods can of course be attempted. Since the United States has used all of these devices, it provides a good test case for comparing them.

Some of the approaches can provide lasting adjustment by altering basic income and price relationships between the United States and other countries. Devaluation and successful incomes policies are the best examples. Other approaches, particularly the selective steps aimed at specific international transactions, but also the policy mix, only suppress disequilibrium temporarily or provide additional means of financing the deficits.[1] They may represent adequate policy if the major need is simply to buy time while underlying factors—such as trends in prices and productivity—are moving to restore balance

1. For a lucid presentation of the distinctions among "adjusting," "suppressing," and "financing," see Fritz Machlup, "Real Adjustment, Compensatory Corrections, and Foreign Financing of Imbalances in International Payments," in Robert E. Baldwin, et al., *Trade, Growth and the Balance of Payments* (Chicago: Rand McNally, 1965).

anyway, but they provide little lasting adjustment themselves. Buying time may even be beneficial if underlying factors fail to restore equilibrium, provided the eventual adjustment is not much costlier than it would have been at an earlier stage. The costs of particular policies must therefore be compared with their effectiveness in assessing their overall impact on U.S. adjustment, and hence on the gains of avoiding adjustment for U.S. deficits via dollar financing.

This analysis takes no position as to whether the exchange-rate changes of 1971–73 have restored equilibrium in the U.S. balance of payments. It need not do so, because the one certain feature of the external position of any country is that it will periodically move into disequilibrium, on either the surplus or deficit side, and hence have to face the perennial issues of (a) adjust or finance and (b) how to do either. The United States is no exception to this rule. The changes of the early 1970s may throw the United States into substantial surplus, or the shortcomings of internal U.S. policy may throw it back into sizable deficit. In any event, the costs of the different adjustment alternatives—and the benefits of avoiding them—will be at least as important to the United States as they have been in the past.

Any improvement in the current account,[2] with the United States at full employment, requires an equivalent reduction of domestic absorption, freeing additional U.S. production for exports of goods and services or simply reducing the consumption of imports. There would be no reduction in gross national product or increase in U.S. unemployment, however, because the reduction in domestic expenditure would be fully offset by the increase in net sales to foreigners. In actual practice, of course, payments adjustment may well commence when there is domestic unemployment, so the initial effect can be an increase in U.S. output. In that case, however, there is still a *potential* reduction in U.S. domestic expenditure which will

---

2. It is not axiomatic that a U.S. balance-of-payments deficit must be reduced through an improvement in the current account. In principle, lasting improvement could be achieved in the capital account alone. This analysis will focus on the current account, however, for several reasons. First, any measures which achieve lasting adjustment will do so via *both* the current and capital accounts; there are no such measures which in practice operate *only* on the capital account. Second, the United States (like most countries) focuses attention on its current account position in determining whether it has achieved payments equilibrium. Third, we saw in Chapter 5 that the current account (plus long-term portfolio flows) is the most important component of the payments position of a key currency country. Fourth, the analysis can be presented far more easily in terms of the current account (though the same conclusions are derived when capital flows are included).

be realized when full employment is eventually achieved. Hence there would always be a minimum cost of external adjustment equivalent to the foregone domestic consumption of goods and services, which might take place immediately or be delayed until the achievement of full employment.

In addition, most adjustment measures work at least partly by affecting relative prices between the adjusting country and the rest of the world. Adjustment for the United States would require a reduction in relative U.S. prices to improve its competitive position, turning against it the international "terms of trade"—the relationship between the prices it receives for its exports and the prices it pays for its imports. This represents a second cost which is almost certain to play a part in any adjustment, by varying degrees depending upon the nature of the adjustment measures.

Adjustment can be pursued either by engineering a reduction in *total* domestic expenditures, with an *indirect* effect on external transactions, or through measures aimed at changing international flows *directly*. Either method requires an initial effect greater than the targeted *net* improvement in the balance of payments because of the "feedback" effects from other countries. Any increase in net U.S. foreign earnings reduces net foreign earnings of other countries below what they would otherwise have been, depressing foreign incomes directly and reducing their expenditures in the United States. Such effects may also lead to contractionary policies in some other countries, because of the unfavorable effects of the U.S. moves on their balance-of-payments positions. In addition, particular U.S. policies could be emulated—or retaliated against—by other countries which perceived unfair, or simply unfavorable, effects on their own economies.

One careful econometric study estimated that U.S. exports in the early 1960s fell by 40 to 100 per cent of any decline in U.S. imports.[3] A similar study performed by the Agency for International Development produced average feedbacks of around 70 per cent for improvements in the U.S. current account vis-à-vis Europe and Japan, and even higher ratios for the most of the less developed countries with which the United States has close economic relations.[4] In addition, about 80 per cent of any improvement in the U.S. current account

---

3. Rolf Piekarz and Lois Ernstoff Steckler, "Induced Changes in Trade and Payments," *Review of Economics and Statistics*, Vol. XLIX, No. 4 (November 1967), p. 54.
4. Charles D. Hyson and Allan M. Strout, "Impact of Foreign Aid on U.S. Exports," *Harvard Business Review* (January-February 1968), pp. 63–71.

was historically offset by a deterioration in its capital account, or vice versa.[5]

The two econometric studies, however, assume that foreign countries would not let their reserves fall in the face of declines in the growth of their exports to the United States. This means that they would all take steps to counter the net payments effects on them of any U.S. actions, and the United States could gain only by increasing its share of their reduced level of foreign exchange expenditures. Assuming instead that countries would let their reserves fall (or rise less) to "permit" the U.S. improvement, which is probably more realistic for most industrialized countries at least in the short run, later versions of the AID study revealed ratios of about 60 per cent for Canada, 50 per cent for Japan, 40 to 60 per cent for most of the LDCs, but only 20 to 30 per cent for most of Europe. Since the time of the study, the increase in Japan's reserves would probably make it much more willing to "permit" U.S. adjustment and reduce its ratio closer to the European level. The weighted average feedback in this study is thus close to the lower end of the range of the Piekarz-Steckler approach.[6] But even using these lower estimates of the feedback effect, most U.S. measures would have to aim at improving its trade balance initially by about double the targeted net gain.

This discussion suggests that adjustment policy has three basic objectives. The first, of course, is to achieve the necessary adjustment itself. The second is to limit the reduction of domestic absorption as closely as possible to that needed actually to achieve the necessary transfer of production into net exports. The third objective is to find the measures whose net impact on the balance of payments most closely approximates their gross impact, to minimize changes in the flow of economic activity, and hence the level of world welfare, by directing them at countries most able and willing to accept the corresponding effects on their own payments positions.

Throughout this chapter, we will assume for illustrative purposes that the aim of the different adjustment alternatives analyzed is to improve the U.S. balance of payments by about $5 billion. Virtually all of the relationships to be discussed are linear, in any event, so the

---

5. Fritz Machlup, "The Transfer Gap of the United States," *Banca Nazionale del Lavoro Quarterly Review*, No. 86 (September 1968).

6. And the methodology by which Machlup reached his very high feedback effect is thrown into question by David Morawitz, "The Effect of Financial Capital Flows and Transfers on the U.S. Balance of Payments Current Account," *Journal of International Economics*, Vol. 1, No. 4 (November 1971), pp. 418–20.

reader can adjust the magnitudes discussed if he regards as larger or smaller the balance-of-payments improvement which is needed at any particular time. They are also reversible if the objective were to reduce a surplus instead of a deficit; opposite measures would be used, "costs" would become "benefits," and vice versa. We will also assume that the United States seeks primarily to improve its current account, especially its trade balance, since such a structural objective has clearly been present in recent policy steps and in the payments policies of most of the other industrialized countries as well. Data for 1972 will be used throughout.

Slowing Growth

Achieving a $5 billion improvement in the current account through internal deflation would require a massive contraction of the U.S. gross national product on the order of magnitude of at least $60 billion. Such a contraction would improve the trade balance through the reduction in U.S. imports resulting from the decline in domestic economic activity itself, and through the improvement in the U.S. competitive position generated by the resultant dampening of price increases. If the United States were experiencing "overfull" employment and excessive inflation, such action would of course be called for on purely domestic grounds and would help the balance of payments without representing any new policy target. Here, however, we are discussing a slowing of growth undertaken solely for balance-of-payments reasons and *beyond* that "needed" by the domestic economy.

Merchandise imports, including transportation costs, accounted in 1972 for about 5 per cent of U.S. gross national product.[7] The income elasticity of demand for imports in the United States is about 1.5, and has been even higher in recent years—reaching 2 or even more.[8] It is unclear whether these higher elasticities were a

7. Imports of all goods and services accounted for about 6 per cent of gross national product. This analysis is limited to merchandise imports—on a CIF basis, since transportation payments relate directly to the level of imports— because the other current account items respond to different variables, e.g., foreign travel payments are determined by the disposable personal income or total consumption expenditures of U.S. residents, and interest and dividends payments and receipts by the stock of assets on which they are paid and current interest rates.

8. H. S. Houthakker and Stephen P. Magee, "Income and Price Elasticities in World Trade," *Review of Economics and Statistics*, Vol. LI, No. 2 (May 1969), pp. 111–25, derive U.S. income elasticities for imports ranging between 1.42 and 1.68 for the 1951–66 period, i.e., a percentage change in imports is 1.42–1.68 times the percentage change in GNP, or national in-

purely cyclical phenomenon, caused by the temporary (if prolonged) overheating of the U.S. economy, or whether they resulted from structural changes in the U.S. propensity to import. Even with an income elasticity of demand of 2, however, a reduction of over 5 per cent of U.S. gross national product—about $60 billion on the basis of the $1,150 trillion GNP in 1972—would still be needed to get a $6 billion reduction in gross U.S. imports through income effects, and a net reduction of $3 billion after applying the feedback ratio discussed above. Such a relationship would imply a marginal propensity to import of 10 per cent of changes in U.S. gross national product, almost twice the present average propensity to import and even higher than the actual performance of any year in the late 1960s and early 1970s, when import rises were extremely sharp. The required GNP cut of 5 per cent, or $60 billion, is thus a quite conservative estimate.

Such a 5 per cent reduction of the gross national product could be expected to reduce the annual rate of U.S. price increases by about 2 percentage points.[9] Such a reduction in U.S. prices could in turn provide an additional gain of at least $2 billion in the trade balance.[10] Combined with the import cutback of $3 billion due to the income effect, this would achieve the targeted net gain of $5 billion.

We simply cannot predict the effects of such a cutback in growth on the rest of the U.S. balance of payments. Foreign travel expenditures would presumably drop, and the reduced earnings of American firms would reduce their financial capacity to invest abroad. On the other hand, investment in the United States (by both American and foreign firms) would be deterred by the reduced pace of economic

---

come. Mordechai E. Kreinen, "Price Elasticities in International Trade," *Review of Economics and Statistics*, Vol. LIII, No. 4 (Nov. 1971), correctly notes that there may be sharp differences between trend and *cyclical* income elasticities of demand, which are very important for short-term forecasting and policy. We are here concerned with long-term effects, however, and the elasticities used are accurate for such purposes. The OECD trade model uses 1.5.

9. George L. Perry, "Changing Labor Markets and Inflation," *Brookings Papers on Economic Activity* 3, 1970, especially p. 433.

10. F. Gerard Adams and Helen B. Junz, "The Effect of the Business Cycle on Trade Flows in Industrial Countries," *Journal of Finance*, Vol. XXVI, No. 2 (May 1971), especially p. 264. They append (p. 267) the updated OECD trade model, which includes the U.S. income elasticity of demand for imports cited in the previous paragraph. No feedback adjustments had to be made to these price elasticities because they come from general equilibrium models. Feedbacks had to be applied to the income effects because the income elasticities derive from partial equilibrium models.

activity. The direction of short-term capital movements is unclear; tighter monetary conditions might be sought to achieve the targeted disinflation, while the slackness of the economy would certainly tend to produce lower interest rates.

The effects of such a policy might be tempered by recognition that the cutback was a one-shot affair, with normal growth to be resumed after realization of the desired effect, and by "achieving" the reduction in GNP over several years. Indeed, this would have to be a corollary of such an effort to avoid massive cutbacks in investment and hence severe damage to the U.S. competitive position in the process. But a reduction in gross national product of 5 per cent, even if achieved over time, would increase the aggregate unemployment rate by about 2 percentage points.[11] The black unemployment rate could be expected to rise by about twice as much. The GNP loss would be equivalent to a full year's real growth.[12]

Normal growth could then resume for the future—but the loss of income could only be made up at a pace which enabled the gains for U.S. price competitiveness of the initial and subsequent improvement in price competitiveness to recapture for the balance of payments the income effects of moving back to full employment. If other countries did not react to the U.S. move by lowering their rates of inflation, preservation of the implied level of unemployment would enable the United States to maintain a rate of inflation 2 percentage points below its full employment norm and hence to improve its trade balance by about $2 billion more each year—in

11. Using Perry's modification of Okun's Law, which indicates that the percentage GNP gap is about 2.7 times the excess of the unemployment rate above 4 per cent. See George Perry, "Labor Force Structure, Potential Output, and Productivity," *Brookings Papers in Economic Activity 3* 1971. pp. 555–58.

12. The reader will recall that U.S. unemployment did rise by over 2 percentage points from 1969 to 1971, but that the current account deteriorated sharply instead of improving. This particular rise in unemployment was a result of the need to dampen the inflationary excesses of the previous years, which may have produced "overfull" employment. In addition, it was accompanied by a steady continuation of price inflation, further erosion of the U.S. competitive position, and increasing overvaluation of the dollar as a result of the previous U.S. inflation, as well as a slowdown in foreign growth rates which reduced net U.S. exports significantly. The analysis in the text assumes a starting point of full employment with reasonably stable prices, equilibrium exchange rates, maintenance of full employment throughout the rest of the world, and the "successful" implementation of a policy of cutting growth for balance-of-payments purposes. These assumptions are of course never met in the real world, and they probably bias the estimates in a "favorable" direction—in practice, a *larger* deflation would probably be needed to achieve the targeted gain in the balance of payments, as would be suggested by the 1969–71 experience.

addition to the one-shot gross gain from moving to a higher level of employment. The increasing gains on the price side would permit a gradual move back to full employment—which could be completed after eighteen months, if it could be done without letting prices rise beyond the level to which they had been cut via the increase in unemployment. The cumulative loss of output to the United States over the period of two and a half years would be at least $150 billion at 1972 levels of GNP. If cutting back growth were the only adjustment alternative, the value to the United States of dollar financing for payments deficits would clearly be so great that it would be worth preserving at almost any cost.[13]

In addition, such a policy would undermine the growth criterion for a key currency, although it would help achieve the criterion of relative price stability. More important from a key currency standpoint, however, such a policy would wholly violate the national independence criterion. Indeed, it illustrates why that criterion is so important—because adjustment based on cutting growth and inducing unemployment would be politically untenable in an economy large enough to have a key currency in the first place, and hence would not be credible as a policy alternative. It was unsustainable even in Britain in the 1920s, and it would certainly be unsustainable in the United States in the 1970s.

The Policy Mix

Because straight cutbacks in growth would be so costly, two other types of macroeconomic policy have been adopted in numerous countries to help deal with payments imbalances: the so-called "policy mix" approach, and the use of incomes policies. Since the cutback approach would be even more costly for the United States than for other countries, because its economy is the least open of any in the non-Communist world to international transactions, these approaches have been widely proposed.[14]

13. A much higher estimate of the cost to the United States of adjusting via internal policy—$100 billion to achieve a $5 billion improvement—is derived by H. Robert Heller and Mordechai E. Kreinen, "Adjustment Costs, Currency Areas, and Reserves," in Willy Sellekaerts, ed., *Essays in Honor of Jan Tinbergen* (London: Macmillan, 1972). However, they use the much lower U.S. import elasticities of the early 1960s, and make no allowance for the improvement in the U.S. competitive position stemming from the improved price competitiveness corresponding to higher employment.
14. Heller and Kreinen, *op. cit.*, conclude that, to achieve an identical improvement in the balance of payments, the United States would have to reduce GNP (in percentage terms) three times as much as Japan would have to, three and one-half times as much as Germany, four times as much as Canada, and about seven times as much as Britain or Italy.

In its simplest form, the policy mix approach under a fixed exchange rate would assign monetary policy solely to the pursuit of external equilibrium and fiscal policy solely to the pursuit of internal equilibrium.[15] For a deficit country, the objective would be to attract capital inflows and discourage capital outflows by raising interest rates relative to other countries. Stimulative fiscal policy would then be employed to offset the contractionary effect of such a monetary policy on the domestic economy and avoid any undesired reduction in GNP. Surplus countries could, similarly, lower their interest rates to induce net capital outflows and offset the inflationary domestic effect by tighter fiscal policy.

It has now been demonstrated that, in practice, the approach would almost certainly be much more complicated.[16] First, foreign interest rates are deeply affected by U.S. interest rates, and it is highly dubious that wide differentials could exist for very long—at least in the absence of direct controls to reinforce the mix. At a minimum, foreign countries would have to cooperate by actively keeping their rates down, in turn risking inflation or tightening their fiscal policies sufficiently to avoid such effects; like most international economic policies at this time in history, the mix cannot be effectively applied by one country alone. But fiscal policy is not sufficiently flexible, either in the United States or abroad, to be used in such a way.[17] Even if it were, the United States would hardly be willing to base its tax rates and government expenditures on the needs of the balance of payments.

The force of all these problems with policy mix approach becomes even clearer when we assess the magnitude of the changes in monetary and fiscal policy that would be necessary to achieve the targeted objective. There are two competing views of how best to explain interest-sensitive movements of international capital. Enjoying wider support at present is the "stock-adjustment" approach, which suggests that the main effect of changes in interest rates is to produce one-shot shifts in the division between domestic and foreign assets in national portfolios. The alternative "flow" model postulates that any given interest rate change triggers a steady flow of capital toward

---

15. The classic presentation is in Robert Mundell, "The Appropriate Use of Monetary and Fiscal Policy for Internal and External Stability," *IMF Staff Papers*, Vol. IX (March 1962), pp. 70–79.

16. See especially Ronald W. Jones, "Monetary and Fiscal Policy for an Economy with Fixed Exchange Rates," *Journal of Political Economy*, Vol. LXXVI, No. 4, Part II (July–August 1968), pp. 921–43.

17. Largely for this reason, Michaely, *op. cit.*, p. 63, found virtually no actual use of the policy mix in the entire 1950–66 period, despite much discussion of its virtues.

the country whose rate has increased, which continues as long as the new differential continues. The stock-adjustment model concludes that these capital movements are determined by *changes* in interest rate differentials, while the flow model concludes that they are determined by the *level* of interest rate differentials.

The differences between the two views are not as great as they appear.[18] Conceptually, the stock-adjustment model does include a continuing flow effect, from the net additions which accrue over time to private wealth in growing economies. Empirically, one study concludes that stock and flow adjustments actually accounted for 45 per cent and 55 per cent, respectively, of actual short-term U.S. capital outflows during 1959–67.[19] The most sophisticated version of the stock-adjustment model suggests a quarterly flow of about $350 million toward the United States from a rise of one perecntage point in short-term U.S. interest rates, in addition to a one-shot stock shift of about $3.4 billion over five quarters. A major study based on the flow concept concludes that each percentage point by which U.S. short-term interest rates exceed those in the United Kingdom generates *annual* flows toward the United States of $600 million, but it was based on the much smaller magnitudes of capital movements which prevailed in the early 1960s and was limited to short-term capital.[20] It appears reasonable to conclude that, in the absence of speculative or other temporarily dominant considerations, net capi-

18. And are indeed reconciled in Thomas D. Willett and Franceso Forte, "Interest Rate Policy and External Balance," *Quarterly Journal of Economics*, Vol. LXXXIII, No. 2 (May 1969), pp. 242–62.

19. Normal C. Miller and Marina v.N. Whitman, "The Outflow of Short-Term Funds from the United States: Adjustment of Stocks and Flows," in Fritz Machlup, Walter S. Salant, Lorie Tarshis, eds., *International Mobility and Movement of Capital* (New York: Columbia University Press, 1972), pp. 253–86. They also conclude, however, that stock-adjustment dominates the total effect on short-term flows of any *single* change in interest rates, and they reach a similar conclusion for long-term U.S. portfolio flows in "A Mean-Variance Analysis of United States Long-Term Portfolio Investment," *Quarterly Journal of Economics*, Vol. LXXXIV, No. 2 (May 1970), esp. pp. 193–94, which also concludes that virtually all of U.S. long-term portfolio adjustment shifts represent stock-shifts and that 80 per cent take place within one year.

20. The stock-adjustment effect is from William H. Branson and Raymond H. Hill, Jr., "Capital Movements Among Major OECD Countries: Some Preliminary Results," *Journal of Finance*, Vol. XXVI, No. 2 (May 1971), esp. pp. 283–85. The flow effect is from Jerome L. Stein, "International Short-Term Capital Movements," *American Economic Review*, Vol. LV, No. 1 (March 1965), pp. 40–66. All the recent empirical work indicates that numerous factors besides interest rates, such as trade flows and domestic economic variables, have important effects on these capital movements; here we are interested only in the effects of interest rates, however.

tal inflows to the United States might rise by roughly $1 billion annually from each percentage point rise in U.S. short-term interest rates relative to foreign interest rates.

However, increases in U.S. interest rates sharply increase interest payments to foreigners.[21] Every percentage point rise in U.S. rates increased payments on the outstanding stock of dollar balances by perhaps $700 million in 1973, since interest-bearing foreign deposits in the United States amounted to over $70 billion at the end of 1972. The entire interest cost of the new money attracted by the higher rates must also be added—say, $50 million or so for every $1 billion inflow. So the *net* gain to the U.S. capital account from every percentage point increase in domestic interest rates is about $250 million—not $1 billion. This implies that U.S. rates would have to rise by about 20 percentage points to achieve a payments improvement of $5 billion. Such a rise is of course inconceivable.

"Even" an increase of 10 percentage points in U.S. interest rates would generate a direct deflationary pressure of about $50 billion.[22] With a multiplier of 2, a tax cut or increase in government expenditures large enough to counter a potential GNP decline of almost $100 billion would be needed. Assuming a tax multiplier of 1.5, the required tax reduction would be about $70 billion. Assuming a government expenditures multiplier of 2, the required increase in government expenditures would be at least $50 billion.[23] Either implies a huge government budget deficit that would have to be maintained over time, swelling the federal debt by $100 billion–$150 billion every couple of years. The required magnitude of changes in both interest rates and government expenditures are thus clearly outside

---

21. See Thomas D. Willett, "Official Versus Market Financing of International Deficits," *Kyklos*, XXI, 1968. See also the related arguments (and some others) against the policy mix approach in W. M. Corden, "Monetary Integration," *Princeton Essays in International Finance No. 93*, April 1972, pp. 30–32.
22. David J. Ott and Alliot F. Ott, "Monetary and Fiscal Policy: Goals and the Choice of Instruments," *Quarterly Journal of Economics*, Vol. LXXXII, No. 2 (May 1968), especially pp. 323–24. They questioned, even at that time when foreign holdings of dollars (and hence the U.S. interest cost) were much smaller, "whether directing fiscal policy toward domestic objectives and monetary policy toward external objectives is really a viable policy under present circumstances."
23. In both cases, the numbers cited are minima because they include only first round effects. The increase in government expnditures, for example, would have some import content and would require a further tightening of interest rates, which would in turn require further increases in government expenditures to eliminate the payments deficit entirely.

the political and psychological boundaries imposed on these policy tools in the U.S. society.[24]

It is also unlikely that monetary and fiscal policies could move in diametrically opposed directions, especially in the magnitudes just suggested, without drastically altering the shape of the overall economy. There would be a dramatic shift from investment, housing, and local government expenditures to consumption. For example, an increase of mortgage rates by 10 percentage points could bring the housing industry to a total standstill. Even if possible, such a shift would add further pressure to the balance of payments because the import component of consumption is about twice the import component of investment,[25] and hence would require an even greater tightening of monetary policy.

In addition, the decline in investment would lower the effective rate of growth of the economy.[26] One result would be an improvement in the balance of trade, at least in the short run; to that extent, the magnitudes outlined above are overstated. At the same time, however, a sharp decline in the rate of investment would hurt the U.S. competitive position—particularly since it relies heavily on innovation and technological leadership. This would hurt U.S. trade over the longer run, and it would also reduce the incentives for foreign investment in this country and increase the export of U.S. capital.

Finally, offsetting foreign responses to such a change in the U.S. policy mix would be impossible to avoid. Such astronomical U.S. interest rates would obviously put tremendous pressure on foreign rates, and require drastic expansionary monetary policy by other central banks if major feedback effects were to be avoided. As there

24. Mundell himself recognized explicitly, over a decade ago, that "the current mixture of monetary and fiscal policy . . . might necessitate larger changes in interest rates and budget deficits than are politically feasible." See his "On the Selection of a Program of Economic Policy with an Application to the Current Situation in the United States," *Banca Nazionale del Lavoro Quarterly Review*, No. 66 (September 1963).

25. Ott and Ott, *op. cit.*

26. Empirical estimates of the interest elasticity of business investment range from −0.1 to −0.5. Even at the lower end of the range, an increase of interest rates by 10 per cent—more than doubling the present rate—could cut investment by 10–25 per cent. See Myron Ross, "Operation Twist—A Mistake In Policy" *Journal of Political Economy*, Vol. LXXVII, No. 4, Part II (July–August 1968), pp. 811–13. It would be theoretically possible, though extremely difficult in practice, to avoid such effects by carrying out the compensating fiscal expansion wholly through investment-inducing measures such as cuts in corporate income taxes or new investment tax credits.

would clearly be such feedbacks, the United States would have to tighten its monetary policy even more to achieve the targeted balance-of-payments improvement, and relax its fiscal policy even more to retain the targeted GNP.

The policy mix approach would also carry several costs related specifically to the key currency role of the dollar. Basing U.S. fiscal policy on the balance of payments would represent as drastic a violation of the "aloofness" criterion required for a key currency as would straight deflation. The reduction in economic growth would undermine the dollar's roles. The required monetary tightening would sharply reduce U.S. capital exports, especially at short term. Placing reliance on interest-sensitive capital inflows to achieve equilibrium would represent acceptance of a payments structure that included basic, and perhaps even current account, deficits; this would hurt, not improve, the most important U.S. liquidity ratios. Like direct cutbacks in growth, such a structure might not be widely regarded as tenable and would shake rather than improve confidence in the dollar.[27]

Hence the cost of eliminating the U.S. payments deficit solely through the policy mix approach would be enormous, and is impossible in any practical sense. Within more reasonable bounds, the approach could induce a modest reduction of the deficit or combine with other instruments to achieve full elimination thereof, although it would still not be clear that doing so would strengthen the international role of the dollar. If the U.S. adjustment alternatives were limited to internal deflation and/or the policy mix, retention of the financing power of the international roles of the dollar would still be worth paying a very high price.

Incomes Policy

A third policy instrument which the United States could use in an effort to achieve payments equilibrium is incomes policy. Such a policy aims to shift the Phillips curve inward by coercing or persuading business and labor to restrain their price and wage increases within the context of a given level of overall demand. Success of such efforts would improve the country's competitive position, and

27. Alexandre Lamfalussy, "Limitations of Monetary and Fiscal Policy," Chapter 10 in William Fellner, Fritz Machlup, and Robert Triffin, *Maintaining and Restoring Balance in International Payments* (Princeton, New Jersey: Princeton University Press, 1966), pp. 157–60. He notes that speculative outflows might be induced as a result of such a policy approach and the public reaction to it, swamping the interest-induced inflows and hence frustrating even the immediate objective of the mix approach.

hence its balance of payments, without the loss of output and employment which would result from a reduction of aggregate demand.

Such efforts have already been made in several countries, including the United States from 1962 to 1966 and again from August 1971. The U.S. guideposts in the earlier period appear to have significantly damped the growth of wages, by about 1 percentage point in 1964 and almost 2 percentage points in 1965, and to have helped hold price rises in the 1961–65 period to 0.5–1.5 per cent below expected levels.[28] There is evidence that incomes policy helped restrain wage increases in Britain, particularly during the first postwar Labor government in 1948–50 and the mandatory freeze of 1966–67, but a clear impact on prices has been discerned only in the brief freeze period.[29] The results in other countries, including Canada, are not very encouraging. The record to date is ambiguous, though it gives at least some encouragement for the effectiveness of incomes policy as an adjustment measure for the United States.

For domestic political reasons, mandatory controls can be either very tough for a short time or mildly restrictive over a long period, but not very tough for an extended time. Even assuming a degree of compliance by industry and labor, voluntary cooperation cannot be expected to produce dramatic improvements in price stability. And even when controls are very tough, it takes a while for the effects of wage and price restraints to work their way through the economy to affect the external balance. So incomes policy can be expected to have a major effect only over an extended period of time. But if an incomes policy were to succeed in holding down the rate of price increase by 1 percentage point per year, the U.S. balance of trade might improve by at least $1 billion for each year of such a result.[30] A successful incomes policy of this magnitude could thus by itself achieve the targeted balance-of-payments improvement in about five years.

28. See George L. Perry, "Wages and the Guideposts," *American Economic Review*, Vol. LVII, No. 4 (September 1967), esp. 899.
29. See David Smith, "Incomes Policy," in Richard E. Caves, ed., *Britain's Economic Prospects* (Washington, D.C.: Brookings Institution, 1968), esp. pp. 132–35.
30. Adams and Junz, *op. cit.* No feedbacks need be calculated, because the price elasticities used in their study derive from a general equilibrium model and hence include such effects. A more recent analysis by Junz and Rhomberg, *op. cit.*, would provide a more optimistic estimate of the gains to the United States; an improvement in the trade balance of as much as $3 billion annually after four years, reducing to perhaps three years the period of needed restraint to achieve the targeted overall improvement—but Houthakker and Magee, *op. cit.*, provide a less optimistic estimate.

Incomes policy could thus be viewed as part of a long-term program of adjustment for the United States, as indeed it was in August 1971. Furthermore, its effectiveness appears to depend heavily on the cyclical position and certain structural features of the domestic economy. In an inflationary environment, when incomes policies are most needed and most likely to be launched, they are least likely to succeed. (On the other hand, such a situation usually represents a "non-dilemma" case from the standpoint of the balance of payments, with incomes policy an adjunct to a policy of domestic restraint. In such a case an incomes policy would not be considered as an additional *adjustment* measure adopted for external reasons in the sense of the present analysis. Such a policy might thus do better when it *was* adopted "purely" to help the balance of payments.) They are also more likely to succeed where unionism is more highly centralized than in the United States, so that a decision by top union leadership to cooperate does in fact lead to real cooperation.[31] Finally, foreign perceptions about the effectiveness of adjustment measures are as important, in at least the short run, as their actual effectiveness; thus any measure with as long-term a payout as incomes policy, and with as checkered a past history, will probably not be even as convincing where it counts as might be justified.

The main economic costs of incomes policy are the reduction in efficiency associated with any controls over market behavior and the effects on income distribution. Both are likely to be relatively small if the policy has a short life span, but could become significant if it were pursued for a sufficient time to have the desired balance-of-payments effects and to convince foreign (and domestic) observers that it would do so. On the other hand, an incomes policy may *add* to economic efficiency if it effectively injects the public interest as a countervailing force to the concentrated power of big business and big labor, which have themselves distorted the economic system. It is true that the more visible industries and unions are more susceptible to pressures for restraint than the less visible, but their potential for monopolistic behavior—and for resisting governmental pressure—is also greater. Balance between restraint of prices and wages can achieve reasonable equity under an incomes policy, which may be

---

31. Eric Schiff, *Incomes Policies Abroad* (Washington: American Enterprise Institute, April 1971), p. 4. Jurg Niehans, "Wage and Price Guideposts in the Context of Balance of Payments Adjustment," Chapter 13 in Fellner *et al.*, *op. cit.*, pp. 171–76, adds that incomes policies are most likely to succeed in countries where industry and labor are acutely aware of the importance of maintaining export markets, a characteristic not widely present in the United States at this point in history.

politically necessary even at the cost of some reduction in the effectiveness of the policy in achieving its basic goals. It is also conceivable that the major dose of publicity which is a necessary component of a successful incomes policy could improperly reduce the needed attention to fiscal and monetary policy,[32] and it is certainly true that incomes policy can only work in the context of reasonably effective anti-inflationary macroeconomic programs. An alert and skillful executive branch could presumably avoid being lulled to sleep simply by its own incomes policy, though the Congress might use the existence of such a policy to justify higher levels of spending than were consistent with price stability.

In short, incomes policy provides a modest but relatively low-cost instrument to help achieve payments equilibrium. Its problems concern effectiveness and perceptions of probable effectiveness, since it is desirable on domestic anti-inflationary as well as on external payments grounds. And it would not appear to violate any of the basic criteria of key currency status.

Direct Controls on Current Account

The United States could also attempt to improve the current account through measures aimed directly at the specific transactions which comprise it. The most likely possibilities are export subsidies, such as preferential financing for exports by the Export-Import Bank and tax advantages like the Domestic International Sales Corporations (DISCs) authorized by law in late 1971, and import restrictions, such as the 10 per cent surcharge of late 1971.[33]

To achieve a net current account improvement of $5 billion, any of these measures would of course require a like reduction in domes-

---

32. Herbert Stein, "Unemployment, Inflation, and Economic Stability," in *Agenda For the Nation* (Washington, D.C.: Brookings Institution, 1968), p. 285, suggests that this occurred in the United States after mid-1965. The view is shared by many members of the monetarist school of economic thought; see, for example, Milton Friedman, "What Price Guideposts?" in George P. Shultz and Robert Z. Aliber, eds., *Guidelines, Informal Controls, and the Market Place* (Chicago: University of Chicago Press, 1966), esp. pp. 37–38.

33. Despite the enthusiasm for exchange-rate changes in the United States in the early 1970s, such direct controls must be regarded as a real policy option for the future. As indicated in the text, some are still in place. The Trade Act of 1974 provides explicit Congressional authority to apply import surcharges again in the future, and the U.S. proposals for monetary reform presented to the Annual Meeting of the IMF in September 1972 envisaged the possibility of such controls. And, as in the interwar period, it is possible that the experience of flexible exchange rates will generate much opposition to them for the future.

tic expenditures. Import surcharges may actually improve the terms or trade of the countries applying them, however, and export subsidies may not hurt the terms of trade much because they work at least partially by inducing greater promotional efforts instead of direct price cuts. There would be an additional cost, however, from the loss of economic efficiency resulting from the protection or subsidization of domestic industry—though these losses would be minuscule, since the foreign sector of the U.S. economy is so small.[34] Current account controls, or indeed any selective controls over particular international transactions, would thus be much less costly to the U.S. economy than cutting growth or altering the policy mix.

A subsidy of about 10 per cent to all exports would probably be needed to achieve the required $5 billion net improvement in the U.S. trade balance, if it were the only policy adopted.[35] A tariff surcharge of about 8–10 per cent, applied to *all* imports, would be necessary to achieve the same improvement purely through a reduction in imports.[6] From the standpoint of U.S. adjustment, an import

34. All studies of the efficiency gain from improved allocation of resources through such measures as tariff reductions find that they are exceedingly small, even in economies much more open to international transactions than the United States is. It is thus quite likely that the efficiency cost from increasing tariffs (or similar barriers) would also be quite small. For a review of the literature, see Harvey Leibenstein, "Allocative Efficiency and 'X' Efficiency," *American Economic Review*, Vol. LVI, No. 3 (June 1966), esp. pp. 392–93. For a theoretical analysis, see Harry G. Johnson, "The Costs of Protection and Self-sufficiency," *Quarterly Journal of Economics*, Vol. LXXIX (August 1965), pp. 356–72.

35. Assuming a foreign price elasticity of demand for U.S. exports of −2, a 10 per cent subsidy would enable U.S. firms to cut the dollar price of their exports by 10 per cent and expect a rise of about 20 per cent in the volume of their sales (denominated in dollars), for a net value gain of about 10 per cent from the 1972 level of about $50 billion. No feedback effect need be deducted, since the elasticity of −2 is derived from general equilibrium analysis.

36. Using a price elasticity of demand for U.S. imports of −1.3, a surcharge of about 8 per cent would reduce the volume of imports by about 10 per cent —about $5 billion at the 1972 level of about $50 billion. If the dollar prices of foreign goods did not rise by the full amount of the surcharge, and hence support such a volume cutback, it would be an indication of a reduction in prices by the foreign sellers which would provide nearly as much help for the U.S. balance of payments by turning the terms of trade in its favor. If the foreign sellers *fully* offset the surcharge, it would have to be set at 10 per cent to achieve the targeted $5 billion gain. I assume no increased government spending, or tax cuts, to offset the increase in government revenues from the surcharge. This calculation gives results similar to the Nixon ad-

surcharge would probably be preferable to export subsidies on economic grounds because its effectiveness would be less uncertain, because it would turn the terms of trade in favor of the United States, whereas export subsidies would deliberately turn them against it;[37] and because it would generate tax revenue and thus contribute to the needed reduction in domestic expenditure, while export subsidies would work in the opposite direction unless new taxes were levied to finance them—which would add to the political costs of the step. The efficiency loss created by either measure would be $4–5 billion.[38]

If both an export subsidy and import surcharge were adopted simultaneously, each could be placed at about 5 per cent and produce the net $5 billion improvement. Such a combined approach would be the equivalent of a devaluation of like amount on the trade account alone, except that the import surcharge would result in increased tax payments to the U.S. government whereas devaluation would lead to increased dollar payments to foreigners. It would avoid the distortion between export- and import-competing industries which would otherwise be caused, but would provide a broader overall distortion between traded and nontraded goods. Hence it would have a slightly higher efficiency cost than an export subsidy or import surcharge alone, but still in the range of $4–5 billion.

These selective controls on current account transactions are unlikely in practice to have the economic effects outlined. The international trading rules of the GATT flatly aim at complete prohibition of export subsidies. The laws of many countries—including the United States—require the application of countervailing duties against them. The United States did use countervailing duties against French export subsidies in 1968–69, and threatened to do so when Canada contemplated subsidies to offset the U.S. import sur-

---

ministration's estimate of a $2 billion annual drop in U.S. imports as a result of the 10 per cent surcharge levied from August 15 to December 20, 1971 on about 50 per cent (the most price-elastic portion) of all imports.

37. See James E. Meade, *The Balance of Payments* (London: Oxford University Press, 1951), pp. 309–13.

38. Comprised of a consumption cost of 0.032 per cent of GNP and a production cost of 0.34 of GNP, assuming that elasticities of substitution of both production and consumption are unity. Derived from Johnson, *op. cit.*, pp. 361, 365. This figure is supported by the estimated effects of the DISC export subsidy: it would cost about $4 billion in budgetary terms, a rough but reasonable measure of its welfare effect, to increase net exports (allowing for the usual 50 per cent feedback effect) sufficiently to meet the $5 billion adjustment target used in this analysis.

charge in late 1971. Domestic political pressures are likely to be even stronger in most countries against foreign export subsidies than against foreign import barriers—as in the far greater U.S. concern over the sales tactics of "Japan, Inc." in the U.S. market than over Japan's own barriers to U.S. exports—because "unfair import competition" is always more visible than "unfair barriers to exports," and because lost exports can generally be more readily offset by other exports or even by increased domestic sales. Domestic politics exert pressure on governments to emulate new foreign export subsidies, if they do not force retaliation against them, as when the preferential credit facilities adopted for exporters in a few European countries in the early 1960s sparked a credit race throughout the industrialized world. So export subsidization of any significant size for any significant period of time is unlikely to produce changes in relative export positions, though it is likely to reduce world welfare in the process.[39]

Import surcharges are also unlikely, in practice, to have the economic effects outlined above. First, it is unlikely that they will be applied uniformly to all of a country's imports, because many imports are insensitive to price changes and a surcharge would simply add to internal price pressures without reducing the volume of imports. This means that a higher level of surcharge would be needed to reach the targeted balance-of-payments gain, and that the efficiency costs would be higher because distortions would be created among imports as well as between imports and the rest of the economy.

Second, they have been tolerated without retaliation only when clearly limited to temporary periods of time.[40] As long as the surcharges are perceived to be temporary, however, their effects are likely to be quite limited: importers will simply postpone rather than cancel

39. Possible gainers from such mercantilist competition are the developing countries, which get their imports more cheaply as a result. However, this gain is probably more than offset by (a) the unfavorable impact on their own exports, which are vital for their growth and which already have great difficulty breaking into new markets since they cannot afford to enter the subsidy race, and (b) the inducement to import more than they should and hence add to their already sizable debt burdens, a concern which has caused the IBRD to call attention to the *unfavorable* developmental aspects of the export credit competition.

40. Import surcharges are illegal under the GATT. However, virtually all observers agree that they are less bad than import quotas, which the GATT permits as an emergency balance-of-payments measure. The GATT did not try to roll back any of the three uses of surcharges by major countries (Canada, Britain, United States) in the last decade.

their purchases,[41] foreign suppliers apparently absorb a significant portion of the added costs in order to maintain their market shares, and domestic suppliers do not re-orient production to substitute for imports anyway. Against an originally estimated impact of $560–840 million annually, the U.K. surcharge of 1964–66 is estimated to have had a *maximum* annual effect of only $170–280 million, or 1–2 per cent of imports at the time.[42]

Third, import surcharges (and the "border tax" measures Germany used in 1968 on the surplus side) have always been viewed in practice simply as efforts to avoid eventual exchange-rate changes, which would become necessary anyway, rather than as substitutes for them. Adoption of such measures has thus tended to undermine, rather than strengthen, confidence that currency rates will remain unchanged; it may therefore accelerate imports into a deficit country, on the view that a devaluation will eventuate and have an even greater price impact than the surcharge, and accelerate speculative capital movements against it.

If a surcharge were ever presented as being permanent, it would almost certainly trigger foreign retaliation and hence lose most of its potential net balance-of-payments gain. This is so both because import restrictions are generally deemed highly inappropriate as a means to achieve payments adjustment,[43] and because they would be viewed as offsetting the reciprocal tariff concessions extended to the offending country during earlier trade negotiations.[44]

41. For strong evidence that British importers reacted this way in response to the U.K. surcharge, see Richard Marston, "Income Effects and Delivery Lags in British Import Demand: 1955–67," *Journal of International Economics,* Vol. 1, No. 4 (November 1971), esp. p. 391.

42. John Johnston and Margaret Henderson, "Assessing the Effect of the Import Surcharge," *The Manchester School of Economic and Social Studies,* Vol. XXXV, No. 2 (May 1967), pp. 89–110. This estimate, however, understates the effect to the extent that foreign suppliers did reduce their prices and enable the British to improve its terms of trade temporarily. And part of the poor result of the U.K. surcharge may have stemmed from the failure of overall economic policy to slow inflation and hence obtain the full price differentials on imports originally intended with the surcharge.

43. Working Party 3 of the OECD, *The Balance of Payments Adjustment Process,* August 1966, p. 23, records the international consensus that measures directly affecting the current account "cannot be justified unless quick results are essential, and unless at the same time more fundamental action is taken to restore durable equilibrium."

44. The European Community frequently noted during the life of the U.S. surcharge that it represented a "unilateral U.S. annulment of all tariff concessions extended by the United States in the postwar period," for which the United States had obtained reciprocal foreign concessions.

All of these shortcomings of surcharges have eventuated in each of the three cases in which they have been adopted in the post-convertibility period: by Canada in 1962, by the United Kingdom in 1964–1966, and by the United States in 1971. Each covered only part of the country's imports. Each had much smaller trade effects than anticipated, largely because foreign sellers absorbed much of the temporary price differentials. And each was subsequently replaced by devaluations to achieve payments equilibrium.[45]

Direct Controls on Government Expenditures

The balance-of-payments effects of government programs, mainly military arrangements and foreign aid, can also be reduced by expenditure-reducing or expenditure-switching. Expenditure-reducing in the military field could mean either an overall cutback in U.S. force levels, part of which would affect overseas expenditures, or a cutback specifically in overseas force levels not compensated by a buildup in forces maintained at home. Expenditure-reducing on aid would mean further cuts in the magnitude of the program. Military expenditure-switching would mean reducing foreign-exchange costs without reducing deterrent or combat capability by redeploying forces from overseas to home bases, by increasing procurement in the United States to maintain forces overseas, or by getting other countries to pay some of the costs previously borne by the United States. Expenditure-switching on aid could mean further procurement shifts to U.S. suppliers under the U.S. aid program and/or increased U.S. exports financed by the aid programs of other countries.

As with all other potential adjustment measures, the net gain to the balance of payments from reduced military expenditures would be significantly less than the gross gain. General feedback effects would cut the gain by perhaps 50 per cent, especially in Asia (outside Japan). In this particular case, specific feedbacks would produce a higher percentage because the military offset agreements with

45. This is not strictly true of Canada, which adopted its import surcharge at the same time it devalued; the measure was designed primarily to reinforce the new parity and was lifted as soon as it became clear that the new parity would hold. The United States adopted its surcharge as part of a program explicitly aimed at achieving a dollar devaluation, and dropped the surcharge only when it succeeded in negotiating an acceptable realignment. France also adopted a surcharge in late 1968 after refusing to devalue, despite the agreement at the Bonn Conference that it would do so, but quickly dropped it in response to the protests of its EC partners. All three of the objections cited apply equally to the "reverse surcharge" (and "reverse subsidy") adopted by Germany in lieu of revaluation at that same time.

Germany would either collapse completely or be reduced proportionately with the U.S. expenditures. Other U.S. military sales would decline due to the reduced leverage of the U.S. military presence, the reduced incentive for other countries to standardized their military equipment on U.S. lines, and the consequent pressure to build up defense industries to support national defense capabilities (which would assume greater importance with the hypothesized reduction in U.S. forces).

Overseas military cutbacks would thus have to be quite sizable to provide significant net balance-of-payments improvement for the United States.[46] Such cutbacks would imply major changes in national security policy, barring major changes in the world political situation[47]—and it seems clear that the balance of payments should not determine basic national security policy, whatever changes may on their merits be needed in that policy.

Expenditure-switching offers some opportunity for balance-of-payments savings, but only of a modest magnitude. The 50 per cent "Buy America" preference of the Department of Defense for U.S. goods cut gross balance-of-payments costs by about $50 million in 1963–64, at an estimated welfare cost to the United States of about one-half that amount.[48] The gross savings probably rose in later years, but at a very high cost/benefit ratio. The broader possibility of pulling U.S. troops back from Europe, without reducing the level of the military commitment to NATO, would probably be extremely costly in budgetary terms because of the need to increase airlift and sealift capabilities, pre-position supplies to await the troops, etc.[49] It could also be costly in strategic terms by reducing the credibility of

46. Morawetz, *op. cit.*, p. 426, concludes that 68 per cent of any reductions in U.S. military expenditures abroad are offset by reductions in U.S. exports. His result is not statistically significant, however.

47. Although some military strategists argue that NATO could maintain an adequate capability for conventional defense with at least two fewer U.S. divisions. This could produce gross balance-of-payments savings of at least $500 million annually—but mainly in Germany, where the feedback effects would be high. For a summary of the strategic arguments, see Morton H. Halperin, *Defense Strategies for the Seventies* (Boston: Little, Brown and Co., 1971), pp. 107–12.

48. Norman S. Fieleke, "The Buy-America Policy of the United States Government: Its Balance of Payments and Welfare Effects," *New England Economic Review* (Boston: Federal Reserve Bank of Boston, July-August 1969).

49. For an excellent analysis of these costs, and of the critical distinction between the burden-sharing and balance-of-payments aspects of international defense economics, see Edward R. Fried, "The Financial Cost of Alliance," Chapter 5 in John Newhouse, *U.S. Troops in Europe* (Washington, D.C.: Brookings Institution, 1971).

the U.S. deterrent and the likelihood of engagement of U.S. forces, since flying them into a crisis situation could exacerbate rather than calm a possible military confrontation.

The most promising possibility, from the U.S. standpoint, is for the NATO allies to pick up a share of U.S. costs in Europe, perhaps through transforming present U.S. bases into joint allied bases in both military and financial terms. However, European budgetary and political pressures also render this approach unlikely to provide major net gains for the U.S. balance of payments. The fundamental conclusion therefore remains that major balance-of-payments gains can be achieved in the military area, at reasonable budgetary and welfare costs, only through sweeping changes in national security policy or the overall world political situation—neither of which provides much concrete hope for U.S. international monetary policy.

The same conclusion holds, even more emphatically, for U.S. bilateral foreign aid expenditures. Virtually all this aid is now tied to U.S. goods and services, and probably costs no more than 20 cents on the dollar even after allowing for "substitution" effects.[50] Of this "net loss," some is recouped through feedback effects— which are particularly high in this area, because most aid-recipient countries spend most of their foreign exchange and many spend large parts of it in the United States. Virtually total elimination of bilateral aid would thus be necessary to get significant balance-of-payments gains.[51] The only way to achieve further expenditure-switching would be to revive the "additionality" approach, but the costs of tying are already quite high to the recipients—estimates range from 12 per cent to 30 per cent as the reduction in the real value of aid caused by tying.[52] The only possible source of a signifi-

---

50. Aid-financed exports might be purchased by foreign countries even in the absence of any aid, so the aid financing may merely "substitute" for cash receipts which the United States would receive anyway and free up foreign exchange for the recipient country to spend elsewhere. Vigorous U.S. efforts to assure "additionality" of aid-financed exports reportedly saved only about $35 million over 4 years, however, according to former AID administrator William S. Gaud, and the policy was abandoned early in the Nixon administration. For the best analysis of this issue, see Charles D. Hyson and Alan M. Strout, "Impact of Foreign Aid on U.S. Exports," *Harvard Business Review*, January-February 1968, pp. 65–66.

51. Morawetz, *op. cit.*, p. 246, concludes that U.S. aid (bilateral and multilateral) produces U.S. exports of a slightly greater magnitude than the aid itself. His result is not statistically significant, however.

52. See the summary of studies of the subject, and an analysis of the Colombian case, in Thomas L. Hutcheson and Richard C. Porter, *The Cost of Tying Aid: A Method and Some Colombian Estimates*, Princeton Studies in International Finance No. 30, March 1972, pp. 5, 34–39.

cant U.S. payments gain in the aid field appears to be an increase in U.S. exports financed by other donor countries.

Multilateral aid is untied and leads to slightly greater U.S. balance-of-payments outflows. However, each $1 of U.S. aid channeled through the International Development Association now levers $2 of aid from other donors, thus going far toward achieving burden-sharing objectives. In addition, U.S. tying would be emulated immediately by all other major donor countries, reducing the real value of IDA aid by the same 10–30 per cent already cut from the value of most bilateral lending. Such a move would undercut the broad aid and foreign policy objectives of Republican and Democratic administrations, both of which have moved steadily toward increasing the role of the multilateral lending institutions as channels for U.S. aid to lower income countries.

In sum, drastic changes in U.S. foreign policy would be necessary to achieve major reductions in the balance-of-payments costs of U.S. government expenditures through sharp reductions in gross military or aid outlays. There are severe limits on the savings which could be achieved by changing the pattern of expenditures at their present levels, because much has already been done and the attendant costs are very high. The government account is unlikely to provide much help as a flexible adjustment tool, though it could of course again make relatively minor contributions to ad hoc balance-of-payments programs as it did in the 1960s. And major foreign policy changes for balance-of-payments reasons would be one of the surest ways to undermine the world political role and national independence criteria of a key currency country.

Capital Controls

The capital account is the final component of the U.S. balance of payments where selective measures could be applied, and have been. It includes numerous types of capital: U.S. direct investment abroad and foreign direct investment in the United States; transactions in domestic and foreign stocks and bonds, both new and outstanding issues; bank loans and borrowings, both long- and short-term. Controls over such flows are permitted under the Articles of Agreement of the IMF, in contrast to the general prohibition of controls on current account transactions, on the theory that capital controls carry smaller economic and political costs. They have in fact been invoked by virtually all countries.

The United States has acted directly on virtually all parts of its capital account. "Operation Twist" has periodically sought to dampen liquid capital outflows without reducing domestic investment, by raising short-term interest rates and simultaneously lowering long-term rates. The Interest Equalization Tax raised the cost to foreigners of selling most new and outstanding foreign securities in the United States from 1963 through 1973, and of raising long-term bank loans there from 1965 as well. Voluntary restraints limited loans to foreigners by banks and non-bank financial institutions from 1965 through 1973. And restraints existed over most capital exported by American direct investors through 1973, on a voluntary basis from 1965 and on a mandatory basis from 1968. Numerous other means of applying such controls could be found in the practices of other countries, operating either through market forces or by direct controls over the transactions themselves.

It is often argued, however, that only fundamental changes in prices or incomes can achieve true adjustment and that capital controls can at best suppress a payments imbalance. And it is certainly true that capital flows, like trade flows, derive fundamentally from income and price relationships among countries. On the other hand, additional structural factors—such as different tax structures and incentives for domestic investment, and the state of development of capital markets—play important roles in determining capital flows. There is thus no conceptual reason why lasting adjustment cannot be achieved through the capital account, either by market-oriented measures to separate national capital markets (as with the IET, or in Britain's "investment dollar" market) or by physical controls over the flow of money itself.

It is almost certain, however, that capital controls have little net effect if applied piecemeal only to particular components of the capital account. The United States did achieve gross reductions in the capital outflows covered by its various balance-of-payments controls: perhaps $400 million in the stock-shift (and some continuing flow) out of foreign securities through the Interest Equalization Tax,[53] $400 million annually in reduced term bank loans to foreigners through the IET plus the voluntary restraints, $2 billion of

---

53. William H. Branson, "Monetary Policy and the New View of Inter-national Capital Movements," *Brookings Papers on Economic Activity* 2, 1970, pp. 247-48, finds a *gross* stock-adjustment effect of $429 million for the IET in 1964-74 (but does not make any estimate of the ongoing flow effect). F. J. Prachowny, *A Structural Model of the U.S. Balance of Payments* (Amsterdam: North Holland, 1969), derived a gross effect of about $1 billion, but Branson in his review of Prachowny's book, *Journal of International Economics*, Vol. 1, No. 4 (November 1971), p. 479 criticizes Prachowny's technique and concludes that Prachowny's own equations really suggest a stock-shift of $365 million.

stock-shift plus $1 billion to $2 billion annually in reduced short-term bank claims on foreigners through the voluntary restraints.[54] But the original IET cutbacks on portfolio outflows were fully offset by increases in term bank loans, before they became subject to restraint themselves eighteen months later.[55] And an outflow of term loans just prior to their coverage explains at least the first year's reduction below expected levels.[56] So there are even doubts about the net effect of controls applied fairly comprehensively to U.S. capital. Leads and lags in trade financing alone could completely overwhelm controls over "normal" capital flows. The doubts become even greater when we consider foreign capital, which can move in opposite and hence offsetting direction. Reduced capital outflows, especially if they include export credits, may also feed back via reduced merchandise exports.

The increase in foreign borrowing by U.S. direct investors, occasioned first by the vountary and then the mandatory control programs, may have had a somewhat greater net effect on the balance of payments. Indeed, it may have corrected a market imperfection by heightening foreign awareness of the desirability of buying U.S. securities—foreign purchase of U.S. equities *rose* at the same time that U.S. firms were increasing their own offshore borrowing. These increases may have totaled as much as $500 million annually in 1966–67, $2 billion in 1968, and $1 billion annually in 1969–70.[57] There is no *a priori* reason why this type of borrowing could not continue indefinitely, though, as noted in Chapter 5, changes in U.S. holdings of long-term assets and liabilities have some importance in determining the U.S. liquidity ratios which undergird confidence in the dollar—so that such borrowing could be regarded as part of the dollar overhang and thus a threat to the dollar rather than a support for it.

54. Branson, *op. cit.*, pp. 246, 249, and 259; Prachowny, *op. cit.*, p. 115.
55. See Richard N. Cooper "The Interest Equalization Tax: An Experiment in The Separation of Capital Markets," *Finanzarchiv*, Vol. XXVII, No. 3, p. 469. Prachowny, pp. 114–16, concludes that the IET achieved a cumulative net gain to the U.S. balance of payments of $277 million over its first three quarters but that *no* net gain remained by the end of 1964.
56. Branson, *op. cit.*, p. 249.
57. For a nonquantitative discussion, see H. David Willey, "Direct Investment Controls and the Balance of Payments," in C. P. Kindleberger, ed., *The International Corporation* (Cambridge: MIT Press, 1970), esp. pp. 106–8. Morawetz, *op. cit.*, pp. 426–27, concluded that the *net* gain to the U.S. balance of payments of controls over all private *U.S.* capital outflows was 40 per cent of the gross cutback. If the offsets to the controls over bank and portfolio lending were as high as indicated in the text, then the offset to the shift in direct investment financing must have been quite low.

Over the longer term, however, effective capital controls may actually hurt the balance of payments of the country applying them. A real deflection of net bank borrowing to foreign sources would raise foreign interest rates relative to U.S. rates. This would increase the incentives for other capital to move abroad, reduce the yield criterion for a key currency, undermine the capital exporter criterion directly, and impede adjustment of the U.S. current account.[58] If one believes that there is a long-term equilibrium level of foreign investment desired by U.S. firms and banks, portfolio theory suggests that it will be reached later if not sooner and that any short-term gains from controls would be lost unless they are maintained indefinitely. Foreign investment is bound to have a positive effect on a country's payments position (and net welfare) over time, in purely financial terms, if the return on the investment plus the net trade effect is greater than the interest costs of the financing for any payments deficit which might result.[59]

Intense debate rages over direct investment on this point. Multinational business claims that such investment is recouped for the balance of payment within two or three years, because U.S. exports are increased and investment income (including earnings on previous investments as well as on the new investment) is boosted sharply. Organized labor claims that foreign direct investment represents a loss of exports fully equivalent to the buildup in production abroad, thereby hurting the balance of payments by that amount, in addition to the cost of the investment itself. In reality, the answer probably differs sharply for different investments, with the aggregate effect somewhere in between. Foreign direct investment does produce generous income returns for the U.S. balance of payments in later years; but we do not know the effect on domestic productivity and perhaps increased inflows of foreign capital if the money had been invested at home instead. Foreign direct investment does generate some increase in U.S. exports to set up the new production facility abroad and to supply it with intermediate inputs, but it also displaces some exports by substituting production from the new foreign plant. The best studies so far suggest that such investment, on average, pays off *at best* in balance-of-payments terms only after

58. Meltzer, *op. cit.*, p. 200.
59. For a sophisticated elaboration of this analysis see Peter H. Lindert, "The Payments Impact of Foreign Investment Controls," *Journal of Finance*, Vol. XXVI, No. 5 (December 1971), pp. 1083–1100.

about 9 years for the United States,[60] and 14 years for Briain[61]—although both are based more on assumptions than on analysis of what might have happened in the absence of the foreign investments by the firms, and can thus only be regarded as suggestive of the possible real effects. A high policy premium on short-run effects could thus justify measures to control direct investment for external payments reasons.

It must be recognized, however, that the capital controls instituted and expanded by the United States from 1963 through 1968, and maintained thereafter though liberalized, were intended to find additional financing for its deficits and to convey the impression that it was "doing something" about its balance of payments, rather than to achieve real adjustment. Indeed, there is some justification in regarding the program as a kind of issuance of "Roosa bonds" by U.S. firms rather than the government. The direct investment controls affected the sources of financing for such investment, not the level of investment itself; the bank program had little net impact on the balance of payments; and the IET exempted the biggest borrowers (Canada and the World Bank). The main goal was psychological: to allay the foreign suspicion that the United States regarded its balance of payments with benign neglect, and to show that it was indeed prepared to "defend the dollar" by initiating "adjustment." One may even suspect collusion in this effort by sophisticated foreign monetary officials, who fully recognized that under the prevailing system the United States had no acceptable adjustment option and there were no sources of additional liquidity other than the dollar. It would otherwise be impossible to explain the contrast between the cacophony of foreign demands that the United States apply capital controls in the first place, and maintain them, with the total absence of criticism of their loopholes and the meagerness of real results—despite the development of persuasive evidence of such meagerness by numerous American analysts![62]

60. Gary C. Hubauer and F. Michael Adler, *Overseas Manufacturing Investment and the Balance of Payments*, Treasury Department Tax Study No. 1, Washington, D.C., 1967, esp. pp. 59–71 and 92.
61. W. B. Reddaway, J. O. N. Perkins, S. J. Potter, and C. T Taylor, *Effects of U.K. Direct Investment Overseas: An Interim Report*, 1967, as translated into pay-back terms by Hufbauer and Adler, *op. cit.*, p. 92.
62. One might object to the analysis in this chapter on the grounds that I consider each policy option separately, in terms of its effectiveness and costs in achieving the entirety of the hypothesized adjustment, whereas in practice several such measures are almost always linked. The criticism is correct, however, only if combining the measures leads to a greater net benefit from them

The U.S. controls thus cannot be regarded as models for adjustment via the capital account. As already noted, comprehensive controls—either through the market mechanism, or more probably through exchange regulations—are necessary to achieve results. The French and Japanese models are much more relevant. Operating through direct exchange controls, both have been effective throughout the postwar period in limiting capital outflows and regulating inflows, though their effects cannot be quantified because there is no base against which to estimate flows which might have occurred in the absence of the controls.

Comprehensive controls of this sort would, however, be exceedingly difficult to apply in the United States. The vast size of the country and its population means that any such control network would have to be massive and very costly to run. The ready existence of Eurodollar and Asia-dollar markets and of vast unpoliced borders with Canada and Mexico makes doubtful the effectiveness of even a comprehensive network. At a deeper level, the abhorrence of such pervasive control imbedded in American traditions would render any such approach a major political liability to any government which tried to institute it under existing law, and make it equally difficult to get Congressional authorization to do so with new legislation. The effectiveness of such measures is further clouded since feedback effects on comprehensive U.S. capital restrictions might be higher than the average feedbacks, because of their close relationship to future income and, in some cases, to U.S. exports and foreign investment in the United States. It thus seems quite likely that the United States would have to shut off gross capital outflows of at least $10 billion to achieve the targeted net gain of $5 billion, which would mean virtually total cessation of U.S. capital exports and hence be very difficult to achieve both administratively and politically.

Finally, it is likely that the U.S. capital controls undermined the key currency roles of the dollar. Some of the controls covered non-

---

than the sum of the individual measures themselves. In defense of such a view, it is true the U.S. government (unlike the British) was extremely skillful in packaging its balance-of payments measures throughout the 1960s and thereby *seeming* to do much more about "the problem" than was really the case. This U.S. approach certainly promoted the success of the "conspiracy" alluded to in the text by providing more ammunition with which U.S. and foreign officials could defend U.S. policy than isolated individual measures would have. There is no analytical reason to believe, however, that the measures had any enhanced real effect because they were packaged.

resident funds, in particular the outflows of U.S. agencies of foreign banks and the foreign direct investment of U.S. subsidiaries of foreign companies, and thus undermined to some extent their free convertibility. They limited foreign access to the U.S. capital and money markets. They promoted the development of rival markets. They induced foreign withdrawals of dollar deposits related directly or indirectly to dollar credits. And by presaging an eventual devaluation, they constituted recognition of a payments problem but were ineffective in solving it.

On the other hand, the effects of these steps on the *dollar* have been at least partly offset by the distinction between dollar holdings *abroad* and foreign holdings *in the United States*, which is made possible by the existence of the Eurodollar market. International use of the dollar, particularly for private transactions purposes, has expanded at an increasingly rapid pace during the very period when the U.S. capital controls were being applied and extended. The main reason is that the controls have not been very effective. But they have also promoted the development of the Eurobond and Eurodollar markets themselves. In fact, the existence of these expatriate dollar markets may actually enhance the international attractiveness of the dollar since they couple most of the economic virtues of the currency with total independence from political control by the U.S. government.[63] Indeed, the Eurodollar market originated partly because Eastern European countries sought precisely this combination of advantages and independence; and its virtues to wealthy oil sheiks who oppose the United States over Israel—not to mention supposedly apolitical central banks—are obvious.

Complaints that the controls have undermined the international role of the New York capital and money markets are understandable, and indeed correct to some degree. However, as noted in Chapter 7, U.S. banks have been quick to seize much of the Eurodollar business—on which profits are higher—through setting up foreign

---

63. Ralph C. Bryant, *op. cit.*, Chapter 11, pp. 56–62, outlines five differences between Eurodollar holdings and balances in the United States. Three are favorable to Eurodollars—generally higher interest rates, fewer risks of blockage or other controls, and greater proximity to many foreigners. Two are favorable to balances in the United States—greater negotiability and liquidity of the investment media—although further development of the Eurodollar market will probably erode both U.S. advantages, e.g., by providing a wider range of maturities and by permitting checks to be written directly on Eurodollar accounts. Another Eurodollar advantage not noted by Bryant is the fact that it is far easier to avoid paying taxes on Eurodollar interest than on interest earned in the United States.

operations of their own.[64] We must not confuse the roles of the dollar with the roles of New York. Indeed, such a confusion has long existed in Britain between the international roles of sterling and the scope of business for London banks; it contributed importantly to the anachronistic British effort to retain sterling's roles despite the rush of "the City" into *Eurodollar* financing.

If one discounts future earnings at a high rate, in seeking balance-of-payments improvement in the short run, controls over capital flows (including direct investment) are thus a relatively attractive adjustment option. They are the one type of control permitted under governing international law, seldom trigger retaliation or emulation, and arouse far fewer domestic political and foreign policy problems than any other mode of adjustment. On the other hand, the U.S. controls over portfolio and direct investment became quasi-permanent, and any reductions in net investment which resulted probably levied net losses on the cumulative payment position over the decade of their existence. More important, however, truly effective U.S. capital controls would probably require a comprehensive exchange-controls regime, which would run deeply against the basic orientation of society and probably have some negative effect on world welfare. As it would also render more difficult the maintenance of the international roles of the dollar, by covering nonresident dollar holdings comprehensively, one cost of these roles is to add to the shortcomings of seeking adjustment via comprehensive capital controls.

Exchange-Rate Changes

The final adjustment option for the United States is exchange-rate changes. Like controls, the economic costs of this type of adjustment can be limited to the reduction in domestic expenditure which must be shifted to meet foreign demand in order to achieve the needed improvement in the balance of payments. Devaluations are thus decisively less costly in income terms than either cutting growth or changes in the policy mix, with their massive impacts on employment and/or the structure of the domestic economy, though they are no less costly in these aggregate terms than controls which alter the balance of payments directly. If the United States were to move

64. Before the U.S. controls were instituted in 1965, 11 U.S. banks had about 200 foreign branches. By the end of 1971, 91 U.S. banks had 583 such branches.

again into a sizable payments surplus, revaluation would be cheaper than adjusting through additional domestic inflation or by changing the policy mix through easing · interest rates and raising taxes or cutting government expenditures, though no cheaper in these terms than unilateral tariff cuts. Devaluations do turn the terms of trade against a country, like most other adjustment options (except import surcharges), although this is an exceedingly small cost for the relatively closed U.S. economy. In addition, the reduction in national income caused by the deterioration in the terms of trade will achieve part of the reduction in domestic expenditure required to achieve adjustment anyway; it thus represents no *additional* reduction in domestic expenditure, although it does represent a loss to GNP and national income. Finally, exchange-rate changes affect all components of the balance of payments equally, thereby avoiding the costs of uneconomic resource allocation which accompany direct controls over trade and capital movements.

Exchange-rate changes cannot be effective in changing domestic absorption, of course, without complementary domestic macroeconomic policies. If full employment at the time of devaluation is assumed, domestic demand must be restrained sufficiently to permit the price effects of the devaluation to produce the needed reduction in domestic absorption. The task is easier if underutilized resources exist in the economy, but even then macroeconomic policy cannot permit excessive increases in demand. Exchange-rate changes are particularly attractive in "dilemma" cases, such as the United States faced in 1971, where the needs of the domestic economy call for measures which would exacerbate the balance-of-payments problem, where additional measures aimed specifically at the external imbalance are clearly needed, and where domestic unemployment is likely to be part of the "dilemma" and thus provide a relatively favorable environment in which to carry out a successful devaluation.

Every 1 per cent devaluation of the dollar can be expected to provide a net gain of more than $1 billion in the U.S. trade balance, at present levels of trade, over a period of two to three years.[65] Addi-

---

65. Using, as earlier, a foreign price elasticity of demand for U.S. exports of -2 and a U.S. price elasticity of demand for imports of -1.3. In dollar terms, the improvement would come primarily through an increase in exports. This estimate is slightly higher than the official U.S. and international consensus of 1971, which foresaw an $0.8 billion trade gain for the United States from each percent of U.S. devaluation, and is higher than suggested by the Houthakker-Magee elasticities. It is significantly lower, however, than suggested by the Junz-Rhomberg analysis cited earlier.

tional gains would result in some of the service items, particularly tourism, which is quite sensitive to such price changes.[66] On the other hand, there would be balance-of-payments losses for such price-inelastic items as U.S. military expenditures overseas. The effect on capital flows, even of a longer-term nature, is uncertain: dollar devaluation reduces the profitability of foreign relative to U.S. investment, but most large firms appear to base their investment decisions on long-term calculations of market growth and few long-term investment plans would appear likely to change very much from small exchange-rate changes.[67] (The higher initial dollar cost of investing overseas is offset by the higher dollar return on future profits, and thus represents little if any deterrent.) On balance, the United States would probably gain at least $1 billion annually, after several years, from every 1 per cent devaluation of the dollar. A 5 per cent devaluation would thus be required to achieve the $5 billion payments improvement used as a guidepost throughout this chapter. The U.S. terms of trade would deteriorate by about $2–$3 billion as a result, producing an equivalent reduction in national income.[68]

66. Price elasticities of foreign travel were found to be quite high (3.4 for expenditures, 2.2 for receipts) for Germany in Jacques R. Artus, "The Effect of Revaluation on the Foreign Travel Balance of Germany," *IMF Staff Papers*, Vol. XVII, No. 3 (November 1970), pp. 602–19. The German expenditure elasticity cannot be taken to mean much for U.S. travelers, but the receipts elasticity is at least suggestive since a significant proportion of German receipts come from U.S. travelers. An earlier article, which studied the effects on tourist receipts of seven exchange-rate changes in the late 1950s, also discovered high price elasticities. See Andrea S. Gerhis, "Effects of Exchange-Rate Devaluations and Revaluations on Receipts From Tourism," *IMF Staff Papers*, Vol. XII, No. 3 (November 1965), pp. 365–84.
67. John Borcich, "Capital Flows, Devaluation, and the Balance of Payments," *Canadian Journal of Economics*, Vol. V, No. 2 (May 1972), pp. 227–36, concludes in his pioneering analysis of the effects of devaluation on the capital account that a devaluation which leads to both an improvement in the trade balance and reduced unemployment will also produce a reinforcing improvement in the capital account, especially in the short run. His model envisages a small country without significant external liabilities, however, and thus may not apply to the United States.
68. See Harry G. Johnson, "The Welfare Costs of Exchange Rate Stabilization," *Journal of Political Economy*, Vol. LXXIV, No. 5 (October 1966), pp. 512–18. Kreinen and Heller, *op. cit.*, estimate that every dollar of U.S. adjustment achieved through devaluation costs the United States 64 cents of income via the deterioration of its terms of trade—contrasted with 95 cents for Canada and $2–4 for all other major countries tested. However, they use the extremely low Houthakker-Magee elasticities, and their formula indicates that the cost to the United States would be only about 44 cents if the higher elasticities used in the text are included instead.

There were several major problems, however, which precluded the use of exchange-rate changes by the United States throughout most of the postwar period. All of them related to the existing international roles of the dollar, to the hopes of U.S. officials for preserving those roles, or to both.

The first was the simple (but powerful) technical problem that, while it could alter the official price of gold, the United States could not unilaterally alter its exchange rate vis-à-vis other currencies. Most other countries intervened in the exchange market with dollars, so they had to change *their* intervention points to effectuate a *U.S.* parity change. To be sure, other countries could maintain their intervention points only by changing their own parities (in terms of gold or any other numeraire) by the same amount as the United States changed the dollar parity. This would require majority approval of the IMF Executive Board, which the United States could fight. Nevertheless, it was still quite easy in the late 1960s to envisage a majority of the weighted votes in the Fund combining to approve each other's emulative parity changes, just as vested-interest majorities form frequently in the GATT to override U.S. objections to new EC preferential agreements. At a minimum, the United States would be uncertain about the effective change in its exchange rate which would result from changing its parity since it could not know *how* much others would let the dollar devalue, even assuming they would not emulate it altogether. Its great weight in the world economy would make other countries reluctant to accept parity changes for the dollar anyway, but the intervention currency role of the dollar provided a ready way for other countries to emulate and thus represented a significant handicap to U.S. adjustment via the exchange-rate mechanism.

This opportunity for other countries to frustrate a U.S. devaluation, though it stemmed from the dollar's intervention currency role, was rendered more likely to occur in practice by its reserve currency role. Dollar-holding countries would take a loss on the local-currency value of their reserves if the United States devalued against them.[69] They might thus emulate the U.S. move to prevent such

69. Aliber, *op. cit.*, p. 53, writing in 1966, argued that the concerns of other countries for their competitive positions were far more important than their fear of capital losses in determining their reluctance to let the United States devalue (though he recognized that the proposition could not be tested). He may have been right at that time, but it was also *at that time* that the United States was most concerned about losing the perceived benefits of the dollar's roles—especially financing for U.S. deficits and the direct and indirect political effects of a dollar-based system—which devaluation would have

losses.[70] It was at least partly because of these problems that the United States chose in August 1971 to apply the import surcharge and try to negotiate a new exchange rate for the dollar, rather than simply devaluing unilaterally (as it was permitted to do under the Articles of Agreement, since the move was by less than 10 per cent of its original postwar parity) to effect the realignment which it wanted,[71] and again in early 1973 felt that it had to negotiate a parity realignment before deciding on its own policy steps.

From the standpoint of achieving effective adjustment, however, the system was even worse for the United States than just precluding it from devaluing by itself. On balance, the other major countries used their active intervention and parity-changing options to actually force an implicit *revaluation* of the dollar throughout the 1960s —while the United States was running sizable payments deficits and being told by some of these very same countries to "put its house in order." The amount of this dollar appreciation was somewhere between 1 and 5 per cent, depending on the method of calculation[72] —which probably hurt the U.S. trade balance by amounts ranging between $1 billion and $5 billion annually by the end of the period.

---

risked. In any event, the confidence of the major foreign countries in their competitive position grew sharply in the later 1960s, as the U.S. trade balance deteriorated. So, while I believe that the devaluation constraints of the roles of the dollar alone were a much more important factor even in the earlier years than does Aliber, they clearly became more important after about 1967–68.

70. The importance of this factor is noted by one of the closest observers of national policies in this field, Milton Gilbert, *op. cit.*, p. 6, who contends that gold-bloc countries tried to avoid dollars precisely so that they would not face this additional complication in the face of a U.S. devaluation.

71. Brandon, *op. cit.*, p. 220, supports this view when he notes that "there was general agreement within the Administration that . . . other countries enjoyed a disconcerting whiphand over the dollar."

72. The lowest calculation of the implicit U.S. appreciation was 1.15 per cent against the other industrialized countries, in IMF, *The Role of Exchange Rates in the Adjustment of International Payments Imbalances* (Washington, D.C., 1970), p. 39. Including a number of less developed countries (ruling out only the 18 which devalued by more than 25 per cent), Edward Howle and Carlos F. H. Moore, "Richard Cooper's Gliding Parities: A Proposed Modification," *Journal of International Economics*, Vol. I, No. 4 (1971), p. 433, derived an appreciation of 3.1 per cent. Looking only at the Group of Ten, but using different weights than the IMF, Cooper, "Comment on the Howle-Moore Analysis and Proposed Modification of Cooper's Gliding Parity System," *ibid.*, p. 438, got a figure of 3.4 per cent. The highest estimate was 4.7 per cent, using weights based on trade with the United States rather than world trade shares, by Fred Hirsch and Ilse Higgins, "An Indication of Effective Exchange Rates," *IMF Staff Papers*, Vol. XVII, No. 2 (November 1970), p. 475.

The basic asymmetries in the system's adjustment process were central to this development, but the roles of the dollar both generated foreign demand for the U.S. currency—which became increasingly unsustainable because of the resulting divergence between the exchange rate of the dollar and the international competitive position of the U.S. economy on current account—and added to the scope for other countries to force such an effect on the United States. The dollar's roles provide one benefit in that they tilt the burden of *initiating* adjustment onto others, but the United States may very well suffer net costs as a result of the higher levels of payments deficits —or perverse "adjustment"—which result.

A further problem related to the broader policy aspects of the international roles of the dollar—primarily the reserve currency role, but also the intervention and vehicle currency roles to some extent. As indicated in Chapter 5, maintenance of each of these roles under the Bretton Woods system required confidence in the fixed-price convertibility of the dollar. U.S. parity changes, or even widespread expectations that the United States would consider parity changes, could thus have undermined the dollar's international roles even if the new parity promised to achieve payments equilibrium. The dash of numerous countries from the sterling area *after* the devaluation of 1967 was partly due to their renewed realization that a key currency could be devalued (as well as to lack of confidence in the new rate itself and underlying factors previously discussed), just as Britain's re-pegging in 1925 to the pre-World War I parity was largely motivated by a desire to retain foreign allegiance to sterling even though it was known that adjustment to it would be difficult. Resort to parity changes for adjustment would thus risk the benefits which the United States might otherwise obtain in the future from a continuation of these roles, which appeared to most U.S. officials at least until 1971 as outweighing the costs of the roles to the country as a whole. Only with the onset of major domestic problems which could be helped by devaluation were American officials ready to take this risk.

Next among the constraints, it was widely though that devaluation of the dollar would cause serious difficulties for the entire monetary system. It would cause major problems of liquidity, confidence, and even technical market intervention since the system had come to rest so largely on the dollar. One direct effect could be to enhance the role of gold, and hence set back the progress which had been made through the years in moving to a more rational base for world finance. Another, as just noted, could be a *subsequent* flight from the dollar toward other reserve assets and private transactions currencies—and the continued speculation against the dollar after the devaluations of both 1971 and 1973 seemed to bear out this fear. We will see in the next chapter that the United States has a major economic and political stake in the effective functioning of the monetary system, and we traced in Chapter 4 some of the political considerations which would lead it to assume a leadership role in promoting such a system in the first place. Accordingly, systemic considerations surrounding the roles of the dollar have also been an inhibition to devaluation. A conviction that the entire system was no longer stable, and required basic reform anyway, thus became necessary before most U.S. officials were ready to devalue the dollar.

The final problem was broadly political and relates almost wholly to the reserve currency role. Countries which had acquired and held uncovered dollars in their reserves would of course suffer a capital loss from a dollar devaluation. Some of them—particularly Canada, Germany, and Japan—were among the closest allies of the United States, and at least part of their willingness to hold dollars was due to overall alliance politics and explicit urging (especially in the case of Germany, with its public pledge in 1967 not to buy U.S. gold). Dollar devaluation could thus be read as a betrayal of their confidence, and cause internal political problems for governments which had cooperated with the United States in this way. As a result, many U.S. officials regarded the maintenance of the dollar exchange-rate as a matter of fundamental national honor (not unlike the way in which other officials regarded the commitment to Vietnam). At a minimum, this obligation forced the United States—like Britain before it—to *appear* to make every effort to avoid devaluing: by accepting financing, even under unfavorable terms; by extending exchange-value guarantees; by trying alternative adjustment options first. This concern loomed menacingly when the contemplated dollar devaluation was large, such as a doubling or tripling of the official price of gold as contemplated earlier in the 1960s for liquidity reasons. It could also become severe if frequent parity changes were contemplated for the dollar, since under such circumstances the United States could hardly ask others to accumulate unguaranteed dollar reserves without engendering serious political problems when it changed the dollar exchange rate.

The capital losses suffered by dollar holders as a result of the 1971 devaluation were protested only by the lower income countries. It did not have any serious impact on the industrialized dollar holders because the capital loss caused by the move was relatively small and could be fully offset by the interest on the dollar balances accumulated over just a year or two, and because the overriding political implications of "sharing the adjustment burden" prompted even the biggest dollar holders actually to call for a small dollar devaluation as part of the realignment package. In addition, some of these dollar reserves were guaranteed against a U.S. devaluation under swap arrangements or sales of Roosa bonds.

But all of these factors meant that the dollar's roles produced a deep-seated and fully understandable schizophrenia in the minds of American officials: Are the potential but uncertain[73] adjustment gains of devaluation worth the risks of (a) the potential gains from the dollar's roles in the future, (b) upsetting the entire monetary system, and (c) endangering some important political relationships? This schizophrenia has even pervaded U.S. thinking on the desirability of revaluations by other countries—which "denigrate the stability of the dollar" by devaluing it relative to the currency being revalued—and on increasing the flexibility of exchange rates in the system, as well as on whether the dollar itself should be overtly devalued. When Canada decided to float its currency in May 1970, high-level views within the U.S. government ranged from support for maximum appreciation of the Canadian dollar (to provide the maximum benefit for the U.S. competitive position) to "telling them they can't do it" (because of the implied devaluation of the American dollar). This psychological effect, which has frequently led to immobilism or ineffectual "adjustment" efforts that represented futile attempts to achieve partial de facto devaluation on a specific portions of the balance of payments, is one of the greatest costs of the dollar's roles to U.S. international monetary policy.[74]

Summary and Conclusion
The analysis of this chapter clearly indicates that neither cutbacks in domestic growth (beyond the anti-inflationary needs of the domestic economy) nor the policy mix approach can be regarded as real adjustment alternatives for the United States. The GNP cost of deflation is simply far too high—roughly $60 billion to achieve a net payments gain of $5 billion. The mix would create huge distor-

---

73. The adjustment gains were uncertain not only because of the unpredictability of foreign reaction, which was in turn partly due to the international roles of the dollar, but also because of the usual economic imponderables such as price elasticities. These uncertainties are no greater than those surrounding other adjustment alternatives, but may be a greater force for immobilism when added to the other uncertainties noted in the text which were peculiar to the devaluation option.

74. Since it was such financial concerns which permitted the dollar to become so overvalued by 1971 and cause significant losses of jobs for Americans, perhaps the Treasury Department and the Federal Reserve Board, rather than U.S. trade negotiators, should be accused of "selling out U.S. interests to the foreigners."

tions in the economy—such as 15 per cent interest rates and additional budget deficits of $100 billion—if it were expected to carry the major part of such an adjustment.

All of the other adjustment alternatives carry much lower GNP costs, probably of no more than $4–5 billion annually. (All these costs are in addition to the needed reduction of $5 billion in domestic expenditures—not GNP—if the adjustment is to come from an improvement in the current account.) Although the estimates are not sufficiently precise to have much confidence in ranking them within that range, it seems likely that the efficiency costs of current account and government controls ($4–$5 billion annually) might be slightly higher than the terms-of-trade effect of devaluation ($2–$3 billion) and the earnings foregone through capital controls (much less). The efficiency costs of incomes policy are highly uncertain. These differences are probably sufficiently small, however, that policy choices among them should be based on other considerations.

The major consideration is their efficiency in actually achieving adjustment. Only comprehensive controls over the entire balance of payments could bear any promise of achieving adjustment, and they would raise both major administrative and political problems. But neither comprehensive capital controls nor a uniform export subsidy/import surcharge scheme would probably be effective alone, because of feedback effects on the current account and retaliation-plus-emulation from abroad, respectively. Incomes policy is highly uncertain and depends very much on both domestic political and economic conditions. Partial capital controls are demonstrably ineffective.

Thus devaluation is probably the most effective among the adjustment policy options whose GNP costs could be considered acceptable to the United States, and in addition it is the only measure (besides incomes policy) which approaches equilibrium through basic changes in relative prices. The success of the Canadian, French, and American devaluations (as long as they were coupled with proper domestic policies, of course) in eliminating their payments deficits provides recent evidence of the effectiveness of exchange-rate changes, especially when contrasted with the ineffectiveness of the controls over specific international transactions adopted by those same countries to try to avoid devaluing.

The most effective adjustment measures, however, also violate most sharply the attributes required of a key currency country.[75]

75. As recognized by Treasury Secretary Henry H. Fowler in his important Grenada speech of May 27, 1966: "This [the reserve currency role of the dollar] is a very heavy responsibility, one that *prevents us from always doing just as we might like to do.*" Italics added.

Comprehensive exchange controls would directly violate the safety and liquidity requirements. Devaluation would directly violate the preservation of price stability of the asset, and also appears to undermine confidence in the future preservation thereof simply because it demonstrates that a change in the parity of the key currency can take place. Within the broad category of limited selective measures, both current account and capital controls are probably less consistent with the needed key currency attributes than are controls over government programs, because the former usually presages devaluation and the latter violates key currency criteria directly. Indeed, next to incomes policy, which violates no key currency attributes, government account controls are probably the least costly from this standpoint—but it will be recalled that they provide little hope for major improvement in the balance of payments short of basic changes in U.S. national security policy.

In addition, the effects of the actual existence of the key currency role have severely constrained the United States from using the devaluation option. The conclusion of this section is clear: the financing provided for U.S. payments deficits by the international roles of the dollar have been of very high cost to the United States, because those very roles have themselves severely limited its capability to adjust its payments position effectively. The psychological decision-making problems which derive from all of the dollar's roles, the political problems which derive primarily from the reserve currency role and led the United States to exhaust all alternatives before considering devaluation in 1971, and the technical problems which derive primarily from the transactions/intervention function fused to inhibit severely the willingness and ability of the United States to devalue—the only economically effective means of adjustment which was politically acceptable both at home and abroad. In addition, the dollar's roles discouraged the use of comprehensive capital controls, which, although less effective than devaluation, is the only other adjustment device that is politically acceptable both at home and abroad. These are among the most critical dilemmas of the dollar for U.S. international monetary policy.

The dollar's roles thus forced the United States to make every effort to avoid adjustment, because the only effective alternatives were so costly. As a result, it took advantage of the financing opportunities provided by those roles, and took numerous steps to buttress and prolong them. When adjustment did seem necessary, the dollar's roles meant that the United States could confidently adopt only ineffective capital controls, politically dangerous current account controls, or a highly uncertain incomes policy. Other countries could talk about deflation or changes in the U.S. policy mix, but both were politically impossible for the United States in any significant degree. (This of course excludes the non-dilemma cases of 1968 and 1971 when the tax hike and incomes policy, respectively, were needed for purely internal anti-inflationary reasons.)

The dollar's roles thus provided both a major benefit for the United States, by enabling it to avoid cutting growth or sharp structural change for payments reasons, and levied a heavy cost by relegating it to adjustment impotence. A continuation of the dollar's roles would extend this situation into the future. The United States must therefore insist that at least the major countries agree to make effective U.S. adjustment possible, either by eliminating the roles of the dollar or by accepting the dollar even in a system in which its price can change frequently.[76] The United States must get control of its exchange rate to really possess the adjustment option, and doing so raises basic questions about the international roles of the dollar. In the best of all worlds for it, the United States would have either the adjustment or the financing options for use when unemployment and inflation, respectively, are the chief domestic economic problems. But this would be seen abroad as further enhancing the asymmetry of the system in favor of the United States, and would be impossible to achieve in practice.

The resolution of these issues thus goes to the heart of reform of the overall international monetary system. The potential scope for dollar financing for U.S. deficits and better scope for adjustment depend critically on the nature of the system. Two more ingredients are therefore needed before we can reach policy conclusions. One is an analysis of how the various candidates for systemic reform would handle these questions. But this must wait until Part III, with the final chapter of this section completing the basis for judging the reform options—rounding out the costs and benefits to the United States of the dollar's roles—by analyzing the interests of the United States in an effective monetary system and how the international roles of the dollar have both added to, and subtracted from, such effectiveness in the past.

76. Robert Mundell agrees: "The U.S. is powerless to correct its deficit short of forbidding other countries to buy or use dollars. . . . Only by creating a substitute for the dollar . . . can the U.S. correct its balance of payments." See his analysis in "A Plan for a New European Currency," in Johnson and Swoboda, eds., *The Economics of Common Currencies*, esp. p. 155. We will see in Chapter 11 that it was precisely such a view which has been one basis of Jacques Rueff's long-standing advocacy of eliminating all use of key currencies in favor of "a return to the gold standard."

10

The U.S. Interest in the International Monetary System

In addition to their direct and indirect economic impacts, as analyzed in the preceding three chapters, the international roles of the dollar affect the United States through their influence on the entire system. An analysis of this raises two basic questions: Does the United States have an important national interest, economic or political, in an effective international monetary system? Do the dollar's roles contribute to, or detract from, the maintenance of such a system?

The U.S. Economic Interest in an Effective System
The international economy is functioning effectively if it promotes optimum economic progress in the national economies which it comprises. In general, it can best do so by permitting the maximum international flow of goods, services, and the mobile factors of production —capital, management, labor to a lesser degree—which are motivated by market conditions.[1] On the other hand, the international economy is dysfunctional if it contains widespread restraints on these transactions. The prototype is the 1930s, when sharp limitations set by most countries on international trade and capital flows deepened the Great Depression.

1. For the moment, this begs the question of which flows are motivated or discouraged by "real" market conditions and by market distortions (e.g., differential tax treatments) or market imperfections (e.g., lack of knowledge concerning foreign demand). It also leaves open whether the international costs of particular types of flows, such as short-term capital movements, exceed their international benefits. It is based on *global* welfare considerations, recognizing that the national welfare of individual countries can be imposed by the adoption of an "optimum tariff" or "optimum capital restrictions"—if no one else emulates or retaliates. And it makes the usual assumption that microeconomic dislocations for particular groups can be effectively countered either through macroeconomic full-employment policies or microeconomic policies tailored to the specific problems.

An effective monetary system is a necessary underpining for an effectively functioning international economy. Inconvertibility of national currencies is the most pervasive restraint on international transactions; as noted in Chapter 3, the maintenance of convertibility was an inviolable policy goal before World War I and its restoration was the major objective of the Bretton Woods system. However, countries will accept the risks of convertibility—despite its potential gains—only if they have faith in the existing monetary mechanism. This in turn requires that they be assured of some combination of international reserves and adjustment procedures which will provide a high probability that they will not have to retreat quickly back to inconvertibility (like Britain in 1947), or adopt domestic deflation or a panoply of other controls to preserve convertibility at an unacceptably high cost (like Britain in 1926).

A country with inadequate reserves or access to credit will have to adjust its payments deficits quickly. Hence it will be unable to rely on underlying gains in its competitive position, or even on small changes in its exchange rate. One option is excessive devaluation, in an effort to get large real effects and to make the new rate credible to speculators so as to reverse the previous flow of liquid capital, but this is often costly to national economic objectives (such as price stability). A likely course then is direct controls over its international transactions; controls are widely perceived to be the most rapid possible way to adjust—which in fact may be true if the controls are sufficiently widespread to be effective.

An inadequate adjustment process has similar effects. Payments problems cumulate if early attention is not paid to them. As a result, they become increasingly intractable in both economic and political terms. A small amount of deflation to correct a small deficit may be acceptable, but large-scale deflation certainly is not. A failure to move exchange rates at an early stage creates a problem; governments become publicly committed to the existing rate, and concerns over "admitting defeat" (for a deficit country) or for "solving the problems of others" (for surplus countries) add greatly to the increased real economic effects of larger shifts, which are already formidable.

The history of the postwar period clearly supports these conclusions. Pervasive exchange and trade controls were maintained to protect the balance-of-payments positions of virtually all countries until 1958, when a number of the major industrialized nations made their currencies convertible.[2] Even after that time, however, the major

2. Even the major European countries did not accept the convertibility obligation of Article VIII of the IMF until February 1961, and Japan did not do so

deficit countries resorted first to controls in all dilemma adjustment cases which they faced while trying to preserve fixed parities as soon as they have concluded that further financing was unavailable and adjustment was therefore necessary.

The chronic deficit countries of this period were the United States and Britain. The United States started to adopt controls over its overseas government transactions in 1959–60; sought to influence private capital flows in 1961 and began to control outflows in 1963; tightened those controls in 1965 and 1968, and contemplated a tax on foreign travel by Americans in 1968; and adopted a temporary import surcharge and permanent export subsidy in 1971, before finally devaluing in 1971 and 1973 by sizable amounts. This cumulative development of an overvalued dollar, by accelerating the growth of imports and of foreign investment by U.S. firms, played a major role in promoting unemployment and the growth of protectionist trade pressures domestically, which nearly succeeded in subjecting a wide range of U.S. imports to quotas through the "Mills bill" of 1970 and gave rise to the concerted pressure for protectionist trade and investment policies manifest by the submission of the Burke-Hartke bill.[3] Britain progressively tightened its capital controls in each of its payments crises from 1961 through 1966, and imposed an import surcharge and export subsidy in 1964, before finally devaluing in 1967. France responded to its 1968 payments crisis by instituting a wide range of trade and capital controls, before finally devaluing almost a year later. The one partial exception was Canada, which devalued and imposed an import surcharge simultaneously to remedy its payments deficit in 1962.[4]

Similar results are evident on the surplus side. Germany was the chronic surplus country throughout the 1960s. Time after time, it tried to use controls to stop capital inflows: especially before its small revaluation of 1961, to forestall the need to do so again in

until April 1964. Only Mexico (1946), the United States (1946), Canada (1952), and several Central American and Caribbean countries, some of which have honored their obligations mostly in the breach, had done so previously. As of this writing, there are still only 32 countries which have moved to Article VIII status.

3. See C. Fred Bergsten, "Crisis in U.S. Trade Policy," *Foreign Affairs*, July 1971, and Paul A. Samuelson, "International Trade for a Rich Country," *Morgan Guaranty Survey*, July 1972, esp. p. 7.

4. Italy also imposed capital controls in 1964. However, the purpose of the controls was primarily to halt the masking of its ongoing payments deficit through inflows of Eurodollars. Italy adjusted by dampening the growth of its domestic economy, which was the proper step in such a non-dilemma case.

1964, and to quell the crises of 1968. It took numerous steps to promote capital exports and agreed to "offset" the bulk of U.S. and U.K. military expenditure in Germany. In 1968 it even altered its border tax rebate system, increasing the tax burden on exports and reducing the burden on imports, in an effort to head off the revaluation which eventually came a year later. Other smaller surplus countries, notably Switzerland and Austria, took similar steps.

The country most recently in chronic surplus, Japan, seemed for a while to be replaying in the 1970s the German effort of the 1960s. It sought to counter pressure for continued revaluations by liberalizing old deficit-suppressing controls and creating new surplus-reducing controls, mainly on capital inflows but increasingly on trade as well. The prolonged maintenance of undervalued exchange rates in all these countries—which was a self-reinforcing process, because domestic industries expanded their capacity to take advantage of the export opportunities provided in part by undervaluation and then lobbied with even greater vigor against revaluation—intensified their competitive advantages in world trade and hence exacerbated political pressures for protectionist trade controls in the United States and elsewhere.

Even with the advent of greater flexibility of exchange rates in the early 1970s—*due* to that phenomenon, according to some—controls continued to proliferate. Surplus countries sought to avoid "excessive" appreciation of their currencies by checking capital inflows, and the United States maintained its controls over capital outflows to avoid charges that it was "unfairly" enhancing its competitive position by encouraging further dollar depreciation. The theoretical substitutability of controls and exchange-rate changes gave way in practice to complementarity, due to continued disagreement over the proper structure of national payments positions and the fundamental goals of the international economy.

It is thus clear that an ineffective international monetary system generates controls over international transactions, most of which reduce world economic welfare. The relatively smooth pre-1914 system largely avoided such controls. The chaotic non-system of the 1930s certainly generated them. The system that prevailed in the 1960s, which is usually given high marks despite its periodic crises, did so; the level of world controls declined briefly after the advent of general convertibility in 1958, but soon began to grow again. And they continued to grow despite the advent of exchange-rate flexibility in the early 1970s.

In addition, an ineffective system generates excessively large and hence unnecessarily jarring exchange-rate changes. As noted in Chapter 9, such changes finally become inevitable because controls provide no fundamental adjustment for underlying disequilibria. Because they are so long delayed, and the disequilibria which they must correct are so large, the needed magnitude of exchange-rate changes becomes quite uncertain. As a result of the uncertainty and the need to convince speculators that the move finally adopted will be definitive, devaluations tend to be excessive and promote new undervaluations—as in the French cases of 1958 and 1969, and the British case of 1967. Similarly, revaluations tend to be inadequate and permit continued undervaluation—as in the German cases of 1961 and 1969, and the Japanese case of 1971. Under flexible rates there have also been wide gyrations: sterling rose and fell by about 10 per cent after it floated in mid-1972, and the dollar fell and then rose by a like amount against some currencies within a few months in 1973. Exchange-rate changes under both the Bretton Woods and floating rate systems may thus fail to correct existing imbalances smoothly, and even create new ones, thus providing an environment in which controls are likely to continue to proliferate. The next issue is whether such controls, excessive exchange-rate changes, and persistence of exchange-rate disequilibria have significantly adverse effects on the United States.

The Economic Interest of the United States in the World Economy
The conventional wisdom in this area runs as follows. The United States is less reliant on international trade than any other country in the world except the Soviet Union and the People's Republic of China. Exports and imports of merchandise were each about 5.5 per cent of GNP in 1973, and the addition of exports and imports of services brings each ratio only to about 8 per cent. Few U.S. firms need foreign markets to maintain production runs of adequate scale to achieve maximum efficiency. The size of its market is so large that, aside from a few agricultural commodities and raw materials, the United States is relatively self-sufficient and could survive a sharp drop in most imports.

Until August 1971, U.S. balance-of-payments policy was based on this perceived high degree of self-reliance. Unlike all other countries, the United States was willing to let its exchange rate—a key element of its international competitive position—be determined by others, and indeed to let the effective exchange rate of the dollar appreciate throughout the decade despite the persistence of payments deficits and, after 1964, a declining trade surplus. Alone among the major countries, it devoted no significant budgetary resources to export promotion or to serious efforts to deal with structural unemployment resulting from imports.[5]

However, this policy prevailed in a period which will undoubtedly prove to have been unique in U.S. history. During the first 10 to 15 years of the postwar decade, the United States had little real international competition; it thus viewed an open world economy as the only support needed for its domestic economic objectives.[6] Subsequently, just as such competition began to develop in the early 1960s with the creation of the EEC and the economic revival of Japan, the United States emerged from recession and began a spectacular period of economic growth. Unemployment fell steadily from 1962 until 1969; corporate profits rose steadily from 1961 through 1966, and remained at that record level through 1969. Such economic success meant that U.S. economy had little need to concern itself about a competitive international environment until the early 1970s, when that environment for the first time coincided with high unemployment and excessive inflation at home. The dramatic reversal of U.S. international economic policy in August 1971 was the manifestation of these changed circumstances.

These circumstances, however, are likely to be normal in the future, and they have revealed the underlying importance of the international economy to the U.S. economy. Despite its small share in the overall economy, foreign trade is huge in absolute terms—by far the largest of any country in the world. Exports and imports of goods each reached $70 billion by 1973, and exports and imports of services added over $25 billion to each total. Exports of merchandise provided jobs for about 2.6 million Americans, imports sustained another 1 million jobs,[7] and foreign investment added perhaps an-

---

5. The *concept* of adjustment assistance for U.S. firms and workers hurt by imports was incorporated in the Trade Expansion Act of 1962, a major breakthrough which overcame violent opposition to its "socialist" implications and passed the House Ways and Means Committee by only one vote. However, not a single case of assistance took place until 1969, due to the tightness of the statutory requirements and their rigid implementation by both the Tariff Commission and the Kennedy and Johnson administrations. Such assistance takes places in most other industrialized countries in the normal course of their overall industrial and manpower policies.

6. Revisionist historians, such as Joyce and Gabriel Kolko, *American Foreign Policy, 1945–1953*, argue that U.S. policy in the early postwar period was dominated by concern for U.S. economic objectives. This view fails completely to recognize the political importance attached to a liberal world economy by U.S. postwar planners, as discussed in the next section. The Kolkos note correctly, however, that such concern for U.S. economic interests as did exist primarily took the form of promoting a world economic system based on currency convertibility and free trade—not of export subsidies and other direct supports for U.S. business.

other 250,000.[8] Investment in foreign plant and equipment by U.S. firms exceeded $16 billion in 1972 alone, and the (grossly understated) book value of these investments approaches $100 billion—and are only about one-half of total U.S. foreign assets. Sales by the foreign affiliates of U.S. manufacturing firms alone exceed $80 billion. U.S. liabilities to foreigners far exceed $100 billion. International securities transactions by Americans totaled about $35 billion in 1971.

In addition to these massive absolute figures, the share of international transactions in some U.S. aggregates is impressive. Exports amount to about 13 per cent of total goods production. Imports provide a similar share of the goods available to U.S. consumers; they have already become critical for some key individual commodities, most notably oil, and may soon become equally critical for a wide range of raw materials.[9] More than 15 per cent of total plant and equipment expenditures of U.S. firms is now made abroad, and for manufacturing firms this figure is about 20 per cent. All of these figures are growing; for example, foreign investment by U.S. firms has been rising twice as fast as domestic investment for over a decade.

Indeed, U.S. dependence on the world economy may, in aggregate terms, now be almost as great as the dependence of the two other economic power centers, the European Community (taken as a group) and Japan. Exports represent less than 10 per cent of the GNP of each, compared with 6 per cent for the United States. But the U.S. ratio has been growing far faster than the EC and Japanese ratios. And U.S. firms are far more reliant on foreign investment than European and Japanese firms, so adding profits to the calculation for each might go far toward eliminating the remaining difference.

For individual sectors and firms, much higher percentages abound. Earnings from foreign operations now contribute a major share of U.S. corporate profits.[10] About one-third of U.S. farm acreage pro-

7. Andrew F. Brimmer, "Imports and Economic Welfare in the United States," Remarks before the Foreign Policy Association, New York City, February 16, 1972. Imports also pre-empt domestic jobs, of course, although Brimmer concluded that foreign trade on balance generated 750,000 U.S. jobs even when the trade balance dipped into deficit in 1971.
8. Raymond Vernon, "A Skeptic Looks at the Balance of Payments," *Foreign Policy* (Winter 1971–72). The *net* employment effect of direct investment is much less clear.
9. C. Fred Bergsten, "The Threat From the Third World," *Foreign Policy*, 11 (Summer 1973), pp. 102–24.
10. Lawrence B. Krause, "The International Economic System and the Multinational Corporation," *Annals*, Sept. 1972, p. 96, notes that before-tax foreign profits amount to 20–25 per cent of U.S. after-tax profits. Available data do not permit an accurate comparison of foreign to domestic after-tax profits, but they are widely estimated in the 10–15 per cent range in the aggregate and much higher for many individual firms.

duces for export. Exports account for about 27 per cent of employment in the construction machinery industry, 15 per cent in engines and turbines, 14 per cent in aircraft, and 13 per cent in office and computing machines. More than one-half of the sales and profits of numerous firms now derive from their international activities.[11]

Finally, at the broadest level of macroeconomic policy, international transactions can play an important strategic role for the United States. The increasing overvaluation of the dollar contributed to a decline of almost $10 billion in net U.S. exports from 1964 to 1971, reducing GNP by that amount and perhaps eliminating 500,000–750,000 jobs annually by the end of the period. The subsequent depreciations of the dollar added several percentage points to the U.S. inflation rate, and were a major factor in its dramatic rise in 1973–74. Import restrictions were costing American consumers perhaps $20 billion annually in the early 1970s[12] and raising the overall U.S. price level by a similar amount. The competitiveness of the American economy, which is its chief driving force toward greater economic efficiency and maintaining a low level of unemployment, would decrease perceptibly if domestic textile firms had to pay much more for their foreign machinery or if auto manufacturers had to pay much more for the foreign components in their compact cars, and if firms no longer had to compete at all in the world marketplace. Trade flows are particularly important to the United States because of shifts in the structure of the labor force, which make it much harder to restrain inflation while maintaining full employment in the 1970s: inflation rates tend to be 1.5 percentage points higher at full employment than they were even a decade ago.[13] This requires the imagina-

11. Eighty-six multinational firms with consolidated sales of $85 billion in 1970, polled in early 1972 by *Business International*, indicated that about 27 per cent of their 1970 sales were made outside the United States. From 1966 to 1970, foreign sales rose by 82 per cent compared with 23 per cent for domestic sales. 22 per cent of their gross investment budgets were spent outside the United States in 1970, compared with 18 per cent in 1966. 31 per cent of new fixed assets were installed in foreign affiliates in 1970, and 24 per cent of their increase in new fixed assets took place outside the country over the entire 1960–70 period.

12. C. Fred Bergsten, "The Costs of Import Restrictions to the American Consumer," in Robert A. Baldwin and B. David Richardson, *International Trade and Finance* (Boston: Little, Brown, 1974), as modified by the analysis of the consumer costs of U.S. tariffs in Stephen Magee, "The Welfare Effects of Restriction on U.S. Trade," *Brookings Papers on Economic Activity* 3, 1972, pp. 645–708.

13. George L. Perry, "Changing Labor Markets and Inflation," *Brookings Papers on Economic Activity* 3, 1970, pp. 411–41; Charles L. Schultze, "Has the Phillips Curve Shifted? Some Additional Evidence, *Brookings Papers on Economic Activity* 2, 1971, pp. 452–67.

tive use of new selective policies, as on incomes and manpower, to supplement macroeconomic fiscal and monetary policies to achieve the twin goals of full employment and price stability.

Liberal trade pursued under equilibrium exchange rates is such a policy. The avoidance of an overvalued dollar avoids additional difficulties in reducing the stubbornly high rate of unemployment. It would also avoid the inflationary shocks of ultimately sizable devaluation. And avoidance of an undervalued dollar would avoid unnecessary inflationary effects. An elimination of present U.S. trade restrictions could offset some of the increase in prices caused by the structural shifts in the labor force. In addition, it would have a lasting effect by increasing the competitive pressures on American firms and workers. On the other hand, renewed overvaluation of the dollar could complicate further the effort to restore and then maintain employment, and increasing restrictions on international trade would add to the inflationary tendencies in the United States.

Since about 1968, the Executive Council of the AFL-CIO has adopted a view directly contrary to the analysis just offered. This view asserts that a liberal international trade and investment regime *hurts* the American economy by robbing it of jobs through excessive growth of imports of goods produced at "unfair low wages" abroad and through the "export of jobs" by U.S. multinational corporations.[14] The AFL-CIO has sought relief from both evils through legislation.

On imports, it is clear that the AFL-CIO argument is totally erroneous. More barriers to imports will increase U.S. unemployment, rather than reduce it. The reasons for this are (1) a reduction in imports from foreign countries means that their incomes drop, so they are unable to buy as much U.S. merchandise, and (2) other countries would retaliate against such increased U.S. barriers, directly or indirectly, on at least a dollar-for-dollar basis. There would thus be no net increase in the U.S. export balance, and the level of both exports and imports would be lower. This could even cost American jobs, because U.S. exports are on the average more labor-intensive than U.S. imports; an average dollar's worth of exports produces

14. For the most thorough exposition of this approach, see Stanley R. Ruttenberg and Associates, *Needed: A Constructive Foreign Trade Policy*, a special study commissioned and published by the Industrial Unions Department, AFL CIO, October 1971. The paper supports the elimination of dollar overvaluation and the achievement of an improved monetary system to avoid such overvaluation in the future; it does not disagree with the analysis in the text on this issue, but regards such steps as wholly inadequate to meet the "real problems" which it perceives.

more jobs here than a dollar's worth of imports eliminates.[15] In addition, the higher prices resulting from import barriers reduce the overall purchasing power of Americans, because a larger share of their incomes has to be used to buy the restricted goods, and hence reduces demand for domestic productions and jobs.[16]

The fallacy of the employment argument for protectionism is best exposed by simply referring to the situation of 1968 and 1969, when there coexisted the lowest rate of unemployment since the Korean War and the lowest trade surpluses in the 1960s. (To be sure, inflation was accelerating and the overall economic situation was far from perfect at that time; nevertheless, the correlation between full employment and a small trade surplus was clear.) Imports were rising dramatically while unemployment was falling dramatically. The high rate of activity of the U.S. economy, which generated such job growth, also generated major pressures on the price level—which were mitigated at least partially by the surge of imports. And it was this high rate of domestic economic activity plus the increasing overvaluation of the dollar accompanying it, rather than any fundamental decline in U.S. competitiveness or "unfair foreign trade practices,"[17] which caused imports to grow so rapidly. Indeed, the switch to a protectionist stance by the AFL-CIO at a time when aggregate unemployment was at its lowest level in twenty years clearly suggests that other reasons—such as a desire to avoid any changes in the *structure* of production, with the dislocations for individual workers which accompany them—dominated its decision to take this position. Such job changes are a real problem, to be sure,

15. Lawrence B. Krause, "How Much of Current Unemployment Did We Import?" *Brookings Papers on Economic Activity* 2, 1971, esp. pp. 421–25, concludes that each $1 billion of additional exports from the first quarter of 1970 to the first quarter of 1971 created 111,000 jobs, while each $1 billion of additional imports over the same period displaced 88,600 jobs. Brimmer, "Imports and Economic Welfare in the United States," pp. 11–17, updates earlier Department of Labor data and concludes that each $1 billion of exports in 1971 produced an average of 66,000 jobs while each $1 billion of imports produced an average of just under 65,000 jobs. The marginal analysis of Krause is of course more relevant, since policy issues deal with changes from current levels. See in addition the enormous literature since 1953 on this so-called "Leontief paradox."
16. Based on an assumption that imports are about 10 per cent cheaper than domestic goods, Brimmer, "Imports and Economic Welfare in the United States," concludes that consumers have about $4 billion more to spend as a result of the imports and, since about 90,000 domestic jobs are created for every $1 billion of consumer expenditures, that 360,000 jobs are created.
17. Indeed, U.S. nontariff trade barriers rose sharply during the 1960s while foreign trade barriers declined. This means that the U.S. trade position was probably helped, not hindered, by changes in commercial policies.

and must be met through the maintenance of aggregate full employment and an effective program of adjustment assistance.

In addition, one must conclude that the Executive Council of the AFL-CIO has now come to support protectionist trade policies, reversing its traditional liberal stance, at least partly because the AFL-CIO no longer accurately represents the overall American labor force. Its constituent unions represent less than 20 per cent of all American workers, and even this sample is highly skewed.[18] Manufacturing workers constitute over 43 per cent of the membership of the AFL-CIO, but only 26 per cent of the total labor force. They are thus "over-represented" by 67 per cent or a ratio of about 5 to 3, in the organized labor movement. Nonmanufacturing workers are correspondingly "under-represented," comprising 74 per cent of the total labor force but only 57 per cent of the AFL-CIO. The differences at this broad level are even sharper if allowance is made for the unusual degree of unionization of contract construction workers; eliminating them from the total of "nonmanufacturing" workers reduces that category's share of AFL-CIO membership to 40 per cent. This skewness between the manufacturing and nonmanufacturing sectors has major implications for trade policy, since it is American manufacturing workers who compete directly in international trade and thus seek protection, whereas services workers, whose product does not compete internationally, have the greatest interest as consumers in maximizing trade flows.

The skewness of the AFL-CIO representation on trade issues becomes even clearer, however, from disaggregated data. First, the two industries which are most vocal about their problems with imports are the two major manufacturing industries most "over-represented" in the AFL-CIO, apparel and steel. Second, virtually all other industries which have pleaded for protection from imports are heavily over-represented in the AFL-CIO: petroleum refining workers have a representation ratio of 200 per cent; leather and leather products workers, of which shoe workers are the great majority, also have a ratio of 200 per cent; glass workers are in a broader group with a ratio of 189 per cent; even workers in the food industries, within which meat, dairy and sugar have traditionally been protected sectors, have a ratio of 126 per cent. Third, the major components of the labor force with a major interest in liberal trade, as

18. See the table in Bergsten, "The Costs of Import Restrictions to the American Consumer," *op. cit.*, pp. 14–16; it develops "representation ratios," which compare the share of each industry group in the labor force as a whole with its share in the AFL-CIO.

consumers whose output does not face import competition, are the grossly under-represented services workers, with representation ratios ranging from 6 per cent to 38 per cent for exceedingly large components of the labor force. Fourth, those manufacturing industries which continue successfully to expand their export markets are not heavily represented: the export-oriented professional, scientific, and controlling instruments workers have a representation ratio of only 50 per cent, and are the worst represented of all manufacturing industries; nonelectrical machinery, the industry in which the United States has its largest—and a rapidly growing—trade surplus ($7 billion in 1970), has a ratio of only 108 per cent, one of the lowest for a major manufacturing group; the chemical industry, with a growing surplus which exceeded $2 billion in 1970, has a ratio of only 114 per cent; transportation equipment, which in the AFL-CIO comprises mainly aircraft workers, whose trade surplus reached $2.5 billion in 1970 and was growing fast, has a ratio of only 88 per cent. The only exception to the pattern is electrical machinery, with a smaller though sizable ($1 billion in 1970) trade surplus and a representation ratio of 208 per cent; however, a significant portion of that industry has been threatened by rapidly growing imports of radios, television sets, other consumer electronic products, and components, and the industry is thus split internally concerning trade policy and does not take an industry-wide position on the issue.

The composition of AFL-CIO membership, due to its contrast with the make-up of the total labor force, thus goes far to explain the Federation's new position on trade. Indeed, shifts in representation ratios since 1961 add to the explanation: the textile and leather goods workers increased their ratios from 176 per cent to 203 per cent, the glass group grew from 160 per cent to 200 per cent, the group dominated by chemical workers declined from 123 per cent to 104 per cent, and the transportation equipment group dropped sharply from 303 per cent to 88 per cent as the United Auto Workers (who have maintained a basically liberal trade position) left the Federation. So the AFL-CIO can hardly be expected to represent accurately the view of all labor, at least on the issue of international trade policy.

On international investment, the net economic effect on the United States is far less clear. Organized labor has not proved its assertion that foreign investment by U.S. firms represents the "export of jobs" that could otherwise be retained for American workers. But neither have the corporations proved their contention that such investment keeps them from losing out entirely to foreign firms and saves at home by enabling them to supply their foreign plants with American-made components, preserve U.S. management positions, and repatriate earnings which ultimately produce additional jobs for Americans. Their demonstration that they have expanded their domestic employment at a faster pace than the national average at the same time that their foreign investments have been rising sharply (the main line of their defenses)[19] proves nothing about whether those investments themselves added or subtracted jobs in the United States.

What is needed is a detailed comparison between the job effects of U.S. foreign investments that have actually taken place and the job effects of the most likely alternative course of events had those investments not occurred. So far, all broad-scale analyses have been based purely on (explicit or implicit) *assumptions* about alternative developments.[20] Similar analysis is needed to obtain better understanding of the balance-of-payments effects of these investments, which depend critically on whether, on balance, they increase or decrease the U.S. trade surplus.

Thus we do not now have an analytical basis for judging the merits of foreign investment from the standpoint of U.S. national interests. It is probable that such an analysis will show the United States needs a set of policies to enable it to deal with problems caused by specific investments, just as it has policies (the escape clause, countervailing duties, antidumping duties, adjustment assistance) enabling it to deal

19. 121 firms queried by the U.S. Chamber of Commerce increased their domestic employment by 31.1 per cent from 1960 to 1970, compared with the national average of 12.3 per cent. In addition to the fundamental irrelevance of this argument as noted in the text, these firms accounted for only 17.3 per cent of total manufacturing employees and may have represented a very biased sample, and *their* employment growth included growth through mergers which did not create employment growth in the *overall* American economy. See the Chamber's "Multinational Enterprise Survey," February 1972.

20. There has been one effort adopting this methodology, but it was primarily limited to a number of relatively simply cases in which the market was motivated by high foreign tariffs. It did, however, include one case where U.S. investment abroad to produce radio components admittedly cost U.S. jobs in the short run but allegedly saved jobs after five years because imports wholly produced abroad would otherwise have seized the U.S. market. In addition, this study focused solely on single-firm effects, and did not include aggregate macroeconomic effects in the particular markets. The study estimated, on the basis of rather limited evidence, that U.S. foreign investment in 1971 generated about 600,000 jobs—250,000 in main offices of U.S. multinational enterprises, and perhaps another 100,000 for associated "supporting workers." It made no effort, however, to set against these the jobs that might be *lost* by foreign investment substituting for U.S. exports. See Robert R. Stobaugh and Associates, "U.S. Multinational Enterprises and the U.S. Economy," January 1972.

with problems caused by specific trade flows, and that the merits of any policies which subsidize foreign investment (such as several features of the tax code) are dubious. But it is highly improbable that such analysis would suggest an interest in checking all, or even the bulk, of the foreign investments that take place in response to market incentives. And it is also clear that there is emerging an important need for new international rules to check the rising tendencies for host countries to such investments to place strict controls on their performance, which tilts the benefits generated by the investments away from the home country of the firms—most frequently, the United States.[21]

It thus seems clear the United States has important economic interests in preserving a world economy in which controls over international transactions are minimized, and in which exchange-rate equilibrium is maintained. Huge amounts of American output and investment and large numbers of jobs are involved. Particularly at the margin, these international transactions are of major importance to particular sectors of the economy. They are of overwhelming importance to individual U.S. firms and groups of workers. The relative importance of all these transactions is growing steadily, and will continue to do so, barring a major onset of controls or general international instability. The United States as a whole relies less on these transactions than do other countries, but they nevertheless play an extremely important role in its economy and any serious cutbacks therein could retard domestic welfare.

Perhaps equally important to such a substantive outcome is continued confidence in it. Fears that international economic cooperation was about to collapse, and fears over the uncertainties that would result, clearly dampened the investment plans of U.S. firms and overall economic expansion during the crisis triggered by the U.S. actions of August 1971.[22] The international monetary system must be sufficiently effective to preserve confidence in the world economy if it is to foster optimum economic progress in all countries, including the United States, and avoid crises of ever-deepening importance.

The U.S. Political Interest
The United States sponsored the creation of a liberal world economic order in the aftermath of World War II largely for political reasons.

21. C. Fred Bergsten, "Coming Investment Wars?" *Foreign Affairs*, October 1974.
22. As testified by Arthur Burns, Chairman of the Board of Governors of the Federal Reserve System, in his statement before the House Committee on Banking and Currency, March 2, 1972, p. 5.

Postwar planners read the history of the interwar period as suggesting close links among factors such as the collapse of the world economy and international economic relations, national economic chaos (including both mass unemployment and runaway inflation), and the political rise of totalitarian governments of both Right and Left, which together led to war. An essential step in avoiding a repetition of those disasters was the creation of a liberal world economy that would reverse the experience of the 1930s. The Bretton Woods system and the GATT were born primarily of that impulse.

Subsequent U.S. international economic policies had a similar basis. The Marshall Plan and the Point IV program sought to prevent political instability, particularly as fomented by Communists, in the war-torn and underdeveloped countries. The economic unification of Europe was to make it impossible for Germany and France to go to war for a fourth time within a century, as well as to strengthen the non-Communist alliance against the totalitarian threat. Even the Kennedy Round of tariff reductions and the creation of Special Drawing Rights (SDR) fit the same pattern. All these steps were viewed as serving U.S. economic interests, but their major motivation was political. This is borne out by the major role played by the foreign affairs bureaucracy throughout postwar U.S. foreign economic policy.

Such broad political concerns continue to play a major role in U.S. foreign economic policy, if in a somewhat different way due to the changed international political and economic milieu. As repeatedly indicated, international economic transactions are far more important to all other non-Communist countries than they are to the United States; most countries rely critically on a smoothly functioning international economy for the maintenance of satisfactory economic progress at home.

International economic issues are thus extremely important in political terms in virtually all countries. Exchange rates, balance of payments, and trade issues have played major roles in recent elections and governmental shifts in Britain, Germany, and Japan. And it appears that a devaluation under the rules of the Bretton Woods monetary system roughly doubled the chance that a ruling group in a lower income country would be removed from power, and roughly tripled the likelihood that responsible finance ministers would lose their jobs.[23]

In view of their crucial political effects *within* countries, these

23. Richard N. Cooper, "Currency Devaluation in Developing Countries," *Princeton Essays in International Finance*, No. 86, June 1971, pp. 23–29.

issues are necessarily crucial in relations *among* countries. They therefore assume an important role in U.S. relations with virtually all countries. The degree of importance depends, of course, on the presence or absence of other issues in these relations; security and political issues still generally dominate economic issues in U.S. relations with Germany, while the paucity of other issues places economic matters in the forefront of U.S. relations with Canada, Mexico, and many lower income countries.

In recent years, however, economic issues have been assuming an ever larger role in overall U.S. relations with most of the other industrialized countries as well. American pressure for a better military offset agreement contributed to the fall of the Erhard government in Germany in 1966. The possibility that the Mills bill would pass the Congress in 1970 brought expressions of deep concern from scores of countries and thinly veiled hints of retaliation, including retaliation against U.S. investment abroad, by a few of the most powerful. The minicrisis triggered by Germany's decision to float the mark in May 1971, which appeared to many as an anti-U.S. move,[24] encouraged Senator Mansfield to press finally for a vote on his legislation to cut U.S. troop strength in Europe by 50 per cent—which a swing of only nine votes in the Senate would have carried. The numerous expressions of U.S. concern over the economic policies of the European Community, particularly the Common Agricultural Policy (CAP) and the proliferation of preferential trading pacts, has added to the serious doubts in Europe about U.S. attitudes toward the Continent, including the credibility of U.S. defense commitments. America's relations with Japan were seriously clouded by the textile negotiations of 1969–71, which led to the breakdown of trust and communication between the two countries that underlay the "Nixon shocks" on China and broader economic issues in mid-1971. Most clearly of all, the unilateral measures of August 1971 promoted economic issues to the top of the intra-alliance agenda. British Prime Minister Heath even refused to meet President Nixon at the summit to discuss the President's forthcoming trips to Peking and Moscow until the United States took steps to end the crisis which had resulted from the American actions.

The incidence of these economic clashes is likely to grow in the

---

24. Reflecting the U.S. schizophrenia about all exchange-rate changes caused by the roles of the dollar, outlined in Chapter 9. Despite the help which the move was bound to provide for the U.S. balance of payments, the Treasury first sought to prevent it and then commented on it in extremely chilly terms.

future as international economic interdependence continues to grow. Indeed, the growth of interdependence is likely to be impeded only by the imposition of controls over international transactions, which could themselves cause major political problems. This is not to say that free international trade and capital flows will not cause international political frictions. In fact, as noted, the accelerated growth of interdependence carries with it the seeds of additional conflict. Freedom for U.S. firms to invest abroad raises foreign policy problems directly, because some foreigners think that they are "losing control over their own economies" as a result, and because it contributes to the protectionist push by American labor. The extremely rapid growth of some trade flows, such as Far Eastern textiles into the United States, improve the chances for the omnipresent protectionist pressures to succeed. We have already discussed how unlimited international flows of liquid capital can greatly complicate domestic monetary policies.

Questions are thus raised over the optimum rate of growth of international transactions, which go far beyond the scope of this book. International agreements to regulate optimum growth might be helpful, on balance, in *reducing* political tensions in some cases. They would have to be based on the specific trade or capital flows involved, however, and not—with the possible exception of short-term capital movements—on international monetary considerations. And they would have to be agreements within the framework of international codes, rather than *unilateral* measures by which one country sought to export its internal economic problems.

A second caveat on the impact of international economic transactions on overall international relations is bureaucratic. In most governments, foreign offices and perhaps defense ministries remain primarily responsible for political and military relationships, while finance and commerce ministries are primarily responsible for economic relationships; and often the twain meet only when issues rise to sufficient importance to engage the attention of the chief of state and, in parliamentary systems, the cabinet as a whole.

This caveat is receding in importance, however, as more international economic issues rise to the highest level, especially in Europe, where EC issues—by nature economic—are now among the primary foreign policy concerns of heads of all member states (and some nonmember states as well). It is also the case in Japan, where economic objectives are a major determinant of overall foreign policy. It was dramatically clear in the United States during the monetary negotiations of late 1971, when President Nixon asserted a major personal role in international economic policy and Secretary of the Treasury Connally at least temporarily dominated overall policy toward the major allies.

Despite these caveats, it remains generally true that restrictions on international trade and capital flows are on balance likely to cause significant political difficulties among countries and that this likelihood is rising rapidly. It is curious, in a sense, that the achievement of payments adjustment through internal economic policies or exchange-rate changes generates much less international political difficulty than do controls, even if the targeted payments shift is similar. But there appear to be three reasons why this is so: the former, by definition, take effect on a global basis and do not include the regional and/or product discrimination which is almost inherent in the latter; restrictions break explicit international rules; and, most important, restrictions are widely (and rightly) perceived to be ineffective stopgap measures, which at best will resolve the underlying problem temporarily and at worst will actually accelerate the difficulties.

Prolonged maintenance of disequilibrium exchange rates will also cause international political problems. I have already noted that dollar overvaluation in the late 1960s played a major role in promoting protectionist sentiments in the United States; its policy of "benign neglect" of its balance of payments and lack of effort to maintain an equilibrium exchange rate was fundamentally inconsistent with its effort to maintain a liberal trade policy. To the extent that dollar overvaluation contributed to the lengthy period of U.S. deficits, it also helped lead to widespread charges that the United States was absorbing real resources from the rest of the world "in return for pieces of paper." Similarly, the prolonged undervaluation of the German mark and Japanese yen, and in some periods the French franc, produced bitterness that these countries were exporting unemployment by unfairly enhancing their international competitive positions.

A smoothly functioning monetary system, which minimizes resort to controls and disequilibrium exchange rates, thus helps avoid the development of international political problems. Indeed, the optimum monetary system from this viewpoint would be one to which foreign policy in all countries could remain totally oblivious. For a while, political leaders in most countries *could* remain largely oblivious to it, because the United States was prepared to accept a payments position which was the residual of the policy targets of other countries. As noted above, the United States is unlikely to pursue such a policy again, at least in its relatively pure pre-1971 form—even if it never again feels a need to lash out unilaterally as in August 1971. Thus the monetary system will become a matter of political disinterest only if it is improved sufficiently to avoid the contentiousness produced by controls and disequilibrium exchange rates. The United States thus has broad foreign policy, as well as economic, interests in promoting such improvement.

The Impact of the Dollar in Achieving an Effective Monetary System
The next question is whether the present roles of the dollar foster or hinder the kind of international monetary system in which the United States has these economic and political interests. No *a priori* answer can be based on history. As shown in Chapter 3, key curren cies played a major role—for private transactions purposes, for official intervention in the exchange markets, and as a reserve asset—in the reasonably effective systems which existed prior to 1914 and in the 1950s, as well as in the systems which broke down in the 1920s and the 1960s.

Indeed, it can be argued that existence of one or more key currencies was the inherent *reason* for the success or failure of the different systems; alternatively, that the systems *permitted* the success of the key currencies or doomed them to failure; or that both the systems as a whole, and the roles of key currencies in them, were determined by the underlying conditions of the national economies at the time, and the ability and willingness of the major countries to cooperate sufficiently to make the international system work. I lean toward the last of these three possibilities, for the short run, since the sharply contrasting historical results suggest that no definitive generalizations can be drawn about the inherent short-term effects of key currencies. Moreover, as noted in Chapters 4–6, key currency systems could work if the center country was meeting the criteria adequately, and would flounder only if it was not, and its ability and willingness to do so depended on its political and economic position *relative* to other countries at a given time. However, a number of inherent inconsistencies in key currency systems were also noted, and it is quite possible that the pre-1914 system would have broken down in a few years even without the onset of war, just as the system of the 1950s became unstable in the 1960s. For the longer term, the use of key currencies is thus probably an unstable basis for an effective world economy. I will try here to analyze how each of the three present roles of the dollar affects the outlook for an effective international monetary system for the near future, in broad terms, and the next section will do so with greater precision as it examines the specific reform options.

Transaction currencies reduce the costs of international transactions. Technically, markets could be created to permit direct conversions between all of the more than 5,000 pairs of existing national currencies. This would be much more costly and cumbersome, however, than using one or several currencies as media of exchange through which most transactions take place—and hence reducing the number of exchange markets, in the case of a single transactions currency, to one fewer than the total number of individual currencies (about 150 at present). Further transaction costs are saved if the medium of exchange can also be used as a temporary store of value. The costs are minimized if a single currency plays this role, but the losses are relatively small if several do so instead.[25]

On the other hand, the existence of large balances of national currencies for international transactions purposes complicates intergovernmental monetary arrangements, as we saw in Chapters 7 and 8. These currencies can move rapidly into official hands when interest rates shift or confidence in them weakens, as occurred on a massive scale for sterling in the mid-1960s and for dollars in the early 1970s. Monetary authorities then take the exchange risk of holding the currencies, in the absence of guarantees of their value, or add to the pressures on the reserve center and on the system as a whole by seeking to convert them. So ways must be found to deal with this problem of transaction currencies if it is not to offset, at least partially, the benefits of such currencies for private international finance.

The next question is whether the dollar needs to be the sole transactions currency, or at least one of the major such currencies. Chapter 6 concluded that the dollar has two major advantages for such a role: the fact that it is the currency of the monetary area with the largest share of international trade and capital flows, and that it rests on the world's most effective money market. On the other hand, world confidence in the stability of its exchange rate and its ability to remain aloof from international pressures are less certain. On all four criteria, the relative dominance of the United States is clearly declining; as a result, its monopoly over the transactions currency role has already disappeared and its relative share will probably continue to decline.

However, there appears to be no other national currency which possesses the attributes to *fully* replace the dollar in private international transactions, except at sizable economic cost and inconveni-

25. For further elaboration, see Richard N. Cooper, "Eurodollars and Reserve Dollars: Asymmetries in the Monetary System," *Journal of International Economics*, September 1971.

ence to money markets. Indeed, it would be technically possible to replace the dollar in this role only by an international agreement requiring all foreigners to exchange their dollars for other currencies, and levying stiff sanctions against those who did not, with the dollars then disposed of in whatever way was chosen for the outstanding reserve dollars. The United States could greatly discourage the transactions use of the dollar by unilateral measures such as subjecting foreign dollar balances to exchange controls or imposing negative interest rates, on them, as several European countries have done. But private international finance will clearly continue to function more smoothly if the dollar remains an active transactions currency. The policy need is to find means to deal effectively with the disturbing effects of shifts in dollar (and other transaction) balances into official reserves.

The *intervention currency* role of national currencies also saves transactions costs, but is not technically necessary. Adoption of freely flexible exchange rates, of course, could eliminate the need for intervention currencies. A fixed-rate system could also be maintained without market intervention, however, by use of a clearing system as in the Federal Reserve System or the European Payments Union of the 1950s (with or without its credit-extending features). Monetary authorities would simply obtain currencies needed by their nationals from the clearing mechanism, and supply those which it received in excess of the needs of its nationals; countries whose currencies accrued to the mechanism on balance would either receive a credit or have to buy them back with its reserves. This would in turn require very narrow exchange-rate margins, essentially the spread between the buying and selling rates needed to permit private banks a profit on foreign exchange dealings, which would represent a significant cost for such a system.[26]

On the other hand, elimination of intervention currencies would have some of the merits of eliminating reserve currencies, to which we turn in a moment, since the line between the two is very fuzzy and in practice depends on the shifting sentiments of monetary authorities about the potential intervention needs they may face in the coming months or even years. Since the intervention currency role is a major factor in inhibiting effective changes in the exchange rate of the dollar, as outlined in Chapter 9, it also disturbs the effectiveness of the entire system in promoting prompt adjustment.

On balance, the intervention currency case is much like the transactions currency case: it saves transactions costs and permits greater

26. *Ibid.*

flexibility of financial operations, but should be retained only if ways can be found to mitigate its adverse systemic effects. If a role is retained for intervention currencies, the continued use of the dollar —though as a declining share of the total—would add to the savings.

The necessity of the *reserve currency* role is both easier and more difficult to judge. It is easy to say that national currencies are no longer needed for this purpose, because the progress in monetary thinking and in international economic cooperation has now produced a viable alternative in SDRs. The international community can now create international money, tailored to its precise needs and without the economic and political liabilities of national currencies for international purposes, just as individual countries create national money tailored to their national needs. Indeed, it is much easier to create new reserve assets, which can be done through intergovernmental agreement, than to create vehicle currencies, which rely on market forces and hence are subject to all of their inertia.

The difficulties lie in history, psychology, and the basic economic objectives of most countries. Reserve currencies have been sought and held for at least a century. Many countries continue to hold them, for the various reasons spelled out in Chapters 4–6. In the past, however, these currencies have been the *only* way for the system as a whole to achieve enough expansion of liquidity—to offset the phase-out of silver in the late nineteenth century and the perennial shortages of gold since then. Now, SDRs have been created and their use *could* be expanded sufficiently to obviate any need for further growth of reserve currency balances—and even to replace most or all of the existing balances.

One key problem is psychological: whether countries will be willing to rely this heavily on a new asset which has no intrinsic value in private markets. If they are willing, an SDR system can be created and the reserve currencies replaced. If not, then gold and reserve currencies, including some new ones, will continue to compete. Or a middle course could evolve, with countries willing to expand their use of SDRs but unwilling to rely on them fully, in which SDRs would continue to move gradually to supplement reserve currencies, with or without new rules to govern the relationships among the several assets and with the eventual balance among them left indeterminate. These issues will be discussed in detail in Part III.

Perhaps the most fundamental issue, however, is whether the monetary system can exist without stewardship of the type provided by the United States through the roles of the dollar (and by the United Kingdom through sterling in an earlier period). Through the dollar, the United States could run payments deficits which enabled other countries to achieve their payments goals—and, in many cases, could take overt policy actions (such as extending loans) to help others avoid payments problems even while exacerbating its own. In this milieu, the United States paid relatively little attention to its trade balance and permitted other countries to achieve their national (and often mercantilist) trade-balance objectives. In a world in which dollar financing were unavailable to it, the United States could no longer afford to play such a role even if it wanted to. I will later suggest a new kind of leadership role for the United States, focused on facilitating world adjustment rather than obviating the need for it. But it is clear that it will be much more difficult to achieve stability in such a system, and major adjustments in both technical arrangements and ways of national thinking will be required to make it work.

The systemic interests of the United States lie in a cooperative and effective resolution of these issues much more than in the nature of any specific solution. This interest could be served by a resolution which enthroned the dollar as a reserve currency, dethroned it, or pursued some middle course. From the systemic standpoint, however, the United States clearly need not push even for maintenance of the existing roles of the dollar, let alone any future growth thereof. Indeed, its interest is in the solution which provides the greatest promise that the reserve role chosen for the dollar—including a zero reserve role—will maximize the effective functioning of the system, including effective adjustment options for it. There are a variety of technically viable liquidity solutions, but the success of any of them rests on the international cooperation underpinning their implementation. On this criterion, the chief desideratum from the U.S. standpoint should be the general acceptability of the solution.

Systemic Political Problems

Aside from these specific effects of its roles as transaction, intervention, and reserve currency, the international status of the dollar raises three political problems, domestically and internationally, which add difficulties to the functioning of the international monetary system. The first is that the dominance of the dollar in private money markets means that every foreign exchange crisis in which money flows into another country involves the dollar, even if the U.S. balance-of-payments position is strong. An example was the prolonged crisis in 1968–69 centering on the strength of the German mark and the weakness of the French franc. The United States was in official settlements surplus throughout this period. Nevertheless, the crisis was widely portrayed as implying dollar weakness since much of the movement from France to Germany went through the dollar—purchases of marks were portrayed as "selling of dollars," despite the fact that there was virtually as much "buying of dollars" as people sold French francs. The same thing occurs under floating rates: the appreciation of the mark and its satellite currencies in mid-1973 was trumpeted as a "weakening of the dollar," despite the fact that the dollar did not depreciate at all against the currencies of many of its major trading partners (Canada, Japan, Britain, etc.).

Internationally, the pervasiveness of the dollar's roles also exacerbates the politics of monetary difficulties. The size of the United States makes it a convenient target for criticism in any case, but the dollar's roles certainly augment the image of other countries "importing inflation" or "importing deflation" from the United States—and those roles often provide some reality for the image. The dollar often provides a scapegoat which helps some foreign officials, and many private foreigners, evade real problems and needed solutions to them.[27]

Greater maturity would, of course, largely obviate these problems. Unfortunately, neither in the United States nor abroad, can it be attained very rapidly, if ever, on issues of this degree of complexity. Indeed, the increasing politicization of international monetary issues, especially in the United States, could easily make the problem worse —a little knowledge being a very dangerous thing in such matters. The very sterility of the SDR would help defuse monetary problems politically and hence solve them constructively.

A second political problem of the dollar's roles for the system is that the United States is responsible for the value of the bulk of the reserve assets of other countries. It obviously has a major responsibility for the value of the dollars themselves. But it also sets the official gold price by determining the gold-dollar relationship. (As long as the value of SDRs was tied to gold, the United States controlled that price too.) Only the holdings of non-dollar foreign exchange by monetary authorities are immune from this U.S. control. Indeed, one of the major issues surrounding the exchange-rate realignment of late 1971 was whether it should occur wholly through parity revaluations by other countries or partly through an increase in the gold parity of the dollar, because of the differential impact of the two methods on the value of foreign (and hence world) reserves.

---

27. For a remarkably candid admission of this effect, see "The Eurodollar Market and its Controls," an address by Guido Carli, Governor of the Bank of Italy, to the Swiss Institute of International Studies, Zurich, February 14, 1972.

The third political problem is the widespread international perception that the roles of the dollar provide the United States with extra political leverage over individual dollar-holders, and we have seen in earlier chapters that it does possess leverage through its ability to finance balance-of-payments deficits and to break up the entire system. In addition, it can block the holdings of foreign parties. The United States used this leverage against the Axis powers in World War II and against the Asian Communist countries in the early postwar period, and contemplated using it to pre-empt the threatened Arab withdrawals of dollars during the Middle East crisis of 1967. It could also be used to retaliate if foreign countries expropriated U.S. property without adequate compensation.

However, we have also seen that the "leverage" of being able to run payments deficits also carries costs which now exceed the benefits of the "leverage." The ability to break up the system and to block particular balances is usable only *in extremis,* and it is hard to imagine its use against major dollar-holders. Doing so would clearly jeopardize any future international use of the dollar, and would be self-defeating if attempted on any sizable scale. In addition, countries can now easily avoid this risk—and many, including some Communist and Arab countries do so—by holding their dollar balances in the Eurodollar market where U.S. legal controls cannot reach them. And we saw in Chapter 8 that other countries may have more leverage over the United States than it does over them by using their dollar reserves to force U.S. attention to its aggregate payments position or specific issues which the converting country regards as important. So it is unclear in the abstract in which way the international leverage runs, and it should not be regarded as very important in determining the future of the international monetary system. But the perception that the United States possesses such leverage adds to the international political problems caused for it by the roles of the dollar.

Summary and Conclusion

The United States has major economic and political interests in the maintenance of an international monetary system that will effectively prevent a proliferation of controls and the frequent development of disequilibrium exchange rates. In relative terms, the overall economic interest may still be less than that of most other countries, although it is of vital importance for several key sectors and for a large number of individual firms and workers. In addition, the relative importance of the world economy is growing for the U.S. economy as a whole, while it is stable or even declining for Japan and the European Community as a unit, the other major economic powers. In absolute terms, the U.S. interest is far greater than that of any other individual country.

The U.S. foreign policy interest in an effective world economic system is also growing. The share of international economic relations in overall relations is rising rapidly. Security and other issues of "high politics" are declining in importance with the demise of the Cold War, and the broad "solutions" to them—mutual deterence by the superpowers, NATO and the Warsaw Pact for the alliances— are well entrenched. At the same time, international economic transactions are becoming increasingly important to the domestic economies, and hence the domestic politics, of all other countries as well as of the United States—and the broad "solutions" to them, based on sharp changes in power relationships, have been thrown into doubt and remain to be worked out.[28]

The achievement of an optimum international monetary system requires continuation of the transactions currency and intervention currency roles of the dollar. Each helps minimize the international transactions cost of doing business, thereby promoting an optimal level of trade and capital flows. However, the dollar can increasingly share these roles with other national currencies. Indeed, such sharing could help the system, not least because other countries would thereby be induced to accept greater responsibility for its effective management. Complete elimination of the dollar from these roles would jar both private international finance and the official intervention system—which will in practice exist under flexible as well as fixed exchange rates—causing serious dislocations and costs for the former and requiring sweeping and exceedingly cumbersome changes in the latter.

Both roles, however, raise major problems for public international finance when the dollars move into reserves because of the real "confidence" problems which result and because of the political problems, within the United States and internationally, which they raise. Both the United States and the system are thus subjected to serious costs from these roles of the dollar as long as no means exist to deal effectively with such shifts. Indeed, the costs of the shifts can at times be greater than the ongoing benefits which derive from the transactions and intervention currency roles, and hence raise questions—particularly from a U.S. national standpoint—as to whether

28. For an overview see C. Fred Bergsten, *The Future of the International Economic Order: An Agenda For Research* (Lexington, Mass.: D. C. Heath and Co., 1973), esp. Chapters 1 and 7.

their continuation should be permitted, let alone facilitated. At a minimum, it is clear that the systemic benefits of these roles can only be optimized by the development of new arrangements to take care of the shift problem.

On the other hand, the creation of SDRs means there is now no economic requirement for preserving the reserve currency role of the dollar. Indeed, there is a strong economic case for eliminating it. The political calculation is less certain, since some countries would regard the elimination of the dollar's reserve role as extremely positive while others would regard it as extremely negative. (The weighted average of these countries in terms of U.S. foreign policy interest is highly uncertain, both because few of them have well-defined views on the subject and because no such weighting from the U.S. side is very feasible.) But the greatest uncertainty is psychological, since the SDR is a new asset with no market value of its own, and since the same monetary psychology which led to the global buildup of dollar balances in the postwar period has been demonstrably at work for at least a century.

If SDRs cannot completely replace the dollar, however, new rules must be found to eliminate the systemic problems which the reserve currency role has caused in the past and would doubtless cause again in the future. Thus, reform in this area is clearly needed if the United States is to permit the dollar to go on playing any reserve currency role, purely from the standpoint of the systemic results—which, in this case, are strongly reinforced by the national effects on the United States itself. We therefore turn to the options for reform, and the effect of each on the national interests of the United States.

Part III
Policy Alternatives and Reform Proposals

11

Eliminating the Dollar

There are two broad approaches to international monetary reform which would result in the complete elimination of the dollar's *reserve* currency role. The first would eliminate the need for *any* international reserves by assuring rapid adjustment through the adoption of freely flexible exchange rates or a "return" to the automatic rules of the "gold standard." The second approach would eliminate only the use of the *dollar* as a reserve asset, substituting gold, SDRs, or some new national currency for both the dollar balances now outstanding and for any future buildup which might otherwise occur. In the political typology of Part I, freely flexible rates or a "gold standard" would represent a return to an unmanaged international system; the substitution of a new national currency for the dollar would mark a resumed domination of the system by a single country; and an SDR approach would seek to rely consciously on collective international management.

No intervention currency would be needed under freely flexible exchange rates; and the dollar would probably be replaced in its intervention role by any other national currency which took its place as a reserve currency. The intervention role could also be eliminated within the framework of a basically fixed-rate system, however, in favor of an international clearing arrangement in which all countries would temporarily hold all other currencies before clearing them through some new institutional mechanism. Short of such dramatic systemic changes, the intervention currency role of the dollar could also be eliminated by substituting other national currencies for it in foreign working balances, or by instituting private use of the SDR and then making it the intervention currency. The private *transactions* role of the dollar could be eliminated only by a total collapse of private international financial relations, or by substituting other national currencies or a world money for it.[1]

1. All of these approaches are here couched in the extreme form which would be necessary to *eliminate* the different roles of the dollar. All could, of course, be pursued in more moderate form to simply reduce the dollar's roles, and

There are three ways in which any of these systemic changes could evolve. They could be negotiated internationally, particularly as regards the reserve currency role. The options discussed in this chapter are basically of this type. Second, they could simply evolve through the operation of market forces, in the absence of either international or unilateral U.S. actions to the contrary, in response to a failure by the United States to meet the key currency criteria developed in Part II.

Or, third, the United States could pursue them unilaterally by adopting policy measures designed to eliminate the attractiveness of the dollar as a key currency. At a minimum, it could eliminate some of the incentives offered to foreign official dollar-holders in the past: exemption from the interest-rate ceilings of Regulation Q, exchange-rate guarantees through Roosa bonds and the swap network. Or it could go further, as several European countries have done to try to blunt the international use of their currencies, actively to discourage foreign dollar-holdings by denying any interest payments to foreigners or even charging them to hold dollars in the United States, or doing so indirectly by levying high reserve requirements against the foreign deposits held in U.S. banks. It could actively promote a steady and sizable depreciation of the dollar to induce foreigners to convert their dollars into real U.S. assets—if it were at some point faced with widespread domestic unemployment and the economies of other countries were sufficiently strong to accept such a depreciation. The ultimate step would be a prohibition on foreign deposits, as Japan has done to a large extent and as Germany has done on an extensive range of German assets.

Such steps would certainly discourage international use of the dollar. However, they would be blunted to a significant extent by the existence of the Eurodollar market, where foreigners could hold dollars outside the jurisdiction of such U.S. steps. The several European countries which have sought to discourage a key currency role for their currencies have discovered that this is a significant barrier to their efforts. To make its moves even partially effective, the United States would have to apply its own controls to the deposits of Euro-

---

some of those variants will be discussed in Chapter 13. For example, the need for reserves would be totally eliminated only under a system of *freely* flexible exchange rates in which national monetary authorities completely abstained from intervening in the markets. The intermediate option of managed flexibility, under which rates float but are subject to official intervention, and which prevailed both in the 1930s and after March 1973, will be analyzed in Chapter 13.

dollar branches with their U.S. head offices—or seek international agreement to close down the entire Eurocurrency markets.

Whether a unilateral U.S. effort to eliminate the dollar as a key currency succeeded wholly or partially, however, something would have to take its place: either an adjustment system which obviated the need for official reserves, or a financing system which provided a substitute for the dollar, or some combination thereof. The desirability of such a move thus depends on the nature of the replacement, and the means of getting there raises primarily tactical (though by no means unimportant) issues. The focus of this analysis must therefore be on the potential replacements for the dollar.

Freely Flexible Exchange Rates

The first approach that would completely eliminate the dollar as a reserve currency is the adoption of a system of freely flexible exchange rates by all countries, with no official intervention by monetary authorities. Such a system would also eliminate the use of the dollar as an intervention currency, since no intervention would be necessary.[2]

The basic argument for flexible exchange rates is that they would permit market forces to maintain balance-of-payments equilibrium by automatic adjustment of the price relationship between national currencies in response to the market supply and demand for each— and, unlike the adjustment rules of the gold standard, that they would do so without forcing domestic economic policy (and hence full employment, the maintenance of relative price stability and economic growth) to conform to external financial needs. Indeed, the use of flexible rates to achieve external adjustment would enable monetary and fiscal policy to concentrate more directly on domestic economic objectives. This would be of particular importance for monetary policy, since it is both more constrained than fiscal policy by fixed exchange rates and is a far more flexible policy instrument than fiscal policy in most countries.

2. A system of managed flexibility, which would permit some intervention by monetary authorities, is another possibility. This would retain the dollar as an intervention currency, however, and some observers even argue that larger reserves would be required under such a system. See, for example, Roy Harrod, *Reforming the World's Money* (London: Macmillan, 1965), Chapter 2, and James Meade, "Bretton Woods, GATT and the Balance of Payments: A Second Round?" *Three Banks Review*, December 1952, pp. 3–22. Another possibility is a system in which some major exchange rates did float freely, but in which some countries maintain fixed parities against one or another of the major currencies. These approaches will be considered among the "intermediate options" in Chapter 13.

Fixed exchange rates represent a subsidy to international traders and investors by reducing their risks at least in the short run. The costs of the subsidy are borne by society as a whole, because the country must maintain a higher level of reserves and adopt adjustment policies which may produce an inequitable distribution of these costs.[3] And the advocates of flexible rates argue that they are the best route to world economic integration, with its benefits in optimizing global resource allocation, because the practical alternatives to it are (a) direct controls over international transactions and (b) periodic jumps in exchange rates, which are far more disruptive of international trade and capital movements than are the relatively smooth fluctuations which they would expect from an autonomously flexible rate.[4] Finally, fully flexible rates are alleged to eliminate the problems of international and national decision-making in both the adjustment and the liquidity areas, thereby eliminating one major source of international economic (and frequently political) tension. They do this partly by "bottling up" excessive inflation or deflation in the countries where it originates, thereby minimizing the internation repercussions thereof.

There are of course rebuttals to these points. Domestic monetary and fiscal policy is truly freed of external constraints by flexible rates only if (a) the country involved is not so open to international transactions that the flexible exchange rate dominates its economy; (b) it is wholly indifferent to the structure of its balance of payments, since tight money can lead to capital inflows which in turn appreciate the exchange rate and produce a decline in the current account; and (c) the reduction in domestic employment triggered by such appreciation is welcome because of an initial state of overheating of the economy, or the increase in domestic prices triggered by depreciation is acceptable because of an initial state of relatively stable prices. Some of the present and proposed controls over international trade and capital movements are motivated by concerns wholly apart from the balance of payments; thus even the achievement of more effective payments adjustment might not be sufficient

3. See, e.g., Anthony Lanyi, "The Case for Floating Exchange Rates Reconsidered," *Princeton Essays in International Finance,* No. 72 (February 1969).

4. The classic theoretical exposition is by Milton Friedman, "The Case for Flexible Exchange Rates," in his *Essays in Positive Economics* (Chicago: University of Chicago Press, 1953). For a comprehensive updating, which stresses the superiority of flexible rates over the practicable alternatives at this point in history and their advantage in freeing internal macroeconomic policies, see Harry G. Johnson, "The Case for Flexible Exchange Rates, 1969," in Bergsten, *et al., Approaches to Greater Flexibiltiy of Exchange Rates,* pp. 91–111.

to eliminate them. And advocates of flexible rates can be viewed as adopting too readily a second- or third-best strategy, retarding the admittedly uneven progress toward the first-best of global economic integration, which could continue if financing for payments imbalances were adequate to forestall resort to controls and even if some of the exchange-rate changes do finally eventuate.

The case for fixed exchange rates is based on the view that they are needed to maximize international economic integration, which in turn is needed to provide optimum allocation of the world's resources.[5] Flexible rates are viewed as increasing the costs and risks of international transactions so much that they will be seriously retarded, and as prompting speculative capital flows that will disrupt the international economy. Thus any subsidy that fixed rates extend to particular sectors of a society are fully justified by the overall national gains from trade. Moreover, flexible rates may also exacerbate the problems of domestic economic policy in "non-dilemma cases," where internal and external policy objectives can both be met by proper internal policies. In such cases, the use of flexible rates to solve a payments deficit will intensify the difficulties of checking inflation at full employment. Generalizing this argument beyond "non-dilemma" cases, some observers feel that the requirements for maintaining a fixed exchange rate are one of the few remaining disciplinary bastions against rampant inflation. And "elasticity pessimism" sometimes throws doubts on the effectiveness of exchange-rate changes in achieving balance-of-payments adjustment.[6]

5. See especially Charles P. Kindleberger, "The Case for Fixed Exchange Rates, 1969," *The International Adjustment Mechanism* (Federal Reserve Bank of Boston, 1969), an explicit rebuttal to the Johnson paper cited in the previous footnote. Arthur B. Laffer, "Two Arguments for Fixed Rates," in Harry G. Johnson and Alexander Swoboda, eds., *The Economics of Common Currencies* (London: Allen and Unwin, 1973), stresses that truly fixed rates promote equilibration of nominal as well as real rates of interest, which would contribute to maximizing world economic welfare.

6. Technically, exchange-rate changes will not even work *in the right direction* to achieve equilibrium unless the sum of the country's price elasticity of demand for imports plus the price elasticity of demand of the world for its exports exceeds one, the so-called Marshall-Lerner condition. The higher these elasticities, the greater is the *degree* of the effectiveness of exchange-rate changes in achieving balance-of-payments shifts. We saw in Chapter 9 that there is still lively debate over the magnitude of these elasticities, but widespread agreement that they are large enough to satisfy the Marshall-Lerner condition for at least the industrialized countries, so that we can be confident that exchange-rate changes will work in the expected direction. The absence of the Marshall-Lerner condition in the case of most of the oil-exporting countries is the primary reason why changes in exchange rates can *not* be relied upon to adjust the payments imbalances triggered by the massive rise in oil prices in 1974.

There are persuasive answers to most of the arguments for fixed rates. The basic criticism is that there is no possibility under present conditions of achieving truly fixed rates; thus its advocates are really supporting a system of "rates fixed until further notice," as Fritz Machlup has so aptly described it. The significant differences in economic conditions and policy preferences among countries, outlined in Chapter 2, assure that true policy harmonization is a chimera at this time in history—even within the European Community, the most closely knit grouping of sovereign countries. Exchange rates therefore *will* change. But we have seen in earlier chapters that exchange-rate changes in the postwar period have been inordinately delayed and that controls have proliferated as a result. World economic integration may thus have been impeded, rather than enhanced, by the effort to maintain fixed exchange rates.

In addition, flexible rates may not raise the costs and risks of international transactions if the alternative is a regime of infrequent but large jumps in parities and widespread controls to defer them. In addition, exchange risks at least on short-term transactions can be hedged through forward markets, and as long-term depreciation of a currency will simply be the external result of excessive internal inflation, the long-term investor will come out roughly even in terms of foreign exchange. There is no empirical evidence that short-term capital flows have been more destabilizing under flexible than under fixed rates, and there are sound theoretical reasons to expect them to be stabilizing instead. Nor is there evidence that trade and international investment are deterred by flexible rates. And there is no reason to assume that flexible exchange rates will produce greater wage and price increases than will periodic changes in parities. It is true that "unnecessary" exchange-rate changes may take place in non-dilemma cases, but the proponents of flexibility argue that this simply adds marginally to the requirements for internal policy and is a price worth paying for assuring rate changes in dilemma cases.

In addition, national monetary authorities may be no more disciplined by balance-of-payments deficits under fixed rates, which can be hidden through reserve losses and even more so by foreign borrowing, than by steady depreciation of the exchange rate and the resulting real economic effects on the population. For a key currency country which can maintain a fixed rate by building up liabilities in its own currency, *flexible* rates are almost certain to generate more "discipline." The discipline argument is weak, in any event, in a world where virtually every country will resort to controls and/or a large devaluation rather than deflate its domestic economy unnecessarily. The absence of any regulated control of the growth of international liquidity means that changes in the world money supply are determined by the economic and political power of individual countries and may not be right for reaching any systemic goals or for any individual country in the system—to which exchange-rate changes may be the only effective response. Finally, virtually all econometric studies of the issue conclude that price elasticities in international trade are now quite high, so that over time exchange-rate changes will provide major changes in a country's balance of payments.

At the same time, however, we have limited evidence of how freely flexible exchange rates would work in practice. Our only postwar experience with a lengthy float is Canada, from 1950 to 1962 and again since 1970, but we can learn little of wide application from it because Canada was the sole floater in a fixed-rate world during the earlier period and because its proximity to the United States makes its economy a very special case. The short-lived German float of 1969 was purely transitional to find a new parity. The numerous floats of 1971, including the German and Dutch moves which antedated the U.S. suspension of convertibility, were also part of an effort to find a new equilibrium structure of fixed rates rather than to maintain an existing equilibrium situation. The floats from early 1973 have not proceeded long enough, at this writing, to provide a basis for any firm judgments, though through their early months they certainly appeared to be reducing the impact of speculative capital flows, promoting major adjustment of the two chronic imbalances which had previously existed (the U.S. deficit and the Japanese surplus), and co-existing with a flourishing level of international trade and investments. So political leaders, as well as monetary authorities and private financial communities, have ample grounds for caution in approaching freely flexible exchanges.

Intellectual refinement of the issue now suggests that the case for "freely flexible rates" does not apply to all countries at all times, nor that total flexibility is even necessary to achieve most of the virtues of the basic approach. The theory of optimum currency areas, though not very helpful in identifying such areas in practice, demonstrates that flexible rates are the right policy only for countries which are not heavily dependent on the international economy and that fixed rates are preferable between countries which are; between countries which are prepared to harmonize their policies and provide resource transfers to backward "regions"; and among countries where there is a high degree of factor (in addition to product) mobility.[7] In addi-

7. Ardent supporters of flexibility, such as Friedman, and ardent supporters of fixed rates, such as Triffin, agree that rates should be flexible between large

tion, however, even countries which are relatively open to the world economy may want to float at times when their main trading partner(s), to whom they normally peg their currency, is inflating or deflating excessively, relative to world trends. We have shown that exchange-rate changes are needed primarily in "dilemma" cases—depreciation of the exchange rate would make it more difficult to counter domestic inflation, and appreciation would make it more difficult to reduce unemployment.

In practical terms, it is also clear that few countries would agree to abstain from intervention in the exchange markets. This was one of the major lessons of the 1930s, when the mercantilist objectives of virtually all countries combined with their reading of the effects of truly free floats in the early 1920s to foster active and aggressive intervention policies. In late 1971, the United States and Germany explicitly called for free floats but themselves contributed to the universal practice of "dirty floats." From March through September 1973, the beginning of the most recent experiment with "free floating," market intervention by monetary authorities reportedly totaled $14 billion!

It would be folly for only some countries to float freely, since the countries which intervened would effectively set the exchange rates of the currencies which did not—and the latter would almost certainly have their own objectives undercut as a result and might gain no extra freedom for their domestic economic policies. At a minimum, it is clear that the risk of such behavior would require active international surveillance of the market activities of the major monetary authorities, and possibly a set of rules to govern such activities, so it is inconceivable that "freely flexible rates" would in fact eliminate the need for national or international decision-making on international monetary issues. The practical policy possibilities for the near future, as well as the strongest intellectual case, lie within the range of options for limited exchange-rate flexibility, which will be analyzed in depth in Chapter 13.

---

and relatively self-sufficient economic blocs, and fixed within them. Indeed, Kindleberger questioned whether such a situation should be viewed as a modified version of flexible rates or a modified version of fixed rates; perhaps this semantic uncertainty will help achieve agreement on such an approach, since both schools could claim victory for their basic principles. The three major articles on optimum currency areas, which we shall discuss in detail in Chapter 13, are: Robert Mundell, "A Theory of Optimum Currency Areas," *American Economic Review*, Vol. L, No. 4 (September 1961), pp. 657–65; Ronald McKinnon, "Optimum Currency Areas," *American Economic Review*, Vol. LIII, No. 4 (September 1963), pp. 710–21; Peter Kenen, "The Theory of Optimum Currency Areas: An Eclectic View," in Mundell and Swoboda, eds., *op. cit.*, pp. 41–60.

It should also be noted that, in practice, countries would probably not abolish their reserves even if they did agree to adopt freely flexible rates, despite the fact that they would not need them for market intervention under such a regime. Most countries would want to hold at least some reserves for "war chest" purposes, against the contingency of some future disaster (such as war or famine—or a dramatic increase in oil prices!) in which a stock of internationally accepted money would be needed to make purchases of crucial importance to national welfare, and because they might not be confident that free flexibility would last.[8]

Under a system of freely flexible rates, the United States, like all other countries, would adjust its payments position through changes in its exchange rate. This would be a major gain to the United States from the adoption of such a system, since, as we saw in Chapter 9, its adjustment options have been severely limited by the constraints placed on exchange-rate changes by the international roles of the dollar at the same time that it needs to be able to use the exchange rate to achieve adjustment more than does any other country. At the same time, the total elimination of the reserve and intervention currency roles of the dollar, plus the total systemic reliance on adjustment rather than financing under flexible rates, would eliminate any U.S. option of financing deficits through foreign accruals of dollars. The gains to the United States from this particular reform option, as we will see in the case of the other options as well, depend in significant part on the outlook for dollar financing of U.S. deficits (and the broad costs of relying on such financing) in the absence of any negotiated change in the system. If the outlook were dim, then the U.S. gain from a system which moved to reliance on adjustment via the method by far the most congenial to the United States would be extremely high—especially since U.S. owned reserves are far smaller, relative to its level of international transactions (let alone the dollar overhang), than the reserves of virtually all other major countries.[9]

The net effect of such a system on the transaction role of the dollar is indeterminate. The ability of the United States to maintain that role would be strengthened because it would no longer need to institute controls over international transactions to achieve payments equilibrium. And adjustment via the exchange rate would almost certainly mean improvement in the U.S. current account and higher economic growth, relative to the adjustment actions which the

---

8. Both Harrod and Kindleberger, in the works cited, predict that strong market tendencies would push countries back toward fixed parities even if they consciously set out to fluctuate freely.

9. See Table 2, Chapter 2, p. 35.

United States might take under fixed rates, strengthening the most important liquidity ratio and better maintaining the economic dynamism criterion. On the other hand, the elimination of the intervention currency role would eliminate the present advantage for the dollar which results from the fact that it can fluctuate by only one-half as much toward any other currency as can any third currency. The elimination of the reserve and intervention currency roles would weaken foreign private interest in holding dollars, since the holders would no longer have their own central bank as a fixed-rate buyer for any dollars they wished to sell. All these effects would probably be swamped by the outlook for the exchange rate of the dollar in terms of the several other most important currencies, however, which can certainly not be predicted in advance.[10]

Fluctuations of the dollar exchange rate, mainly through changes in the terms of trade, would affect the level and distribution of U.S. national income. But since the foreign sector is a small part of the total economy, these effects would be small in terms of overall GNP. On balance, the United States might therefore gain more than most countries from the ability to pursue domestic economic policies without restraint from a finite level of reserves (gross or net) and a faulty adjustment process. Of course, it would free itself of any constraints caused by the reserve currency role, such as the need to run deficits on the official reserve transaction definition or pay higher interest rates to keep foreign officials from correcting dollar balances, by virtue of the elimination of this role.

The Gold Standard
The second proposal for international monetary reform which could eliminate the reserve currency role of the dollar would be a "return" to the gold standard as it is alleged to have existed prior to 1914.[11] Such a system had two fundamental components: gold was the *sole* international reserve asset, and countries were to achieve payments adjustment through the "automatic" reaction of their economies to changes in their gold holdings. The adjustment effect assumed that

10. Lord L. Robbins, "The International Monetary Problem," *Journal of Political Economy*, Vol. LXXVI, No. 4, Part II (July-August 1968), p. 2, predicted that "In a world of freely fluctuating currencies, there would be a permanent incentive to make contracts in terms of the currency expected to fluctuate least."
11. In fact, as we saw in Chapter 3, sterling and other national currencies had become important components of world reserves during at least the last two decades of that period. The discussion here follows the textbook model of how the gold standard supposedly worked, which is what its few remaining supporters advocate.

each country's domestic money supply was tied rigidly to its gold stock, so that the gold losses caused by payments deficits produced immediate deflation and the gold inflows caused by payments surpluses caused inflation. Countries would in practice anticipate these gold flows and try to head them off through changes in interest rates —upward in deficit countries, downward in surplus countries—which would have similar effects on their economies.

The specific policy proposal most often associated with "a return to the gold standard" is a sizable increase in the official price of gold. Different proponents of this step, however, have two very different objectives in mind. Some see the resultant increase in world liquidity as the primary purpose, to provide additional reserves to all countries —particularly the reserve centers—and hence to *reduce* the adjustment pressures in the system.[12] Others would increase the price of gold only to enable the reserve centers to "pay off" the overhangs of their currencies. They regard the institution of *much tighter* "gold standard" adjustment rules as the objective of reform, and have little interest in the entire liquidity issue.[13] In fact, the effect on both liquidity and adjustment of an increase in the official price of gold *by itself* is indeterminate.

The crucial requirement of any "return to the gold standard" to achieve a better adjustment process is international agreement that national monetary authorities would never again add dollar (or other national currency) balances to their reserves. Only such agreement would result in the certain elimination of the ability of key currency

12. Sir Roy Harrod, *Reforming the World's Money* (London: Macmillan, 1965), esp. Chapter 3, and Ian Shannon, *Gold and the American Balance of Payments* (Chicago: Henry Regnery, 1966). Milton Gilbert, *op. cit.*, advocated an increase in the price of gold throughout the 1960s to enable the United States to restore equilibrium to its balance of payments, but his views will not be considered here because they were aimed at reforming neither the liquidity nor adjustment arrangements of the system as a whole.

13. The most notable and persistent proponent of this thesis is Jacques Rueff; for his most complete statement on adjustment, see *Balance of Payments: Proposals for the Resolution of the Most Pressing World Economic Problem of Our Time* (New York: Macmillan, 1967). His disinterest in providing additional world liquidity through his proposed increase in the official price of gold is demonstrated by his companion proposal that the gold revaluation profits be used to retire debt and extend large-scale aid loans to the less developed countries—a "gold link." See his statements in Randall Hinshaw, ed., *Monetary Reform and the Price of Gold: Alternative Approaches* (Baltimore: Johns Hopkins Press, 1967), p. 42. There is of course a third motive behind pleas for an increase in the official price of gold: capital gains for gold holders, be they private citizens or monetary authorities. This motive, however, will not be analyzed here.

countries to finance payments deficits by increasing their liabilities, the means by which proponents of this approach would hope to achieve a better adjustment mechanism for the system as a whole.[14] The reserve centers could contribute to the implementation of any understanding to end their reserve currency roles by erecting controls or forbidding interest payments on deposits by foreign monetary authorities, or even by levying charges on them, as has in fact been done at times by several European countries on *all* foreign balances held in their banks. Similar restrictions would have to be placed on Eurodollar deposits as well, however, to avoid evasion via that route.

From the standpoint of this adjustment objective, it would in fact be irrelevant whether the dollar overhang was eliminated or not, since the crucial consideration would be the agreement to avoid *future* increases in dollar reserves.[15] Thus the proposed increase in the official price of gold is *not* an integral element of a "return to the gold standard." Furthermore, the world could agree to avoid any future buildups of reserve currency holdings at the same time it was *demonetizing* gold, either through turning completely to SDRs or freely flexible exchange rates. And it could eliminate the dollar overhang through means other than an increase in the gold price, as will be discussed in the next section. So it is essential to distinguish clearly between the adjustment and liquidity motives of "a return to the gold standard."

In fact, in the absence of such an agreement on future dollar buildups, the reserve currency role of the dollar could be revivified by a sizable increase in the official price of gold—as indeed happened after the increase in 1934. Such a step would drastically improve all of the U.S. liquidity ratios, which, as noted in Chapter 5, were the key underpinning for foreign confidence in continued fixed-price convertibility of the dollar, even if the gold revaluation profits were used to convert outstanding dollar balances. Indeed, an increase in

14. Rueff's position was clarified in his debate with Triffin and Bernstein at Bologna in early 1967. There he stated that he did not rely on automatic adjustment to result from adoption of the gold standard, but rather on the incentives to countries to adjust if they knew that they would have to finance any deficits by selling gold. He does not blame the United States and the United Kingdom for the development of the gold exchange standard, and in fact concludes that they "are its victims." See his statements in Hinshaw, *op. cit.*

15. Rueff obviously has no desire to force the United States to refinance its past deficits with gold, since he calls for gold revaluation which would enable it to do so "without tears." The overhanging dollars would have to be sterilized, through one of the options discussed below, to assure that such pressure would not be brought on the United States.

the official price of gold without a corollary agreement on future dollar balances might therefore fit into the options for increasing the reserve role of the dollar![16] So the entire Rueff proposal is inconsistent on two fundamental points: its adjustment objective could only be achieved by international agreement to eliminate the reserve currency roles of the dollar for the *future*, and could even be *undermined* by the proposed increase in the official price of gold in the absence of such agreement; and there would be no need to convert the dollar overhang into gold, and hence to raise the official price to permit such a payoff, once the basic agreement was reached to avoid future dollar buildups. In short, "gold standard" adjustment could be achieved without reliance on gold for liquidity, and gold could be relied on for liquidity without the adoption of "gold standard" adjustment rules.

Our discussion of "the gold standard" must therefore distinguish carefully between these two aspects of the approach. The adjustment rules of the gold standard would rely solely on internal deflation and inflation to eliminate payments imbalances. The preservation of truly fixed exchange rates and the total avoidance of direct controls over international transactions would be corollary "rules of the game." However, we have already seen in Chapter 9 that the costs of such adjustment would be intolerably high for the United States. It is also clear that adjustment via domestic macroeconomic policy would be costlier than adjustment via the exchange rate for most major countries.[17]

In addition, Michaely, in his comprehensive study of the domestic policy responses of the major countries during 1950–66 to payments imbalances—in reality, a test of whether they were willing to live by gold standard adjustment rules—discovered that no country ever moved its fiscal policy consistently even in the *direction* called for

16. Giovanni Magnifico, *op. cit.*, p. 128, suggests that, even *with* such an agreement, private dollar holdings might grow rapidly and in fact take the place of the previous growth in official holdings, thereby frustrating the whole adjustment objective of the gold standard approach even if the United States were in *official settlements balance*. He sees such a development as simply an extension of present trends for central banks to encourage such holdings by their private sectors.

17. Heller and Kreinen, *op. cit.*, p. 11, conclude that the ratio of costs from income adjustment to costs of exchange-rate adjustment is roughly 5 : 1 for Canada, 3.5 : 1 for Japan, 3 : 1 for the United States. On these calculations, only the very open Swiss and Swedish economies, and, surprisingly, the Italian economy would experience greater costs from adjusting via the exchange rate. They did not, however, study the even more open Dutch and Belgium economies, nor the closed economy of France.

by external considerations; that only the United Kingdom and Japan moved their monetary policy consistently in such a direction; and that only France, Belgium, the Netherlands, and possibly Italy did so occasionally.[18] From the standpoint of the relative costs of different adjustment policies just mentioned, we would have expected such behavior of Belgium, the Netherlands, and Italy because they are so open to international transactions. The surprising behavior of Britain, Japan, and France can be explained mainly by the fact that their payments imbalances were often of the non-dilemma variety so that their internal economic needs called for the same policy approach as did their balance of payments. In addition, both France and (eventually) Britain devalued when the non-dilemma cases became dilemmas, and both applied pervasive controls over their international transactions; so it is obvious that neither carried the gold standard rules to the *extent* needed to achieve adjustment. Michaely also discovered that even the *directional* response to monetary policy to external considerations weakened from the 1950s to the 1960s. Bearing out that trend, the British in 1972 made it clear that they would not subordinate domestic policy to the maintenance of "an unrealistic exchange rate,"[19] and when Japan acquired massive reserves instead of the $2 billion it held as late as 1967, it no longer needed to subordinate its domestic policy to external considerations.

The reasons for this antipathy to gold standard adjustment rules in all but the most open modern societies, or in cases where such policies are called for by domestic needs anyway, are obvious. The level of domestic unemployment or inflation which would be needed to provide the sole cure for payments deficits and surpluses, respectively, would create huge economic costs and thus be politically unacceptable in modern societies. Governments and monetary authorities already have great difficulty in achieving their numerous economic policy targets, and they could hardly afford to give up three of their policy instruments—the exchange rate, selective controls, and external financing—as called for by the gold standard. So the adjustment objective of the gold standard option is clearly unacceptable to most countries. It would be completely unacceptable to Americans because it would shackle the United States with the most costly of all adjustment alternatives while eliminating the financing potential of foreign buildups of dollar reserves. Fully per-

18. Michaely, *op. cit.*, esp. p. 62.
19. As revealed in their rapid decision to float sterling in June 1972 and the statement of Chancellor of the Exchequer Anthony Barber, Annual Budget Speech, March 21, 1972.

ceiving this reality, some advocates of a "return to the gold standard" have done so as part of an effort to sharply reduce U.S. international monetary power by simultaneously denying it the financing for deficits available from the roles of the dollar and the adjustment which could be available from exchange-rate changes.

For the liquidity aspect of the "gold standard" approach, we shall assume a corollary agreement to avoid future buildups of reserve dollars to make clear that this option really would eliminate the dollar as a reserve currency, at least at the margin. Two sub-options then merit discussion.

One is the Rueffian approach of a sizable revaluation of gold, the proceeds of which could be used to "pay off" the reserve currency overhangs and hence *fully* eliminate the reserve currency role of the dollar. This approach creates *annual* additions to world liquidity only to the extent that it induces some combination of (a) increases in new gold production, (b) reductions in private gold consumption due to the higher prices, (c) net private dishoarding, and (d) net sales by Communist countries to reap capital gains. On the basis of 1973 conditions, the official gold price would have to be raised to almost $350 per ounce to enable the United States and Britain to pay off fully the dollar and sterling overhangs with no net reduction in their gold (plus SDR) reserves.[20] Such an increase would carry the official price far above the price in the free market, which had never exceeded $200 per ounce by the end of 1974. Monetary authorities might then decide on a new two-tiered system to avoid a new "golden avalanche"—to keep private holders from dumping their gold on monetary authorities and creating major inflationary difficulties in countries where gold is widely held. Net private dishoarding could not then be counted on to add further increments to national monetary reserves.

On the other hand, the authorities might feel confident of their ability to sterilize such effects and thus permit private dishoarding. In that situation, one cannot predict whether private investors and speculators would become net sellers of gold to take their profits, as occurred after the near-doubling of the price in 1934, or net buyers in anticipation of further price increases in the future, given the confirmation of the view held previously by some that the monetary authorities would eventually have to accept a rise in gold prices to

20. American gold and SDR reserves totaled about $14 billion in early 1973, against estimated foreign dollar reserves of perhaps as much as $100 billion. British gold and SDR reserves were under $2 billion, compared with sterling liabilities to official holders of over $7 billion.

"solve" their international monetary problems. It seems most likely that the short-run effect would be dishoarding and a further increase in international reserves, beyond the one-shot increase from the gold revaluation itself.[21] The combined effect would be equal to the amount of SDR creation, at an annual rate of $5 billion, which would otherwise take place over a period of 70 years.

The very long-run effect would be determined by whether companion steps to the gold-price rise provided credibly definitive improvements in the monetary system. If they did, and were seen to be working over the course of the succeeding years, then renewed gold speculation could probably be avoided indefinitely; if they did not, and new systemic problems were to arise, the demonstration effect of the gold-price increase would doubtlessly prompt expectations that it would occur again, and hence breed new speculation. Assuming the preservation of a two-tiered system, such speculation would have no significantly damaging direct effect on the international monetary system. However, it could well eat up all current gold production, as it began to do in the mid-1960s, and cut off any net additions to world reserves at that point. It could thus help push the system into another crisis situation, self-fulfilling its own prophecy of a further rise in the gold price.[22] But the advent of any such new crisis involving the liquidity aspects of the system would probably be far in the future in view of the huge increases in reserves which would take place at the onset of the new regime. Indeed, this is a second key reason—along with the need to enable the United States and Britain to use the profits to redeem fully their outstanding liabilities—that any increase in the official price of gold would have to be huge.

The second sub-option is periodic small increases in the official price of gold to provide periodic growth in world reserves—perhaps

21. In 1967, prior to the inauguration of the two-tiered system, some experts thought that as much as $10 billion of gold could be added to monetary reserves by a mere doubling of the official price. See the statements by William J. Busschau and Michael Spieler in Hinshaw, *op. cit.*, pp. 115 and 119.
22. Some proponents of this approach, including Rueff, argue that changes in general price levels would generate changes in the profitability of gold production and hence change in the appropriate direction the amounts of new gold made available to monetary authorities. In *Historical Appraisal, op. cit.*, Triffin has, however, demonstrated that such an effect did not even occur in the supposedly halcyon nineteenth century days of the gold standard. It is even more difficult to believe that it would operate in today's environment of downward price rigidity and emphasis on full employment. Triffin's doubts on this score were supported by the gold experts at the Bologna Conference, including William J. Busschau and Michael Spieler; see *ibid.*, Chapter 9.

a "crawling peg" for gold.[23] This would provide the answer to the world liquidity problem—modest, periodic infusions rather than large one-shot jumps with uncertain follow-up—which is now widely accepted as needed. On the other hand, it would be more likely to promote speculation in gold by assuring steady if slow appreciation of its capital value. This would occur despite the continued interest-rate advantage of other assets; that advantage has existed throughout the postwar period and has not prevented periodic outbreaks of gold speculation. Such a step alone would not reduce by very much the perceived possibility of the large rise in the gold price which motivates much of the speculation, if indeed it did not actually heighten that perception by accepting the concept of increases. This view might be strengthened by the realization that small changes in the gold price would provide no way to deal with the dollar overhang, but that a large change would. Such increased speculation would add to the pressures on the official price of gold, so renewed agreement to maintain a two-tiered system would have to be part of any such monetary reform.

These two approaches to raising the gold price for liquidity reasons would distribute additions to world liquidity on the basis of national gold holdings at the time the scheme went into effect. The United States would thus achieve the greatest single share of the increase, since it holds over one-fourth of world gold reserves. This would, however, represent a share only slightly higher than it would get under any SDR scheme based on IMF positions. A much larger share of the total increase in reserves would go to the Group of Ten countries, than under the SDR approach, however—38 per cent and less than 20 per cent, respectively. The less developed countries would get only about 15 per cent of total liquidity creation, compared with about 25 per cent under the SDR scheme. The main gainers, relative to the SDR scheme, would be the continental members of the Common Market—each of which would get about twice as much. If the United States were to use its revaluation profits to redeem all foreign dollar reserves, then France, Switzerland, the Netherlands,

23. Kiyoto Miyata, "A Proposal to Increase the Price of Gold," *Banking* (Osaka), No. 176 (1962), and Paul Wonnacott, "A Suggestion for the Revaluation of Gold," *Journal of Finance*, Vol. XVIII (March 1963), pp. 49–55. The U.S. devaluations of 1971–72 and 1973 were carried out through relatively small changes in the gold price, but were motivated solely by the need to realign exchange rates. They were certainly not aimed at increasing world liquidity, though they did help avoid the reduction in world liquidity which would have occurred if the realignments had been achieved solely through foreign revaluations.

Japan and Italy would join Germany in having larger reserves than the United States has—and the United Kingdom, Canada, and Belgium would move close behind. The European Community as a whole would then have reserves ten times as large as those of the United States. (See Table 15.)

From the standpoint of the dollar, a small increase in the official price of gold, particularly of the "crawling peg" variety, would whet speculation *against* the dollar and do little to improve its position. The effect of a large price increase depends on how it would be carried out and what followed. There are three possibilities. Such an increase, without any use of the revaluation profits to redeem foreign dollar reserves and with no resumption of dollar convertibility into U.S. reserve assets, would of course be wholly beneficial to the United States—and therefore unacceptable to other countries, although some of them would then be put in the position of opposing the move which they had supported for so long!

The second approach is for the United States to use all or most of its revaluation profits to redeem foreign dollar reserves. This would leave it with a much weakened reserve position relative to other major countries. German reserves would alone become about triple those of the United States. As noted, the reserves of the enlarged EC would be almost ten times as great. The United States would wind up on a much shorter reserve leash than the other major countries and so would not only lose its "aloofness" but also become more prone than most countries to forced exchange-rate changes or a resumption of inconvertibility. The international use of the dollar would decline sharply, even in the absence of an explicit agreement to that effect, despite the improvement in the U.S. liquidity ratios which would result. So this approach would leave the United States with far smaller reserves than the other major countries have, continued adjustment constraints, and no financing capability through the dollar. It would thus represent the worst of all worlds for the United States and be completely unacceptable.[24]

---

24. The United States could of course use the gold revaluation proceeds to redeem the foreign dollar reserves over a long period of time rather than immediately. It would then enjoy the sharp increase in reserves from the gold revaluation and have additional time to adjust to any continuing deficits, but with the requirement for eventual amortization making it clear that such adjustment would have to occur eventually. Rueff himself provided the basis for such a variant by suggesting, in an interview in *U.S. News and World Report*, December 11, 1967, pp. 56, 69, that the continental European countries lend part of their gold revaluation profits to the United Kingdom

Table 15

RESERVES OF MAJOR COUNTRIES AT END OF 1974, AND IF OFFICIAL GOLD PRICE WERE RAISED TO $340 WITH ENTIRE DOLLAR OVERHANG THEN REDEEMED
(In millions of dollars)

	At end–1974				If official gold price were raised to $340 and dollar overhang converted			
	Gold	FX	SDR and IMF position	Total	Gold	FX	SDR and IMF position[a]	Total
Belgium	1,807	2,197	1,341	5,345	16,653	—	1,341	17,994
Denmark	78	656	201	935	1,280	—	201	1,481
France	4,325	3,753	773	8,851	38,353	—	773	39,126
Germany	5,040	24,016	3,343	32,399	64,336	—	3,343	67,679
Ireland	19	1,146	102	1,266	1,298	—	102	1,400
Italy	3,535	3,185	221	6,941	31,465	—	221	31,686
Netherlands	2,328	3,495	1,136	6,958	22,119	—	1,136	23,255
United Kingdom	899	4,945	1,095	6,939	12,137	—	1,095	13,232
Total EC	18,031	43,393	8,212	69,634	187,641	—	8,212	195,853
Canada	941	3,781	1,104	5,825	11,309	—	1,104	12,413
Japan	905	11,347	1,268	13,519	18,587	—	1,268	19,855
Switzerland	3,565	5,446	—	9,011	33,966	—	—	33,966
United States	11,826	5	4,226	16,058	15,000[e]	—	4,226	19,226[e]

FX—Foreign exchange

[a] Assumes no change in valuation of SDR and reserve positions in the IMF.

[e]—U.S. figure can only be estimated, due to the imprecision of published figures for world dollar reserves—which, under these assumptions, would be converted into U.S. gold at the revalued price.

Source: *International Financial Statistics*, April 1975.

The third case, the only one which might be politically acceptable to most of the major countries, including the United States, would envisage no redemption of the overhang, but full convertibility for all outstanding dollars. This would help the U.S. liquidity ratios although it *could* in practice lead to conversions, which would move the result toward that of the second case. Most important, however, such a "solution" would simply replicate the system which existed before August 15, 1971, with all its uncertainties. By roughly equating U.S. assets and liabilities, it would in fact most nearly replicate the mid-1960s phase of the postwar system, which, as noted earlier, was the riskiest phase for both the United States and the system as a whole. And the renewed competition between a dollar strengthened in absolute terms and one or more European currencies greatly strengthened in both absolute and relative terms could add greatly to the confidence problems of the system as a whole.

Such a measure should thus be adopted from a systemic standpoint only if it were accompanied by an agreement to avoid the creation of additional reserve balances of any national currencies in the future. But such an agreement would eliminate any deficit-financing potential for the United States from the reserve currency role of the dollar while leaving the overhang outstanding. In addition, the relative strengthening of other countries, along with the great increase in their relative weight in the world economy, could greatly reduce the vehicle currency role of the dollar. Since Chapter 7 concluded that the United States should get out of the reserve currency business altogether unless it could get additional dollar financing of at least $2.5 billion annually, and since there is no offsetting systemic benefit, it seems clear that an increase in the official price of gold would be disadvantageous to the national interests of the United States even if there were a politically feasible means by which such an increase could take place.

There is another political reason why even this variant of the gold-price increase is unacceptable, however. Especially after their reserve increases of the early 1970s, it seems dubious that skewing the distribution of additional liquidity in favor of the industrialized countries—particularly those in continental Europe which have run persistent payments surpluses—would be acceptable to the rest of

---

to permit it to redeem all the sterling balances, repaying the loans to the Europeans over a 20- or 25-year period. Such an operation would amount to a funding of that part of the sterling overhang by the European loans. This type of funding could be used for the outstanding dollar balances as well, since the gold revaluation profits of the continental Europeans would easily be large enough for them to make such loans to the United States.

the world. The less developed countries (which hold less than 10 per cent of world gold reserves) and some of the major countries which hold little gold (Japan, Canada, and recently Britain) could certainly be counted on to oppose the needed amendment to the Articles of Agreement of the IMF and block such a step.[25] Indeed, the less developed countries will probably insist on some kind of "link" between new liquidity and development assistance to give them an *increased* share of new reserves as a price for their agreement to any overall reform scheme. They would be particularly opposed to an increase in the official price of gold because all of their debts to the IMF are valued in terms of gold. So the political liabilities of any of the possible approaches render an increase in the price of gold as highly undesirable, and as unlikely an "answer" to the global liquidity problem as to the global adjustment problem.

Adoption of an International Reserve Asset

An alternative method to eliminate the dollar as a reserve currency would be to substitute completely a truly international asset for it. Such a new international asset could be used to replace all *existing* currency balances (and perhaps other reserves held by monetary authorities) *and* as the sole source of future liquidity, thereby eliminating altogether the use of national currencies as international reserves.[26] It has no direct bearing on the adjustment process, although this liquidity solution would also increase the pressure on the United States to adjust by prohibiting further expansion of the reserve currency role of the dollar.

An "international asset" is a medium of exchange created and distributed by international agreement, and acceptable to the monetary authorities of all members of the system in settlement of their

25. It would also be objectionable to some to provide windfall gains, through a gold price increase, to South Africa and the U.S.S.R., the two leading producers, and to private gold speculators who have contributed to the problems of the monetary system in the past.

26. An international asset could also be used less ambitiously, in two ways. It could become simply a source of *future* liquidity to *supplement* whatever amounts of gold and national currencies become available, without any explicit change in *existing* currency balances or the role of other reserve assets. This is the present role of the SDR, under which the dollar overhang remains a component of the international monetary system and national currencies remain a potential source of future liquidity. Or an international asset could be made available for *optional*, rather than mandatory, conversion of both outstanding and new reserve currency holdings, which could also produce only a partial consolidation thereof. Both of these approaches, which would modify but not eliminate the dollar's reserve currency role, are considered in Chapter 13.

payments imbalances. The Special Drawing Rights created through the IMF since 1970 are such an asset. At the outset, however, this discussion will not differentiate among the various types of international assets which have been proposed—SDR, Composite Reserve Units (CRUs), claims on a Reserve Settlement Account, etc. They all possess the same basic characteristics, and their differences in detail, while of great importance in some contexts, are not critical to a conceptual appraisal of a reformed monetary system in which such an asset played a (or the) central role.

Robert Triffin and Edward M. Bernstein have for many years made proposals which could effectively eliminate the dollar as a reserve asset by basing the international monetary system on an international reserve asset.[27] The idea in its simplest and extreme form would be for member countries to deposit all of their present reserves—including gold, SDR, dollars, sterling, other national currencies, and perhaps even claims on the IMF—into an internationally managed account, in return for which they would receive claims on the account. The need for reserve growth would be met by annual creation of SDRs, as in 1970–72, but new SDR allocations would be promptly deposited in the international account and increase the holder's claims on it. No increase in other reserve assets would be permitted. Claims on the account would then become the sole asset used in settlement of payments imbalances among member countries. The objectives of the proposal are to remove the risk of instability inherent in any monetary system comprising more than one type of money, particularly when at least one type (gold, in this case) begins to acquire a growing scarcity premium, and to provide the basis for complete international control of the expansion of international reserves. Countries could not then exercise a preference for one reserve asset over another, and the danger of a competitive race for gold (or any other asset) would be avoided.

The claims could be "backed" by the gold, dollars, and other assets

27. Triffin's published explanations of his approach are numerous, starting with *Gold and the Dollar Crisis* (New Haven: Yale University Press, 1960). Bernstein is associated with several approaches to international monetary reform. His idea referred to here was mentioned as early as May 1961 in "The Adequacy of United States Gold Reserves," *American Economic Review*, Vol. LI, No. 2, p. 446 and has been most completely explained in "The Outlook for Gold—Midyear 1967," a privately circulated publication of Model, Roland and Company, Inc., pp. 27–29. The Triffin and Bernstein proposals are broadly similar in their effects on the role of the dollar, and this analysis will differentiate between them on specific points only where the difference would critically affect either the international monetary system or the dollar's roles therein.

which they had replaced. However, the international community created SDRs without any such "backing," and it is clear that none is needed. The asset, like the SDR, would derive its value from the agreement of the countries participating in the scheme to provide usable currencies for them, supplemented if necessary by agreement of the participants (as in the SDR case) to provide alternative assets to a country with net acquisition of SDRs if it opts out of the scheme or if the scheme were liquidated.[28]

A less sweeping approach would be for member countries to deposit in the international account only the reserve currency component of their reserves, retaining their gold and other present assets in addition to their claims on the new account.[29] The overhang of dollar balances could thus be consolidated, and there would presumably be agreement that countries would no longer accumulate balances of national currencies in their reserves. The scheme would avoid the risk of conversions of overhanging dollars into U.S. assets, and prevent renewal of the same problem through the further accumulation of dollars by foreign monetary authorities—precluding future financing for U.S. deficits by foreign accumulations of dollars in the process. The chief demerit of this approach relative to consolidation of *all* reserve assets—that it would leave open the risk of destabilizing shifts between gold and the new asset—could be obviated (as was done with the SDRs) by simply declaring the new asset inconvertible into gold.

An important technical question is whether outstanding reserve assets should be consolidated in a new account, as Bernstein and Triffin have proposed or into SDRs themselves. A new account might open a wider range of options for the consolidation operation, partly because it could carry a different interest rate than SDRs. On the other hand, creation of a new asset would require negotiation of a whole set of new rules, and it would represent the creation of a second international money only a few years after the historic and difficult step of creating one international money, which could well

28. Tangible "backing" might be more important psychologically in the case of the exchange of old assets than in the case of the creation of new reserves, but could of course be readily provided by the assets which were exchanged.

29. Such an internationalization of a *single* reserve asset could also be used for gold. Countries could deposit their gold holdings in an international account to permit intervention in the private gold market without reducing monetary reserves in the process, retaining their reserve currency balances as at present. Some of the pre-March 1968 suggestions for changes in gold pool procedures were along these lines, such as the proposal of Robert Mundell to replace gold reserves by "gold certificates" of a fixed value and then use the real gold in market transactions without affecting the value of monetary reserves.

detract psychologically from both. It would present the strange spectacle of creating additional reserves through one international money (SDR), which would immediately be converted into another (the new account). The following discussion assumes that the consolidation is into SDR, although the only differences between the two techniques would be technical except where noted.

Three specific aspects of any scheme which would consolidate the dollar overhang are of particular importance to the United States: the disposition of the dollars converted into the special issue of SDRs, interest payments on those dollars, and any guarantees which might be required on the converted dollars. Chapter 8 pointed out that the United States would gain from the elimination of the threat of the overhang to its existing reserves or to the exchange rate of the dollar, and hence to its domestic economic policy and foreign policy, and also it would then be assured of reserve increases when it ran payments surpluses in the future. Chapter 7 concluded that the overhang does levy sizable net interest costs on the United States; Chapter 10, that systemic stability would be promoted by the elimination of the overhang; and, most important to the United States, Chapter 9 argued that the elimination of the overhang would facilitate American use of the exchange-rate mechanism to initiate balance-of-payments adjustment. But the United States has to set the costs of the terms of the dollar consolidation against these gains in determining whether its national interest would be served by such a step.

There are four basic options for dealing with the amortization issue:

1. The dollars could be retained by the IMF and redeemed by the United States, with its reserve assets, on a fixed schedule; the duration of the schedule would determine how "tough" this option would be on the United States.
2. The United States could redeem the dollars only when it ran payments surpluses.
3. The dollars could be retained indefinitely by the IMF as "consols" with no maturities.
4. The dollars could be returned to the United States and eliminated altogether from the system, which would have the same economic effect as perpetual consols but different technical effects on the operation of the scheme.[30]

30. Bernstein explicitly calls for "monetization" of the outstanding dollar balances, i.e., no amortization. He would treat them as a "fixed fiduciary issue of reserves"; see "The Outlook for Gold—Midyear 1967," p. 28, and his references to the same concept in Hinshaw, *op. cit.*, pp. 76 and 162. Triffin

American amortization of the overhang on a fixed schedule could impart a deflationary bias to the world economy. The United States would need to build its reserves under any of these approaches which eliminated the possibility of dollar financing for future deficits, since its reserves relative to the level of its economic transactions are among the lowest of the industrialized countries. Any dollar repayment obligation would thus increase the magnitude of the payments surpluses which are likely to be sought by the United States. To be sure, this target could be met through sufficient annual creation of SDRs (or other new reserve assets)—it would represent circular reasoning to force the United States to "pay off its past debts" and then give it the money to do so, but this approach might be politically more palatable to other countries than letting it "get away" without amortization, and others would of course get more new SDRs in the process. The United States would of course need full assurances that the needed amounts of additional SDRs would in fact be created.

Without such a guarantee, amortization of the consolidated dollars could produce major systemic problems. Reconciliation of the mercantilistic trade and payments objectives of other nations has been extremely difficult in the past, with the United States playing an essentially passive and accommodating role. It will become extremely difficult even with the United States aiming for surpluses to build its reserves. And it could become unmanageable if the United States aimed at sufficiently higher surpluses to achieve the desired reserve growth and also pay off debt. It is quite possible that $30 billion of the outstanding dollars could be consolidated, so that even a 50-year amortization schedule would add $600 million to the annual U.S. payments target.[31] The United States would have to reduce its

_____

calls for amortization at a rate not exceeding 2 to 5 per cent a year (to be postponed when such amortization was "deemed in conflict with the general stabilization objectives of the IMF") or, if negotiable, only when the United States was running balances of payments surpluses in the future and amortization became an alternative to U.S. gold purchases. See "Contingency Planning," pp. 135 and 143.

31. The British surplus target might also have to rise by $100 million to pay off the $5 billion of sterling which could come in. On the present distribution formula, an *extra* $2.5 billion of SDR would have to be created annually to provide the United States with enough *extra* reserves to meet the amortization schedule without having to take reserves away from other countries. Britain would get an extra $250 million, more than enough to cover its amortization needs. From the standpoint of the reserve centers, this approach would be identical to raising the official price of gold sufficiently to enable them to redeem their liabilities; it would be very different for most other countries, however, because of the difference in the distribution of additional SDR allocations and gold revaluation profits.

domestic demand by a multiple of that amount or by maintaining a more depreciated exchange rate; and other countries would have to accept the corresponding deficits and hence pressures on their level of output and employment. The longer the amortization period, of course, the smaller would be these burdens in any single year.

Amortization solely from the proceeds of autonomous U.S. payments surpluses would not have such additional deflationary effects. However, if amortization took *all* these proceeds, it would eliminate the incentive for the United States to run surpluses. To avoid this result, amortization of this type would have to be made only from U.S. earnings above an agreed trend growth. Such growth might be set at 5–6 per cent annually, which we have seen earlier was the growth needed for total world reserves under the Bretton Woods system; if this norm were adopted for annual SDR creation, the U.S. amortization obligation could be to redeem dollars held by the IMF with any reserves which it accrued beyond the amount of its own annual SDR allocations.[32]

The United States would, of course, strongly prefer to avoid any amortization of the consolidated dollars. This arrangement would also be in the interests of the system as a whole. As just noted, any requirement for amortization will cause systemic problems. In addition, the countries converting their dollars into SDRs would by definition be getting an asset which they preferred to the "old" dollars. There is thus no reason from their standpoint, or from that of the system, why the United States should amortize. Some might argue, however, that the United States should not "get away with" the past appropriation of real resources from the rest of the world accomplished through its payments deficits. A partial answer is that many of the dollars were the result of foreign demand for reserves and exports rather than U.S.-generated supply; moreover, many of the dollars which *were* supply-generated resulted from expenditures (such as those for NATO) which were in the interest of other countries as well as the United States. A complete answer would have to include a concurrent U.S. assurance against the re-creation of a new overhang by agreeing to finance its deficits in the future entirely with reserve assets.

On the interest-rate issue, there are five basic approaches:

1. To treat the new SDRs as "initial allocations," on which no interest is paid;

32. An additional problem with any amortization requirement for reserve currencies, if gold were consolidated into SDRs at the same time, is that there is no one to redeem the gold. This would require different treatment, which might make it more difficult to negotiate the scheme.

2. For the United States to pay the IMF amounts equal to its payments of interest to the holders of the new SDRs at the standard SDR interest rate;

3. For the United States to pay the IMF amounts equal to the "normal" U.S. debt service burden on the consolidated dollars (current U.S. market rates on the debt instruments which were originally consolidated, some "average" current U.S. interest rate, some average U.S. debt service level in the past, or simply some negotiated rate agreeable to all), with this rate passed on to the holders of the special SDRs, and with lower rates continuing to apply to regulate SDRs;

4. For the United States to continue its "normal" payments, with the present rate prevailing for all SDRs and the difference used to amortize the dollar "principal";

5. For some new use to be found for this difference.[33]

Avoiding interest payments altogether on the new SDRs would of course maximize the financial savings to the United States and be extremely attractive to it. And there is some logic in treating these SDRs as "initial allocations," since in fact they are newly created additions to the stock of SDRs to serve an agreed international monetary purpose. On the other hand, there would be technical problems in treating these SDRs as "initial allocations" rather than as "net use" by the United States, particularly with regard to the need for someone to bear ultimate liability for them in the unlikely event of liquidation of the SDR scheme.[34] Attempting to do so would of course intensify opposition on "moral grounds" to the entire consolidation scheme.

The alternative of further increasing the interest rate on all SDRs, sufficiently to equate it with the interest rate on dollars, has the advantage of avoiding the benefits which now accrue to net users by virtue of their being able to finance their payments deficits at interest rates below market levels. It could also make surplus countries more willing to finance their surpluses, rather than demand that deficit countries adjust to them, by increasing the financial return on the additions to their reserves. And it would make SDRs more attrac-

33. All of these approaches are consistent with returning the consolidated dollars to the United States. The special issue of SDRs would be treated as a "net use" of SDRs by the United States and a "net acquisition" by other countries, with any interest paid through book transfers as under the present SDR scheme anyway. The Fund need not hold any actual dollar instruments.

34. No one bears a liability to redeem initial allocations of regular SDRs. On the other hand, net users of SDR do bear a liability to redeem, with acceptable assets, the net acquisitions of SDR which surplus countries accepted in lieu of other assets.

tive and hence increase their acceptability as a substitute for the dollar.[35]

However, such higher rates for SDRs have serious disadvantages. Countries would acquire an exchange-value guarantee by converting their dollars into SDRs, and would thus profit significantly if they were to receive market interest rates as well. It is true that higher interest rates plus the guarantees on "net acquisitions" of SDRs would make payments surpluses even more attractive than they are now, but few major surplus countries determine their policies on the basis of interest earnings on their reserves. Hence they are not likely to reduce their preferences for adjustment by deficit countries as a result, even if this were a desirable objective. More important, to the extent that a higher interest rate did determine the policies of surplus countries, it would further increase their reluctance to take adjustment initiatives. And higher SDR rates would make payments deficits even costlier, so such a change would exacerbate further the adjustment bias of the system against deficit countries, whereas a key objective of reform is to reduce this bias.

The alternative of paying a higher interest rate on the special issue of SDRs than on regular SDRs is also undesirable. In fact, this approach would require the creation of a totally different asset to avoid insuperable technical problems when the SDRs shift hands, and we have already concluded that this would undermine rather than enhance the postulated movement toward reliance on a single international asset for world liquidity.

The two viable choices are thus (a) U.S. payments to the Fund equal to the interest rate paid to SDR holders, at or near the present 5 per cent, or (b) higher payments based on some notion of a "fair" burden for the United States, with a decision as to how to use the difference. (For reasons already outline, there is no utility in using the difference to "redeem" the U.S. debt.) The United States would of course strongly prefer option (a), which would reduce the costs to it of the reserve currency role outlined in Chapter 7 in return for its giving up the benefits of that role. Since the United States has unilaterally abrogated redemption of the dollar overhang into its reserve assets, thereby eliminating two of the chief costs of the dollar's roles by seizing the opportunity to achieve adjustment via the exchange rate and pre-empting threats to U.S. policy from dollar conversions, the interest-rate issue will in fact be one of the key elements of U.S. concern in any negotiated settlement of the entire monetary reform question.

35. See Fred Hirsch, "SDRs and the Working of the Gold Exchange Standard," *IMF Staff Papers*, Vol. XVIII, No. 2 (July 1971).

The most promising variant of option (b), and the most likely to develop strong political support within the IMF, is to seize this opportunity to forge a link between the SDR system and development finance. The difference could be granted to the World Bank, to augment the lending capabilities of its International Development Association. Consolidation of $50 billion, with SDR rates remaining at 5 per cent and U.S. interest obligations set at 8 per cent, would generate $1.5 billion annually for development. The "burden" of this aid would be shared by the previous holders of the dollars, who gave up their interest earnings in return for the gold-value guarantee and systemic effects of the SDRs, and the United States, which would actually be paying the interest and which otherwise might have seen its interest burden reduced. Some of the lower income countries may insist on some form of "aid link" if they are to go along with any overall reform program, and this seems the best way to do so that is consistent with the basic monetary needs of the world as a whole.

As this approach would eliminate any reduction of U.S. interest payments, it might obviate one potential major gain from getting rid of the overhang. However, there would be a saving to the United States of equal magnitude if the aid to developing countries provided through this device were simply to substitute for aid which it would have extended anyway (e.g., through regular appropriations to IDA). Even if the new U.S. contribution were only a partial replacement for aid which would otherwise have been extended, there would in effect be some cutback in U.S. foreign expenditures as a result of this particular handling of the interest-rate aspect of a dollar consolidation.

The final consideration is whether the United States will have to extend a guarantee on the value of the asset into which outstanding dollars are converted. If the conversion is into SDRs, the United States would presumably have to provide whatever guarantee applied to SDR. So it would assume an additional cost contingent on any future dollar devaluations, which could increase U.S. inhibitions against such action. The guarantee would only have to be made good in the event of a liquidation of the scheme, however, or withdrawal from it of individual countries with "net acquisitions."[36] In addition,

36. It would thus be somewhat analogous to the requirements of the charters of the IBRD, IADB, and ADB under which a devaluing country must be prepared to make available extra units of its currency to preserve the original value of its capital contribution. Since this capital is simply callable, however, it requires no immediate real contribution—and probably none in the future either, since the callable capital represents backing for borrowings by these institutions in the private capital markets and could be called only in the unlikely event that they were dissolved.

the guarantee would now cost the United States less since the SDR are now defined in terms of a basket of national currencies, of which the dollar is only a part, instead of in terms of gold, any revaluation of which equates fully to dollar devaluations. It is thus unlikely to cause much real cost to the United States—and stands in sharp contrast to direct guarantees on foreign dollar holdings, like those Britain extended on sterling under the Basel arrangements, which have to be made good in full immediately upon the act of devaluation.

The United States will therefore doubtlessly have to extend guarantees on all consolidated dollars, and should be willing to do so. This will raise at least the contingent costs to it of any consolidation operation, however, and make it less willing to agree to "tough" amortization and interest rate provisions. From its national interest standpoint, it should seek to come as close as possible to no amortization and no interest payments. Its actual position on these particular issues would of course be determined by the desirability of the overall reform package from the U.S. standpoint.

None of the schemes proposed for consolidating the dollar overhang includes private dollar holdings within its purview. However, the one major agreement of this type which has actually been negotiated, the Basel arrangements for sterling, provided "funding" for conversions of private as well as official sterling balances in sterling area countries. In addition, Chapter 2 concluded that private dollar-holdings are at least as volatile as official balances, and Chapter 8, that the private overhang can add to the pressure for monetary authorities to seek dollar conversions. Finally, there could be a secular decline in private foreign demand for dollars under any of these options for eliminating the reserve currency role of the dollar, so that dollars outstanding at the time the new regime started could shift permanently into official hands—either leaving these officials "stuck" with them, or requiring the United States to use its reserve assets to refinance old liquidity deficits immediately, both of which would violate basic principles of any such reform approach. Thus there is a strong case for making private dollar balances outstanding at the time of any agreement to eliminate the dollar's reserve currency role eligible for consolidation into SDRs, whenever they move into official hands.

The dollar could continue to be used as an intervention currency by central banks, even if it were eliminated as a reserve currency, if a basically fixed exchange rate system would continue under which central bank intervention was necessary. Countries could thus retain their dollar working balances. They could, however, sell any excess dollar accumulations to the United States for U.S. reserves. If their stock of international currency became depleted, they could buy additional amounts from the United States or from the IMF.[37]

The dollar could also retain its role as a private transactions currency. The removal of the threat of massive official gold conversions would sharply improve the U.S. liquidity ratios and could well increase foreign private demand for dollars, as long as foreign central banks remained ready to buy any unwanted dollars for local currency. (The foreign central banks presumably would become more willing to do so, since they could then immediately convert the dollars.) On the other hand, the need for rapid U.S. adjustment to payments deficits would increase the likelihood of dollar devaluation or controls, and could deter private holdings at some periods of time.

This whole approach would require much more rapid adjustment on the part of the United States, since it would proscribe further increases in foreign official dollar holdings. Indeed, some observers feel that such a proscription would alone go far toward improving the international adjustment process, as outlined earlier in this chapter in discussing the case for a "return to the gold standard." Our analysis in Chapter 9 demonstrated that more active U.S. adjustment requires independent improvement in that process, however, though it also demonstrated that elimination of the international roles of the dollar would be an integral step in permitting such improvement. To the extent that a shift to an international reserve asset successfully met all or part of the world's liquidity needs and led to improved confidence in the functioning of the system, it would improve the atmosphere in which such new adjustment arrangements could be developed.

Consolidation of *all* present reserve assets, including the outstanding official dollar balances, and agreement to proscribe any renewed expansion of such balances would produce total reliance on the new international asset as the sole source of owned reserves. Amounts of new liquidity would clearly be regulated by international agreement in response to the agreed needs of the international community for additional reserves. There would be an equal degree of certainty in the case of *dollar* consolidation alone as long as the proscription for the future applied to *all* national currencies, and as long as interna-

---

37. The initial amount of dollar deposits in the IMF would probably take care of each country's needs for intervention currency for a long time to come. Even if countries view as much as 15 per cent of their reserves as working balances, the $50 billion which might be deposited (even without considering the additional $5 billion or so of sterling) would not be exhausted until total reserves rose far above present levels.

tional agreement precluded purchases of gold by national monetary authorities. Membership in a system which was to eliminate the dollar's reserve currency role could only be universal. If membership were limited and some countries did not consolidate their dollar balances through the funding or monetizing operation, then the dollar would not be eliminated as a reserve currency.

Another major question is how new quantities of the international asset would be distributed. One possibility is to follow the original pattern of the SDR and to distribute in proportion to each country's quota at the IMF. Another is for the management of the international account to make loans or open-market purchases at its own discretion in the financially strongest countries ("to preserve the full liquidity of its members' deposits")[38] as needed to support the adjustment process, but also in IBRD bonds to help finance international development. A third possibility would be to channel all, or at least a larger part, of the new reserves to the less-developed countries where they are needed most, directly or through IDA. The LDCs would be expected to spend a large part of their new liquidity, and it would thus be earned (rather than received "gratis") by the industrialized countries.[39]

Replacement by a New Reserve Currency

Finally, the dollar could be eliminated as a reserve currency by retaining the gold exchange standard but substituting another national currency or currencies for it. In practice, this is of course a real option only if some other currency were to qualify for the role. To see whether such a possibility exists, we can compare the outlook for the major national currencies—the German mark, the Japanese yen, sterling, the French franc, the Swiss franc, and the Dutch guilder—with the attributes required for key currency status as outlined in Chapters 4–6. In this context, we will have to make some forecasts of the evolution of European monetary unification to see whether it might significantly alter the outlook.

First, however, we must note the fact that there has already been, in the last few years, extremely rapid growth in the key currency role of several national currencies. Williamson reports that information available to the staff of the IMF indicates that the proportion of

---

38. Triffin, *Gold and the Dollar Crisis*, p. 118.
39. See, for example, Maxwell Stamp, "The Stamp Plan—1962 Version," *Moorgate and Wall Street* (Autumn 1962) pp. 5–17; Edward R. Fried, "International Liquidity and Foreign Aid," *Foreign Affairs*, October 1969, pp. 139–49; and Roelf L. Haan, *Special Drawing Rights and Development* (Leiden: H. E. Stenfert Kroese N.V., 1971).

Table 16

EXTERNAL LIABILITIES OF REPORTING EUROPEAN
COMMERCIAL BANKS IN DOLLARS AND OTHER
FOREIGN CURRENCIES, 1966–71
(In per cent)

	Dollars	Marks	Swiss francs	Sterling	Guilders	Other	Memorandum: total amounts (in $ million)
1966	80.0	5.3	6.6	3.8	0.4	3.9	18,460
1967	80.7	7.4	6.2	3.6	0.4	1.6	22,450
1968	79.6	8.9	6.8	2.4	0.7	1.6	33,760
1969	81.3	8.2	7.1	1.4	0.6	1.4	56,380
1970	78.0	10.7	7.6	1.2	0.7	1.7	75,290
1971	72.3	15.2	7.9	2.2	0.9	1.5	97,390
1972	73.0	14.8	6.7	1.7	1.3	2.5	131,930
1973	68.2	16.8	8.9	2.5	1.2	2.4	191,430

Source: Bank for International Settlements, *44th Annual Report*, June 10, 1974,
p. 162.

Table 17
INTERNATIONAL AND FOREIGN BOND ISSUES:
PUBLIC OFFERINGS AND PRIVATE PLACEMENTS: 1970–73
(In millions of dollars)

	Dollars	Marks	Guilders	Other*	Total
1970	1,961	601	310	123	2,994
1971	2,241	860	268	487	3,756
1972	3,864	1,232	473	922	6,491
1973	2,390	990	190	520	4,090

*Includes Luxembourg francs, Danish krone, Australian dollar, French francs, etc.
Source: Bank for International Settlements, *44th Annual Report*, June 10, 1974,
p. 176.

foreign exchange reserves held in the "new" reserve currencies increased from 5–6 per cent in 1964 to about double that figure by March 1973, and grew by another 4 per cent or so in the rest of 1973—which would bring the amount to almost $20 billion.[40] Ac-

40. John Williamson, "Increased Flexibility and International Liquidity," a
paper presented to the Williamsburg Conference of the Bürgenstock Group,
May 1974, p. 11. These numbers are a good bit higher than those published as "identified" holdings of "new" reserve currencies in the IMF
Annual Report 1974, p. 32; the difference presumably comes from the
large "residual sources of reserves" shown in the published data.

cording to other sources, the growth of this source of reserves approximated $10–12 billion in 1972 alone.

The growth was most pronounced for the German mark. Indeed, the Deutsche Bundesbank reported in early 1973 that, although data in this area remain imperfect, it appeared that the mark had passed sterling as the world's second most used reserve currency.[41] This would imply mark reserve holdings approaching $10 billion by that time. Such an estimate fully conforms with widespread reports of mark holdings by central banks.[42] As Tables 16 and 17 show, it also conforms with BIS estimates that the mark component of the Euro-currency and Eurobond markets has been rising rapidly, exceeding 15 and 20 per cent, respectively, by 1971. The IMF estimated that the mark and Swiss franc accounted for 12.1 per cent of all "private international liquidity" at the end of 1973, up from 2.0 per cent and 2.5 per cent, respectively, in 1964; their methodology is consistent over time, and thus these numbers probably characterize accurately the growth of the roles of the mark and Swiss franc, but biases the absolute numbers downward.[42a]

In fact, one can interpret the decision of six European Community members and three non-EC countries in March 1973 to maintain fixed exchange rates (within narrow margins) among each other, and to flex together vis-à-vis the rest of the world, including three other EC members, as the de facto creation of a mark area. The primary motive of five of the EC members (Germany itself, Denmark, the Netherlands, and Belgium-Luxembourg, partly through their monetary tie to the Netherlands) and the three non-members (Austria, Sweden, Norway) for the action was their close link to the German economy. The motive of France is more complicated, and relates to its preferences for fixed exchange rates and European monetary unity as well as its close and growing ties to the German economy. How-

41. The $10 billion estimate is derived by the Bank for International Settlements, *43rd Annual Report*, 18 June 1973, p. 121. The $12 billion estimate is in the *Report of the Deutsche Bundesbank for the Year 1972*, p. 36.

42. E.g., Federal Reserve Board Chairman Arthur Burns, in responding to Congressional questions about the sources of exchange-market speculation in early 1973, reported that "German officials have indicated, according to news reports, that some foreign central banks, notably those of some Middle Eastern countries, accounted for a significant portion of the rise in non-resident deposits [of marks]." The total rise of such deposits was almost $4 billion. Hearings before the House Subcommittee on International Finance, on H.R. 4546, March 6–21, 1973, p. 149.

42a. Because they do not include foreign deposits in Germany and Switzerland directly, but only in the Eurocurrency markets. See IMF, *Annual Report 1974*, pp. 43–44.

ever, France departed the new grouping in early 1974 and its character as a mark zone then became clear.

Data are even less readily available on the international use of other national currencies. The BIS data reveal that several have been rising steadily, the share of the Swiss franc has become significant (about 9 per cent in 1973) in the Eurocurrency markets, and the French franc and Dutch guilder have become significant in the Eurobond market (almost 8 per cent each in 1972).[43] In addition, one can infer a rising reserve role for these currencies, taken together, from the wide and growing gap in IMF data between (a) reported holdings of all reserve currencies and (b) reported liabilities of the United States and Britain, even after allowing for the statistical discrepancy resulting from the practice of holding reserve currencies in the Euromarkets rather than directly in the country of issue.[44]

The most obvious shortcoming of any of these candidates for reserve currency status is political. None of them comes anywhere near to playing the world role of Britain in the nineteenth and even twentieth centuries, or of the United States after World War II or even World War I. Britain probably still has the largest world role of any of these political middle powers, but that role continues to recede rapidly and its overseas attentions appear likely to be increasingly limited to Europe. Japan is bound to play an increasing role throughout the developing world, but even its regional efforts will continue to be hobbled for many years by the legacy of World War II. French overseas influence will remain confined to the franc zone, and perhaps the Middle East. Germany's international policy is confined largely to Europe, and its leadership potential is constrained even there by the lingering hostilities fostered by two world wars. And all of these countries, particularly exposed and non-nuclear Germany and lightly armed Japan, remain heavily dependent on the United States for their own ultimate security.

If no individual country is likely to assume a sufficient political role for its currency to completely replace the dollar, is it possible that the expanded European Community could do so as a unit? At

43. See also the strong evidence for "currency transformations" from dollars into marks and guilders and "probably" also into Swiss francs, derived from analysis of Eurobank data as early as 1970 by Robert Z. Aliber, "The Impact of External Markets for National Currencies on Central Bank Reserves" in Johnson and Swoboda, eds., *op. cit.*, esp. pp. 192–95.

44. It will be recalled that "U.S. liabilities to official foreigners" include only dollars held *in the United States* by national monetary authorities. Dollars held by those authorities in the Eurodollar market show up as "U.S. liabilities to foreign commercial banks," the intermediaries who hold the direct claim on the United States.

present, the EC countries seem little interested in such a role and have been unable to achieve meaningful cooperation even toward a neighboring area with such importance to them as the Middle East. Neither French nor British foreign policy appears aimed at submerging national autonomy to a Community stance. Indeed, much of the present U.S. disenchantment with the EC is a result of its failure to develop politically as it has economically, and this failure undermines its capacity to take burdens off U.S. shoulders economically as well as politically.

The EC could achieve a global political role in the traditional sense only by dramatically building up its military power, in any event, which is extremely unlikely both because the members perceive little military threat from the Soviet Union (or anyone else) and because tremendous budgetary expenditures would be required for them to develop a credible nuclear or conventional capability. Indeed, the sharp re-orientation of national spending patterns necessary for them to achieve world political status could even undermine some of the economic attributes that could propel them toward key currency status.

However, the whole nature of international politics has been changing in a direction which will, at the same time, reduce the importance of the "world political role" criteria for key currency status and enhance the capacity of a united Europe (or even the major European countries or Japan alone) to meet it. In a period of relative détente, a country may no longer require vast military might to enjoy political power. Conversely, great economic strength may provide a larger measure of political power than was the case in at least the fifty years from Sarajevo through the coldest years of Cold War. So the European countries, especially acting together but even alone, and Japan, may well "qualify" for key currency status even without the traditional trappings of political power.[45]

Economically, Germany and Japan are clearly powerful enough to be key currency countries. (Table 18 arrays the data on each of the criteria to be discussed.) No single country is of course nearly as large as the United States in terms of GNP or other domestic economic indicators, though several (including Germany) now approximate the United States in terms of per capita income. The level of German trade flows has now moved quite close to the U.S. level, however, and Germany has passed beyond as an exporter of manufactured goods. Japan, still a distant third, is closing the gap rapidly

45. Robert Mundell, in Johnson and Swoboda, *op. cit.*, p. 170, argues that this is so "because Europe has become a security area, a war-free domain."

Table 18

SOME KEY CURRENCY ATTRIBUTES OF MAJOR COUNTRIES

| | GNP (1973) (In $ billion) | Exports (1973) | Openness (Exports/GNP) | Reserves (end-1974) ($ billion) | Increases in GNP deflator (per cent) | | | Growth in GNP per capita (1960-71) average, per cent | Size of capital market (1966) ($ billion) | No. of security issues traded (end-1965) | Basic cost of a $100 share transaction (1966) |
					1959-71 average	1972	1973				
France	243	37	15.2	8.9	4.4	6.0	7.3	4.6	33	3,384	$1.30
Germany	345	68	19.7	32.4	3.6	5.9	6.0	3.7	39	3,903	$1.12
Japan	396	37	9.3	13.5	4.8	4.7	12.0	9.6	31	1,986	na
Netherlands	67	24	35.8	7.0	4.8	8.9	8.0	3.9	na[a]	2,770	$1.86
Switzerland	40	13	32.5	9.0	4.4	9.1	8.2	2.7	na	1,010	$0.19
United Kingdom	165	31	18.8	6.9	4.2	7.7	8.9	2.2	218	9,431	$2.25
Memo: EC	1,055	100	9.5	69.6	4.1	6.4	7.6	3.7	328[b]	21,065[c]	nr
Memo: United States	1,295	71	5.5	16.1	2.8	3.2	5.4	3.0	642	4,398	$1.80[d]

na—not available.   nr—not relevant.

[a] Netherlands stock market capitalization was $8 billion. No figure available for bond market.

[b] Excludes Netherlands and Belgian stock markets, and total capital markets of Denmark and Ireland.

[c] Excludes Denmark and Ireland. Overstates total because same issues are quoted on several markets, and total is derived by simply summing the number of issues traded on the individual national markets.

[d] U.S. cost would be only $0.99 per $100 on a transaction of $5,000, the average size for the New York Stock Exchange.

Sources: IMF, *International Financial Statistics*. IBRD, *World Bank Atlas*, 1973. OECD, *Economic Outlook* 15, July 1974. OECD, *Capital Markets Study* (Paris 1967), pp. 197–98, 212.

with its tremendous growth. The level of U.S. capital flows doubt-lessly still exceeds those of both countries, except perhaps for brief periods of speculative activity, but that gap has also declined, partly due to the U.S. controls over capital exports. Switzerland and the Netherlands export fairly sizable quantities of capital, but both are very small in the context of overall world economic transactions. On this "national size" criterion, the uniting of Europe makes a major difference: its joint GNP still reaches only about one-half the U.S. level, but its trade as a group with the rest of the world far exceeds that of the United States and its reserves dwarf the American. Thus a united Europe would have considerably more "positive power," than the United States on international economic issues, if less "negative power."

The same conclusions apply to the aloofness criterion. Although Germany is a fairly open economy, its domestic economic policy has been largely independent of external considerations throughout the postwar period.[46] On the other hand, it has now revalued several times to help ward off inflationary pressures. And its political expo-sure, as long as any vestiges remain from the Cold War, renders it vulnerable to external political events—as when money fled Germany in the wake of the Soviet invasion of Czechoslavakia in 1968, despite the imminent economic need for revaluation. Japan is the least open of the other major economies in terms of trade-to-GNP ratios, but literally must import to live and has traditionally regarded the for-eign sector as of crucial strategic importance for its economic well-being; hence it is very sensitive to external events. France is also relatively closed to external pressures. However, it is a smaller econ-omy; has had to devalue numerous times in its history, including three times in the recent past; and has maintained a degree of aloof-ness only by tight controls over its international transactions, a major violation of another important key currency attribute. Switzerland and the Netherlands, as highly open economies, also fail to qualify on this score. Once more, a united Europe is by far a better prospect: less than 10 per cent of its aggregate GNP depends on trade outside its membership, a figure approaching the 6 per cent of the United States. Such a Europe would have a significant extent of "negative power" in the world economy.

Britain and Japan have both maintained pervasive controls over international use of their currency throughout the postwar period,

---

46. Michaely, *op. cit.*, p. 62, found that only Germany among the major coun-tries joined the United States in entirely ignoring the balance of payments in formulating its monetary and fiscal policy during 1950–66.

and even before, which represents a major drawback to their accepta-bility as reserve centers. This would be true even if the controls were lifted at some point, because history (which reflects fundamental national attitudes) would indicate that they might be rapidly re-instituted if trouble developed. Germany probably ranks best on this criterion, due to its well-known antipathy to controls and a favorable balance-of-payments outlook which reduces the likelihood of a need for such measures. Indeed, Germany's only post-convertibility con-trols have been over *inflows* of capital, to keep the mark from becom-ing even more widely used as an international currency. Switzerland and the Netherlands also dislike controls, and many of those which they have applied have similarly aimed at limiting capital inflows and their international roles; but both are so open to the world economy that they have frequently been forced to control outflows as well, and they will undoubtedly have to do so again in the future.

The nature of any joint EC policy toward controls is uncertain. Its economic strength and German preferences suggest that it would eschew them. However, its policy could be dominated by the French proclivity for controls and the British willingness to use them, espe-cially since Germany has recently begun to accept controls more readily as well.

On the other hand, the importance of this criterion has waned with the evolution of the Eurocurrency markets. A variety of na-tional currencies can now be used in international finance wholly outside the jurisdiction of the countries which issue them. Indeed, the mark has become the world's second key currency despite tight German controls against capital inflows. National controls over the international use of a currency are thus no longer an overwhelming deterrent to their use. For this very reason, opposition by govern-ments to key currency roles for their currencies is inadequate to stop them from assuming such roles (albeit on a smaller scale than if their governments supported such developments, or were at least neutral to them).[47]

Britain ranks next to the United States as a capital market. It is

47. Most countries have voiced such opposition. J. J. Polak of the IMF reported in 1967 that "The multiple reserve currency approach [which we shall con-sider in Chapter 13] did not . . . find support if for no other reason than that the position of a reserve center failed to appeal to countries that so far had been spared this particular blessing." See Herbert Bratter, "Alchemy in Rio," *Interplay*, Vol. I, No. 4 (Nov. 1967), p. 23. Under the IMF procedures governing SDR transactions, only the three existing reserve currencies—the dollar, sterling, and the French franc—have been declared "fully convertible in fact." See the *Annual Report of the IMF*, 1970, p. 31.

far ahead of all other countries on this criterion, and is even far ahead of the United States in terms of the number of issues traded. Hence it has attracted a sizable share of the early "petrodollar" reflows. Switzerland has the lowest transactions costs, but is a relatively small market. Germany and Japan rank much more poorly (relative to the United States and Britain) in this regard than in any other, partly because both lack a sizable public debt and have relied predominantly on their banking systems for financing internal growth in the postwar period. The EC aims to create a unified capital market on the road to monetary unification, and might be able to do so by pooling the financial strength of Britain and the Netherlands with the underlying economic strength of Germany and perhaps France. It would still be only about half as large as the U.S. market—about in line with the relative GNP relationship—but would have enough absolute magnitude to function as both a depository for foreign funds and an exporter of capital.

Beyond these "structural" characteristics, we found in Chapter 5 that the most important varying economic criterion for a reserve center was its liquidity ratio. In looking first at the narrowest ratio, between reserves and liquid liabilities to foreigners, the United Kingdom is in the weakest position—although its ratio improved dramatically with the buildup of its reserves in 1970–71 and would be improved further by any consolidation of the sterling overhang which might be negotiated. All the other major countries have solid ratios on this definition, since reserves have risen sharply in recent years and their currencies have been little used internationally until recently. As of early 1973, the level of their gross reserves placed Germany and Japan at the top of the list. Germany had higher gross reserves but larger external liabilities, since German firms and banks had borrowed huge amounts of foreign capital in recent years to combat the tight monetary policy of the Bundesbank. In addition, Japanese exchange controls had frustrated most foreign efforts to build up yen balances whereas foreign mark balances have been rising rapidly. The EC reserves, taken together, would swamp Britain's sterling liabilities (and French liabilities to the franc zone, which are "safe" anyway) and provide an imposing set of ratios. In addition, a pooling of EC reserves would mean that these countries would no longer use reserves to settle imbalances among themselves, and hence probably reduce the need for reserves of the individual members.[48] An even larger share of their holdings would thus be

48. Richard N. Cooper, *Sterling, European Unification, and the International Monetary System*, British–North American Committee, March 1972, p. 16.

available as "backing" against foreign claims on them, and the EC would begin its reserve currency life with an even more impressive balance sheet than did the United States after World War II.

Complete data are not available on the broader liquidity ratios of the major countries that include all of their foreign investments (with perhaps less weight accorded to foreign direct investment) and liabilities to foreigners. On this basis, however, the U.K. position was positive by about $7 billion at the end of 1969, and improved further by the end of 1971.[49] Excluding direct investment, Germany had net claims on the rest of the world of about $12 billion at the end of 1970.[50] Its reserves more than accounted for the positive net balance, however, and Germany is doubtlessly a net recipient of foreign direct investment (over $4 billion from the United States alone) which would reduce its net position.

In fact, all the major countries, except the United States, Britain, and Japan, are still probably net importers of foreign capital and hence present a stronger liquidity ratio on the narrower basis than on this broader concept. They have used their current account surpluses more to build their reserves than to build their foreign investments. One implication of their accepting key currency status would probably be a reversal of this pattern, to make their currencies more readily available abroad while still building their liquidity ratios as more broadly defined. This would help solve the world payments problem by providing more capital exports from the industrialized countries to finance both the trade surpluses which they seek and the import gaps of the developing countries. At present, in any event, the liquidity ratios of these countries are quite strong on either basis.

Liquidity ratios change with annual balance-of-payments positions, especially current account positions. Again, Germany is widely regarded as likely to maintain sizable payments surpluses, based on solid current account surpluses, in the coming years. Britain and perhaps France are less certain, as is Japan due to the energy crisis. A joint EC is also uncertain, with the interplay between its traditionally "weak" currencies (sterling, French franc, Italian lira) and its traditionally "strong" currencies (mark, guilder, Belgian franc).

Finally, the outlook for the internal economic attributes of the major countries underlies the outlook for the external attributes.

49. Excluding both U.K. direct investment abroad and foreign direct investment in Britain would cut its net foreign asset position roughly in half. For the data, see HMSO, *United Kingdom Balance of Payments 1970*, p. 46–47.
50. Monthly Report of the Deutsche Bundesbank, May 1971, p. 31. Conversion into dollars at the early-1972 central exchange rate.

Germany continues to be regarded as the paragon of *relative* price stability, despite the escalation of its prices in *absolute* terms in the recent past, and is likely to continue to grow well. Japan's consumer prices will continue to rise rapidly, but its wholesale and export prices are likely to remain relatively stable and its dynamic growth, even if considerably lower than the hectic pace of the 1960s, should still outdistance all others by a sizable margin. On the other hand, there is no firm evidence yet that Britain will be able to emerge from its syndrome of low growth and rapid inflation despite EC membership. France is likely to grow well in the 1970s, but its price performance remains suspect. Switzerland and the Netherlands are somewhere near the middle in both categories.

The EC, as a group, again presents an uncertain picture. Will German (and perhaps Dutch) price stability dominate French-British-Italian inflationary tendencies? Will Britain be a drag on the growth of the Community, or will the Community provide the needed impetus for improved British performance? These basic imponderables are impeding the willingness of the member countries to move decisively to monetary and economic union. Political determination to renew the momentum of European integration may override these concerns, but it will not determine their economic outcome. The inevitable compromises would probably place the expanded EC on a growth and price path not too dissimilar from that of the United States, the other sizable customs union in the modern world.

In sum, no individual country seems likely to qualify to play a reserve currency role of sufficient magnitude to fully replace the dollar.[50a] Germany comes closest on most of the basic economic criteria, both external and internal. However, it still operates under major political constraints, has relatively weak capital markets, and is not sufficiently aloof to external economic and political forces.

50a. Richard N. Cooper, "The Future of the Dollar," *Foreign Policy* (Summer 1973), goes much further. He makes an "unconditional forecast" that "At the end of the decade the position of the dollar will not be very different from what it is now," and that "there is at present no clear, feasible alternative" (pp. 4-5). At the same time, however, he recognizes that "other national currencies, and especially the German mark, will play a greater relative and absolute role as international money" (p. 4); that recent data indicate "the growing use of the mark, the yen and possibly other currencies as official reserves" (p. 10); and that "other currencies are increasingly held by foreigners as well [as the dollar]" (p. 20). Cooper never defines the "position of the dollar," but his recognition of the rising role of other currencies supports the analysis of this chapter, and appears to me to represent a rather marked change in that position.

Japan suffers from the same shortcomings, particularly its lack of economic security, and also has a demonstrated proclivity to apply controls.[51] The only other serious national possibility is Britain, based on its superior capital markets, but its political role has moved in a direction which is opposite from what is needed and its economic outlook is far more uncertain than the outlook for most of the other major countries. France, Switzerland, and the Netherlands simply have too many limitations to qualify on a national basis.

Two subsidiary conclusions emerge. One is that some of these national currencies, particularly the mark, if not strong enough to fully replace the dollar, are likely to be quite strong and hence could come to play important regional roles as reserve currencies or *share* global reserve currency status with the dollar. We will turn to these possibilities for moderating the international roles of the dollar in Chapter 13.

The other conclusion is that a monetarily united Europe would even more assuredly play such regional and partial global roles, and is the *only* possibility for fully replacing the dollar as a reserve asset. If it were able to blend British capital markets, German price and external payments performance and dislike for controls, and French political pretensions, it would represent a formidable competition. Its effort to limit intra-EC exchange-rate flexibility to one-half the flexibility permitted by the wider margins authorized on a global basis in the Smithsonian Agreement of late 1971 would already eliminate the advantage of greater exchange-rate stability heretofore held by the dollar (all other things equal) as an inherent function of its transaction currency role.[52] The use of EC currencies for interven-

51. As of late 1973, before the energy crisis erupted, Japanese thinking appeared to be evolving rapidly toward acceptance of a key currency role for the yen. See Ichiro Takeuchi, "International Monetary Problems and Japan," *Pacific Community*, Vol. IV, No. 4 (July 1973), pp. 630–32, and Goro Koyama, "Reconstructing the International Monetary System," *ibid.*, p. 640.

52. This is another concrete way in which the Smithsonian Agreement tended to reduce the international roles of the dollar in the long run. Previous to the widening of the margins on a global basis, the EC had planned only to reduce its internal margins to 1.2 per cent from the previous level of 1.5 per cent. This would have reduced, but by no means eliminated, the "exchange-rate fixity" advantage of the dollar. With a total margin of 4.5 per cent agreed in December 1971, however, the EC was able to retain a much wider internal margin than it had planned before (2.25 per cent) and thus raise fewer potential conflicts among its members, but also fully eliminate this particular advantage of the dollar. And if one particular EC currency became the dominant vehicle for intra-EC intervention, it would *ipso facto* achieve the greatest "exchange-rate fixity" of all currencies because it would flex only one-half as much as the other EC currencies.

tion purposes by other EC members, to keep each inside the "snake" inside the tunnel, would enhance their usability as key currencies. Parts I and II revealed the dynamism of the process: once a currency becomes key, a self-reinforcing process is begun by which that currency increasingly meets the criteria needed to retain such status. Even if EC monetary unity has no intention of qualifying the currencies of its members for broader international use, it is bound to have that result.

Even with such "success," however, what would be the claim on the EC which other countries would hold? The mark would dominate economically but would hardly be acceptable politically to France. Sterling would dominate financially, but would probably also be unacceptable to France and now carries a legacy of economic suspicion anyway, the eradication of which would require generosity by the Continental countries to back sterling with their reserves to a virtually unimaginable degree. France will be important politically, but is unlikely to achieve economic leadership. Indeed, the only politically acceptable national currency which also meets at least some of the economic attributes is the Dutch guilder, particularly if it were to remain linked in an even tighter intra-EC monetary union with the Belgian franc. In addition, the Dutch price and balance-of-payments performance is more likely than either the German or British to be modal, and thus representative of the Community as a whole.

It is more likely, however, that this intra-EC political difficulty and economic uncertainty would be reconciled by creating a synthetic money in the same way the world has reconciled the same difficulties by creating the SDR.[53] To do so, EC countries could pool some or all of their reserves and issue a new asset which would represent a claim against the pool. Such an asset would doubtlessly be viewed as providing greater assurances against both devaluation and revaluation than any single EC currency, both because it would be based on the performance of a number of widely differing economies and because of the bureaucratic immobilism which hampers all

53. For proposals to this end, see Robert Triffin, "Report on the Creation of a European Reserve Fund," presented to the Action Committee for the United States of Europe, Dec. 1969, and Bela Balassa, "Monetary Integration in the European Common Market," in Alexander Swoboda, ed., *Europe and the Evolution of the International Monetary System* (London: Allen and Unwin, 1973).

Community-wide decisions. This asset could be held in the reserves of countries outside the EC, just like the SDR.

However, it could be used for intervention purposes only if it became widely used in the private capital markets of Europe. A decision .to permit such use could only be based on the momentous decision to begin a process leading to the eventual substitution of such an asset for all present national EC currencies; otherwise the new asset would simply represent a potentially destabilizing competitor to those currencies. National exchange rates could fluctuate around the new unit during the transition period, but the leverage of such changes over the respective national economies would decline as the EC unit assumed an increasing share of transactions within them. Eventual monetary unity for the EC would require a European-wide capital market, based on a truly European currency, because the elimination of national money markets would require such a market if only to provide financing for budget deficits of member governments (or the Community as a whole, at perhaps an even later stage).

Even if such a potential substitute for the dollar were to develop quickly enough to make this a viable option for monetary reform in the near future, there would be numerous systemic objections to it. Chapter 4–6 revealed a number of inherent contradictions in any international system based on national currencies that could be expected to develop with the passage of time, however solid in economic terms was the starting position of, say, the expanded EC. It is doubtful that even a "united" Europe would be able to provide the leadership which is a major systemic advantage of relying on a key currency, in view of the inevitable continuation of national differences within Europe and the resulting difficulty of reaching decisions there. The best that could be said for the approach is that, like a sizable increase in the official price of gold, it could provide a new liquidity mechanism which might meet world needs without running into major problems for some intermediate period of time.

But even the short-run advantages of key currency status which the new reserve center(s) would obtain would probably be objectionable partly on the grounds that the United States would continue to bear the major responsibility for the defense of the non-Communist world while being at a disadvantage in such an economic arrangement. The reasons are that the exchange-rate immobility which would in all probability both promote the acceptability of a new European asset and derive from its new international role would run directly counter to the U.S. need for greater flexibility of exchange rates to improve its own adjustment potential, as developed in Chapter 9;[54] and that the United States would no longer have a dollar-financing option open to it. On the other hand, if the assumption of key currency status propelled Europe into payments deficits, as it did both Britain and the United States in the past, it might restore some of America's international economic power over the longer run —at the cost of renewed systemic and perhaps political instability. Finally, this approach provides no means for consolidating the dollar overhang. It is inconceivable that the EC would exchange its own currency for dollar balances, in essence taking over the exchange risk of holding dollars in return for only the possibility—which might never exist—of net interest-rate earnings on a portfolio of dollar assets and liabilities in their own currencies. (If the United States were willing to give guarantees on the dollar balances, it could of course do so directly to the dollar holders rather than to some intermediary "funder" such as the EC.)

This option, in its extreme form, therefore is both unlikely and has little to commend it. An increase in the international use of additional national currencies does, however, merit close attention in two different ways: as regional assets in *all* of the key currency functions, and as global assets in the vehicle currency functions. We consider these intermediate options in Chapter 13.

Eliminating the Intervention Currency Role

Two of the options for eliminating the reserve currency roles of the dollar—a "restoration" of the gold standard in the adjustment or liquidity sense, and total reliance on SDR for liquidity purposes—would retain the intervention currency role of the dollar.[55] A regime of freely flexible exchange rates, on the other hand, would eliminate this role too because it would eliminate any market intervention by

---

54. It is quite possible that a united Europe would be much *more* prepared to adopt systemic reforms to promote greater flexibility of exchange rates between it as a unit and the rest of the world than have been the individual European countries, if only because the EC as a unit would be so closed to outside transactions that the economic costs to it of external flexibility would be small. However, such willingness would be much more likely to evolve if some solution were found for the liquidity problem other than reliance on its own new currency—for the several reasons, outlined in Chapters 5 and 8, which prompt reserve centers to oppose exchange-rate changes.
55. Theoretically, a pure gold standard could include market intervention in gold by national monetary authorities. In practice, however, this would once again subject the system to instability due to private gold speculation (in either direction, depending on the relationship between the official price and market considerations).

national authorities. There are three other options for eliminating the intervention currency role of the dollar, all within the context of a system of basically fixed exchange rates, to which we now turn: adopting a clearing mechanism in lieu of market intervention by monetary authorities, substituting other national currencies for the dollar in this role alone, and permitting private holdings of SDRs and then using them for intervention as well as reserve purposes.

An International Clearing Union would operate on the model of the Federal Reserve System within the United States, the European Payments Union of the 1950s, and the intervention practices instituted by the EC countries in 1972 to narrow the margins among their currencies. The Union would declare fixed buying and selling rates for all pairs of currencies. Central banks in all countries would meet the needs of their commercial banks for particular currencies by drawing them from the Union, and would deposit in it balances of currencies sold to them by their commercial banks as being excess to their needs. The Union would then clear all currencies periodically, with countries required to buy up any excess of their currency that accumulated in the Union with their reserve assets. Countries whose currencies were needed by the Union would sell them to it for these assets provided by others. Clearance could take place either daily or less frequently, if short-term credit were extended automatically through the Union.

The difference between buying and selling rates would have to be small, or else private markets would develop with rates fluctuating within that spread and profits made at the expense of national monetary authorities. This would require a return to fixed exchange rates, and even a *narrowing* of the band around parities from the width decided in December 1971; it would thus either force a closer coordination of national monetary policies, or induce even larger movements of interest-sensitive capital than we have seen in recent years. Since such policy harmonization is extremely difficult, such a step would in practice have to be coupled with a sharp expansion of the use of the swap network to regulate such flows, new controls over them, or an agreement simply to ignore their international effects. Even then, however, there could be adverse effects on some domestic economies, as we saw in Chapter 7, which would represent a significant cost of such a move. Thus the adoption of the Clearing Union approach would carry significant costs for the system.[56]

56. For a more complete discussion see Richard N. Cooper, "Eurodollars and Reserve Dollars: Asymmetries in the Monetary System," *Journal of International Economics*, Vol. II, No. 4 (September 1972), pp. 325–44.

The replacement of the dollar as an intervention currency by another national currency, or by several, would also raise problems. The use of additional currencies would intensify the risk of destabilizing shifts among different assets, although the magnitude of this risk might not be great if countries limited their holdings strictly to working balances which they could not easily reduce. Since no other currencies equal the market attributes of the dollar, because of the far greater size of the United States than any other present currency area and its superior capital markets, transactions costs would be raised. An offsetting advantage would be the greater involvement in the international economy that would be forced upon the countries whose currencies began to play important international roles, and the wider diffusion of responsibility for the maintenance of the system that would result.

SDRs could replace the dollar as an intervention vehicle only if wide private markets developed for them.[57] This would in time require widespread private use of the asset running into many billions of dollars, since official working balances alone total at least $5 billion and private markets would have to be many times larger to absorb transactions of significant size without undue price fluctuations. But such a volume of SDRs, issued by the IMF, would undermine the monetary sovereignty of national authorities. Hence it is highly unlikely to occur much before the day when a true world central bank becomes responsible for the entire world money supply. In addition, permitting private holdings of SDR would replicate part of the problem with gold which existed before the creation of the two-tiered system in 1968 and the problem with the dollar which has continued to exist. Private buying or selling of the asset could jeopardize its price stability, thereby jeopardizing its value as a medium of exchange between national monetary authorities.[58] So this approach is both unwise and unlikely.

All of these approaches aimed specifically at the elimination of the

57. Robert Mundell, "A Plan for a World Currency," in *Next Steps in International Monetary Reform*, Reuss Subcommittee, September 9, 1968, pp. 25–28, explicitly proposed that a new international unit (which would subsume SDRs) play an intervention currency role. However, he failed to address the ways in which this could be done and the problems it would raise.

58. The other part of the problem with gold was its dual use as a commodity and as money. Even without commodity use, however, the value attached by the private market to any international money can differ sharply from the value attached to it as a reserve asset by the monetary authorities who determine its rate of creation—hence jeopardizing its price stability, on the analogy of either the "dollar shortage" or the subsequent "dollar glut."

intervention currency role of the dollar—achieving full "symmetry" between it and other major currencies—would be costly in both narrowly financial and broad systemic terms. They would thus be pursued only if other countries deem elimination of the dollar's role as extremely important for political reasons, or if the United States decided that it had to take measures to eliminate the dollar's intervention currency role because it seriously handicaps the ability to change the U.S. exchange rate (as we concluded in Chapter 9) and because no better answer to that problem was available.

Eliminating the Transaction Currency Role
Virtually the same options are available for eliminating the transactions currency role as for eliminating the intervention currency role, and the same general conclusions hold.

In this case, however, the only option for eliminating the international need for *any* national currencies is complete inconvertibility of all currencies into each other. *All* private international transactions would then require use of an International Clearing Union, as outlined in the last section, to provide needed foreign currencies and convert into local currency all foreign currencies earned in international operations. The Union could provide swing credits to individual *countries*, but there would be few private transaction balances and international exchange would be severely hobbled, and much more costly, as a result. Such a system now exists within Eastern Europe, where currencies are inconvertible and the International Bank for Economic Cooperation has since 1964 provided multilateral clearing of the bilateral balances of members of the Council for Mutual Economic Assistance. Such a system is of course much more compatible with the planned economies of the countries involved than it would be with market economies.[59]

The dollar could also be replaced as a transaction currency by other national currencies. Sterling is generally thought still to finance a considerable share of world trade, and several European currencies and the Japanese yen have probably been financing an increasing

59. The creation of this multilateral clearing mechanism in Eastern Europe in fact represented major progress from the previous system of rigid bilateral balancing among these countries. Indeed, it is technically similar to the clearing arrangements under the European Payments Union in Western Europe in the 1950s. However, its basic objectives and parallel moves on trade policy are vastly different, since the EPU was a "halfway house" on the road to full convertibility of currencies and multilateral trade while the IBEC has evidenced no such objectives. See Henry Francuz, "The International Bank for Economic Cooperation," *IMF Staff Papers*, Vol. XVI, No. 3 (November 1960), pp. 489–501.

share, at least for the last few years. But, as in the intervention currency case, sizable costs and inconveniences to traders and investors around the world and in the United States would result from any effort at *total* substitution of those currencies for the dollar. Indeed, it would probably be technically impossible to eliminate the dollar without completely shutting down the Eurodollar market. Such a drastic step could be contemplated only if the United States concluded that the policy costs of this role—the threat of collapse of the private overhang, the net interest costs of the private balances, and the systemic instability they can (but need not) generate— became great enough to offset its systemic benefits.

Finally, a truly international money could theoretically be used to finance private international transactions. This would require an even broader use of such an asset than would be needed to permit it to play an intervention role, as outlined in the last section, which would further erode national monetary sovereignty and revive all the monetary problems which arrive when a single asset is used widely for both private and public international finance. It can be envisaged only in the far distant future when a truly world government manages a truly world monetary and economic policy, if ever.

Summary and Conclusions

There are four possible types of international monetary reform which would completely eliminate the dollar as a reserve currency: freely flexible exchange rates, "a return to the gold standard" for adjustment and/or liquidity purposes, and replacement of the dollar either by a new international asset or by a different national currency (or currencies). The dollar's use as an intervention currency would also be eliminated under a regime of freely flexible exchange rates or by the adoption of a different national currency (or currencies) in its place, and could be eliminated in addition by substituting an International Clearing Union for the present intervention system under fixed rates, but would probably be preserved under a move limited to relying henceforth on an international reserve asset for liquidity purposes and under the adjustment or liquidity version of the gold standard (or both). The dollar's use as a transactions currency among private traders and investors would probably continue under any system, though it could also theoretically be eliminated by moving to complete reliance on a Clearing Union for *all* international financial transactions or by substituting other national currencies (or even an international asset) for private use.

Any of the four systems would confront the United States with policy choices fundamentally different from those it has faced in the past. Under the system which existed prior to August 1971, the

United States could in principle (1) finance its deficits (a) partly through using its gross reserves but (b) mainly through increasing its dollar liabilities; (2) adjust its internal economy, in ways which might or might not be contrary to its domestic needs, to adjust its balance of payments indirectly; (3) adopt measures aimed at specific external transactions; or (4) attempt to change its exchange rate. In practice, it tried to maximize (1b), used (3) to support (1b), resorted reluctantly to (1a) if (1b) and (3) did not do the trick, largely avoided (2), and avoided (4) totally.

Under a gold standard adjustment system, the United States would be expected to use (2) and undergo (1a) if necessary; (1b) would no longer be possible, and (3) and (4) would be outside the rules of the game. Under a system based wholly on an international asset, or a gold standard liquidity system, the United States would no longer have resort to (1b) and could only chose among (1a), to the extent possible in light of its reserve level, (2) and (3); (4) would still be difficult unless the intervention currency role were eliminated as well. Under a gold exchange standard based on some other national currency, or currencies, the United States would no longer have resort to (1a) but could choose among all of the other options. Under freely flexible exchange rates, (4) would result automatically, with some indirect effects on the U.S. domestic economy, and there would be no need for either (1) or (3).

Under any of these alternatives, U.S. policy-makers would thus have at hand a significantly changed set of policy instruments and targets. In any of the four cases they would lose one instrument which has heretofore been available: use of the dollar's reserve currency role to enable them to avoid being forced to take any adjustment action or losing owned reserves. They could also forego one target—maintenance of "confidence in the dollar" sufficient to prevent a collapse of the overhang—but we learned in Chapter 8 that the risk of collapse is not sufficiently serious so that this gain would go very far in offsetting the loss of dollar financing. These would in fact be the *only* target/instrument effects of the international asset and gold standard liquidity options, which therefore would be costly to the United States on balance from this standpoint.

In the pure gold standard adjustment case the United States would also give up the instrument of selective external measures, or even the possibility of exchange-rate changes,[60] without gaining any new

60. An alternative formulation would be that it would adopt at least one new policy target: no restrictions on international transactions. It could be viewed as also adopting the policy target of "no exchange-rate changes," but this would not be much different from the U.S. approach (and potential) under the gold exchange standard.

instruments in return. The result would clearly be added conflict among U.S. policy objectives. To avoid this problem, one could envisage a gold standard system without the target of complete freedom for international transactions, although the basic objective of such a scheme is to assure adjustment through internal policy measures.

With flexible rates, the policy-makers would gain a new instrument: variability in the exchange rate. Alternatively, they might be viewed as giving up the target of a fixed exchange rate, although they might adopt instead a new target relating to the direction and degree of change in the exchange rate which they wished to see. They would also give up the instrument of selective controls over external transactions, which might otherwise be used to mute adjustment via the exchange rate and thus does represent some policy cost. On balance, however, the targets/instruments equation would be markedly improved by this option.

In the case of substituting other national currencies for the dollar, with no other changes in the system, the United States would lose its financing instrument but gain in its place the instrument of initiating exchange-rate changes. It would also gain in its ability to use the controls instrument, which is now somewhat inhibited by key currency requirements. This trade-off would depend upon how much the United States decided it preferred adjustment via the exchange rate to financing via the dollar, given the realistic possibilities for both.

Among the four alternatives considered individually, the pure gold standard would most adversely affect the balance between policy instruments available to U.S. authorities and their policy targets. The shift to an international asset by itself would also represent a net loss in this regard, although a smaller one. The substitution of other national currencies for the dollar, because it would eliminate the intervention as well as the reserve currency role, would provide a favorable trade-off. And adoption of freely flexible exchange rates would probably most improve the balance between instruments and targets in practical terms.

This discussion also illustrates the systemic effects of each of the four alternatives. The gold standard in its pure form requires full and virtually immediate internal adjustment to changes in each country's external position; it would leave the liquidity issue unresolved, which is consistent with its theoretical operation but would be highly dangerous in practice. Freely flexible exchange rates themselves provide adjustment, wholly through the external accounts, and would obviate the liquidity problem. Adoption of an international reserve asset would solve the confidence and liquidity problems, but by itself makes no direct contribution to a solution of the adjustment problem. Adoption of new key currencies would have no favorable systemic effects and could even create added confidence problems. Combinations such as flexible exchange rates for adjustment combined with an international asset for liquidity purposes are thus possible, and indeed necessary to achieve optimum monetary reform.

12

"Crowning" the Dollar

Having examined the several options for eliminating entirely the international roles of the dollar, we turn now to the opposite extreme to consider the options for basing the international monetary system entirely on the dollar. This would require reliance on the dollar for additions to world reserves, and either complete unavailability of other reserve assets or, at least, inconvertibility of dollars into them. It would also require that no other national currency be so convertible, since any such currency might then rival the attractiveness of the dollar as a reserve asset.

There are three broad ways in which a pure dollar standard could be installed. The first is through *force majeure*: unilateral U.S. maintenance of inconvertibility of the dollar into U.S. reserve assets, with a dollar standard resulting from the absence of any viable alternatives to either its reserve or vehicle currency roles. This would represent a resumption of national dominance of the monetary system. The second is through negotiated agreement for the United States to extend, and other countries to accept, guarantees on all foreign dollar holdings on the model of the dollar-value guarantees extended by the United Kingdom to sterling area monetary authorities in 1968 in return for their pledges to maintain a certain percentage of their reserves in sterling. This would represent international organization of the system. The third is through U.S. action that maintained beyond any doubt the attributes required of a key currency country, as outline in Chapters 4–6, with full and free foreign acceptance of the dollar as a result. This would represent an unorganized system, relying on the interplay of market forces.

All of these approaches focus on the liquidity and confidence aspects of international monetary reform. None deals explicitly with the adjustment process. In fact, however, their effects on the process would differ sharply. The first two would permit the United States to follow a policy of pure "benign neglect," even more so than it did during the twilight phase of the gold exchange standard, while the third would require *more* effective U.S. adjustment while providing it with fewer instruments with which to do so. These options do not rule out concomitant improvements in the adjustment process, but the first two imply that the United States would avoid any active adjustment initiatives, and all three rule out its adopting an active exchange-rate policy.

A Dollar Standard by Force Majeure

The United States placed the world on a virtually pure dollar standard by suspending the convertibility of the dollar into U.S. reserve assets in August 1971. On the liquidity side, gold had obtained such a scarcity premium—with the free market price well above the official price, and little new gold finding its way into national reserves—that it was essentially buried at the bottom of the reserve stocks of virtually all countries, to be used only when all else failed.[1] Sterling area countries could and would continue to use sterling, but its dollar-value guarantee made it functionally equivalent to the dollar. All major countries sought to return to fixed exchange rates as soon as a new "equilibrium" level could be negotiated. Once that was done, via the Smithsonian Agreement in December 1971, virtually all countries began settling virtually all of their payments imbalances in dollars (or dollar equivalents).

Countries then had no choice but to accept dollars to finance any payments surpluses they were running. The United States would not convert dollars into any of its reserve assets, and dollars were not convertible into other assets at the IMF. The only alternative was for countries to take adjustment measures to reduce or eliminate the inflow of dollars. Some, such as France and Belgium-Netherlands, did so at first by maintaining two-tiered exchange markets and letting the "financial rate" for their currencies appreciate above the ceiling of the new band. Some, such as Germany and Japan, did so by instituting new market disincentives to capital inflows or physical controls over them. The reductions of some European interest rates might have been motivated at least partly by a desire to ward off

---

1. Data on national gold holdings on August 13, 1971, are not available. From the end of the third quarter through early 1973, however, the only significant gold sales recorded in *International Financial Statistics* (June 1973) were small shifts from Belgium to the Netherlands as part of the settlements system included by these gold bloc countries in the payments union which they instituted in the fall, sales by countries running payments deficits which had no other assets to use (South Africa and Argentina), and small shifts under the EC settlement scheme initiated in mid-1972. Even within the EC scheme, however, Italy was quickly permitted to settle its debits completely in dollars to keep it within the system.

more dollar inflows. All major countries then floated their exchange rates against the dollar in early 1973.

As a result the United States appeared to achieve the best of all monetary worlds: unlimited financing via the dollar for its deficits, adjustment initiated by others when they were unwilling to accept dollars any longer. But it immediately became clear that such a situation was far from an unmixed blessing for the United States. The further depreciation of the dollar—labelled "the third devaluation" by French President Pompidou—went far beyond what even the most ardent advocates of U.S. action had in mind. Indeed, it added significantly to the inflation which was already "public enemy number one," and led to calls for action to *strengthen* the exchange rate of the dollar. In addition, the general instability which resulted probably added to world inflation, and weakened the resistance of the world economy to its next shock—the energy crisis.

Even in a more structural sense, the viability of this system relies wholly on the absence of alternatives to the dollar, both as a reserve asset and as a vehicle currency, and on alternative adjustment mechanisms. To carry the *force majeure* strategy to its logical extreme, the United States would seek to block any additional creation of SDRs or any sizable increase in the official price of gold[2]—both of which it can do through its veto power in the IMF. It would also have to block any breakdown of the two-tiered gold system to be sure of maintaining the pure dollar standard, since new gold could otherwise start coming into national reserves again.[3] It would have to block the international use of other national currencies, which it clearly cannot do. And it would have to stop others from floating their exchange rates, which it obviously cannot.

Thus the United States could keep the world on a dollar standard by *force majeure* only if two conditions are met: if market forces did not "elect" new rivals to the dollar, and if other countries were unwilling to act to get off the standard. Overwhelming evidence has already developed that neither would be met.

We have seen in Chapters 4–6 how the United States no longer

---

2. The small increases of 1971–72 and early 1973 left the official price well below the market price, and did little to enhance the possibility of renewed reliance on gold as a reserve asset.

3. On the other hand, South Africa and other sellers—while they continue to want a guaranteed price floor, as they now have at the IMF—would obviously be reluctant to sell very much gold at the lower official price. So gold could probably work its way back into the system in a major way only with *both* a breakdown of the two-tiered system and a sufficient increase in the official price to bring it closer to the market level.

meets the key currency criteria as well as it did in the past, and in Chapter 11 how several other currencies now rival the dollar on most of those criteria. We have also seen how several of those currencies are already being used to a significant degree, and at a rapidly expanding pace, in international finance. In fact, the process has developed so far that it would no longer be accurate to characterize even the financial side of the monetary system at the time of this writing as anything approaching a "pure dollar standard"; it is much more akin to a "multiple reserve currency" system and moving ever more rapidly in that direction. So it is quite clear that the market can be expected to "elect" new key currencies, as it is indeed already doing. The process could be stopped only a concentrated effort by the countries whose currencies were involved. Such an effort is highly unlikely if the alternative to use of their currencies is a *force majeure* dollar standard; in fact, they would then be almost certain to support this, or some other, alternative means of reforming the monetary system.

In addition, steps were taken in 1973 and 1974 to resuscitate the monetary roles of both gold and SDRs. In November 1973, the two-tiered gold system was formally abandoned, opening the door to revaluing it closer to the market price for settlement purposes and hence reviving its monetary use. This trend developed further in 1974, when it was agreed that gold reserves could be valued at market-related prices, first as collateral against foreign loans and then (in December, at the meeting of Presidents Ford and Giscard d'Estaing in Martinque) in the reserve statistics published by each country. Similarly, the method of revaluation of SDRs was altered, temporarily by an IMF decision in November 1973 to break its link with the dollar via gold, and in mid-1974 to tie it to a basket of major currencies instead. Hence there was movement on all fronts— new key currencies, gold, SDR—to provide monetary alternatives to the dollar, and the life span of the *force majeure* dollar standard turned out to be quite brief.

Even more important than these financial developments is the clear willingness, and ability, of most major countries to break out of the dollar mold by floating their exchange rates. Chapter 2 discussed how the costs of initiating balance-of-payments adjustment are additional to the actual economic costs of adjustment. Surplus countries would have to suffer additional inflation and distortions in their policy mixes, because of the need to ease monetary policy, if they maintained fixed parities in the face of nonadjustment by the United States of its payments deficit. They would suffer competitive losses vis-à-vis *all* (or most) other countries if they were forced to revalue because the United States would not devalue. The difference in who takes an exchange-rate action also affects the valuation of reserves, and the persistence of a pure dollar standard would give the United States total control over the form of world reserves and the major voice in determining the amount thereof. All of these economic effects raise the political costs to the initiating country. Most countries faced a similar economic situation throughout most of the postwar period, but the nominal convertibility of the dollar and the periodic U.S. balance-of-payments "programs" gave at least the appearance of a U.S. adjustment effort. But even under that system, with its significant differences from a *force majeure* world, the international monetary system reached a crisis stage when some countries (e.g., Germany and Japan) felt strong enough to resist U.S. pressure —and a growing number clearly feel strong enough to resist it in the future.

Even when viewed in broad systemic terms, there is a strong case for sharing the adjustment initiative. World inflation will accelerate if U.S. price performance exceeds the world average and other countries do all the adjusting to a U.S. deficit by letting their own prices rise more rapidly. A U.S. monetary policy unrestrained by the balance of payments, and relied upon to carry the load of domestic stabilization policy because of inadequate fiscal tools, can cause huge flows of international capital (as in 1969–71) which are disruptive to the world economy. The allocation of world resources will suffer if a failure to share the adjustment initiative produces deadlock; hence increasing controls over international transactions, as we saw in Chapter 10, would quite likely be the case. Sharing of these initiatives is also a political necessity in a world of relatively equal economic powers into which we have already moved. It is both good economics and good politics—and perhaps necessary to get adjustment—for the dollar exchange rate to change when the United States is out of line toward most other major currencies, as in 1971 and again in early 1973.[4]

An active U.S. adjustment policy does raise risks of overdetermining the system, since all countries would then presumably be pursuing national balance-of-payments targets and it would be a great coincidence if these targets were consistent with each other. (In the past, as I have noted repeatedly, the absence of an active U.S. payments policy or even a serious payments target obviated much of

4. A number of these points are made by John Williamson, "The Choice of a Pivot for Parities," *Princeton Essays in International Finance*, No. 90 (November 1971), pp. 8–15. He concludes by asking: "Is neglect benign? To Americans, yes. To America's partners, no. Their loss exceeds her gain."

this problem.) These can only be met by developing a set of international rules to guide the adjustment process. The "redundancy problem," which calls for only $n-1$ currencies to change their exchange rates actively in a world of n currencies, can be resolved by permitting the dollar parity to move actively against a gold/SDR pivot—which would become the international $n+1$ currency permitting all national currencies to move actively. (These possibilities are discussed in detail in the concluding chapters.)

The proponents of a U.S. balance-of-payments policy of "benign neglect" favor it in large part because they sincerely believe that it would produce the best international monetary system, or at least provide an optimum U.S. role under the system that existed when they made their proposal—which was well before August 1971.[5] They are right if such a policy is compared with rigid international adjustment as under the gold standard or in a world of zealous national competition for reserves and exports with competitive depreciations and proliferating controls. Other alternatives exist, however, as outlined throughout this book, although it is worth remembering that some form of dollar standard may well be better, from a global standpoint, if none of the alternatives is agreed to be better and negotiated.

Once other countries were ready to act to stop a *force majeure* dollar standard, they had several choices. They could simply declare a higher gold price for transactions among themselves, presumably somewhere near the free market price, and resume purchases from gold producers. (They could also resume intervention in the private gold market to maintain equilibrium between the official and free market prices, though this would expose them to future gold losses as in 1967–68 and would not be necessary.) Declaration of such a gold price without IMF approval would represent a violation of the

5. See especially Lawrence B. Krause, "A Passive Balance of Payments Strategy for the United States," *Brookings Papers on Economic Activity: 3, 1970,* pp. 339–60, and Gottfried Haberler and Thomas D. Willett, "A Strategy for U.S. Balance of Payments Policy," American Enterprise Institute, Feb. 1971. Both analyses are based on the critical assumption that the United States could not change its exchange rate even if it wanted to, from which logically follows support for "benign neglect" for the reasons developed in Chapter 9. In fact, Krause regarded his approach as growing out of the "relative weakness" of the United States, and his proposals did not add up to a very passive approach anyway. He would have had the United States seek a modal rate of inflation, sell off its reserve assets when necessary, actively promote greater flexibility of exchange rates and sufficient SDR creation, and help other countries in crisis situations (including the institution of U.S. controls), and let other countries influence U.S. policy.

Fund's rules, however, and the countries involved might wish to avoid this. In that case, they would have two alternatives. They could create a synthetic reserve asset like the SDR for circulation among themselves or they could designate one or more national currencies other than the dollar to become their key currency.

It is quite likely that one of these alternatives, helped along significantly by market forces, would emerge if the United States were perceived to be seeking indefinite extension of a pure dollar standard. The United States' removal in early 1974 of all controls over dollar transactions could indeed be read as an effort to restore a dollar standard by signaling its ability to neglect its balance of payments totally and at the same time eliminate one of the inhibitions to the dollar's use.[6]

In such a case, *other countries* might well levy an increasing number of controls over dollar transactions and hence reduce its conformance with the criteria for a vehicle as well as a reserve currency. Indeed, the controls against capital inflows imposed by most major countries in recent years amount to controls over the dollar. Some countries would probably also let their exchange rates appreciate against the dollar periodically, as in fact several have been doing, thus reducing its fulfillment of the key currency criterion of "fixed-price" convertibility into other national currencies and indeed undermining its attractiveness by forcing its depreciation. Other national currencies would thus have an opportunity to become more attractive than the dollar, and we saw in Chapter 11 that a number had the potential to do so—at least for vehicle currency use on a global basis and for all uses on a regional scale. Since monetary authorities would certainly build working balances in any currencies which became widely used in the private markets, any such currencies would erode both the transactions and intervention roles of the dollar. Paradoxically, therefore, market forces alone would probably lead to a relative reduction in the vehicle currency role of the dollar under this scenario even if the U.S. action retained for it a primary reserve currency role. This is precisely what happened just before and after August 1971, when private foreign dollar holdings declined to very low levels while official holdings rose to record peaks and continued to climb.

It is more difficult to judge whether the reserve currency role would also be reduced, because conscious decisions by national monetary authorities and the requisite political will would be required. Under

6. Some of the U.S. proposals for monetary reform to the Committee of Twenty, between September 1972 and June 1974, also seemed designed to reinforce the roles of the dollar.

the scenario just outlined, they would certainly build working balances in other national currencies and some would also hold reserve balances in them. On the other hand, the creation of a truly synthetic money to be used by the private sector as well as by monetary authorities would represent a total commitment to a single world (or regional) currency and is highly unlikely.

The authorities of a region (or all of the world apart from the United States, for that matter) could, however, find a middle course by creating a "regional SDR" which would be used only for settlements among monetary authorities willing to hold it—as indeed the European Community seeks to do on its road to monetary union. It would be used solely at the margin, since by hypothesis the United States would be unwilling to participate in any consolidation of the dollar overhang and other countries would be unlikely to undertake such an operation by themselves. Thus the dollar overhang would remain intact in foreign hands, drawing interest (in dollars), and usable in settlements only with the United States and any countries which formalized their membership in the dollar area.[7] A combination of this approach for reserve assets and the growing use of national currencies other than the dollar for vehicle purposes could reduce sharply the dollar's international roles at the end of a scenario designed by the United States to crown it!

One crucial variable in the likelihood of this scenario would be the U.S. balance-of-payments position. If the United States were in surplus, or even in small deficit, there would be far less economic and political opposition to a dollar standard. Nevertheless, continued U.S. inconvertibility even under such circumstances would breed widespread resentment among others who *were* still playing by "the rules of the game," both legal and informal. Some individual countries would doubtlessly run large surpluses periodically, and acquire large additional dollar balances, even if the U.S. position were in overall surplus.

In addition, it is highly probable that the United States would slip into sizable deficit, at least periodically, as virtually all countries do. Some countries might then deeply resent the ability of the U.S. to avoid adjustment, particularly if they viewed the policies which

7. The issue of how non-dollar countries could use inconvertible dollars was raised early in the dollar-inconvertibility period during the EC negotiations on how to settle the imbalances which were expected to develop when they began to maintain their exchange rates within a band narrower than their band with the dollar. Even in the absence of an alternative European asset, they limited the role of the dollar in such settlements to its share in the reserve assets held by the deficit country at the time the scheme was instituted.

produced the U.S. deficits as harmful to their own interests. In addition, however, the United States might then wish to adjust for internal reasons, as in 1971, or to avoid adverse foreign reaction to the dollar standard, as in the 1960s. But under the "successful" dollar standard phase of this option, the United States could only adjust to such deficits by devaluing with full foreign cooperation—since other currencies would be pegged to the dollar, and foreign countries would have full control over their decisions to add dollars or take steps to reduce the influx of them. The negotiated approach of late 1971 and early 1973 would have to be repeated under conditions in which other countries would be far less sympathetic to U.S. objectives. Needless to say, the probability of obtaining cooperation would be low in a system based on unilateral U.S. inconvertibility. Thus the United States could only adjust quickly by adopting comprehensive controls, which themselves would accelerate the demise of the dollar standard, or by the extremely costly deflation or policy mix approaches. So it would be back in the box of the gold exchange standard, with even less likelihood of foreign cooperation and successful achievement of adjustment.

This long discourse on the probable unfolding of events under a U.S. effort to achieve a dollar standard by *force majeure* has been necessary to lay the foundation for an analysis of its benefits and costs for the United States. If it "worked," it would represent a purified version of the partial dollar standards which existed throughout the postwar period. It would provide unlimited financing for U.S. deficits or force other countries to take all the adjustment initiatives, and hence fully remove any external constraint on U.S. domestic economic policy. It might thus appear to give the United States the best of all possible monetary worlds.

In fact, however, it would not. The United States might not like the specific adjustment measures that other countries would take—including controls over U.S. capital flows and controls over the dollar—or even the direction of that adjustment, e.g., if other countries sought to export their inflation to the United States by letting their exchange rates appreciate. Such a system would not *help* the United States to initiate adjustment when it wanted adjustment, and it would probably further impede that possibility. It would provide no definitive resolution of the major problems of the international monetary system, and would weaken rather than strengthen the adjustment process by permitting disequilibria to build up as U.S. deficits were financed rather than eliminated.

It would also engender foreign hostility and undermine U.S. foreign policy objectives. One cannot judge in the abstract whether this cost to foreign policy would outweigh the gain from eliminating the balance-of-payments constraint on foreign policy expenditures, such as military costs abroad and foreign aid. There would probably be a net gain vis-à-vis countries in which the United States has large foreign policy expenditures and which have limited concerns about "dollar hegemony," such as Japan and perhaps Germany, and a net loss vis-à-vis countries in which it has few such expenditures but which care a great deal about the politics of international money, such as France and perhaps Britain.

If the system did degenerate, the United States would reap even greater foreign policy problems, which could have a major impact on its national security, for the reasons outlined in Chapter 10. It would continue to pay interest on the overhang, which could hardly be consolidated under this totally noncooperative approach. It would suffer from the weakening of the entire system, perhaps replete with national currencies competing for financial superiority, competitive exchange-rate actions by major countries, a broken cross-rate for gold, and widespread proliferation of controls. It could, however, still get either dollar financing or adjustment by other countries, depending on *their* choices. And it could try to adjust via the exchange rate by assuming the unaccustomed position of actively intervening in the exchange markets; other countries might not let it succeed, however, and the result could be a competitive depreciation race, as in the early 1930s, or a competitive appreciation race in a world of widespread inflation. In short, this would be an exceedingly high-risk strategy for the United States to follow, with very high potential costs.

A Guaranteed Dollar Standard

Many of the problems of the *force majeure* approach could be avoided, and many of the gains to the United States of a dollar standard preserved, if the United States were to guarantee the value of foreign-held dollars against any U.S. devaluation.[8]

There is a recent precedent for such action. In 1968, the United Kingdom agreed to guarantee the dollar-value of all reserve sterling held by sterling area countries beyond 10 per cent of their total reserves (presumably a proxy for their working balances). In return,

8. Such an approach has been advocated by William Fellner, "The Dollar's Place in the International System; Suggested Criteria for the Appraisal of Emerging Views," *Journal of Economic Literature*, Vol. X, No. 3 (September 1972), esp. pp. 751–55; and Gottfried Haberler, "Prospects for the Dollar Standard," in C. Fred Bergsten and William Tyler, eds., *Leading Issues in International Economic Policy* (Lexington, Mass.: D. C. Heath, 1973).

those countries pledged to maintain a "Minimum Sterling Proportion" in their reserves, the percentage of which was negotiated with each country and has never been revealed.[9] The Basle Agreement was supposed to help phase out at least the reserve currency role of sterling, but the guarantees preserved and even expanded the role instead.

We concluded in Chapter 5 that fixed-price convertibility is the major requirement for a key currency, over a longer time horizon for official than for private holders. There would be no convertibility in a pure dollar standard, because there would be nothing to convert into; but convertibility would not be needed, because a fixed price for the dollar in terms of other currencies would be assured by a U.S. extension of guarantees—the cost of any devaluation to foreign dollar holders would be fully offset by payments of the guarantees.

However, some foreign countries do not reject unlimited additions to their dollar reserves simply because they fear that the asset may depreciate in the future. This *is* the sole concern of many countries, particularly those in the dollar area which for competitive reasons would usually expect to devalue with the dollar, and is a major concern of all. But some also reject dollars because they dislike either the economic or foreign policy consequences of U.S. payments deficits, and wish to be able to convert dollars into U.S. reserves to express this displeasure and try to force a change in U.S. policies. It is thus apparent that dollar guarantees would not, by themselves, suffice to make all countries willing to hold all dollars they might accumulate in the market.

The United States could assure total foreign acceptance of the dollar only by providing both a guarantee and full convertibility into U.S. assets—in which case, however, the resulting system would not be a pure dollar standard because the United States as well as other countries would be able to hold large amounts of other reserve assets and add to them at the margin. Indeed, even the Basel arrangements of 1968, which the British negotiated with their backs to the wall, did not provide sterling area countries with both a guarantee and full convertibility; it offered them a choice between *either* retaining convertibility privileges for their sterling *or* receiving a dollar-value

9. *The Basle Facility and the Sterling Area*, Command 3787, Oct. 1968. Twenty of the agreements were for five years. The rest were for three years, and 33 were renewed in 1971—with a 10 per cent reduction in the MSP required to retain the dollar-value guarantee. Several countries left the sterling area and gave up the guarantees during 1972–74, and the whole arrangement lapsed at the end of 1974.

guarantee on it. Conversely, by giving guarantees the United States could obviate foreign opposition to its devaluations on asset-valuation grounds, but this would not give it a free hand on adjustment because other countries might still resist such moves because of the impact on their competitive positions.

These problems underlie the case against guarantees made in 1962 by Robert Roosa, then Under Secretary of the Treasury for Monetary Affairs.[10] He cited three reasons why the United States should not offer any such guarantees: they were said to rest upon a contradiction, because the United States would expect the guarantees to free its policies from balance-of-payments constraints whereas the recipient of the guarantee would expect it to accept precisely such constraints; they would require constant negotiation with a host of countries; and they would force the United States into a "strait-jacket of additional obligations" to maintain the credibility of the guarantees. Indeed, Roosa expected that other countries would attach conditions concerning U.S. policy to their acceptance of the guarantees, and concluded that the United States would be better off to give up the key currency role than to undergo such an operation. Other critics have raised additional arguments: private dollars could be turned into central banks to take advantage of the guarantee;[11] even U.S. dollars might "fly" abroad to seek the guarantee; and other internationally held currencies would come under attack because they would be converted into dollars to get the guarantee.

Whether countries would expect any more "balance-of-payments

---

10. Robert V. Roosa, "Assuring the Free World's Liquidity," *Business Review Supplement*, Federal Reserve Bank of Philadelphia, September 1962.

11. See, for example, Sterie T. Beza and Gardner Patterson, "Foreign Exchange Guarantees and the Dollar," *American Economic Review*, June 1961, pp. 382–85. However, few private dollars (including U.S.-owned dollars) are likely to be turned in to central banks to gain access to the guarantee. The yield on the assets received by the depositors in return would doubtlessly be lower than what they could receive elsewhere, including the yield on unguaranteed dollars, since central banks would not pay high rates of interest on dollars which earned a lower rate of interest for them from the United States because they carried a guarantee. This factor should also deter Americans from exporting dollars simply to acquire the guarantee, and foreigners from switching into dollars from other currencies to do so. If the possibility of private conversions were regarded as a problem despite all these factors, the monetary authorities could simply agree not to pass on their guarantee to private holders and so eliminate any possibility for them to take advantage of it. For a convincing refutation of some of the other technical points made by Beza and Patterson, see Peter Kenen, *op. cit.*, pp. 69–70.

discipline" on the part of the United States after a gold-value guarantee than before would depend on whether they approved of U.S.
policies. If they did, then they should be quite satisfied because they
would be assured of full compensation in terms of their international
purchasing power even if the United States devalued. These countries could in fact have the best of both worlds: interest-earning dollars (though perhaps at a lower rate in view of the guarantee), and
full compensation for holding dollars if devaluation ever did occur.[12]

The Basel guarantees for sterling were fully credible, judged by
the buildup of sterling reserves by sterling countries after they were
extended, despite the U.K. decision to float sterling in mid-1972 and
its temporary dip below the guaranteed price. The success of the
U.K. guarantees were largely due to the disinterest of sterling countries in trying to "discipline" Britain for the inflationary consequence
of its policy on the system, coupled with their far greater concern
for their own narrower economic interests—such as their exports to
Britain and their borrowing from it. In short, the concern about
sterling which motivated these countries to begin "diversifying" from
it in 1968 was based on asset-valuation rather than policy-disapproval
considerations. Indeed, some of their conversions and threats thereof
may have been based on objections to the adjustment measures
which Britain *did* or might take, such as restricting capital flows to
sterling area members, rather than to any *failure* to adjust.

On the other hand, countries which cared about U.S. policy, as
well as about possible losses in the value of their reserve assets, might
fulfill Roosa's prophecy of insisting on "better" U.S. performance as
a condition for accepting the guarantees and subject the United
States to recurrent negotiations to monitor that performance.[13] These
problems could be avoided if the United States were simply to make
a blanket offer of guarantees to all countries, asking them simply to
notify it of the amounts which they held and which were to be

12. George N. Halm has suggested that Roosa's failure to distinguish between
U.S. pledges to avoid devaluation and gold-value guarantees to make up the
costs to others of a devaluation may explain why his objections do not apply
to the latter. See Halm, "Gold-Value Guarantees," *Weltwirtschaftliches
Archiv*, Band 95, Heft 2 (1965), pp. 168–69. Halm focused his disagreement
with Roosa on the asset-valuation concern of dollar holders rather than
their desire to alter U.S. policies, although he later recognized that Roosa
did emphasize the latter.
13. By doing so, they would in effect be insisting that the United States pursue
the third dollar-standard option—that of assuring market acceptability of the
dollar—in addition to extending guarantees. The British were able to avoid
these costs because of the purely asset-valuation motivations of sterling area
countries just outlined.

guaranteed, and making clear that it would undertake no negotiations on related issues. This approach would alleviate any negotiating problems, but it would not satisfy countries concerned about U.S. policies and would thus by itself be unlikely to generate a pure dollar standard. It seems highly likely that the EC countries, particularly if they were able to act as a unit on the issue, would be unwilling to accept a dollar standard and the elimination of any external constraints on U.S. policy simply in return for guarantees on a portion of their reserve assets.

It must also be noted that, despite his arguments against guarantees, Under Secretary Roosa presided over a significant extension of them by the United States and even lent them his name. In 1962, the United States began to issue "Roosa bonds" denominated in foreign currencies to countries which wanted guarantees against a dollar devaluation and were willing to limit their convertibility privilege by accepting maturities varying from 18 to 27 months on the related debt instruments.[14] Four gold bloc countries (Austria, Belgium, Italy, and mainly Switzerland) and Germany purchased these securities during the 1960s. The largest amount outstanding at the end of any year was $1,750 million at the end of 1969—about 15 per cent of total U.S. liabilities to foreign monetary authorities at that time.

In addition, Roosa persuaded the Federal Reserve System to inaugurate the swap network, under which foreign holdings of dollars triggered by U.S. drawings were also guaranteed against a dollar devaluation. The maximum year-end net drawings of the United States under the network were about $1.5 billion at the close of 1967, which together with the $1 billion of Roosa bonds then outstanding meant that over 15 per cent of total U.S. liabilities to foreign monetary authorities were guaranteed against a dollar devaluation at that time as well. In addition, U.S. liabilities under any borrowing from the General Arrangement to Borrow—also negotiated by Roosa—would carry a full gold guarantee.[15] Clearly the United States has made initial excursions into extending exchange-rate guarantees, as circumstances required, much as the British did prior to their formalization

---

14. A few of the bonds were truly inconvertible for their full maturities, and so were treated in the U.S. balance-of-payments statistics as reducing the liquidity deficits. Most could be converted back into liquid dollar instruments within a few days, however, although they would of course lose their guarantee in so doing. In addition, the United States sold large amounts of *dollar*-denominated "Roosa bonds," which carried interest rates above market levels but no value guarantees.

15. Milton Gilbert, *The Gold-Dollar System*, p. 9.

in the Basel arrangements.[16] Indeed, the 1971–72 devaluation required the United States to make good its guarantees in amounts of about $145 million for the Roosa bonds and $200 million for the swaps, implying outstanding totals of about $1.8 billion and $2.5 billion at the time of devaluation, respectively.[17]

This discussion reveals that there are five important issues that must be decided in any system of guarantees:

1. Is the guarantee to be paid off in gold itself at an assured fixed price, as in the Tripartite Agreement of 1936, the General Arrangements to Borrow, and one special deposit at the IMF? In dollars, to maintain the gold value of the guaranteed dollars, as in all other debts to the IMF?[18] In dollars, but only to maintain the local currency value of the dollars guaranteed, as on Roosa bonds and swap drawing?

2. Is it to apply whether the creditor revalues or the debtor devalues? Or only when the debtor devalues, as with the Roosa bonds, swaps, and Basel arrangements?

3. Is the guarantee to cover only official balances? Or private holdings too, as was partially true under the Basel arrangements for sterling?

4. Are the guaranteed assets to carry market interest rates? Or some lower rate to take account of the financial value of the guarantee?

5. Are the guarantees to be extended formally, as in all the cases mentioned so far, or informally through market intervention to prevent a discount on the forward exchange rate as done by Britain in 1964–67?

The objective of a guarantee, based on the responsibility of foreign monetary authorities to avoid losses of their nations' wealth, is to protect them against losses in the international purchasing power of their dollar reserves. A second objective, in view of the "tyranny of the accountants" cited in Chapter 5, is to avoid a decline in the value of these dollar reserves in terms of the local currency of the countries involved. A third objective of some monetary authorities, in addition, is to avoid foregoing any increases in the value of their

---

16. Cohen, *op. cit.*, p. 228, describes these developments.
17. Statement of Treasury Secretary Connally before the House Banking and Currency Committee, March 1, 1972, pp. 7–9.
18. A SDR-value guarantee is now another alternative. It was the same as a gold-value guarantee in practice as long as the SDR maintained *its* gold-value guarantee.

reserves that they might achieve by holding the asset which is least depreciated (or most appreciated) after any parity change.

Each of these objectives by itself requires different types of guarantees. The first could be met simply by a guarantee against devaluation of the dollar in terms of the foreign country's currency. As long as the United States set the official price of gold by pegging the dollar to gold, or by pegging the dollar to a gold-value guaranteed SDR, this amounted to a one-way gold-value guarantee. The second would require a two-way guarantee in terms of the local currency to cover any revaluation of it as well. The United States has previously opposed guaranteeing a foreign country against any local currency losses accruing from its own revaluation on the grounds that any such action is "its own business" from which it should not expect to profit. Such a view is clearly anachronistic, however, since exchange-rate changes of major currencies are everybody's business. Even more important, one-way guarantees further the devaluation bias of the system by adding to the interest of surplus countries, as a group, in getting deficit countries to initiate any needed exchange-rate changes, whereas one of the key objectives of monetary reform is to eliminate, or at least reduce, this bias as discussed in Chapter 10.[19] The third objective would require a guarantee in terms of the value of the asset considered least likely to depreciate, which has traditionally been gold but might now be the mark or some other national currency expected generally to appreciate against gold.

Any particular currency, however, might depreciate, no matter how strong it looked at the time the guarantee was set. The dollar valuation of the guarantees extended by Britain on sterling reserves in 1968, and renewed in 1971, turned out to be a poor choice for the holders very shortly. Thus a gold-value or SDR-value guarantee, which would amount to the most likely proxy for a two-way guarantee against any loss of international purchasing power or local-currency equivalent for dollar holders, would be best equipped to carry out the objective of crowning the dollar via this route.[20]

19. This is less a problem when the unit of guarantee is neither the currency of the holder nor the currency of the issuer of the guaranteed asset. For example, the dollar-value guarantee given to sterling countries by the United Kingdom came into play only if Britain devalued, not if the United States revalued. Even here, it would presumably try to pressure the United States to revalue instead of devaluing itself, but the problem would probably be much less a bilateral U.S.-U.K. affair than would be the confrontation between the United States and a group of surplus countries, as in 1971.

20. It might seem paradoxical to achieve a pure dollar standard by providing a new gold-value guarantee, but there is no logical objection to the step and some psychological justification for it. An SDR-value guarantee is now even

A pure gold guarantee would of course provide coverage equal to a gold-value guarantee. However, such a guarantee would not be credible for either the United States or Britain, if extended to all dollar or sterling holders, since neither has sufficient gold to redeem all of its outstanding liquid liabilities at the present official price. A gold guarantee is not necessary anyway, because it would simply assure a dollar holder that he could get enough gold—through exercising the guarantee at the gold-dollar price which prevailed before any dollar devaluation—to maintain the dollar value of his reserves. A gold-value guarantee provides the same assurance. Gold guarantees could of course be extended on a limited value of U.S. dollar liabilities, as under the GAB, or even to all the dollars held by a limited number of countries, as under the Tripartite Agreement in 1936;[21] the effect is to give the privileged party a first claim on the limited gold stock of the guarantor.

The third issue is whether the guarantee should cover private as well as official dollar balances. "Coverage of private balances" has two different meanings: extension of the guarantee to private holders of dollars, or extension to dollars held by private foreigners at the time the guarantees went into effect if they subsequently moved into official hands. The 1968 arrangement for sterling adds to this confusion, because its dollar-value guarantee and minimum sterling proportions apply only to official sterling, whereas the Basel funding facility covers private as well as official balances outstanding at the time of the arrangements.

It would be unthinkable for the United States to extend any kind

---

more likely, since SDRs have been tied to a basket of currencies and the official price of gold has become meaningless. However, protection against a general increase in the official price of gold would require a gold-value guarantee (though such an increase would be inconceivable in the context of moving to a pure dollar system). In any event, general changes in the gold (or SDR) prices would presumably be made only for systemic liquidity reasons, and there would be no reason for the United States to underwrite the profits of others from them. So a gold-value guarantee should be extended only with the proviso that it would not apply in case of a "uniform increase in par values," per Article IV, Section 7, of the IMF Agreement.

21. Under the Tripartite Agreement, any country planning to devalue had to give 24-hour notice to other participants in the Agreement. This would give them time to convert into gold their balances of the currency about to be devalued. It was thus not technically a "guarantee," but had the same effect. The Agreement was originally made by the United States, Britain, and France and subsequently joined by Belgium, Netherlands, and Switzerland—basically the gold bloc that still exists.

of guarantee to private foreigners, if only because they would then be-treated better than U.S. residents. In addition, it would be unjusti-fiable to extend such a guarantee to private foreigners and continue paying them market interest rates; but doing so could only be avoided by issuing a completely new dollar instrument carrying the guarantee and a lower rate of interest, which would be tantamount to creating a second international dollar and would actually undermine the currency.

There is no reason not to guarantee dollars which move into official hands from private balances, however, perhaps with a small excep-tion for working balances as in the 10 per cent exemption in the Basel arrangements. Virtually all official dollars were initially acquired from the private sector, and it makes little difference, in terms of seeking stability for them in foreign reserves, whether they were first held for some lengthy period by private foreigners. If they moved into reserves due to speculative fears, it would probably be precisely a time when the guarantees were most needed to preserve stability. The dollars would probably move back into private hands when the speculative flurry ended. On the other hand, a secular move of pri-vate dollars into official hands would represent a permanent addition to official reserves and thus require the guarantees to assure stability. So the guarantees should cover all foreign official dollars, including those which come in as a result of declines in foreign privately held dollars, just as was argued in Chapter 11 that any consolidation of the dollar overhang into SDRs should also provide a place for dollars held privately at the time the arrangement took effect.

The issue of interest rates is more difficult. Certainly the guarantee is worth a great deal, and the holder of the guarantee hardly deserves market interest rates. If he did, he would be treated better than do-mestic residents.[22] In addition, interest rates are increased by the inflationary expectations of the market for a given currency, which in turn anticipate any future devaluation thereof, and no holder should expect a guarantee against a devaluation if he profits from expectations of events which would cause it. Market interest rates,

---

22. Although the U.S. government *has* discriminated in favor of foreign dollar-holders in the past (a) by exempting foreign official holders from the interest-rate ceilings of Regulation Q, (b) until 1971 by exempting all foreign deposits from the Federal Reserve requirements and FDIC insurance charges, and (c) by paying rates above the market to persuade foreign monetary authorities to buy dollar-denominated "Roosa bonds."

or rates at least higher than on SDRs, might be justified for the United States if they induced foreign monetary authorities to forget their desire for conversions into U.S. reserve assets to try to force it to adjust. We saw in Part II that few large official holders are very interest-sensitive, however, so it is doubtful that many could be bought off in this way from trying to exert leverage over U.S. policy.

In fact, it can be argued that gold-value guarantees should eliminate all interest on dollar balances. The capital value of the dollars would then assuredly be fully as good as gold. In addition, it costs money to store gold and dollars have a convenience value for market transactions. So gold-value guaranteed dollars would be better than gold in purely financial terms. The national interests of the United States would of course be maximized by a maximum reduction in the interest paid on foreign dollar reserves. The issue is complicated by the existence of SDRs, which have a gold-value guarantee but also pay 5 per cent interest. On the other hand, as they have no direct market use, they are less convenient than dollars.

A major question is whether foreign officials would have a choice between unguaranteed dollars at market interest rates and guaranteed dollars with lower rates.[23] With such a choice, many dollar area countries—which would generally expect to devalue along with the United States, and hence bear no local-currency losses from a dollar devaluation—would choose the former, while most gold bloc countries would choose the latter. This would amount to creating two classes of dollars, but would not raise the problem cited above—two classes of dollars for *private* holders—since the United States could justifiably insist that all dollars eligible for the guarantees, and therefore to receive the lower rate of interest, be held with the Federal Reserve System so that it could at all times know the size of its contingent liability.

Another option would be to pay market interest rates on all foreign official dollars but deduct from any guarantee payoff an amount equal to the interest earned on each guaranteed dollar. If interest rates had been averaging 5 per cent, the guarantees would be made good on a 10 per cent devaluation only for those dollars held less than two years—and the full 10 per cent compensation would be paid only on those dollars acquired in, say, the quarter before the

23. Both classes of dollars would have to be inconvertible into U.S. reserve assets under this pure dollar standard option. The Basel arrangements gave sterling holders virtually the best of all worlds by permitting them to choose between convertible sterling at market interest rates and inconvertible sterling with dollar-value guarantees at market interest rates.

parity change. This would have the desirable adjustment effect of inducing the guarantor to move promptly. (It would, however, undercut an objective of those countries which accepted a dollar world in order to *avoid* adjustment by the United States.) On the other hand, it would reduce the potential value of the interest earnings on the dollar balances—but they would suffer an offset only when the dollar was devalued, and would never be offset by more than the amount of a devaluation. Of course, some partial offset between interest earnings and devaluation compensation could be negotiated. In the event of guarantees, this approach seems best designed to handle the interest-rate issue.

Finally, the United States could extend "informal guarantees" by intervening in the forward exchange markets to prevent a sizable discount on dollars for future delivery, as the British did in 1964–67.[24] This enables foreigners to sell their dollar holdings forward and thus insure themselves against devaluation losses. It could even be a profitable business for the U.S. authorities as long as no devaluation takes place.

Such "informal guarantees," however, are much more appropriate for *private* than for official foreign balances. Private traders and investors are used to covering forward and regard the costs of doing so as part of their normal business expenses. Monetary authorities are *not* used to doing so and would undoubtedly view the costs as an important offset to the advantages of holding the dollars—at a minimum, reducing the value of the resulting guarantees. In addition, this approach could be much more costly for the United States than extending formal guarantees, since it would cover private as well as official dollars—depending on whether devaluations were sufficiently spaced to reap enough profits to offset the periodic losses.

Thus intervention in the forward markets, covering mainly foreign private dollars, would be most appropriate as a *supplement* to formal gold-value guarantees on foreign *official* dollars. We have already concluded, however, that such guarantees are sufficient to preserve systemic stability and that private dollars need to be covered only as

---

24. See Cohen, *op. cit.*, pp. 185–87. IMF rules do not require member countries to defend their currencies in the forward exchange markets. The forward rate for currencies expected to be devalued can thus fall far beneath the lower spot margin and cause losses for holders or earners of that currency— even if it is not eventually devalued, if the holders sold in fear thereof. So intervention to maintain the forward rate at any higher level represents a subsidy, or kind of guarantee, to these holders.

they enter official reserves.[25] So there would be no need for the United States to add this "informal guarantee" to the formal gold-value guarantees of official dollars to achieve a pure dollar standard through this option.

Under such a system, the guarantees would presumably apply to the overhang. Net U.S. interest costs on the present level of dollars would be sharply reduced if a lower interest rate were paid on the guaranteed dollars and if most of the outstanding dollars took advantage of the offer. This would significantly reduce the current net cost of the dollar's roles to the United States, derived in Chapter 7. The United States would also gain from the removal of any threat of collapse of the overhang, which we decided, in Chapter 8, was modest but not zero. The additional cost would be the contingent cost of a dollar devaluation—which could amount to $2 billion, if $40 billion from the overhang were guaranteed, on the 5 per cent devaluation which we concluded in Chapter 9 would be required to achieve the assumed target of a $5 billion improvement in the U.S. balance of payments. If the arrangements included an offset between interest rate payments and guarantee payoff, as recommended above, even this cost would be netted against the interest which the United States had paid anyway.

Even a guarantee payoff need not be much of a cost in real U.S. resources, however, because the bulk of the markup would go to countries with large reserves and they would probably never use it anyway. There would be some cost to the administration which sought Congressional authorization to extend the guarantees, and to any administration which had to seek appropriations to make good on them, but these do not represent national costs which should deter pursuit of the policy if it were to make sense otherwise. In addition, the dollar value of the U.S. gold (and SDR) stock would be *increased* by any dollar devaluation, and provide a partial offset

---

25. To be sure, this is true for the United States only because the dollar is the chief intervention currency and as long as it defends any parity for the dollar by converting official dollars into U.S. reserves rather than by active intervention in the exchange markets—since private dollars cannot place direct pressure on U.S. reserves. It is not true for the United Kingdom, which would only defend its currency via market intervention and whose reserves thus would be drained directly by private transactions, as discussed in Chapter 5. The British policy of intervening in the forward markets was therefore arguably defensible from their standpoint in 1964–67, whereas it could not make sense for the dollar unless the United States too were to commence defending a dollar parity through active market intervention.

to the accounting loss rendered by the payoff on the guarantees.[26]

Whether this option would help or hurt the United States depends crucially upon whether it would ease or tighten the devaluation constraint which has existed with the previous roles of the dollar. The gold-value guarantee would make devaluation easier by eliminating any foreign opposition to it which was motivated by balance-sheet considerations, and it would obviate any U.S. reluctance to "penalize cooperative dollar holders." However, any costs of making good the guarantees might dissuade the United States from devaluing. The net result of these conflicting considerations is uncertain, but would be likely to reduce the devaluation constraint.

The British were certainly not constrained from devaluing by the sterling guarantees, and it is probable that the reduction of the foreign problem would outweigh the domestic political problem of making good on the guarantees. Foreign opposition to dollar devaluation could still be intense because of the effect on national competitive positions and hence on domestic employment, and the continued intervention currency role of the dollar would still enable them to block a U.S. move; but these problems will plague a U.S. devaluation under any monetary system, so elimination of the asset-valuation problem is probably as much as any reform scheme can do to improve the situation from the U.S. standpoint. This form of dollar standard would also quiet the problem of systemic confidence by eliminating the risk of shifts out of dollars, but it would leave the need for new liquidity to be met erratically by U.S. payments deficits where better alternatives clearly exist.

The United States would also have to pay compensation for a dollar devaluation, however, if the overhang were consolidated in the IMF, for SDR or in a new Reserve Settlement Account, since these claims would almost certainly carry gold-value guarantees. Foreign-held SDRs would continue to be convertible into dollars at the pre-1971 dollar exchange rate. They would thus represent an increased claim on U.S. resources, just as the augmented dollar balances would if the dollars themselves were guaranteed. In the SDR case, however, the United States would have to provide additional dollars only for

26. The costs of the guarantees cited are of course in addition to the obligations to the IMF and international development institutions under existing arrangements, which required appropriations of about $1.6 billion to make up the 8 per cent devaluation of 1971–72. It would encompass the $345 million cost then incurred on Roosa bonds and swaps. The revaluation of the U.S. gold and SDR holdings in 1971–72 amounted to almost $1 billion. American drawing rights at the Fund rose by an additional $575 million.

SDRs actually presented to it in the normal course of SDR business, which would be a small part of the total. It would be held liable to make good the guarantee on the rest of the SDRs in case of need, but the need would occur only if the whole scheme collapsed or if individual members withdrew from it. An administration would still have to seek appropriations to make good on the guarantee, as in 1972, but could accurately point out that actual payment of compensation was unlikely ever to occur. So the overhang would be treated in essentially the same way under both approaches, though with less potential *real* cost to the United States under the SDR approach.

The basic difference between the two approaches is that dollars *newly* acquired by foreign monetary authorities would be inconvertible into U.S. assets but eligible for the gold-value guarantees under this dollar standard option, whereas they would be convertible into U.S. assets but unguaranteed under the international asset option, as developed in Chapter 11. The United States would thus gain new financing flexibility under the former option in return for the contingent costs of compensation on the ensuing buildup of additional dollars in the event of any future devaluation. For precisely this reason, this option will not appeal to some countries, which, for both economic and political reasons, do not want the United States to have such a privilege. We thus turn to the only dollar standard option which might meet their concerns as well.

A Market-determined Dollar Standard
The dollar, like sterling before it, was originally "elected" a key currency by market forces. A world political role was a necessary precedent for such election, and subsequently reinforced the market's choice. But the United States neither forced the dollar on the rest of the world nor provided widespread guarantees of its value to induce others to hold it. If the dollar were again to meet the necessary criteria, a pure dollar standard could emerge once more.[27]

The main criterion would be assurance of fixed-price convertibility for the dollar for as far ahead as anyone could see. This would require a U.S. declaration to renounce devaluation as a policy instrument and policies to permit achievement of that objective, probably including *inter alia* a return to a system of fixed exchange rates.

27. The criteria are set out in Chapters 4–6. Restoring a dollar standard by this approach was proposed as a longish "interim solution" by Gunther Ruff, *op. cit.* His analysis agrees with that of this section, but he concludes with advocacy of a dollar standard from a global standpoint, while I conclude with opposition from a U.S. national standpoint for reasons that will shortly become apparent.

There would have to be full foreign confidence that the United States had both the will and the capacity to stick to this aim. With such confidence, foreigners would no longer need the option of trying to force policy changes on the United States by converting their dollar acquisitions into U.S. reserves. Dollar inconvertibility could thus be maintained *de jure*, though more probably *de facto* to avoid the appearances of asymmetry which raise political problems.

There would be one difference from that period, however. The huge dollar overhang would mean that the U.S. liquidity ratio, defined narrowly as the relationship between reserves and foreign official (or all) dollars, would be highly unfavorable. Even if current U.S. performance were exemplary, the overhang would remain a potential threat to both the United States and the system as a whole. This option would probably be inconsistent with consolidating the overhang through a special issue of SDR or a sizable gold revaluation, and there would be no incentive for the United States to convert the overhang into a long-term obligation with fixed maturities. So, to achieve a pure dollar standard, the United States might have to combine the gold-value guarantees of the option just discussed with meeting fully the political and economic attributes of key currency status. The two steps together should obviate any needs of other countries to convert their old or new dollars into U.S. reserves, since by hypothesis they would be assured against improper U.S. policy actions *and* against any potential losses on their holdings.

As shown in Chapters 4–6, a key currency can achieve and maintain its position only by meeting certain attributes *relative* to other currencies and, in the case of the reserve currency role, other potential reserve assets (mainly gold and SDR now) as well. For example, it could maintain such status with a spotty record of price stability in a world with no serious rivals but might not be able to do so with a better price record in the face of stiff competition. There are thus two routes to a market-determined dollar standard: exemplary performance by the United States, or inept performance by its rivals.

Under present conditions, achievement of a market-determined dollar standard would require much better U.S. performance than ever before on many of the key currency criteria, because of the greatly improved position of other currencies, the continued attraction of gold, and the emergence of a new rival reserve asset in the SDR. As noted throughout Chapters 4–6, the relative U.S. position has *declined* in terms of almost all of the key attributes. Politically, the United States world role has receded with the emergence of new power centers; the reduced political value of the nuclear arsenal, in light of the Soviet achievement of nuclear parity and a marked re-

duction virtually everywhere of the perception of active threats to
world security; and the re-orientation of U.S. concerns toward domestic issues. Indeed, the United States now seeks actively to share
its political power with its major allies. So the political hegemony
of an earlier day is gone, presumably forever, barring another world
cataclysm from which the United States were somehow to emerge
relatively unscathed.

The same trends are even clearer in the economic area. On the
size criterion, the U.S. share of international transactions has declined significantly and the European Community with its numerous
associates represents a much larger factor in world trade; Germany
alone has reached the U.S. level of exports. The devaluations of
1971–73 would require a better U.S. performance in the future than
in the past, because they demonstrated that the United States can
and will seek such a step. The internal economy is no longer aloof to
external transactions either; important sectors are increasingly reliant
on them. Aloofness in foreign policy has also been reduced, as first
became apparent in the 1960s in the running debates with Germany
and other allies on military offset arrangements and the steady tightening of the conditions on aid loans, and then became obvious with
the New Economic Policy in 1971. At the same time, the adverse
shift in the U.S. Phillips curve caused by structural changes in the
labor force now makes it *more* difficult for the United States to
achieve relative price stability, at acceptable levels of unemployment,
than was true even a decade ago. This reduction in aloofness also
prompted the United States to institute a number of selective controls over foreign access to dollars. Even in the area of effective capital markets, where the United States maintains a huge lead, Europe
has been catching up. And we have also seen, in Chapter 11, how
the U.S. liquidity ratio is now significantly inferior to that of all
other potential key countries, and how one or two others now have
larger reserves even in absolute terms.

The renewed world focus on economic *security*, exemplified by
the energy crisis, has restored some of the earlier U.S. power position in both economic and political terms because it is relatively self-
sufficient in most economic sectors. Nevertheless, it would be harder,
and more costly, for the United States to meet fully the key currency
criteria now than it would have been in the past. Recognition of this
difficulty would understandably prompt foreign officials to insist on
playing an active role in the formulation of U.S. economic policies
and perhaps foreign policy, if they were to have full confidence in
the results—as required for this option to be agreed to in the first
place, and for it to work thereafter. For precisely this reason, Kindle-

berger and others have frequently suggested converting the Federal Reserve Open Market Committee into an Atlantic (plus Japan and OPEC?) Open Market Committee to provide for a fully coordinated U.S. monetary policy. This would be a necessary but probably insufficient step, however, since even a U.S. monetary policy fully agreed upon by the key foreign countries would not assure foreign acceptance of U.S. policy and results in all of the areas just cited.

In short, the United States would have to go very far in submerging its sovereignty in economic and foreign policy to achieve this kind of pure dollar standard. By explicitly giving up the exchange-rate instrument and controls over *foreign* capital, it would remove the possibility of *effective* adjustment except through internal measures. It would probably also have to give up at least the choice of controls it would apply over U.S. capital—some other countries might welcome some capital controls, particularly over direct investment, but object to others. It would subject its domestic economic choices to active foreign surveillance and would probably have to achieve a price performance that met the average of the major countries.

We saw in Chapter 9, however, that the costs of adjusting other than through the exchange rate or controls are exorbitant. And this option would provide only limited financing for U.S. deficits, since there would need to be at least rough international agreement on the equilibrium level of the U.S. balance of payments that was "allowed." To be sure, less financing might be needed to turn the *direct* effects of the dollar's roles into a net benefit because of the possible reduction in net interest costs from the extension of gold-value guarantees on the overhang. But the United States would have to walk a tightrope in its external accounts in two senses. Its official settlements position would have to be weak enough to avoid fears of appreciation of the dollar, but strong enough to avoid criticism of excessive deficits. And it would need to maintain current account (though not necessarily trade) surpluses to strengthen its liquidity ratio on the broader concepts developed in Chapter 5. In short, U.S. policy would become tightly circumscribed in such a system, both by a reduction in policy instruments and by much tighter definition of external policy targets. If the United States did *not* meet these requirements, and foreign confidence in the new arrangements withered, the result would parallel the degeneration of the gold exchange standard in the mid-1960s and once more become subject to likely collapse because of dissatisfaction on the part of the United States, other countries, or both.

It will be recalled that a market-determined dollar standard could also be achieved by a lack of competition for the dollar from other sources, as well as from exemplary U.S. performance. We saw in Chapter 11 that no other national currency is now in a position to replace the dollar as a global reserve asset, though a united EC unit might eventually do so, but that some currencies are increasingly challenging it at least on a partial basis. Nothing could be done by the United States to prevent these trends; a reversal of its traditional support for European integration would be more likely to accelerate that movement than to derail it.

On the other hand, the United States could take unilateral steps in an effort to undermine gold and SDR. Such opposition to SDR would be simple, since the United States has sufficient voting power in the IMF simply to block any allocations and any changes in its characteristics that would make it more attractive.

Gold is more difficult, however. Historically, most countries have eliminated gold as a domestic rival to their paper currency by making it illegal for their private citizens to hold the metal, a step the United States took in 1934. Several approaches to eliminate the international use of gold were proposed in the early and middle 1960s. Fritz Machlup suggested an international agreement which would have done so by gradually reducing the price which monetary authorities would pay for gold purchased either from each other or from private sellers.[28] (This was the period when there was a single market for private and official gold.) This scheme was a non-starter, both because it would either have forced capital losses on all monetary authorities and corresponding *reductions* in world liquidity, *or* crowned the dollar if they had sold all their gold to the United States—in which case it would have suffered *all* of the capital losses, which might have been unacceptable to it. This "downward crawling peg" for gold could now be combined with SDR creation to achieve any desired level of total world reserves and avoid any net losses to monetary authorities. However, offsetting the effect on reserves through SDR creation would run contrary to using the approach to achieve a pure dollar standard.

The most elaborate proposal to crown the dollar by cutting down gold was the Despres Plan of 1965–66.[29] The United States would

28. Fritz Machlup, "Comments on the Balance of Payments and a Proposal to Reduce the Price of Gold," *Journal of Finance*, Vol. XVI (1961), pp. 186–93. Machlup's objective was not to crown the dollar, but simply to provide an answer to the problem of private gold speculation which plagued the system at the time of his proposal.
29. Emile Despres, "Statement" in *New Approaches to International Policy*, Reuss Subcommittee, September 9, 1966, pp. 39–42, based on a paper which he circulated privately in April 1965.

rescind its commitment to *buy* from foreign monetary authorities any gold which they acquired after the announcement of the new U.S. policy. (In fact, the United States would be willing to buy only one-third of the gold held *on* that date by major gold-holding countries, offering unlimited credits equal to the other two-thirds, however, in order not to *reduce* drastically the value of their international reserves.) This would supposedly make clear that gold derived its value primarily from its assured convertibility into dollars at a fixed price, and eliminate it as a serious contender to the dollar as a result. The United States would continue to *sell* gold at a fixed price, and thereby maintain its obligation to "defend the dollar" in this way. The Despres Plan thus differs sharply from the *force majeure* route to a pure dollar standard, which would give foreign official holders no alternative to their dollar balances.

It is conceivable, though dubious, that such a scheme would have actually moved the world close to a pure dollar standard when it was proposed by Despres in 1965.[30] Proposals to strengthen the dollar by deliberately weakening gold have a strange ring historically, because the market-determined sterling and dollar systems of the past both developed with no such steps—indeed, they developed while the interconvertibility of gold and the dominant key currency of the day was unassailable. Despres himself admitted that the scheme would not be credible if announced at a time when the United States was losing gold. It would be even more dubious today, when the market price for gold stands well above the official price. As noted above, some key countries simply do not want a dollar standard. And gold could be demonetized unilaterally by the United States only if other countries stood idly by and let it happen, for several reasons.

---

30. Its last real chance probably came in 1963–64, when the gold pool *bought* $1.4 billion to keep the market price for gold from falling below $35 per ounce. Elimination of the U.S. buying commitment (and the gold pool) might then have instituted a two-tiered system, since the gold bloc might not have been able to form a buying pool by itself, with a sharp plunge in the market price below the official price. Monetary authorities might then have scrambled for dollars, as the safest available asset. Such a U.S. move would have been buttressed by the sharp improvement from 1960 through 1964 in the U.S. trade and current account balances and the near-elimination of the official settlements deficit in 1964. Such an outcome in 1963–64 might well have avoided the gold rush of 1967–68 and the large losses to private speculators from the U.S. (and other countries') gold reserves, by setting up a two-tiered system for gold four or five years earlier, but it is doubtful that it would have prevented the most important subsequent developments, such as the sterling and later dollar devaluations.

First, the IMF Articles of Agreement probably require the Fund to buy gold at its official price. The United States has opposed such an interpretation of the Articles, but the Fund agreed to provide a floor at $35 per ounce—under certain conditions, to be sure—for South African and other new gold production after the United States limited its buying commitment to gold already in official reserves after the institution of the two-tiered system in 1968. American opposition to a Fund floor in the postulated circumstances, however, would engender foreign bitterness even additional to that caused by the move to crown the dollar itself, and would probably threaten a breakdown of the Fund.[31]

Second, any group of other countries, such as the European Community or even the smaller gold bloc within and near it, could announce that *it* would buy gold at the official price and essentially replace the United States in guaranteeing a floor. The entire EC, at a minimum, would probably do so because of the political strength within it of gold bloc countries and because it would be difficult even for the dollar countries within the Community not to oppose such a unilateral U.S. effort to crown the dollar. They would almost certainly move in this way if they could not get the IMF to provide a floor, and would in fact be creating a regional substitute for the global system based on the Fund. A group of this size would certainly be willing to buy gold from each other, and perhaps even resume buying from the private market, on the assurance that they could always re-sell it to each other to finance payments imbalances.

Third, the premium for gold in the free market over the official price now provides great psychological support, and some real support, for any such opposition to demonetize or even reduce the official price of gold.[32] And the outlook for supply and private demand for gold suggests that extremely large sales of monetary gold would be necessary to keep the market price from remaining above the official price and rising steadily.

Despres sought acceptance of his proposal by other countries by recognizing that the United States would have to coordinate its monetary policy with them under the resulting dollar standard. As just noted, however, this would place major constraints on the U.S. econ-

31. Despres regarded these problems as "matters of technical detail which raise no insuperable difficulties."
32. Despres assumed that his proposal would itself trigger the institution of a two-tiered market, which did not then exist, because foreign monetary authorities would be unwilling to buy gold from the market if they could not be assured of selling it to the United States. He made no firm forecast of the market price, but implied that it would decline below $35 per ounce.

omy. In fact, it would be forced to adopt the policy mix approach discussed in Chapter 9—and suffer the very high costs which could result if foreign demands for a tight U.S. monetary policy coincided with periods of high U.S. unemployment, as could easily have happened in 1970–71. In any event, foreign acceptance of a dollar standard, which would be required for the Despres approach to work, could seemingly be more easily obtained without the actions on gold which are central to the Despres Plan.

There have been other suggestions for crowning the dollar by way of demonetizing gold. The United States could deliberately sell off all of its gold. Or it could try to trigger a collapse of confidence in gold simply by indicating a willingness to use it freely to finance U.S. payments deficits, or even to convert dollars from the overhang.[33] Or, more modestly, the United States could discourage foreign official holdings of gold by widening the margins around the gold parity of the dollars—or at least using the presently allowable margins of ±1 per cent—and thus inflicting a loss equal to the total width of the band on foreign monetary authorities when they sold to the United States any gold which they had bought from it at an earlier time.[34] All of these approaches could now run into the same problems as outlined above regarding the Despres Plan, however, and would probably also prevent the United States from building its own reserves by buying gold from others, since others would not sell gold to the United States if they could never buy it back or do so only at a significantly lower price.

It is thus highly unlikely that the United States could crown the dollar by undermining the market attractiveness of gold. It certainly could not undermine the attractiveness of other national currencies. And the positive efforts needed to achieve a market-determined dollar standard would levy extremely heavy costs on the U.S. economy and foreign policy. It is not a very attractive option.

33. Despres, *op. cit.*, p. 13, took this position in 1966: "If our obvious pain in undergoing gold losses disappeared, the whole situation would be utterly transformed." William McChesney Martin, former Chairman of the Federal Reserve Board and widely respected throughout the international monetary community, indeed stated frequently in public that the United States would sell its gold "down to the last bar" to defend the dollar. This obviously did not eliminate some appetites for gold. And the private gold price *rose* sharply in early 1972 in the face of hints leaked by the U.S. Treasury that it might again start selling gold in that market.
34. Robert A. Mundell, *The International Monetary System: Conflict and Reform* (Private Planning Association of Canada, July 1965), pp. 39–43. Mundell also hoped to get some adjustment flexibility by widening the gold points, with several major currencies pegging to gold instead of to the dollar.

Summary and a Comparison

There are three different means by which the dollar could become the center of a new international monetary system. From the standpoint of the United States, all three would have the advantage of providing at least some dollar financing for its payments deficits and hence enabling it to avoid the costs of forced adjustment. The guarantees approach would be best on this count, because it would remove completely any foreign concerns about the future value of dollar balances they accrued. The *force majeure* system could turn out the same way, in principle, although under it dollars would be accepted less graciously. The market-based system would be least generous in this regard, and would in fact permit dollar financing only to the extent it was negotiated internationally.

However, none of these "pure" results would be likely in practice. We saw in our analysis that some countries would seek to convert their dollars even if the dollars were guaranteed, because they did not like U.S. policy. Some countries (and the market) would simply not accept a *force majeure* dollar standard, with the possible exception of a period when the U.S. balance of payments was very strong and little, if any, dollar financing was needed. And the United States would probably be unable to maintain the market-oriented approach itself because of the heavy constraint on its own policy objectives.

In any event, the market-based system would preclude the United States from devaluing or implementing effective capital controls to achieve adjustment, and would constrain domestic economic policy. It could apply controls under the *force majeure* system and manage its domestic economy with little heed to the balance of payments— but any effort it made to change its exchange rate could be frustrated by other key countries, given the uncooperative milieu implied by such a system, and its interests could be adversely affected by the exchange-rate changes initiated by others. Both effective devaluation and controls would be possible only under guarantees, and the domestic economy would be unconstrained. Controls would not be needed for balance-of-payments purposes under this approach, however, and devaluation—if needed by the United States for domestic reasons, and justifiable internationally—would be rendered more costly by the need to pay off the guarantees. The real economic costs of redeeming the guarantees might not be very great, however, and only this approach to a dollar standard would permit devaluation to take place effectively at all.

America's net interest payments rise with the level of foreign dollar balances, and would probably rise fastest with the theoretically unlimited financing approaches of gold-value guarantees and *force ma-*

jeure. The *force majeure* approach would be more likely to induce controls on U.S. capital exports, especially by other countries, so U.S. liabilities might grow more slowly under it than under a system of gold-value guarantees alone. In addition, lower interest rates would be paid on the overhang if it were guaranteed. Guarantees could also be offered in tandem with the market approach, under which U.S. liabilities rose more slowly.

Thus U.S. net interest payments would probably rise least under a combination of the market system and gold-value guarantees, because of the limited growth of U.S. liabilities plus the reduction of payments on the overhang. The outcome on this criterion among the three pure options is indeterminate. The straight guarantees option would be most likely to minimize these costs, despite the relatively unlimited expansion of dollar liabilities which it would make possible, because the overhang is so large relative to the likely growth of additional dollars in the future.

The key question, of course, is whether any of these approaches are viable on a global basis. The *force majeure* approach would undoubtedly be unacceptable to a number of key countries and would therefore trigger foreign reaction which would terminate the dollar standard at least for them— and levy major costs on overall U.S. foreign policy as well. The guarantees approach would be acceptable to those countries whose only concern about the dollar was the stability of its economic value to them, but would be unacceptable to those which did not want the United States to be relieved of all policy constraints through its balance of payments. Only the market-oriented option, particularly if combined with the guarantees, is likely to be acceptable to virtually all other countries—but it would probably not be acceptable to the United States.

We might expect an obverse rank correlation between the systemic viability of the options and their net benefit to the United States. Indeed, the market-oriented approach, which has the greatest systemic potential, is far too costly for the United States to consider (whether or not combined with guarantees). However, the gold-value guarantee ranks at the top from the purely U.S. national standpoint, and second—decidedly better than *force majeure*—from the systemic standpoint. *Force majeure* is the only serious rival from the U.S. standpoint and is systemically unstable. So the United States should pursue the gold-value guarantee approach, and seek to minimize the policy constraints which others might require to accept the guarantees and the resulting system, if it wished to impose a pure dollar standard on the international monetary system.

13

Intermediate Options for Changing the International Roles of the Dollar

Between the extremes of eliminating or sharply expanding the international roles of the dollar lie three options for change in the international monetary system which provide a kind of middle use of the dollar. All three are modified, less extreme variants of options considered in Chapter 11: adoption of *limited* exchange-rate flexibility; use of a truly international asset as the sole or at least major source of additional reserves for *some countries*; and the use of additional national currencies as international reserve assets, *along with* the dollar, in a move to a "multiple currency reserve" system. These proposals are not mutually exclusive. Limited exchange-rate flexibility is addressed primarily to the adjustment problem, while the other options are addressed primarily to the confidence and liquidity problems. Thus, they could logically be adopted in combination. None would deal definitively with the dollar, as would those discussed in the previous chapters, but they would affect the dollar significantly and so can be judged on the basis of American national interests.

LIMITED FLEXIBILITY OF EXCHANGE RATES

Flexibility of exchange rates can be limited, relative to the model of full flexibility for all countries discussed in Chapter 11, in five different ways. First, the *amount* of flexibility can be limited: both to the amount of flexibility around a given parity (or "central rate") at any point in time, and to the changes in parities (or "target zones") themselves in any given time period. These limitations could either be determined de jure by new international rules amending the articles of Agreement of the IMF, or de facto by informal agreement to implement the existing Articles more flexibly to let rates float, subject to market intervention limiting the extent to which they were actually to move. Second, parities could flex only in *certain situations*, such as the dilemma cases in which the fiscal and monetary policies needed to pursue domestic economic targets exacerbate

430

rather than eliminate the simultaneous external disequilibrium. Third, flexibility could be limited to *upward* exchange-rate moves only—perhaps to counter the devaluation bias of the system and to avoid fears that frequent downward changes would erode completely the "discipline" of the balance of payments.[1] Fourth, the number of countries which flex their rates can be limited—perhaps to those whose economies are relatively closed to external transactions. Finally, even those countries which generally elect not to flex might adopt different exchange-rate policies at *different times*—perhaps as a transitional device to help them find a new equilibrium parity, or for a longer time if the center to which they usually peg their rate failed for a period to maintain a reasonable degree of price stability. These five types of flexibility can be combined; for example, a limited number of countries could opt for limited movement of their exchange rates to meet dilemma problems when the major country to which they usually pegged their exchange rates was inflating excessively. We turn now to an analysis of each type of limitation.[2]

Limited Degrees of Flexibility

The most circumscribed approach to limited amounts of flexibility is to widen the band around fixed parities from the narrow margins which were permitted before August 1971,[3] and perhaps from the

1. These first three types of limitation are advocated by William Fellner, "A 'Realistic' Note on Threefold Limited Flexibility of Exchange Rates," in Bergsten *et al.*, *Approaches to Greater Flexibility of Exchange Rates*, pp. 237–44. An asymmetrically widened band, to permit greater fluctuation only on the upside of a given parity, is proposed by George Chittenden, "Asymmetrical Widening of the Bands Around Parity," *ibid*, pp. 245–50.

2. Conceptually, there is a sixth possibility: limitation of flexibility to *certain classes of a country's international transactions* under one or another system of multiple exchange rates. Indeed, the French and Benelux two-tier exchange-rate systems comprised at one time an essentially fixed rate for current account transactions and an essentially flexible rate for capital movements. This approach is best viewed as one means of limiting selected international transactions, however, rather than as a mode of achieving more flexibility of exchange rates.

3. The IMF Articles of Agreement limited the margins to 1 per cent on either side of parity. In practice, the major European currencies bound themselves in the European Monetary Agreement to maintain margins of ±0.75 per cent. (Only Switzerland, which is not an IMF member, maintained wider margins at ±1.75 per cent.) These margins prevailed, however, only against the intervention currency—in most cases, the dollar. Thus any two nonintervention currencies could fluctuate against each other by twice these amounts. In practice, however, the fluctuation of any major currency against any other major currency seldom if ever approached the possible limit of 1.5 per cent. IMF. *The Role of Exchange Rates in the Adjustment Process* (Washington,

2.25 per cent on each side which was adopted "temporarily" in December 1971, to some broader range.[4] Fixed parities would be retained, but rates would be allowed to fluctuate within this zone. Official intervention would occur when one end of the band was reached, just as has traditionally occured at the extremes of the much narrower limits around parity. Intervention might also take place within the band in an effort to smooth out underlying trends, and possibly to combat undesirable speculation as well. Suggestions for the width of the band have ranged from 2–3 per cent on either side of parity[5] to as much as 7.5 per cent.[6] This variant is usually proposed primarily as a means to help reduce the volume of liquid capital flows—by making destabilizing speculation more costly and stabilizing speculation more rewarding—and thus help meet the confidence problem, although some of its proponents feel that it would help improve the adjustment process as well.

The second approach would have countries, either by their own unilateral decision or in response to internationally agreed rules or suggestions, maintain exchange-rate parities but change them gradually by a series of small adjustments.[7] Some have suggested a limit of 2 or 3 per cent per year for such alterations, perhaps carried out in monthly, weekly, or even daily steps. The rates would not fluctuate except within a small range around parity. Such a system, which is variously referred to as the "sliding" or "gliding parity," or "crawling peg," would seek to make exchange-rate changes more feasible by replacing the large one-shot changes characteristic of the Bretton Woods system with a series of small changes taking place over sufficient time to minimize speculative interest and political problems. The changes could either be triggered automatically under

---

D.C., 1970), pp. 12–22. The narrow margins incorporated in the IMF and EMA Articles apparently date back to such historical factors as the cost of transporting gold (when exchange-rate margins were really the "gold points" at which it became profitable to transport gold) and the British desire to defend the $2.80 parity chosen in 1949 at a round number (2 cents on either side).

4. For the most complete development of this approach see George N. Halm, *The "Band" Proposal: The Limits of Permissible Exchange Rate Variations*, Princeton Special Papers in International Economics, No. 6, January 1965.
5. IMF, *op. cit.*, p. 74.
6. Robert Mundell, "The Gold Herring," in *The United States Balance of Payments*, Hearings before the Reuss Subcommittee, Part 3, November 12–15, 1963, p. 547.
7. The earliest complete statements of this proposal were by James Meade, "The International Monetary Mechanism," *The Three Banks Review*, No. 63 (September 1964), pp. 3–25, and John H. Williamson, "The Crawling Peg," *Princeton Essays in International Finance*, No. 50, December 1965.

formulas previously agreed, remain totally up to the discretion of national authorities, or be presumed (but not forced) to occur when certain criteria are met. The maximum amount of the permitted changes might be limited, or left open but presumed to be much smaller than was normal in the past. The band and sliding parity approaches could also be combined to permit both wider exchange-rate fluctuations around parity and small moves in parities themselves.

These options have been seriously considered throughout international monetary history. Widening of the gold points, the gold standard equivalent of today's exchange-rate margins, was a frequently used tool prior to 1914.[8] Britain reportedly sought to widen the band to 3–5 per cent on either side of parity during the negotiations for the European Monetary Agreement in 1955.[9] As early as 1965, the Reuss Subcommittee urged the administration thoroughly to examine the permissible limits of exchange-rate variations and concluded that "the time may now be ripe for a modest broadening of the present limits of exchange rate variations."[10] And the Group of Ten decided to adopt wider margins, at least temporarily, as part of the Smithsonian Agreement of December 1971.[11]

The primary objective of any increased flexibility in exchange rates is an improvement in adjustment. Since rate changes have been often resisted until all other possibilities are exhausted, the adoption of a system which would permit such changes to occur more fre-

---

8. Arthur Bloomfield, *Monetary Policy Under the International Gold Standard* (New York: Federal Reserve Bank of New York, 1959), pp. 52–55.
9. Robert Triffin, *Europe and the Money Muddle* (New Haven: Yale University Press, 1957), pp. 225 and 282.
10. In *Guidelines for Improving the International Monetary System*, August 30, 1965, pp. 19–21.
11. In fact, the United States had already adopted a limited combination of the band and sliding parity approaches if one views the Interest Equalization Tax as a partial dollar devaluation. The "portfolio investment dollar" created by the IET could fluctuate between zero and an effective cost to the borrower of one and one half percentage points per annum, depending on the state of the U.S. balance of payments and interest rate differentials between the U.S. and foreign money markets. The effective rate for the "portfolio investment dollar" thus moved within a band bounded on one end by the basic dollar rate and on the other by a rate depreciated by 22.5 per cent. The "portfolio investment dollar" did not fluctuate, but was adjusted from time to time by the authorities. Conceptually, it was a parity for a limited class of transactions—and thus a partial substitute for changes in the overall dollar exchange rate, which were then deemed difficult for the United States to achieve unilaterally, as outlined in Chapter 9—sliding within a band by discretionary U.S. decisions.

quently would provide countries with a major new policy instrument, relative to the Bretton Woods system. The more flexibility permitted under any variant of the flexible rate approach, the more scope is given to the new policy instrument. As described in Chapter 11, full flexibility of rates would assure complete adjustment of payments imbalances (and hence eliminate the need for any international reserves). It would thus release domestic economic policy (and foreign policy) from some of the constraints of defending a fixed parity. Adoption of any of the limited flexibility variants would provide less new adjustment potential, but still more than existed under the Bretton Woods system. How much more would depend on the limits chosen.

The band of 2.25 per cent on either side of parity adopted in December 1971 provided about three times the scope for daily rate changes that existed previously. Such a broadened range would allow the relationship between any pair of currencies (except a pair including the intervention currency) to change by 4.5 per cent if each started at parity and reached opposite support points. A subsequent full reversal of these positions would amount to a shift of 9 per cent from the first set of extreme positions, since each could then move 4.5 per cent (of original parity) from ceiling to floor and vice versa —although instances of such reversals from one end of the band to another, by two currencies simultaneously, have been extremely rare in practice.[12] Similarly, a sliding parity of 3 per cent per year would permit an initial annual shift of up to 6 per cent for any pair of nonintervention currencies and then a move of 12 per cent of the initial amount if the directions of the slides were both reversed.

One anticipated result of the broadened scope for spot exchange-rate movements is a dampening of international movements of liquid capital. With the previous narrow margins and infrequent but sizable parity adjustments, speculators against a fixed parity faced a maximum loss of 1.5 per cent if they bet on devaluation of a currency at its floor and the rate then went to its ceiling instead, whereas they stood to realize a substantial gain if proved right because devaluations tended to be sizable.

Similarly, speculation that a parity would not be devalued could

---

12. The EC countries decided in early 1971, and again in early 1972, to limit fluctuations between their currencies around existing parities to one-half the possible fluctuation of each of them vis-à-vis the currencies of nonmembers. Even this degree of flexibility represented an increase in the absolute magnitude of intra-EC fluctuation which was possible prior to December 1971, but it reduced each of the magnitudes mentioned in the text by 50 per cent for purposes of intra-EC fluctuation.

produce a maximum profit of only 1.5 per cent even if the rate bounced all the way from its floor to its ceiling—since revaluations never occurred in such situations. As a result, simple mathematical calculations encouraged betting against a parity and discouraged betting on it.

Even under the mild widening of the band of December 1971, these calculations changed a great deal. A speculator could then lose 2.25 per cent if he bet against a currency even at its central rate and it rose to its ceiling, and could gain a like amount if he bought a currency at its floor and it regained even its central rate. He could lose and gain 4.5 per cent respectively, under the conditions specified in the previous paragraph. The essentially one-way option of the past had already been significantly changed. Stabilizing speculation should clearly dominate destabilizing speculation if the bands were widened even further, under any return to fixed parities, and especially if a system of sliding parities were added—since the potential gains to speculators even if they guessed right on a parity change might be no more than the potential risk if they guessed wrong, and with the spot rate moving from one extreme to the other within the widened margins around an unchanged parity.

A second result is an increase in the scope for independent national monetary policies. Purely interest-sensitive (i.e., nonspeculative) capital movements are motivated largely by *covered* interest-rate differentials, the difference between national interest rates *after* taking into account the forward exchange rate between the currencies involved. For example, much higher German interest rates will not induce U.S. funds to move to Germany if the forward discount on dollars is even greater. Under the narrow margins of the past, however, forward exchange rates could not provide very large premia and discounts[13]—so interest rate differentials could not be very large without triggering huge flows of funds. These flows could then undermine the domestic monetary policy of the countries involved, as we saw in Chapter 7. A widening of the margins for spot rates would permit wider forward premia and discounts, which in turn would permit correspondingly wider interest-rate differentials to be maintained effectively.

The widened band plus the sliding parity would also prove extremely useful in helping restore and maintain international pay-

13. Legally and technically, forward rates did not have to be maintained within the prescribed margins; only spot rates did. However, expectations of a parity change would be sharply enhanced if any monetary authority let its forward rate stray very far outside the margins for any period of time. In practice, forward rates were thus also constrained.

ments equilibrium. The increasingly high degree of price sensitivity which permeates international transactions today provides a basis for optimism concerning the adjustment impact of price changes within such a range.[14] A review of the adjustment requirements of individual countries in the post-convertibility period suggests that a sliding parity of 3 per cent, plus a band of like width on either side of parity, might have been sufficient to promote equilibrium significantly (assuming that proper domestic measures were also used in "non-dilemma" cases where domestic and external objectives were both served by similar macroeconomic policy.)[15]

Simulations of the effects of such a regime on the German undervaluation and British overvaluation of the 1960s support this conclusion. If Germany had adopted in mid-1964 a band of ±3 per cent and a sliding parity of up to 2 per cent annually and coupled this with a stability-oriented monetary and fiscal policy, it could have achieved payments equilibrium, avoided the recession of 1966–67 (because tight money would not then have been needed to fight inflation), and held internal price rises to about 1 per cent annually into 1969, when this study was made.[16] This compares with the huge payments surpluses and 3.5 per cent rate of inflation which actually occurred, in addition to the recession. From the standpoint of the monetary system as a whole, such results would have avoided the speculative waves of 1968 and 1969 that eventually led to the 10 per cent revaluation of the mark and would have considerably eased the pressure on the contemporary deficit countries—Britain, France, and the United States.

In the British case, the free "investment dollar" exchange rate—which provides a market test—depreciated at an annual rate of 4.5

14. For a general statement of the increased responsiveness of international trade to small price changes, see Richard N. Cooper, *The Economics of Interdependence: Economic Policy in the Atlantic Community* (New York: McGraw Hill, for the Council on Foreign Relations, 1968), esp. Chapter 3. See also the elasticity estimates presented in Chapter 9. And a system of "trotting pegs" has worked effectively in Brazil and several other developing countries, although the analogy between them and the industrialized countries, which are the focus here, cannot be pushed too far.

15. To prevent small parity changes from forcing changes in the market exchange rate, and unsettling the foreign exchange markets, the *total* band must be substantially wider than the maximum parity change. See Harry G. Johnson, "A Technical Note on the Width of the Band Required to Accommodate Parity Changes of Particular Size," in Bergsten *et al.*, *op. cit.*, pp. 280–81.

16. Herbert Giersch and Wolfgang Kasper, "A Floating German Mark: An Essay in Speculative Economics," in Bergsten *et al.*, *op. cit.*, pp. 345–55.

per cent from early 1962 until the onset of particularly intense speculation in mid-1967, with short-term fluctuations occurring (with one
exception) within a "band" of ±5 per cent.[17] These quantitative
results overstate the rate of devaluation and short-term fluctuation
required for sterling itself, because restrictions on capital exports were
progressively tightened during the period under review, the supply of
dollars available to this market was constantly reduced because one-
fourth of all gross sales of foreign securities had to be converted into
sterling (at the official exchange rate), and the maintenance of an
overvalued rate for all other transactions forced all speculation against
sterling into this market. So a British downward crawl within roughly
the same bounds as the German upward crawl might have met the
problem of sterling effectively as well.[18]

The U.S. situation is more conjectural. As early as 1962, some
analysts believed that the dollar was overvalued by anywhere from
4.5 to 22 per cent.[19] In 1968, Machlup estimated that the dollar was
overvalued by about 4 per cent,[20] and the numerous partial devaluations of the dollar which had occurred by that time amounted to

17. Wolfgang Kasper, "The Floating British Pound: A Postscript in Non-
Speculative Economics," unpublished paper presented to the Tarrytown
Conference of February 1969.
18. In addition, it can be argued that the British devaluation of 14.3 per cent
in 1967 was excessive. Just prior to that move, Richard N. Cooper in Richard
G. Caves, ed., *op cit.*, concluded that a devaluation of 8 per cent would
have sufficed. The sizable British surpluses of 1969–1971 and the willingness
to revalue against the dollar by about 8 per cent in 1971 appeared to support
this view, although the 1971 change in Britain's effective exchange rate represented a small devaluation. However, the U. K. external balance bene-
fitted from heavy domestic unemployment and huge U.S. deficits throughout
the same period, and a new devaluation was needed in 1972.
19. John E. Floyd, "The Overvaluation of the Dollar: A Note on the International Price Mechanism," *American Economic Review*, Vol. LV, No. 1
(March 1965), pp. 95–106 concluded that the overvaluation was probably
less than 4.5 per cent and certainly no more than 10 per cent. Jaroslav Vanek
derived a 15 per cent overvaluation through the use of econometric techniques in "The Balance of Payments, Level of Economic Activity, and the
Value of Currency: Theory and Some Recent Experiences," Three Lectures
Presented at the Graduate Institute of International Studies in Geneva, 1962.
Hendrik S. Houthakker's conclusion that the overvaluation in March 1962
was about 22 per cent was based simply on the use of German Statistical
Office data in a purchasing power parity calculation. See his "Exchange Rate
Adjustment" in *Factors Affecting the United States Balance of Payments*,
Compilation of Studies Prepared for the Reuss Subcommittee, 1962, pp.
287–304.
20. Fritz Machlup, "The Transfer Gap of the United States," *Banca Nazionale
del Lavoro Quarterly Review*, No. 86 (September 1968), p. 237.

the equivalent of an overall devaluation of about 1.5 to 2 per cent.[21] The 15 to 20 per cent dollar devaluation which finally did occur in 1971–73 thus represented a further deterioration of about 10–15 per cent. Any initial overvaluation as well as the subsequent deterioration could thus have been handled within the postulated limitations.

There are three major questions about the effectiveness of these possibilities for limited amounts of exchange-rate flexibility in considering whether they would have been superior to the adjustable peg system in the past: (1) Would the rate changes which did occur have taken place more smoothly? (2) Would additional adjustment or confidence problems, such as rate changes which did not take place but *should* have, have been met through rate fluctuations? (3) If so, would adjustment via the rate have been more desirable than what actually did occur?

There is a good possibility that the answer to all three questions is yes. Under the adjustable peg system, exchange-rate changes were treated as a last resort, especially if key currencies were involved. Thus they were both very large in size and delayed in coming at all. The expectation of such changes can touch off massive unsettlement in the exchange markets and threaten the stability of the entire system. As a result, meaningful international consultations on rate changes, as prescribed by the Articles of Agreement of the International Monetary Fund, entail very heavy costs. They cost the British a billion dollars or so of reserves in 1967 and induced Britain to move without notice to anyone the next time it had to, in 1972; they exacerbated the difficulties surrounding the German and French disequilibria in 1968 when the consultations at the Bonn Conference failed to produce the needed parity changes; and the dollar devaluation of 1971 was engineered only by suspending the operation of the entire system and risking a complete breakdown of international economic cooperation.

A devaluation has been widely considered as a blow to national prestige and an admission of policy failure,[22] and as "giving in to the

21. The figure is derived by crudely applying the degree of devaluation to the weight of that category in total U.S. international transactions (itself a crude number since only *net* figures are available in some categories) before the "devaluation"; e.g., the 15 per cent "devaluation" via the IET is applied to the first-half-of-the-1963 level of security purchases from countries subsequently covered by the tax and the 1964 level of term bank loans to those countries.

22. For a typical evaluation, contrast the attitude of former President Lyndon B. Johnson toward the devaluation of sterling in 1967 ("a heavy blow") and his grudging admiration for de Gaulle's refusal to devalue (even after France had agreed to do so at the Bonn conference) in 1968. *The Vantage Point* (New York: Holt, Rinehart and Winston, 1971), pp. 315–21.

speculators." It was a step taken only well after a disequilibrium had developed and after other measures, normally of a restrictive nature but sometimes (even in "dilemma" cases) inconsistent with domestic economic objectives, had been attempted. Revaluations were also resisted steadfastly, because they hurt the competitive position of exporters—who are politically powerful in many countries—and because they represent "solving the other fellow's problem."[23] The IMF Articles exacerbate these problems by requiring a demonstration of "fundamental disequilibrium" before a parity change is justified, and then requiring the problem to be solved in a single move.

The exchange-rate changes which did eventually take place were thus larger, and created more of a shock, than would have been necessary had they been taken earlier in the adjustment process. Such sizable changes have profound effects on the level and distribution of income within all economies, the more so the more open they are to international trade and capital movements. A government is seldom so satisfied with the state of its domestic economy that it wants to risk such shocks. And a government may not even have much confidence in the expected impact of a parity change, given the uncertainty of forecasting but even more so the uncertainty of how other countries will react to its move. This was a particular problem for the United States, since the conventional wisdom at least as late as 1968 suggested that virtually all countries would fully emulate any U.S. devaluation.[24]

These shortcomings could be remedied by a system of sliding bands. Small exchange-rate changes would have far smaller economic effects within countries than the large changes which characterize the adjustable peg system. They could, in fact, become normal instruments of economic policy—much like the small changes in the discount rate now utilized by the Federal Reserve System, or the small changes in prime rate utilized by many large banks. Sectors of the economy affected by international transactions would have less to fear, and hence political opposition to rate changes would decline. Governments would have less concern for losses of prestige or "capitulation to other countries." Perhaps most importantly, the wider band would permit spot exchange rates to fully anticipate the small

23. The most extreme resistance of this type came from Germany in the late 1960s, notably from Finance Minister Franz Josef Strauss but also endorsed by Chancellor Kiesinger and his CDU government.
24. For a lucid analysis of these shortcomings of the adjustable peg system in terms of the decision-making process, at both the national and international levels, see Stephen N. Marris, "Decision-Making on Exchange Rates," in Bergsten *et al.*, *op. cit.*, esp. pp. 77–80.

changes in parity—so the authorities could even blame "the market" for having caused the change to take place.

Smaller changes would also reduce the level of speculative capital flows between countries. We have already seen that the wider margins would by themselves reduce both speculative and interest-sensitive movements of liquid funds. The substitution of small for large parity changes would reinforce this effect by sharply reducing the size of the quick gains now available to the speculator. International consultation on rate changes would become possible, and would greatly improve the chances for knowing how other countries would respond, and hence for predicting the net outcome of the exercise.

It is likely that the rate changes which did occur would have taken place more efficiently had they done so by flexible movement within a band and through much smaller parity changes. Massive capital inflows to Germany, in large part out of the United Kingdom, preceded *and* succeeded each of the German revaluations, because speculators first anticipated that such a change would become necessary eventually and then anticipated that the change itself had been insufficient. Similar inflows drowned Japan, Canada, and several smaller countries in a flood of foreign exchange in 1970–71. Massive speculation cost the British dearly between late 1964 and the November 1967 devaluation, and additional speculation against sterling—plus a massive wave of gold speculation—continued thereafter. The actual French devaluation of 1969 was carried out amidst considerable calm, but only after the franc had been buffeted by repeated attacks during the second half of 1968. The dollar, of course, was subjected to widespread speculation in 1971 and again in 1973.

These flows carry three kinds of costs for the countries undergoing them. Domestic economic policy is undermined directly (especially for surplus countries) by the need to take policy actions to convince the markets that no parity changes are forthcoming. Governments and central banks in both surplus and deficit countries lose money from the national treasuries to speculators.[25] And deficit countries increase their interest payments to foreigners to finance the deficits which pile up awaiting eventual corrective action.

An earlier parity change would have reduced these problems in three ways. It would have smoothed out the changes over time and kept the country closer to its long-term equilibrium path. It would have reduced the expectation of further large changes beyond what

---

25. Cohen, *op. cit.*, concluded that Britain lost about $500 million in this way in 1964–67.

did occur. And, by beginning the adjustment process earlier, it would have reduced the total amount of adjustment needed. All three improvements would have sharply reduced the speculators' opportunity for sizable quick profits. Virtually every serious dilemma case has been eventually reconciled by a parity change, even under a system where such moves were so strongly resisted, so it is clear that the only issue is *how* best to effect such changes—not *whether* such changes will or will not take place.

Periodic flurries during the 1960s shook confidence in such currencies as the Canadian dollar, Swedish crown, and Italian lire, in cases where no rate changes were eventually needed. In some cases the speculative flurries were reversed, after some use of reserves, with no harm done. In other cases, however, the unnecessary reserve fluctuations which occurred induced the countries concerned to adopt policy measures unrelated to their basic external or domestic position. Had these flurries been able to work themselves out through slightly larger movements of the exchange rate, such policies would not have been necessary. In addition, and perhaps more importantly, the fact that the potential loss to speculators would be multiplied several-fold by the very existence of the broadened band suggests that the amount of speculation would be reduced by the very existence of such a system.

The case of the United States supports the same conclusion. To the extent that its deficits coexisted with underutilization of domestic resources, as occurred in at least the 1958–63 period and again in 1970–71, such flexibility would clearly have been desirable from the adjustment standpoint. Such adjustment was very much an *international* problem and clearly required adjustment by *both* Europe and the United States, since *both* sides of the imbalance were in large part "dilemma" cases—Europe's overfull employment plus payments surpluses mirroring the U.S. unemployment and deficits. The two periods differed sharply, however, in two ways: in 1958–63, the U.S. deficit was much smaller, and the current account (and especially trade) surplus was rising sharply, with U.S. prices much more stable than prices abroad. Exchange-rate changes in 1958–63 would thus have represented European acquiescence to an even bigger U.S. current surplus, whereas foreign cooperation with the devaluations which did occur in 1971–73 simply enabled the United States to rebuild its current surplus to some extent.

Nevertheless, there is reason to think that greater flexibility would have effectively promoted adjustment even in these most difficult cases. American willingness to change the dollar parity would certainly have increased European willingness to change their parities.

for the largely political but also economic reasons outlined earlier, as in fact it did in 1971 and 1973. And earlier adjustment of this disequilibrium via the exchange rate would have been far superior to the events that actually unfolded, especially the controls which proliferated as a result (and which played a major role in threatening to reverse the whole liberal tenor of postwar U.S. trade policy) and the political frictions (such as the constant U.S.-German hassles over offsets) which accompanied them.

There is thus at least a good chance that most of the necessary parity adjustments of the 1960s and early 1970s would have been carried out sooner, requiring smaller changes, under a system of sliding parities and a wider band. By taking effect gradually, there would have been less disruption, and less private speculation would have been attracted. As a result of the strongly reduced likelihood of speculation, countries would presumably have been less reluctant to let rates move. Counterproductive domestic policies, and especially external restrictions, could have been reduced if not fully avoided. In short, the adjustment process would have had a new tool which, compared with the role open to the exchange rate in practical terms during that period, could work more smoothly, less drastically, and with less harm to other objectives of national policy.

There remains the case where a really sizable parity adjustment is needed, triggered by a major event to which the needed response is outside the range of any conceivable band or which a sliding parity could not reach in any reasonable period of time. In such instances, a sizable adjustment of parity might still be required. Frequent large adjustments would destroy the credibility of the sliding parity system, and revive the problems of destabilizing speculation when the limits of the (even widened) band were reached. Indeed, some view this problem as sufficiently serious that such a system would not work unless large parity changes were absolutely forbidden.

However, such events are highly unlikely. The only candidate in recent years was the wage explosion in France instituted by the "events of May 1968." Even in that case, many observers feel that subsequent developments demonstrated that the 11 per cent devaluation which resulted a year later was excessive and perhaps even unnecessary. If such cases were to occur, however, at least a significant part of the needed change could still take place sooner and more gradually within the band than is the case today, and small parity changes could begin at once. Any further changes in parity could then be smaller, both because the earlier partial adjustment would have reduced the magnitude needed later and because part of the change would have already taken place within the band. The net result would be less destabilizing speculation and greater acceptability to national authorities.

A final problem with the sliding parity approach, by itself, is that widespread expectations that the parity would slide in one direction for some fairly lengthy period into the future would require a compensating interest-rate policy to prevent destabilizing capital flows. Interest-sensitive (not speculative) money would certainly flow out of depreciating currencies unless the announced degree of depreciation were offset by higher interest rates. A maximum depreciation of 3 per cent per year would require an interest rate higher by the same amount than prevails in any other comparable money markets. Thus the sliding parity approach could *reduce* the autonomy of monetary policy as an instrument to help meet the needs of the domestic economy, whereas a basic objective of limited rate flexibility is to free other economic instruments, including monetary policy, to concentrate on domestic policy targets.

This constraint may not be too great in practice, however.[26] In many cases, an overvalued exchange rate results from domestic inflation which would require high interest rates anyway. In any event, the relevant comparison is not with a system in which interest-rate constraints are absent, but the adjustable-peg regime—and it is likely that the constraint is less under the sliding parity, primarily because this approach holds promise of achieving adjustment of existing imbalances more effectively. In addition, international movements of interest-sensitive funds are motivated by *changes* in differentials, not by their absolute levels, as shown in Chapter 5. The commencement of a downward crawl would indeed trigger capital outflows, all other things being equal, but the volume of outflows would decline as the rate of crawl declined; and inflows—perhaps amounting to most of the funds that originally flowed out—would result from a cessation of the crawl and would not require a reversal of the downward movement.

In addition, we have already seen that widening the band discourages interest-sensitive flows and expands domestic monetary autonomy. It would thus provide a countervailing force to help combat any interest-rate constraint which resulted from the institution of a

26. This discussion draws heavily on Thomas D. Willett, "Short-Term Capital Movements and the Interest-Rate Constraint Under Systems of Limited Flexibility of Exchange Rates," in Bergsten, *et al., op. cit.,* pp. 283–94. He also notes that it should be easier to maintain a *consistently* higher level of interest rates, as could be required under a steadily crawling peg, than the highly *variable* rates which could be required under an adjustable peg which periodically require large changes.

sliding parity. So, the combination of the sliding parity with the widened band would serve to reduce conflict and produce an improved exchange-rate regime.

If all this is so, why not go the whole way to fully flexible rates? One reason, already noted, is simply that monetary authorities are more likely to accept *some* rate flexibility than *total* flexibility. Their widespread intervention since the general abandonment of parities in March 1973, albeit almost wholly in a constructive rather than competitive vein, pays vivid testimony to this conclusion.[27]

There are at least six major economic reasons why their view is correct, however. First, as already discussed, exchange-rate changes are the proper adjustment tool only in dilemma cases. They actually exacerbate the problems facing economic policy in non-dilemma cases.

Second, limited rate fluctuations would not have as much inhibiting effect on international transactions as would full flexibility, given the uncertainties which full flexibility might conjure up in the private sector and the greater cost of forward exchange which might result. This is particularly true because the creators of forward exchange markets, who play a critical role in enabling businessmen to purchase insurance against these uncertainties, would have both a smaller and more clearly defined task to perform.

Third, the presence of limits should reduce destabilizing capital flows, since the limitation on the potential profits for speculators against an existing rate is a major factor in the radical change from the adjustable peg system in the calculations which they face. In addition, the presence of the limits should encourage stabilizing speculation by increasing confidence that large parity changes will not occur. These two factors suggest that speculation will be more stabilizing under limited flexibility than under full flexibility, though both would be far superior to the adjustable peg on this criterion. This might in turn reduce the need of the authorities to intervene in the exchange markets, and hence reduce the need for official reserves.

Fourth, limited flexibility "undermines" the "discipline" of fixed rates less than does full flexibility in view of the limits on the amount of adjustment which can be achieved through the exchange rate in any short period of time. To the extent that the external sector in fact exercises "discipline" on internal policies, it will certainly do so

27. One early test of the use of reserves (i.e., the amount of intervention) under flexible as opposed to fixed rates found "modest economies," for the industrial countries, due to reduced use by Germany and the United States, but actual increases for the other developed and developing, countries. See Williamson, "Increased Flexibility and International Liquidity," *op. cit.*, pp. 4–10.

more in a regime under which the exchange rate may not achieve the total adjustment needed at a given time. Fifth, limited flexibility has less inflationary potential, partly because the rate itself can move less. But also labor will probably be willing to absorb small and frequent exchange-rate changes more easily, without demanding fully offsetting wage increases, than the large and abrupt changes which are the hallmark of the adjustable peg system.

Finally, and most important, "freely flexible rates" would be much more likely than limited flexibility to produce uncoordinated and even competitive market intervention by national authorities—"dirty floating," as it was so aptly labeled by German Economic and Finance Minister Karl Schiller in 1971. The 1971–73 experience was a vivid reminder that the political and economic forces which prompted such actions in the 1930s were by no means dead, despite the far better economic conditions enjoyed by all countries today. The risk of competitive policies in the exchange markets, which tilted the Bretton Woods system too far in the direction of discouraging all exchange-rate changes, must still be taken seriously into account in the search for an optimum monetary system.

Limited flexibility thus appears superior to full flexibility. We have just discussed one such approach: a combination of widened margins around parities and more frequent changes in the parities themselves. Another approach would encompass nominal devotion to freely flexible rates but with full recognition that national authorities would intervene to limit the degree of actual rate fluctuation. What are the differences between the two, and which (if either) appears superior from the standpoint of improving the functioning of the overall monetary system?

The major difference between the two approaches is the presumption on which each is based. A regime of "managed floats" presumes exchange-rate flexibility, while a regime of "gliding bands" presumes exchange-rate fixity. In either case, however, international rules would be needed: to assure against "dirty floating" in the former case, to assure adequate but not excessive flexibility in the latter. The objective of such rules, in either case, would be to trigger (or permit) appropriate rate changes and discourage inappropriate ones. Their nature would thus be central to either approach to limited flexibility.

One reason why rates have changed so infrequently in the past is that it is so difficult to tell when an imbalance represents "fundamental disequilibrium." There are always cogent arguments why the present imbalance is considered "only temporary" and, given time and the "proper use" of some more reserves, that balance will be re-established at the existing parity. So some observers doubt that sliding parities would in practice alter very much the actual frequency of exchange-rate changes unless they were triggered automatically by predetermined formulas. Similarly, predetermined formulas could be utilized to identify and check "dirty floating."

There are numerous bases for such formulas, such as the actual movement of spot exchange rates[28] or of reserves over some recent period.[29] The application of any such formula could then be mandatory on the country in question (Houthakker and Marsh), discretionary within some range but mandatory beyond it,[30] a basis for IMF intervention to force such a change if overall conditions warranted (Triffin and Hirsch), or presumptive only (Cooper).

No mandatory rules are likely to be adopted, simply because countries regard the exchange rate as such an important instrument of national sovereignty. There is a good economic reason for their reluctance to accept any *simple formula* based on a single variable, however, since no formula can accurately indicate at all times whether changes are needed. For example, currency depreciation may not be needed when a payments deficit coincides with excessive domestic inflation; indeed, it would exacerbate the domestic problem in such a non-dilemma case. Similarly, currency appreciation to adjust a payments surplus which coincided with high domestic unemploy-

28. For example, J. Black, "Proposal for Reform of Exchange Rates," *Economic Journal*, June 1966, pp. 28–95, which suggests that parities should change when the spot rate has changed by a given amount over a given time period. Analogously, a "managed float" could be permitted to set limits, based on the recent moves in its spot rate, beyond which it would not have to float.

29. This is the approach favored in the official U.S. reform proposal, announced in September 1972, which is presented in detail in an annex to the *Annual Report of the Council of Economic Advisers*, 1972, pp. 160–74. For the underlying analysis, see Hendrik Houthakker, "Some Reflections on the International Monetary System," speech given at the University of Bonn, April 16, 1969; Donald B. Marsh, "The Fixed-Reserve Standard: A Proposal to 'Reverse' Bretton Woods," in Bergsten *et al.*, *op. cit.*, pp. 261–69; Richard N. Cooper, "Sliding Parities: A Proposal for Presumptive Rules," *ibid.*, pp. 251–59; Robert Triffin, "How to Arrest a Threatening Collapse into the 1930s," *Bulletin of the National Bank of Belgium*, November 1971, p. 24. The various proposals incorporate different definitions of "reserves," different time periods during which the changes are to be measured, different amounts of reserve change needed to trigger parity moves, and different amounts and frequency of these moves. They all would trigger parity changes when reserve movements exceed a predetermined level. The "managed float" analogy would be a limitation on the amount of reserve changes permitted.

30. Thomas D. Willett, "Rules for a Sliding Parity: A Proposal," in Bergsten *et al.*, *op. cit.*, pp. 271–74, and Fred Hirsch, "The Exchange Rate Regime: An Analysis and a Possible Scheme," *IMF Staff Papers*, July 1971.

ment would make restoration of full employment even more difficult. Rules based either on reserve changes or spot exchange rates alone, if they applied to the United States, would have triggered depreciation of the dollar in the early 1960s and appreciation of the dollar in 1968–1969—though most observers would have called for opposite changes in view of the sharp growth in the current surplus from 1959 to 1964 and its rapid subsequent decline.

On the other hand, even major countries have already given up a great deal of sovereignty in the exchange-rate area. External economic pressures have forced exchange-rate changes in a number of cases. All the major parity changes of recent years—Britain in 1967, France and Germany in 1969, the United States and others in 1971 and 1973—were the subject of at least some international discussion, and the amounts of each may have been largely determined by the tolerance expressed by other major countries in those discussions. In fact, all recent changes have been based on the growing recognition that exchange rates are relationships between pairs of currencies and cannot be determined solely by any one country. (The United States, of course, has had little sovereignty over its own exchange rate because of the intervention role of the dollar and its passivity in the exchange markets.) Advocates of firm rules as a basis for parity changes respond to criticism of such rules by noting that domestic policy can compensate for any perverse internal effects thereof, and by arguing that rules are absolutely essential to assure more effective use of the exchange-rate mechanism. They note that the quicker response to disequilibria would also reduce the extent of any interest-rate constraint.

In principle, all of these responses are correct. The basic problem, however, is the intellectual difficulty of finding adequate rules on which to base a formula. Advocacy of simple rules simply underestimates the great difficulty already facing domestic policies in virtually all countries in achieving the complex of internal economic goals. The exchange rate has sizable economic effects, especially in economies more open to international transactions than the United States is, so the degree of additional complication caused by its perverse movements could be quite significant. As a result, countries would be even less willing to accept rules if they bound them to move their parities in non-dilemma as well as dilemma cases. On the other hand, the availability of an extra policy instrument which could help reconcile dilemma cases—without requiring perverse changes in domestic economic policy—should be gratefully accepted and implemented. Thus there is every reason to expect that countries would adhere to rules which focused on dilemma situations, although even here one could not be certain that small and frequent parity changes would not on occasion start off in a wrong direction and require subsequent reversal.

In practice, however, the problem is further complicated by the presence of purely *internal* economic dilemmas. Countries, like the United States and Britain in the early 1970s, frequently face a combination of high unemployment and excessive inflation. (There is no problem with the opposite "dilemma" of full employment and price declines.) A country might want to devalue to correct a payments surplus, in light of its inflation, but fear exacerbation of its unemployment.

Such problems can be solved only by bringing three policy instruments into play, since three separate economic objectives—full employment, price stability, and payments balance—are being pursued. Some would argue that monetary policy could be targeted solely on price stability and fiscal policy on full employment, with the exchange rate to take care of the balance of payments. However, we saw in Chapter 9 that part of the reason why mixing fiscal and monetary policy could not meet simple dilemma cases was the practical difficulty and sizable structural effects of using them in opposite directions. For the same reasons, they cannot be targeted on two separate domestic goals, especially when pursuit of the goals requires policy action in opposite directions. Indeed, "domestic macroeconomic policy" can be better thought of as single policy instrument rather than two separate instruments. In practice, it will generally be aimed at whichever of the two domestic problems is regarded as more serious at a given time or more susceptible to macroeconomic solutions.

The third instrument (exchange-rate policy being the second) must therefore be selective policies aimed at the other domestic problem. If macroeconomic policy focuses on restoring full employment (which would be proper if unemployment was due primarily to lagging domestic demand, and/or inflation had become primarily a cost-push rather than demand-pull phenomenon), incomes policy and other selective devices will have to lead the battle against inflation. If macroeconomic policy is aimed at checking inflation, because demand is excessive or unemployment is basically due to structural problems in the labor force, manpower programs will have to deal with much of the unemployment need.

A final consideration in adopting a proper combination of policies is the openness of the economy in question. As noted earlier, the comparative advantage of exchange-rate changes as an adjustment instrument is greater the more closed is the country. The comparative advantage of macroeconomic adjustment grows with the degree of openness of the country. Thus a relatively open economy with a payments deficit and an internal dilemma would be more likely to devalue to deal with the deficit and unemployment, while relying on selective (incomes) policy to cope with inflation.

This discussion indicates further why simple rules for exchange-rate changes, limited to indicators of the external payments position, are inadequate. There are too many different domestic situations which can correspond to any external position and which call for a different combination of policy responses, including exchange-rate moves. Analysis of individual cases will continue to be needed.

At the same time, however, the complexities highlight the difficulty of both achieving international agreement on a set of rules in the first place and implementing them after they are agreed. The initial agreement would obviously have to be negotiated among the key countries. But this leaves unanswered the crucial question of *who* will take the lead in implementation.

No individual country would be in a position to police the rules. Indeed, the United States never dominated this area vis-à-vis major countries even during its period of greatest hegemony. It could dictate parity changes, and then only devaluations, only to countries so heavily dependent on foreign aid that they had no choice. It failed miserably in its most overt effort to force a parity change on a major country: revaluation of the German mark at the Bonn conference in November 1968. It felt increasingly *victimized* by the devaluation bias of the system during the 1960s. And it achieved a realignment in 1971 only by devaluing itself, taking advantage of the floats already instituted by most of the other key currencies (with the notable exception of Japan) to get additional revaluations by a few others, and even then using extreme leverage (particularly the import surcharge) which threatened to undermine the broader interests of the United States itself. Changes in the exchange rate have remained a very real exercise of national sovereignty.

Nevertheless, exchange-rate changes have clearly become a matter of international concern, and the amounts and timing of such changes have become subjects of intense international discussion. All of the discussions have been ad hoc, however, based on analysis gathered rapidly (if at all) in response to the crisis of the moment. Yet, by hypothesis, any new regime of limited exchange-rate flexibility would be based on a set of rules adopted internationally. Only an international body could thus take the lead in their implementation, if actors others than the involved country are to play a systematic role on the issue.

The obvious candidates are Working Party 3 of the OECD or the Group of Ten, and the IMF, probably via the Interim Committee (of Twenty) which represents a de facto steering group within it.[31] In the negotiated realignment of late 1971, both the IMF and OECD secretariats provided important analyses of the needed changes, but the major negotiation took place in the Group of Ten. The previously important parity changes could not be discussed over any extended period, and any formal discussions took place (as at Bonn) at hastily called sessions of the Group of Ten. A case can be made for maintaining such flexibility in the future.

On the other hand, an internationally agreed code should have a designated custodian. This is the case for all existing codes. It is necessary to assure efficient procedures both for dealing with individual problems and for developing the kind of common law which will have to play a crucial role in this field.

On membership grounds, both the OECD and IMF would qualify.[32] Working Party 3 is perhaps marginally superior to any present IMF body on this score, since *all* of the key industrialized countries, the major actors in any exchange-rate realignment, are represented individually at all times. (The Interim Committee at the IMF excludes several industrial countries, including Switzerland, which is not a member of the IMF.)[33] Working Party 3 could also lay a strong claim to the function because its business is the adjustment process, and it has developed considerable experience in dealing with these problems of the major countries. Its Report on the Balance of Pay-

---

31. I exclude the BIS, since governments are—rightly—even less likely to turn these decisions over to an international organization of central bankers than to an international organization in which they provide the national representation themselves. I lump together Working Party 3 and the Group of Ten, since their membership is virtually identical and since they have worked on the same issues under the two different institutional hats for many years.

32. It is even conceivable that the less developed countries would *prefer* the OECD, to keep the rules from applying to them.

33. It is often charged, especially by U.S. officials, that the EC is over-represented in the OECD (and Group of Ten). Such charges are fully understandable, since it is indeed frustrating to confront a large group of countries which either take no position (because they cannot agree among themselves) or a rigidly common position (when they can). For this reason, as well as others outlined elsewhere in this book, early achievement of the monetary integration in Europe is highly desirable, since one representative could then speak for Europe. In fact, such a representational change should be made as soon as Europe agrees to maintain internally fixed exchange rates. Pending that day, however, the importance of each of these countries to the global structure of exchange rates condemns any organizational arrangement to including them if it is to deal effectively with the issue.

ments Adjustment Process in 1966 is the nearest precedent to presumptive rules heretofore agreed by any international body, even though it falls far short of the rules considered here and virtually fails to integrate exchange-rate mechanisms into its code.

In broad terms, the OECD has focused more explicitly on the interrelationship of national balance-of-payments positions while the IMF has directed its attention primarily to the problems of individual countries. The OECD has more experience than the IMF in dealing with trade measures, an advantage if such measures were to play a major role either as an alternative adjustment technique or as a means for forcing compliance from countries called on by the international rules to make exchange-rate changes. The OECD suffers from its use of unit voting, as opposed to the weighted voting of the IMF, but formal voting has not heretofore been important in either organization and would probably be even less important in such a sensitive area, at least for many years. The meetings of Working Party 3 have always been attended by top policy officials of the member governments, in contrast to the more technocratic qualifications of the Executive Directors of the IMF, but the Interim Committee of the Fund was created to deal with precisely that question.

In addition, the IMF has five major advantages over the OECD. Exchange rates are at the core of its purpose, whereas Working Party 3 is only one part of a much larger organization devoted to a far wider range of issues. Its universal membership would permit a broader application of the rules than would the OECD. Its constitution already provides legal authority for it to apply pressure for adjustment to deficit countries, through withholding credit from them, and to surplus countries, through the "scarce currency" clause. It has built up a great deal of operational experience in recommending exchange-rate changes through its active role in helping guide the policies of less developed countries.

Most significant, however, it is a creator of international liquidity through both SDRs and its regular credit operations, whereas the OECD has no important liquidity functions. If the SDRs were to assume an even more important role in world liquidity, or if a new international asset were created for consolidation of the overhang, the role of the IMF would grow correspondingly. The crucial link between adjustment and liquidity has been stressed throughout this book, and the initial SDR agreement itself "assumed" that SDRs would be created only if the adjustment process were improved so as to limit the resort to new liquidity to meet international monetary problems. It thus makes sense to lodge the two functions in the same institution. Credits to an individual country should be closely linked to the adjustment policies of that country as the IMF now does—but with the crucial exception of active consideration of exchange rates for the major countries. Liquidity creation for the system as a whole should take full account of progress in improving the adjustment process and the prospects for improving it further. In this context, countries would be forced to face the trade-off squarely: to accept larger additions to world liquidity if they refused to permit improvements in the adjustment process, and to support improvements in the adjustment process if they disliked sizable liquidity growth.

One elaborate scheme has been proposed to remedy the present organizational shortcomings of the IMF to take on such a task.[34] To avoid the problems caused by universality, it would authorize the creation of panels limited to countries with common interests. This would permit the Group of Ten, for example, to become a formal part of the IMF structure. The interests of other countries would be protected, however, by permitting representatives of other panels to participate fully in the discussions of any panel and by requiring the approval of a sizable weighted majority of the *entire* Fund membership for major policy actions. To avoid the problem of inadequate levels of representation, it would permit member countries to designate high-level officials to sit on the panels instead of the permanent Executive Directors. The panels would first consult on the balance-of-payments relationships among the countries represented, such as Working Party 3 does now. However, changes in reserves beyond some agreed norm would trigger a "special review" of a country's policies—or such a review could be forced by a simple majority vote of the panel even without such reserve changes. As a result of the reviews, the panel could informally recommend specific actions to the country in question. But it could also make formal recommendations to the Board of Governors of the Fund, which would become effective if approved by 70 per cent of its total voting power.

Finally, to increase the probability of improving the adjustment process, it might be necessary to authorize the international community to apply sanctions against a country which disobeyed any new rules or failed to observe any presumptive guidelines. At present, the Fund already has the authority to withhold its regular

34. "Long-Term International Monetary Reform: A Proposal for an Improved International Adjustment Process," A Report by the Panel on International Monetary Policy of the American Society of International Law (Washington, Feb. 1972). The panel included the U.S. Executive Director of the IMF and the Assistant General Counsel for International Affairs of the Treasury Department.

credits from deficit countries which fail to adopt acceptable policies. It can also declare as "scarce" a currency of a persistent surplus country, and authorize discrimination against its exports by the other members. Credit has indeed been withheld in numerous cases, even from such major countries as Britain and France, pending their acceptance of a sufficient adjustment program. On the other hand, the "scarce currency" clause has never been used.[35] The clause is faulty in concept anyway, because a surplus country can avoid its adjustment impact simply by providing more of its currency to finance its surplus.

The existing authorities provide a basis for meaningful sanctions to back up any new exchange-rate rules, however. The Fund could adopt a firm policy of denying credit to any country failing to make the prescribed parity changes, unless that country could demonstrate to the satisfaction of a bulk of the membership that its problem was temporary or that it had taken sufficient action in other areas. For surplus countries, the scarce currency clause calls for publication of a Fund report on the need for action by the country if it neither lends nor adjusts. Such publication would undoubtedly launch speculation that would help force the needed revaluation or termination of inappropriate intervention to take place. (The denial of credit would have the same effect on deficit countries, and the Fund could also be empowered to issue reports on them.) Indeed, as the markets themselves would continually analyze the economic situation of individual countries in terms of the agreed criteria, to try to anticipate exchange-rate moves as much as possible, the very existence of agreed rules should speed the decision-making process in member countries to comply with them.

More ambitious sanctions could of course be envisaged. Import controls according to the procedures of the present scarce currency clause are a possibility, but are unsatisfactory. They may hurt the countries *applying* them by adding to their inflations; they are difficult to administer, since the origins of trade flows are so difficult to detect without an elaborate customs system to police them; and they could presumably not be used within a customs union or free trade area. In addition, using trade measures for payments purposes in this way might encourage the use of trade measures as a substitute

35. Some would argue that the United States launched the Marshall Plan at least partly to avoid such discrimination against the dollar, so that the scarce currency clause was "successful" at least indirectly. The United States already tolerated near-universal discrimination against its exports at the time, however, so it is dubious that this consideration was very important to a decision made on much broader grounds.

for exchange-rate changes, whereas we saw earlier that such measures have proven totally ineffective as adjustment devices in the past and give additional impetus to the omnipresent threat of purely protectionist trade barriers.

Within the financial area alone, member countries could be called upon simply to stop intervening in their own markets to keep other currencies from breaking through their margins. This would both add to the speculation against a currency, by letting it actually pierce its ceiling or floor in some markets, and reduce the volume of reserves mobilized to combat it. In addition, the IMF itself could be authorized to enter the exchange markets to force rates in the needed direction—although this would be costly in revaluation cases, since the Fund would sell back the revalued currency at a price lower than it was bought, and is thus not very practical. The Fund could expand its sanctions against uncooperative countries by denying them SDR allocations, although this would not pinch surplus countries very hard because they would be earning reserves through their surpluses anyway. And, as originally proposed by Keynes for his Clearing Union in 1943, countries with excessive creditor balances could be *charged* interest on the excess.

This issue of international rules also arises with regard to the permissibility of official intervention within the wider exchange-rate margins, a limited case of the general issue of intervention in a no-parity regime, as already discussed. Intervention simply to smooth out market trends raises no problems. But intervention to counter the trend, as indeed practiced by some countries even within the narrow margins which prevailed until August 1971, would undermine the basic objectives of widening the band. The reluctance of countries to foreswear such intervention will of course vary directly with the amount of the widening, and one possibility is to limit the prohibition on intervention to a narrower "inner band" while permitting intervention within the rest of the broader band.[36]

However, there are also strong technical arguments against intervention in a world with a great number of freely moving rates. It would be exceedingly difficult to coordinate market intervention effectively.[37] Would London or New York (or Washington) deter-

---

36. Lawrence B. Krause, *Sequel to Bretton Woods* (Washington: Brookings Institution, 1971), pp. 35–36, proposed an "inner band" of ±1.5 per cent within total margins of ±3 per cent.

37. This is, in fact, one of the major arguments against even limited rate flexibility advanced, e.g., by Triffin, *The Evolution of the International Monetary System: Historical Reappraisal and Future Perspectives*, Princeton Studies in International Finance, No. 12, p. 39.

mine the dollar-sterling rate if each was free to move in terms of the other? What if countries disagreed where their cross-rate should be? The specter of the competitive depreciations of the 1930s begins to appear. And the dollar could fluctuate within the margins as much as other currencies only if (among a number of changes from present practice) infra-marginal intervention was avoided by all countries. No management within the band, plus full management at the limits, thus appears to be the best solution from the standpoint both of adjustment and of permitting more autonomous domestic monetary policies by discouraging interest-sensitive capital flows.[38]

Objections may be raised on the grounds that rate flexibility has taken place thus far without any such problems arising. The reason was that the United States did not intervene to maintain the exchange rate of the dollar *against other currencies*, and that most other major countries intervened for their own currencies *with dollars*. The "dollar exchange rate" was thus the *residual* of the transactions of all other major countries, and cross-rates were aligned by arbitrage through the dollar. It was noted in Chapter 11 that a restoration of this intervention system is possible—but that the United States should be willing to accept it only if it were to receive the international support needed to protect it against the costs of the intervention role of the dollar discussed in Chapter 10. So intervention within the band is technically possible, if conceptually undesirable.

Another possible limitation on flexibility is to permit *upward* movements of parities only. As discussed in Chapter 2, one of the most significant weaknesses of the Bretton Woods adjustment process was the asymmetrical pressure it placed on deficit countries relative to surplus countries. There were far fewer pressures, from both internal and external sources, to revalue than to devalue. The ability of the United States to adjust suffered from the resulting devaluation bias of the exchange-rate regime.

In addition, upward flexibility would presumably avoid some of the dangers feared from downside flexibility. Deficit countries would not be given a new "soft option" which could relieve them from the "discipline" of the balance of payments. Inflation in individual countries, and in the world as a whole, would not be accelerated by frequent devaluations. Indeed, world inflation would be dampened if a

38. Unless an *international* body were given authority to do *all* the market intervening necessary to smooth out undue fluctuations in rates. Meade would prefer just such an international body, but recognizes that it is a nonstarter politically. See his "Exchange Rate Flexibility," *op. cit.*, pp. 17-18.

greater share of the adjustment burden could be borne by revaluations than by devaluations. The risk of fostering competitive depreciations, which dominated thinking at Bretton Woods and remains important today, would be avoided.

The main objection to this approach is that it leaves unresolved the need to improve the system for countries which need to devalue. Large disequilibria could still build up, which would lead to the usual problems for the deficit countries themselves. In addition, however, these problems could put major pressure on the system—especially if the major countries were running deficits—and hence undermine the credibility of maintaining both the slower rate of appreciations of surplus countries and the (even widened) margins around parities. The past devaluation bias should not be replaced by a revaluation bias. This issue is particularly important for the United states, and will be considered further in our analysis of the effects on it of limited flexibility of exchange rates.

Who Should Flex?

The final possible limitation to flexibility is its geographical scope. The earliest debaters on fixed versus flexible exchange rates argued (at least implicitly) that all countries should adopt one regime or the other. However, further reflection has led even the most ardent supporters of flexible rates (e.g., Friedman) to admit that fixed rates were superior for some countries, and the most ardent supporters of fixed rates (e.g., Triffin) to recognize that flexible rates were better for at least some groupings. A refined search then began for the criteria on which the decision to fix or flex, for an individual country, should be based.[39]

Four criteria have been proposed. The first in genealogy suggested that an optimum currency area—the area within which exchange rates should be fixed, and whose unified rate should flex toward the rest of the world—should be based on a high degree of labor mobility, where production could respond rapidly to changes in demand and sizable unemployment could be avoided without a need for

---

39. For a brilliant synthesis of the literature, on which this explanation draws heavily, see Marina V. N. Whitman, "Place Prosperity and People Prosperity: the Delineation of Optimum Policy Areas," in Mark Perlman, Charles J. Leven, and Benjamin Chinitz, eds., Spatial, Regional and Population Economics: Essays in Honor of Edgar M. Hoover (New York: Gordon and Breach 1972).

exchange-rate changes.[40] Since labor is generally highly immobile internationally, and even within some countries, this meant that the optimum currency area should be very small.

A second proposal, which supports the first, is based on our earlier conclusion that exchange-rate changes are needed in dilemma cases but may be mistaken in non-dilemma cases. It notes that small and open economies are more likely to face dilemmas, because external disturbances have a far greater impact on their economies: an increase in foreign demand for their products leads them to the dilemma situation of full employment and payments surplus much more readily than it would for a large and closed economy, which is much more likely to be dominated by internal developments. Therefore, small and open economies are more likely to need flexible exchange rates.[41]

The third proposal reached the opposite conclusion: that an optimum currency area is very large and relatively self-sufficient.[42] This is so largely because the value of money, in achieving efficient allocation of economic resources, is maximized by increasing the size of its domain—and fixed exchange rates represent the closest international approximation to a common currency within a single country. In addition, exchange-rate changes are relatively effective in achieving external adjustment in such economies because their small foreign sectors typically imply much higher price elasticities than do small open economies,[43] and because the impact of exchange-rate changes on domestic prices is small enough not to vitiate their adjustment effects. By contrast, a small and open economy cannot use flexible rates as effectively, because inflationary costs offset a large part of the effect on the external balance. In any event, the cost of adjust-

---

40. Robert A. Mundell, "A Theory of Optimum Currency Areas," *American Economic Review*, Vol. LI, No. 4 (September 1961), pp. 657–65. Peter B. Kenen, "The Theory of Optimum Currency Areas: An Eclectic View," in Mundell and Swoboda, eds., *op. cit.*, pp. 41–60, supports this view by arguing that a large and diversified economy does not need flexibility because it can absorb the shocks caused by changes in external demand through shifting resources rapidly from one sector to another, whereas a small and open economy cannot and thus does need a flexible exchange rate.
41. Whitman, *op. cit.*, p. 13.
42. Ronald I. McKinnon, "Optimum Currency Areas," *American Economic Review*, Vol. LIII, No. 4 (September 1963), pp. 717–25.
43. See especially Guy H. Orcutt, "Exchange Rate Adjustment and the Relative Size of the Depreciating Bloc," *Review of Economics and Statistics*, Vol. XXXVII, No. 1 (February 1955).

ing through internal policy changes are less for such a country.[44]

The fourth possible criterion is the degree of compatibility between the policy objectives and the economic structures of the countries involved.[45] Different rates of inflation are impossible within a currency area. Therefore, differences in national Phillips curves, or in the preferences of different countries for locating on their respective Phillips curves (i.e., their choice between unemployment and inflation), will produce a higher level of unemployment than each would seek if not a member of a currency area. The significance of these rates of unemployment—or, alternately, the size of the transfers among members of the currency area to avoid them through the equivalent of domestic "regional policies"—varies positively with the differences in national Phillips curves and national choices on the inflation-employment trade-off. The ideal currency area would thus comprise countries with identical Phillips curves and identical views on this trade-off.[46]

This final criterion resolves the contradiction between the first two criteria and the third, at least partially, by suggesting that the "feasible currency area"[47] should be neither excessively large nor excessively small. On the one hand, such an area should be large enough that the money it uses promotes efficient utilization of its resources. It should also be large enough that the costs to units within the area of adjusting to "external" imbalances through altering domestic policy exceed the costs of adjusting through changing the exchange rate. On the other hand, it should be small enough to make it feasible for countries to align their Phillips curves, align their policy preferences along their respective Phillips curves, or adopt "regional policies" to avoid undue economic hardships to areas hurt by the formation of the currency area. As always, either adjustment or financing is possible; though *within* a currency area, which may also be a customs union and/or economic union, the choices of exchange-rate changes

44. For empirical evidence, see Heller and Kreinen, *op. cit.*, who found that adjustment via domestic policy was less costly than adjustment from exchange-rate changes for Italy, Sweden, and Switzerland, but more costly for the United States, Canada, Japan, Germany and Britain.
45. Whitman *op cit.*, pp. 18–25 and James C. Ingram, "Comment," in Mundell and Swoboda, *op. cit.* A somewhat similar argument was made much earlier by Nobel Economics Prize winner Ragnar Frisch, "On the Need for Forecasting a Multilateral Balance of Payments," *American Economic Review*, Vol. XXXVII, No. 4 (September 1947), pp. 535–51.
46. For empirical support, see G. C. Archibald, "The Phillips Curve and the Distribution of Unemployment," *American Economic Review*, Vol. LIX, No. 2 (May 1969), pp. 124–34.
47. An apt term coined by Max Corden in his *Monetary Integration*.

and direct controls are ruled out and the only options are financing or adjustment via the domestic economy, i.e., more inflation or more unemployment.

Nation-states are obviously the minimum optimum currency areas for political reasons (even though theory suggests that this is not always true in purely economic terms.) Thus the operational question is what countries should combine to optimize the combination of exchange-rate fixity among themselves and at least a limited degree of flexibility toward the rest of the world. The criteria just analyzed suggest that. the combination should be large and self-sufficient enough so that exchange-rate flexibility will be an effective tool of external adjustment without causing undue domestic disturbances; if it does not do so, then adjustment via the domestic economy may be less costly even in dilemma cases. In addition, however, the countries must either have quite similar economic structures or the political will to take compensating action.

The de facto dollar area which developed in the postwar period, as described in Chapter 3, was based on financial transfers and, to some extent, on similar policy preferences. Member countries financed U.S. deficits by accumulating dollars, and the United States provided (official or private) financing when the members were in need. The members all sought to avoid adjustment; the outer countries because they feared the effects on their competitive positions or national security (if U.S. troops were withdrawn), the United States because it placed broad foreign policy concerns above its narrowly defined economic interests. The sterling area was similarly based.

For the future, however, currency areas are unlikely to be based on such unlimited financing or convergence of goals, for reasons outlined throughout this book. Thus, different sets of economic criteria will have to underlie any such groupings.

In practice, only a few pairs of important industrialized countries appear to have very similar Phillips curves (see Table 3).[48] A high degree of political determination to choose points on each national Phillips curve consistent with a common area-wide rate of inflation, or to effect "regional" transfers, would thus be necessary for any of these countries (except the United States and Canada) to form a currency area. The only grouping of major countries where such will may exist is the European Community.[49] But sizable intergovern-

---

48. Erich Spitaller, "Prices and Unemployment in Selected Industrial Countries," *IMF Staff Papers*, Vol. XVIII, No. 3 (November 1971), esp. p. 550.

49. Based on the experience of the 1960s, the EC could presumably achieve a common rate of inflation of about 3.5 per cent if member countries were willing to accept the following rates of unemployment: Belgium, 3 per cent;

mental transfers, mainly from Germany to the others, would be necessary for even this particular currency area to have a chance to work. It is for precisely this reason that Germany has insisted that "economic integration"—i.e., convergence of national Phillips curves or alignment of national trade-offs at a level of price stability accepta- ble to Germany—parallel fully the progress toward monetary union; and it even forced agreement to abandon the latter effort if by 1975 there is no progress on the former.

Two caveats should be registered, however. One is that the on- going process of economic integration within the EC is presumably reducing the differences in the national Phillips curves of the member states.[50] Increased mobility of labor and capital between the coun- tries should have such an effect. So far, however, the four large members (Germany, Britain, France, Italy) remain relatively self- sufficient, as measured by their dependence on trade even with other member countries, and there appears to be no convergence of rates of price increases nor of preference functions among EC members.[51] The second caveat is that *some* fluctuations in exchange rates be- tween the member country currencies, albeit of smaller magnitude than the fluctuations permitted toward the rest of the world, will be

---

France, 2.25 per cent; Germany, 0.7 per cent; Italy, 3.6 per cent; Nether- lands, 1.4 per cent; Britain, 2.4 per cent. However, the implied unemploy- ment rates might be intolerably high for all of the countries except Germany and the Netherlands; for example, Belgium projected unemployment at 1.7 per cent for 1970–75; France, 1.6 per cent; and Italy, 3 per cent.

50. Bela Balassa, "Monetary Integration in the European Common Market," in Alexander Swoboda, ed., *Europe and the Evolution of the International Monetary System* (Leiden: A. W. Sijthoff, 1973), concludes that: "It would appear that, given the intercountry differences in the transformation and the preference functions, the attainment of the optimal combination of growth, employment and price stability in the individual Common Market countries is not compatible with balance of payments equilibrium under fixed exchange rates." Balassa proposes that adoption of a limited form of exchange flexibility *within* the EC would help rather than retard progress toward economic unification. For an expression of the Italian concern that any EC monetary integration include an effective "regional" policy, see Giovanni Magnifico, *European Monetary Unification for Balanced Growth: A New Approach*, Princeton Essays on International Finance, No. 88 (August 1971).

51. Balassa, *ibid.* The medium-term national programs for 1970–75 encompassed price deflator rises varying from 2.2 per cent for Germany to 4 per cent for Belgium and the Netherlands—leading to a cumulative price difference of over 10 percentage points over the period. However, there has been since the early 1950s a steady increase in intra-EC trade relative to national income for the *original* EC members (*not* for Britain), though no corresponding decline in their openness vis-à-vis non-EC countries; see Ronald J. McKinnon, "The Dual Currency System Revisited," in Johnson and Swoboda, eds., p. 86.

permitted in the early stages of their monetary unification and hence relieve some of the strains on national policy choices.

Many other countries, of course, are so small and open to the world economy that adjustment of the internal economy is a more effective policy instrument for them in pursuing external equilibrium under almost any conditions than are exchange-rate changes. They face something of a dilemma, however, because few of them have similar Phillips curves or policy preferences with the major countries to which they might fix their exchange rates. But under some circumstances they may be able to receive transfers from those countries through the private capital markets, government aid programs, or preferential trade arrangements.[52]

Under a generally more flexible international exchange-rate regime, each country would have to decide whether to fix its rate to some major currency or to take advantage of the new opportunities. The choice might differ over time, depending on the performance of the center country or countries. Economic conditions in the center are rapidly transferred to an outer country under fixed rates, whereas the outer country can insulate itself from policy errors or undesirable performance in a center (or other) country through flexible rates. The stability of pegging to the dollar, even if it is regarded as an overriding benefit in most instances, loses much of its appeal if U.S. inflation exceeds a rate which is tolerable to the outer country. Since the outer country has too little economic weight to force the United States to accept more unemployment, to regain an acceptable price level, it can avoid the inflationary pressures only by breaking its link to the dollar. Those countries closest to a reserve center—and hence most likely to link to its currency during normal times—also feel such pressures soonest and with greatest impact and are most likely to break away. Canada decided to float for precisely this reason in 1970.

In the final analysis, a country will make a political choice as to whether the economic gains of fixing its exchange rate in terms of some other currency, or more formally joining a monetary area, is worth the loss of national sovereignty that is involved. The foregoing analysis has demonstrated, however, that one must distinguish between real and nominal sovereignty, just as one distinguishes between real and nominal interest rates. A small country which is very open

52. Preferred access to the London capital market and tariff preferences were the main inducements to join the sterling area in the 1930s, and to remain in it until the recent erosion of both with British entry to the EC. Virtually all sterling countries, through their concurrent membership in the Commonwealth, also had preferred immigration rights into the United Kingdom itself and thus a small degree of labor mobility.

to the world economy has little real economic sovereignty; thus it "gives up" little or none by abstaining from the exercise of even limited flexibility of exchange rates. On the other hand, a large and closed economy would give up a great deal of real sovereignty by disdaining the exchange-rate option. In the case of the European Community, the possible loss of real sovereignty is very real. At least three members of the Community—Germany, Britain, and France—are sufficiently large and closed economies, even in terms of their EC partners, that they can use the exchange rate as an effective tool of adjustment. All three have in fact done so in recent years. So they will have to place heavy weight on the political objectives of monetary integration, and the long-term efficiency effects of creating such a unit, to be willing to undertake the steps necessary to make it work.

Effects on Liquidity

As previously noted, none of these approaches to limited exchange-rate flexibility addresses directly the question of the amount of reserves. Their basic aim is to improve the adjustment process. But liquidity and adjustment are perfect substitutes in at least the short run: the more of one, the less needed of the other. This principle suggests that a shift to greater exchange-rate flexibility would reduce the world's needs for reserve holdings if it were successful in its stated objective of improving adjustment.

Since countries would presumably adopt any modified exchange-rate system only if they thought that it would improve the adjustment process, they should simultaneously conclude that their need for reserves would be less than it would otherwise have been. However, some countries might lack confidence that the regime of greater rate flexibility would endure, and so wish to continue to build reserves against a possible return to less flexibility when the level of their international transactions or payments imbalances might be a good bit higher.[53] Such an attitude might assure a short life for the attempt

53. This question is complicated because some advocates of exchange-rate flexibility, especially of these limited varieties, view it as a "second best" way-station to a world of unalterably fixed rates (not rates "fixed until further notice," as at present) at a later stage when economic integration among at least the major countries has proceeded to the point where adjustment to imbalance will take place through coordination of national policies. (Some others view limited flexibility as a way-station to full flexibility). Such improved coordination should also minimize the need for reserves, however, since adjustment (of a different type) would by hypothesis be much more effective than in the past. The obvious way to reconcile short-run flexibility and reduced need for reserves, with long-run fixity of parities even if the latter were felt to require large reserves once more, would be a large-scale one-time creation and distribution of international assets at the time the change to the latter system was made.

to use rate flexibility in a self-fulfilling way, since countries could obtain reserves only by braking appreciation of their exchange rates and hence frustrating the basic objective of the system (unless sufficient reserves were increased for the system as a whole, e.g., via SDR creation, to satisfy these desires).

There is a minority dissent from the view that greater exchange-rate flexibility will reduce the need for international reserves. While admitting that the need for reserves to cope with *basic* deficits will be reduced, this view holds that an even greater increase in reserves will be required to cope with strictly *temporary* deficits.[54] The reason given is that private capital movements play a major equilibrating function under a system of fixed parities in cases where exchange-rate fluctuation stems from purely temporary phenomena and where there is no uncertainty about the basic parity, by entering the market as the rate approaches its limits due to the small risk and potential gain involved. With a flexible rate system, however, such capital might not appear because of uncertainty about how far the rate might go before it was reversed. For the same reason, monetary policy and other techniques of official management could not be used because uncovered capital movements would take the bait only if the inducements were so great as to entail unacceptable domestic costs. The authorities, in addition, would want to minimize such fluctuations because of their inhibiting effects on international transactions and internal economic developments. They would therefore intervene to prevent much fluctuation, and would need *more* reserves to do so than under fixed parities because of the absence of private resources coming into play.

This reasoning might conceivably be correct with regard to freely flexible rates, but it simply does not apply to the sliding band variant. The private forces which have operated at the narrow margins in the past would then operate at the wider margins, and we concluded above that private activity would be *more* stabilizing under such a system. Even if there were official management within the band, the argument that greater reserves would be needed underestimates greatly the ability of the private money markets. It assumes that the official monetary authorities can see better what is temporary

---

54. See Roy Harrod, *Reforming the World's Money* (New York: St. Martin's Press, 1965), pp. 45–50, and James Meade, "The International Monetary Mechanism," *op. cit.*, p. 13. Harrod (p. 51) admits that such a comparison rests wholly on personal judgment, and is primarily interested in arguing against a glib assumption that greater rate flexibility reduces the need for reserves. He deals only with the case of rates theoretically free to fluctuate completely.

and soon to be reversed than can the private market, whereas there is no evidence to support such a view.

It is of course impossible to judge definitively how much the reduction in needed reserves might be, just as it is impossible to say how large reserves should be or how much they should grow under a system of fixed parities. It would be no more logical to say that a three-fold widening of the band would reduce to one-third the need for reserves (or need for growth therein) than it is to say that, in the absence of such a change in the tools for adjustment, reserves should grow *pari passu* with world trade. We can be sure only that the need should decline relative to what would otherwise have been the case.

The Effects on the Dollar

Two major considerations are often cited as militating against any possible interest in greater flexibility of exchange rates on the part of the United States.

The first relates to adjustment and runs as follows. Greater movements of exchange rates would produce more depreciations than appreciations because of the greater pressures on deficit than on surplus countries, because of the general reluctance of countries to lose reserves or risk deterioration of their competitive positions, and because it would lead to a relaxation of the "discipline" of fixed rates. These exchange-rate movements would take place against the dollar, because of its role as the pivot currency of the system. The dollar would, thus, become increasingly overvalued and the competitive position of the United States would steadily deteriorate.

The second relates to confidence and liquidity. One important reason for the past attractiveness of the dollar, in its various international roles, was the widespread perception of the stability, relative to other currencies, of its price in terms of other currencies. (Its price stability in terms of gold is also important for some monetary authorities.) Increasing flexibility of exchange rates would destroy this stability and, hence, jeopardize both future increases in foreign dollar holdings and the huge volume of outstanding dollar assets. Introduction of such flexibility could, thus, pre-empt an important source of financing for any future U.S. balance-of-payments deficits.

These two considerations contradict each other and reflect the same schizophrenia about the effect of exchange-rate changes on a key currency discussed in Chapter 9. If American adjustment is prejudiced by depreciations against the dollar greater than would be called for by relative price changes, the resulting appreciation of the dollar with regard to a weighted average of all other foreign currencies could only result from the willingness, or even desire, of both official and private foreigners to increase their dollar holdings. In turn, this appreciation—or even a widespread perception that such appreciation was likely—would *increase* the attractiveness of the dollar as a financial asset. It would thus enhance the likelihood that dollar accruals abroad would provide financing for any American payments deficits prompted by the added appreciation of the dollar.

Conversely, any actual or expected net depreciation of the dollar beyond what would be called for by relative price changes—which might stem from foreign distaste for dollars and, in turn, discourage foreign holdings—would contribute to an improved competitive position for the United States and to an improvement in its balance of payments. The United States would thus need less balance-of-payments financing, and need be less concerned about any decline in the attraction of the dollar to foreign holders which results. It would thus benefit from either the adjustment *or* the confidence-liquidity effects of greater exchange-rate flexibility.

However, the benefits to the United States from a system of greater exchange-rate flexibility would depend importantly on how such a system would work in practice. In turn, the U.S. choice between seeking better adjustment for itself or renewed financing potential from the dollar would be crucial in deciding how to set up that system. The risk of a new depreciation bias against the dollar, and hence a perverse adjustment effect on the United States, could be reduced if the dollar could fluctuate more freely along with other currencies. This raises seven possible ways, encompassing either flexibility via "managed floats" or a via a return to a regime based on parities or central rates:

1. The dollar could remain the market and parity pivot (perhaps resuming convertibility into U.S. reserves at a fixed price) with all other currencies free to fluctuate more freely in terms of the dollar. This makes sense systemically since only $n-1$ currencies can fluctuate consistently in a world of "n" currencies (or currency areas). It would represent the smallest change from the Bretton Woods system, in which discrete parity changes and flexibility within the margins took place in terms of the dollar.

2. A mixed system could be adopted, in which the dollar remained the *market pivot* but SDRs or gold became the *parity pivot*. Dollars would remain the pivot currency against which other currencies fluctuated within the wider margins. However, the parity of the dollar *and* the parities of other currencies would be denominated in terms of some common numéraire, presumably SDR, against which all could change by small amounts. Changes in the dollar parity could thus proceed without con-

comitant changes in the parities of others, and changes in cross-rates would presumably proceed automatically from the changes in parities.

3. Either SDRs or gold could become the parity pivot, as in the previous option, but the dollar could also share the role of market pivot with at least several of the other major currencies. If intervention were effected by each country for its own currency in all major exchange-rate markets instead of going through the dollar, the dollar could then fluctuate about as much as any other currency both in terms of its parity and within the margins around a given parity. This is the approach implicitly suggested in the reform proposal made by the U.S. Secretary of the Treasury George Shultz in September 1972, and subsequently considered by the Committee of Twenty under the heading of "multi-currency intervention."

4. A currency other than the dollar could become the pivot of the system, with all other currencies, including the dollar, free to fluctuate more freely with respect to it. This is not a practical option at present, because, as Chapter 11 showed, no other currency is a plausible candidate for the center role on a global scale.

5. All currencies, including the dollar, could be free to fluctuate more freely in terms of gold, with market intervention carried out in gold. This would require reintegration of the official and private markets for gold, including legalization of private gold holdings everywhere. It would almost certainly require a massive initial increase in the price of gold, even from present market levels, to enable present holders of dollars to acquire enough gold to use for intervention purposes without completely draining the reserves of the United States and other larger holders, with the effects outlined in Chapter 11. Under this option, the value of world reserves would be subject to sizable fluctuation as the price of gold and of any national currencies held in reserves fluctuated relative to each other, thus injecting a new element of instability into the system.

6. All currencies, including the dollar, could be free to fluctuate more freely in terms of Special Drawing Rights, with market intervention in SDRs. This approach is only a theoretical possibility at present, since SDRs can be held only by monetary authorities. Any extension of its use to include the private sector would run into the problems discussed in Chapter 11.

7. The concept of market intervention could be abandoned altogether and replaced by frequent clearing of balances among

central banks, as also outlined in Chapter 11. Central banks could accumulate all other currencies with an assurance that any net balances would be converted periodically. There would be no need for an intervention currency.

The effects of greater exchange-rate flexibility on the dollar would depend on which of these options were chosen. In Chapter 11 we reached certain conclusions about the effects on the dollar of replacing it with a different national currency or with SDR, and of a sizable increase in the price of gold, which need not be repeated here. This analysis will consider only the *additional* effects on the dollar of adopting limited flexibility of exchange rates under the different possible approaches.

Under option 1, each of the fluctuating countries would define its currencies in terms of the dollar and intervene in the exchange markets in dollars, as they have in the past. The United States would remain passive with regard to both parity changes and market intervention, which would obviate the international coordination problems that could be caused if the monetary authorities of the key currency country and of other countries had different ideas about the proper exchange rates between their currencies. The dollar could fluctuate vis-à-vis any single currency in the markets only half as much as could any other currency in the markets, and it would still be difficult for the United States to initiate parity changes.

Even with such a passive exchange-rate policy, the United States would certainly not be indifferent to the exchange-rate movements that occurred in a world of greater flexibility. The reasons were stated above: the United States could get either more adjustment or more financing, and might frequently prefer more adjustment. And each of the various biases of the Bretton Woods system against the dollar should be removed, or at least mitigated, if greater flexibility of exchange rates were to work in practice as outlined in theory, even without active changes in the dollar parity.

The system would be based on rules or presumptions under which a surplus country would have the same responsibility to permit appreciation of its currency as a deficit country would have to permit depreciation of its currency. The same rules or presumptions would assure that the *amount* of the appreciation was sufficient to remove the disequilibrium. Further, they should reduce the *amount* of currency depreciations by making an earlier start on the removal of disequilibrium and therefore reducing the extent of the adjustment needed. The rules should provide countries with a high degree of confidence that depreciation could continue until a new equilibrium rate was reached, and so reduce the need to overshoot the mark. They should also reduce the "follow-the-leader" tendency to devalue, because any rate could begin to move as soon as disequilibrium became apparent, and because greater flexibility would de-dramatize and de-politicize changes in rates and make countries less reliant on justifying changes in their own rates by linking them to similar changes in other countries.

In terms of adjustment, the United States would thus benefit to some degree from the reduction in the amounts of depreciation of other currencies and perhaps in the number of such depreciations. This suggests that the United States should prefer a symmetrical system of greater flexibility to an asymmetrical system that permitted only upside flexibility. The great benefit for the United States, however, would come from the elimination (or any reduction) of the revaluation-devaluation asymmetry of the Bretton Woods system.

In practice, of course, the United States might not be able to count on the rules or presumptions working as well as they should in theory. It would therefore strengthen the probability that it would achieve needed adjustment promptly and adequately if it could actively move the dollar parity as well, even if it continued as the market pivot against which other currencies intervene, as would be the case under option 2. The depreciation bias against the dollar within the exchange-rate margins, even if they were widened to as much as ±5 per cent, would be small over time relative to the problem caused for the United States if it could not actively change the dollar *parity*. In addition, any bias within the wider margins would hurt the U.S. balance of payments, and hence increase the likelihood that devaluation of the dollar parity would be called for by the parity rules or presumptions, thus offsetting the initial adverse effect on U.S. adjustment. So the mixed approach of option 2, with the dollar remaining as passive market pivot but with a potentially active parity policy against one other numéraire, would protect the United States fully.

The United States could go even further, however, and also insist on as much flexibility for the dollar to fluctuate freely as was enjoyed by any other currency. This could theoretically be done through substituting some other intervention asset for the dollar, as in options 4–6, but we saw in Chapter 11 that none of them was feasible. It could also be done by abandoning the intervention system altogether, which we saw in Chapter 11 was possible but costly. It could be largely done, at the least cost, through option 3 which will be discussed in the last section of this chapter, since it would represent at least a partial step toward a multiple reserve currency system.

The adoption of an active parity policy by the United States, even without any changes in the intervention role of the dollar, would represent a significant change in the operation of the international monetary system.[55] The dollar and *all other* currencies would declare their parities in terms of SDR, and the United States along with all others could change its parity in terms thereof. The dollar parity could move as much against any currency as any pair of other currencies could move against each other, removing the historical asymmetry where the dollar could move only half as much and enabling the United States to get more adjustment. The SDR pivot would help the United States combat the devaluation bias, which could well remain in the attitudes of other countries even under presumptive rules. It would make exchange-rate changes politically easier, and hence much more likely, in cases when the dollar is out of line against most other countries since the United States could then more easily move itself instead of waiting for a large group of others. In short, it would give the United States sovereign control over its exchange rate for the first time in at least forty years.

Such a change would also benefit the system as a whole. America's sharing of the burden of *initiating* adjustment would meet legitimate foreign complaints that the United States was malignantly neglecting its balance of payments through the one policy tool, the exchange rate, the costs of which are acceptable to it in both economic and political terms. And it would provide better systemic results, if U.S. price performance were non-modal or if changes in U.S. monetary policy would otherwise trigger huge and unsettling capital flows.

A comparison between the effective adjustment which the United States would have achieved under a passive and active parity policy has been simulated for 1960–69.[56] Assuming a formula-variant sliding

55. This issue was first raised by Stephen Marris, "The Burgenstock Communique," *op. cit.*, pp. 47–50, and was labelled the "Marris heresy" since changes in the dollar parity were regarded as heretical even at that late date. It has been most thoroughly analyzed by John Williamson, "The Choice of a Pivot for Parities," *Princeton Essays in International Finance*, No. 90 (November 1971). Williamson then believed that SDRs were likely to retain their gold-value guarantee for at least the immediate future, so refers to "gold/SDR" as the alternative pivot to the dollar.

56. Edward Howle and Carlos F. J. Moore, "Richard Cooper's Gliding Parities: A Proposed Modification," *Journal of International Economics*, Vol. II, No. 4 (November 1971), pp. 429–36. Cooper, in his comment, pp. 437–42, accepted the Howle-Moore modifications with some qualifications.

parity based on reserve changes, the United States would have achieved an implicit depreciation of less than 2 per cent if only the other countries had crawled, whereas it would have depreciated by an additional 14 per cent had it moved on its own. Both figures can be compared with the implicit *appreciation* of 3 per cent for the dollar which actually occurred during that period. One striking result is that, under an active parity policy, the dollar would have depreciated by small and frequent changes by an amount virtually equal to the devaluations actually negotiated in 1971–73 after many crises and costly adjustment failures. In addition, the earlier start provided by the gliding parity· might have reduced the total move which was needed. So the United States would get both *more and quicker* adjustment from adopting an active parity policy under any new exchange-rate regime.

A major question concerning the interest of the United States in a system of greater flexibility is whether it would lead monetary authorities to seek to disgorge their present dollar holdings, or avoid dollar accumulations in the future, or both. The better adjustment of any American disequilibrium which would derive from greater flexibility should better assure all countries about the continued convertibility of the dollar. If it occurred under option 1, with the dollar parity in terms of SDR remaining basically fixed, such adjustment would reduce even further the possibility of a change in the dollar price of other reserve assets, the only narrow financial reason why monetary authorities may have been uneasy over their holdings of dollars. And by helping adjustment, greater flexibility would eliminate the possibility of U.S. controls over its international transactions in the future—improving still further the attractiveness of the dollar.

On the other hand, the value of the dollar in terms of a weighted average of other currencies would depreciate even under option 1, relative to the Bretton Woods system, if the United States tended basically toward deficit. This decline would be very slow under any of the variants of greater flexibility, however, and of itself might not have much negative effect on holders of dollars. At any given time, of course, such a weighted average value of the dollar could be appreciating. Despite recent problems, the United States has a better long-term record of price stability than any other country. And any anticipated depreciation of the dollar, even in terms of a single other currency, could be offset by increasing its interest yield. The major problem for the dollar, as both a vehicle and a reserve currency, could occur if one or two of the flucuating currencies exhibited a strong bias toward appreciation relative to the dollar. (The mark and the yen might represent such cases.)

Under any of the other options, the dollar could also depreciate steadily against SDR and gold. This could renew the interest of foreign monetary authorities in gold, although the large spread which already exists between the market and official prices, and the small magnitude of the changes in the gold-dollar parity, probably minimize the potential importance of this risk. And the United States could again try to use interest-rate differentials to prevent any adverse effects of such depreciation on foreign dollar-holdings. However, we learned in Chapter 6 that the holdings of foreign monetary authorities—unlike those of private foreigners—are not very interest-sensitive, and one of the econometric studies cited there concluded that the outlook for the private gold price influenced monetary authorities positively. In addition, such an interest-rate constraint could carry sizable costs for the United States—more so than the constraint vis-à-vis other national currencies, since in that case other countries could also move their interest rates to achieve at least part of the required differential and hence share the costs. The only safe course, if the United States wanted these additional adjustment benefits, would be to eliminate the reserve currency role of the dollar for those countries which did not plan to move their parities with the dollar in most instances.

The U.S. interest in the different routes to greater flexibility must also be considered from the standpoint of the effective functioning of the entire international monetary system. We have already seen that the adjustment process would work better under a SDR pivot, because it would provide both better sharing of the burden of initiating adjustment and average changes in exchange rates against some norm other than U.S. economic performance, thereby minimizing the total amount of exchange-rate changes which would have to take place.[57] In addition, exchange-rate changes should be easier to initiate for the United States than for virtually all other countries, since its economy is the least open of all to the international economy and the political costs should be lightest; thus the inclusion of a U.S. ability to initiate changes would probably increase the degree of flexibility which would actually exist in the system by more than a proportional amount. The experiences of 1971 and 1973 lend strong support to this conclusion.

On the liquidity side, Chapter 11 concluded that there would be

57. Howle and Moore *op. cit.*

sizable systemic costs in replacing the dollar as a vehicle currency with other national currencies or by SDRs or by abandoning the intervention system, and that replacing it with gold would be extremely disruptive. On the other hand, replacing its reserve role with SDR would be acceptable and perhaps even desirable. Option 2 would move clearly in this direction by preserving the intervention role of the dollar but pegging the dollar and all other currencies to some different numéraire, presumably SDR, which would enhance further the attributes of such an asset for reserve purposes.

From the systemic standpoint, the choice among options 1, 2, and 3 for greater flexibility of exchange rates depends upon a judgment as to the importance of preserving the intervention currency role of the dollar, and the likelihood that this role would be jeopardized by limited flexibility and/or by significantly expanding the use of other national currencies for intervention purposes. From the point of view of the narrower U.S. desire for better adjustment, the choice would depend on a comparison between the faith one had in getting *other* countries to adhere to any set of flexibility rules or presumptions and thus provide adjustment for the United States *indirectly*, and the likelihood that an active U.S. parity policy and/or equal scope for dollar flexibility within the margins would increase the chances for effective adjustment. If the United States had full faith in other countries' abiding by the rules, it could accept option 1— essentially a return to the dollar-centered system of the past, but with other countries obliged to adjust promptly when their payments positions moved into disequilibrium. If the United States wanted to be able to change its own parity actively, because it doubted that others would actually conform to the rules or because its own disequilibria might not show up adequately in the sum of other countries' disequilibria, it should pursue option 2. If it doubted that the new adjustment rules would assure even its own ability to alter the dollar parity when necessary, it might, in addition, insist on option 3 to permit the dollar to fluctuate around existing parities as much as any other national currency.

This critical choice for U.S. policy has been developed from the standpoint of a system of fixed parities, operating within wider margins and under new rules or presumptions to promote more rapid changes in those parities, when needed. The same choice would have to be made by the United States, however, under a system of managed flexibility in which no parities (or central rates) existed. Indeed, the choice then becomes difficult because options 1 and 2 collapse into a single option: continued dollar intervention as the operating mode of the system, with no "escape" for the United

States through its being able to change its parity in terms of an SDR numéraire (since no parities exist). The only sure route to equal adjustment opportunity for the United States would then be option 3, multi-currency intervention, perhaps with the United States prepared to intervene actively in the markets along with other currencies, if necessary. In a world of managed flexibility, the United States would thus either have to be *very* confident that the rules governing intervention would work effectively, or insist on a multi-currency intervention system which enabled it to intervene in the markets with other national currencies.

Political Considerations
Finally, what of the politics of a system in which other currencies moved more freely around the dollar, perhaps enhancing the appearance of the dollar as the lodestar of the system and its bastion of stability, as in option 1?

They might not be so bad. In light of our analysis of optimum currency areas, only a few currencies might in practice fluctuate more freely; other countries would retain their present fixity (to the dollar or some other currency) just as the dollar would retain its fixity (to gold or SDR). Other countries would gain a further degree of flexibility in their adjustment policies, which they could use to fend off unwanted dollars. Greater flexibility of exchange rates would "bottle up" inflation or deflation to a greater extent within its country of origin, thus reducing the possibility that Europe would have to "import inflation" from the United States or that the latter could "export unemployment" to the rest of the world.

There is one other probable political gain to other countries vis-à-vis the United States in such a system. Given the relatively small impact of foreign transactions on the American economy, it is highly doubtful that the United States will ever permit balance-of-payments developments or foreign authorities to exercise overriding influence over its domestic policy. The exchange rate of the dollar has a much smaller impact on the American economy. American authorities should, thus, be prepared to accept much greater foreign influences over the exchange rate than over domestic policy. Any system that increased the influence of exchange rates in the adjustment process should enhance the influence on the United States of foreign developments and foreign authorities.

On the other hand, the mechanics of option 1 would remain quite similar to those of the Bretton Woods system. It would be seen as increasing the asymmetrical position of the dollar. By contrast, option 2 would place the dollar on an equal footing with all other currencies regarding parity changes. It would retain some asymmetry, however, in that the dollar would remain the market pivot within the margins around a given set of parities. Only option 3, which would equate the dollar with other currencies in terms of both parity changes and market fluctuations, would eliminate all asymmetries of the Bretton Woods system. These political considerations, on balance, seem to influence the choice in the direction of option 3—which would also achieve maximum flexibility for the dollar. Option 2 ranks second on both these counts, though it is probably the best choice for the optimum functioning of the system as a whole.

LIMITED DOLLAR CONSOLIDATION VIA AN INTERNATIONAL ASSET

Chapter 11 described in detail how the dollar's reserve currency role could be eliminated if a truly international unit were adopted as the sole reserve asset held by all countries, or if such an asset were used to replace at least the outstanding dollar balances and prevent the creation of any additional dollars. References were also made to modified versions of the basic approach, which would be less sweeping.

One possibility is simply to continue the original SDR scheme, with no explicit provision for other reserve assets. SDR amounts would be created on the basis of rough judgments about global reserve needs and the portion of those needs which would be expected to be met by increases in other reserve assets, primarily dollars but also gold and other national currencies. The creation of SDRs itself would be expected to meet the desires of most monetary authorities to build their reserves, and thus obviate any need for dollar increases (and U.S. payments deficits).

Reliance would thus be placed on market forces to limit the growth of dollar reserves as a result of foreign demand for them. However, there would be no effective constraints on dollar growth due to deficits resulting from U.S. policies and performance. So world reserves could grow by much more than the amount of SDR creation (or by much less if the United States were to run a sizable payments surplus financed by reducing its dollar liabilities). This is, of course, the main argument for the more comprehensive liquidity options—such as ruling out increases in reserve assets other than SDRs. Without a more sweeping approach, or at least improvements in the adjustment process which would avoid any "supply-generated" U.S. deficits, the aggregate liquidity outcome of a limited move away from the dollar would be highly uncertain.

There is one way to reduce this uncertainty without going over to full reliance on SDRs, or any other non-dollar asset. Instead of adjusting the amount of SDR creation by *ex ante* judgments about the likely course of growth in other reserve assets, which may turn out to be wildly wrong (as in the first "basic period"), adjustments could be made *ex post* to achieve the desired total of global growth of total reserves. Upon having decided that annual reserve increases of $5 billion were needed for global reasons, for example, SDR allocations of $2 billion could be made at the end of a year in which national reserves of other assets climbed by $3 billion. If the growth of other assets *exceeded* the desired global total, there would be no SDR creation—and the overage could be deducted from allocations in the succeeding year(s) to "catch up."

This approach would effectively equate world liquidity growth with the agreed desire of the IMF community. However, it would raise major distributional problems. To put the case most simply if most extremely, there would be no SDR distribution—and no reserve growth at all for other countries—if Japan and Germany together increased their dollar balances by $5 billion and everybody else (except the United States) was in payments balance.[58] Even in the absence of such an actual result, it would always be possible; uncertainty about adequate reserve growth could thus still motivate countries to run extremely aggressive balance-of-payments policies. In short, this approach would vitiate much of the gain from the basic SDR scheme.

An alternative technique would be to make SDR allocations as at present, but then to deduct from members' balances in the Special Account any non-SDR buildup in their reserves after each year (or other chosen time period). This would meet the distributional problem of the previous alternative, and of the original mode of SDR allocation by offsetting the growth of non-dollar reserves on a *country* rather than *global* basis. It would not be certain to achieve a full offset, and hence global reserve growth precisely equal to the desired amount, because individual countries might build their reserves by an amount greater than their SDR allocation, which would represent the maximum compensating deduction that could be made. However, such situations could develop only if SDR allocations were very low *and* the surpluses of individual countries were very high. The likelihood could be reduced even further by basing the deductions on a moving average of both SDR allocations and non-SDR reserve

58. This assumes that world liquidity is defined in terms of *gross* reserves, and that U.S. liabilities are not netted against them. If they were, U.S. deficits might not affect SDR allocations at all and this approach would be meaningless.

growth over several years, because most countries swing between surplus and deficit—or at least between surpluses which exceeded their SDR allocations and surpluses which are smaller—over such periods. An analysis of 1966–70, on the assumption of annual SDR allocations of $4 billion, indicates that actual reserve growth would have exceeded the *five*-year target by only $1 billion—5 per cent—under this national deduction formula.

In practice, most countries would of course avoid deductions from their SDR holdings by converting all of their non-SDR reserve accumulations into SDRs. The primary effect of this option would therefore be to provide a powerful disincentive to any buildup of dollar (and gold, or other national currency) balances. Hence it is really one method for achieving the aim of Chapter 11, rather than only *limiting* the dollar's roles as considered here. And that aim could be achieved much more simply by a flat prohibition on future dollar buildups than by such a complicated scheme. We again see that significant problems arise in any attempt to maintain a pluralistic reserve system, rather than going wholly over to some single asset. Indeed, we have now seen that there is *no* feasible way both to permit a multiplicity of growing reserve assets and to achieve full control over the growth of world liquidity.

A New Alternative: Optional Consolidation

The shortcomings in the extreme consolidation approaches outlined in Chapter 11, and in the original SDR scheme, suggest a modified alternative which would achieve international control of the growth of total reserves, respect the different views of different countries about the composition of their reserve assets, yet also avoid any systemic problems from the coexistence of the different assets. An "optional consolidation" plan for doing so could include the following features:

1. All IMF member countries[59] would be invited to deposit as much of their outstanding reserve dollars (and their balances of sterling and other national currencies, and perhaps their gold as well[60]) *as they wished* at the IMF. It would be up to each to

---

59. Special technical provisions could be made to take care of Switzerland, the only sizable dollar holder not an IMF member. It might be better, however, to use the limitation as an inducement to Switzerland finally to join the Fund—and to the several Fund members which have not joined the SDR scheme to do so.

60. For a discussion of the merits of including gold in any reserve consolidation scheme, see Chapter 11.

decide how many dollars to keep for working balance purposes, debt repayment needs, etc. Dollars held on the base date for the scheme could be deposited either immediately or at some later date.

2. In return for whatever dollars they decided to deposit, countries would receive additional SDRs, which could be used at any time to finance payments deficits directly or to reconstitute their balances of dollars or any other currency from the IMF.

3. The dollars deposited in the IMF would be treated as a fixed fiduciary issue of reserves, *or* the United States would redeem them in the future when it ran balance-of-payments surpluses, *or* it would redeem in annual amounts agreed in the negotiation. U.S. interest payments on the dollars would also be negotiated. (Both issues are discussed in Chapter 11). The United States would guarantee the gold- or exchange-value of the dollars which are deposited.

4. With respect to dollars *not* deposited in the IMF, countries would pledge not to use them except when needed to finance future balance-of-payments deficits, i.e., when they met a "needs tests" as under the original SDR rule. The dollars would not be convertible into U.S. reserve assets. Thus countries could not change the *composition* of their reserves by exchanging dollars which they retained for other assets (unless some country other than the United States volunteered for such a transaction).

5. Any dollars accruing currently to countries which did not wish to hold additional dollars, but not new to the system as a whole, could be placed by them in the Fund in exchange for additional SDRs. This would protect the United States and the system against conversion of outstanding dollars that happened to shift from dollar to non-dollar countries, which could occur frequently under the "needs tests" of paragraph 4.

6. (a) All IMF member countries, whether or not they converted their outstanding dollars into SDRs at the outset, would declare how many *additional* dollars, either in absolute terms or as a percentage of their reserve gains, they would be willing to accept in the future; i.e., they would declare a holding limit (annual or longer term, say, five years) for the dollar portion of their reserves. They could specify that they would hold no additional dollars or that they would place no limit on their future accruals. Dollars accruing to them beyond the levels which they had specifically agreed

to hold would be immediately converted into U.S. reserve assets.[61]

(b) Dollars accruing initially to dollar-holding countries, and then shifting to non-dollar countries, could be so converted. Dollars not converted at once by dollar-holding countries could never be converted *by those countries*. The declaration of the *accruing* country would dominate. The United States could thus not *count* on any permanent dollar financing from increases in its dollar liabilities under the new regime, even if dollar countries ran temporary payments surpluses.

(c) A country could at any time change its position on whether it would hold or convert newly accruing dollars, but could not begin to implement the new approach for some period of time, say, six months, after it has been announced, to give the United States time to adjust to the changed situation. Countries could thus opt into or out of, or shift their relative membership in, the different parts of the SDR-dollar system.[62]

7. Dollars held by private foreigners on the base date of the new system, which subsequently shifted to authorities which were unwilling to hold unlimited amounts of dollars, would also be eligible for deposit at the IMF. In the absence of such a provision, U.S. reserves could be drained by a collapse of the private overhang. This approach follows the precedent of the

61. I leave open for the moment whether *all* dollars, or only dollars arising from certain components of their payments positions (the current account or basic balance, for example), would be eligible for these conversions.

62. Sir Roy Harrod, in an effort both to *increase* the reserve currency role of the dollar (and sterling) and to free domestic monetary policy in the United States (and United Kingdom) from constraints imposed by fear of withdrawal of foreign-held balances, proposed a different kind of "optional consolidation." Harrod would have the IMF open lines of credit to the United States equal to any fall in its gold holdings, i.e., a compensatory loan for any U.S. reserve losses due to dollar conversions, similar to the Basel arrangements for sterling which are linked specifically to changes in the outstanding level of sterling balances. If any such credits were outstanding after three years, the loan would have to be amortized by the United States over twenty years. See pp. 154–58 of his *Reforming the World's Money* (New York: St. Martins Press, 1965). The two major differences between his scheme and the one proposed here are that (a) the United States would have to use its owned reserves over a twenty-year period to redeem overhanging dollars presented to it, and (b) it would have no more idea than it does now about the possible scope of future dollar financing of any deficits it might run and, correspondingly, the world would have no idea of the probable contribution of the dollar to overall increases in international liquidity.

1968 arrangements for sterling, under which Britain could draw on the Basel credits to finance any conversions from private as well as official holdings in sterling area countries.

In essence, the authorized special creation of SDRs would be large enough to reserve a place for all foreign-held dollars, official and private, outstanding at the time the system was instituted, whether they were converted at once or with some delay, and whether they were converted by the original holder or by some other country. The result would be a world of countries stretched along a "dollar use continuum": at one extreme would be those countries, if any, that rejected the dollar entirely; at the other extreme those, if any, which decided to retain all their outstanding dollars and hold all those accruing to them in the future. In the middle would be those countries, probably the vast majority, which opted to hold some but not all outstanding and future dollars. It would thus put into actual practice the explicit, differentiated revealed asset preferences of all countries.

The scheme is complicated, which is perhaps its major drawback. It might therefore be helpful to spell out in detail how it might work under different situations. In doing so, we will distinguish between "old" dollars, which were outstanding at the time the scheme began, and "new" dollars, which would be created thereafter as a result of future U.S. deficits (in its current account, basic balance, liquidity, or official settlements position—whichever was decided as the reference point).

If there were no "new" dollars acquired by monetary authorities, there would be no technical problems. "Old" dollars could be converted into the special issue of SDRs either by the countries which held them at the commencement of the new scheme, at that time or later, or by other countries which acquired them through running payments surpluses. The absence of "new" official dollars would be verified by the IMF records on dollar holdings of each monetary authority—which are already submitted annually, but which should perhaps be submitted more frequently to permit checking on the dollar situation.

The first complication arises if "old" private dollars move into official hands and hence become "new" official dollars. It is a complication only because the data on private foreign holdings are less complete than the data on official holdings. Thus some estimation might be required of the level of private dollars outstanding both on the base date of the scheme and at subsequent intervals. The problem here is technical rather than conceptual.

The greater conceptual problem comes with the creation of "new" dollars. There would not even be a problem here if the "old" dollars did not change hands at the same time that "new" dollars were emerging. Indeed, there is no problem in determining the global liability of the United States even in this case, because the total growth of reserve dollars can be easily calculated by comparing the amount held at any given time with the level on the base date. An individual surplus country, however, may acquire both "new" dollars from a U.S. deficit and "old" dollars from the overhang held by other countries. There is thus a question of what part of *its* dollar inflow could be converted into U.S. reserve assets, and what part into the special issue of SDRs.[63] If the United States were to use only SDRs to finance its deficits, this would not even be an issue to the surplus country from a portfolio standpoint because it would get SDRs for *all* of the dollars it acquired.

However, there is a significant difference from a U.S. standpoint. The United States would not have to finance as much of its current deficit with reserve assets if it were decided that non-dollar surplus countries had acquired mostly "old" dollars, with some portion of the "new" dollars going to dollar countries, in contrast to a determination that the surpluses of dollar countries were financed wholly by "old" dollars from other dollar countries, with the current U.S. deficit fully offset by "new" dollar holdings of non-dollar holders. This determination could have an important bearing on both U.S. reserve losses and on foreign desires that the United States adjust rather than finance, if in fact dollar holders turned out to be very significant surplus countries.

Conceptually, it is impossible to trace bilateral flows of dollars to see whose surplus was caused by whose deficit without resorting to a complete set of exchange controls. At best, the problem could be approached by developing a global payments matrix which estimated the marginal effect of each country on the payments position of each other country. One could then say that, over time, x per cent of any French surplus was likely to have resulted from a British deficit. Data do not even permit the development of such a matrix at this time, however, and a *trade* matrix alone—which could be developed— would not be very helpful.

The only solution is thus fairly arbitrary. In any time period, it

---

63. Dollars which are "new" after the base date can also shift from one country to another. However, they are always "new" dollars convertible into U.S. reserve assets for the purposes discussed, and thus raise no additional complications for the working of the scheme.

would be easy to calculate the global increase of "new" dollars and any net decline of "old" dollars beneath the level willingly held at the start of the period. The two together would equal the buildup of unwanted dollars in other countries. Each surplus country could then take a prorated share of its dollar conversions from the United States, and get the rest through the IMF from the special issue of SDRs. For example, if Germany is in surplus by 100 and Japan by 50, the United States is in basic deficit by 100, and all other countries are in basic balance, Germany gets 67 and Japan 33 of U.S. reserve assets and each can turn in the rest of its surplus dollars for the SDRs that were created at the outset of the new regime. This formula could be applied by the IMF with the data regarding reserve-asset compositions of national reserves now reported to it annually (on an extremely confidential basis) by member governments.

To be sure, this device is not fully satisfactory. However, the problem arises in *any* limited consolidation of the overhang, whether "new" dollar creation is permitted or not. And *limited* consolidation will probably prove necessary to get any consolidation at all, unless *all* countries are forced to convert *all* of their dollars at the outset— which seems politically less feasible than achieving agreement on this arbitrary formula for dividing up subsequent conversions.

This approach could be adopted in a much less politically charged atmosphere than the extreme options of either Chapter 11 or 12. The countries converting their overhanging dollars at the outset would be able to receive an alternate asset which (by hypothesis) they would consider more attractive than dollars without jeopardizing the stability of the system. The United States could thus be much more relaxed about a wider group of countries "foresaking the dollar." Countries opting to convert their outstanding dollars could, if they desired, agree to accept some additional dollars in the future. They would not have to make a once-for-all choice. Countries not converting their overhangs, the closest equivalent to the existing dollar area, could place a ceiling on the amount of dollars they would agree to accrue in the future. Countries could at any time opt to switch their reserve asset preferences, and the United States would not suffer gold losses through their liquidations of dollars outstanding on the base date at such time. Countries would be arrayed across a spectrum from "total SDR holders" to "total dollar holders," rather than divided into sharp categories, and no explicit "dollar area" would emerge.

This approach would not solve the adjustment problem, although any parallel discussions on this question might well effect national decisions regarding their dollar balances. For example, if greater exchange-rate flexibility were instituted along the lines outlined. in the previous section of this chapter, countries would have to agree to add to their dollar balances if they wanted to peg to the dollar and hence avoid appreciation of their currencies when they were in payments surplus. On the other hand, this approach would probably increase the adjustment pressure on the United States by sharply limiting its access to dollar financing. The United States might thus support it only in combination with some assured improvements in the adjustment process both for other countries and for itself.

This approach does not take care either of the need to assure additional reserves, or of regulating their growth. It does provide scope for dollar increases, as well as SDR creation, and thus leaves total growth indeterminate (unless one of the reserve adjustment approaches discussed at the end of the last section were adopted). The importance of this indeterminacy would depend on whether a significant number of important countries opted for dollar increases. If only a few smaller countries made such a choice, it could be assumed that their cumulative payments surpluses, if any, would be so small over time as not significantly to undermine the rate of growth of world liquidity desired by the international community. On the other hand, dollar accruals by even a few persistent surplus countries could distort the desired trend. The only way to avoid this risk, however, is to force all countries to avoid dollar buildups in the future, as outlined in Chapter 11.

The effect on the dollar's reserve currency roles would thus also be indeterminate, and could go in either direction. More countries would be eligible to convert outstanding dollars and foreswear future dollar accruals, but all could opt to hold onto all or part in each category. At a minimum, however, the United States would be fully protected against the entire dollar overhang and would be on notice that it could face conversions from any "new overhang" that might develop, even if countries accumulated dollars for a while before passing them on to countries which wanted to convert them.

A MULTIPLE RESERVE CURRENCY SYSTEM

The third "middle ground" alternative is to adopt *additional* national currencies for use as international reserves to supplement the dollar. This could be done by using either a number of national currencies globally or different national currencies in different regions. Like the option just discussed, this approach would deal only with the confidence and liquidity aspects of the international monetary problem. Although it would have an effect on the adjustment process, it would not deal with it per se.

The approach is based on the concept that the responsibility for providing a large percentage of the expansion of international liquidity is now too heavy a burden to be borne by the dollar, but that no other currency (or currencies) can fully replace it. In addition, the present reserve currency countries are thought in some quarters to have the "unfair advantage" of being able to finance balance-of-payments deficits without losing owned reserves. One answer to both problems would be to use additional national currencies in a similar role.

There is already a significant and growing holding of a few of these currencies by foreign monetary authorities, particularly the mark, so the approach would build on existing patterns. It would get a boost from European monetary integration, under which each EC member has agreed to hold at least working balances in the currencies of all other members.[64] The "burden" of providing international liquidity would thus be shared, and those industrialized countries which agreed that their currencies could be used for such purposes would have "opportunities" equal to the United States and United Kingdom to finance deficits by expansion of their liquid liabilities. Thus world liquidity could rise whether the United States was in deficit and Europe in surplus, or vice versa, and the threat to expansionary domestic and foreign economic policies by either trying to protect its gross reserves would be obviated at least to some extent.

In 1962, the United States offered to hold European currencies to finance future U.S. payments surpluses as a contribution toward developing such a system.[65] No European country responded affirmatively however, although it was reported that the approach was discussed in late 1962 both in the Monetary Committee of the EEC and the Basel group of central bankers.[66] (The U.S. proposal fore-

---

64. Governor Carli of the Bank of Italy, in his Annual Report for 1972, indicated that Italy aimed to hold 20 per cent of its reserves in EC currencies. Italy is one of the world's biggest reserve holders, and this alone would mean reserve status totaling at least $1 billion for the other EC currencies.

65. See Robert Roosa, "Multilateralizing International Responsibility," address before the 9th Annual International Monetary Conference of the American Bankers Association, Rome, May 17, 1962, reprinted as Chapter 4 of his *Dollar and World Liquidity* (New York: Random House 1967), pp. 57–59. Roosa hedged his offer very carefully, however, by adding that the United States would not expect to make any commitments to hold particular currencies, that its holdings would be comparatively small, and that in any case implementation of such a system should not reduce balance-of-payments discipline for any countries.

66. Fritz Machlup, *Plans for Reform of the International Monetary System*, Special Papers in International Economics, No. 3, revised March 1964, p. 29.

saw *global* use of several currencies. The new possibility of using EC currencies for intra-EC intervention would focus on *regional* use of such currencies, although it would almost certainly accelerate non-regional holdings as well.) In practice, the United States did begin holding foreign currencies about that time, but only in small amounts and with exchange-value guarantees, under the swap network or related credit arrangements.

One problem with the U.S. proposals for a multiple currency system in the early 1960s was that no other countries were yet able to meet the criteria spelled out in Chapters 4–6 to play significant key currency roles. Indeed, one is thereby justified in wondering whether the U.S. proposals were aimed more at legitimizing the international roles of the dollar, by "internationalizing" the key currency approach, than at developing a truly new system. In any event, it soon became clear that a system using several reserve currencies would have all the liabilities of a system based on a single reserve currency.

In addition, such a system would require rather specific rules to avoid a perverse effect on confidence and the amount of total reserves, the very problems it attempts to solve. This is a hazard simply because the likelihood would increase sharply that the Gresham's Law problem would arise. The presence of additional reserve assets raises the possibility of frequent moves from one currency to another if the stability of any of them comes under question. Unless full and virtually equal confidence was maintained in all the currencies involved, destabilizing shifts in reserve preferences and hence sharp declines in total liquidity could easily arise. The basic objective of the scheme—that international liquidity could rise as a result of balance-of-payments deficits in the various participating countries—could only eventuate if in fact there were imbalances within the group, and hence at least a serious risk that confidence would wax and wane among the various currencies.[67] Barring some further sys-

---

67. It is conceivable, of course, that any such imbalances would be clearly recognized as temporary and hence no cause for selling of the currency by monetary authorities. The persistence of deficts and surpluses, at least since 1958 however, does not provide much assurance that this would in fact be the case. The multiple currency reserve system, in short, would require a great improvement in the adjustment process to work effectively. (Such improvement in the adjustment process could, of course, reduce the need for liquidity provided by the additional reserve currencies.) It makes no contribution toward that goal, however, and all participating countries might even be more tempted to run deficits if they could finance them without losses of owned reserves. Even if official holdings did not shift, it would be quite possible that private movements in the currencies would become large enough, given their new international use, to precipitate crises.

temic arrangements, the system would thus suffer from a fundamental contradiction which would compound the inherent shortcomings of a system based on a single key currency.

A final and important distributional point, particularly since we now have a universal SDR, is that "first use" of all the new liquidity generated by the adoption of more national currencies as international reserves would go to the highly industrialized countries. The result would be exactly the opposite of the approach which seeks to "link" reserve creation and development financing: the developing countries would have to "earn" all of their reserve increases, while the industrialized countries would be the ones able to run "deficits without tears."

Most proponents of this approach soon recognized the confidence problem outlined above, and devised systematic arrangements to protect against it.[68] Participating countries would have to hold or transfer the various reserve currencies in fixed proportions to gold and their other reserve assets. For example, a participating country might settle three-sevenths of a deficit in gold, two-sevenths in its own currency (hence creating international liquidity to that extent), and two-sevenths in other foreign currencies. Or minimum holding (or transfer) limits might be required, to assure that liquidity would be increased, and/or maximum holding (or transfer) limits adopted to avoid too much relaxation of discipline on participating countries. Even this rigid approach does not deal with the possibility of shifts *among* the various foreign currencies, and one could imagine highly complex holding or transfer ratios with places required for each of the half-dozen or so currencies involved. The exchange rate and probably gold values of the national currencies involved would have to be guaranteed to insure their acceptability.[69] And some observers felt that each country would have to make its currency convertible into gold, just as the United States did, to ensure its acceptability as a reserve asset.[70]

68. See John H. Williamson, "Liquidity and the Multiple Key Currency Proposal," *American Economic Review*, Vol. LIII, No. 3 (June 1963), pp. 427–32, and S. Posthuma "The International Monetary System," *Banca Nazionale del Lavoro Quarterly Review*, No. 66 (September 1963), pp. 239–61.
69. See Williamson, *op. cit.* As pointed out in Chapter 12, the U.S. government has resisted general extension of any such guarantees to official dollar holdings though it has done so for specific and limited types of foreign balances. It would be difficult to envisage other countries offering such guarantees if the United States were unwilling to do so.
70. For example, Friedrich A. Lutz, "The Problem of International Liquidity and the Multiple-Currency Standard," *Princeton Essays in International Finance*, No. 41, March 1963, pp. 13 and 15.

In fact, realization of such needs was a major factor in the early death of the multiple reserve currency approach as a serious policy possibility. It became apparent that it would be much simpler to create an *international* reserve asset "backed" proportionately by various national currencies than to use the national currencies themselves as reserve assets. The international approach would provide true multilateralization and at the same time avoid many of the problems cited above. The multiple currency reserve approach can in fact be best viewed intellectually as a step in the evolution of thinking toward a truly international asset, which has finally emerged in the form of the SDR. In practical terms, however, it might nevertheless emerge in response to market forces—with all the problems here cited—in the absence of progress toward expanded use of the SDR.

It has already been noted that EC monetary integration might include the use of additional national currencies solely for intervention purposes. On a global basis, it would be possible to eliminate one of the key asymmetries in the system by a basic change in the market intervention rules, which would also encompass using a variety of additional intervention currencies.

At present, countries are obligated to defend their own exchange rates, and those of all other countries, *in their own territory*. This system has underlain the development of the intervention currency role of the dollar to maximize efficiency by intervening in one currency in all markets. In turn, it has forced national authorities to accumulate dollars in preventing their own currency from appreciating, and then to make the increasingly difficult policy choice of what to do with the dollars. To avoid facing countries with this choice, an alternative intervention approach would be to require all countries to intervene *in all exchange markets*, at least in the major currencies, when their own currency reached its floor. For example, the United States would have to sell marks *in Germany* when the dollar reached its floor there, and France would have to sell sterling *in London* when the franc reached its floor there. This would obviously require the United States and France to maintain balances in marks and sterling, and indeed in all currencies in which intervention to defend their exchange rates would be necessary. All such currencies would thus become intervention currencies. Foreign countries would continue to hold dollars for intervention in New York, but its share of their total working balances would drop sharply under this approach.

The United States (and others) would acquire needed currencies from the issuing countries, or the IMF, in return for acceptable assets (or a liability to be paid off in acceptable assets). Countries could agree to accept each other's currencies in return, but this would raise all the problems of multiple reserve currencies just outlined. Indeed, this particular proposal is usually seen as a way to reduce the intervention currency role of the dollar along with its reserve currency role, and implies that the United States—like all others in the past—would finance its deficits with reserve assets or through global credit facilities available to all on similar terms.

This approach would go far toward eliminating the asymmetry of the dollar in the present intervention system. It therefore appeals both to those foreigners who wish to end such asymmetry, essentially for political reasons, and to those Americans who wish to get as much flexibility for the dollar as is now enjoyed by other currencies (per option 3 in the discussion of how to achieve greater flexibility of exchange rates, above). However, this approach also eliminates the efficiency gains of using a single currency for such purposes. In addition, the scheme could obviously not call for each of the 125 IMF members to intervene in the markets of all 124 other currencies; most countries would in fact have to continue using the traditional intervention currencies, mainly the dollar, so a dual system would emerge (and perhaps carry significant political overtones as well as economic complications). However, if large-scale reduction of the intervention currency role of the dollar became a widely shared objective, then this option would have to be considered alongside the option of substituting an international clearing union for market intervention altogether, which was developed in Chapter 11.

The Effect on the Dollar

Adoption of a multiple reserve currency system would have two specific effects on the dollar. First, it would sanction continued existence of the dollar overhang and expansion of the dollar's use as a reserve currency by all countries. In this sense it is more "liberal" toward the dollar than any of the other alternatives considered so far for limiting the dollar's use. Second, it would provide new competition for the dollar. Several additional currencies would be designated as reserve currencies, and accumulation of them would presumably accelerate.

Countries holding these *new* reserve currencies would obviously want to use them for market intervention, and hence the dollar's role as an intervention currency would decline at least proportionately. Monetary authorities would need suitable investment media for their holdings, which would encourage further development of money markets in the countries whose currencies were involved. Such development would presumably enhance their position relative to the U.S. money market, and would probably improve the competitive positions of their currencies against the dollar as a vehicle currency. In a broader sense, such improvement might be expected to generate additional external borrowing from these markets and hence relieve the U.S. balance of payments of the short-term costs of heavy lending to foreigners—but simultaneously undermine the key currency attribute of the United States as a capital exporter. We have already seen that this approach would generate systemic instability. Thus the availability of other assets, assuming that their international use did evolve as outlined here so that they would become real competitors to the dollar, would seem to have a negative impact on the dollar's present international roles.

SUMMARY AND CONCLUSION

Each of the three approaches to limited reduction of the international roles of the dollar aims at a different problem: limited flexibility of exchange rates at improving the adjustment process, limited consolidation of the dollar overhang primarily at the confidence problem, and the international use of additional national currencies at the growth of liquidity for the future. Thus all three, or only two of them, could be meshed in any overall reform effort.

One result could be a division of the world into two or three large monetary areas. Our discussion of optimum currency areas suggested that greater flexibility of exchange rates might in practice lead mainly to greater flexibility among a dollar area surrounding the United States, a sizable area centered on the expanded European Community, and possibly a yen area centered on Japan. Of course, large countries whose economies were not dominated by any one of these centers—such as Australia and South Africa—might retain national flexibility. Others, even those as closely linked to a major economy as is Canada to the United States, might well disengage from their usual pegging to a center currency if the economic performance of the center country faltered toward either excessive unemployment or excessive inflation.

The decisions of countries on this exchange-rate question would influence their decisions on whether to consolidate their overhanging reserves. Countries which pegged to the dollar would need dollars for intervention purposes and would suffer no loss on their dollar holding, in terms of their own currencies, from a dollar devaluation. If they were motivated by some of the positive aspects of holding dollars, such as its interest yield, they might opt to hold at least some of their "old" dollars. If they did not want the United States to adjust, they might also retain at least some of any "new" dollars they acquired. Indeed, some might even sell some of their gold to the

United States, as Canada has done in the past, and there should be no systemic objections to such "reserve pooling" by dollar countries since the United States would have to convert these "new" dollars if they moved into countries which did not want them.

Additional national currencies would probably play an increasingly important role in such a world. This would certainly be true for intervention purposes, since intra-European intervention would take place primarily through present EC currencies or some new European unit, and intra-yen area intervention would take place through the yen. The traditional market influences would then induce member countries to hold the center currencies in their reserves. Each center country could then hold intervention balances of each other center, and would have to do so under the proposal for each center to intervene in *all* markets to defend its currency at the floor of the band. On the other hand, the present practice of relying on the dollar for intervention purposes, with the United States remaining passive in the markets, could continue.

The result would be a very rough tripartite world aligned quite differently from the world which emerged under the Bretton Woods system. The gold bloc would become a gold/SDR (or perhaps mark) bloc encompassing most of Europe and surrounding areas, including some present dollar countries. The dollar area would be smaller in size, a natural result of the objective of limiting the international roles of the dollar. A new yen area might emerge. The sterling area would finally dissolve in name as well as fact, with the members moving into one of the other areas or maintaining an independent position.

Adjustment among the areas and for individual unaligned countries would take place primarily through the greater flexibility of rates. Adjustment by countries within the broad areas would take place primarily through changes in their domestic economic policies, with occasional exchange-rate changes as well—probably even within Europe, for many years. Private financial flows could of course ease the requirements for adjustment both within and among areas, and the reserves of each area could be augmented by periodic creation of SDRs. The international roles of the dollar would be sharply reduced, though remain paramount within a smaller dollar area and still be used globally for vehicle purposes.

A particular source of uncertainty in the outlook for such developments, however, is that the politically feasible currency areas for adjustment purposes cut diametrically across the de facto currency areas of the recent past. Within the Common Market, Germany has been a premier dollar country; France and the Netherlands were

clear gold adherents; and Italy and Belgium were somewhere in between, though leaning toward gold. And U.K. external transactions
remain about equally oriented toward Europe and North America,
leaving its position "as ambiguous as ever."[71] Japan has been *the*
premier dollar holder among the industrialized countries, but should
be a prime candidate for more frequent exchange-rate changes and
to play an independent role as a key currency center. (Indeed, the
two leading candidates to become key currency countries—Germany
and Japan—were the two most significant "members" of the previous
dollar area.)

In addition, the positions of a number of secondary countries
would be quite uncertain in such a world. Australia has switched
from sterling toward the dollar, but its trade ties are increasingly
with Japan. It is often assumed that all of Latin America would
"join" a dollar area, but only four Latin American countries (Pan-
ama, Dominican Republic, Mexico, Haiti) sell more than 50 per cent
of their exports to the United States. Ten Latin countries, including
Brazil, Argentina and Chile sell more (often much more) to Europe
than to the United States, though their services and capital accounts
are more oriented toward the United States, so they might join the
"European" monetary zone or remain independent. In addition, most
Latin American countries oppose any such trend toward North-South
blocs, partly for political reasons and partly because Latin America's
own integration might therefore be impeded.[72] Such "obvious" members of any yen area as Taiwan and Indonesia trade more with the
United States than with Japan, and might avoid a yen area for political reasons. Thus diversity rather than conformity may well be the
emerging pattern. Politically this is a desirable outcome in a period
when mercantilist pressures could push monetary areas toward becoming trade blocs tempted to adopt new trade restrictions to intensify the gains internal to each.

71. McKinnon, *op. cit.*, p. 87. In "Taking the Monetary Initiative," *Foreign
Affairs*, July 1968, I foresaw the evolution of a world of greater exchange-rate
flexibility in which the United Kingdom might flex on its own rather than
peg either to the dollar or the Continent; so far, that prediction has been
borne out despite British membership in the Common Market, which was
not foreseen at that time.
72. See Alexander Kafka, "Optimum Currency Areas and Latin America," in
Johnson and Swoboda, *op. cit.*, pp. 210–18.

14

The Need for Reform of the International Monetary System

The U.S. decision of August 15, 1971, to suspend the convertibility of the dollar into U.S. reserve assets signalled the final collapse of the monetary system created at Bretton Woods. As a result, the world stood very close to a pure dollar standard based on U.S. *force majeure*—a system which, we saw in Chapter 12, is unstable and unviable. Indeed, evidence of that instability was not long in coming: renewed and persistent crises, frequent runs on the dollar and its further depreciation, an accelerating erosion of confidence around the world in the basic fabric of international economic cooperation, and the accelerated tendencies toward widespread international use of European currencies and the Japanese yen to rival the dollar. The dollar standard proved to be short-lived, and was repudiated by virtually all major countries in early 1973 when they decided to move instead to a regime of flexible exchange rates, obviating the need to accept additional dollars. The subsequent acceleration of world inflation, and the onset of the energy crisis in late 1973, intensified both the spread of exchange-rate flexibility and the use of new key currencies.

These events have already forced major changes in the international monetary system. Some of these changes provide healthy progress toward lasting reform. The advent of more flexible exchange rates marks a dramatic step toward a more effective adjustment process, as developed in Chapters 9 and 11. The attractiveness of Special Drawing Rights as a reserve asset has been enhanced by shifting its valuation base from the official price of gold (and hence, in practice, the dollar) to a basket comprising a weighted average of sixteen national currencies, and by raising substantially the interest rate payable on net SDR accumulations. Significant progress has been made at the technical level, mainly through the work of the Deputies of the Committee of Twenty, in developing specific proposals

491

for implementing a number of the needed reforms, including several proposed in this book.[1]

But a number of key issues remain wholly unresolved. Market developments are intensifying problems in several areas. And even the reforms which have taken place raise major new difficulties themselves.

The liquidity problem has, if anything, become more serious and more difficult. The debate over the proper amounts of international reserves has been further complicated, on the one hand, by the need to finance huge payments imbalances between oil exporters and oil importers and, on the other hand, by the continuation of rapid world inflation. Regarding the form of reserves, the consensus of the late 1960s toward basing the monetary system on SDRs has apparently evaporated. World dollar balances are rising again. Balances of other national currencies are rising even faster, accelerating the trend toward a multiple key currency system—which we saw in Chapter 11 was perhaps the least stable financial basis for the world economy.

In addition, gold reserves are now in the process of being revalued. Indeed, the Martinique agreement of December 1974 effectively authorized countries to do so. As a result, as soon as the majority of the major countries emulates the immediate revaluation by France, gold will again by the leading component of world reserves. Even if countries do not formally mark up the value of their gold stocks, any move to "unfreeze" gold reserves—to enable major holders of gold (like Italy and France) more easily to finance their oil-induced payments deficits—will provide its *de facto* revaluation. No country could sell gold at $42.22 when the market price is four times higher; and no country would buy gold at such a price unless it was assured, by the seller and as many other countries as could be induced to agree, that it could re-sell at a similar level. Hence, total world reserves will rise sharply, obviating even further the need to create more SDRs and adding to the difficulties of asserting international control over the stock of internationally usable money. And the distributional effects of such a reserve rise will be highly inequitable, as we saw in Chapter 9, particularly against the developing countries, most of whom hold very little gold and have been seeking a *higher* share of future increases in world liquidity; hence this method of raising reserves will intensify the likelihood of political conflict over international monetary matters.

Market developments are also reviving the problem of the dollar

1. See the Annexes to the Outline of Reform, Committee of Twenty, published as a Supplement to the *IMF Survey*, June 17, 1974, pp. 198–208.

overhang. For a short period, in 1973 and especially 1974, the issue seemed to disappear. For most oil-importing countries, concern about their dollar balances was replaced by the sudden fear that their reserves, recently viewed as excessive, might be inadequate to pay for their oil imports. As a result of the rise in oil prices, however, the overhang immediately began to change hands. And, predictably, the new surplus countries soon began to raise the same doubts about their dollar reserves that the previous surplus countries had expressed for so long—particularly once the dollar again began to depreciate in late 1974.

Indeed, the politics which now underlie world economic arrangements suggest that the overhang may be a far greater problem in the future than in the past. Its old holders were traditional allies of the United States, but many of the new holders are potential adversaries—as was explicitly the case during the oil embargo of October 1973–March 1974. Hence the new surplus countries, fearing the possibility that their dollar balances might be frozen in a renewed crisis, are likely to seek to convert an important share of their oil earnings into other assets. This would in turn both weaken the dollar, via a partial collapse of the overhang as analyzed in Chapter 7, and intensify directly the trend toward a multiple currency system since most of their conversions would be into "safe haven" assets, notably the Swiss franc and German mark. Indeed, the depreciation of the dollar in late 1974 can best be explained in these terms.

Even the basically positive reforms which have taken place since 1971 have also raised problems. The flexible exchange rates are subject to unilateral management by national authorities, which risks policy conflict and, particularly in a world combining deep recession and high rates of inflation, could thus easily give way to competitive efforts. The higher interest rates on SDRs, as noted in Chapter 9, may further skew the initiative for adjustment measures toward deficit countries because they increase the cost of running deficits and the benefits of running surpluses.

Overarching these specific problems is the virtually total failure of the Committee of Twenty to make any significant progress, despite its initial mandate to negotiate fundamental and comprehensive reform of the monetary system and twenty-one months of effort. Aside from the "interim" arrangements adopted regarding SDRs, noted above, its "program of immediate action" and "Outline of Reform" are presented only as "the general direction in which the Committee believes that the system could evolve in the future." Substantively, the proposals for "The Reformed System" either avoid the key issues—for example, by calling vaguely, and already somewhat anachronistically, for an "exchange rate regime based on stable but adjustable par values and with floating rates recognized as providing a useful technique in particular situations"—or focus solely on procedural matters.

In summarizing the efforts of the Committee, Chairman C. Jeremy Morse of its Deputies cited four reasons why "the original aim of a complete design of reform [is] not going to be achieved": the breakdown of fixed exchange rates, the rise in oil prices, the acceleration of inflation, and a "lack of political will."[2] Yet, as indicated throughout this book, these developments and the underlying causes of each are the very reasons why comprehensive monetary reform is necessary, and why a failure to achieve such reform will prove increasingly costly in both economic and political terms.

This book has developed in detail the shortcomings of the Bretton Woods system and why basic reform was needed, from both the global and purely national U.S. standpoints, well before the American actions of 1971. This chapter summarizes these problems, and Chapter 15 will then present a specific set of proposals to achieve reform.

The international monetary system is simply not effectively performing its basic task: maximizing the contribution which international economic activity can make to the advancement of national economic and political objectives. The enormous growth of world trade and financial movements concealed the shortcomings of the system for many years, but they are now crystal clear. Having achieved the initial postwar economic objectives of currency convertibility and a multilateral trading system, the world must now attune its monetary system to the far more complex challenges of the current era.

National economies are constrained unnecessarily by the absence of an effective adjustment mechanism, and by periodic shortages or excesses of world liquidity. Exchange-rate changes are by far the most effective way of adjustment, particularly in dilemma cases where the needs of the internal economy call for macroeconomic policies that would exacerbate the external disequilibrium rather than promote its elimination. However, they were exceedingly difficult to execute under the Bretton Woods system. Excessively deflationary and inflationary policies were thus frequently forced upon countries by external considerations. To avoid such internal effects, there was

2. C. Jeremy Morse, "The Evolving Monetary System," an address to the International Monetary Conference in Williamsburg, Virginia, June 7, 1974, excerpted in *IMF Survey*, June 17, 1974, pp. 186–89.

increasing resort to controls over international transactions. These controls rarely helped in solving the underlying payments problem; they usually permitted exchange-rate disequilibria to cumulate and *increased* the welfare costs of the adjustment which was ultimately required. When exchange-rate changes finally became unavoidable, there was a strong tendency for deficit countries to have to make them—and then overdo them, in order to avoid the early repetition of the entire unhappy cycle. Both this proliferation of controls and the tendency toward excessive depreciations when parity changes were finally made raised serious problems for trade policy and international politics. The prevalent adjustment mechanism in the system was basically faulty.

The increasing adoption of managed exchange-rate flexibility since early 1971 has provided significant improvement. Yet, as we saw in Chapter 11—and as was the case in the 1930s—this approach also raises fundamental problems. Risks of competitive exchange-rate competition and concerns over balance-of-payments structures replace the risks of competitive non-revaluation and aggregate imbalance which prevail under fixed rates. In the absence of multilateral surveillance of the entire exchange-rate regime, based on agreed international norms and guidelines to implement them, the adjustment process will remain unstable.

Liquidity uncertainties render the situation doubly dangerous. Partly because of the uncertainties of the adjustment process, countries fear that periodically they will have to face sizable deficits in their payments position without reserves sufficient to finance them, or perhaps even to give them time to adjust in an orderly way. This heightens the caution surrounding domestic policies, as well as the proclivities toward controls. It also promotes competitive exchange-rate depreciations—which may be easier to accomplish in a world of "managed floats"—although countries may also wish to avoid the inflationary effects of depreciations and hence seek to finance deficits rather than let their exchange rates fall even when afforded the opportunity to do so by the prevailing system. The problem is deepened further by the desire of most countries to achieve payments surpluses, to build their reserves against the day when they face deficits.

Both proclivities are greatly magnified by the rise in oil costs. These costs simply cannot be accommodated by changes in exchange rates. Neither the price elasticity of world demand for oil, nor of most of the OPEC countries for imports of goods and services, are high enough to make exchange-rate changes effective in this particular instance. The rise in oil prices has produced a fundamental deterioration in the collective payments position of the oil consuming countries, which can be restored only when the oil producing countries, several years in the future, become able to absorb the real goods and services which their new liquid wealth can buy. The problem is similar to the German transfer problem after World War I, or indeed the "dollar shortage" after World War II, when the contemporary surplus countries could not—or, through policy measures, would not—absorb enough exports from the contemporary deficit countries to enable them to restore payments equilibrium, at least for a number of years. The resulting pressure on the entire system intensifies the need for effective liquidity and adjustment arrangements.

At the other extreme, a few persistent surplus countries continue to fear that liquidity creation will be excessive and force them to inflate or revalue, hurting their competitive positions. Thus they seek to limit the growth of reserves, adding further to the pressure on the system and on the majority of its members.

As a result of all these shortcomings in international monetary arrangements, the frequency of "crises" remains high, despite the de facto reforms which have taken place. Even the crises prior to August 1971, none of which seriously disrupted the basic flow of economic activity, levied high costs on individual countries. The crisis of the fall of 1971, which made no progress toward solution for at least three months after the U.S. actions of August 15, brought the world perilously close to a breakdown of confidence in the future of international economic cooperation—confidence being the real international underpinning of the postwar economic prosperity, rather than any particular system derived from that cooperation—and hence undermined investment plans and economic confidence across the globe. The energy crisis is the latest example, at the time of this writing. Each succeeding "crisis" reinforces the system's inadequacies and reduces the proclivities of individual countries to place high value on adhering to it.

If all of the crises had occurred for the same reason, they would be less disturbing since some single reform could then prevent their recurrence. But they have occurred for very different reasons, which points to the need for sweeping change. The energy crisis of 1974 revived concerns about the adequacy of world reserves and the quality of the liquidity system and made clear that exchange-rate changes were no panacea for handling balance-of-payments disequilibria. May–July 1973 reminded us of the instability generated by the dollar overhang and the structural evolution toward a multiple key currency system. February–March 1973 and August 1971 vividly demonstrated the inadequacy of the adjustment process (especially when the U.S. balance of payments is directly concerned), the instability of the dollar's roles in the system, and the effects of unregulated liquidity creation. May 1971 pointed to the need for wider exchange-rate margins, better coordination of at least the timing of national economic policies, and more comprehensive international machinery to deal with interest-sensitive capital flows. The trauma of sterling from 1961 through November 1967, the problems of the mark in 1961, 1968–69 and 1971 and the franc difficulties of 1968–69 highlighted the need for improved means to adjust national parities. The generalized floats from March 1973, and the Canadian floats of 1950–62 and 1970 to the present, reveal the need for international rules to govern exchange-rate changes when they do take place. The spectacular rise in the gold price in early 1973 and late 1974, and the systemic upheaval of late 1967 through early 1968—which led to the institution of the two-tiered gold system, the final agreements on Special Drawing Rights, and the Basle arrangements for sterling—displayed vividly the "confidence" problem which arises from the existence of several competing reserve assets, and the inadequacies of the existing liquidity mechanism. (So, too, did the 1960–61 difficulties with gold, though to a much lesser degree.) The events of 1967–68 also focused the inadequacy of the adjustment process, especially when the U.S. balance of payments is directly concerned. Similarly, the minicrisis of late 1964 through early 1965 made clear the trouble which could be caused for the system by the political maneuvering of a middle power.

Each of these problems is likely to foster continual crises if left unsolved. Each succeeding crisis is likely to be correspondingly larger in magnitude, in view of the growth of internationally mobile funds and the greater market knowledge of international opportunities. Each is likely to increase the probability that truly serious economic and political problems will result. Even if this probability remains small in absolute terms, it can no more be ignored by responsible policy-makers than can other possibilities with equally small odds; the small probability that the Soviet Union will attack Western Europe has not undermined allied determination to maintain NATO or U.S. determination to spend huge amounts of money to maintain a credible nuclear deterrent.

The failure to reach agreement on a new monetary system is likely to generate increasingly serious political problems among its members. There is no agreement on how to control the trade-off between adjustment and liquidity in the system as a whole, or what modes of adjustment should dominate, or on how liquidity should be created.

There are fundamentally different national attitudes toward these issues, given the fundamental differences in national goals and capabilities described in Chapter 1. After an apparent convergence of views in the late 1960s toward limited exchange-rate flexibility and reliance on SDRs, the strength of these differences began to reassert itself as the systemic vacuum emerged. Individual countries are emboldened to try again to win support for ideas once thought dead, such as restoring gold as the financial basis of the world economy or again constructing a viable dollar standard.

Surplus countries generally attempt to force deficit countries to initiate adjustment, but no surplus country has the power to force adjustment unless a particular deficit country loses reserves beneath a level which it views as its absolute minimum. Deficit countries try to force surplus countries to initiate adjustment—and U.S. deficits have certainly contributed to adjustments in the exchange rate, and perhaps even price level, in Europe and Canada. But even the United States does not have sufficient power to force such changes, as was amply demonstrated by the refusal of France to adjust at all in 1971 except as a result of U.S. actions fully acceptable to it and negotiation at the highest political level. Surplus countries fearing inflation want deficit countries to adjust by deflation, while deficit countries facing unemployment want surplus countries to inflate or revalue. Despite the initial agreements on SDRs, total changes in world liquidity remain completely unregulated and subject to disagreement between surplus and deficit countries. In addition, some countries are perfectly willing—some even eager—to finance their surpluses by accruing dollars and hence obviating adjustment pressure on the United States, whereas other countries are not only unwilling to do so themselves but deplore this abstention by others from forcing "discipline" on the reserve center. Some would really prefer to "return to gold," while others continue to see SDRs as the only viable means for restoring a truly international monetary system.

A final political effect of the inadequate adjustment and liquidity mechanisms is the risk of increasingly pervasive national controls over international capital movements and trade, and competitive exchange-rate moves—all of which impinge directly on the national economic welfare of other countries. For example, the onset of protectionist trade policies in the United States in the early 1970s was closely related to the adverse effect on U.S. competitiveness of the growing overvaluation of the dollar in the late 1960s. The resulting conflicts among nations will grow in importance as economic interdependence opens national economies increasingly to international exchanges, and as foreign economic policy becomes a larger element in overall foreign policy consideration in all countries, including the United States. Indeed, controls *have* proliferated since the advent of more flexible exchange rates, despite the predictions of economic theory to the contrary.

The shortcomings of the system were obscured for most of the postwar period with the neglect by all parties of the U.S. trade and payments position. Payments deficits and a laissez-faire U.S. policy toward its trade balance provided an economic umbrella—not unlike the nuclear umbrella which the United States raised in the defense area—under which other countries could achieve their basically mercantilist goals of reserve increases and trade surpluses. In August 1971, however, the United States joined the mercantilist race—and the underlying politics suggest that it will stay on this course, even if not as aggressively as in the first manifestations thereof. At an earlier time, when the United States still held its dominant power position, the system might have adjusted to this change in American goals simply by accommodating them—by forcing others to modify *their* goals. Now, however, the clash of national goals coexists within a framework of relatively equal national capabilities among the United States, Western Europe, and Japan—not to mention the oil exporting countries.

The adjustment-liquidity trade-off and the methods by which adjustment is achieved and liquidity created are thus resolved in today's international monetary system largely by the exercise of market forces and national power. Yet the nature of this power is also unclear. Is it based on the size of a country's economy? On its economic openness? On its reserve level? On its current balance-of-payments position? On its overall political and military position in the world? Power to change the system differs from power to operate within a given system. In any given circumstance, different factors dominate the outcome. It is thus completely unclear whether individual payments problems will even *be* resolved, let alone *when* or *how* resolution will occur.

The U.S. Interest in Monetary Reform

The United States, of course, shares these global interests in monetary reform. It is clearly in the U.S. national interest for the monetary system to promote maximum world welfare, avoid crises, avoid uncertainties which may disrupt international economic transactions, and avoid the exacerbation of overall international relations which an ill-functioning monetary system could foster. Despite the small share of international transactions in the overall American economy, huge amounts of money are involved— about $100 billion in both exports and imports, hundreds of billions of dollars' worth of foreign investment—and they are of critical importance to a large number of U.S. industries, firms, consumers, and groups of workers. The broad interest of the United States in these global goals probably exceeds that of most countries, in view of its leadership responsibilities within the non-Communist world.

In addition, however, the United States has specifically national interests in the international monetary system. Some of these interests parallel those of other countries, though they differ in degree because of national differences. Some are different in kind, because of the unique world role of the United States and its resulting goals for the system as a whole.

All nations wish to minimize the external monetary restraints on the pursuit of their internal economic, and hence political, objectives. The United States is no exception.[3] In fact, this national goal is probably more prevalent in the United States than in any other country, with the possible exception of the Soviet Union, for three reasons.

First, the foreign sector plays such a relatively small role in the American economy that it could hardly be permitted to determine national economic policy. Other countries, with economies more open to international transactions, simply must give more weight to their payments positions in developing their domestic policies. The only necessary caveat is that international transactions *are* of great absolute importance to the U.S. economy, so it would be as impossible for economic policy to ignore the world economy as to be dominated by it.

Second, its leadership of the non-Communist world remains so important to the maintenance of world security that the United States cannot permit its foreign policy to be seriously deflected by external monetary considerations. Most of its allies shared this view for at least most of the post-1945 era, and most still share it today.

Third, the ability of the United States to avoid being forced to adjust its balance of payments for so long is deeply embedded in this country. Any significant change from that situation would come as a deep shock to most Americans, and could have far-reaching implications for the political willingness to continue playing a constructive world role, economically as well as politically. Among the

3. An exception must frequently be made for individual cabinet ministers or central bankers in individual countries, who seek to employ the "discipline" of the balance of payments to buttress their cases for economic restraint in intra-governmental decision-making councils. "All nations" here means the ultimate political view in most countries at most times.

most cryptic cases in point are the near-miss of the Mansfield Amendment to halve U.S. troops in Europe in early 1971, triggered by the
"attack on the dollar" symbolized by the German float and the inex-
plicable failure of the U.S. government warmly to welcome that
move, and the major threat of protectionist trade legislation, which
was originally given impetus by the overvaluation of the dollar and
would derive continued support from any aggressive monetary competition between the United States and other major countries.

The broad national goal of avoiding policy constraints from the external sector is readily translated into specific international monetary
policy goals. First, the United States wants an effective adjustment
system so that its internal economic objectives, be they primarily
full employment or price stability at any particular time, are not
undermined by external events. Second, the United States wants sufficient financing for itself to avoid being forced to adjust with undue
haste to any external imbalance which it may run. Third, it wants
to maximize the net benefits to it from the international roles of
the dollar.

Given the inevitable limits on liquidity, and indeed the costs of
perpetuating payments disequilibria, an effective adjustment process
is necessary. The United States and other countries face two issues
in this context: *what measures* are used to achieve adjustment? *who*
initiates the action?

From the standpoint of the United States, or any other individual
country, two adjustment cases must be distinguished. The first is
when the United States *wants* to adjust, perhaps because an overvalued exchange rate has produced domestic unemployment and
pressures for protectionist trade policies (as in 1971), or because an
undervalued rate has intensified inflation (as in 1973). The second
is when the United States is *forced* to adjust, because its imbalance
raises serious problems for others—"exporting inflation or unemployment"—even though the domestic consequences thereof are quite
acceptable, even desirable, to the United States.

In both cases, the United States has a major interest in the
method by which adjustment occurs, particularly when it must act
itself. We have seen, in Chapter 9, the sharp variation in costs to
the United States, ranging from very high costs for domestic macroeconomic policy changes to relatively low costs for exchange-rate
changes. Accordingly, the United States wants to be able to turn to
the exchange rate to effect adjustment, whether in pursuit of its
own internal goals or in response to external pressures, or to the
combination of the two which often occurs in practice.

The United States similarly has an interest in the mode of adjustment when other countries initiate the action. The effect on the United States of German adjustment differs whether Germany chooses to eliminate a payments surplus by revaluation, internal inflation, reduction or imposition of its own capital or trade controls, or other measures. For example, German adjustment through controls over capital inflows would probably affect the United States differently than would equivalent adjustment through the trade account, since the United States is the leading single source of capital flows to Germany whereas it is only the third largest trading partner (and since the real costs of capital controls would probably be less than the costs of ·changes in trade patterns). Revaluation might be deemed injurious to the roles of the dollar, whereas German imposition of controls over capital inflows would be seen as enhancing the dollar as an international currency. German border tax changes would help U.S. trade without making U.S. military expenditures there more costly in dollar terms, as would revaluation. In addition, the costs to the United States would differ whether a country adopted import-restricting measures alone, or measures affecting both exports and imports—be they macroeconomic policy or exchange-rate changes.

No generalization is thus possible about what measures the United States would prefer to see other countries take. To get an effective exchange-rate option for itself, however, it would certainly have to accept such an option for others. And since access to effective exchange–rate changes is the single most important U.S. objective of monetary reform, that option will certainly have to be available to all countries.

All countries share in the costs and benefits of international adjustment, regardless of which country initiates action. For example, the United States bears real welfare costs when Germany revalues its currency, even though the United States has "done nothing," because German goods and services (and other foreign goods, to a lesser extent) are now more costly to Americans.[4] However, in cases where it does not want to adjust for international reasons, the United States would generally prefer to avoid initiating action itself if it can get adequate action from others. The real costs to the United States of international adjustment are probably less if other countries trigger the development, because the effects are then diffused throughout the

4. American goods, along with other foreign goods, are then of course more competitive with German goods, so the net welfare effect for the United States turns on whether unemployment or inflation is the greater problem, in both the short and long runs.

world and the United States "suffers" less from them. In addition, as the real economic effects of adjustment are much more obvious in the initiating country than in a country to which change is transmitted through the world economy, the political risks of initiation are high and argue strongly against it to that country's government unless they serve internal purposes. This is less apparent in a country relatively closed to the world economy where the effects are not as noticeable, but it may still be true for the United States with its history of relative aloofness to responding to international disturbances and the absence of public familiarity with the periodic need to do so.

If an adjustment initiative is unambiguously *beneficial* in domestic political terms, the United States would then be quite willing, even eager, to initiate action. In such cases, however, there is significant risk that the action will be a beggar-thy-neighbor policy of significant cost to other countries, which will therefore trigger emulation and retaliation and wind up with little net adjustment effect and sizable costs in the broader sense. In addition, such a scope for domestically oriented U.S. action would permit other countries to act likewise, with potentially adverse effects on the United States. Thus the only reconciliation appears to be a system which *permits* adjustment initiatives only when they are clearly called for by a country's *external* position, and indeed *requires* such initiatives when the external position calls for them.

America's liquidity objectives in international monetary reform must be conditioned by the fact that, compared with those of other countries, U.S. gross reserves now stand quite low relative to all of the standard variables—annual imports, potential variations in exports, overall payments positions, etc.—without even allowing for any future conversions of the present "overhang" of outstanding dollar balances. A return to convertibility for the dollar into U.S. reserve assets would probably require a sharp increase in those reserves. In the past, the acceptability of dollars to the rest of the world meant that the United States needed *fewer* owned reserves to finance its payments deficits. On the other hand, the stability of this situation depended at least partly on the adequacy of U.S. reserve assets as "backing" for foreign-held dollars, which called for *additions* to the reserve stock both to protect against collapse of the "overhang" and to promote further dollar accruals. In view of the decline in the international acceptability of the dollar, and the emergence of real alternatives to it, it is virtually certain that the United States will seek to avoid further declines in its reserves, and indeed seek increases in them, either because dollar financing will no longer be as available or because more reserves will be needed to make it available. This will presumably call for increases in global reserves, since it is difficult to envisage an increase in reserves granted to the United States alone by other countries, (e.g., via a special allocation of SDR *to the United States*) without a return to a growing key currency role for the dollar *and* foreign acceptance thereof.

As for the reserves of other countries, the U.S. bias is to err on the high side in calculating the level which could be generally deemed "adequate" for them from the American standpoint. The inflationary effect of increased world reserves is probably smaller on the United States than on any other major country, whereas countries more open to the world economy understandably fear the inflationary consequences for them and are thus much more concerned with avoiding such impulses, as could occur from excessive creation of international liquidity. In addition, given its steady deficits of the past, the United States would prefer the pressure on surplus countries generated by excessive liquidity to the pressure on deficit countries generated by inadequate liquidity, which would compound the devaluation bias against the dollar of the Bretton Woods exchange-rate regime. So U.S. interests call for sizable growth in world reserves.

There is, of course, the usual trade-off between these liquidity and adjustment objectives: more liquidity for the United States means less need for an effective adjustment process, and vice versa. The ability of the United States to finance its payments deficits through foreign-held dollar accumulation for so many years rendered unnecessary any deep interest in improving either the liquidity mechanism or the adjustment process. It was only with the onset of foreign concern over additional dollar holdings that the United States began actively to seek, first, new modes of creating international liquidity through Special Drawing Rights and, second, improved adjustment (both by individual countries, as in the pressure placed on Germany to revalue in 1968, and by improving the functioning of the system as a whole through greater flexibility of exchange rates). And it was only with the onset of stubborn domestic unemployment, in an era when foreign competition was sufficiently tough to add visibly to that unemployment, that the United States began actively to seek an improved adjustment process for domestic economic reasons.

The choice between liquidity and adjustment is a difficult one, raising issues both of principle and of how in practice each can be achieved. At one extreme, the United States would obviously prefer unlimited liquidity through the internationally approved creation of Special Drawing Rights, which would carry none of the economic and political problems of dollar financing, to the very costly adjustment of its own payments deficits via contraction of the domestic economy. At the other extreme, it would prefer adjustment through changes in exchange rates by other countries to financing for U.S. deficits through foreign accumulations of dollars which might be converted into U.S. reserve assets in the near future. These extremes are not the choices faced by policy-makers in the real world, however, and there is no single answer as to whether the United States should prefer financing or adjustment.

Total financing for any payments deficit of the United States would enable it to appropriate real resources from the rest of the world, which would add to its real wealth and be particularly helpful in combating internal inflation. On the other hand, it would shield the economy from external competition and lessen U.S. competitiveness, and could lead to dollar overvaluation with unfavorable employment and trade policy effects. Adjustment *via exchange-rate changes* would have the contrary effect of enhancing aggregate U.S. competitiveness and boosting total U.S. employment, though at the same time requiring more rapid microeconomic adjustment to changes in the structure of production. The prospect that adjustment would become a more frequent response to payments disequilibria than financing would add to the pressures on U.S. industries to improve their competitive position.

The optimal strategy for the United States is therefore to seek a situation in which it can get payments financing and increased imports if the domestic economy is running at full employment with major inflationary pressures, and depreciation of the dollar if unemployment is the major domestic problem. The problem is that in some cases this flexibility would intensify U.S. deficits (and world inflation) and in others, U.S. surpluses (and world recession). Other countries would therefore be unwilling for the United States to have it both ways at all times. If they let it have financing via a dollar standard, we saw in Chapter 12 that they could impede its getting adjustment. And if they let it have effective adjustment via the exchange rate, we learned in Chapter 5 there would be a concomitant reduction in its ability to play a key currency role and hence to get dollar financing.

The policy conclusion is that the United States should seek maximum flexibility in policy to be able to pursue either course as far as possible in light of the peculiar needs of particular times. This conclusion is not as trivial as it sounds, since the United States has not had such flexibility in the past. Since it is highly probable that less dollar financing will be available to the United States in the future than in the past, it should thus have a cardinal interest in getting both new modes of adequate liquidity creation and—even more important, since any such creation is likely to provide the United States with less financing than did the dollar's roles—a significant improvement in the adjustment process both for other countries and for itself.

This conclusion for U.S. policy is reinforced by considering its power position. In the past, the United States was able to dominate a fixed exchange-rate system by virtue of its large reserves and dollar-financing capability, as well as by its underlying economic and political strength. Both sources of international monetary power have now diminished sharply, with U.S. reserves far below those of the European Community as a unit, below those of Germany alone, and only slightly above those of Japan. Thus a system based relatively more on adjustment than on financing will also conform more to present U.S. monetary capabilities. On the relative power concept, such adjustment needs to be based on greater flexibility of exchange rates since its relatively closed economy provides U.S. policy with little leverage over the balance of payments via domestic demand policy, but significant leverage via the exchange rate. Accordingly, the changed power position, as well as the change in policy objectives, argues strongly for U.S. support for a high degree of exchange-rate flexibility in any future monetary system.

The United States also seeks to maximize the benefits to it of the dollar's international roles, and to minimize their costs. The main benefits are the potential financing for U.S. payments deficits, the political leverage which they bring in some cases, and the related financial benefits which accrue mainly to private American citizens. The costs are the limitations on the ability effectively to initiate adjustment via changes in the dollar exchange rate, the only effective way the United States *can* adjust; the contingent threats posed by the dollar "overhang" to domestic economic and foreign policies, which would be realized only if actual sales took place but which could be costly anyway if there was widespread belief that such sales were a serious possibility; the very high interest payments on this "overhang," which amount to a net cost of about $3 billion per year; the political leverage which others enjoy over the United States as a result of the overhang's existence; and the broad political effects of a dominant dollar when changes in the overall world position of the United States mean that it must move toward greater sharing of international responsibiliies in all fields.

The United States thus has both broader and narrower sets of objectives vis-à-vis the future international roles of the dollar. In broad terms, the United States should promote dollar roles which enhance an effective exchange-rate adjustment system, its primary objective in monetary reform for the reasons just indicated. Ideally, it would like to maintain some potential for dollar financing as well, but we have seen that this is largely incompatible with the overriding adjustment goal. These broad goals suggest a U.S. effort to reduce markedly, if not eliminate, the key currency roles of the dollar.

In narrower financial terms, the United States has a major interest in reducing as much as possible the costs to it of the existing dollar overhang and any additional dollar balances which might emerge in the future. At present, the United States pays market interest rates on the outstanding dollars. It extends exchange-rate guarantees on only a small share of them. And the dollars have essentially infinite maturities as long as the dollar remains inconvertible into U.S. reserves, but could once again represent a very immediate conversion threat if dollar convertibility were restored. An optimum reform for the United States would cut the interest-rate burden, avoid any maintenance-of-value guarantees, and avoid conversion. The available options on these issues were outlined in Chapter 11, where we also concluded that the most desirable outcome, which was also politically feasible, would point to a sharp reduction if not elimination of the future roles of the dollar.

Beyond these "purely economic" objectives, the United States has global political and economic objectives which also critically affect its stance on international monetary issues—"milieu goals," as they are called by political scientists. Continued leadership of the non-Communist world requires a continued broad interest in preserving the economic and political strength of allies from Germany to Japan, which in turn requires an effectively functioning international monetary system to underpin an effectively functioning world economy. Disarray in the monetary system could easily spill over into disarray in world trade and investment generally, with international political difficulties and weakening of the system of alliances as the inevitable result.

The key currency roles of the dollar add significantly to the U.S. interest in an effective monetary system, since all international monetary problems involve the dollar, and hence the United States. There can be no "dollar problem" when the system is healthy.[5] So

5. Some observers also believe that there can be no systemic problem as long as the dollar is healthy. This was probably true in the dollar-centered world of the 1950s and even early 1960s, but it is certainly not true in the polycentric monetary world in the early 1970s.

the overriding U.S. interest in avoiding policy constraints is served importantly by effective operation of the entire system, as well as by its specific effects on the United States directly.

A related consideration is that, because a key currency country does inherit such systemic interest, the U.S. interest is served if other currencies play a similar or supportive role alongside the dollar within an agreed and widely understood, not an antagonistically competitive, framework. A greater sharing of international monetary responsibilities by other countries is a likely concomitant of key currency status, even if it is limited to a private transactions role; hence such status for others is in the U.S. interest. But there are risks in moving toward such a multiple key currency system, as developed in Chapter 11 and referenced at the outset of this chapter. And dollar hegemony has its merits for the United States, while duopoly or multipolar monetary power raise well-known problems of coordination and potential rivalry.

But dollar hegemony is no longer a viable option. The vital need for the United States, as for the system as a whole, is to bring into balance the true power positions of individual countries or groups of them and their roles in the international monetary system—through means, such as SDRs and joint surveillance over the exchange-rate regime, which avoid the risks of a multiplicity of international key currencies. Troublemakers for the monetary system, like France in the late 1920s and gain in the middle 1960s, are generally those whose true power is not accurately reflected in their positions in the system—just as troublemakers on the broader world scene have frequently been countries whose power aspirations have been frustrated by the dominant political powers of the time. It is clearly dangerous, to the dominant power and to the system as a whole, to fail to align power and responsibility.

It is extremely difficult to do so, however, during a period when international power relationships are unsettled. Hegemonial periods —such as those dominated by the United Kingdom in the early nineteenth century and the United States in the early postwar period —are relatively free of uncertainty, due to the dominance of a single power. Non-hierarchical periods—such as the interwar years, when the United Kingdom lost its leadership role and the United States and France competed for the rights of leadership without expressing much willingness to accept its responsibilities—are particularly dangerous. They call for maximum international cooperation to resolve the underlying uncertainties, treading between the Scylla of attempting to preserve an anachronistic hegemony and the Charybdis of passing power to those unprepared to exercise it effectively.

We are now in such a period. U.S. dominance of the non-Communist world is over, both politically and economically, for both international and domestic reasons. The relative might of the United States, though it will remain large forever and probably always preserve an effective veto power, will continue to decrease, particularly in the world economy. Thus, as we saw in Chapter 4–6, the dollar simply can no longer play the key currency role it played in the past.

At the same time, Europe, and especially Germany, is regaining its traditional world role. Japan's assumption of the leadership of Asia is only a matter of time, and its main rival is China—not the United States. The power of the Third World is rising rapidly, and the U.S. role there is likely to continue its relative decline.[6] The "new nationalism," so prevalent throughout both the industrialized and developing worlds, assures that these new capabilities in other countries will be translated into demands for new rights to influence the range of issues subject to international interaction.

In consequence, the United States should now actively seek a greater management role in the international monetary system at least for the countries of Western Europe, as a unit if they prefer or individually if not, Japan, and some of the most important of the developing countries (especially the oil exporters). Resistance to the trends leading inexorably in this direction would be folly, and would create additional tensions and conflict rather than cooperation. Over time this would lead to financial, and broader economic, disturbances, which could then in turn feed back negatively on overall political relations. An effort to maintain, or re-establish, dollar hegemony would be the epitome of such a mistaken effort and would lead over time to a *forced* reduction of the dollar's roles, the worst outcome for the United States both economically and politically. Furthermore, a reduced international financial role for the dollar may be a necessary concomitant of the reduced world political role sought by most Americans, since the United States might otherwise be frequently tempted to maintain excessive security and other commitments abroad to protect an exposed financial position.

This is the major lesson for the United States from the historical experience of the United Kingdom. An unwillingness to recognize that fundamental changes in Britain's world position precluded any possibility of maintaining sterling's pre-1914 roles disastrously pervaded British economic and foreign policy for over forty years, from

6. See C. Fred Bergsten, "The Threat from the Third World," *Foreign Policy*, No. 11 (Summer 1973) and "The Response to the Third World," *Foreign Policy*, No. 17 (Winter 1975).

the return to an overvalued gold parity in 1925 through the costly effort to avoid devaluation in 1961–67. Sterling's lame duck position contributed significantly to the sterling crises which have permeated virtually the entire postwar period, with sizable costs both to the United Kingdom and the system as a whole, and to the perpetual weakness of the British economy. When finally forced to negotiate the international roles of its currency in mid-1968, Britain did so with its back to the wall and emerged with arrangements which maximized their costs, and minimized their benefits, to Britain. It was an object lesson in the absence of foresight and a victory for inertia predicated on unanalyzed nostaligia. It is noteworthy that foresight was absent not only in Britain but in other countries, and the United States must avoid the temptation of accepting the blandishments of *other* countries to preserve an excessive role for the dollar—whether such blandishments are motivated by a sincere belief that a dollar world is desirable, or by a Machiavellian effort, based on the same conclusions reached in this book, to keep the United States under pressure through an overextension of its international financial position.

The United States could never be constrained as badly by the roles of the dollar as was the United Kingdom by the roles of sterling, even if it and the world were to repeat the errors of the past. The United States is much bigger and its economy is less reliant on the world economy. The rest of the non-Communist world will probably continue to rely much more heavily on the United States for broad security and political support than did Britain's allies, at least beyond the Napoleonic period. But this difference in degree should not mask the similarity in kind, and it cannot hide the absolute magnitudes of the problems which could develop.

The Relationship Among the Specific Problems

There are thus several key areas in which improvement is needed in the international monetary system, from both the global and U.S. standpoints. The most important is the adjustment process, which must incorporate active and politically acceptable means for changing exchange rates that are at the same time as immune as possible from competitive intervention for nationalistic reasons. The system must be assured of adequate but not excessive liquidity, in a manner which is based on an international consensus regarding amounts and form, respects the different proclivities of countries to hold their reserve in various forms, and supports the improvements in the adjustment mechanism. The long-term confidence problem must be resolved by removing uncertainties over possible changes in the portfolios of national monetary authorities. The short-term confidence problem arising from huge international capital flows must be met both by reducing the incentive for such flows and by assured, coordinated official response to them.

These four basic problems are closely interrelated. An effective liquidity mechanism can promote more effective payments adjustment, and a better adjustment mechanism can relieve liquidity pressures. Improvements in both mechanisms will go far toward easing short- and long-term confidence problems. The uncertainties of the official confidence problem clearly exacerbate the private confidence problem. Institutional improvements are needed to implement all of the changes, particularly strengthening the role of the IMF on liquidity so that it can exercise enhanced influence on adjustment.

The dollar's international roles pervade each of these issues, and the U.S. interest in them. The dollar's impact is clearest on liquidity: the possibility of unlimited foreign accumulation of dollars provides a major source of new liquidity, but in a wholly uncertain manner which undermines the objective of international control of the growth of international reserves and in a form which is increasingly unstable. The impact is also clear on the confidence issue: the omnipresent possibility of a collapse of the dollar overhang poses a basic systemic instability since such efforts could lead only to excessive depreciations of the dollar, another U.S. suspension of convertibility if the United States had previously returned to a fixed parity, draconian balance-of-payments measures, or a huge increase in the official price of SDR/gold—each of which would be disruptive to the system as a whole. On the institutional issue, the dollar's roles are the main instrument through which the United States has exercised its stewardship of the monetary system, and neither the IMF nor anyone else can accede to this position unless those roles are correspondingly diminished.

In addition, the dollar's roles add significantly to the problems of the adjustment process. They render it difficult for the United States to initiate adjustment in the only economically effective manner which is feasible in its domestic politics—changes in the exchange rate of the dollar—even in a world of managed flexibility of rates. The reserve currency role contributes to this impasse: it renders U.S. policy-makers inherently schizophrenic on the desirability of adjustment, because foreign dollar-holders are reluctant to accept frequent depreciation in the value of their dollar reserves, and because the United States would attempt to avoid imposing such costs on them. The intervention currency role may be equally important in this regard, because it means that other countries must abstain from the markets or change their intervention prices to permit an effective change in the U.S. exchange rate—even under a regime of managed flexibility, where others are actively intervening. The dollar's overall international status also exacerbates the unwillingness of other countries to change their exchange rates, because more frequent changes by others would enhance the image of the dollar as "the sole bastion of the system"—despite the significant decline in the relative power position of the United States, the decidedly unstable path of its economy in recent years, and the long persistence of balance-of-payments deficits. Finally, the dollar's widespread use and inevitable involvement in all international monetary events makes it a chief target of criticism during most short-run disturbances, whether or not it actually contributed to causing them, and thus compounds the political implications of international monetary developments.

Two major conclusions emerge. The first is that all of the inter-related issues must be considered together if definitive progress on reforming the system is to be achieved, or indeed if any one of them is to be handled satisfactorily. Indeed, the *de facto* revaluation of gold reserves is a clear indication of the errors which can be made when monetary reform is implemented piecemeal. The second is that such considerations must explicitly include the dollar's international roles if reform is to be truly comprehensive.

These conclusions are buttressed by their implications for the United States, without whose agreement there can be no negotiated and orderly improvement of the system. The United States has a major national interest in negotiating the dollar's international roles, both because they increasingly exert real economic and political costs on it and because of its broad interest in the success of any comprehensive effort to improve the international monetary system. But the United States must have several major national objectives in the reform negotiations. It cannot expect to match the balance-of-payments financing received from the dollar in the past from any other method of meeting world liquidity needs. Hence it must insist that enough liquidity for the system as a whole and an improved adjustment process—including adequate liquidity for itself, and improved means for it to initiate adjustment—be included in any package in which it voluntarily gives up some or all of that financing benefit, especially if it remains saddled with the real and potential costs of the dollar overhang. And it should no longer permit the intervention use of the dollar if doing so hamstrings its own adjustment options or if periodic "crises"—which are bound to continue to permeate even an improved monetary system, though hopefully to a much lesser degree—are permitted to levy significant economic and political costs on the United States.

The Bases of Reform

The systemic reform which will meet the problems outlined in the preceding sections must be based on five principles. The first is that the new system must be managed internationally. The two alternatives to international management are unviable. No single country, including the United States, can now manage the system alone. And a completely unmanaged system is too likely to be unstable, through competition among several national currencies (and gold) for liquidity supremacy and unregulated (and even competitive) exchange-rate changes and proliferating national controls, to command confidence that it will not seriously erode the economic benefits of international exchange and foster major political problems as well.

International monetary power as well as responsibility for the system must be effectively shared, and effectively exercised. This requires coordinated action among all countries, but primarily the United States, the expanded European Community, Japan and some of the leading powers of the Third World. Such coordination can best be assured through institutionalization, primarily through a reformed International Monetary Fund. Its potential for international burden-sharing could serve a major national interest of the United States.

The second principle is that, within this framework of international management, individual nations must maintain sufficient sovereign authority to meet the needs and aspirations of their peoples. Different countries have very different economic and political priorities, which are a major source of present tensions in the world economy. Yet it would be politically naive to attempt to force all countries into any single policy mold. The new monetary system must accommodate diversity.

In addition, the new system must restore national sovereignty in some areas where it has been absent. As a result of the dollar's international roles, the United States had little sovereign control over its own exchange rate under the Bretton Woods system. Because of the intervention currency role, it still has less sovereignty over its exchange rate than do other countries under a regime of managed flexibility. Some other countries, as a result of the dollar's roles, have had little sovereign control over the growth of their reserves and imperfect control over the growth of their domestic money supplies. Again, the future of the dollar is central to achieving improvement of the basic system.

There is obvious tension between these first two principles. Complete international management cannot co-exist with unbridled national autonomy. Any set of proposals for reform must provide a reconciliation, finding ways in which international management can be effective without undermining national autonomy and that autonomy can be exercised without upsetting other countries or the system as a whole. The specific suggestions in Chapter 15 seek that reconciliation by building on a third and a fourth principle.

The third principle is that international liquidity arrangements should henceforth be based primarily on Special Drawing Rights, with the holding of other reserve assets—gold, dollars, and other national currencies—permitted only *under new rules to prevent adverse effects on the system*. SDRs are created and managed internationally, and are thus the proper vehicle for monetary primacy. Reliance on them will best enable the international community to determine the appropriate growth of *total* world reserves, over which it has no control at present. The primacy of SDRs will strengthen the role of the IMF and help institutionalize the needed international management. National currencies are nationally managed, and gold is unmanaged; hence neither is appropriate as a primary monetary vehicle in the world of the foreseeable future. But some countries will still wish to hold and even accumulate these other assets, and they will be needed for vehicle purposes. Thus there should be scope for them in the system, as long as they do not destabilize it or undermine its other objectives, such as improving the adjustment process. Adherence to this important caveat adds further to the case for relying heavily on SDRs.

The fourth principle is that the needed improvement in the adjustment process should come primarily from flexibility of exchange rates, managed within a framework of internationally agreed guidelines and with sanctions available to the international community to support the guidelines if needed in extreme cases. Exchange rates link national economies and should be the primary focus of international management of the relations among those economies. The adoption of flexible rates by most major countries in early 1973 is a major step toward implementing that concept. But only with a set of agreed guidelines, and with an international surveillance mechanism (such as the IMF) to continuously recommend where and how they should apply, can individual countries both derive international support for exchange-rate changes they wish to make and have reasonable assurance that their own positions will not be jeopardized by exchange-rate changes which other countries ought not to make. We have seen that this principle can be implemented either through a system of nominally flexible exchange rates, with national intervention in the markets subject to such multilateral surveillance, or through a system of nominally fixed exchange rates (within wide margins) that can change frequently in response to such guidelines.

The United States should benefit greatly from this reform in adjustment. Either approach would enable it to initiate adjustment by neutralizing the ability of other countries to frustrate any such U.S. initiative through their use of the dollar for intervention purposes. And such a code should enable the entire international community to bring sufficient pressure to bear to avoid at least such gross disequilibria as the undervaluation of the Japanese yen in 1970–71. Marshalling the entire community for such an endeavor would obviously ease the political problems for all the countries taking such a stand, a particular benefit for the United States since it has heretofore attempted to police the world monetary system unilaterally.

At the same time, guidelines are not firm rules. Even when the guidelines appear to call for an exchange-rate change, or to bar intervention in the exchange markets, a country can argue that the guidelines do not apply or that it is taking other actions—including changes in domestic economic policy or selective controls over its international transactions—which are better equipped to restore equilibrium. National sovereignty over both the timing and, especially, the means of adjustment will thus be preserved. But the development of an international code against which national behavior is judged would provide a major step forward.

The fifth principle is the most important. It is simply that real cooperation among the major power centers is essential to any lasting monetary reform. The maintenance of such cooperation must be the cardinal objective of the United States and all other countries.

This point would have appeared superfluous and banal just a few years ago, but is critically central today. Worldwide confidence in international monetary cooperation almost broke down in the fall of 1971, when the greatest crisis of the postwar period seemed further from solution on November 15 than when it began on August 15. It was this primordial concern, rather than fears of specific problems such as import surcharges and dirty floats, which produced near-panic in boardrooms and bourses around the world. And there has been continued uncertainty about the future of the monetary system, and new crises, ever since—especially since the onset of the energy crisis in late 1973. The high degree of stability and predictability of the Bretton Woods system has been replaced by widespread instability, unpredictability and great uncertainty about the future—over the shape of the monetary system, and whether the major countries will cooperate sufficiently even to reconstruct anything which can be called a system. Once shaken to its roots, particularly by the action of its mightiest member, confidence in the system is not easy to restore. A renewed commitment to international economic cooperation is thus a necessary underpinning of any progress toward restoring world monetary stability.

The Urgency of Action

There are three reasons why reforms based on these principles should be pursued with urgency. First, the disparity between international monetary relationships and the underlying political realities is likely to continue to widen in the next few years. The expanded European Community will continue to play a growing role in the world economy, even if its efforts toward further integration (including monetary union) continue to stagnate, and European currencies (especially the mark) will in any event increasingly challenge the dollar throughout the world. Japan will increasingly assert the power which its capabilities make possible. The oil exporters, and other countries of the Third World, are rapidly evolving in a similar direction. The adjustment of political relations between the United States and the rest of the industrialized world and parts of the developing world, which is already underway and being consciously promoted, must have its monetary corollary. The 1971 crisis made it clear that these essentially political problems could begin to affect adversely the overall relations among the countries involved and foster truly serious economic problems, with disastrous effects on the functioning of the international economy and hence national economic welfare around the world. The energy crisis has restored a measure of U.S. power, relative to its more dependent allies in Western Europe and Japan, but this only slows the trend toward the equalization of world economic power, rather than reversing it.

Second, a number of key features of the system are under review, even aside from the new uncertainties caused by the radical change in U.S. policies. Further allocations of SDRs, and the reconstitution provision and other changes in their governing rules; amendments to the IMF Articles to reconcile the managed floats which began in early 1973; monetary unity in the European Community; the role of gold in the system, and its official price; continuing pressure to restore at least limited convertibility of the dollar into U.S. reserve assets—each of these is integral to a solution of the overall international monetary problem, but can be handled rationally only in the context of fundamental overall reform.

Third, the international monetary world may evolve unconsciously in highly dangerous directions if a new system is not consciously negotiated. A failure to negotiate new adjustment rules could easily produce increasing national use of uncoordinated selective controls and exchange-rate changes, whether under the guise of managed floats or efforts to retain par values. A failure to negotiate new liquidity arrangements will imply to many a U.S. effort to preserve a de facto dollar standard based on a dollar inconvertible into U.S. reserves, and a European effort to counter it by permitting (or even promoting) widespread international use of one or more European currencies. The result could well be a global multiple reserve currency standard, one of the worst of all the reform options which (as we saw in Chapter 13) was carefully examined and then dismissed by virtually all observers over a decade ago.

A related possibility is the development of monetary blocs *in an atmosphere of hostility toward each other*. In all monetary systems in history, smaller countries have tended to coalesce around major poles of power. The potential for such blocs clearly exists today, most notably in Europe but also in the Far East, partly because the United States, the expanded EC, and Japan are *all* relatively closed to the world economy. However, we also concluded that such blocs— or "monetary areas," to use the less perjorative terminology which is appropriate in such circumstances—could be a constructive step toward establishing an effective global system *if they developed within a framework of constructive cooperation with each other*. In the absence of such cooperation, however, the formation of powerful economic units could intensify the costs and dangers already outlined as inherent in an unregulated system. We turn now to a set of proposals to reform the monetary system constructively to avoid the onset of such developments.

15

The Reform of Adjustment and Liquidity

ADJUSTMENT

The adjustment problem lies at the heart of the international monetary sytem. It is at once the most important and the most difficult issue to resolve in paving the way for an effective and smoothly functioning world economy. As with the liquidity and confidence issues, the United States and the dollar's roles are critical elements in its solution.

Greater Flexibility of Exchange Rates

The only effective and politically practical way to provide an effective adjustment process in the near future is to use exchange-rate changes for that purpose. Domestic macroeconomic policies will continue to focus on domestic economic needs, even when they run counter to the needs of the balance of payments. Selective controls over international transactions are inefficient, delay real adjustment, increase the magnitude of the adjustment eventually needed, and carry major political risks. Better international coordination of both domestic macroeconomic policies and controls over international transactions is desirable and should be pursued, but cannot be expected to yield major results at this time. In short, the exchange-rate mechanism must be the center of meaningful action in this area.

Exchange rates need to move early in the adjustment process and therefore by smaller amounts than under the Bretton Woods system. They should be regarded as a normal policy tool. Through earlier and smaller changes, they could prevent the cumulation of disequilibria and the resultant deepening of both domestic political problems and likely international repercussions, which render proper action increasingly difficult.

The bias at Bretton Woods was to make exchange-rate changes *more* difficult because of the understandable preoccupation with the competitive depreciations of the 1930s. The risk of competitive depreciations is still with us—as has been clear since August 15, 1971, and especially since the adoption of nominally full flexibility in March 1973 was joined by global recession in late 1974—and changes in the exchange-rate regime must provide safeguards against it. In addition, the advent of inflation as a major ongoing problem in virtually all of the industrialized countries, and the efforts of numerous countries to export it in recent years through both monetary and trade measures,[1] raises the specter of competitive appreciation. But the Bretton Woods system, as it evolved, provided no effective means for inducing countries to change their exchange rates by proper amounts when such changes are needed. It was especially weak in bringing pressure to bear on surplus countries, and therefore provided no answer to the central problem of the competitive undervaluation of currencies. Meaningful reform of the adjustment process must ease the domestic political problem of changing exchange rates, and must exert effective international pressure on countries to move when necessary to achieve payments equilibrium and avoid such moves when they are not.

There are two ways to achieve such reform. The first would retain the focus of the past, exchange-rate parities, but provide for much wider margins around the parities and for effective means to change them. The second would be to continue to avoid fixed parities, with new rules to govern the inevitable intervention by national authorities in the floating-rate markets which result.

Under the first approach, the Articles of Agreement of the International Monetary Fund would be amended to encourage earlier, hence smaller and probably more frequent, exchange-rate changes. Technically, amendments to the International Monetary Fund Articles are not necessary to achieve this, but they could explicitly eliminate any barriers to such action by making clear that (a) parity changes should be used in cases of *impending* as well as *actual* "fundamental disequilibrium," and (b) a single change need not remove the *total* disequilibrium all at once.[2] These changes would be desirable even if no amendments to actively promote exchange-rate changes were adopted, partly because discussion of the amend-

---

1. For an analysis of such efforts through trade policy see C. Fred Bergsten, *Completing the GATT: Toward New International Rules to Govern Export Controls* (Washington: British North American Committee, 1974).

2. For example, a country might want to devalue by stages to enable it to dismantle gradually its import or capital controls, which demonstrated the existence of a fundamental disequilibrium. Or it might be willing to keep its interest rates high to pull in sufficient liquid capital to finance such a policy.

ments would in itself help the evaluation of basic attitudes toward using the exchange-rate mechanism.

In addition, the Articles of Agreement should be amended to permit countries to widen the margins within which their exchange rates may fluctuate daily, to 5 per cent on either side of parity. One objective of this move would be to dampen the volume of interest-sensitive international capital movements to help deal with the "private" confidence problem. More importantly, wider bands would help the adjustment process in four ways. They are necessary to permit smooth implementation of smaller and more frequent parity changes, to avoid the need for spot rates to move discontinuously when parity changes take place. The wider scope for exchange rates to move freely could itself have a modest adjustment effect if a spot rate remained significantly away from its parity for an extended period of time. Bands of this width would obviate the need for "transitional floats" to find new parity levels, thus reducing the opportunity to use uncertainty as an excuse for competitive depreciation or appreciation. And a consistent deviation from parity by the spot rate would make it politically much easier for a government to change its parity, since doing so would then merely represent "ratification" of a change already instituted and maintained by market forces.

New Guidelines for Adjustment

But further steps would be needed to assure adjustment under a regime of nominally fixed rates. One major impediment to revaluations in such a system is the legitimate fear of an individual country contemplating such action that no other countries will revalue in concert with it (even if they should do so) or move at later times when their payments situations require similar action. The prolonged impasse over choosing new parities in the wake of the U.S. moves of August 1971 is a telling illustration of this problem. The quick agreements reached in February 1973 did little to change this picture, and may have intensified the problem for the long run, because the parities so quickly agreed upon lasted less than a month and had to give to widespread floating, the results of which differed markedly from the rates which had been negotiated.

Similarly, a major impediment to orderly devaluation is the fear that too many other countries will move and effectively offset much of the impact. Under the Bretton Woods system, individual exchange-rate action left a country exposed—economically, especially in cases of revaluation; politically at home; and internationally, especially in cases of "excessive" devaluation or "inadequate" revaluation. These were major reasons for the unwillingness of countries to initiate exchange-rate changes, especially revaluations.

Under any system, each country needs a reasonable degree of assurance that other exchange rates will change when they need to do so, but not otherwise. This assurance requires a threefold procedure that makes clear the point at which there is a need for exchange-rate changes, indicates the magnitudes needed, and sharply increases the probability that rates will move by the "right amount" when the need exists. The United States has a particular interest in this issue because the continued use of the dollar as the major intervention currency means that other countries will also continue to be able to nullify effective changes in the exchange rate of the dollar by maintaining their interventions points.

One answer would be for the international community to agree on a set of criteria to indicate when changes in parities should take place. The alternative would be agreement to abandon permanently the notion of exchange-rate parities, with rates left free to fluctuate and the new set of criteria to provide a basis for judging the permissibility of intervention in the markets by national monetary authorities. In either case, the criteria would be the basis for judging the acceptibility of action proposed, taken, or not taken by individual countries. In the parity system, of course, there would exist a bias toward fixity; in the non-parity system, a bias toward flexibility. The choice between them rests essentially on one's preference between those biases.

The criteria themselves could be either very complex or very simple. Ideally, one needs to know the outlook for all the key aspects of a country's internal economy and balance of payments to make a definitive judgment concerning the accuracy of its present exchange rate. In practice, of course, the outlook for all these variables is quite uncertain. No single set of past indicators—such as movements in the spot exchange rate or changes in reserves—could provide an analytically adequate or politically acceptable guide for the future. Reliance must therefore be placed on the most recent economic indicators available, and the best judgments concerning the future, on a broad enough array of variables to permit a comprehensive view. In an intensive study of recent history to see which variables did in fact accurately predict the need for exchange-rate changes, the IMF staff concluded that changes in the basic balances and overall reserves of countries had been the best leading indicators, and had in fact foreshadowed the need for exchange-rate changes quite well. The use of such objective indicators appears to be quite feasible.

The primary guideline should be that exchange-rate changes are generally needed to reconcile dilemma cases where the internal macroeconomic policies required to cope primarily with unemployment or inflation would exacerbate an existing imbalance in the basic payments position. This would call for revaluations or appreciation in cases of rapid inflation coupled with basic payments surpluses, and devaluations or depreciation in cases of high unemployment and basic payments deficits. I would focus on the basic balance, which includes trade in goods and services and long-term capital flows, because exchange-rate changes are inappropriate responses to movements of liquid capital not related to underlying economic trends that will affect the basic balance itself. Indeed, the massiveness of such flows can now frequently dominate a country's entire balance of payments, and hence would dominate changes in its exchange rate if overall balances (or reserve changes) were the focus.

In this particular instance, the focus on the basic balance is reinforced because most countries are sufficiently mercantilist to look to the basic balance, or even the current account or trade balance, as the major indicator of the state of this external financial position. Indeed, few countries would be willing to accept changes in their trade balance caused by exchange-rate changes that were in turn caused by liquid capital movements not based on underlying economic trends.

But it would be virtually impossible to focus on the current account or trade balance alone, for two reasons. Since most major countries seek steady surpluses rather than balance in their current accounts, trying to use it as a basis for the adjustment guidelines would abort the whole exercise by requiring a negotiated agreement on the appropriate level of the surplus for each country, which would probably be impossible. Second, such a focus would exclude direct investment, which is one of the most politically sensitive items in the balance of payments of the United States (and of other countries, to a lesser extent), as well as an item of rapidly growing economic impact. The focus on the basic balance is also supported by the conclusion of Chapter 5 that, perhaps with direct investment excluded, it is the focus of monetary authorities in assessing the attractiveness of individual key currencies. Some technical problems in defining the basic balance consistently among countries would have to be worked out through consultation between national governments under the leadership of the IMF, because national data differ as to coverage and timing, and even because one country's short-term capital outflow may become another country's long-term capital inflow. But overcoming differences in data is only one small part of the increase in international collaboration which will be needed to make any monetary system work in the future.

If countries choose to give priority to balance-of-payments equilibrium in setting their domestic policies, as some countries with particularly open economies probably would at times, they would not need to take exchange-rate actions. (This is a key reason—along with the uncertainty of any set of statistical indicators, political impracticability, and the desirability of avoiding exchange-rate changes in non-dilemma cases—for not trying to institute automatic parity changes.) Any countries which choose to link their exchange rates to each other, perceiving themselves to constitute an optimum currency area (as described in Chapter 3), could do so as long as the group as a unit conformed to the new international criteria. Otherwise, there would be a presumption that exchange rates would change until the dilemma case is resolved.

In practice, it is not always easy to distinguish between dilemma and non-dilemma cases. Not only are the normal forecasting problems involved, but the growing simultaneous existence of high unemployment and rapid inflation has blurred the traditional conceptual distinctions. Realistic guidelines must therefore deal with all possible combinations of the level of employment, the rate of price change, and the position of the balance of payments.

In targeting macroeconomic demand management policy on the level of employment, selective measures such as incomes policies on prices and manpower policies on structural employment problems, and the exchange rate on the external position in dilemma cases, the tabulation on page 524 assigns a course of action in each of the eight possible economic circumstances. The eight combinations represent segments on a continuum not marked off by clearly separable points. Accordingly, individual countries might have different policy responses to situations which, defined in these broad terms, were equivalent, thus reflecting *inter alia* their degree of openness to the world economy and the relative weights which they attach to the different policy targets. (Parentheses around a policy response indicate that the need for it is uncertain and would depend on the particular circumstances of the country concerned.)

Cases 1 and 8 are the classic non-dilemma situations where changes in macroeconomic policy meet both the internal and external needs of the economy, although selective measures might be pursued if needed to guard against losing the one positive element (full employment in Case 1, price stability in Case 8) in each situation. Cases 3 and 6 are the classic dilemma situations where the internal

Economic Outlook	Open or Closed Economy	Demand Policy	Selective Policy	Exchange Rate
1. Full employment, rapid inflation, payments deficit	Both	Restraint	(Manpower policy)	. . . .
2. Full employment, stable prices, payments deficit	Open	Restraint	Manpower policy	. . . .
	Closed	. . . .	(Incomes policy)	Devaluation
3. Full employment, rapid inflation, payments surplus	Both	. . . .	(Manpower policy)	Revaluation
4. Full employment, stable prices, payments surplus	Open	Expansion	Manpower policy	Revaluation
	Closed	. . . .	Manpower policy	Revaluation
5. Unemployment, rapid inflation, payments deficit	Open	. . . .	Incomes policy	Devaluation
	Closed	Expansion	Incomes policy	Devaluation
6. Unemployment, stable prices, payments deficit	Both	. . . .	(Incomes policy)	Devaluation
7. Unemployment, rapid inflation, payments surplus	Open	Expansion	Incomes policy	. . . .
	Closed	. . . .	(Manpower policy)	Revaluation
8. Unemployment, stable prices, payments surplus	Both	Expansion	(Incomes policy)	. . . .

and external needs of the economy cut in opposite directions, and hence require exchange-rate changes to eliminate the payments dis-equilibrium, again perhaps with additional selective measures to avoid harmful effects on the positive element (full employment in Case 3, stable prices in Case 6).

Much more difficult are the intermediate Cases 2, 4, 5, and 7. In Cases 2 and 7, the classic demand-management approach (along with complementary selective policies) is called for in open econ-omies, but exchange-rate changes are prescribed for closed economies because the leverage of demand-management policy is so small that internal economic objectives would be subjected to excessive costs if it were used to eliminate external disequilibrium. Cases 4 and 5 are the trickiest. Domestic expansion is needed to offset the deflationary effects of appreciation of the exchange rate in an open economy in Case 4, and to augment the battle against unemployment in a closed economy in Case 5, since depreciation carries so little leverage in such a situation, whereas appreciation would not have much slowing effect in a closed economy nor would depreciation need help from demand-management policy in reducing unemployment in an open economy.

The broad guidelines indicate the policy actions which individual countries should take when confronting particular policy situations. Additional guidelines are needed, however, to indicate which countries should initiate the adjustment process, or play a greater role in it, when several face disequilibrium. These additional guidelines need to be based on the overall world economic situation, as shown in the tabulation on this page.

If the basic world economic problem at a given time is inflation, one set of guidelines should prevail. In cases where both surplus and deficit countries face non-dilemma situations, the deficit countries should restrain their internal economies to achieve all or most of the needed adjustment. If both sets of countries face dilemma situations, appreciations by the surplus countries should dominate the process. If the surplus countries are in dilemma and the deficit countries in non-dilemma situations, the mix of appreciations and internal re-

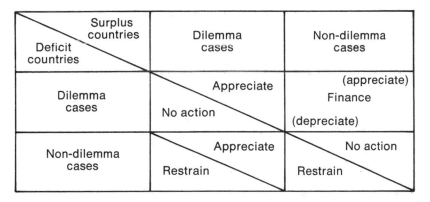

GUIDELINES FOR INITIATING ADJUSTMENT

straint measures should be based on the weights of the respective countries in helping to combat inflation. If the surplus countries are in non-dilemma situations and the deficit countries in dilemma, the respective expansions and depreciations should be mixed to minimize their inflationary effects; in such cases, financing of the imbalances might be more desirable from a global standpoint than adjustment.

If the basic world problem is unemployment, an opposite set of calculations applies. The surplus countries should expand their economies if both face non-dilemma situations. The deficit countries should depreciate if both face dilemmas. If the surplus countries are in non-dilemma cases and the deficits in dilemma, the internal expansions and depreciations should be mixed to maximize impact on world jobs. And if the surplus countries are in dilemma and the deficit countries in non-dilemma cases, the respective appreciations and internal restraint measures should seek to minimize adding to world unemployment; financing might prove particularly appropriate in such situations.

This analysis reaffirms the impracticability of relying on any simple indicators like spot exchange rates or reserve changes to guide changes in rates. The existence of such difficult situations requires that general guidelines, such as those proposed, be supplemented with detailed analysis of the specifics of each case. The primary need is to combine agreement on guidelines, institutionalization of an international process of consultation through which they will be applied, and willingness on the part of national authorities actually to apply them as normal tools of economic policy. Clearly, the IMF would have to play a major role in the new process, which adds importantly to the case for moving toward reliance on SDRs for liquidity purposes so that the Fund, as manager of the asset, will be able to exercise greater authority over the adjustment process.

National governments will have to make some internal rearrangements to facilitate more frequent exchange-rate changes. Concern for bookkeeping losses on the valuation of their reserves may deter countries from revising their exchange rates, especially when they hold foreign exchange. The perception by key currency countries of this "cost" to others has added to their reluctance to initiate parity changes. These concerns about adjustment thus buttress the case for minimizing the use of national currencies as international reserve assets. But even for the working balances of national currencies that are likely to remain under any system, national governments will have to permit their monetary authorities to establish contingency funds against losses caused by any depreciations of key currencies which might be needed. In such a contingency fund, the authorities could place profits from appreciations of the same or other key currencies, interest earnings on their reserves, the profits they normally make from exchange-market intervention (which could increase with the widening of exchange-rate flexibility), and any other earnings. In addition, the United States has a unique need for Congress to authorize the President to change the exchange rate of the dollar, at least up to some ceiling amount as was done in the Gold Reserve Act of 1934, without getting congressional approval each time—which would be ridiculous if changes are to be small and relatively frequent.

International Sanctions

The international community should also agree on concerted measures to take against countries which failed to act in accordance with the agreed criteria and could not justify their derogation. At present, the international community can bring pressure on a deficit country to adjust by refusing to extend credit to it. More active use of this lever should suffice for dealing with failures to devalue.

In addition, the Articles of Agreement empower the International Monetary Fund to bring pressure on a surplus country by declaring its currency "scarce" and authorizing members to discriminate against it. The scarce-currency clause does not force adjustment, however, since a country can escape its sanctions simply by providing unlimited financing. In practice, it has not been used to provide either adjustment or more financing.

There is at present no agreement on sharing the cost of adjustment or responsibility for initiating it. Adoption of criteria establishing a need for exchange-rate action, as proposed above, would partially fill this gap. It would then be possible to undertake sanctions against offenders.

The sanctions themselves should be carefully graduated. As a first step, after a staff analysis that showed a country was not acting according to the criteria and after discussion of the situation, the Managing Director of the Fund should inform the offending country of the judgment and consult with it concerning the reasons for the improper action and the possibility of remedial steps. A second step could be the publication of a Fund report citing the "offense," analogous to the report called for under the scarce-currency clause, which would generate both exchange-market and international political pressure on the "offender." Under a parity system, such Fund publicity could be supported by an instruction to all countries to stop intervening in their markets to prevent the appreciation of the violator's currency, as they are otherwise obligated to do under the

Articles of Agreement. This would in essence float the currency in question upward in all of its external markets, unleash massive demand for the currency in its own market as arbitrageurs sought to profit from the different prices for it, and bring massive pressure on the offending country to revalue as indicated.

Still failing action, other countries could be empowered to apply discriminatory trade and exchange measures against an offending surplus country, up to an amount equaling the amount by which its exchange rate should change. One possible measure against surplus countries would be higher tariffs on imports from them, perhaps by an amount double the needed exchange rate since the tariffs would apply to only one-half the trade balance and much less than one-half the country's international transactions.[3] But such a step would penalize the countries applying the sanctions by raising their costs, and would be impossible to apply among members of a customs union or free trade area. The credible existence of such threats, like any good deterrent, should however render their actual use unnecessary. The emergence of sufficient national will to authorize such changes in the system should go far toward achieving an effective adjustment process.

The Effects on the United States

These new criteria and sanctions would apply to the United States as well as to all other countries. The only difference would be that, in implementing a parity change under a system of nominally fixed rates, the United States would continue to need the active cooperation of other countries. The continued role of the dollar as intervention currency would require others to change their intervention points against the dollar to permit the change in the dollar's value, in terms of the new SDR numéraire, so as the be translated into effective changes in exchange rates between the dollar and other national currencies. This is the objective of the concerted measures.

The process for implementing the criteria, however, should assure that the desired result would occur and hence greatly benefit the United States. When currencies other than the dollar moved in re-

---

3. This would consciously violate the GATT most-favored-nation rule. Such violation would be proper, since the rule often leads to inappropriate use of trade measures to secure payments adjustment. For example, the United States was required to apply its surcharge in August 1971 against all countries though its objective was payments adjustment through revaluations from only a very few.

sponse to the criteria, they could be assured that only those other currencies (if any) meeting the criteria at the same time would move with them. They would no longer need to fear that their actions would be offset by others. The United States would be assured that other countries would similarly take the necessary complementary action to permit effective changes in the exchange rate of the dollar, since the rules would not authorize them to move with the dollar. Unless the United States were to get such assurance, it should take the steps necessary to bar the continued use of the dollar for intervention purposes.

Indeed, the United States should become a frequent user of the improved exchange-rate mechanism, reversing its earlier postwar role in which it steadily rejected any effort to change its parity. The reason is that the United States has a triple comparative advantage in changing its exchange rate. First, such changes are the most effective way for it to achieve payments adjustment by a greater margin than for any other country, because (a) the U.S. economy is so relatively closed to the world economy that macroeconomic policy changes have little leverage over the external accounts and (b) the country is so big that the comprehensive controls needed to achieve effective adjustment by that route are almost impossible administratively. Second, exchange-rate changes are much easier to implement in the United States than in other countries (economically and therefore politically) because its economy is so closed and hence the exchange rate has such a relatively small impact on the society as a whole. Third, exchange-rate changes are likely to be much more effective in achieving adjustment if initiated by the United States because the closed nature of the economy reduces the likelihood that the domestic economic shifts needed to make good on the changes will be consciously offset by those affected, e.g., demands for offsetting wage increases by organized labor.

The exchange rate of the dollar can change only if the dollar price of Special Drawing Rights and the official price of gold are allowed to change. Changes in the official price of gold are generally undesirable but would be tolerable in the context of the overall reform program proposed here. The dollar might as frequently move up as down against SDRs or gold, of course, so that the official price of gold might move down as often as it moved up. Even when the dollar depreciated, however, the move would be very small under the new exchange-rate regime—not nearly enough in a year to make up for the earnings foregone by holding gold instead of interest-bearing assets. And the resulting price could still be so far below the price in the free market that it would have little effect there. In fact, large changes would be even less likely than at present because the new system would be effectively meeting both the liquidity and adjustment problems and hence obviate any need for a sizable increase in the official price of gold. One major objection to an increase in the price of gold for liquidity purposes is that it would have to be very large to achieve its objectives, which would carry major psychological, inflationary and political consequences, whereas any such increase for adjustment purposes could only be very small—even smaller than in 1971 and 1973.

Most important, however, the liquidity focus of the new system should clearly be Special Drawing Rights. Given enough consolidation of outstanding reserves, along lines shortly to be spelled out, they could leap immediately to first place among existing reserve assets. At the margin, Special Drawing Rights would provide the bulk of the growth of world reserves, and perhaps all of it. The main objection to an increase in the official price of gold was always that it would imply a return of gold to the center of the international monetary system, a costly reversal of the historical evolution of money. This objection does not hold in a context which clearly elevates Special Drawing Rights to the center of the system. From the standpoint of the United States, the cost of gold-price increases under such a new system would be worth the flexibility which they would provide for changing the dollar exchange rate—the same preference which the United States revealed at the Smithsonian Agreement in December 1971, and again in February 1973.

The proposed changes in the exchange-rate regime would produce a dramatic improvement in the adjustment process. Under a return to fixed parities, the wider bands would permit much greater flexibility around a given parity and the more frequent changes in parities would keep the band moving as needed. Under a no-parity regime, rates would float continuously and intervention would be limited by international agreement. During the negotiations leading to the adoption of either alternative, agreement would be reached on the key international issue of when individual countries would be expected to initiate adjustment and on how the adjustment burden would be shared. The adoption of an active exchange-rate policy by the United States would go far toward meeting both its adjustment problem and the international political problems of adopting greater flexibility. Furthermore, the new regime would greatly reduce the key domestic problem of justifying exchange-rate changes to national electorates, and thus go far to remedy the most fundamental problem of the international monetary system.

Full Flexibility

A no-parity regime of managed floats would probably be superior to limited flexibility of parities if all major countries grouped into two or three large monetary areas, within which rates were fixed but between which they flexed. (Such areas might center on the United States, the expanded European Community or Germany alone, and perhaps Japan.) In that situation, each area would be so economically self-contained that it would approximate an "optimum currency area." Full flexibility would not represent a significant threat to internal stability of the areas, even in non-dilemma cases. Coordination of intervention practices would be relatively easy because of the small number of actors. If such monetary groupings were to be rapidly formed, full flexibility might indeed be the best mode of adjustment reform.

Such a coalescing of countries into huge monetary areas is highly unlikely, however. The EC has been unable to achieve any significant degree of monetary unity, and even its plans for such unity have left open the possibility of exchange-rate changes within the Community until much later in the evolution of their monetary union, as they must because of the sharp differences of economic performance and policy preferences among the members. The mark zone which has emerged instead leaves at least two major European countries—the United Kingdom and Italy—floating on their own. Japan may continue to peg to the dollar for prolonged periods, and few countries are likely to peg soon to the yen. Numerous middle-sized countries, such as Australia, India, and the larger Latin American countries, divide their trade among the two or three potential monetary centers and would thus be reluctant to peg to any one of them. Even some of the countries which border the potential centers, such as Canada and Switzerland, have recent histories of independent floats. The basic differences in national objectives and capabilities suggest that the monetary system of the 1970s must accommodate wide diversity. Thus it is probably not yet ready for freely flexible exchange rates, and there will be continued pressures to return to a regime of "stable but adjustable parities." A regime of limited flexibility, of either type just discussed, is thus the preferred solution.

THE REFORM OF LIQUIDITY

The Growth of Reserves

There are two central liquidity issues: the size of world reserves, and their composition. Despite the sharp increase in their dollar holdings in 1970–73, few industrialized countries view their reserve levels as excessive—particularly in light of the steep rise in their bill for oil imports. The ratio of world reserves to world trade and the ratio to the respective trade of most individual countries remain below— often far below—where they were in the 1950s or even a decade ago. Furthermore, the ratios targeted by most countries have risen sharply because the huge flows of liquid capital which have permeated the system can wipe out even seemingly massive reserves in literally a few days. Britain's loss of one-third of its reserves in a single week in June 1972, from the highest level by far which they had ever reached, was only one recent example. Also, each country perceives its minimum needs to be rising as the scale of its international transactions rises.

Countries usually resist *any* reserve losses, since such losses are widely regarded as indicating a basic weakness in their currency and hence may cumulate. In order to avoid even temporary reserve losses, each country needs assured annual increments to its owned reserves, sufficient in amount to preclude the adoption of policies inimical to its own domestic requirements or to the rights of other countries under the international trading and payments rules. This means that the system as a whole needs assured annual increments roughly equal to the sum of these needs. At the same time, the system should not create excessive amounts of new liquidity, since doing so would enable some countries to resist adjustment too long, drain real resources away from others, and foster world inflation. As in the determinants of adjustment measures, the overall world economic situation—whether the chief problem of the moment is inflation or unemployment—should play a major role in decisions on amounts of liquidity.

Individual countries obviously have different ideas as to what constitutes "adequate" or "excessive" increments in their reserves and those of other countries, and how such "adequacy" is determined. At a minimum, it seems clear that countries want to maintain the level of their real reserves; this requires annual increments in their nominal reserves roughly equal to the rate of world inflation, which has been running well above 5 per cent annually in recent years. Since world reserves totaled $78 billion at the end of 1969, even before the sizable increases of 1971–72, this alone would call for annual increments of at least $4 billion in nominal reserves.

In addition, countries appear to want increases in their real reserves at least to match their expectations of increased swings in their payments positions measured in *absolute* magnitudes. We saw in Chapter 2 that such swings, measured by variance in export positions, grew in the past by about 6 per cent per year. This is a lower figure than the growth of world trade or even the growth of world gross national product (in money terms), two other variables frequently viewed as determining national desires for reserve growth, and it may be overly conservative under a system of fixed parities, for a variety of reasons.

In any event, it can never be shown conclusively that an extrapolation of the past will provide a "proper" level of reserve growth for the future. Indeed, some of the ills which troubled the system as long ago as the early 1960s have often been attributed to inadequate reserve levels and the resulting competition for the "suboptimal" level of the reserves that were coming available. On the other hand, some analysts charge that excessive international liquidity has contributed significantly to recent, excessive rates of world inflation. It is also true that holding reserves represents a real cost in terms of foregone consumption.

Perhaps more important, however, is the reduced need for reserves which might be expected to accompany implementation of the proposals outlined for improving the adjustment process, and indeed the greater flexibility of exchange rates which has already developed. Better adjustment should mean less need for financing. However, as we saw in Chapter 11, it has been cogently argued that *larger* reserves will be needed even under a regime of *freely* flexible exchange rates—theoretically the most assured route to effective adjustment—than under fixed rates because liquid capital flows may be more destabilizing during some periods of time under such a regime. In addition, and closely related, the adjustment effects of exchange-rate changes may take a good deal of time—at least two or three years—to come to pass. Moreover, there may be increased strategic need for assured reserve growth under a more flexible exchange-rate system, because under such a regime countries could otherwise use the excuse of meeting their reserve needs to intervene in the markets and brake appreciation of their currencies in frustration of its basic objectives. Finally, because of a lack of confidence that flexibility would persist, they might scramble for position against a return to a more fixed-rate system. It would thus be a mistake to assume that the initial institution of a more flexible adjustment system would dispel the need for assured reserve growth, and the events of 1971–74 fully support such doubts.

The value of analyzing past developments, even under a different adjustment process, is that they reveal the realized desires of national monetary authorities. Over a sufficient period of time, it is difficult to imagine that these actual results would differ greatly from the countries' aims since there was ample opportunity to change policy to alter the outcome, except perhaps for the United States (which would presumably have *raised* the total). In addition, monetarist theory posits that the demand for money—including demand at the national level—is one of the principal determinants of economic behavior; it may therefore be inaccurate to regard national reserve growth as simply the residual effect of numerous other policy actions taken for wholly unrelated reasons. In any event, to minimize the need for sharp policy adjustments to future payments imbalances, whatever the adjustment process, most major countries clearly like large reserves more than they dislike the costs of holding them.

The membership of the International Monetary Fund concluded in 1969 that world reserves should grow by $4 billion to $5 billion annually during the first Special Drawing Rights allocation period in 1970–72, or 5.1 to 6.4 per cent based on the level of world reserves at the end of 1969. The international community has thus explicitly ratified a rate of growth quite similar to its actual performance for most of the postwar period, and such a rate seems a good guide for minimum reserve creation in the future. This is of course a long-term figure. Until all reserve creation is firmly regulated, the growth of unregulated assets can bring the global total for any single year well below or above the desired long-term trend.

The big question, of course, is who will do the regulating. The growth of liquidity can be unregulated, regulated by national authorities in a position to do so, or regulated internationally. The historical trend has been clearly moving from unregulated reserve creation under the gold standard, through national reserve creation (by key currency centers, "willing" and "unwilling" holders) under the several incarnations of the gold exchange standard, toward the international regulation of Special Drawing Rights. The logical culmination is full international regulation, which would provide the best solution to the economic needs of the system and meet the crucial political issues underlying it.

Special Drawing Rights, the only internationally manageable reserve asset, should thus immediately become the primary source of growth of world reserves. They should be created in sufficient magnitude to increase the total by 5 to 6 per cent annually, the rate of growth suggested both by the record of the past and by the collective decision of the international community in the first SDR allocation period. Such reserve growth should help improve the adjustment process by assuring countries that their reserves will grow steadily without the need of aggressively having to seek payments surpluses. It would thus dampen the tendency toward controls and the devaluation bias of the Bretton Woods system, which forced deficit countries to initiate adjustment much more frequently than surplus countries, without significantly increasing the risks of world inflation.[4]

Adequate reserve growth is an essential element of monetary reform for the United States. Its reserves are now among the lowest of any industrialized country, relative to their respective levels of international transactions. If the United States were to restore convertibility of the dollar into U.S. reserve assets, or especially if it were to go further and agree to finance all or most of its payments deficits with U.S. assets, it would have to be assured of an adequate and growing level of reserves with which to do so. Creation of SDRs in the magnitudes mentioned here would provide the United States with $1 billion to $1.5 billion of new liquidity annually in helping meet the need. For both narrowly national and broad systemic reasons, the United States should thus insist on firm agreement on the rate of future SDR allocation as an integral part of any overall monetary reform.

Consolidation of the Overhang

Annual SDR creation in these magnitudes is by itself inadequate, however, to give the world assurance of sufficient but not excessive liquidity growth. If there were no other changes in the reserve system, countries would also be able to build their reserves by acquiring other reserve assets—mainly dollars but also gold, sterling, and, increasingly, marks and other national currencies. In addition, if the United States were to resume some form of convertibility obligations while the dollar overhang remained outstanding, conversions of dollars into U.S. reserve assets could lead to sharp reductions in world liquidity—as they did in 1947 when the restoration of sterling convertibility, in the face of the sterling overhang, had to be abandoned after six weeks. International regulation of these other assets, both existing and prospective, is therefore needed to achieve effective international control over the total level of world reserves. Such steps are also needed to solve the official confidence problem, which stems from the unstable relationships among multiple reserve assets.

4. Only 70 per cent of gross SDR creation can be counted as owned reserves until the "reconstitution" rule is changed, however, because 30 per cent must be "reconstituted" within five years and represent medium-term credit instead. This rule would bite harder as SDRs move beyond their early years because it requires that countries maintain a 30 per cent balance, averaged over the previous five years, at all times. If reconstitution remains in force, Special Drawings Rights should be created at a gross annual rate of 7 to 8 per cent, so that the unfettered 70 per cent will meet the word's need for 5 to 6 per cent annual increments of owned reserves.

Such regulation must, however, recognize that it is neither politically possible nor technically necessary to force countries to adopt uniform patterns of reserve-holding, such as reliance on a single asset or harmonization ratio, and that countries have legitimate reasons for maintaining different portfolio mixes. It must reconcile these principles with the principle that the individual countries cannot be permitted to trigger systemic instability by shifts in their reserve portfolios.

Each country should therefore be given two choices with respect to its current reserve holdings of dollars, sterling, gold and any other foreign currencies.[5] It could convert them into Special Drawing Rights, of which a special issue equal to the total of world reserves, *plus* private holdings of foreign currencies outstanding at the time of the agreement, would be authorized for this purpose. Or it could hold on to them, agreeing to use them only when necessary to finance a payments deficit just as countries can now use SDRs only when they meet such a "needs test." If it chose this second option, however, it would have no right to convert the dollars into other U.S. reserve assets. Convertibility of the outstanding dollar balances would be restored, but only into SDRs through the creation of new SDRs at the IMF.[6]

A country could, at any time in the future, exercise its option to convert into the specially created Special Drawing Rights the dollars which it had continued to hold when the new scheme went into effect. Similarly, when dollars retained by an individual country after the beginning of the new scheme shifted to another country as financing for a payments imbalance, the receiving country could convert them into the specially issued Special Drawing Rights. In

---

5. All parts of my proposal encompass all existing reserve assets, except SDRs themselves and automatic drawing rights at the IMF (gold and supergold tranche position), except where specified to the contrary. For simplicity of presentation and because they are likely to be affected in far greater amounts than the other assets, I will henceforth refer in the text only to dollars.

6. The details of the proposal outlined in the next several pages are presented in Chapter 13, pp. 476–81. This approach would not be as restrictive on the use of outstanding dollars as were the "minimum sterling proportions," which sterling area countries had to agree to maintain to receive Britain's dollar-value guarantee of their sterling balances in 1968, on the use of outstanding sterling. Those rules required not only the equivalent of a "needs test" for using the sterling but that it be used only in proportion with the other reserve assets of the sterling country. Countries which chose to maintain their dollar holdings under the approach proposed here could use them "off the top of the pile" to finance deficits, but neither would they receive exchange-rate guarantees on them.

sum, the special issue of Special Drawing Rights would be large enough to consolidate *all* of the outstanding reserves in the international monetary system on the date of entry of the new system. An opportunity would be indefinitely available for conversion of all reserve balances of dollars, gold, sterling, and other currencies outstanding at that time. The actual conversion could take place either at the outset or later, whether by countries holding the assets at the outset or by countries which earned them later on.

In addition, a place would be made for private holdings of dollars outstanding on the base date, just as the 1968 Basel agreements for sterling provide that Britain could obtain loans from the Basel participants (the Group of Ten, excluding France, plus Austria and Norway) to finance declines in private sterling balances held in sterling area countries. If such private dollars moved into official reserves, they too could be converted into the special issue of SDRs. Otherwise, foreign official holders might have to accumulate unwanted dollar reserves and the United States would still have a sizable potential liability as a result of the dollar's roles in the past.

In practice, few conversions of dollars held privately on the base date would probably become necessary. Private foreign-held balances dwindled sharply during the monetary uncertainties of 1971–73, because of declining confidence in the dollar and growing confidence in other currencies, and may well remain at a relatively low level at least until negotiations on basic reform clarify the roles of the dollar in the system and U.S. policy clarifies the outlook for its future stability. In the past, net dollar conversions by private foreigners into other currencies, which move dollars into official hands, occurred mainly as a result of temporary shifts in interest-rate differentials and other reversible causes, and did not reflect the basic balance-of-payments positions of either the United States or the foreign country involved. They were generally held by the foreign monetary authorities simply as working balances, with the anticipation that private demand for the dollars would soon reverse the movement, or swapped to the United States to obtain a temporary exchange-rate guarantee.

In the future, however, a secular shift away from the dollar as a vehicle currency could parallel the proposed shift away from the dollar as a reserve currency, even if there is some renewed buildup of private dollar balances after the uncertainties of the early 1970s are reduced. (Indeed, part of the recent move away from the dollar doubtlessly represents a stock-adjustment by private foreigners based on the sharp changes in the ability of the United States, on the one hand, and Germany and other industrialized countries, on the other, to meet the key currency criteria.) In that event, the reduction of private dollars would represent as much a "collapse of the overhang" as the desired reduction of official dollars, and should be treated equally as a legacy of the past. Another reason for protecting the private dollars is the need to maintain their contribution to the efficiency of private international transactions, which would be undermined if the private sector ever had reason to worry that monetary authorities would be unwilling to buy dollars from them for fear of having to hold on to the dollars themselves.

The United States has three particular interests in consolidating the dollar overhang. First, the elimination of potential quick claims on U.S. reserves obviously removes a major constraint on policy, including potential further depreciation of the dollar. Foreign dollar holdings far exceed U.S. reserves. In addition, elimination of the overhang facilitates an increase in U.S. reserves in the future. In the absence of consolidation, future U.S. payments surpluses might well be financed through reductions in its dollar liabilities; with consolidation, the United States could earn SDRs or other assets with its surpluses. For this reason alone, future deficits in the basic U.S. balance of payments could be financed by reserve assets only with a consolidation of the overhang; without it, the United States might lose reserves over time even if its basic payments position was, over time, in balance or even in surplus.

Finally, consolidation is essential to achieve the proposed adjustment reform, including the adoption by the United States of an active exchange-rate policy. We have seen how the several international roles of the dollar add severely to the constraint on U.S. adjustment via the exchange rate. These constraints would be much greater in a future regime of greater exchange-rate flexibility because of the continued uncertainty of foreign monetary authorities about the value of their dollar balances. Foreigners would thus be much more likely, in such a system, to use the leverage afforded them through use of the dollar for intervention purposes, to frustrate U.S. exchange-rate initiatives. In addition, we saw in Chapter 12 that other countries are virtually certain to reject a world which permits the United States to adjust when it wants, either by its own action or via theirs, and to finance via the dollar when it wants. In short, continuation of a major reserve currency role for the dollar is inconsistent with an active exchange-rate adjustment policy by the United States and the cooperation needed from other countries to implement a regime of effective exchange-rate flexibility.

Consolidation would affect only the *composition* of the reserves of other countries, not their magnitude. As countries could choose either to convert their dollars or to hold them, they should have no economic objection to this optional consolidation approach. Their only objection could be to a reduction in leverage over the United States which they feel might occur; but the leverage is not very real if the alternative, as is likely, is indefinite continuation of total inconvertibility of the overhanging dollars into U.S. reserves.

Some dollar holders might dislike the new de jure limitation on the use of their outstanding dollars. However, most countries which actively seek to hold dollars have little if any desire to see the United States adjust. They regard their interest earnings as an adequate offset to the risk of capital loss from dollar depreciations, and are likely to avoid any capital loss by depreciating along with the dollar anyway. These countries are unlikely to worry much about being unable to convert their dollars into U.S. assets. In any event, they have gotten used to both de facto and de jure inconvertibility over a number of years, and the new situation would merely formalize such a state, thereby eliminating the uncertainties and unilateral U.S. actions which have previously surrounded it. They would be under no U.S. pressure to continue holding dollars, and the option to convert them freely into the special issue of SDR would always be available.

The Terms of Consolidation

The overhanging dollars converted by present holders into the special issue of Special Drawing Rights should remain indefinitely in the International Monetary Fund, in the form of dollar claims on the United States with no maturities ("consols"). There should never be any "retirement" of the dollars by their amortization into U.S. reserve assets.

A large part of these dollar reserves were accumulated abroad during a period when they were the only available means to provide the necessary increases in world liquidity. Almost $17 billion were acquired through 1958, when the only "dollar problem" was that other countries could not get enough of them. Almost $42 billion were acquired through 1969, when most countries were still willing and even eager holders of most of their dollars, and alternative reserve and transactions assets (in the form of SDRs and other national currencies) were not yet available. During these periods the dollars served a major international function, with sizable benefits for other countries as well as for the United States. Consolidation of these dollars without U.S. amortization could be viewed as representing a partial foreign repayment of Marshall Plan grants and ongoing military expenditures, since they would lift a potential repayment burden which those grants and expenditures helped to cause. Furthermore, such a "reverse Marshall Plan" would have dramatic political benefits for relations between the United States and its allies, without any cost to the "reverse granters" who would simply be exchanging one reserve asset for another.

It can of course be justifiably argued that some of the more recently acquired dollar reserves have been accumulated reluctantly, and that this portion should be paid off by the United States rather than written off through international action. However, it would be impossible to determine what portion should be treated as "unwanted," in any event, and other countries would differ sharply on the issue. In addition, even in recent years, U.S. military expenditures (net of military sales and other offset devices) for collective security purposes have accounted for much of the basic U.S. deficit—even excluding expenditures related to Vietnam.

More fundamentally, the real gainers from dollar consolidation are the countries holding dollar reserves: they could then acquire an asset which their exercise of the conversion option demonstrated that they preferred. Since the suspension of convertibility in August 1971, they could convert none of their dollars. Even before that action, most countries could convert only a small percentage, if any, in view of the excess of foreign dollar holdings over U.S. reserves—or by virtue of explicit agreement, as in the case of Germany. Such an arrangement therefore would not represent "aid to the United States," in any sense of transferring real resources to it, because the alternative is continued inconvertibility of the dollar into U.S. reserves, and because real U.S. resources could be bought with the SDRs just as with the dollars which were converted into them.

In addition, a repayment requirement would push the United States toward striving for even larger payments surpluses in order to make repayments while continuing to build its owned reserves. The abrupt U.S. decision to join the mercantilist race already raises major new problems for the world economy, which are further heightened by the massive deterioration in the trade balances of the oil importing countries, caused by the rise in the price of fuel. A repayment obligation would probably raise the U.S. surplus target by an equal amount. Such an outcome would make the adjustment process all the more difficult by intensifying the international scramble for trade surpluses and reserves, thus running counter to the most important single objective of this overall reform scheme. In seeking to create a viable international monetary system for the future, this whole proposal would let bygones be bygones in dealing with the legacies of the past in return for suitable quid pro quos for the future, as included in several parts of the scheme discussed below.[7]

The avoidance of amortization requirements would greatly enhance the acceptability of the overall approach to the United States, and help persuade it not to pursue the dollar standard alternative. If amortization *were* required, the United States might well choose to continue taking its chances with the outstanding balances, probably by indefinitely maintaining the suspension of convertibility for at least those dollars.

The United States would of course have to guarantee the SDR value of the dollars which remained in the International Monetary Fund. The guarantee would require the United States to make additional dollars available to the Fund if the dollar were devalued (in terms of SDR, the new numéraire). The amounts would be sizable since $50 billion might easily be consolidated in the Fund and every 5 per cent devaluation of the dollar would generate a U.S. liability of $2.5 billion to it. Such guarantees could add to U.S. reluctance to change the dollar exchange rate, whereas one of the objectives of the reform scheme is to make such changes easier.

However, the guarantee could be made good simply by an increase in U.S. contingent liabilities to the Fund, rather than by actual cash transfers. The Fund would actually have to use the dollars only to redeem SDRs of any country leaving the scheme and, perhaps, to provide working balances to countries which run short of dollars for that purpose. Only in the case of complete liquidation of the SDRs would the United States have to make good its guarantee. Congress would have to authorize the guarantee payments any time the dollar depreciated for some agreed period of time, but few actual appropriations would ever be needed. Moreover, the increase in the dollar value of U.S. reserve assets which results from dollar depreciation

---

7. If it proved politically impossible to avoid U.S. amortization of the consolidated dollars, these competitive and deflationary pressures could also be avoided by increasing annual SDR allocations by a sufficient amount to enable the United States (and Britain) to make annual payments without running higher surpluses. If $50 billion were to be amortized over 100 years, this would mean creating about $2 billion extra SDRs annually if the United States continued to get about 25 per cent of SDR allocations. (The United States, of course, would want full assurance that these SDRs were additional to those which would have been created anyway—which would strengthen the case for firm agreement on the amounts of SDR creation proposed above as an integral part of the whole reform package.) This would provide additional reserves to all countries, however, not just the United States and United Kingdom, and substitute an inflationary bias for the deflationary bias which would otherwise stem from the U.S. need for larger surpluses. It thus adds to the argument in the text for simply avoiding an amortization requirement.

would provide at least part of the needed amounts, as it did in 1971–73, and would provide a full (or greater) offset if the United States were successful in building its SDR holdings over time. The same accounting procedures recommended above for all countries in a world of greater exchange-rate flexibility would take care of any real problem in the United States as well.

The case against amortization is strengthened by the symmetry which only this approach can provide among the assets to be eligible for conversion into the special issue of Special Drawing Rights. There is no one to amortize gold, which should be treated just like dollars in the optional consolidation. It can of course be argued that gold is money and dollars are credit (to the United States), but there has been no operational distinction along these lines throughout the postwar period. In addition, gold for many years derived much of its monetary value from its assured convertibility into dollars rather than vice versa. Gold and dollars would be treated symmetrically in other parts of this proposal, and should be so treated here. Equal treatment for gold and the dollar would make U.S. participation in the overall scheme much more likely.

To strengthen the symmetry, the United States could agree to convert most or all of its gold into the special issue of SDRs. This would also mollify possible foreign concern that consolidation would enable the United States to preserve its gold holdings when they had previously been pledged explicitly to convert the dollars. Moreover, it would be the only way for the United States to convert into SDRs an amount of reserves, or share of its total reserves, roughly equivalent to the amount or share converted by other countries. This would be desirable psychologically, and it would also increase the SDR holding limits on the same scale for the United States as for other countries (if that rule remained in force).

We saw in Chapter 11 that there are five basic ways to deal with the interest-rate obligation on the dollar balances to be levied on the United States. The two viable choices are (a) U.S. payments to the International Monetary Fund equal to the interest rate paid to SDR holders, or (b) higher U.S. payments based on some notion of a "fair" burden for the United States, with a decision as to how to use the difference. Under the second option, the difference could be granted to the World Bank to augment the lending capabilities of its International Development Association. Consolidation of $50 billion, with U.S. interest obligations set at three percentage points above SDR rates, would generate $1.5 billion annually for development. At the same time it would finance exports from the industrialized countries, helping them to realize their trade balance objectives. The "burden" of this aid would be shared by the previous holders of the dollars, who gave up their interest earnings in return for the gold-value guarantee and systemic effects of the SDRs, and the United States, which would actually be paying the interest and which otherwise might have seen its interest burden further reduced. Some of the lower income countries may be reluctant to go along with an overall reform program as outlined here unless there is something specific in it for them, and they could easily have enough votes to block the needed amendments to the IMF Articles of Agreement. Their major plea with respect to monetary reform has been for such a "link," and this would be one way to provide it consistent with the basic monetary needs of the industrialized world. In addition, continued payments of interest by the United States at the higher rate should make it easier to win acceptance of the generous amortization provision proposed above, and hence avoid major new competitive and deflationary pressures on the world economy.

The Composition of Future Reserve Growth

To avoid the re-creation of an undesired dollar overhang, all countries should declare publicly what policies they will follow in determining the composition of net additions to their reserves in the future. At one extreme, they could opt to add only Special Drawing Rights. At the other, they could opt to add only dollars. In the middle, they could opt to hold in dollar form some portion of their additions, such as whatever percentage they need for working balances, or some *absolute* annual increment, with Special Drawing Rights to make up the rest. Countries themselves would declare publicly their holding limits for dollars, as some have done privately in the past. They could change their declarations for the future at any time, but all of their assets would be governed by the rules in effect under their declarations at the time the assets were acquired.

The prime need is to remove the uncertainty surrounding the possibility of shifts among reserve assets. The uncertainty stems from the unfettered opportunity for national monetary authorities, at any point in time, to hold several different assets and shift among them indiscriminately. One way to eliminate the uncertainty would be to eliminate all but one asset from the system. But this would also eliminate the flexibility of monetary authorities to choose different portfolio compositions. The confidence problem can also be solved, without eliminating the freedom of national choice in composing reserve portfolios, by eliminating the possibility of shifts among assets once they are in the portfolios.

A method of doing so for the existing overhang of gold, dollars, sterling, and other currencies has been proposed in preceding pages: countries could alter their existing portfolios by increasing the Special Drawing Rights portions thereof, but would otherwise have to hold on to all their existing assets except to finance their balance-of-payments deficits. A similar arrangement is needed to handle reserve additions: countries would declare *in advance* what (if any) part of their reserve increases they would acquire *and maintain* in the form of dollars. Once having acquired "new dollars," these countries could use them only to finance payments deficits under a "needs test" similar to that which governs the use of SDRs. Most other increases in reserves would be financed through the acquisition of Special Drawing Rights, either in the annual allocation process or from other monetary authorities in the settlement of current imbalances. The only additional possibility would be gold transfers, directly between countries and indirectly via the International Monetary Fund.

The resulting system would still be imperfect. It would be unclear, in advance, how much liquidity would be added to the system through accumulations of key currencies because the payments positions of countries opting to build their balances in this form would be impossible to predict with certainty. (Gold additions would also be uncertain.) Preserving the freedom for individual countries to acquire different reserve assets makes it impossible to control fully the growth of world liquidity without additional rules. One response would be to welcome such a means of providing needed elasticity in world growth, recognizing that U.S. basic deficits did not necessarily represent any economic disequilibrium. Or one could simply accept it as a relatively inconsequential shortcoming of a significant overall systemic improvement, which could be ignored because most of the industrialized countries (which normally run the bulk of the world's payments surpluses) would presumably opt to add dollars only as needed for working-balance purposes, limiting dollar financing for U.S. deficits. The only means for reconciling the objectives of (a) total control of liquidity creation and (b) permitting continued diversity of national reserve portfolios is to deduct the amount of the non-SDR reserve accruals of each country from its SDR allocations, which was examined in Chapter 11 but is not recommended because it would be so restrictive that it would in practice vitiate objective (b).

Under this approach, there would be a technical problem of how to handle shifts of "new dollars" from the dollar-holding countries which initially accrued them to non-dollar countries which did not want to retain them. There are two options. The dollars could be made eligible for consolidation into SDRs—not into U.S. reserve assets—if they remained with the original "willing" holder for some sustained period of time, perhaps 3 to 5 years, before shifting to an "unwilling" holder. These dollars would then be seen as part of a new overhang reflecting U.S. deficits of the past rather than of the present. Such an approach would be based on the new principle that U.S. sales of reserve assets may have to equal, but can never exceed, the current deficit in the U.S. basic balance. Under this concept it would be unfair to the United States to "charge" it with the outstanding dollars on a delayed basis just because the original surplus country which wanted dollars had moved into deficit. The conversion into newly created Special Drawing Rights would then be the only way to meet the asset preference of the new holder of the dollars without reducing world reserves by reducing the reserves of the United States.

Many supporters of an overall reform proposal along these lines will wish to make a complete break between dollars accumulated before and after its institution, however, with all the former and none of the latter eligible for consolidation through Special Drawing Rights. The notion of automatic financing for future overhangs through the open-ended creation of more SDRs, and hence financing for current U.S. deficits on a delayed basis, could well prove unacceptable. The United States should therefore accept an obligation to convert into its assets all new dollars accruing to "unwilling" dollar holders, as a result of its basic deficits, whether immediately or after a time lag. Prudence would then dictate that the United States treat only a small percentage of new foreign dollar accruals (if any) as certain to *remain* in dollar form, and build its reserves *pari passu* against them.

"Crowning" SDRs

A number of changes are needed in the rules governing Special Drawing Rights to enable them to become unquestionably the central reserve asset in the reformed monetary system. The basic objective of the changes is to make the SDRs at least as attractive as the other reserve assets with which they will continue to compete. Amendments of the IMF Articles will be needed to implement several of the reforms already proposed, and the opportunity should be seized to compete the evolution of SDRs to full status as international money. Two key steps in that direction were already taken in 1974: valuing the SDR in terms of a weighted average of the most important national currencies, and raising its interest yield from 1.5 to 5 per cent.

As already noted, the reconstitution rule should be abolished, if only to avoid the need to increase by more than 40 per cent[8] the amount of SDR allocation required to meet a given world desire for increases in owned reserves. The present reconstitution rules could also subvert the objective of avoiding non-SDR increases in world reserves, because the United States would normally reconstitute by expanding its dollar liabilities in the first instance and U.S. (and world) reserves would thus rise to the extent that the dollars were not then converted into American reserves.[9] The desirability of using new SDRs to replace outstanding balances of other reserve assets greatly strengthens the case for eliminating reconstitution because countries would be understandably reluctant to convert a fully transferable asset into one which had such limits on its use. In general, the abolition of reconstitution would equate SDRs fully with gold and dollars, which are subject to no such requirement, and eliminate the connotation of "credit" rather than "moneyness" that reconstitution clearly conveys to the SDRs. The IMF Articles call for reconstitution to be reviewed before the end of the first basic SDR period in 1975 and it can be eliminated by an 85 per cent vote of the Fund's Board of Governors without an amendment to the Articles.

The rule obligating countries to hold SDRs only to an amount equal to three times their net cumulative allocations should also be eliminated. Though several loopholes exist and no real problems have emerged, this rule could jeopardize the use of SDRs by deficit countries in cases where payments surpluses were heavily concentrated, as the few surplus countries reached their holding limits. This concern takes on increasing importance as SDRs fill a larger share of each country's total reserves, as they would after a consolidation exercise. No such "holding limits" exist now for other reserve assets (although some countries have privately declared limits for building dollar balances). Indeed, combining the elimination of the SDR holding limits with the proposal made above requiring countries to declare publicly their holding limits for further dollar accruals would make SDRs at least marginally superior to dollars as a reserve asset in this regard.

Next, the authority to cancel allocations should be removed from the SDR rules. It is certainly consistent with the basic objective of

8. Since 30 per cent of SDR allocations must be reconstituted, only 70 per cent can be treated as owned reserves and the growth allocation must be increased by about 43 per cent—30/70—to achieve a given target.
9. Fred Hirsch, "SDRs and the Working of the Gold Exchange Standard," *IMF Staff Papers*, Vol. XVIII, No. 2 (July 1971), p. 239.

using SDRs to regulate the total growth of world liquidity to permit reduction, as well as increase, in the amount of SDRs outstanding. The only conceivable contingency under which allocations should be cancelled is an unexpectedly sharp increase in other reserve assets, which would, however, be highly unlikely under the overall reform scheme proposed here. In practice, it is almost inconceivable that the rule would ever be applied anyway, if only because a large number of less developed countries would have to approve giving back resources, some of which they might have already used. Cancellation of SDRs was never proposed despite the huge buildup of dollar reserves in 1970–73. Since the possibility of cancellation detracts at least marginally from the moneyness of SDR, and since gold will always command commodity value and reserve currencies will always command real resources in the country of issue, the objective of at least equating SDRs with all other reserve assets argues strongly for removing the provisions for cancellation from the Articles.

Even without any of these changes, SDRs should immediately become the numéraire of the monetary system in which all national currencies, including the dollar, are denominated. The United States and Germany took this step in 1973. SDRs should replace gold and the dollar in that role, which is psychologically important. The IMF denominates drawings on it in SDRs, and is publishing its statistics in terms of SDRs as well as in traditional dollar form.

Gold

The role of gold in the monetary system would continue to decline gradually under these proposals, all of which remain applicable after the revaluation of official gold reserves by monetary authorities which began in early 1975. Gold should continue to shrink as a proportion of total reserves, albeit from a much higher level after the revaluation, which means that further upward revaluations should not be permitted even if the market price trended higher over time. Its share would decline in absolute amounts with each increase in IMF quotas (since 25 per cent of all quota increases must be paid in gold). It would also lose its role as partial numéraire in the system to SDRs, and the dollar would resume convertibility into all U.S. reserve assets rather than into gold alone.

Monetary authorities would continue to eschew gold purchases from the private markets. Gold could continue to flow into monetary reserves via the IMF, undermining in principle the objective of bringing total liquidity growth under the control of the international community, but it would do so only in very limited amounts. In addition, it would do so wholly through the IMF, which could determine at least the timing of the movements. Two of the principles underlying these proposals—permitting national choice of reserve assets and treating present reserve assets alike—argue for permitting small increments of gold to persist, since some countries clearly continue to want to hold gold and since some increases in dollar balances would also be permitted.

One of the two provisions of these reform proposals which relate operationally to gold is the authorization of special SDRs into which national monetary authorities could convert their present gold reserves. I have already suggested that the United States so convert a large share of its gold. In addition, to add to the likelihood of gold conversions, it would be desirable to leave the converted gold in the physical possession of the converting countries and simply earmark it to the Special Account of the IMF. The rationale is that gold is held partly for "war chest" purposes, as a hedge against a complete breakdown of the international system, and its physical location is an important consideration to some monetary authorities.

Payment of interest on these gold-generated SDRs is much more difficult than on dollar-generated SDRs, since there is no one, like the United States for the dollar overhang, to pay "net user" charges on them. One solution would be to treat all of the specially issued SDRs, whether converted into gold or dollars, as "initial allocations" bearing no interest. However, as noted, other countries would be unlikely to agree to such a total elimination of U.S. interest payments on its dollar liabilities. The alternative of paying interest on dollar-generated but not gold-generated SDRs is equally unattractive, because it would create two classes of SDRs and would also create an asymmetry between gold and dollars in the overall scheme.

The best solution is for the IMF to finance the interest payments on gold-generated SDRs by selling some of the gold in the private market. It would then invest the currencies acquired and use the interest on them to pay the "net acquirers" of these SDRs. The Fund would need to sell only a fraction of the gold converted into SDRs, both because SDR interest rates are below rates that would be paid on the national currencies acquired by the Fund and because the Fund would sell at the higher market price the gold which it acquired at the official price. The Fund would draw proportionately from the gold deposited by each country to make the sales.

To meet the concerns of gold holders, the Fund should be authorized to make gold sales in the private market only to the extent that they would not threaten to drive down the price excessively. Many monetary authorities fear that a significant reduction in the market price would jeopardize, at least psychologically, the value of their gold reserves. For analogous reasons it remains desirable to avoid a wide premium for the market price and such sales would, of course, contribute to doing so. They would also provide a marginal saving of real resources by holding down the price of commodity gold.

The second aspect of these proposals which relate to gold is the general impact of greater exchange-rate flexibility on its official price. Frequent changes in the exchange rate of the dollar, for example, directly change the official price of gold. Since such changes are small, however, we concluded earlier that they would have little adverse effect on the system in view of the clear focus on SDR throughout these reform proposals. There would probably be little danger, in such circumstances, even in a more sizable uniform increase in the official price of gold to enhance once more its usability as a reserve asset, although the preferred course would be IMF gold sales, as just proposed, to reduce the spread between the official and market prices by reducing the latter.

The Effect on the United States and Dollar Convertibility

As part of the new regime, the United States would henceforth define any parity for the dollar in terms of SDRs instead of gold. More importantly, if the new exchange-rate regime were based on adjustable parities (rather than managed floats), it would stand ready to convert into U.S. reserve assets all dollars generated by deficits in its basic balance after the new system—which included an effective adjustment process based on presumptive indicators and international guidelines, assured creation of adequate world reserves, and optional consolidation of the dollar overhang—was instituted. No such rules would apply if the system were based instead on managed flexibility of exchange rates, without any declaration of parities (or "central rates").

It will be recalled that assets outstanding in the system but not converted into the special issue of SDRs, or any new assets acquired in the future, could be used only to finance payments imbalances and not to change reserve-asset compositions. Automatic U.S. sales or purchases of gold, without regard for the payments positions of the United States and the other countries involved, would be inconsistent with this basic approach. Thus the United States need not buy gold from, or sell it to, official comers at a fixed price. And the United States would no longer need to maintain gold convertibility to promote a reserve currency role of the dollar. It would be limiting that role sharply by agreeing that countries could convert their outstanding dollars into the special issue of SDR, and by avoiding any pressure on countries to accumulate unwanted dollars in the future. If, nevertheless, countries still accumulated dollars, they would obviously not be motivated by the prospect of gold convertibility.

The United States would fit into any new parity system by financing deficits in its basic balance of payments in two ways. It could convert unwanted foreign accruals of the dollar by selling its gold and Special Drawing Rights both to foreign countries and to the International Monetary Fund, and by using the proceeds of borrowing from other countries and the Fund. Second, it could intervene directly in the foreign exchange markets with foreign currencies obtained in any of these ways; it is doubtful that much active U.S. intervention would be needed in practice if the dollar remained the principal intervention currency, but it might be if other countries failed to live up to their new adjustment obligations and the United States therefore had to insist on a multi-currency intervention scheme. The United States could still sell dollars, or lend to other countries, to meet their need for intervention currency balances although the IMF could do so as well and would probably increasingly share this central role in the system's settlements mechanism. As already indicated, the United States should convert some of its gold into the special issue of SDRs since the two could be used interchangeably and SDRs would pay a significant interest return.

Flows of Liquid Capital

Finally, the swap network should be modified to deal decisively with any undesired international effects of flows of interest-sensitive liquid capital. These flows cause two sets of difficulties: internal management problems for countries whose economies are significantly affected by them, and international monetary problems stemming from the large payments imbalances that develop temporarily as a result. These problems point to the need for measures both to reduce the magnitude of the flows and to offset their effects on national economies and on the world economy as a whole. Some of the effects on national economies will have to be mitigated by the affected countries themselves by adding to the array of policy instruments available to them, such as open-market operations and improved fiscal policy tools, to manage better their own economies.

Managed flexibility of exchange rates, or even widening the margins around exchange-rate parities to 5 per cent on either side, as proposed in the discussion of the adjustment process, is the most important single step to reduce the incentives for these interest-sensitive capital movements. Either approach would increase the likelihood of fluctuations in both spot and forward exchange rates, thereby adding uncertainty to the calculation of the speculator (who faces very little uncertainty with narrow margins), reducing the amount of potential profit for even the successful speculator against an existing parity, and inducing stabilizing speculation by enlarging the profit potential of the speculator who guesses correctly that the long-term trend of the rate will differ from its short-term direction. Even the slightly wider bands adopted in December 1971 can take part of the "credit" for the failure of dollars to flow back to the United States after the Smithsonian Agreement, and the sharply reduced level of liquid flows attracted by the "dollar crisis" of May–June 1973 can be largely attributed to the existence of floating rates.

I have also mentioned the need for improved consultations on domestic policies among the major industrialized countries. There is a particular need for consultation over the timing of changes in national monetary policies to avoid creating needless incentives for interest-sensitive flows of funds. Countries might also be able to coordinate their manipulation of long-term and short-term interest rates, including rates in the Euromoney markets, as was done in "Operation Twist" of the early 1960s in the United States to moderate the incentives for interest-sensitive movements without disturbing basic investment decisions—especially by raising short-term rates and moderating long-term rates in deficit countries.

Additional steps are needed, however. The reforms proposed for dealing with the liquidity, "official" confidence, and adjustment problems would all deal solely with *basic* payments positions; it would be silly for countries to change their parities, or for new Special Drawing Rights to be created, or for the United States to finance deficits with reserve assets, because of purely interest-sensitive or speculative capital movements which are temporary and likely to be reversed. Indeed, countries would need massive levels of owned reserves—far above the levels discussed above—if they had to finance liquid flows as well as basic imbalances. These flows should be recycled, which requires three changes in the existing swap network, the management of which might also be centralized in the IMF rather than in the Federal Reserve Bank of New York.

The first change is an extension of the maturities of the swaps, from the present 3–6 months to 18–24 months. The definition of "temporary," which governs the kinds of capital movements that the swaps cover, would be broadened to include those movements motivated primarily by interest-rate differentials, and such differentials can easily cause flows for at least as long as eighteen months in perfectly "normal" cases. The second is to continue the expansion of the size of the network, which even at its 1973 level of $18 billion would be inadequate to handle flows to and from particular countries. To assure that it would be large enough to handle all possible circumstances, particularly those emerging in light of the buildup of liquid petrodollars, the network should be expanded to at least $50 billion. Finally, the longer-term duration of the swaps, and the legitimate uncertainty as to whether the covered flows are caused *solely* by temporary interest-rate differentials, indicate a need for full exchange-rate changes by the country whose outflows have caused the need to activate them.[10]

10. This change will also help reduce the asymmetrical adjustment bias of the Bretton Woods system, since surplus countries would then receive compensation for the change in value of their foreign-exchange assets when their currencies appreciated, as well as when the currency of the deficit country depreciated.

16

The New World

The monetary system that would emerge from these reforms combines a dramatic increase in international management with continued scope for the realization of unique national interests by sovereign governments. International management would be exercised collectively by the leading monetary powers, not dominated by the United States or any other country. Correspondingly, the system would more accurately reflect the political and economic realities of the 1970s and beyond.

International control would be established over both the liquidity and adjustment mechanisms. The international community would effectively control most of the creation of world reserves through the SDR system, and would avoid the risk of a destruction of world reserves through expanding the SDR system to consolidate the dollar overhang. It would have a major voice in determining the initiation and implementation of adjustment: maintaining constant surveillance on the underlying (as opposed to the transitory) elements in current payments imbalances, making continual judgments as to whether countries were abiding by the agreed rules, and bringing concerted pressure to bear if such presumptions were ignored by the country or countries involved.

There would be a direct link between the decision-making on adjustment and liquidity because the criteria would trigger pressure for exchange-rate changes, or proscribe national intervention in the exchange markets, only when, *inter alia*, reserves changed relative to the agreed trend increase. This agreed increase would be both the basis for, and mainly the result of, decisions on the size of Special Drawing Rights allocations. To deal with any problems caused by large movements of liquid capital, which could still be sizable, the international community would also cooperate collectively by consulting closely on the timing of changes in monetary policy and actively using the augmented swap networks.

In fact, the institution of this international consultative process on some of the most vital issues of national sovereignty would be one of the most important effects of the whole reform. The present degree of cooperation, which has often been effective at the periphery in responding to crises and providing emergency financing, would evolve into meaningful engagement on the central issues of adjustment and liquidity creation. The central institutional role of the International Monetary Fund would be greatly enhanced by the new regimes for liquidity and adjustment, in itself a major advance in internationalizing world economic management. The Fund would provide the key monetary forum in which all countries (including the Communist countries, if they chose to join), but especially the United States, Western Europe, Japan and some of the leading Third World powers could work together to build the community which is essential for the constructive management of overall relations among them in the years ahead.

Major problems would still remain, national goals and capabilities would continue to vary, crises would still occur, ad hoc solutions would prevail in many instances, and political disagreements would recur. But the proposed changes would produce major improvement. Devoting international attention primarily to exchange-rate changes would turn the focus of the debate from domestic economic policies —largely an ineffectual debate because these policies will continue to be determined overwhelmingly by domestic needs in most countries— to the means of adjustment which most directly affect other countries and which should be most susceptible to coordinated effort. The multilaterally managed flexibility of exchange rates would enable such efforts to take place with less fear of arousing unsettling waves of speculation, and the improved swap networks will help deal with those that do occur. These changes should permit a reversal of the accelerating trend toward increased controls over selected international transactions by virtually all countries. The reduced roles of both the dollar and gold will remove much of the emotional element from discussions of liquidity and confidence matters; the antiseptic Special Drawing Rights would become the basic numeraire in the system and its major reserve asset.

National governments would, at the same time, retain their basic prerogatives. But untrammeled practices would be modified to avoid disruption to the system as a whole, and no country could cause major systemic problems without clearly violating the rules of the game. They could choose their reserve-asset composition with complete freedom, with three exceptions: no purchases of gold directly from gold producers; no assurance of gold purchases from the United States; and no assurance of dollar purchases from the United States in exchange for gold. (All of these exceptions exist today; two of them existed at least de facto before August 15, 1971, and the latter two would still be possible in particular cases if the United States were willing.) Under the new regime, gold would continue to recede in importance as a monetary asset, although it could still be held and acquired by countries which wanted to do so through the International Monetary Fund or from countries willing to sell it.

Aside from the exceptions, countries could freely determine the composition both of their existing reserve stock and of future additions to it. They would gain several extra degrees of national freedom, relative to the era of dollar inconvertibility inaugurated in August 1971. For their outstanding reserves, they could move from any or all of their present assets into Special Drawing Rights. For new reserves, they could add either Special Drawing Rights, dollars, or whatever reserve asset the United States and other countries would use to finance their basic deficits. To finance liquid capital movements, surplus countries would have a free choice between holding the currency originally acquired through market transactions, or swapping it for their own currency and fully avoiding any exchange-rate risks. At the outset of the new scheme most major countries would probably convert their reserve currency holdings into Special Drawing Rights, and retain their gold. Over time, however, the combined virtues of the Special Drawing Rights might well result in actual use of most of the special issue to replace most assets outstanding in the system at the time the new option was instituted. It is unlikely that many, if any, private dollar balances would be turned in to the monetary authorities, and then converted into the special issue of SDRs, though the growth of private dollar holdings may slow down from its trend rate of the past as other national currencies assume a greater transactions role.

On adjustment, individual countries could opt either to "join" the regime of flexible exchange rates, or peg to another major currency which in turn would flex. They would, of course, retain their present options of using domestic policies or selective measures aimed directly at international transactions to seek adjustment of payments imbalances, and in fact could point to such measures in defending themselves against charges that they were violating the rules. If they failed to adopt any adjustment measures, however, they would face the possibility of action from the international community to induce them to move their exchange rates—moves which would be politically much easier to make under such an exchange-rate regime.

Many countries at this stage of history would probably opt for national exchange-rate flexibility. Members of the European Community might well seek to narrow the margins within which their exchange rates would differ, but for many years they will probably need a system of small and frequent internal changes to enable them to stay together against the rest of the world. A few lower income countries might peg to the dollar during periods when the United States was maintaining reasonably stable prices. (Only such countries devalued with the dollar in 1971 and 1973.) But the key "members" of the de facto dollar area that existed prior to August 1971, including Germany and Japan, would be unlikely to do so. Some of them have closer economic and even political ties elsewhere, and all would face political difficulties in explicitly pegging to the dollar in the new regime. Canada and several Latin American countries have demonstrated a preference for floating by themselves, even under the Bretton Woods system. Japan would probably move by itself, but it is hard to see any significant number of countries that might peg to the yen. Some sterling area and franc zone countries might retain their pegs to sterling and the French franc, but the sterling area is rapidly disintegrating and is virtually limited to the remaining dependencies and near-colonies, like the franc zone.

There would probably be close relationship between the choices which countries made on their exchange-rate regimes and on the composition of their reserve assets. Countries pegging to the dollar might opt to hold some or all of their reserves, old and new, in dollar form. The main advantages would be higher rates of interest, savings of transactions costs, and offsets to dollar liabilities—mainly for countries which themselves would follow virtually any depreciation of the dollar and hence suffer no losses (in domestic currency) from any shifts in the exchange rate of the dollar. The "new" dollar area would thus primarily comprise lower income countries geographically proximate to the United States and look much more like the franc zone, or the sterling area under the Basel arrangements, than like the widespread area which had developed heretofore.

The position of the United States would be dramatically different under the new monetary regime. The dollar would probably remain the world's chief private transaction and official intervention currency, and would be strengthened in those roles by the reduction in its reserve currency status and the new safeguards for that status. Other currencies would doubtlessly capture a growing share of both functions at the margins. The United States should welcome their doing so, within the negotiated and cooperative framework proposed here, because this should move the issuing countries toward exercising more responsible leadership in the monetary system. A sharp reduction in the reserve currency role of the dollar would restore the balance between the true international power position of the United States and its roles in the world's monetary system. The United States would still be the single most important country by far, but would henceforth operate as one of several key partners in directing the system's activities and would consult with increasing closeness on all international economic issues. Since no individual country or group could effectively fill the role of balancer which the United States maintained throughout the postwar period until August 1971, true internationalization of that process through the IMF and other international organizations will be necessary.[1]

These changes in the dollar's roles would have a profound impact on the international financial policy of the United States. It would still have to maintain the attributes required of a vehicle currency: confidence that convertibility into other national currencies will be maintained at reasonably stable prices, at least in the short run, and reasonable proximity to balance-of-payments equilibrium and price stability; the preservation of efficient capital and money markets; and, politically, the maintenance of a sufficient world role to assure others that it would not capriciously abrogate its currency's transaction functions. Payments equilibrium would be easier to maintain under the new regime, and the other goals are desirable for purely domestic reasons as well. In short, this list adds little to the requirements for national policy.

Furthermore, the United States would no longer have to maintain the additional requirements of a reserve currency, which *do* place it under extra constraints: international political dominance, assumption of primary responsibility for the functioning of the monetary system, assured convertibility into all other assets (including gold) used as reserves in the system, maintenance of a ratio between reserve assets and liquid liabilities deemed "adequate" by the most conservative wing of opinion in the world financial spectrum, avoidance of exchange-rate changes and comprehensive controls over international transactions, and probably a balance of payments comprised of current account surpluses plus net capital exports. The United States would be rid of any threats from the dollar overhang or any risk that it would be re-created in the future. It would, in sum, stop the slide in the benefit-cost ratio to it of the international roles of the

1. For the immediate future, however, Germany as the home of the world's second key currency might have to play a special leadership role alongside the United States. See "The United States and Germany: The Imperative of Economic Bigemony," Chapter 23 in *Toward a New International Economic Order: Selected Papers of C. Fred Bergsten, 1972–1974* (Lexington, Mass.: D. C. Heath and Co., 1975).

dollar—a ratio which has long since turned negative and certainly would continue so in the future—by sharply reducing the role itself and placing its remaining portion on a fully protected basis.

Under the new regime the United States would get annual unfettered SDR allocation of perhaps $1.5 billion annually. (It would also get at least temporary dollar financing for any basic payments deficits if countries opting to accumulate dollars rather than Special Drawing Rights ran payments surpluses. But it should build reserves *pari passu* with the bulk of such increased dollar holdings since they could later shift to other countries which would not hold on to them.) It could get recycling credits under the augmented swap network to finance short-term capital outflows which added to its official settlements deficits.

Beyond these sources of financing, the United States would have to adjust its payments position. To adjust, however, the United States could now change its exchange rate—the only economically effective way which is also politically feasible at home. It would now be assured of the cooperation of other countries when the agreed criteria pointed to the need for a U.S. change, which would mitigate the risk that the continued key currency roles of the dollar might abort the effort. The adjustment initiatives required of the United States would of course be reduced by the increased pressure that the new system would place on other countries to change their exchange rates in cases where they were clearly in positions of pending disequilibrium of their currencies. And the United States could call on stronger defenses for the dollar at times of heavy international movements of liquid funds, from the larger and longer-duration swaps which would then be available.

All these gains to the United States, moreover, are well matched by the gains to other countries in the overall package. Indeed, other countries stand to gain more from the basic improvements in the monetary system in view of their greater dependence on international economic transactions. The sharp reduction in the risk of systemic breakdown is in itself a major incentive for all countries to adopt such an approach. And their willingness to engineer a "reverse Marshall Plan" by agreeing to avoid amortization of the outstanding dollar balances could be a major breakthrough in generally improving U.S.-European, and U.S.-Japanese, relations—without any real cost to them.

Other specific gains would also be obtained. The veto rights of the European Community over SDR allocations in the International Monetary Fund decision-making process would enable its members together to achieve truly equal power with the United States on liquidity issues, with the elevation of Special Drawing Rights. Moving the international community as a whole, through the International Monetary Fund, toward the center of decision-making on exchange rates would achieve a similar result; other countries would obtain a much more meaningful way to influence the balance-of-payments policies of the United States, because the exchange rate is clearly a less sensitive matter to it politically than is its domestic economic policy. Other countries would also get unconditional exchange-rate guarantees on the expanded swap network, and the encouragement of the United States in moving their currencies toward key currency status if they wished to do so or were unable to stop trends in that direction.

Finally, the United States would be making some very basic concessions concerning its own role in the world. It would be sanctioning a sharp diminution in the international role of its currency and giving up some of the prestige that role carries. More tangibly, in any return to a parity system, it would explicitly accept responsibility to finance the bulk of any deficits in its basic payments balance with U.S. reserve assets. In achieving scope for its exchange rate to change, the United States would also be accepting the possibility of small increases in the official dollar price of both gold and Special Drawing Rights.

The package should thus be negotiable, despite its breadth and far-reaching implications. With the rules of the game in suspense since August 1971, the opportunity to do so should be seized.

17

An International Monetary Fund for the Twenty-First Century: Experience and Lessons from the 1990s*

The Case for Systemic Reform

In its recent report, the Bretton Woods Commission—convened by Paul Volcker and composed of leading financiers, businessmen, former government and central bank officials, and academics from a wide range of countries—correctly concludes that "the costs of extreme exchange rate misalignment and volatility are high. . . . When exchange rates are misaligned, resources are misallocated. . . . Exchange rate misalignment adds to protectionist pressures in one major country after another. . . . The governments of the major industrial countries should give a high priority to international monetary reforms aimed at reducing large exchange rate fluctuations and serious misalignments."[1]

The most dramatic recent misalignment was of course the massive overvaluation of the dollar in the first half of the 1980s. The resulting decimation of American trade competitiveness led the Reagan administration, to quote its own secretary of the treasury, James Baker, "to grant more import relief to U.S. industry than any of its predecessors in more than half a century."[2] Free traders in Congress despaired that "the

---

*This chapter is based on the author's presentation at the conference "Fifty Years after Bretton Woods: The Future of the IMF and World Bank," Madrid, September 29, 1994, sponsored by the International Monetary Fund and the World Bank to mark the fiftieth anniversary of these institutions. The views expressed are those of the author and do not necessarily reflect the views of individual members of either the Board of Directors or the Advisory Committee of the Institute for International Economics.

1. Bretton Woods Commission, *Bretton Woods: Looking to the Future,* Report of the Bretton Woods Commission, July 1994.
2. Remarks before a conference sponsored by the Institute for International Economics, September 14, 1987.

Smoot-Hawley Tariff itself would pass by an overwhelming majority" had it come to the House of Representatives floor in the fall of 1985. The infamous Super 301 provisions of the American trade law, and American "aggressive unilateralism" more broadly, are part of the trade policy legacy of that particular currency misalignment.[3]

The most recent case is Japan. The yen reached an equilibrium level (about 120:1 against the dollar, the equivalent in real terms of about 100:1 today) at the end of 1987, and, largely as a result, Japan's global current-account surplus dropped to a mere $35 billion (1.2 percent of its gross domestic product, or GDP) in 1991. But the yen was permitted to weaken by 30 percent in 1989–90, despite continued improvement in Japan's international competitive position, producing the huge renewed surplus that triggered sharp trade reactions elsewhere—including the "managed trade" onslaught from the United States and comprehensive automobile quotas in the European Community (EC). The sharp appreciation of the yen that inevitably followed has traumatized much of Japanese industry and, in the continuing (and inexplicable) absence of significant fiscal stimulus despite continued budget surpluses, has extended the country's recession through a record third year. Japan has thus received a double hit from the latest misalignment.

The currency misalignments that developed in Europe are even more widely recognized. The crises of the Exchange Rate Mechanism (ERM) of 1992 and 1993, though different in nature from the dollar and yen episodes, have had equally profound (or even greater) effects on the economies of the countries involved and on the global financial system. Unemployment levels in Europe have been much higher for much longer due to the effort to preserve disequilibrium parities in the face of major changes in the underlying economic fundamentals. Most notable of these changes was German reunification, but differential inflation in Italy and elsewhere, and sterling's entry to the system at a clearly overvalued rate, were also influential.

Any international monetary system that permits such large and recurrent disequilibria, with such major economic costs, is a failure. The only relevant question is whether a better system can be constructed intellectually and implemented operationally.

The Search for Stability
Both extremes have been tried. Fixed exchange rates were attempted at the global level under the original Bretton Woods system and in

3. The central role of currency misalignments in fostering trade protection is demonstrated empirically in Enzo Grilli, "Macroeconomic Determinants of Trade Protection," *The World Economy* 11 (September 1988): 313–26.

Europe during the second phase (1987–92) of the European Monetary System (EMS). Both times, they broke down because they became too rigid and could not accomplish needed parity changes on a timely basis.

Flexible exchange rates have existed for the past twenty years. Implemented in nearly pure form in the first half of the 1980s, they permitted the largest misalignment of all time for a major currency. Both "pure systems" have clearly failed.

Hence governments have constantly sought a better regime. It is fascinating to note that much of today's discussion of international monetary reform echoes the discussion that occurred, at least outside official circles, around the time of the collapse of fixed rates in the early 1970s. Now, as then, the focus is on intermediate systems. They were then referred to as "wider bands" or "crawling pegs" or some combination of the two.[4] Today's proposals for "crawling target zones" are largely an amalgam of such ideas. This similarity of thinking occurs across more than two decades, despite the enormous changes that have occurred in the underlying economic and political landscape—the huge increase in capital mobility, the dispersion of economic power around the world, and the end of the Cold War.

There was of course no agreed monetary reform in the early 1970s. But the new de facto regime of freely floating rates had a very short half-life, as governments immediately revealed their preference for something better. At the regional level, Europe adopted the "snake" in the early 1970s and the EMS more recently, and now seeks full Economic and Monetary Union (EMU).

At the global level, coordinated intervention strategies were adopted in the late 1970s and again in the middle 1980s—most dramatically, with the Plaza Agreement in 1985, when the G–5 explicitly admitted that its previous "benign neglect" and reliance on national "convergence" had failed to produce equilibrium exchange rates. Even more ambitiously, the G–5/G–7 created a system of target zones—which they called "reference ranges"—in the Louvre Accord in 1987.[5]

The Louvre bands were too narrow, and its rates were set prematurely and hence did not last long, because the dollar had not yet

4. See Chapter 13 of this volume and C. Fred Bergsten, George N. Halm, Fritz Machlup, and Robert Roosa, *Approaches to Greater Flexibility of Exchange Rates: The Burgenstock Papers* (Princeton, N.J.: Princeton University Press, 1970).

5. The definitive account is given by Yoichi Funabashi in *Managing the Dollar: From the Plaza to the Louvre* (Washington: Institute for International Economics, 1988).

completed its needed correction. But the major industrial countries have been operating a system of de facto (or "quiet") target zones since that time:

1. The trade-weighted dollar has been relatively stable since 1987, confined to a range within 10 percent on either side of its late–1987 base.
2. The dollar-DM rate has fluctuated between about 1.40:1 and 1.80:1 during the past five years, with repeated intervention to preserve both ends of the range.
3. The dollar-yen rate for most of the period ranged between 120:1 and 160:1 (though, as already indicated, the yen became significantly undervalued at that level and hence broke into a new range in 1993–94).

Moreover, the European Monetary System responded to its crisis of 1993 not by abandoning or realigning its parities but by sharply widening the margins around them. This largest regional arrangement also thereby created a system of de facto target zones, which so far have quite an encouraging record.

Both the global and the key regional monetary arrangements are thus coalescing into an intermediate regime. Such a regime would seek to incorporate the virtues of the two extreme systems: first, limitation of volatility and thus business predictability for fixed rates, and second, responsiveness to market changes for flexible rates. It would also try to avoid the vices of the two extreme systems: first, excessive rigidity and thus periodic misalignments for fixity, and second, extreme misalignments and volatility under flexibility.

But the present de facto target zone system, while it is a decided improvement over the failed extremes of the past, still embodies significant weaknesses. Some of the ranges are so wide that costly misalignments can still occur. There is no orderly mechanism for adjusting the ranges to respond to changes in economic fundamentals, as revealed in the recent case of the yen. The markets are not confident that the ranges will be maintained and are constantly tempted to bet against them. Implementation depends almost wholly on the individuals who are in office at a given time and has no institutional locus (or even memory).[6] The present regime should thus be

6. In *Managing the Dollar*, Funabashi, *ibid.*, documents the rapid dissolution of the policies implanted by Baker-Miyazawa-Stoltenberg as soon as that triumvirate departed from office. Even more clearly, systemic rules are needed to avoid extreme and disruptive policies such as those fostered by Beryl Sprinkel in the first half of the 1980s.

viewed as a temporary way station en route to lasting reform rather than as a satisfactory terminus.

Adopting Announced Target Zones

The best step would be to convert the present de facto regime into a de jure system of announced target zones among the major currencies. The zones could start at +/–10 percent around notional midpoints, determined by calculating the exchange rates needed to produce and maintain sustainable current account positions—a wholly realistic objective within the prescribed margin of error.[7] The zones would be kept under constant review, with changes in bilateral nominal rates as needed to hold real rates constant and with more substantial changes in response to large external shocks (such as the sharp changes in world oil prices in the 1970s or German unification more recently).

It is nonsense for officials to reject target zones on such grounds as "our limited resources do not permit us to cope with the $1 trillion of daily activity in the currency markets." The vast bulk of the daily currency flow is self-balancing, reflecting routine steps by market participants to rebalance their portfolios following normal financial transactions. While very large sums will move if the market is convinced that the authorities are trying to defend a disequilibrium rate, net market movements for most currencies on most days are quite small.

Indeed, a credible target zone regime could convert present destabilizing private flows into stabilizing flows in the future.[8] As long as the zones were set properly and defended effectively, private capital movements would help maintain rather than disrupt them. When rates approached the edges of the zones, speculators would know that they could make little money pushing further in that direction but that there was substantial scope for profit from reversing course. Governments and central banks, in their pursuit of economic and financial stability, would gain much more from these stabilizing properties of an effective monetary system than they would lose by giving up their present ability to surprise the market on occasion—

7. As demonstrated in the several papers reflecting the state of the art regarding such calculations in John Williamson, ed., *Estimating Equilibrium Exchange Rates* (Washington: Institute for International Economics, September 1994). It is also noteworthy that the United States and Japan have been able largely to agree in their current Framework Talks on the proper current account surplus for Japan (1 1/2–2 percent of its GDP), despite their acrimonious conflict on virtually everything else.

8. See Paul Krugman, "Target Zones and Exchange Rate Dynamics," NBER Working Paper 2481 (Cambridge, Mass.: National Bureau of Economic Research, 1988).

and they would of course retain that ability for intramarginal intervention.

There is also strong empirical evidence that coordinated, announced intervention in the exchange markets can effectively defend exchange-rate targets—even when the intervention is sterilized and hence conducted without changes in monetary policy. Dominguez and Frankel, using previously unavailable German and American intervention data, show that publicized intervention can be extremely potent.[9] A study by the research staff of the Banca d'Italia, using even more extensive intervention evidence from all G–10 and EMS countries, reaches even stronger conclusions: that all seventeen episodes of concerted intervention from 1984 to early 1992 were "definitely successful," that in no case was intervention steamrollered by the market, and that all but one of the major turning points in the dollar-DM and dollar-yen rates since 1985 have been "exactly coincident" with episodes of concerted intervention.[10]

The combination of wide bands and effective intervention suggests that macroeconomic policy, including monetary policy, would not often have to be devoted to external purposes under a credible target zone system. Hence monetary and fiscal policy could largely retain their focus on domestic policy targets.

In the cases in which domestic policy had to be altered, however, the alterations would generally go in directions that would be quite healthy from the long-term standpoint of the country in question (as well as the world economy as a whole). Improved international policy coordination could in fact promote better domestic policy coordination, a problem for most of the major countries despite their sophisticated policy regimes. A target zone system could on occasion reduce the short-term flexibility of macroeconomic policy in participating countries, but, in practice, would primarily reduce these countries' flexibility in making policy errors, as indicated in some of the most spectacular recent cases of such error:

1. A target zone system, in addition to calling for intervention that would have limited the final (and totally irrational) stage of the appreciation of the dollar in 1984–85, would have pushed the United States to restrain its run-up in interest rates in the early 1980s through less fiscal expansion—surely a desirable outcome

9. Kathryn A. Dominguez and Jeffrey A. Frankel, *Does Foreign Exchange Intervention Work?* (Washington: Institute for International Economics, 1993).
10. Pietro Catte, Giampaolo Galli, and Salvatore Rebecchini, "Concerted Intervention and the Dollar: An Analysis of Daily Data," in Peter B. Kenen, F. Saccomanni, and F. Papadia, eds., *The International Monetary System* (Cambridge, Mass.: Cambridge University Press, forthcoming).

and one that many Americans now seek through far more artificial and arbitrary devices such as balanced budget amendments and legislative procedures à la Gramm-Rudman-Hollings.

2. A target zone system centered on the end–1987 equilibrium rates would have sought to avoid the sharp depreciation of the yen in subsequent years, thereby pushing Japan to use fiscal rather than monetary policy to expand domestic demand and shielding it from at least the worst excesses of the "bubble economy."

3. A target zone system would have pushed Germany toward appreciation of the DM in the wake of reunification, reducing the need for subsequent sky-high real interest rates that pushed all of Europe (especially *outside* Germany) into prolonged recession.[11]

The relationship between the monetary regime and macroeconomic policy coordination is an issue on which the Bretton Woods Commission and many other analysts make a critical error. The Commission and others argue that governments should first achieve more successful coordination of their macroeconomic policies and then subsequently adopt target zones or some other better monetary regime. Unfortunately, there are no historical examples of such agreements on policy coordination. Hence such recommendations represent pious statements of principle that are destined to remain totally nonoperational.

By contrast, at least two historical examples of monetary systems in turn induced participating countries to achieve a degree of policy coordination. The original Bretton Woods regime of adjustable pegs produced such results to an important extent despite the caveats cited above.[12] So has the European Monetary System, most dramatically in the case of French adjustment to the disastrous effects of its "dash for growth" in 1982–83; but also in its evolution into a much more extensive regime of policy coordination in the 1990s and the subsequent plans for full monetary and even fiscal coordination via EMU. History

11. Some argue that the breakdown of the ERM in 1992 and again in 1993 demonstrates the futility of seeking to manage exchange rates as proposed here. This is incorrect: as noted above, the ERM collapsed because, like the Bretton Woods system in the late 1960s and early 1970s, it failed to adjust its parities in the face of clear changes in the underlying economic fundamentals. The lesson is to avoid defending disequilibrium exchange rates, which (as indicated in the text) are as likely to emerge under floating rates as under fixed rates, rather than to abdicate all efforts to manage currencies.

12. See Michael Michaely, *The Responsiveness of Demand Policies to Balance of Payments: Postwar Patterns* (New York: Columbia University Press, 1971).

suggests that the more feasible progression is from monetary accord to policy cooperation rather than the reverse.[13]

There is a problem of transition in the adoption of any new monetary regime. If the starting point is fixed exchange rates, as under the original Bretton Woods system, a comprehensive realignment is required. Much of the debate in the early 1970s centered on where the new parities should be set.

If the starting point is floating rates, or even de facto target zones like today, it is much easier to launch a new system "around current levels."[14] Any need to jump to new rates could be disruptive and make institution of the new regime substantially more difficult, thus deterring governments from making the effort. Hence governments must look for an opportune moment to launch a system of target zones (or anything more ambitious).

Fortunately, there is widespread agreement that today's exchange rates are close to long-term equilibrium levels. International Money Fund (IMF) Managing Director Michel Camdessus has recently noted that "exchange rates among the key currencies are probably not very far from the professional consensus on the rates that are appropriate."[15] Hence the present moment, unlike most of the past dozen years, would permit a smooth start-up of a new regime. The opportunity should not be wasted.

Target Zones and the IMF[16]

Who would manage a system of target zones? The G–7 is clearly inadequate. It has no staff nor even a secretariat to keep records and produce an institutional memory. Its members frequently disagree on what they said soon after an agreement is reached. No decision-making system, let alone a procedure for resolving disputes effectively, is in place.

13. Guidelines for implementing such policy coordination can be found in chapter 15 of this volume and in John Williamson and Marcus Miller, *Targets and Indicators: A Blueprint for the International Coordination of Economic Policy* (Washington: Institute for International Economics, 1987).
14. As laid out in Funabashi, *op. cit.*, British entry to the ERM at a clearly overvalued rate for sterling is a recent example of the perils of commencing a new regime "around current levels" when the levels are incorrect.
15. Michael Camdessus, "The IMF at Fifty—An Evolving Role but a Constant Mission," an address to the Institute for International Economics, Washington, June 7, 1994, p. 8.
16. This section draws heavily on John Williamson and C. Randall Henning, "Managing the Monetary System," in Peter B. Kenen, ed., *Managing the World Economy: Fifty Years after Bretton Woods* (Washington: Institute for International Economics, September 1994).

The only satisfactory forum within which to manage a new international monetary regime is the IMF. The Fund is the only institution that would permit the needed integration of the decisions by participants in the regime with those of nonparticipants, for example, with respect to the selection of current account targets. Only the Fund could provide a channel through which the interests of nonparticipants could be brought to bear on the decisions of the participants. The IMF already has available the robust staff of economists, analysts, and technicians that would be needed to support the regime.[17]

At the same time, the G–7 industrial democracies account for a substantial majority of world economic activity and will continue to do so for some time.[18] All the countries that are crucial to the initial success of the regime are contained within the G–7. They are the most likely participants in a target zone regime at its outset. They bear responsibility for systemic stability so must play a central role in the management of any successful monetary regime.[19]

The G–7 finance ministers and central bank governors should therefore remain the initial locus in which implementation and administration of target zones are negotiated and discussed. They would establish the targets for the current account balances of the participants in the regime, establish the exchange rates needed to achieve and maintain those positions, and realign the target zones in response to real shocks or new evidence about the need for payments adjustment. Decisions within the G–7 would continue to be taken by consensus. The G–7 ministers might meet quarterly, as they agreed at the G–7 summit meeting at Naples in July 1994, with their deputies meeting as often as necessary.

The finance ministers and central bank governors should, however, draw much more fully on the Fund staff by giving it responsibility, along with the staffs of the national finance ministries and central

17. The Fund staff demonstrates its capability to conduct the required analytical studies in chapter 2 of Williamson, ed., *op. cit.*
18. Recent suggestions that the G–7 share of world output has dropped to little more than 50 percent rely on unrealistically large gross national product (GNP) adjustments for China, India, and other developing countries to incorporate inflated estimates of purchasing power parity rather than market exchange rates.
19. The G–7 should be collapsed into a G–3 as soon as the European Union achieves Economic and Monetary Union and can speak with a single voice on these issues. I shall henceforth refer to the G–7 but hope and expect that EMU will occur within the relevant future, converting the G–7 into a G–3 and thus easing the global coordination task in the same way that creation of the original European Economic Community facilitated global trade negotiations by permitting Europe to speak with a single voice in that venue.

banks, for preparing discussion papers and decision memoranda for G–7 meetings. The managing director, who presently participates only in the portion of G–7 meetings devoted to multilateral surveillance, should be included throughout. He or she should participate in discussing current account targets, setting the target zones, and pursuing any policy adjustments needed to defend them—in order to bring global systemic concerns, and those of the remaining members of the IMF, to the table.

Moreover, the G–7 should seek the approval of the appropriate bodies of the IMF before implementing any decisions that it has taken.[20] As presently constituted, however, the Fund's Executive Board would then have to pass judgment on decisions taken by officials who are much more senior than the executive directors themselves. Hence it would be desirable, when making important decisions about setting up and implementing the new regime, to constitute the Executive Board at ministerial level.

Such a body, called the "Council," has already been provided for by the Second Amendment to the Articles of Agreement (1976) and could be activated by 85 percent of the voting power of the Fund (Article XII, Section 1, Schedule D). By involving the same finance ministers that represent their countries in the G–7, the Council could consult and confer with the individuals responsible for G–7 decisions. The Interim Committee, after its twenty-year "interim," should thus be converted into the "Council," as originally intended in the Second Amendment.[21]

To implement the new regime, and to dramatize the role that the Fund would be playing in managing the global monetary system, the Executive Board itself should be upgraded through the appointment of

20. So should the EMS. However, there is no legal obligation for either the G–7 or the EMS to do so. The Articles of Agreement allow groups of members to create such exchange-rate regimes. The only obligation of such groups is to notify the Fund of changes in their arrangements (Article IV, Sections 2a and 2b).

21. Activating the Council would be a far better way to manage the new regime than relying on the existing Interim Committee or even a strengthened version of the Interim Committee. The Interim Committee, like the proposed Council, meets at ministerial level and has the same representative configuration as the Executive Board. The Interim Committee, however, possesses no formal powers of decision making and was intended solely to provide political guidance to the work of the Executive Board. The Council, on the other hand, would have real decision-making authority within the Fund: it could approve (or reject) decisions taken within the G–7 with all the formal surveillance authority of the Fund, rather than relying on the Executive Board to provide formal approval indirectly.

ministerial deputies as executive directors.[22] Under this change, which would be implemented by each country group or "constituency" within the Fund, the G–7 deputies would be members of the Executive Board, which would be overseeing international monetary matters under the authority of the Council when the ministers were unable to convene (or did not need to do so). The alternate executive directors, who would be appointees at roughly the same level as the current executive directors, would carry on the regular business of the Fund.

The Council would then exercise the Fund's powers of surveillance over the exchange rate arrangements of its members, approving the new regime and decisions taken within it (Article IV, Sections 2b and 3b). The Council would examine and discuss the current account targets of both participants and nonparticipants in the regime, the target zones for the participating currencies, and policy adjustments needed to sustain them. The Council, or the Executive Board meeting under its aegis, would approve realignments, for example.

The Council and the Executive Board could be expected to accept the proposals of the G–7, for whom these decisions would be far more consequential than for the nonparticipants, on most occasions. Approval by the Fund bodies, however, would be much more than a rubber-stamping of the decisions of the G–7, as follows:

1. The Council and the Board could reinforce the majority within the G–7 in exercising peer pressure over miscreants, adding to the prospects for prompt and constructive policy changes when needed.
2. The G–7 would have to consult with the Council and the Board throughout the process, giving them immediate notice of decisions and the right to cross-examine the representatives of the G–7 countries.
3. The accumulation over time of a record of decisions and advice on the part of the Council and Board could contribute both to future decisions by G–7 countries and accession to the regime by others.
4. The G–7 governments do not quite command a majority of the votes within the IMF.

The actual role of the Council or the Executive Board would depend on the type of G–7 decision being approved. General surveillance over the regime and consideration of future policy adjustments that might be required to meet regime targets, for example, could be conducted at

22. As proposed by C. David Finch, "Governance of the International Monetary Fund by Its Members," in Bretton Woods Commission, *op. cit.,* pp. 171–78.

ministerial level. A realignment of the target zones, on the other hand, would require avoidance of any substantial delay between a G–7 decision and its implementation. In this case, the Executive Board could convene on a few hours' notice at the level of the deputy ministers (or even their alternates based in Washington) to approve the decision.

The central banks, acting together in a new committee (the Committee of Central Banks) that would in turn confer with the G–7, and work within the framework of its decisions, should make all operational decisions about intervention and monetary policy adjustments.[23] The central banks should, for example, be given authority to assign intervention responsibilities and extend credits to finance intervention.

Through their participation in the G–7 meetings, and through their new committee, the governors of the central banks should advise the G–7 on the full range of macroeconomic and monetary issues. The committee, in particular, should warn the G–7 when the projected fiscal policies of governments could make maintenance of the target zones impossible without provoking inflationary or deflationary changes in monetary policies in one or more participating countries. The committee should have the authority to propose consideration of a realignment within the G–7.

The advantages of this three-part institutional infrastructure for target zones are several. This infrastructure builds on the meetings of existing and operating institutions: the IMF, G–7, and Basel meetings of central bankers that already take place on a monthly basis. It balances the need for efficiency in decision making with the need for broader participation to enhance legitimacy. It can be implemented without any amendment of the Articles of Agreement of the Fund (or any other "constitutional" changes). It restores the Fund to its original raison d'être of managing the international monetary regime.

Conclusion

At their summit in Naples in 1994, the G–7 heads of government asked, "How can we adapt existing institutions and build new (international economic) institutions to ensure the future prosperity and security of our people?" They inscribed the issue on the agenda of their meeting in Canada in 1995.

.There are a number of needed changes in both categories.[24] But international monetary reform is surely the place to start. The interna-

23. C. Randall Henning, *Currencies and Politics in the United States, Germany and Japan* (Washington: Institute for International Economics, July 1994), chapter 8.

24. For a comprehensive review, see C. Fred Bergsten, "The Case for Reform," in Kenen, ed., *op. cit.*

tional monetary system lies at the heart of the world economy, just as national monetary policies lie at the heart of individual national economies. The present regime is clearly inadequate. A viable alternative is available. There is growing support for such reform, as indicated by the widespread and prestigious participation in the Bretton Woods Commission and the expression of personal views on the topic by the managing director of the Fund himself.[25]

Yet neither the executive directors of the Fund, nor the Board of Governors, nor the G–7 have made any serious proposals in recent years to improve the system. The fiftieth anniversary of Bretton Woods would be an apt moment to begin the process of creating an effective and stable monetary regime for the years, and even the decades and the half-century, ahead. Installation of a central monetary role for the IMF should be an integral element of any such systemic reform. There would be no more apt time to launch the effort than at the annual meeting of the Fund itself, in October 1995.

25. In his address to the Institute for International Economics on June 7, 1994, pp. 7–8.

Index

Adams, F. Gerard, 279n, 287n
Adjustable peg system, and limited exchange rate flexibility, 438, 566
Adjustment, 12–13,
  alternatives for deficit and surplus countries 174, 277–78; change in U.S. approach to, 85–86, 277;
capital controls approach to, 297–304; assessment of option, 304; effect on roles of dollar, 302–3; and foreign direct in investment, 300–1; and payments imbalance, 198, 300; piecemeal application, 298–99; purpose of, 301; U.S. experience not a model for, 300–2; dollar's roles, and problems of, 79–80, 233, 286, 398–99, 511–12; through domestic policy, 39–43 (table), 42; econometric studies of, 276–77; foreign perceptions of effectiveness, 288; via exchange-rate changes (table), 43; under gold standard, 48–51; under "gold-dollar's standard, 85, 87; under "gold-exchange" standard, 57–60; and international monetary power, 39–44; and international monetary system, 19, 375; interwar failure, 57–58; and liquidity, 13–18; mercantilism and, 25; and national goals, 19; open economies and, 20; real economic costs of, 14–15, 332; in reformed monetary system, 375, sharing initiative for, 402; U.S. interest in, 91, 277, 501–3, 504–5

Adjustment *(continued)*
  incomes policy approach to: aims, 281–87; as part of long-term program for U.S., 287–88; economic costs, 288–89
  costs of: policy-mix approach to, 281–86; and U.S. employment, 275–76, 280–81
  direct controls on government expenditures and, 294–97; foreign aid reductions and switches, 296–97; military expenditure reductions and switches, 294–96; undermining key currency roles, 297
  direct controls on current account, 289–94: effectiveness of export subsidies, 291–92; effectiveness of import surcharges, 292–94; efficiency costs of subsidies and surcharges, 290–91; relative cost to U.S. economy, 290
  exchange-rate changes and: constraints on U.S. on using, 307–11; economic costs, 304–5; and ineffective monetary system, 318–19; potential effects, 305–6; new guidelines for 520–27; criteria for, 521; focus on basic balance, 521–23; and general disequilibrium, 525–26; for individual countries, 523–25; internal changes and, 526–27; international sanctions and, 527–28

573

About the Author

C. Fred Bergsten is the Director of the Institute for International Economics, a position he has held since its creation in 1981. He is the author of twenty-five books on international economic issues, including *Global Economic Leadership and the Group of Seven* (1966), *Reconcilable Differences? United States–Japan Economic Conflict* (1993), and *Pacific Dynamism and the International Economic System* (1993). He is quoted widely in the quality press and is a popular public speaker. He also appears often on television news programs and testifies frequently before congressional committees.

He has worked in many capacities with a wide variety of national and international economic and monetary organizations. On the national level, he is currently chairman of the Competitiveness Policy Council, which was created by Congress in the Omnibus Trade and Competitiveness Act of 1988. During the period 1969–71, he served as assistant for international economic affairs to Dr. Henry Kissinger at the National Security Council. He was assistant secretary of the treasury for International Affairs from 1977 to 1981, and functioned as under secretary for monetary affairs from 1980 to 1981. He has been a senior fellow at the Council on Foreign Relations (1967–68), at the Brookings Institution (1972–76), and at the Carnegie Endowment for International Peace (1981).

He is chairman of the Eminent Persons Group of the Asia Pacific Economic Cooperation (APEC) organization, a member of the executive committees of the Trilateral Commission and the Bretton Woods Committee, and a member of the Council on Foreign Relations.

Dr. Bergsten received M.A., M.A.L.D., and Ph.D. degrees from the Fletcher School of Law and Diplomacy. The U.S. Department of the Treasury gave him its Exceptional Service Award, the Department of State presented him with a Meritorious Honor Award, and the government of France awarded him with the Legion d'Honneur.